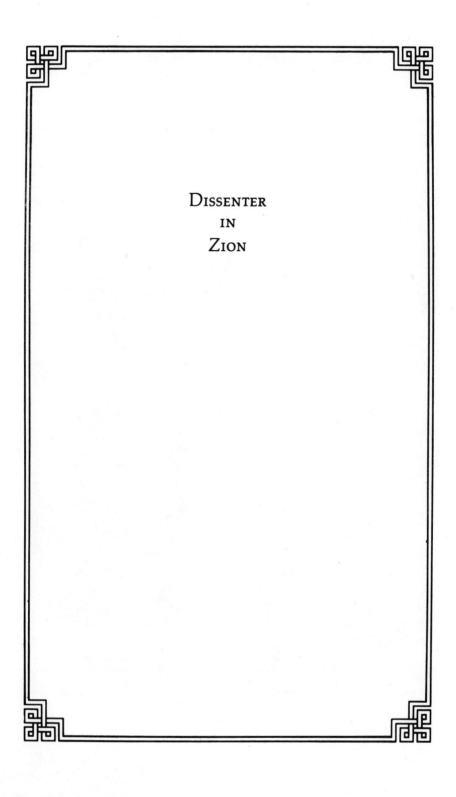

Dissenter
in
Zion

Judah L. Magnes, c. 1946.

Dissenter
in
Zion

From the Writings
of Judah L. Magnes

Edited by
Arthur A. Goren

Harvard University Press
Cambridge, Massachusetts
and London, England
1982

Library of Congress Cataloging in Publication Data
Magnes, Judah Leon, 1877–1948.
Dissenter in Zion.
Bibliography: p.
Includes index.
1.   Zionism — Addresses, essays, lectures.
2.   Jewish-Arab relations — 1917–1949 — Addresses, essays, lectures.
3.   Jews — United States — Politics and government — Addresses, essays, lectures.
4.   Universitah ha-'ivrit bi- Yerushalayim — Addresses, essays, lectures.
5.   Magnes, Judah Leon, 1877–1948 — Addresses, essays, lectures.
6.   Rabbis — United States — Biography — Addresses, essays, lectures.
7.   Zionists — Palestine — Biography — Addresses, essays, lectures.
I.   Goren, Arthur A., 1926–   II.   Title.
DS149.M29 1982   956.94'001   81–7268
ISBN 0-674-21283-5   AACR2

For
Ayalah

Contents

	Preface	ix
	Editor's Note	xi
	Abbreviations	xv
	Introduction: The Road to Jerusalem	1
1	Rebel Rabbi: Judaism, Zionism, and American Life 1900–1910	59
2	Community Builder and Mediator 1911–1916	119
3	Dissenter: Pacifist and Radical 1917–1922	157
4	Jerusalem: Chancellor of the Hebrew University 1922–1935	201
5	The Pursuit of Compromise: Arabs and Jews 1935–1939	307
6	War and the Politics of Dissent 1940–1947	367
7	A Mission of Peace 1948	459
	The Documents and Their Sources	523
	Glossary of Names	527
	Selected Works by Judah L. Magnes	544
	Acknowledgments	546
	Index	549

ILLUSTRATIONS

FRONTISPIECE

Judah L. Magnes, c. 1946
  Courtesy of the Department of Information and Public Affairs, Hebrew University, Jerusalem

FOLLOWING PAGE 306

The Oakland High School baseball team, 1892
  Courtesy of Jonathan and Hava Magnes

Magnes during his student days in Berlin, c. 1901
  Courtesy of Jonathan and Hava Magnes

Magnes in 1907
  Courtesy of Jonathan and Hava Magnes

The Magnes family, c. 1917
  Courtesy of Jonathan and Hava Magnes

Magnes visiting a German military hospital in Poland during his mission for the JDC, September 1916
  Courtesy of Jonathan and Hava Magnes

Magnes speaking at the opening of the academic year of the Hebrew University, November 5, 1933
  Courtesy of the Department of Information and Public Affairs, Hebrew University, Jerusalem

Magnes with members of Kibbutz Ein Gev on the shores of the Sea of Galilee, c. 1940
  Courtesy of Jonathan and Hava Magnes

Magnes visiting Kibbutz Bet Ha'shita, c. 1940
  Courtesy of the Department of Information and Public Affairs, Hebrew University, Jerusalem

Magnes at a conference of British Army medical officers, 1941
  Courtesy of the Department of Information and Public Affairs, Hebrew University, Jerusalem

Representatives of the Ihud Association appearing before the Anglo-American Committee of Inquiry, Jerusalem, March 14, 1946
  Courtesy of the Zionist Archives and Library, New York

Magnes with American Students in his office on Mount Scopus, 1946
  Courtesy of the Department of Information and Public Affairs, Hebrew University, Jerusalem

Preface

Judah Magnes's career anticipated much of the present configuration of Jewish life. Born and raised in California when it was the Western frontier of the Jewish world, he gained fame as a leader of New York Jewry during the years when the mass migration transformed it into *the* Jewish metropolis. Through his endeavors, early in this century, to unify American Jewry, to win broad support for Zionist work in Palestine, and to popularize a vision of a pluralist American society, he helped chart the course of American Jewish development. Then, one of a small number of Americans to do so, he emigrated to Palestine to take part in building the Jewish National Home.

For Magnes, the Return to Zion represented more than a movement of national revival and the creation of a refuge for the homeless. He envisioned a new parity between homeland and diaspora: Eretz Israel would enrich Jewish life everywhere, not replace it. He assigned to the Hebrew University, which he headed, a key place in this design. The Return also possessed a universal significance for him. Zionist pioneers building their collective settlements and creating a workers' society offered an example of social innovation and idealism to the world. But most of all, the prophetic injunction that Zion be redeemed in justice required reaching an accommodation with the other people who claimed the land, the Arabs. Therein lay the supreme moral and political test of Zionism.

This book seeks to distill the essence of Magnes's thought and his responses to the issues of his time. In these writings he often appears as a contentious figure. His espousal of pacifism during the First World War, his criticism of Zionist policy beginning with the Balfour Declaration, and his diplomatic contacts with Arabs and British and American officials provoked accusations of irresponsibility and obstructionism. He held no mandate and was accountable to no one, his opponents charged. Magnes nevertheless continued to speak out, convinced of the rightness of his position. His adversary role tested and strengthened the democratic quality of Jewish life. It also enabled him, in part because he was free of the constraints of the politician and the responsibilities of the officeholder, to perceive the long-range dangers threatening the Zionist enterprise and Jewish survival, dangers that the Jewish people still face. Inspired by the teaching of the Hebrew prophets, in an age of cynicism and cataclysm Magnes refused to surrender to pessimism. He practiced a politics of morality and believed in the power of the dissenting voice speaking out for the sake of Zion.

Since the beginning of my work on the Magnes papers, wars of attrition, the Yom Kippur War, and the threat of more war have formed a contrapuntal theme to my research on the writings of a pacifist. For Magnes, war was obscene, destructive no less to the victor than to the vanquished. He dreaded above all else that war between Jews and Arabs would produce a never-ending spiral of revanchism and bloodshed. And he was tormented by the thought that Israel's youth, forced to learn war and to live in constant readiness for battle, would turn into callous chauvinists. During these years my two sons, Avner and Amos, and their generation reached manhood, learned war, and were exposed to its perils. At the same time, despite stress and storm, Ayalah presided over a joyous home while pursuing her interest in the folk culture and dance of Jews and Arabs. Our sons and their comrades and families bear witness that Magnes's fears that an Israel isolated and besieged would lose its humanity have not been borne out, and yet the alarm he sounded remains disquieting.

A. A. G.

Jerusalem

Editor's Note

The one hundred and forty documents in this book — letters, journal entries, memoranda, notes, and essays — form a minute part of Judah Magnes's written legacy. Of nearly two hundred articles and addresses that he published, twelve appear in the anthology. The unpublished materials included are drawn primarily from the Judah Leib Magnes Papers, which were deposited in the Central Archives for the History of the Jewish People in Jerusalem by his widow, Beatrice Magnes, and his sons David and Jonathan between 1955 and 1977. The collection includes about 2600 files, which occupy ninety-six running feet of shelf space.

The papers reflect Magnes's broad interests. The years of his activities in the United States are represented by correspondence, minutes of meetings, organizational reports, brochures, press clippings, and drafts of addresses connected with his affiliation with the Federation of American Zionists, the American Jewish Committee, the Joint Distribution Committee, the People's Relief, and other organizations. The nearly complete office files of the New York Kehillah, sent to Jerusalem at Magnes's request, form part of the collection. They consist of some 530 files. Magnes's support of Jewish cultural activities — the theater, art, aid to individual scholars, and European and Palestinian Jewish institutions — is well documented, as is his political activity during the First World War, when he supported the People's Council of America and the National Civil Liberties Bureau and wrote and lectured extensively on foreign affairs, the Soviet Union, and civil rights in America. After settling in Jerusalem he added new interests and affiliations to the old ones. The Hebrew University is prominently represented in the collection with about 250 files. Since Magnes conducted much of his political and communal activities from his office at the university, the university files include material dealing with public affairs as well. His continued association with the work of the Joint Distribution Committee and with Hadassah are represented by extensive correspondence and reports, a considerable part of which pertain to the period of the Second World

War, as does his chairmanship of the Scientific Advisory Committee, established under his urgings by the government of Palestine.

The Jerusalem collection is particularly rich in personal letters and journals. Family correspondence begins in 1894, when Magnes left home in California to study at the Hebrew Union College. Letters Magnes wrote to his wife and children on the occasions of their separation were also saved. The category of personal documents includes many hand-written pieces of various lengths, from a single page to twenty and thirty pages, written on notebook paper of all sizes or other kinds of stationery or, less frequently, in notebooks. This miscellany of writings scattered through the collection is an informal record of ideas, experiences, and reflections intended for his personal use. I have therefore used the term *journal* as an editorial convenience in describing them, with the exception of brief, separate items that I have designated *notes*. Magnes's attitude toward maintaining a diary or journal is worth noting. In a letter to his friend Max Schloessinger, who together with the historian Ismar Elbogen had urged him to write his memoirs, Magnes remarked: "The chief difficulty is the unwarranted contempt I have always had for people who thought themselves so important that they wrote autobiographies or memoirs. I grant you that this attitude is not justified because many an autobiography or book of memoirs contains valuable historical material. But it is for the same reason that I have never been able to keep a diary, although I have started over and over again, and have usually stopped after the first two or three days."[1] Magnes was in fact an indefatigable diarist. However, for this private man writing was a highly personal act intended above all else to meet his own needs.

The subject matter of the journals is frequently political: summaries of interviews with officials, drafts of proposals, and reflections on political affairs; or philosophical: thoughts on Judaism and Jewish nationality, Zionism and universalism, and pacifism and revolution. Magnes also took up the pen to find relief at moments of personal stress or to sort out his thoughts when faced with a major decision. One entry, for November 22, 1925, reads: "Feel greatly alone. Alone in my thoughts about Jews and pacifism and Palestine. No intellectual companionship here. Bentwich a government official and therefore not free. I think of inner necessity. I must take to writing. Seek to find and exchange companionship in this way. Beatie comforts me. Love has the following order: (1) of the heart, (2) of the body, (3) of the mind."[2]

Magnes's voluminous correspondence ranged from brief formal letters to lengthy polemical discussions, all characterized by clarity of thought and economy of expression. The letter as a literary form of exposition was a favorite of his. Although he published in the *Menorah Journal*, *The Nation*, *The New York Post*, *Foreign Affairs*, and *Political*

Quarterly, his letters to the editors of various newspapers, particularly the *New York Times,* represent some of his most effective writing. Arthur Hays Sulzberger, the publisher of the *Times* and his admirer, assured him far more space than that department normally allocated.

His brief career as a preacher and his effectiveness as an orator left their mark on his writing. In both capacities the hallmark of his success was a simplicity of style, modesty of presentation, and sincerity of expression. His most important essays, which appeared in the collection of his university addresses, *In the Perplexity of the Times,* bear the marks of this oral tradition.

Magnes usually submitted drafts of his general, nonpolitical articles or addresses during his later years to Professors Leon Roth and Shmuel Hugo Berman, both philosophers, and to Ari Ibn-Zahav, one of the English editors of the Hebrew University publications. Professors Ernst Simon and Martin Buber, Dr. David Senator, an administrator of the university, and Robert Weltsch and Henrietta Szold read drafts of his political articles. Mrs. Magnes read the drafts of all of his articles, and not only for style in the technical sense. On the back of a statement that Magnes drafted in response to the Simpson Report of 1930 on the economic capacity of Palestine to absorb immigration, Mrs. Magnes wrote in pencil, "Don't write too much like a Quaker because you are not addressing 'brethren,' Jewish, Arab or British . . . Don't lecture too much, but warn against 'policy' of supporting politically clever conservatives (election promises). Refer to the political promises before elections—Baldwin, Amery, Churchill."[3]

In his capacity as head of the Hebrew University, Magnes conducted a wide-ranging correspondence in Hebrew. His diaries and journals, though written largely in English, are laced with phrases, sentences, and occasionally entire entries in Hebrew. However English clearly remained his first language. When he prepared addresses for delivery in Hebrew, he most often wrote out the drafts in English and then translated them. The same is true for his political correspondence. (Unless otherwise indicated I have used the English version or draft when available.) From the time he settled in Jerusalem in 1922 he used Hebrew in his public appearances with only rare exceptions, thus renouncing one of his primary gifts—for he was among the most eloquent orators the American Jewish community had known. In the preface to *In the Perplexity of the Times,* he noted that about half the material in the book was prepared in Hebrew and the other half in English. "One of my difficulties in translation," he wrote, "has been that, no matter in what language the material was prepared, I seemed always to be looking out upon two worlds, the English-speaking and the Hebrew-speaking. The unevenness both of style and of thought may perhaps be due primarily to that."

Several considerations guided me in making selections from Magnes's writings: their importance for understanding some of the major trends in twentieth-century Jewish life; their value in shedding light on Jewish affairs from the perspective of the dissenter, a role Magnes proudly played from 1915 to the end of his life; and their intrinsic interest in disclosing something of the odyssey of a remarkable man — American, Jew, Zionist, pacifist, religious seeker, in New York a spokesman for the Jews and in Jerusalem a protester in Zion.

All the selections, with two exceptions, documents 74 and 140, are published in their entirety. In the case of his journals, each item is a complete entry. The orthography and transliterations have been corrected to conform with current usage. One other liberty has been taken with the text: errors in punctuation and obvious lapses in languages — infrequent ones that Magnes would surely have corrected on a second reading — have been emended.

A final word concerning other archival sources. The Western Jewish History Center, which is part of the Judah L. Magnes Memorial Museum in Berkeley, California, has an important collection of Magnes papers. The Louis Marshall, Jacob Schiff, and Felix Warburg Papers, located at the American Jewish Archives, contain many letters from Magnes, a considerable number handwritten. The Israel Friedlaender and Solomon Schechter Papers at the Jewish Theological Seminary of America, the Stephen S. Wise Papers at the American Jewish Historical Society, and the Hannah Arendt and John Haynes Holmes Papers at the Library of Congress all contain substantial numbers of Magnes's letters. The Central Zionist Archives in Jerusalem, the Max Schloessinger, Shmuel Hugo Berman, and Martin Buber Papers, held by the Jewish National and University Library in Jerusalem, the archives of the Hebrew University in Jerusalem, and the Chaim Weizmann Papers in Rehovoth, Israel, are important sources for Magnes. The American Council for Judaism Papers at the University of Wisconsin, Madison, have files covering Magnes's trip to the United States in 1948. The James Marshall papers, in his possession, contain valuable material.

Persons to whom letters are addressed and names that appear with some frequency are identified in the Glossary of Names. Others are identified in the notes following each document. Document sources are given in the section headed "Documents and Their Sources."

1. Judah L. Magnes to Max Schloessinger, March 26, 1942, Max Schloessinger Papers, Jewish National and University Library, Jerusalem.

2. Judah Leib Magnes Papers, 310, Central Archives for the History of the Jewish People, Jerusalem, Israel.

3. Ibid., 383.

Abbreviations of Document Sources

FMWP   Felix M. Warburg Papers, American Jewish Archives, Cincinnati, Ohio

JHSP   Jacob H. Schiff Papers, American Jewish Archives, Cincinnati, Ohio

MP   Judah Leib Magnes Papers, Central Archives for the History of the Jewish People, Jerusalem, Israel

MPWJHC   Judah L. Magnes Papers, Western Jewish History Center, Berkeley, California

SSP   Solomon Schechter Papers, Jewish Theological Seminary of America, New York, New York

JMP   James Marshall Papers, James Marshall, New York, New York

CZA   Central Zionist Archives, Jerusalem, Israel

Introduction:
THE ROAD
TO
JERUSALEM

BEGINNING IN THE EARLY 1900s and until his death in October 1948 Judah Magnes occupied a singular place in Jewish life. His public career, nearly equally divided between New York and Jerusalem, ranged across a broad spectrum of Jewish communal and political affairs. He is recalled as the spirited young Reform rabbi who endeared himself to Zionists, immigrant radicals, and Jewish traditionalists alike while ministering to New York's Jewish elite. Winning the esteem of such disparate groups, he sought to mold a fragmented American Jewry into a democratically organized Jewish community. He is remembered too for his part in organizing overseas relief during the First World War through the work of the Joint Distribution Committee (JDC) and for his outspoken support of pacifist and civil libertarian causes. However, Magnes is best known for his later activities. One of a handful of American Jews who settled in Palestine in the 1920s, he became the principal architect of the Hebrew University and, on its opening in 1925, its head. Soon after he emerged as the most noted and indefatigable worker for Arab-Jewish understanding. In his early years his influence and appeal eclipsed that of his contemporary Stephen S. Wise, who subsequently became a commanding figure in the American Jewish community, a distinction for which many envisioned Magnes to be destined. Instead, at the height of his popularity, Magnes assumed the role of political dissenter and moral gadfly, challenging over the years such recognized leaders of the American and world Jewish community as Louis D. Brandeis, Wise, Chaim Weizmann, and David Ben-Gurion. His candor and political independence were a bane to the established leadership, which assailed his views—shaped by a radical humanism—as politically naïve. Yet few would deny Magnes's boldness in confronting the core issues that troubled world Jewry during his lifetime and ours: Jewish group survival in democratic America; the character and meaning of the return to Zion; and the reconciliation of universal ideals of Judaism with particularistic Jewish aspirations and needs.

For many Magnes's appearance on the American Jewish scene and his swift rise to prominence carried a special significance. To the community's leaders, largely foreign born, he personified the arrival of the "new American Jew." A native-born son of the American West, he stood out as an authentic product of a liberal America, whose ardent, buoyant involvement in Jewish affairs held out the promise of Jewish continuity in an America where rapid acculturation among the young threatened ethnic survival. Growing up in the congenial setting of Oakland, California (he was born in San Francisco on July 5, 1877, and moved across the bay when he was five), young Magnes won distinction in high school as a class orator, editor of the school journal, and star pitcher of the baseball team. In later years admirers as far away as New York and Jerusalem would repeat the story of his athletic prowess, telling proof for them, together with his California birth, of the genuine American. They would point out as well that instead of enrolling at the neighboring University of California, as did most of his peers, the seventeen-year-old youngster chose Cincinnati's Hebrew Union College, Reform Judaism's rabbinical seminary. He became the college's first graduate to originate from west of the Mississippi.[1]

Magnes had acquired a more thorough religious education than was common in the small Jewish centers of the West. He had come to the notice of Rabbi Jacob Voorsanger of San Francisco's Temple Emanu-El, a leading figure in the Reform ministry, who tutored the young man in Talmud, urged him to study for the rabbinate, and became his sponsor.

Judah's parents encouraged him as well. His father, David, a struggling dry goods merchant, no doubt took into consideration the remuneration a successful minister might expect; his mother, Sophie, was stirred by the social standing associated with a prestigious pulpit. But the dominant influence in Judah's decision to study for the rabbinate was the Jewishness of his parents' home.

The elder Magnes was active in Oakland's First Hebrew Congregation, and although no longer Orthodox in observance he retained warm sentiments toward the Hasidic Judaism of his youth. Born in Przedborg, near Lodz, in south-central Poland, he joined his elder brother in San Francisco in 1863 at the age of fifteen. To his children he succeeded in transmitting a sensibility for the religious traditions and culture of his parents' home. "That I am a Jew with all my heart and soul," Judah wrote to his father in 1902, "I now begin to realize is due mainly to you. In spite of the fact that it was ever your endeavor to be a modern American, your Jewish heart and mind spoke more eloquently than anything else." This

1. Norman Bentwich, *For Zion's Sake: A Biography of Judah L. Magnes* (Philadelphia, 1954), pp. 15–18; *Ner*, 7 (September–November 1954), 11; William Schack, "Opening Game in Zion," *Commentary*, April 1949, 380–382; E. R. Bluestone, interview, October 15, 1978.

pride in being a Jew found symbolic expression early in his rabbinical career, when Magnes began using his Hebrew given name, Judah Leib (after his paternal grandfather), rather than Julian Leon, his English given name.[2]

Sophie Abrahamson Magnes, Judah's mother, represented the German-Jewish tradition, although one not far removed from a Polish-Jewish milieu. Her family had originated in Filehne, a small town in the western part of the former Polish province of Posen, annexed for a second time by Prussia in 1815. One of eight children, she and her entire family were brought to San Francisco in the 1860s by her eldest brother. From her mother Sophie imbibed a love for German culture; that and the presence of the Abrahamson grandparents exposed the Magnes children to the German language and culture. Grandfather Abrahamson was Orthodox; when Sophie married she maintained a kosher home. Judah later recalled attending as a young Reform rabbi the cornerstone laying of the Orthodox synagogue of Oakland, named after his maternal grandfather, who had led the traditionalists out of the original Oakland congregation in protest over its reformist tendencies. However, Judah's father and his maternal uncles remained members of the First Hebrew Congregation even after it formally identified with Reform. During the 1890s an uncle, Julius Abrahamson, served as its president. In the case of the Abrahamson brothers their synagogue affiliation fit their social standing: they were leading Oakland merchants, owning one of the city's largest department stores. When David Magnes married Sophie Abrahamson in 1874 he was marrying into one of Oakland's prominent German-Jewish families. Thus the five Magnes children, and particularly Judah, the eldest, were exposed to the cultural heritage of American Jewry's two main constituent groups.[3]

Magnes's formative years were characterized by a harmonious family life. Both parents were young enough on their arrival in California to accommodate easily to the bustling, young society of San Francisco and Oakland. The tensions that marked relations between immigrant parents and their American-born children were absent. In this respect the Magnes children were third-generation Americans. Although the parents often spoke to one another in German, the language of the house was En-

2. Bentwich, *For Zion's Sake*, pp. 11–13; JLM, Journal, August 5, 1922, MP, 329; JLM to father, April 1, 1902, MP, 10b. In writing to his family Magnes signed his letters Leon or Enon, a pet name; he never used Julian. He signed formal letters J. L. Magnes. A few close friends addressed him as "Mag."

3. Bentwich, *For Zion's Sake*, pp. 13–14; JLM to Rabbi Philip H. Langh, September 23, 1945, MP, 217; JLM, diary, May 31, 1901, MP, 293; JLM to family, June 28, 1901, MP, 10b; Fred Rosenbaum, *Free to Choose: The Making of a Jewish Community in the American West* (Berkeley, 1976), pp. 27, 43; Walter Teller, interview, March 25, 1977, MPW-JHC; Ruth Abrahamson to Arthur A. Goren, August 2, 1979.

glish. Sophie's and David's letters to their son were written in fluent English, and David was as avid a baseball fan as his son. For young Magnes public school with its extracurricular activities and religious school, which met on Sundays and weekdays, still left time for the typical youthful ventures of a city boy. Until his father put a stop to it, Judah tried his hand at delivering newspapers. Occasionally, despite parental objection, he slipped away to spend time on the waterfront. He enjoyed attending Salvation Army street-corner meetings and political rallies; it was there, his biographer Norman Bentwich suggests, that he became enamored of the power of the spoken word. After he left for college gossipy letters from all members of the family—from his brother, Isaac, three years his junior; from his sisters, Eva, Tess, and Rosalind, four, six, and fourteen years younger than he; and from his parents—reflected the homely social interests of a middle-class American family.[4]

Within the family Judah clearly held a special place. Parents and siblings alike placed high hopes on their gifted eldest son and brother. They gloried in his youthful triumphs and approved of his most ambitious plans even after his studies at Hebrew Union College and later in Berlin strained the family's resources to the limit, despite the stipend Rabbi Voorsanger had arrangd and the help extended by an uncle. On several occasions he considered interrupting his studies. Each time the family insisted that he continue. When it was possible to do so, Judah spent his summers in Oakland; after he settled in New York, members of the family visited him for extended periods. But letters—frequent, lengthy, and full of advice, admonition, and encouragement—were the main channel of communication.[5]

Oakland, like the Bay region as a whole, was undergoing rapid and intensive change. In 1882, when the Magneses moved to Oakland, it had a population of thirty thousand. Founded thirty years earlier, it had developed into a city only in the last fifteen years. In the course of the next three decades, the population increased fivefold. The newness of the city, its swift growth, and the great distance from the East created a receptivity to innovation and a tolerance for most, if not all, of the elements that made up its multiethnic populace. Like San Francisco, Oakland had a dismal, if less notorious, record of prejudice against Asians. The small Jewish community, however, encountered little if any discrimination. Nor was it large enough to form a residential enclave, even if it had wished to. One index of its acceptance was the publicity given to Jewish social events. The daily *Oakland Times* gave Magnes's bar mitzva de-

4. Bentwich, *For Zion's Sake*, p. 15; JLM to family, 1894–1907, MP, 1–12.
5. Sophie Magnes to JLM, May 6, 1902, MPWJHC; Jacob Voorsanger to JLM, January 3, 1900, MPWJHC; JLM to family, April 12, 1899, MP, 7; JLM to family, October 12, 1902, MP, 10b.

tailed coverage under the banner, "Confirmation of a Bright Oakland Boy—An Excellent Discourse." His departure for Hebrew Union College was similarly noted, and when the newly ordained rabbi returned to deliver his maiden sermon from the pulpit of San Francisco's Temple Emanu-El in August 1900, the event was extensively reported. The *Oakland Inquirer* observed that he was "the first native son to enter the Jewish priesthood." In the Oakland of the last decades of the nineteenth century, Jewish news was shared with the public at large. Ethnic pride came easily.[6]

To those who knew Magnes well, his western upbringing explained his most distinctive traits: his forthrightness, personal courage, and nonconformist bent. His sons, Jonathan and Benedict, ascribed his openness and his uncompromising belief in personal freedom, indeed his anarchic tendencies, to his California origins. On Magnes's seventieth birthday the historian Gershom Scholem, his colleague and coworker at the Hebrew University for over two decades, entitled a tribute to him "*Adam hofshi*—A Free Man."[7] Scholem described Magnes as that rare person, free of dogmas and slogans, who steadfastly pursues a politics of high principle as he understands it, his humanitarian beliefs unshaken by the pessimism of the times. Magnes himself suggested something of the origins of this cast of mind in a letter to his close friend Felix Warburg, the New York financier and philanthropist. Explaining his refusal to accept an honorary doctorate from the Jewish Theological Seminary in 1937, Magnes wrote: "I suppose it is just another form of vanity, but I have never been able to bear the thought of medals and honorary titles—at least, as far as I myself am concerned . . . Perhaps it is because I was born in the far West. I recall how my first teachers used to talk of the glories of the real America—no badges, no titles, no special uniforms, etc. I know it is somewhat different at the present time in America, but I am sure that the true America still feels the same way."[8]

Magnes's independence of mind is evident in his first published essay, which he wrote in his second year at Hebrew Union College when he was not yet twenty. He entitled it "Palestine—or Death," and it appeared in Voorsanger's weekly, *Emanu-El*. The "Death" in the title was the danger of assimilation awaiting American Jewry. The way of assuring "the permanency of . . . Judaism," Magnes wrote, was "a return to the land of our fathers" and the "establishment of a Jewish church and state." The ar-

6. Rosenbaum, *Free to Choose*, pp. 2, 4–7, 25–26; *Oakland Times*, July 6, 1890, p. 5; *Oakland Tribune*, August 10, 1900, p. 2; *Oakland Inquirer*, August 13, 1900, p. 2.

7. James Marshall, "Judah L. Magnes," *American Jewish Year Book*, 51 (1950), 512; Bentwich, *For Zion's Sake*, p. 25; Jonathan Magnes, interview, February 12, 1974; Benedict Magnes, interview, March 15, 1975; Gershom Scholem, "Adam ḥofshi," *Ba'ayot*, 3 (July 1947), 207–210.

8. JLM to Felix Warburg, Feb. 10, 1937, document 81.

ticle was suggestive, indeed daring, but not profound. The Zionist theme was not elaborated. Zionism, in fact, was not yet one of Magnes's major interests. He did depict with great candor the defection of the "advanced Jews"—Reform Jews—from Judaism. Slight as Magnes's first article was —the uninhibited expression of a college sophomore—it was notably devoid of any apologetic note. It pointedly mocked the position of classic Reform Judaism "that says that America is our Palestine, Washington our Jerusalem." For a fledgling rabbinical student to have formulated such views in the anti-Zionist climate of Hebrew Union College and to have published them in the journal of his mentor and patron, who was vehemently opposed to Zionism, was audacious and an intimation of the iconoclasm of the mature man.[9]

Magnes's interest in Jewish matters did not preclude other concerns. In his senior year at the University of Cincinnati, which he attended while studying at Hebrew Union College, he was elected editor-in-chief of the student magazine. When the faculty insisted on censoring student criticism of professors, Magnes led a rebellion that agitated the university for months. Nor did he support the Spanish-American War when it broke out in 1898. The war was "unrighteous," he told his parents. "The nation that had been most blatant in its advocacy of arbitration as a means of settling disputes" had rushed "headlong into a war when there were innumerable chances to avert war. Where are your good Christian ministers with 'peace on earth and good will toward men'? I am ashamed of Rabbi [Marcus] Friedlander [minister of Oakland's First Hebrew Congregation], that he should class himself among the 'fighting parsons.' What a contradiction in terms."[10]

On graduating in 1900 Magnes left for Germany to pursue postgraduate work in Semitics and philosophy at the Universities of Berlin and Heidelberg. For his own intellectual growth and his future career in the rabbinate study in Europe and a doctoral degree promised much. In December 1902 he received his degree from Heidelberg.

For most of this period Magnes lived in Berlin, where he also attended the Lehranstalt fuer die Wissenschaft des Judentums (better known as the Hochschule), the renowned institute for advanced Jewish studies. The intellectual and personal ties he formed with a number of like-minded students at the Hochschule played a decisive role in shaping his spiritual world. His friends growing up in late-nineteenth-century Germany had

9. *Emanu-El*, January 6, 1896, p. 13; Yohai Goell, "*Aliyah* in the Zionism of an American *Oleh*: Judah L. Magnes," *American Jewish Historical Quarterly*, 65 (December 1975), 100–101.

10. Bentwich, *For Zion's Sake*, pp. 19–20; JLM to parents, November 21, December 12, December 23, 1897, MP, 4; January 12, January 16, January 26, 1898, MP, 5; April 22, 1898, MP, 5.

reacted to virulent anti-Semitism on the one hand and widespread assimilation and Jewish self-estrangement on the other by evincing a new-found ethnic loyalty. Jewish studies became an affirmation of their Jewish identity, the cause of Jewish survival their vocation, and the "cultural renaissance of the Jewish people" their special concern. Most were ardent Zionists. Three of them—Arthur Biram, Max Schloessinger, and Gotthold Weil—settled eventually in Palestine. Schloessinger became Magnes's principal aide at the Hebrew University, Weil headed the University's library, and Biram founded the Reali School in Haifa. Emil Cohen, another member of the circle, achieved fame as the so-called Zionist rabbi of Berlin and as one of German Jewry's courageous leaders in the early years of the Nazi regime. Eugen Taeubler rose to a professorship in Jewish history at Heidelberg.[11]

For Magnes this was a heady time of fervent discussions, intensive study of modern Hebrew and Zionist literature, and participation in Jewish organizatinal life. These interests brought him in touch with East European Jews whom he met at the Hochschule, at Zionist meetings, and on visits to their synagogues. Like his German-Jewish friends he idealized the Ostjuden as "complete" Jews who, firmly rooted in their ethnic heritage, were the antithesis of assimilated Western Jewry. "What a remarkable people these poor, starving Jews are," he wrote home after meeting his father's relatives, immigrants from Lodz who were passing through Berlin. "How they cling to life and to hope—what a fine intellectuality they all have, and what a tremendous spiritual power is in them. It is our Talmud Judaism that has kept them alive until this day. God help them if ever in their present condition our cracked-up ideas of 'progress' ever reach them. My fervent prayer is that they be given the opportunity to develop themselves in the land of our fathers, in Palestine. There their great dormant powers will come to life and the world's finest civilization will result."[12]

Thus Magnes's engrossment in Jewish studies and Jewish life became part of an all-consuming Zionism. To his family he wrote:

It is now my whole philosophy. It is my "Lebensprogramm" . . . Since I have become a Zionist my view of life has changed, my view as to my calling has changed, my view as to my future has changed, my hopes, my prayers have changed. The questions concerning the Jewish people—and the Jewish religion is but one of these questions—are the questions that are consuming my days and my nights . . . My Zionism makes me more than

11. Gotthold Weil, "Erinnerungen an die Zeit des Aufenthaltes von Magnes in Berlin," ms, in MP, 132; Judah L. Magnes, Addresses by the Chancellor of the Hebrew University (Jerusalem, 1936), p. 296.

12. JLM to family, November 7, 1901, quoted in Goell, "Aliyah," 103; Bentwich, For Zion's Sake, pp. 27–30.

a preacher or community leader. It makes me a worker for the preservation of the Jewish people as a whole and for their greater glory and better life in their own land.[13]

Much as Magnes grounded his Zionism in Judaism and Jewish culture, he accepted as well the political Zionism associated with Theodore Herzl, the movement's leader from 1897 until his death in 1904. The problem of the hour, Herzl proclaimed, was relief for the oppressed Jews of Eastern Europe, victims of an endemic anti-Semitism, through emigration to an internationally recognized national home in Palestine. Magnes, in a letter to his family written in 1901, echoed Herzl's dictum: only along "political lines," through the organized efforts of the Jewish people, could this "terrible question of life and death be settled once and for all." For American Jewry such a solution had an importance of its own, he wrote some months later. "The Jewish immigration to America is already a danger to the Jews of America. We must endeavor to turn the stream of immigration towards the Orient." (Then, as later, he meant Palestine and the contiguous countries; for Palestine alone would be unable to absorb the thousands who had to leave Europe.) In fact, in the three years before the First World War, as a leading Zionist spokesman he supported efforts to reach a political accommodation with the Ottoman Empire for normalizing and expediting Jewish settlement in Palestine. Politics, he wrote in a eulogy to Herzl, was not the "work of the devil but rather the modern name for that activity which has to do with securing the foundation of government without which spiritual movements are themselves impossible." However, political Zionism constituted no dogmatic truth for Magnes. Writing in 1906 to David Wolffsohn, Herzl's successor as head of the World Zionist Organization, he questioned the exclusive preoccupation of the organization with political activity. Zionism in America, he declared, would grow only if it offered American Jewry a program of practical work in Palestine.[14]

In his support of these various Zionist strategies Magnes revealed uncommon flexibility. Nevertheless, the problem that touched him most deeply continued to be the cultural and spiritual predicament of the Jews: assimilation loomed as the great peril to Jewish continuity. The alarm he sounded in his college essay became the mainspring of his thinking five years later. The Berlin period not only intensified his concern and

13. JLM to family, October 9, 1901, document 1, quoted in Goell, "Aliyah," 103.

14. JLM to family, December 26, 1901, document 2; JLM to family, September 1, 1902, MP, 10b; JLM, "The Ottoman Empire and the Jews," sermon delivered at Temple Emanu-El, March 27, 1909, MP, 448; Cyrus Adler to JLM, May 20, 1909, MP, 732; JLM to Oscar Straus, January 2, 1913, document 16; Evyatar Friesel, Ha'tnua ha'zionit b'artzot ha'brit, 1897–1914 (Tel Aviv, 1970), pp. 127–129; JLM, "Herzl's Influence upon Jewish Students in German Universities," Maccabaean, 7 (August 1904), 105; JLM to D. Wolffsohn, June 19, 1906, CZA, Z 2/379.

broadened his understanding of the problem; it also exposed him to the ideas of Ahad Ha'am, the ideologist of cultural Zionism. Magnes witnessed at close range the impassioned debate that raged within the ranks of the Zionist movement in the years 1900–1902 pitting the cultural Zionists, led by Chaim Weizmann and Martin Buber among others, against Herzl and the political Zionists.

Ahad Ha'am's emphasis on the spiritual rather than the political problem facing the Jews—the plight of Judaism rather than the plight of the Jews—profoundly influenced Magnes. Ahad Ha'am's description of the disintegration and decay of modern Judaism, his discussion of the psychic cost paid by the emancipated Jew alienated from his ethnic roots, which he called "slavery in freedom," and his insistence that the "revival of the national spirit" precede political action and inform the practical work in Palestine appealed to Magnes. Ahad Ha'am's vision of Palestine as a spiritual center that would help sustain Diaspora Jewry also fit Magnes's perception of American Jewry's needs. He found no less persuasive Ahad Ha'am's views on Jewish ethics: the message of the Hebrew prophets, the ultimate expression of the Jewish spirit, annunciated the "universal dominion of absolute justice" and stressed the "predominance of the spiritual life over physical force." (The aphorism Magnes used most frequently in his writing was the biblical verse, "Not by might, nor by power, but by My Spirit.") The bearers of these universal ideals, Ahad Ha'am emphasized, were also Jewish nationalists, keepers of the nation's conscience and believers in Israel's election. A secular nationalist, he nevertheless recognized the place of religion in his notion of Jewish nationality. The links between the Jewish people and its religion were so intertwined that the nonbeliever could participate in religious observance as a national-cultural act, could indeed view it as an instrument of group maintenance. Thus Ahad Ha'am's teachings offered the Reform-trained American rabbi not only a Zionist rationale for working for group survival in the Diaspora but the intellectual resources to deal with broader philosophical problems. As a member of the Reformed ministry, Magnes faced the challenge of reconciling universal ideals with Jewish particularism and religious belief with ethnic allegiance.[15]

On his return to the United States Magnes served as instructor of Bi-

---

15. Magnes was an avid reader of *Ha'shiloaḥ*, the Hebrew literary journal founded and edited by Ahad Ha'am. He also refers to the volumes of Ahad Ha'am's collected essays, *Al parashat ha'drahim* (At the Crossroads), the first three volumes of which appeared between 1895 and 1904; see also JLM, "Discourse [on Ahad Ha'am]," January 20, 1907, ms., MP,. 447; JLM, "Evidences of Jewish Nationality," *The Emanu-El Pulpit*, 3 (December 14, 1907), 1–14; Bentwich, *For Zion's Sake*, pp. 27, 30, 35. For a brief summary of Ahad Ha'am's views see Simon Noveck, "Ahad Ha'am," in *Great Jewish Thinkers of the Twentieth Century*, ed. Simon Noveck (Clinton, Mass., 1963), pp. 34–44, and Leon Simon, ed., *Ahad Ha'am: Essays, Letters Memoirs* (Oxford, 1946), pp. 12–47; Friesel, *Ha'tnua*, p. 87.

ble and acting librarian at Hebrew Union College. His first published article, which appeared in the *Hebrew Union College Annual* of 1904, discussed the poetry of Chaim Nachman Bialik, the poet laureate of the new Hebrew literature. Bialik's work, Magnes urged, was proof that "the Jewish cultural renaissance is a fact which can be disregarded only by those who believe that the creation of distinctly Jewish cultural values ceased with the political emancipation of Jews in a few lands." In America, however, where "Jews were living an unencumbered and healthy life without being troubled with questions of Jewish culture, Jewish misery and the Jewish future," cultural sterility reigned and threatened group survival. Magnes then touched on a second motif that for most of his readers — nearly all Reform rabbis — was especially provocative. "The ideas of a universal religion in the keeping of a given nation and the idea of a national culture, are not mutually exclusive. For, a national culture may have developed a universal religion. National culture is thus the broader term in that it may have expressed itself in numberless other forms, as well as in the terms of universal religion."[16]

Although Magnes condemned classical Reform for denationalizing Judaism, he subscribed to Reform's conception of Israel's universal ethical mission. This Reform component in Magnes's thought allowed him to view the Jewish dispersion as providential. To those who, like himself, believed "that the Jewish people be the servant bringing mankind closer to its idea of brotherhood and righteousness," he jotted down in a notebook, "both are needed — dispersion and concentration . . . Israel is a *Weltvolk*. It must remain among the nations . . . Israel must also seek to deepen its roots, to get soil underfoot." He perceived Zion and Exile and the centrality of Palestine in radically different terms than did European Zionists and Ahad Ha'am. Unlike that of Ahad Ha'am Magnes's Hebrew humanism remained anchored in religious belief. In a sermon delivered in 1909 he declared: "For the Jew there cannot, I think, be a permanent Jewish religion without Jewish nationality, nor can there be, I think, a permanent Jewish nationality without Jewish religion." The import of his religious outlook on his interpretation of Zionism he summarized trenchantly in a 1914 letter to Chaim Weizmann, then in the forefront of the young leaders of the World Zionist Organization. "The despair theory of Zionism," he wrote, "does not appeal to me. I have not despaired of the Jewish people, and I believe in its eternity even without Palestine." Palestine was the cornerstone, but the Jewish people would continue to live without it if need be and continue to develop its culture. However, "with Palestine the people will live better, and develop its culture more hope-

16. JLM, "Some Poems of H. N. Bialik," *Hebrew Union College Annual*, 1 (1904), 177, 186.

fully and with more achievements," he insisted. "We must help one another to be Jews and live as Jews, be it here or there."[17]

To be a Zionist was to be a more earnest and committed Jew pledged to support all manifestations of the group's will to survive. In a formal address entitled "Zionism and Jewish Religion" he declared: "Nor can there be any question that Zionism is doing more than anything else to strengthen the Jewish national consciousness or feeling of peoplehood wherever Jews live throughout the world. Whatever be our interpretation of Jewish history, the basic element of every theory of Jewish life is the continued existence of the Jews, and it is Zionism alone of all Jewish movements which can give a guarantee of the uninterrupted continuance of the Eternal People."[18] In his view the preservation of the Jews as a people transcended all particularistic conceptions of Jews and Judaism.

Precisely this Jewish ecumenicism and his eclectic and undogmatic temper fitted Magnes for the singular role he assumed in the life of the American Jewish community during the decade and a half beginning in 1905. More than any other leader of his time, Magnes had interests that spanned the cultural, social, and ideological chasms dividing the Jews of America. And for a time his catholicity enabled him to win both the confidence of America's Jewish patricians and the adulation of the immigrant masses, to gain the ears of both assimilationists and Zionists, and to raise the prospect of achieving unity and order in Jewish life.

In September 1904 Magnes arrived in New York, called to the pulpit of Temple Israel in Brooklyn. A major consideration in his accepting the Brooklyn pulpit was that it afforded him the opportunity to be part of and take part in the vibrant and variegated Jewish life of New York. What began as a highly successful ministry terminated through mutual consent at the close of his second year with Magnes's resignation. As he explained it he was accused of being "too active in Zionism, too conservative in my Judaism and that I associated too much with revolutionaries." In 1906 he accepted an invitation to become associate rabbi of Temple Emanu-El in New York, the cathedral temple of Reform Judaism, a remarkable distinction for a young rabbi of twenty-nine. That fall he began serving the congregation, which included such eminent German-Jewish families as the Seligmans, the Schiffs, the Guggenheims, the Warburgs, and the Marshalls. For these influential and community-minded leaders, Magnes's public prominence, his eloquence as a speaker, and his

17. JLM, journal entry, December 24, 1922, MP, 190. For a similar comment circa 1904 see note on envelope, MP, 294; *The Emanu-El Pulpit*, 2 (1909), 8; JLM to Chaim Weizmann, June 8, 1914, MP, 838.
18. JLM, *Zionism and Jewish Religion: Address Delivered before the Philadelphia Section, Council of Jewish Women, April 12, 1910* (pamphlet), p. 5, MP, 360.

13

impeccable credentials, from his California accent to his Heidelberg Ph.D., outweighed whatever misgivings his nonministerial activities created. Indeed his downtown interests may well have been viewed as an asset. In the eyes of men such as Marshall and Schiff, noblesse oblige required extending a generous hand to the less fortunate, and self-interest called for stemming the social disorganization of the immigrants and hastening their integration, tasks for which their young minister was eminently qualified. Magnes's prestigious connections, on the other hand, would serve him well in his relations with the immigrant community and give him entree into the larger American and world Jewish scenes.[19]

Two years later his ties with the Jewish elite were further strengthened by his marriage to Beatrice Lowenstein, the sister of Louis Marshall's wife. Beatrice's father had emigrated from Germany in the 1850s and established a large mercantile business in Memphis, Tennessee. Following the Civil War the family moved to New York, where Beatrice was born, the youngest of six children. A woman of marked intellectual independence, she was a tower of strength to her husband, helping him with her keen criticism of his ideas and plans. She was also a jealous guardian of the privacy of their home, protecting him and their three sons—David, Jonathan, and Benedict—from the controversies and tensions of his public life. The modest income Beatrice received from the family inheritance provided financial security and enabled Judah to hold communal posts without compensation for many years.[20]

Soon after his arrival in New York Magnes joined the efforts to aid the Jewish self-defense movement in Russia. In the aftermath of the Kishinev program in April 1903 Jewish socialists and Zionists in Russia began establishing clandestine defense groups, and the call went out to raise funds to supply arms. Although in the United States this support came almost entirely from the radical elements among the immigrants, Magnes quickly emerged as the head of the Jewish Defense Association. On December 4, 1905, he led a parade to protest a new wave of pogroms in Russia. Over a hundred thousand Jews took part in the march from the Lower East Side to Fifth Avenue, while hundreds of thousands watched the procession. His work for the association catapulted Magnes into the front rank of national leadership. He interpreted his success as a mandate to replace the committees of Jewish philanthropists, who were attempting deal on an ad hoc basis with problems of Russian Jewry and immigration, with a democratic national organization, an American Jewish

19. Bentwich, For Zion's Sake, pp. 36-41; JLM to family, November 18, 1905, document 4.
20. Beatrice L. Magnes, Episodes: A Memoir (Berkeley, 1977), pp. 17-24; Bentwich, For Zion's Sake, pp. 42-43; E. R. Bluestone, Jonathan Magnes, Benedict Magnes, interviews.

14

congress. Fearing the loss of their hegemony, the notables of the established community — Schiff, Marshall, and Oscar Straus among others — persuaded Magnes to join them in establishing instead a select committee that would co-opt representative figures from the various sectors of the community. When in the fall of 1906 the American Jewish Committee was formally established, Magnes joined its executive body with the intention of broadening and democratizing it at the first propitious moment.[21]

At the same time that Magnes served on the American Jewish Committee and filled the pulpit of Emanu-El, his involvement in the affairs of Russian immigrants brought him into close rapport with Yiddish intellectual circles. The radical political theorist and publicist Chaim Zhitlovsky, the playwright David Pinski, and the novelist Sholom Asch were close friends and intellectual companions. Magnes attempted to interest uptown donors in a Yiddish art theater, helped the Socialist Zionists establish their journal, the *Yidisher Kemfer*, and was instrumental in the founding of the Yiddish daily *Der Tog*, which he hoped would provide the Yiddish reading public with a respectable, high quality newspaper. Visitors from Europe and Palestine arriving in the United States on fundraising or propaganda missions depended on his guidance, contacts, and friendship. Manya Shochet, who was raising money for self-defense and collective settlements in Palestine; Shmaryahu Levin, a leader of the Russian Zionist movement; and Aaron Aaronson, a Palestinian agronomist, were among the emissaries from abroad with whom Magnes formed lasting friendships. Magnes was little troubled with ideological inconsistencies. On one occasion Solomon Schechter, head of the conservative Jewish Theological Seminary, scolded him for representing the Zionist organization at a memorial meeting honoring the Russian revolutionary hero Gregory Gershuni. Gershuni's revolutionary socialism, Schechter contended, was assimilationist and antireligious and hence opposed to everything the Zionist organization stood for. Similarly, when a group of young Orthodox Jews from the Lower East Side began planning the Young Israel movement, they turned to Magnes for advice and support. Neither they nor Magnes considered the anomaly of a Reform rabbi assisting young Orthodox leaders in organizing an educational program and overcoming the indifference of the Orthodox rabbis.[22]

Contemporaries have described Magnes's psychological impact on the

21. *New York Times*, December 5, 1905, p. 6; Zosa Szajkowski, "The Impact of the Russian Revolution of 1905 on American Jewish Life," *YIVO Annual of Jewish Social Science*, 42 (1978), 64–69, 87–95.

22. Bernard G. Richards, interview, June 24, 1959, William E. Wiener Oral History Library, American Jewish Committee; Bentwich, *For Zion's Sake*, pp. 55, 60–61; JLM to Louis Marshall, April 1, 1915, MP, 1588; Solomon Schechter to JLM, May 25, 1908, March 31, 1908, MP, 115; *Jewish Life*, 33 (January–February 1966), 31–32.

community. One memoirist recalled the response of the established up-town Jews to his charm and grace. "A fairy prince in appearance, a veritable prophet in Israel in the high spiritual and ethical tenor of his fine oratory, he won their admiration. His Jewishness was accepted by them with a ready indulgence; perhaps it was secretly welcomed as vicarious atonement for their assimilation." When a wealthy trustee of Emanu-El approved his daughter's conversion and her marriage out of the faith in a sumptuous Catholic ceremony, Magnes used the pulpit to inveigh against intermarriage. The indignant trustee offered his resignation, and the issue threatened to split the congregation. But Magnes won accolades from religiously indifferent radicals and a vote of confidence from the temple's board of trustees. Years later Schiff wrote privately about Magnes, criticizing his "intense Jewish nationalism" as creating "a grave danger" to many communal causes. What made Magnes particularly dangerous, Schiff continued, was his "magnetism . . . which, perhaps unbeknown to him, hypnotizes many who come into close touch with him." Baruch Zuckerman, leader of the Socialist Zionists, has described how the young East Side immigrants walked uptown to Emanu-El to hear Magnes preach. A student at the Jewish Theological Seminary similarly recalled how fellow seminarians walked down from Morningside Heights to Forty-third Street and Fifth Avenue on the Friday evenings Magnes spoke. "The crowds flocked to hear him," a colleague in the rabbinate remembered, "the press had its reporters present to take down his sermons, and he was lionized on all sides as New York's most gifted Jewish preacher." When Stephen Wise came to New York and founded the Free Synagogue, opinion was divided as to which of the two was the premier preacher.[23]

During the years 1905 to 1915 Magnes was at the peak of his influence. From 1905 to 1908 he was secretary of the Federation of American Zionists, its chief executive officer and most influential spokesman. The significance of the federation far exceeded its size. Although its members numbered only twelve thousand in the years preceding the first World War, it included public figures and young intellectuals who occupied key places in American Jewish life. Zionists dominated the faculty of the Jewish Theological Seminary. Particularly influential were Schechter, Israel Friedlaender, and Mordecai M. Kaplan. Magnes felt especially close to this group, which included Henrietta Szold, a founder of Hadassah, the

23. Morris D. Waldman, *Nor By Power* (New York, 1953), pp. 392–393; *New York Times*, January 30, 1908, p. 4; Jacob H. Schiff to Israel Friedlaender, February 16, 1914, Israel Friedlaender Papers, Jewish Theological Seminary, New York, N.Y.; Baruch Zuckerman, interview, April 9, 1959, William E. Wiener Oral History Library, American Jewish Committee; Herman H. and Mignon L. Rubenovitz, *The Waking Heart* (Cambridge, Mass., 1967), pp. 22, 24–25; Max Raisin, "J. L. Magnes," *National Jewish Monthly* (March 1950), 225.

women's Zionist organization, who like Magnes settled in Palestine in the 1920s. Judged by the polemics in the Yiddish and English-language Jewish press, Zionism was a considerable presence in the Jewish quarter, as was Magnes.

His Zionist activities gained him recognition not only in the United States but in Europe and Palestine as well. He was a delegate to several Zionist congresses (in 1905 he served as English-language secretary of the congress, along with Weizmann as secretary for Yiddish and Joseph Klausner for Hebrew). In 1907 and 1912 he also visited Palestine, where he was received as the key figure of the American movement. Even after he left office his correspondence with Otto Warburg, Menachem Ussishkin, Leo Motzkin, Arthur Ruppin, Bialik, and Weizmann reveal the unrivaled place he held among American leaders in the eyes of the Europeans. In 1914 Shmaryahu Levin, visiting the United States as representative of the World Zionist Organization, confided to Magnes that he wanted him elected to the Small Actions Committee, the movement's highest executive body.[24]

Undoubtedly much of his influence in the Zionist movement as elsewhere stemmed from his access to the uptown philanthropists. Jacob Schiff and his son-in-law Felix Warburg, the heads of Kuhn, Loeb and Company, the preeminent Jewish investment house, and Magnes's brother-in-law Louis Marshall, the prominent lawyer and president of the American Jewish Committee, formed a powerful triumvirate of supporters and admirers. Authoritarian figures with a well-defined notion of where and how they wished to lead American Jewry, they backed Magnes, but with caution. Their commitment to classical Reform made them wary of Magnes's Zionism, though his adherence to cultural or spiritual Zionism made it more palatable than political Zionism, which was anathema to them. Moreover their patrician notion of community stewardship clashed with Magnes's belief in democratic organization. Nevertheless, they saw in Magnes, if carefully monitored and selectively aided, a leader capable of exercising influence in the turbulent world of Jewish affairs. Personal fondness and family ties were certainly elements in the special relationship between Magnes and these three strong-minded men. But Magnes also established excellent rapport with the other leading figures of the German-Jewish aristocracy. Irving and Herbert Lehman, Jacob Wertheim and his son Maurice, Daniel Guggenheim, Cyrus Sulzberger, and Nathan and Oscar Straus were among those who gave Magnes's causes a sympathetic hearing. Indeed the years of Magnes's greatest influence in the Jewish community coincided with the years of German-

24. Bentwich, *For Zion's Sake*, pp. 52–60; Friesel, *Ha'tnua*, pp. 84–85; Herbert Parzen, "Conservative Judaism and Zionism (1896–1922)," *Jewish Social Studies*, 23 (October 1961), 243–250, 259–263.

Jewish hegemony. In the 1920s and 1930s, as a permanent resident of Jerusalem, Magnes would play a subtle but critically important role as host, guide, and interpreter of events to this group.[25]

For Magnes the capstone of these years was his attempt to create a community structure that would encompass the Jewish communal life of New York. United in a democratically governed polity, the Jews would harness their intellectual and material resources and build a model ethnic community. Order and coherence would replace the contention and fragmentation that marked these years of mass immigration. Such an organization would not only alleviate the social and economic problems the newcomers faced and assure a healthy and balanced Americanization, but it would contribute to the general welfare of the city and provide a model for other ethnic groups. The venerable Jewish tradition of community — the European *kehillah* — and American progressive notions of efficiency, enlightened public opinion, and democracy, guided Magnes in his thinking. New York would be the first to create a kehillah, and other cities would emulate it in a grand program to reorder American Jewish life. When in 1909 the New York Kehillah was founded, Magnes was elected chairman. By 1922 the ambitious, innovative experiment was moribund, a victim of apathy, dissension, and its own visionary goals. Yet during its early years it made impressive progress and raised high hopes, largely owing to Magnes's zeal and persuasiveness.[26]

Even in its heyday the Kehillah included only a minority of the Jewish organizations and institutions of the city. However, never had so large and representative a segment of the community joined together into permanent association. Through its representative assembly and bureaus of education, philanthropy, industry, religion, and social morals, communal issues were debated, new ideas and methods were introduced, and the problem of social dislocation, so pervasive in a city two-thirds of whose 1.5 million Jews were newcomers, was confronted. Magnes was the prime mover and commanding figure of the Kehillah: its idealogue, administrator, community spokesman, political mediator, fund raiser, and propagandist. Critics would later claim that his domineering leadership was one cause of the Kehillah's failure. Yet one is hard put to suggest another person who could have undertaken such a task. For a time Magnes, a Reform rabbi, though no longer holding a pulpit, succeeded in bringing together the embittered, demoralized Orthodox rabbis in an attempt to stem the erosion of rabbinical authority and revitalize Orthodox institutions. His outstanding work as labor mediator, together with

25. Arthur A. Goren, *New York Jews and the Quest for Community: the Kehillah Experiment* (New York, 1970), pp. 34–39, 94–96, 207–208, 276.

26. JLM, "The Jewish Community of New York," February 27, 1909, document 8; Goren, *New York Jews*, pp. 3–6, 245–52.

Paul Abelson of the Kehillah's Bureau of Industry, brought him into regular contact with the labor and industrial leaders of the needle trades. Social welfare planning led to the establishment of a philanthropic research bureau and a school for Jewish social workers and the formation of the New York Federation of Philanthropies.

The Kehillah's major effort, funded almost entirely by Schiff and Warburg, was directed toward improving Jewish religious education. The bureau of education, headed by the innovative, resourceful educator Samson Benderly, inaugurated a wide range of reforms guided by the new educational thought, from establishing model schools to producing graded Hebrew-language textbooks. This first communal educational agency marked a new period in the field of Jewish education. In all these activities Magnes succeeded in gathering about him a group of devoted professionals and talented young novices, especially in the field of education. His closest coworkers were Israel Friedlaender, Mordecai Kaplan, Henrietta Szold, and Samson Benderly. They recruited and trained the first cadre of professional Jewish educators — Alexander Dushkin, Isaac B. Berkson, Israel S. Chipkin, and Leo Honor, among others.[27]

Magnes drew upon the American experience and ethos as well as upon Jewish sources and needs to justify an American kehillah. Not only would effective Jewish community organization assure group continuity and lay the groundwork for a Jewish cultural revival, he argued; it would also alleviate the psychic stresses and social disorganization caused by immigration. In a 1909 sermon entitled significantly "A Republic of Nationalities" Magnes declared that "the hiatus between the traditional culture and the new surroundings" was often so great that it led to "degeneracy" because "the chain of tradition had been broken." Generational conflict, the collapse of moral guidelines, and a social morass so evident among the children of the immigrants was the consequence. In these views Magnes echoed the progressive settlement-house workers in arguing for the cultural integrity of the immigrant group.[28]

Group survival, however, was more than a prophylactic measure. Ethnic pluralism was the essence of American nationality. In his 1909 sermon Magnes presented one of the first formulations of what came to be known as cultural pluralism. America was not a "Moloch demanding the sacrifice of national individuality." Democracy and liberty were no less valid for the group than for the individual: "A national soul is as precious and as God given as is the individual soul." Magnes pursued the theme some months later in a harsh critique of Israel Zangwill's play *The Melting Pot*. He rejected its "pernicious message" of ethnic fusion. Using

27. Goren, *New York Jews*, pp. 57–66, 117–123.
28. Ibid., pp. 47–48.

Zangwill's metaphor of America as a great symphony still in the process of being written, he wrote: "[Zangwill's] symphony . . . would be a vast monotone . . . The symphony of America must be written by the various nationalities which keep their individual and characteristic note, and which sound this note in harmony with their sister nationalities. Then it will be a symphony of color, of picturesqueness, of character, of distinction—not the harmony of the Melting Pot, but rather the harmony of sturdiness and loyalty and joyous struggle."[29]

In 1917, in the waning days of the Kehillah, Magnes reformulated the implication of the Kehillah experiment for America: "[It] must be that instrumentality through which the Jews of America exercise self-determination, exercise the right and the privilege of every group to determine what they want to become in this country, what they want to do, what their relationship shall be with one another . . . Rightly used, it will come to be regarded as one of the many group endeavors which may be of aid to the American people in understanding and furthering the development of so complex a unit as America."[30]

The outbreak of war in 1914 profoundly affected the course of Jewish affairs. The Jewish public, alarmed over the fate of millions of European kinsmen, now channeled its best energies into overseas relief and a search for effective ways of rendering political and moral aid to East European Jewry. New movements appeared and new personalities confronted the established leaders. Most notable was the extraordinary growth of the Zionist organization under its new leader, Louis D. Brandeis. Inevitably the Kehillah, and Magnes in particular, became enmeshed in a power struggle. As a key member of both the American Jewish Committee and the newly formed Provisional Executive Committee for General Zionist Affairs, and as the chairman of the Kehillah, he saw his primary role once again as mediator and artificer of unity. But his basic organizational strategy, which in 1909 had appeared constructive and had indeed proven itself in the years that followed, now undermined Magnes's effectiveness.

To achieve a coalition between the established community and the immigrant community, the sine qua non for the success of the Kehillah, Magnes had negotiated an agreement between the Marshall group and the leaders of the downtown community in 1909, making the Kehillah the New York division of the American Jewish Committee. The Kehillah's executive committee served on the American Jewish Comittee representing New York's Jews. It was Magnes's intention that this model

<hr>

29. JLM, "A Republic of Nationalities," *The Emanu-El Pulpit*, 3 (February 13, 1909); "The Melting Pot," document 9.

30. Report to the Ninth Annual Convention of the Kehillah, June 1, 1918, pp. 17–18, MP, 1516.

be followed elsewhere, and in fact a kehillah was established in Philadelphia. Magnes's object was twofold: to create a national system of kehillahs and by their affiliation with the American Jewish Committee to democratize the latter, turning it into the central representative agency of the American Jewish community. So long as the local kehillahs were restricted to dealing with local problems and national and international questions remained the exclusive prerogative of the central body — and this was the proviso of the agreement — the committee leaders saw little threat to their position.[31]

All this changed when a new national Jewish organization came into being, directly challenging the hegemony of the American Jewish Committee. In the fall of 1914 Louis Brandeis lent his support to the creation of a democratically elected American Jewish Congress to represent all of American Jewry in international affairs. Ironically Magnes was among the first to sense the need for extraordinary measures to mobilize American Jewry's full capacity to meet its wartime responsibilities. Repeatedly he attempted to convince the committee to take the lead in sponsoring a congress. As the acrimonious debates and desultory negotiations continued, Magnes's attempts to reconcile the two groups came to naught Forced to choose sides, Magnes supported the American Jewish Committee position.[32]

Loyalty to Schiff and Marshall was surely a factor in his changing his public stance. Their support had enabled Magnes to score his greatest triumphs. Their continued collaboration was essential to the success of the Kehillah and his work for Jewish education. He admired too their utter devotion to the welfare of the community. In their involvement in every major issue and crisis in American Jewish life they had no peers. If they were stubborn and short-sighted in opposing the idea of a congress, Magnes believed that they would accept the idea in time. One could not simply reject the men who had carried the main burden of Jewish leadership. Moreover, by the end of 1915 in Magnes's mind the congress issue had degenerated into a naked power struggle to depose the committee; indeed, in the words of Louis Lipsky, a leading Zionist, the congress would "put the American Jewish Committee out of existence." Mistrust and perhaps envy of Brandeis's meteoric rise to Jewish leadership exacerbated the situation. Brandeis was the newcomer who had been indifferent to Jewish needs while others had accepted the arduous task of Jewish leadership. Then at the first sign of interest on his part the Zionists had made him their chief. If Brandeis's hasty rise to power and his sponsorship of the congress movement were examples of Jewish democracy at

31. Goren, *New York Jews*, pp. 44–56.
32. Ibid., pp. 218–226.

work, then Magnes was determined to expose the demagogy and irresponsibility involved. Thus it was not merely out of past gratitude and current exigencies that Magnes sided with the committee. It was no less his conviction that one had to speak against the crowd when it was wrong. Later his wartime pacifism would bring him into confrontation with the very group he now supported.[33]

In the public's mind, however, Magnes had sided with the autocrats. It appeared as though he who had led the Jewish Defense Association, had graced Zionist platforms with his presence and had created the Kehillah to spread the gospel of democracy and unity in Jewish life had betrayed his most sacred principles. At the 1915 Zionist convention the once great favorite of Zionist audiences was spurned by the rank and file and by their leaders. That summer he resigned from the Provisional Zionist Committee and accused Brandeis and his Zionist followers of fomenting disunity among American Jews. By agitating for a congress, he claimed, they were deviating from the movement's central purpose: concern over Palestine. Rather than devoting themselves singlemindedly to implementing Zionist aims, they were dissipating their strength in Jewish communal politics and alienating potential sympathizers who had reservations about the organizational form, the program, indeed the wisdom of a Jewish congress. It was he, Magnes, who had remained true to the cause.

He also took issue with the Zionist diplomatic policy the goal of which was winning a special political status in Palestine at the conclusion of the war. "I want equal rights for the Jews, no more and no less, in all parts of the world, including Palestine," he wrote to Brandeis in September 1915. All the Jews had a right to ask for, he continued, was the opportunity "to migrate to and settle in and develop their Jewish economic and cultural life in Palestine freely, just as other peoples of the [Ottoman] Empire have the same right." Given the same rights as others — no special political or group preferment — it would be up to the Jewish people to show its creative powers. In July 1916, shortly after Brandeis's elevation to the Supreme Court, the two men participated in a negotiating session sponsored by the American Jewish Committee looking toward a compromise formula on a congress. In the course of the meeting Magnes dramatically rebuked Brandeis for his intransigence in holding to his maximalist position. The incident provoked a furious public counterresponse when the *New York Times* sharply criticized the Justice for failing to maintain a proper judicial deportment by engaging in public controversy. When

33. Ibid., pp. 219, 307; Yonathan Shapiro, *Leadership of the American Zionist Organization, 1897-1930* (Urbana, Ill., 1971), pp. 82-85, 88-92.

22

Brandeis soon after resigned all offices he held in Jewish organizations, many blamed Magnes for forcing Brandeis out of Jewish public life.[34]

It is indicative of Magnes's standing that he continued to play a significant role on the American Jewish scene even after the decline in his influence in 1915 and despite his pacifist activity beginning in 1917. His work on behalf of the JDC was outstanding. At the mass meetings called across the country to raise funds Magnes was the speaker most in demand. In the summer of 1916 he was sent on a four-month mission to Poland to investigate the problem of distributing relief. During the war years he also served on the JDC subcommittee that received reports from overseas and recommended the allocation of funds. His efforts to reorganize and expand the Kehillah failed in the end, but he succeeded in assuring the continued operation of some of its important agencies. However, he lost his position as the popular leader with admirers in all camps. Henceforth he would be not the organizer of men or the mediator between rival interests but the patrician agitator and dissenter.[35]

A second searing experience, the political events of 1917, contributed to the reshaping of Magnes's world of ideas and to his behavior as a public figure. Abruptly in March 1917, as the United States moved toward war, Magnes plunged into American political affairs. To the consternation of friends and the community at large, he took up the causes of pacifism, civil liberties, and anti-imperialism with his characteristic zeal, passion, and abandon. For the next five years, until he and his family sailed for Palestine, he singlemindedly supported these causes while suffering indignities, alienating friends, and jeopardizing his position in the community.

There were few portents that foreshadowed Magnes's sudden turn from Jewish concerns to universal crusades. In all his years in the pulpit, his sermons, unlike those of his contemporary Stephen Wise, dealt exclusively with Jewish themes. As a young man of twenty-one he had rebuked his parents for supporting the war against Spain. On hearing of the assassination of President McKinley, he commented in a letter home, "I cannot say that I am ready to be enraged at the anarchists for it all. In my opinion dishonest men in public office are greater anarchists than those who kill a president once in twenty years." But such flippant remarks reflect at best no more than a youthful anger against injustice rather than his later, full-blown radicalism.[36]

34. JLM to Louis D. Brandeis, June 30, 1915, document 20; Israel Friedlaender to Louis D. Brandeis, September 2, 1915, Friedlaender Papers; JLM to Louis D. Brandeis, September 2, 1915, document 22; Melvin I. Urofsky, *American Zionism from Herzl to the Holocaust* (New York, 1975), pp. 175–179; JLM to Louis Brandeis, July 25, 1916, document 24.

35. Goren, *New York Jews*, pp. 215–218.

36. JLM to family, September 29, 1901, MP, 10a.

Clearly it was his admiration for the Yiddish-speaking socialists, whom he began to know well following his arrival in New York, that proved decisive in fashioning his social radicalism. Their self-help endeavors, particularly the Jewish labor movement, their conviction that czarism could be defeated only by the uprising of the Russian people, and the broad humanitarianism that characterized the best of Yiddish culture in the Jewish quarter appealed to Magnes as they appealed to Brandeis, Marshall, the social worker Lillian Wald of the Henry Street Settlement, and other progressives. In Magnes's case his sympathy for the lot of the immigrant worker and the struggling Jewish trade unions led him to labor arbitration and then, in 1917, to support Morris Hillquit, the socialist candidate for mayor of New York and a leader of the Jewish labor movement. Magnes's abhorrence of czarism, heightened and personalized by his relief mission to Poland, determined in large measure his stand on international affairs. Thus his anticzarism, coupled with his radicalization on social issues, explains much of his sympathy for the Russian Revolution even after others became disenchanted with the Bolshevik regime.

Central to Magnes's radicalism was his pacifism. He interpreted the antiwar sentiment of the Yiddish socialists, which he perceived as indigenous to the Jewish immigrant colony, as rooted in the Judaism of East European Jewry no less than in its political ethos. In October 1917 Magnes told a private gathering of Hillquit campaign workers, "This hatred of all the arts of soldiering, this repugnance for war, this abhorrence of blood spilling that has characterized the Jewish masses, is nothing more or less than a continuance of the great Jewish tradition which exalted the spiritual life of Jacob and condemned the brute force of Esau." In his journal he expanded on what he called the Jewish immigrants' "passion for peace," and in doing so he also wrote of himself. Not only did their "outburst against war" reveal the very essence of the Jewish tradition — Judaism's exaltation of the sanctity of life — but it surged up from the depth of Jewish life and experience. "How many empires have we not seen destroyed, how many cities laid waste; how many battle cries have we not heard, the iron of how many armies pierced our flesh; how many religions and philosophies and ideals and patriotisms have we not seen justifying the slaughter of men."[37]

His antiwar position, the cornerstone of his radicalism, also accorded with Jewish interests as he understood them. With the outbreak of war in 1914 Magnes had taken an adamant stand on neutrality, an attitude shared by most Americans but a dire necessity for Jews. He insisted that

37. JLM, "Remarks, Private Supper for Socialist Campaign Workers," October 18, 1917, MP, 1252; JLM, journal, October 2, 1917, document 26.

the Zionist movement and American Jewry maintain strict neutrality so as not to endanger Palestine's Jews or cripple efforts to aid a Jewish population in Eastern Europe split between the contending armies in the eastern war zone. With the fall of the Czar in March 1917 and the American declaration of war in April, Jewish and indeed humanitarian considerations called for a quick end to the bloodshed. But the war crisis during the early months of 1917 focused his attention primarily on the general issue. Magnes's response proved almost identical to that of a small group of liberal social gospel ministers led by Norman Thomas and John Haynes Holmes, with whom he established close ties. All three, moved by a religious humanism, joined their social reform concerns to a new, aggressive pacifism: the roots of war were to be found in the unjust economic system; only a democratic, anti-imperialist, international radicalism would bring about the just society.[38]

In February 1917, as the United States broke diplomatic relations with Germany and began moving quickly toward war, Magnes plunged into antiwar activities. There was not an important protest meeting in the East in which he did not appear as a principal speaker: February in Washington, March in New York's Madison Square Garden, April again in Washington. On April 5 Magnes was chairman of a conference of representatives of the various peace groups that took place in New York. In the weeks that followed he devoted his time to forming a new, more militant peace movement. At two major pacifist rallies, the first held in New York May 30-31 and the second in Chicago on September 2, Magnes appeared as keynoter. The establishment of the People's Council of America for Democracy and Peace, proposed at the May meeting, was formally completed at the September conference. Conceived as a mass movement of radicals, workingmen, and farmers, the People's Council borrowed its name and its peace program from the Petrograd Soviet, the revolutionary workers' council. Its slogan was: "No forcible annexations, no punitive indemnities, free development of all nations, peoples and nationalities."[39]

Magnes was now collaborating closely with socialists such as Hillquit, Scott Nearing (the chairman of the People's Council), Crystal and

38. JLM to Louis D. Brandeis, May 24, 1915, MP, 755; JLM to Chaim Weizmann, January 24, 1915, MP, 838; Zosa Szajkowski, "The Pacifism of Judah Magnes," *Conservative Judaism,* 22 (Spring 1968), 37; Goren, *New York Jews,* p. 231; C. Roland Marchand, *The American Peace Movement and Social Reform, 1898-1918* (Princeton, 1972), pp. 231-235, 249-259, 263-264, 334-335.

39. *New York Times,* March 25, 1917, p. 1; April 3, 1917, p. 12; JLM, "The People Do Not Want War," March 24, 1917, MP, 1203; Minutes of Conference of Members of Various Peace Groups, April 5, 1917, Emergency Peace Federation Papers, Swarthmore College, Swarthmore, Pa.; *New York Times,* June 1, 1917, p. 1; JLM, *War-Time Addresses, 1917-1921* (New York, 1923), pp. 10-26; Norman Thomas to JLM, June 2, 1917, MP, 1221.

Max Eastman, Jacob Panken, and J. B. Salutsky and social reformers such as Emily Balch, Roger Baldwin, John Haynes Holmes, Louis Lochner, Amos Pinchot, Norman Thomas, Oswald Garrison Villard, and Walter Weyl. Pacifism led to the civil liberties movement, and Magnes became a founder and director of the National Civil Liberties Bureau, predecessor of the American Civil Liberties Union. He participated in protest meetings and in negotiations with the Attorney General to free Eugene Debs, the socialist leader imprisoned for sedition. Magnes addressed meetings demanding constitutional rights for conscientious objectors, called for an "amnesty for political prisoners," and raised funds for the defense of Tom Mooney and Sacco and Vanzetti.[40]

If this was the evil at home, his country and its allies were committing evil abroad. Magnes condemned the peace negotiations as that "gigantic slave market at Paris and Versailles, where whole peoples have been exchanged and bought and sold." He spoke out against the Allied intervention in Russia and demanded that the embargo on medical relief for the Soviet Union be lifted. Like others among the antiwar liberals he saw the Bolshevik revolution as heralding a new epoch. In May 1919, sharing a platform with John Haynes Holmes, Amos Pinchot, Frederick C. Howe, and Lincoln Colcord, Magnes told a Madison Square Garden meeting, "What the Allied governments are afraid of is . . . the power of the Soviet idea, the victorious march of a newer and better social order." In a Chicago address, "The Old America and the New," he described a new America whose political system had turned oppressive and whose economic system had become cruelly exploitive. For the people of Europe not the United States but Soviet Russia now stood forth as "a beacon on the hill-tops, cheering on the agonizing peoples with a light in the darkness, with new hopes and philosophies, with wondrous longings."[41]

Jewish leaders were dismayed over Magnes's political activities. Marshall voiced their distress in a blunt letter to his brother-in-law written June 1, 1917:

> By taking such a prominent position as you are in this agitation, you are jeopardizing other interests . . . which you have no right to imperil. You are the head of the Kehillah. You are a leader of the cause of Jewish education. You are one of the principal workers in the efforts to bring relief to our brethren in the war zone. What right have you, therefore, merely for

40. Marchand, *The American Peace Movement*, pp. 303–306, 309–322; Bentwich, *For Zion's Sake*, pp. 102–107; Scott Nearing to JLM and Morris Hillquit, January 23, 1918, MP, 1236; JLM to Walter Weyl, January 25, 1918, MP, 1335; JLM to Max Eastman, February 5, 1918, MP, 1335; Memorandum of Conference with Attorney General April 17, 1919, MP, 1244; Norman Thomas to JLM, July 28, 1919, MP, 1335; Magnes, *War-Time Addresses*, pp. 63–81.

41. JLM, War-Time Addresses, pp. 45, 89; Goren, *New York Jews*, p. 233.

the purpose of voicing your personal views on a matter as to which the overwhelming opinion of America is opposed to you, to injure these great causes in which you are concerned, and not only injure them, but to injure the Jewish people of America with whom you are so actively identified.[42]

His isolation from the Jewish community grew, and pressure mounted on him to withdraw from Jewish public life altogether. Magnes in fact offered to resign as head of the Kehillah, but it would have only highlighted the community's embarrassment and "raised public issues which it was deemed advisable not to raise." In July 1919, taking stock, he wrote in the privacy of his journal: "I was gratified that during the war I had the z'khut [privilege] and the z'khiya [merit] to have said the things I did, to have taken the stand I did. Would it not have been a disgrace to the Jewish people had none — particularly no Jewish teacher of religion — taken the pacifist and radical stand? Yet I realized that this was harmful to the Kehillah as an organization."[43]

Magnes's pacifist radicalism was inseparable from his approach to Zionist politics. He regarded Britain's issuance of the Balfour Declaration in November 1917, favoring the establishment of a Jewish national home in Palestine, as a calculated move to further imperialistic goals. British promises, therefore, had no real value. Contradictory offers had been made to each side; and had they not been, Britain would not have hesitated to interpret her solemn obligation to the Zionists in whatever way best served her interests. The San Remo Conference in 1920, where the Allied powers assigned the mandate for Palestine to Britain, was "the legitimate heir to Versailles," Magnes wrote to a friend. "Almost every principle of democracy, of self-determination is denied. The fact is that Palestine has five or six times as many Arabs as Jews. You speak of the 'historic rights' of the Jews to offset the claims of the present-day Arab majority. I am aware of the way in which historic rights and strategic rights and economic rights have been manipulated whenever it suited the needs of the conquerors." Magnes rejected the notion of a preferred political status for the Jewish people. "We want free access to the land, free opportunity to develop it and freedom to live the Jewish life in the broadest sense of this term. Nor do we want political privileges to be conferred upon anyone else."[44] Magnes, looking for those with similar views, was drawn to the Socialist Zionists. Jewish pioneers, the Workers of Zion, building a cooperative society in Palestine were demonstrating "the essential harmony between a broad, liberal Jewish nationalism and their deep radicalism." He addressed the meetings of their American sup-

42. Charles Reznikoff, ed., *Louis Marshall, Champion of Liberty*, vol. 2 (Philadelphia, 1957), pp. 971–974.
43. JLM, journal, July 18, 1919, MP, 294.
44. JLM to Dear Friend, May, 1920, document 33.

porters, and when a delegation representing the Histadrut, the federation of Jewish labor, arrived in the United States to raise funds for a workers' bank and settlements, Magnes poured all of his energies into the undertaking. The "workers of Zion," he declared in a public address in 1919, would, he hoped, oppose the Jewish people's becoming "the tail to any imperialist kite" and would "convince the Arab peoples, themselves struggling for freedom and liberty and independence, that we Jews want nothing for ourselves that we are not willing to give to every one." Thus in the midst of jubilation, in the years between the Balfour Declaration and the San Remo Conference, Magnes warned against reliance upon the English and pleaded the importance of the Arab question. His was the only voice in the United States to sound such an alarm.[45]

For the humanist rabbi, social radical, and pacifist internationalist, the times in America were disheartening. In June 1920 Magnes asked to be released from the chairmanship of the Kehillah. Among the reasons he offered the most compelling was a personal one: a desire for "a year without the responsibility for the conduct of any organization" so that he might seek "replenishment of knowledge and inspiration."

> It is my firm belief that a new era in human history is beginning as a result of the war. New forms of life are developing. In this change, it is the Old World which is becoming the New. For this reason, I am anxious to come into direct contact, if this be possible, with the new life that is developing in the Old World. Moreover, the Jews, in their great majority, are at the center of the Old World and new life. And I hope that, by contact with them after these years of their suffering and struggle, I may have a deeper understanding than at present of the Jewish destiny.[46]

Circumstances delayed his departure for two years, and when he finally undertook his journey of replenishment it brought him and his family to Jerusalem. Before leaving he told a farewell gathering: "I am going to Europe and Eretz Israel on a humble mission: to Europe in order to get in touch with the humble scholars, writers, artists, teachers, and students of our people to see if it may not be possible to work out a tentative plan in accordance with which Judaism may continue to strike root and grow."[47] He had two objectives: one was a mission on behalf of the JDC to plan for the reconstruction of Jewish cultural life in Eastern Europe. But his primary goal was Eretz Israel. He was going to Eretz Israel "not as

45. JLM, *War-Time Addresses*, pp. 112–115; JLM, "The Palestine Workers Bank," January 29, 1922; Yehuda Erez, ed., *Igrot B. Katznelson, 1921–1930* (Tel Aviv, 1973), pp. 23–24, 31, 60, 104, 106, 112, 127.
46. JLM to members of the Executive Committee of the Kehillah, June 3, 1920, document 34.
47. Bentwich, *For Zion's Sake*, p. 126.

a leader ... but simply as a Jew ... bound to it not through any political program, but through Judaism, which I cannot conceive of without its roots planted there."[48]

As a perceptive study has shown, Magnes's decision to settle in Palestine was not *aliya* in the classic Zionist sense; it was not a "premeditated decision to make a permanent move to Palestine," nor did it represent a negation of life in the Diaspora. Shortly after his arrival in Jerusalem, in May 1923, he delivered a public lecture vigorously defending the integrity of Diaspora Judaism. "Everyone who lives here in Eretz Israel and works," he concluded his talk, "is helping the Jewish people create spiritual values and is thus aiding the Jewish people to carry out its work in the world. The same is true of those who live and work in the Galut. Where a man can do best for his people is an individual and private matter."[49]

In the first years of the family's stay there were strong pulls to return to the United States. Warburg and others urged Magnes to head a major new fund to advance Jewish educational work in all of its facets. Radical friends—Scott Nearing, Norman Thomas, and Bertha Weyl (Walter Weyl's widow)—wrote to him of how sorely he was needed. Moreover, adjusting to Jerusalem and establishing a home took its toll on Mrs. Magnes's health and spirit despite their warm welcome into government and Zionist social circles. Herbert Bentwich, the English Zionist and attorney general of the mandatory government, and Henrietta Szold, the administrator of the Hadassah health service, became steadfast friends, and there were others. However, Beatrice underwent periods of despondency. She and Judah suffered from a severe case of malaria. Most difficult of all, she saw little prospect for Judah's securing a suitable post that would bring the security and peace of mind she craved. The only way, Magnes wrote, to relieve his wife of "the helpless and hopeless feeling that so often overtakes her" was to establish a home "once and for all" in which she would have "a permanent interest" and where he would settle down in some fixed position. This he believed could happen only in America, "and perhaps the sooner we get to it the better for all of us."[50]

Fortuitously, planning for the opening of the Hebrew University gained momentum shortly after Magnes's arrival. In the fall of 1923 he joined an ad hoc committee that included Ahad Ha'am (then living in Tel Aviv), Bentwich, the veteran Zionist leader Menahem Ussishkin, and the

48. Ibid., 126.

49. Goell, "*Aliyah*," 108, 112; JLM, "Eretz Israel and the Galut," English version of address delivered in Jerusalem, May 22, 1923, document 41, for published Hebrew version see *Hapoel Hatsair*, June 8, 1923, pp. 9–11.

50. Beatrice Magnes, *Episodes*, pp. 76–84; Goell, "*Aliyah*," 112–113; Bentwich, *For Zion's Sake*, pp. 129–130; JLM, journal, June 16–18, August 1–6, 1923, documents 42, 43; JLM, journal, September 10, 1923, MP, 306.

Jerusalem scholars, including the historian Joseph Klausner, the authority on Hebrew poetry and language David Yellin, and the Orientalist Leo Mayer. Magnes's success in persuading Felix Warburg, who visited Palestine in 1924, to establish a $.5 million endowment for the Institute of Jewish Studies led to intensive negotiations between Magnes, representing Warburg and the Jerusalem committee, and Weizmann, representing the Zionist Organization, heretofore the sole sponsor of the university undertaking. In December 1924 the institute was inaugurated, and the following April the opening convocation of the university took place on Mount Scopus, the site of the campus. That September the newly formed board of governors elected Weizmann president of the board, Magnes chancellor, or executive officer, of the university, and Albert Einstein, already a world-renowned scientist, chairman of the academic council.[51]

For Magnes the role was a monumental one. The ideal of the Hebrew University encompassed his many worlds. It was Judaism, humanism, internationalism, Eretz Israel, the meeting of East and West, and the mission of the Jewish people to the world. It was, above all, Ahad Ha'amism, the realization of spiritual Zionism. As Magnes wrote to Weizmann as early as 1913: "Most important of all, the Jewish university must be the heart of that spiritual center which we have been constantly talking of establishing in Palestine. My chief interest in the whole matter lies in the hope that a Jewish university will give to Judaism, as much as to the Jews, new and fresh values." It would also blend the universal and the Jewish. Thus he assigned highest priority to a school of Geisteswissenschaften (humanities), where history, literature, and philosophy would be taken up "using Jewish materials primarily, but by no means exclusively, as the basis of instruction." In Jerusalem, unlike elsewhere, Jewish studies would not be compartmentalized; for there, uniquely, the particular and the universal would be studied as a harmonious whole. Judaism and the Jewish religion would also occupy a prominent place in the school of arts and attract Jewish teachers and ministers from all over the world.[52]

From the outset Weizmann's priorities were different: he felt that precedence should be given to the natural sciences and to the establishment of a medical school, which would meet some of the most pressing needs of the country. He envisioned a number of specialized scientific research institutes, the core of the university, dedicated to pure science but also

51. Goell, "Aliyah," 113–114; Herbert Parzen, The Hebrew University, 1925–1935 (New York, 1974), pp. 2–3; JLM to Julian Mack, November 4, 1925, document 52; David Yellin and Menachem Ussishkin (Jerusalem Committee for the Establishment of an Arts Faculty) to Zionist Executive, September 27, 1923, Chaim Weizmann Papers, Library of the Weizmann Institute, Rehovoth, Israel.
52. JLM to Chaim Weizmann, May 25, 1913, document 17; JLM, Addresses by the Chancellor, pp. 6–7, 16–18, 181–183.

serving the development needs of the yishuv, the Zionist settlement in Palestine. Weizmann in fact had devoted much of his energies to preparing the groundwork for such a university in the years immediately preceding and following the war. Through his efforts the Zionist organization purchased land on Mount Scopus, and it was he who converted Einstein to the idea of a Hebrew university in Jerusalem. The two undertook the first fund-raising campaign for the university in 1921 when they toured the United States and found support for the establishment of institutes of microbiology and chemistry, the nucleus of a future faculty of medicine.[53]

From 1925 to 1935, until Magnes was relieved of direct responsibility for university affairs and elected to the honorary position of president, he was in effect administrator, fund raiser, planner, and academic head. The burden was staggering. He faced mounting pressures to enlarge the research facilities and absorb qualified senior and junior scientists, a situation that became desperate after Hitler's rise to power. Begun with an almost exclusive concern for research, the university soon was called on to expand teaching facilities, increase student enrollment, and offer degree-granting programs. Income, nearly 70 percent of which came from American donors, allowed modest but steady growth in the first years of the university. Then the economic depression of the 1930s thwarted expansion. When many scores of scholars expelled from German universities by the Nazi regime looked to Jerusalem for places, the university absorbed only a small part of those prepared to come. During these years Magnes made periodic trips to the United States to raise money, visits that became increasingly frustrating, and to Europe to attend meetings of the board of governors, where contending interests and personal rivalries hampered the functioning of an already cumbersome governing structure.[54]

Compounding the problem at home was the absence of a university tradition. Scholars drawn from scores of European and American universities brought widely differing academic conventions and standards; questions of status, advancement, and governance became highly charged issues. Personality conflicts exacerbated by Jewish politics, to which Magnes contributed his share, further complicated matters. However, in these early years of the national home, when the yishuv's growth was disappointingly slow, the university despite its small size loomed large as a symbol of national renewal and as an intellectual and spiritual center of the Jewish people. Consequently the chancellor of the

53. Chaim Weizmann to JLM, April 19, 1913, June 15, 1913, December 3, 1913, MP, 838.
54. JLM, *Addresses by the Chancellor*, pp. 20–25, 212–214, 284–285; JLM, journal, March 23, 1932, document 69.

Hebrew University occupied a preeminent position in Jewish public life.[55]

Well before Magnes reentered political life, in the wake of the 1929 riots in Palestine, portents of the difficulties ahead were manifest. Magnes had long since broken with official Zionism and with Weizmann, since 1918 its dominant figure. His supporters and admirers were the wealthy American non-Zionists represented most visibly by Marshall and Warburg. Their philanthropic interest in the university was predicated in no small measure on their faith in Magnes's ability to keep the university free of Zionist domination. Magnes in fact opposed Weizmann's election as president of the board of governors "because he was head of the political Zionist organization." Zionist control, he wrote, "would make of the university something partisan and sectarian, whereas it ought to be the university of all sections of the Jewish people."[56]

For Weizmann the argument was a specious one; Zionism was the movement of Jewish national revival. The Zionist organization, he wrote to Magnes in December 1925, "was the only big democratic Jewish organization through which every Jew . . . can bring his spiritual values and aspirations to bear on the shaping of this new spiritual center . . . Must the influence of a great organization which has constantly to render account of its doings to its adherents and to the public at large be necessarily worse than those of a few men of finance who make big contributions?"[57]

However, the fact that during these years Weizmann sought to win the non-Zionists for an enlarged Jewish Agency — the body designated by the mandate to represent the Jewish people in building the national home — forced him into an uneasy partnership with Magnes, the confidant of Marshall, Warburg, and their friends. Weizmann moreover recognized fully that their aid was essential for the development of the university. He hoped too that this joint endeavor to build the university would go hand in hand with establishing the enlarged Jewish Agency.

The animosity between Weizmann and Magnes went beyond divergent interests and approaches to the university. For Weizmann the university was a cherished offspring; he had been intimately tied to its development from the beginning, until it had slipped out of his hands. Weizmann, moreover, the academician and scientist, regarded Magnes as a "dilettante," as he stated on more than one occasion. Writing to Einstein in July 1926, at the end of the university's first year, Weizmann said: "I

55. Parzen, *Hebrew University*, pp. 7–8, 13–21, 43–57; Bentwich, *For Zion's Sake*, pp. 160–171.
56. JLM to Felix Warburg, April 11, 1924, document 46; JLM to Julian W. Mack, November 4, 1925, document 52.
57. Chaim Weizmann to JLM, December 15, 1925, *The Letters and Papers of Chaim Weizmann*, ed. Joshua Freundlich, vol. 12 (New Brunswick, N.J., 1977), p. 456.

am convinced that your diagnosis of the situation that things cannot go on with Dr. Magnes, and that sooner or later one must definitely get rid of him, is absolutely right. But if you now withdraw your proposal and, instead of urging Dr. Magnes' resignation, now withdraw yourself, what can I do then? I must then stop half-way, because I cannot personally lead the attack against Dr. Magnes in view of my political responsibilities, and the result will be, of course, that Dr. Magnes will remain in power — but this time for good." If Weizmann felt disdain for Magnes, Magnes harbored mistrust for Weizmann. He recognized Weizmann's courage and vision, "but it is his moral quality that is questionable. He is through and through the politician. He is constantly playing a game, very cleverly, and one does not know what he is after."[58]

Discord at the top, academic intrigue within, and moves to depose him from without dogged Magnes in the work of building the university. Einstein, who barely knew Magnes and never visited the university, like Weizmann considered him unqualified to head the institution. He was not a scientist but a theologian, not an independent scholar but the servant of his American donors; he would turn the institution into an American "diploma factory," Einstein insisted. A stream of biased reports by disgruntled academics reached Einstein's ear. The resulting image, magnified by the extravagant expectations both he and Weizmann held for the university, distorted the legitimate differences that existed between them and Magnes. It blinded them no less to the enormous obstacles to be overcome in creating a great scientific center "on the fringe of Asia." Nevertheless, in the ten years of his leadership Magnes built solid foundations for the faculties of science and humanities and directed the growth of the research institutes, which responded to the yishuv's physical and cultural needs ranging from Arabic studies to Judaic and archeological scholarship to malaria control. The nuclei of distinguished departments of mathematics and physics were established. Although Magnes was accused of being autocratic and inaccessible to junior faculty, few denied that he had infused the university with a sense of dignity and purpose. Certainly his contribution to the reputation of the university as a forum for free, uninhibited intellectual discourse was decisive. To Magnes, a dissenter in Zion, this was the essential attribute of the university.[59]

The opening of the 1929 academic year took place in November in the

58. Parzen, *Hebrew University*, pp. 102–109; Chaim Weizmann to Albert Einstein, May 19, 1926, July 19, 1926, May 13, 1928, *The Letters and Papers of Chaim Weizmann*, ed. Pinhas Ofer, vol. 13 (New Brunswick, N.J., 1978), pp. 16–17, 67, 399–400; JLM, journal, February 13, 1928, document 58.

59. JLM to Dear Friend, April 28, 1929, document 63; Albert Einstein to Chaim Weizmann, May 29, 1928, and Albert Einstein to Academic Council and Board of Governors of the Hebrew University, May 29, 1928, in Parzen, *Hebrew University*, pp. 16–20.

shadow of the week-long riots of the previous August, when Arab bands had attacked the Jewish communities of Hebron and Safed and a score of outlying settlements. After eight years of relative quiet the extent and savagery of the killings and pillage shocked the yishuv. The initial response of the Jewish populace was to ascribe the attacks to Arab religious fanaticism and a breakdown of law and order: Muslim leaders had turned a dispute concerning holy day observances at the Wailing Wall into a religious uprising, while British forces were caught totally unprepared. As the weeks passed, the more fundamental question of Arab-Jewish relations, heretofore a matter of little concern, increasingly occupied the public interest. Few, however, cast the problem in terms of the moral dilemma of conflicting and, for each side, just claims to the land. In this setting Magnes used the opportunity of the university's convocation to address himself, for the first time since his arrival in Palestine, to a political issue. To his friend Norman Bentwich he had written in September:

> I feel that unless all of us are unflinchingly honest and intelligent there is but very little hope for our ideals. The most practical policy just now happens to be, so I think, the religious and the ethical and the idealistic policy . . . I begin to feel it to be my duty to speak again after years of silence. After all my "political" activities in Jewish New York with Zionism and the Kehillah, and then after what I went through during the war, I had felt that I had had enough, and I have been all too satisfied to give myself wholly to the university, and to keep away from politics. But I cannot hold my peace any longer.[60]

In his brief address he sounded the themes that he would pursue diligently for the rest of his life. Palestine was a land sui generis, neither Arab nor Jewish but the "Holy Land of two peoples . . . and of three religions." This transcendent fact had to guide the Zionist leadership in seeking an accommodation with the Arabs rather than continuing to depend on British arms. It required concessions. It called for overcoming the rage the yishuv still harbored because of "the intrigues of the instigators of the massacres" and the disappointment that not a single Arab leader "had the common humanity to express his sorrow" over the barbarities perpetrated by his people. Magnes proposed setting Zionist policy on a pacifist course. He called for a politics of morality, if need be at the expense of achieving the political aims of Zionism.

> If we cannot find ways of peace and understanding, if the only way of establishing the Jewish National Home is upon the bayonets of some Empire, our whole enterprise is not worthwhile, and it is better that the Eter-

60. Walter Laqueur, *A History of Zionism* (New York, 1976), pp. 255–56; Bentwich, *For Zion's Sake*, pp. 177–79; JLM to Norman Bentwich, September 13, 1929, MP, 2396.

nal People that has outlived many a mighty empire should possess its soul in patience and plan and wait. It is one of the great civilizing tasks before the Jewish people to try to enter the promised land, not in the Joshua way, but bringing peace and culture, hard work and sacrifice and love, and a determination to do nothing that cannot be justified before the conscience of the world.[61]

The address propelled Magnes into the eye of a storm of controversy that did not abate in the weeks and months that followed. On November 24 the *New York Times* carried a long statement by Magnes explaining his support for a binational government. Under international supervision such a government would be bound to the international obligations stipulated in the mandate that "guaranteed to all elements of the population —the majority as well as the minorities—their equal rights and privileges." Moreover, the fundamental law of the land recognized that "the Jewish people is in Palestine as of right and not of sufferance." This was sufficient to Magnes's mind to enable the Jews "to make a home in Palestine of the kind that Ahad Ha'am pictured, a spiritual and intellectual center for Judaism and the Jewish people, rooted in agriculture, industry, and all kinds of labor." Under such conditions, and at a time when the Jews formed less than a fifth of the population, Magnes favored establishing a legislative assembly; this was a key demand of the Arabs but was opposed by the Zionists.[62]

Magnes further explicated his program in a booklet, *Like All the Nations?*, which appeared in December 1929. Guarantee the Jews immigration, settlement on the land, Hebrew life and culture, he wrote, "and I should be willing to yield the Jewish 'State' and the Jewish 'majority'; and on the other hand I would agree to a legislative assembly together with a democratic regime so carefully planned and worked out that the above three fundamentals could not be infringed." Indeed he would be willing "to pay almost any price for these three, since this price would secure tranquillity and mutual understanding."[63]

But what of immigration, surely the fateful question? Magnes responded with a demographic analysis. Under optimal conditions it would take longer than a generation for Palestine to reach a total population of three million, considered by experts to be the maximum absorptive capacity of the country for the foreseeable future. Suppose through immigration Jews grew to a third of the total, from 160,000 to one million in thirty or forty years. Could one hope for more? "Why talk of 'majorities' and 'state' when even by the wildest stretch of the imagination

61. JLM, *Addresses by the Chancellor*, p. 62.
62. *New York Times*, November 24, 1929, p. 12, and section 2, p. 1.
63. *Like All the Nations?* (Jerusalem, 1930), p. 6.

35

we can hardly picture such a thing within an appreciable period." One day, "perhaps through some miracle in the future the Jews might become a majority." Drought in Palestine might lead to emigration of Arabs; while Jewish colonization might prove so beneficial that the Arab states or an Arab federation would welcome a Jewish majority in Palestine. "But surely no serious practical policy can be built up upon them, and it is a practical policy for the next 10–20–30– years we are after."[64]

In the years that followed, Magnes became the most vocal advocate of a binational state. At the same time he grounded his strategy for Arab-Jewish reconciliation on the principles enunciated in *Like All the Nations?*: avoid the issue of ultimate goals; seek an interim agreement, an armistice, that would not prejudice the ultimate national aspirations of either side. In his discussions with Arabs and with mandatory officials, and in his efforts to mediate between Arab and Zionist leaders, Magnes proposed an agreement for ten years, the first step in the process of making peace. During this period Jewish immigration would be allowed at a rate that would not endanger an Arab majority. At the end of the period, Magnes suggested, Jews would form no more than 40 percent of the population. In 1936, when Magnes reached a tentative understanding with the Arab leader Musa al-Alami, the agreed annual quota was thirty thousand Jews, about half the number that entered Palestine in the peak year of 1935. Magnes's plan included measures to meet Arab grievances connected with land sales to Jews, and it assigned a greater role to Arabs and Jews in governmental administration and policy making, a course in which Magnes placed great stock. Given the breathing space of a period of years of relative peace, he argued, the sharing of responsibility and the advantages of collaboration might placate mutual fears of domination and prepare the way for a further step in the direction of a permanent political solution.[65]

That next step consisted of a binational state in Palestine joined to a federation of Arab states that would include Trans-Jordan, Syria, Lebanon, and Palestine, one of the goals of the Arab nationalist movement. Doubly secure from the fear of Jewish expansionism by the binational arrangement in Palestine—which assured neither people domination over the other—and Palestine's membership in the federation, the Arabs might well agree to unlimited Jewish immigration to Palestine. Moreover, the member states of the federation, underpopulated and requiring capital and Western skills, could be expected to welcome a sizable Jewish

64. Ibid., p. 7.
65. Ibid., p. 8; JLM, memorandum, circa 1932, MP, 2401; Susan Lee Hattis, *The Bi-National Idea in Palestine during Mandatory Times* (Haifa, 1970, pp. 146–148.

immigration. Against the background of the mid-1930s the refugee problem — finding asylum anywhere — had become the urgent matter.[66]

Magnes's approach required reaching an accord with the Arabs through direct negotiations before turning to the British. He viewed London's twists and turns of policy — Churchill's White Paper of 1922, the Shaw Report and Passfield White Paper of 1930, the Peel Commission Report of 1937, and the 1939 White Paper — as determined by two contradictory motives. The British retreat from support of Zionist aspirations reflected growing Arab strength and militancy; yet Britain's moves were tempered by expressions of intent to execute her mandatory obligations to the Jews. Thus alongside the imperialist interest an English sense of fair play and contractual obligation produced genuine albeit sporadic attempts to deal with an immensely complex and volatile situation. Once Arabs and Jews took the initiative into their own hands, Magnes reasoned, British imperialist calculations would recognize the new reality. Then the British could be prevailed on to provide the needed governmental framework, authority, and good will to supervise the necessarily long process of conciliation and final settlement. Magnes's bipartite perception of the British, with all its ambiguity, enabled him, as a staunch pacifist and anti-imperialist, to criticize British policy and maintain at the same time an excellent rapport with His Majesty's colonial secretaries and high commissioners.[67]

The exigencies of the times, particularly the impact of the Second World War, led Magnes to revise certain of his views. In his most important wartime political statement, which appeared in *Foreign Affairs* in January 1943, he questioned his long-held belief that a compromise could be achieved through negotiations between the Jews and the Arabs: "In view of the intransigence of many responsible leaders on both sides the adjustment may have to be imposed over their opposition." To implement an imposed compromise the "association of the United States with Britain" was necessary if Palestine were not to become "a menace to the world's peace." Magnes also amended his stand on the immigration question. Should the Arab federation prove stillborn, political parity of the two peoples in the binational state would be applied to population as well, and as large a Jewish immigration as possible would be admitted in the shortest time possible to mitigate the fate of the thousands of refugees.[68]

66. JLM, "Palestine Peace Seen in Arab-Jewish Agreements," *New York Times*, July 18, 1937, document 83.
67. JLM to Nuri al-Sa'id, February 23, 1938, document 89; JLM, journal, December, 1937-January, 1938, MP, 317; draft of letter, July 1939, MP, 2477.
68. JLM, "Toward Peace in Palestine," January 1943, document 102.

Politically Magnes functioned in an unconventional way: he was preacher, agitator, and negotiator, subordinating his principles to no party and pursuing his own politics of conscience. Although organizations existed that held views similar to his, and he collaborated with them, he appeared on the political scene as an independent figure, insisting that he spoke in no one's name but his own. Even after he helped establish the Ihud (Union) Association in 1942 to advance his binational program and became its chairman, he maintained by and large his freedom of action.

His relationship to the B'rit Shalom (Covenant of Peace) Society further illuminates his complex behavior as moralist and political activist. The society, formed in 1925 with the object of arriving at an understanding between Jews and Arabs "on the basis of absolute political equality of two culturally autonomous peoples," consisted of a small but impressive array of intellectuals and veteran settlers. The society's first chairman was Arthur Ruppin, the German sociologist who since 1907 had headed the Palestine Office, the agency responsible for Zionist resettlement work. Magnes's outlook was especially close to that of a number of academicians in the society who had settled in Jerusalem in the course of the 1920s, most of whom were connected with the university. The most prominent were Shmuel Hugo Bergman, Hans Kohn, Gershom Scholem, and Ernst Simon. All had been born and educated in Central Europe and had come under the influence of the German Jewish philosopher and Zionist thinker Martin Buber. Like Buber they viewed the Arab question as the touchstone of the moral integrity of Zionism. For them, as for Magnes, the return to Zion constituted a spiritual renewal—building a just society imbued with universal significance—no less than a national and cultural rebirth. Magnes participated occasionally in the meetings of B'rit Shalom, commented on the drafts of the political papers that circulated among the members of the group, and contributed to the financial support of the society's publication. Yet he never became a member. In a notation in his diary written several years after the founding of the society he implied that ideological reasons had prevented him from joining. He had wanted a society organized on a genuine pacifist basis "that would seek peace with the Arabs (and with everybody else) not because such a peace was a tactical, practical necessity, but because such a peace was a direct outcome and necessary and logical deduction from the pacifist and Jewish position generally."[69]

Magnes's explanation is not entirely convincing. Much as he believed in moral politics, he well understood that in the real world a dogmatic

69. Hattis, *Bi-National Idea*, pp. 38–58; JLM, journal, September 14, 1928, document 62.

stand vitiated whatever influence the moralist would have. Nor is the assumption tenable that his university position required that he be apolitical, the argument he used in opposing Weizmann's election to the presidency of the university's board of governors. Sufficiently roused, no longer able to hold his peace, he spoke out ex cathedra. Indeed, in November 1929 an infuriated Weizmann inquired about the possibility of using his authority as president to restrain Magnes "from launching out into the political arena and so lowering the standard of the university." Over the next twenty years Magnes would be repeatedly accused of using his high office as a political platform. His replies—that whenever he spoke or wrote on political matters he emphasized that he did so as a private person—were formalistic disclaimers. He certainly knew that in the public's mind he remained identified with the university no matter what he said. It was in fact a source of gratification, for in the larger sense he believed that his public behavior brought credit upon the university. Was not the function of the university to get at the truth in politics as in science and to stand for broad humanistic ideals? As he wrote in 1945, should not his critics instead "rejoice and be proud of the fact that the Hebrew University stands for freedom of speech" and "rejoice also that the President of the University is so ardent an advocate of friendly relations with the neighboring world, and so vigorous an opponent of narrow nationalisms"? The role of politically nonaffiliated chancellor of the Hebrew University was more effective than that of heading a small faction within the Zionist movement subject to the decision of the majority.[70]

However, the role of the political independent also emerged out of the moral calling of the minister in the American social gospel tradition, as it had in his days as a radical pacifist spokesman during the war. The monstrous collective sin of war had compelled Magnes to take to the speaker's rostrum to denounce war and the evils of the social order that produced it. Then as now he acted out of an inner need, the pastor's need to admonish the erring congregation at a moment of crisis. For Magnes the political and the moral were of one piece, a fusion that is the essence of prophetic Judaism and that he insisted guide the return to Zion. One reason for not becoming a member even of B'rit Shalom, he explained, was his fear of being subject to a majority decision that would offend his conscience. The discipline of organization requires compromising one's personal integrity, a condition he would postpone as long as he could.

His politics of conscience expressed itself most dramatically in 1946, when the Anglo-American Committee of Inquiry arrived in Jerusalem at

70. Chaim Weizmann to Harry Sacher, November 19, 1929, *Letters and Papers of Chaim Weizmann*, ed. Camillo Dresner, vol. 14 (New Brunswick, N.J., 1978), pp. 87–89; JLM to Eugene Untermyer, March 25, 1945, document 109.

a crucial juncture in the Zionist struggle for a Jewish state. The Jewish Agency announced that as the body duly recognized by public law as representing Jewish interests in Palestine it alone should present the Jewish case before the committee. Magnes made it known that he intended to give public testimony on behalf of the Ihud, an act many considered traitorous. He and Buber, who since his immigration to Palestine in 1938 had collaborated closely with Magnes, appeared before the committee. They were testifying, Magnes informed the committee, "not in the name of the Hebrew University but as residents of the country, and as Jews who thought it their duty to give voice to a view which though different from the official Zionist program was shared by large numbers of the population."[71]

Magnes expressed his dissenting views not only from the platform and in his political writings. He entered the treacherous field of personal diplomacy, persuaded that patient, informal mediation would bring the sides together. To those who objected to his freelance diplomacy as flouting the policy of the duly elected authorities he replied that his meetings with Arab leaders and British and American officials were private exchanges of opinion. Only when explicitly authorized by accredited bodies would he go beyond these limits. Weizmann accused him of irresponsibility, of undermining the Zionist negotiating position, and "of trying recklessly to force our hand." Magnes's talks, he wrote to Robert Weltsch, editor of the *Juedische Rundschau* and sympathetic to Magnes's views, "could not be considered *unverbindlich* [not binding] in view of his position as chancellor of the university and his connections with American Jewry." The occasion that provoked Weizmann's wrath this time was Magnes's meetings in late October 1929 with H. St. John Philby, an adviser to King Ibn Saud of Arabia, who was in touch with Palestinian Arab leaders. In negotiations with Magnes and with the Mufti of Jerusalem, Philby, whom Weizmann considered an "adventurer," drafted a program for an Arab-Jewish settlement. The program included Arab acceptance of the Balfour Declaration and Jewish acceptance of the establishment of a legislative council on a democratic basis. Magnes deemed the program worthy of consideration. He discussed it with Sir John Chancellor, the high commissioner, brought it to the attention of a Jerusalem member of the Zionist executive, and then strenuously urged Felix Warburg to pressure Weizmann to enter negotiations on the basis of the program.[72]

71. Judah L. Magnes and Martin Buber, *Arab-Jewish Unity; Testimony before the Anglo-American Inquiry Commission for the Ihud (Union) Association* (London, 1947), p. 43.
72. Chaim Weizmann to Robert Weltsch, November 18, 1929, *Letters and Papers of Chaim Weizmann*, vol. 14, pp. 120–121; Hattis, *Bi-National Idea*, pp. 66–70; JLM, *Like All the Nations?*, pp. 34–41.

Although Magnes's first diplomatic initiative proved futile, he continued assiduously to pursue his objective of establishing direct contacts with Arab leaders. (Until 1938, when conditions became too dangerous, the Magnes family even lived in a largely Arab neighborhood.) Magnes established ties with Jamal al-Ḥusayni, the nephew of Hajj Amin al-Ḥusayni, Mufti of Jerusalem and the most powerful Palestinian Arab leader, and with Awni Abd-al-Hadi and Omar Saleh al-Barghuthi, leading members of the pan-Arab Istiqlal (Independence) party. He had an especially warm relationship with Musa al-Alami, a government counsel and Arab adviser to the high commissioner when Sir Arthur Wauchope held the office. These contacts and others were once and sometimes twice removed from the centers of Arab power. His Arab confreres, who recognized his integrity and good intentions, were also fully aware that he represented a small minority in the Zionist camp and that his own readiness for major concessions was rejected by the overwhelming majority of Zionists. Yet Magnes was convinced that his talks with the Arabs proved that an understanding was possible, although more than once he complained to them that not a single moderate Arab leader had declared himself publicly in favor of compromise as he, Magnes, had done. The blame for the impasse Magnes placed on the shoulders of the Zionist leadership, with their unrealistic hopes of achieving a Jewish majority combined with their conviction that the Arabs would never accept a Jewish national entity in Palestine. Thus in Magnes's view chauvinism and pessimism prevented the flexibility needed for compromise.[73]

Strained as the relations were between Magnes and the Zionist establishment, the new leaders who emerged in the 1930s — David Ben-Gurion, chairman of the executive of the Jewish Agency, and Moshe Sharett (Shertok), head of its political department — consulted with him and made use of his good offices. Despite their polarity of views Magnes and Ben-Gurion held each other in high esteem. In 1934, when Ben-Gurion decided to examine personally the possibility of negotiations, he enlisted Magnes's help in arranging meetings with Awni Abd-al-Hadi and Musa al-Alami. Some of the meetings took place in Magnes's home and with his active participation. In September 1934 Ben-Gurion cabled Magnes to join him in Geneva in talks with two important Syrian leaders whom Magnes had met with in the past, Shekib Arslan and Ihsan al-Jabri, but Magnes was unable to make the trip. After the outbreak of the Arab Revolt, the disturbances that began in April 1936 and continued with brief interruptions until 1939, he again arranged a series of meetings between Ben-Gurion and the Arab leader and writer George Antonius. First on his

73. JLM to David Ben-Gurion, March 3, 1938, document 91; JLM to Sol Stroock, June 5, 1938, document 92; JLM, journal, October 1937, May 1938, MP, 317.

own initiative and then in conjunction with an ad hoc committee of five prominent Jews, Magnes soon reached a preliminary understanding with Musa al-Alami. The Jewish Agency found disturbing the fact that Alami could not or would not declare that a responsible Arab body stood behind the understanding; the agency rejected the pivotal paragraph on Jewish immigration that cut the current rate by half, and it fumed over Magnes's acquiescence to Alami's proposal that the Jews voluntarily agree to stop immigration during the course of the negotiations as an indication of good intentions. Magnes saw the episode as a lost opportunity. Arthur Ruppin, a founder of B'rit Shalom, observing the heightened passions brought on by the Arab revolt and Jewish desperation in light of the rapidly deteriorating conditions in Germany, remarked dejectedly, "It is our destiny to be in a state of continual warfare with the Arabs and there is no other alternative but that lives should be lost."[74]

Nevertheless, in the winter of 1937–38, the Jewish Agency agreed once more, despite serious misgivings, to a new peace initiative. Intermediaries sent Magnes a set of negotiating proposals purportedly drafted with the tacit approval of persons close to the Arab Higher Committee, then sitting in exile. The committee, under the leadership of the Mufti, represented the most important center of power among the Palestinian Arabs. Magnes considered the apparent Arab interest in exploring the possibility of direct talks a major accomplishment. The Jewish Agency accepted Magnes's suggestion that he investigate the initiative with a view toward arranging formal talks between the sides.

Magnes, together with the Angelican bishop of Jerusalem, Francis Graham-Browne, and the Jerusalem physician Dr. Izzat Tannous, the Mufti's representative, entered into a labyrinth of negotiations. When the Arab side denied any connection with the set of proposals and offered instead as the only basis for preliminary talks its known stand on immigration, that "the maximum Jewish population should be the present population," the Jewish Agency angrily terminated Magnes's mission. "I thought," Magnes wrote in his diary, "that a meeting was so all important that were I responsible for the Agency I would agree to meet on the basis of any text or no text, provided it be clearly understood that I did not agree in advance to this or that point of the text serving as the basis of discussion."[75] His contacts, including the American Consul in Jerusalem, George Wadsworth, suggested that Magnes meet with the Iraqi foreign minister Nuri al-Sa'id in an effort to salvage the talks. Seeing some glint of hope Magnes went beyond his instructions and conferred with Nuri al-

74. David Ben-Gurion, *My Talks with Arab Leaders* (Tel Aviv, 1972), pp. 33–35, 42–76; Hattis, *Bi-National Idea*, pp. 139, 148–154; Moshe Sharett, *Yoman m'dini*, vol. 1 (Tel Aviv, 1968), pp. 143–147.

75. JLM, journal, January, 1939, MP, 317.

Sa'id in February 1938 in Beirut. Though the meeting was held in good faith and Magnes reported to the Jewish Agency executive on his return from Beirut, the meeting was distorted by the Arabs in order to sow seeds of confusion and contention. Reports reached the British Colonial Office that Magnes had accepted Nuri's condition that the Jews remain a permanent minority in Palestine. In the event the Jewish Agency refused to accept the condition Magnes would urge American non-Zionists to withdraw their support from the Jewish Agency and join like-minded Jews in Britain and Europe in forming an organization prepared to negotiate a peace with the Arabs based on permanent minority status. Magnes hotly denied the reports, presented a detailed written rebuttal to the Jewish Agency, and appeared before its executive committee. The affair embittered relations between him and the Zionist leadership. In all these instances Magnes claimed that the Jewish Agency's rigidity had prevented his following up hopeful signs of Arab willingness to negotiate. He accused Sharett in particular of intentionally stifling the initiatives. In a long reply to Magnes Ben-Gurion wrote reproachfully: "While we do not resort to strategems ourselves, we will not fall victims to those of the other side. We will examine seven times every plan and every proposal that is supported by these deadly enemies of ours. We are not afraid and we do not refuse to meet with them, but we will not rush to fall into their trap. In this entire matter you acted out of good intentions; of that I have no doubt. But intention alone is not enough. It is clear to me that your honest striving for peace is being exploited in order to undermine our position."[76]

The binationalist saw himself by definition as the compromiser and mediator. The humanist and universalist believed compassion and integrity mattered. But beginning in 1937 the realist in Magnes led him to mobilize all the political support he could command.

When the Palestine Royal Commission (the Peel Commission) was appointed to investigate the causes of the Arab revolt, Magnes's activity acquired a new dimension. From November 1936 through January 1937 the commission conducted hearings in Palestine. In July it rendered its report, which concluded that the national aspirations of Jews and Arabs were irreconcilable and recommended partitioning Palestine into separate Jewish and Arab states. During the commission's stay in Palestine Magnes did not testify, though he was invited to do so. "My reluctance to testify has been due," he wrote to Reginald Coupland, the most influential member of the commission and the author of the report, "to my fear lest by some word of mine I might add to the deep suffering of my people here and elsewhere." His testimony would arouse, he intimated, such op-

76. Ben-Gurion, *Talks with Arab Leaders*, p. 194.

position from Jewish sources as to prejudice the final acceptance of his plan. He did, however, send Coupland a memorandum that summarized the tentative agreement reached with Alami in May 1936. He proposed that it form the basis for round-table discussions between Arabs, Jews, and the British. In a situation where neither Arabs nor Jews could achieve their maximalist aspirations, where it is "possible to say that the Jews are right and the Arabs are right," the binationalist formula was the only viable one.[77]

Magnes distributed his memorandum to a number of highly placed political figures and to his non-Zionist friends in the United States. He appealed to Felix Warburg for funds to finance an organization "to fight for the ideas that you and I hold." When Arthur Hays Sulzberger, publisher of the *New York Times*, visited Palestine in February 1937, Magnes won him over to his views. "Our attitude on the *New York Times* when the findings of the Royal Commission become public," Sulzberger wrote in a personal note, "should be predicated upon the Magnes point of view." During June and July Magnes conducted extensive conversations in London, Paris, and Geneva. Following the appearance of the Peel Commission's report the *Times* published a long letter to the editor by Magnes expounding his rejection of partition. In August after the Zionist Congress meeting in Zurich accepted the principle of partition despite serious reservations and strong opposition within the movement, the Council of the Jewish Agency convened. Although the agency was dominated by the Zionists, the antipartition forces, led by Warburg at the head of the non-Zionist faction, made a determined effort to bind the Jewish Agency to negotiate a binational solution. Throughout the months preceding the meeting Magnes and Warburg consulted frequently. At Zurich for the first time in two decades Magnes appeared as an official participant in a representative, public Jewish body and presented the resolution of the non-Zionists to an angry, tense, and in the main hostile audience. He was frequently interrupted, and the chair arbitrarily refused to allow the resolution to be debated. Yet a dialogue of sorts took place.[78]

For a moment the nonconformist patrician returned to the rowdy give and take of Jewish public life and revealed something of his inner self.

77. Laqueur, *History of Zionism*, pp. 514–18; JLM to Reginald Coupland, January 7, 1937, document 79.

78. Arthur Hays Sulzberger, "Personal," February 1937, MP, 200; Sulzberger to JLM, March 13, 1937, MP, 2463; Lacqueur, *History of Zionism*, pp. 518–520; Hattis, *Bi-National Idea*, pp. 167–171; Bentwich, *For Zion's Sake*, pp. 193–194; JLM to Felix Warburg, January 11, 1937, document 80; "List of Those Who Have Read Statement of Dr. Magnes sent to Reginald Coupland," February 22, 1937, MP, 2449; Felix Warburg to JLM, July 6, 1937, MP, 2450.

When his warning that a Jewish state would lead to war with the Arabs was met with scorn, he departed from his prepared remarks:

> Perhaps the man who laughed has not been through what happened last year. I was. My sons were. The sons and the daughters of my friends were. I see some of my comrades from Palestine here who were. It is not a laughing matter for them. My friend Ussishkin and I differ on almost every political question and yet I have rejoiced to find that, on this particular thing, he and I see eye to eye. What is it that connects us in this? It is his fear, it is my fear, and I have no hesitation in telling you that I am afraid, of the consequences of this state in the relations between the Jews and the Arabs. I happen to have been born in a country where people are raised·without fear, and, if I may utter another personal remark, I think that I, personally, have not very much fear. Yet I am afraid for my people, afraid for those tender plants in my country, in that Eretz Israel. I do not want to see the Jewish state conceived and born in warfare.[79]

Earlier in the session his old friend Sholom Asch had turned to him and feelingly described the work of "your young men and women," the Zionist pioneers who "went into a wasteland." Magnes, now citing Asch, responded "I went into that wasteland with them. 'Do you not realize,' Asch said, 'that they have watered that land with their tears and their blood and that they have tilled it with their strength and their life?' I realize that, because I have seen them and I love them for it."[80]

Here indeed was one source of his moral influence: he, the freeborn son of the American West, had followed the young pioneers into the wasteland. He shared with his political adversaries—Ussishkin, Ben-Gurion, in fact the majority of the yishuv—the perils of the troubled land. Having cast their lot with Zion, he and his family would personally pay for what he believed was a wrongheaded policy, one that would lead to the destruction of so noble an enterprise.

The rancor and passion of the debate are understandable, conducted as it was under the shadow of Hitler's increasingly brutal persecution of the Jews. Palestine had become a major refuge for Germany's Jews and the hope of tens of thousands of Polish Jews suffering from anti-Semitic legislation, pogroms, and pauperization. In 1933 the number of Jews who emigrated to Palestine rose to thirty thousand, a threefold increase over the previous year; it climbed to over forty thousand in 1934 and reached a peak of sixty-one thousand in 1935. For Weizmann and Ben-Gurion even a minuscule Jewish state would assure continued if not increased emigration; they saw no alternative. For Magnes this calculation

79. JLM, Address to the Council of the Jewish Agency, August 18, 1937, document 84.
80. Ibid.

was an illusion, false messianism raising hopes for hundreds of thousands that could not be fulfilled. When Magnes claimed that a Jewish-Arab understanding was a prerequisite for mass migration, few listened.

The times were not conducive to moderation and compromise. By early 1938 the partition plan was a dead letter. Impending war induced the British to issue the White Paper of 1939, which was intended to appease the Arab world. It allowed seventy-five thousand Jewish immigrants to enter Palestine over a five-year period, permitted further immigration only with Arab consent, and set a time limit of ten years for the establishment of an Arab state in Palestine. Anger and anguish gripped the yishuv. While the British strictly enforced the immigration quota, the Jewish world helplessly watched as boatloads of fugitives from Nazi-occupied Europe were shunted from port to port, the rescue potential of the yishuv thwarted. Once again the goal of Jewish sovereignty was revived. In May 1942 Ben-Gurion proclaimed Jewish statehood as the immediate goal of the Zionist movement. At a historic conference of American Zionists meeting in New York's Biltmore Hotel over five hundred delegates representing all the Zionist factions demanded "that the gates of Palestine be opened . . . and that Palestine be established as a Jewish Commonwealth."[81]

In Palestine Magnes led the opposition to the Biltmore Declaration. "The slogan Jewish state or commonwealth," he wrote, "is equivalent, in effect, to a declaration of war by the Jews on the Arabs." He quoted an Arab friend as saying that the day the Jews got their state their real war with the Arabs would begin. There were others in Palestine opposed to the Biltmore Declaration. Within the labor movement Hashomer Ha'tza'ir (the Young Guard party), together with a smaller socialist faction, remained committed to a binational state. A considerable number of recent German immigrants considered the call for a state extremist. Those who had belonged to B'rit Shalom, including the university group and such veteran settlers as Chaim Margalit Kalvarisky, Moshe Smilansky, and Rav Binyamin (Benjamin Feldman-Radler), saw the Biltmore Declaration as undermining their continuing efforts to reach an understanding with moderate Arab leaders.[82]

Magnes was in touch with these circles and also with his American friends. After the death of Warburg in October 1937 he turned increasingly to the men of the American Jewish Comittee for support, most especially to Sol Stroock, Maurice Wertheim, Joseph Proskauer, and Mrs. Magnes's nephew James Marshall. (At the end of the war a younger group of AJC leaders became his staunch supporters, among them Alan

81. Laqueur, *History of Zionism*, pp. 521–536, 544–549.
82. JLM, memorandum, August 30, 1943, MP, 2542; Hattis, *Bi-National Idea*, pp. 212–231, 249–258.

M. Stroock, Edward S. Greenbaum, David Sher, and Marshall.) Such key figures in the field of Jewish communal service as Maurice Hexter, Solomon Lowenstein, and Jacob Billikopf constituted an informal council of advisers. Magnes found support too among the Hadassah leadership. During the entire period Arthur Hays Sulzberger kept the pages of the *New York Times* open to Magnes's pronouncements.[83]

In 1939 Magnes had considered visiting the United States for the purpose of establishing the organization he and Warburg had discussed. Three years later the Biltmore program prompted a flurry of renewed interest in Magnes's views. In part this support stemmed form the "sweet reasonableness" of his program, a phrase Henrietta Szold used to describe it. In large measure the interest came from the fear that agitation for a Jewish state would provoke accusations of dual loyalty. For some, American Zionism's aggressive stance — its lobbying in Washington, its mass meetings, and its declared intention to build a Jewish consensus for the maximalist Zionist program — was fraught with danger for American Jewry. Magnes's associate at the university, Max Schloessinger, writing from New York described a meeting of a group of Magnes's warmest supporters "My impression was . . . that these people are primarily concerned with the welfare of the Jewish community in America and are afraid that the existence of a Jewish state in Palestine might endanger their own status, if the world should grow increasingly anti-Semitic. Essentially, it is the same fear that surrounded the Balfour Declaration some twenty-five years ago. To me it was the same ideological stuff that I heard for the first time in my life in 1896 when I came to Vienna as a young student."[84]

Magnes's potentially strong base of support in America never materialized, although some financial help was forthcoming. When the Ihud Association was formally established in the fall of 1942 American money enabled the association to publish its journal, *Ba'ayot*. But there were never enough funds. A projected program of social and cultural work among Arabs and Jews remained unfulfilled. At the end of the war Magnes's supporters implored him to come to the United States to activate a large Jewish public, which they believed would listen to the voice of moderation. He spent the summer and fall of 1946 in the United States. Friends helped him form the American Association for Union in Palestine, but it soon became dormant. When he left for Palestine, he had but

83. JLM to Gladys Guggenheim Straus, October 14, 1937, document 85; Morris D. Waldman to JLM, August 25, 1938, MP, 2463; JLM to Sol Stroock, June 5, 1938, document 92.

84. JLM to Maurice B. Hexter, July 9, 1939, MP, 2464; Roger W. Straus to JLM, September 3, 1942, and JLM to Straus, October 1, 1942, MP, 215; Max Schloessinger to JLM, December 14, 1942, Schloessinger Papers, Jewish National and University Library, Jerusalem, Israel.

a fifth of the $100,000 he had hoped to raise. Magnes did, however, establish personal ties with State Department officials. He met several times with Loy Henderson and his staff of the Near East Division and with Acting Secretary of State Dean Acheson. His views were well known in the State Department, but his position had been greatly enhanced by his appearance before the Anglo-American Committee of Inquiry the previous spring. Indeed, Magnes and his Ihud followers claimed that the committee had implicitly accepted their position: "Jew shall not dominate Arab and Arab shall not dominate Jew," and statehood of any sort was to be postponed. Magnes was encouraged to believe that as the United States became increasingly involved in the Palestine problem it would adopt the binational formula.[85]

In the years 1943 to 1948 Ihud operated as the "loyal opposition," in Magnes's words. Soon after its formation Ihud leaders appeared before the Zionist executive and defended the association's loyalty to Zionism. On the critical question of organizational discipline, Magnes informed the executive: "The recognized national institutions alone have the right to enter upon binding political negotiations . . . On the other hand, Ihud declares that every citizen and every Zionist group has the right of entering into direct contact with Jews and non-Jews for the purpose of clarifying the situation and of exchanging views as to possibilities and of preparing the ground for proposals and plans which are then to be brought before the recognized institutions."[86] Just where "clarifying the situation" and "preparing the ground for proposals" ended, and "binding political negotiations" began had always been the nub of the problem as far as Magnes's establishment critics went.

At the war's end, with the yishuv in a state of insurrection and its underground armed organizations directing a vast network of illegal immigration from Europe to Palestine and striking back at the British, Ihud bore the stigma of disloyalty. Magnes realized this. He understood the mood of "hysteria, helplessness, and rage." But the task of the courageous leader was to reason with the people despite the furor and to pursue the rational, peaceful way toward a solution other than war "even at this late hour."[87]

Magnes's concerns and causes went beyond his political and university interests. He was attuned as few others were to a host of social and

85. JLM to Maurice Hexter, October 5, 1942, MP, 1958; JLM to Alexander M. Dushkin, January 7, 1943, MP, 2192; Bentwich, For Zion's Sake, pp. 257–263; JLM, mimeographed letter, August 27, 1946, JMP; JLM to James Marshall, January 15, 1947, document 114; JLM to Joseph Proskauer, January 17, 1947, MP, 221b; JLM to Maurice Hexter, February 14, 1947, document 116.

86. Hattis, Bi-National State, pp. 266–270; Bentwich, For Zion's Sake, pp. 255–260.

87. JLM, notes, January 3, 1947, MP, 351.

civic questions. He deeply admired the idealism and achievements of the labor movement and the collective settlements, the kibbutzim, and followed closely the ideological controversies that marked their growth. On the other hand he found in the slums of Jerusalem and in the arbitrary power of civil government evils similar to those he had encountered as a social activist in New York. His response was similar. He lectured the university's students on the need to establish settlement houses in the poor neighborhoods of Jerusalem. One such center was established in the Old City, and succeeding groups of students manned it until the fall of the Old City in the 1948 war. He pointed to the absence of American-style community centers for providing the general public with educational and recreational opportunities. Toward the end of his life he used his American connections to lay the groundwork for a YMHA. Much earlier he had joined the Prison Visitors' Committee and the League for the Rights of Man. He interceded on every level of government to alleviate the conditions of prisoners, reduce the harsh sentences imposed on those charged with belonging to the underground defense organizations, and gain the release of political detainees. His standing was such that the government released suspected terrorists on his personal guarantee of their good behavior.[88]

When the war broke out in 1939 he assumed a key role in the war effort and in rescue work. When Hadassah created an emergency committee to supervise its activities in Palestine, Magnes was appointed chairman. Working with Henrietta Szold, Dr. Chaim Yassky of the Hadassah medical services, and Mrs. Ethel Agronsky, he enlarged the organization's social services to include vocational training for girls, youth centers and playgrounds, Jewish-Arab health centers, and occupational therapy for the mentally ill. At the same time Magnes served as chairman of the Middle East Advisory Committee of the JDC. In this capacity he guided the JDC's activities in Palestine, aiding needy religious scholars, providing lunches for schoolchildren, and granting small loans for those who fell between the chairs of the yishuv's self-help institutions.[89]

As the dimensions of the JDC's activities expanded, Palestine turned into a regional center of sorts. With the aid of Harry Viteles and Charles Passman in particular, Magnes supervised a project of sending parcels to Jews in the Soviet Union (a quarter of a million were sent during the war), dealt with Yemenite Jews stranded in Aden, helped in the negotia-

88. Bentwich, *For Zion's Sake*, pp. 165–166, 232–235; *Ner*, 15 (September 1963), vi–viii; Lily Jerusalem to JLM, February 4, 1942, MP, 2100; Yavne, Student Settlement for Youth in the Old City to JLM (Hebrew), April 14, 1947, MP, 2100; Lily Jerusalem to JLM, July 31, 1945, MP, 2311.

89. Index to Minutes of the Sixty-ninth to Eighty-second Meetings of the Hadassah Emergency Committee, June 6, 1944 to May 6, 1945, MP, 2229.

tions that brought to Palestine a thousand Polish Jewish children who had reached Tehran, and directed the dispatch of aid to Greece at the conclusion of the war. These activities brought him into daily contact with the welfare and rescue departments of the Jewish Agency and with the mandatory government. In one instance—rescue activities centered in Turkey—he flew to Istanbul to disentangle differences between JDC, Jewish Agency, and War Refugee Board officials. There he established a close friendship with Ira Hirschmann, the director of War Refugee Board operations in Turkey, and with a group of undercover agents sent by the yishuv to conduct covert rescue operations. These undertakings required him to be in constant touch with the heads of the JDC in New York, of which Paul Baerwald, with whom he had collaborated in JDC work during the First World War, was now chairman, and with the Hadassah organization. Through his persistence he persuaded the mandatory government to create a scientific advisory committee to mobilize the country's scientific skills on behalf of the war effort and served as its chairman. So often portrayed as the dreamer on Mount Scopus, Magnes showed himself to be a man of practical affairs who wielded influence and power.[90]

In 1939 Magnes invited a group of like-minded friends to form a small religious society. It included Martin Buber, Hugo Bergman, Ernst Simon, and Gershom Scholem. The group took the name Ha'ol, "the Yoke": the Yoke of the Coming Kingdom of God. Several lines in Hebrew in Magnes's hand, to be found in the slim file of the society, read: "We are united in the feeling of responsibility toward the life of society in general, and the life of Israel in its land and in the dispersion in particular. This sense of responsibility stems from faith in eternal values whose source is God. We believe in a life of faith which carries a commitment to social action and practical political work, and we reject any attempt to separate the two dominions, which are one in theory and practice."[91]

This creed of the religious social radical is the key to understanding Magnes's behavior and way of thinking. It pervades his public addresses and his more personal, contemplative writings where the political and the religious remain indivisible. The Hebrew prophet who, in the name of the God of Israel, intervenes in the political life of the nation, stands out as his model and inspiration. The bearers of this tradition, however imperfect they may be, when "touched by the living coal from the altar" must speak out and act.

So it had been during the First World War, when Magnes added the voice of his own Jewish social gospel to the Christian, insisting that there

90. JLM, Report to the Jewish Agency Rescue Committee on Visit to Turkey, July 14, 1944, MP, 2144; JLM to Ira Hirschmann, October 10, 1944, MP, 2144; JLM to Paul Baerwald, December 13, 1944, document 107.
91. MP, 2272

was a nonviolent way of changing a competitive, exploitive system that breeds war and despotism. The same conviction led him to mourn Zionism's first political triumph. It is no coincidence, therefore, that when he spoke out again in 1929 his political activity went hand in hand with an attempt to found an association best described as religious. A group of the like-minded, by joining together to clarify and then to disseminate the prophetic meaning of the Return, would perhaps extricate the Zionist movement from the snares of Realpolitik.

With the help of Hans Kohn and Bergman Magnes prepared the guidelines for the group. He posited two religious principles: that those who would join "endeavor to live in accordance with the 'God within' each"; and that the "absolute ethical or metaphysical values must be the real forces determining and directing life." Judaism itself, he wrote, had to become the "central motivating force of the Jewish people," which was still capable of "proving its service to mankind in accordance with the idea of the 'servant of God.' " The association would be committed to social radicalism: "wanting to realize here and now the social ideals of justice and righteousness of the Hebrew prophets." It would stand for nationalism "essentially spiritual and non-violent . . . that would recognize the inner need of every people to develop its cultural heritage and spiritual self."[92]

The association proved stillborn. Yet Magnes remained true to its spirit even in his most politically conventional act, the establishment of the Ihud. In his address to the founding conference he expounded once again his doctrine of the merging in Judaism of the political and the religious. The political problem to be addressed was whether in Eretz Israel the Jews would create "a public life based on justice and mercy" or would "like all the nations, obtain their aims by any and all means." Magnes was not against a Jewish state in principle. ("It would at least place responsibility on *us*," he had written in his journal.) However, the call for a Jewish state fanned enmity between the peoples. "Judaism demands of us finding out whether it is not possible to create something on another basis than force and chauvinism."[93]

Magnes's religious impulses explain too his rejection of the accusation that his policy of reconciliation with the Arab people brought no response from the other side. He believed, indeed, that there were hopeful signs. But more pertinent in understanding his indifference to this criticism is the double standard he used: he expected more from his people. "K'khol ha'goyim beyt yisra'el? [Is the house of Israel like all the nations?] — certainly not," he jotted down in his diary. Its exceptionalism — its obli-

92. "An Association to be Constituted," MP, 2271.
93. JLM, index file, 1942/3, MP, 383; JLM, journal, July 6, 1937, MP, 317.

gation to strive to live up to its Judaic ideals — must be the source of its politics.[94]

Political rhetoric informed with prophetic Judaism made him appear a self-righteous and rigid figure who spoke as if possessed of a higher authority. Yet behind the resoluteness and self-assurance was a religious seeker torn by inner doubts. In a penciled note, one of a number scattered through his papers, he jotted down: "I stand in reverence (or respect) and read and repeat the prayers and am sometimes moved, particularly by the prayers of believers, but I do not *pray*, or at least I do not pray to *Him*. Yet I believe that I should, and others like me, continue to read Psalms and other literature, to ponder, to hope, to complain to Him (just as though there were a Him) to deepen our lives, and perhaps . . ."

And again: "I struggle with myself, with Him night and day. I do not deny that He *is* — how can I? What do I know? I do not deny his power. I deny nothing, nothing. I have not the power, the assurance, the affront of the 'rebel' against Him, surely not the cynicism and the calm of one who is so certain of His wickedness or His impotence in man's affairs that he no longer cares . . .

"I can only read and read and seek and ask — and wait. Perhaps the vision will be vouchsafed to me, too, some day . . . Who are the others for whom this burns as a fire or a light or a hell. I wish I might know them and learn from them and be kindled by them."[95]

There were occasions when the private man shared his quest with others, when he suggested tentatively a way of "conquering pessimism through faith." These occasions were most notably the university convocations held during the war years, when his addresses were in essence sermons. In the long shadow of the disaster unfolding in Europe and uncertainty concerning the fate of the yishuv, the saving remnant, the preacher in Magnes reasserted itself.[96]

Wearing the mantle of the chastiser estranged him from the people, though in the prophetic tradition he was a consoler at moments of great crisis. More precisely many were indifferent to him. His accent, style, and profile — the Reform preacher from America searching for God and calling for moral piety — appeared strange to a yishuv of the orthodox, whether Orthodox Jews or orthodox socialist Zionists for whom survival in a hostile world was the problem. Magnes was aware of this. He told a university audience at a memorial meeting for his old friend Shmaryahu Levin, the Eastern European secular preacher of Zionism, how Levin had

94. JLM, notes, February 12, 1947, MP, 351.
95. JLM, notes, October 24, and 27, 1937, MP, 2424.
96. JLM, *In the Perplexity of the Times* (Jerusalem, 1946), pp. 16–26, 55–78, 104–108; Samuel H. Bergman, *Faith and Reason, An Introduction to Modern Jewish Thought* (Philadelphia, 1961), pp. 146–151.

once taken him to task: "What are you after? You show that you are really an assimilated Jew, that you were not raised 'on the knees of Torah,' if you keep on looking for answers to religious problems. That very search is a sign of your assimilation. A true Jew, one born and bred and rooted in the soil of Tora and the tradition would not have such concern with the solution of the individual's problem, particularly in days such as these when we have such more real tasks to carry out."[97]

Levin was describing the acculturated Western Jew, and in Jerusalem Magnes found kindred souls, understandably, among the German intellectuals, products of an emancipated and enlightened Jewry who in coming to terms with their Jewishness had assimilated the religious socialism of the age. Yet there was a difference. These intellectuals were the products of an Old World skepticism about the possibility of reconciling their ethical ideals with political activism. It was precisely their self-doubt that drew them to Magnes. They were taken by his candor, courage, and self-assurance, indeed by his disarming American innocence. His strenuous pursuit of his ideals — conventional ideals — conveyed moral strength. Scholem called him a man of the nineteenth century, a humanist and a true radical — one who went to the root of the matter — whose authority stemmed from his integrity. Buber attributed to Magnes's persistence in challenging Zionist Realpolitik with moral politics his own return to the political realm after years of withdrawal. Watching Magnes one was obliged to lend a hand.[98]

In early April 1948, seven months before his death and a month before the state of Israel was proclaimed, Magnes received a message through the United States consul in Jerusalem imploring him to come to America. State Department circles and an ad hoc committee of prominent Jews believed that his presence could prove useful in a last attempt to stop the fighting in Palestine. Little time remained before the neighboring Arab armies were expected to invade the country.

The plan to bring Magnes back crystallized among those State Department officials opposed to the UN resolution of 1947 partitioning Palestine into Jewish and Arab states. Their campaign met with initial success in March 1948, when Warren Austin, the chief American delegate to the UN, announced American support for a UN trusteeship over Palestine, a retreat from the position supporting partition. If adopted by the General Assembly the proposal would mean the indefinite postponement of the establishment of a Jewish state. At this point the State Department encouraged the committee of Magnes's supporters to extend a formal in-

97. JLM, *Addresses of the Chancellor*, p. 305.
98. *Baayot*, July 1947, pp. 189–190.

vitation to him. Among its initial members were Lessing J. Rosenwald, president of the anti-Zionist American Council for Judaism; Edward Greenbaum, a New York lawyer; Jerome Frank, a former adviser of Franklin Roosevelt and a judge of the United States Circuit Court of Appeals; Lewis Straus, a financier and a member of the Aromic Energy Commission; and Maurice Hexter. Later James Marshall, David Sher, Alan Stroock, and Edward Greenbaum played the leading role in the committee. All were members of the antipartition minority of the American Jewish Committee at a time when the overwhelming majority of American Jewry supported a Jewish state.[99]

Magnes greeted the turnabout in the American position with elation. When the call came, although he was in poor health he viewed the trip as a necessity. The day his physicians consulted on the advisability of his attempting it he wrote in his diary: "How can I not go and stand before the world and say: Friends, stop the bloodshed. Understanding is possible. This is the moment I have been preparing for all these years."[100]

In the months prior to his decision, despite severe medical restrictions he had continued to deal with public matters. British forces were still in nominal control, but security was rapidly deteriorating. In Jerusalem sporadic fighting escalated into pitched battles; in the Jewish parts of the city water and food were in short supply. From his home Magnes maintained contact with British army headquarters and with officials at the university and at the Hadassah hospital on Mount Scopus, now under siege by the Arab Legion. He intervened with the British to extricate a convoy of the Haganah, the yishuv's main defense group, trapped on the road to Hebron. On April 13 he followed with horror the intermittent reports of the failure, whether through inability or unwillingness, of the British to rescue an ambushed medical convoy on the way to Mount Scopus, an ambush that cost the lives of seventy-six doctors and university workers. He also met frequently with Eliezar Sukenik, a professor of archeology at the university who had come upon goatskin scrolls covered with ancient Hebrew script being sold in the Old City of Jerusalem. Sukenik identified them as biblical and extrabiblical texts copied by a Jewish sectarian group during the time of Christ. After purchasing the rolls with money supplied by Magnes, Sukenik would bring them to

99. Loy Henderson to Acting Secretary of State, April 9, 1948; Henderson to Thomas C. Wasson, April 10, 1948, *Foreign Relations of the United States, 1948*, vol. 5, part 2 (Washington, D.C., 1976), pp. 804–805, 811; Lessing Rosenwald to Mrs. David M. Levy, Lewis J. Strauss, Louis Finkelstein, Julius Ochs Adler, Harold Linder, Edward Greenbaum, Jerome Frank, Horace Stern, April 4, 1948, JMP; JLM to Maurice Hexter, April 6, 1948, MP, 2527; Zvi Ganin, *Truman, American Jewry and Israel, 1945–1948* (New York, 1979), pp. 175–177.

100. JLM, diary, April 16, 1948, MP, 325.

Magnes's home at night, and the two would read the texts that became known to the world as the Dead Sea Scrolls.[101]

On April 22 Magnes, accompanied by his wife and physician, left besieged Jerusalem on his final mission of peace. In New York he plunged into a round of intensive diplomatic talks. His friends formed an informal cabinet, and his hotel room became a virtual office, where he received a stream of diplomats and American Jewish leaders. He met with Muhamed Fawzi Bey, the Egyptian UN delegate; Arthur Creech Jones, the British Colonial Secretary; and Alexandre Parodi, the French delegate to the UN. He was in frequent touch with Ambassador Warren Austin and his staff and with Loy Henderson, Dean Rusk, and Robert McClintock of the State Department. On May 5 he traveled to Washington for an interview with Secretary of State George Marshall and the following day with the President.[102]

As a first step he proposed to Marshall and to the President arranging a cease-fire for Jerusalem. A temporary UN governor, using local Jewish and Arab police, could bring the fighting to an end. World public opinion, he was convinced, would not tolerate Jerusalem's being turned into a battleground and threatened with destruction. The momentum gained by an armistice in Jerusalem could lead to its extension throughout the country. If necessary economic sanctions imposed on both sides would bring the fighting to a halt. With a cessation of hostilities an interim arrangement, the American-sponsored trusteeship plan, could take effect.[103]

Time ran out. On May 15, 1948, with the proclamation of the State of Israel, Magnes's efforts to bring a cease-fire, his support of trusteeship, and his long advocacy of binationalism came to an end. The regular armies of five Arab nations attacked the infant state. His gloomiest prophecies were being fulfilled. As in the past he responded to the moment of great peril with a symbolic act of faith. The day the state was proclaimed he paid a courtesy call on the ailing Weizmann, the president-designate of the Jewish state, to extend his best wishes.[104]

Confronted by a radically new situation Magnes endeavored to find a political formula that would recognize Jewish statehood and allay Arab fears. From June until his death at the end of October he was busy developing the idea of a confederation of Arab and Jewish states with Jerusalem as its capital. During these months Hannah Arendt, the as yet little

101. JLM, diary, January-April, 1948, passim, MP, 325; JLM journal, January–April, passim, MP, 324.
102. JLM, Report to Sponsoring Committee, April 26, 1948, document 128; JLM, journal, May 5 and 6, June 1, 1948, documents 129, 130, 131.
103. JLM journal, May 5, 1948, document 129.
104. Jonathan Magnes, interview, March 18, 1977.

known political scientist, collaborated closely with him. His friends and advisers took steps to establish a formal organization to advance the program. He presented his views to the State Department, to Israeli authorities, and to the UN mediator for Palestine, Count Folkes Bernadotte. Elliot Cohen, the editor of *Commentary* and one of Magnes's advisers, suggested that he publish his proposal. It appeared in the October issue of *Commentary* and proved to be his final public statement, yet another act in his unrelenting quest for peace and political compromise.[105]

Other matters occupied him during his last weeks, even after he suffered a mild stroke in June. He wrote to Ben-Gurion urging him to deal with the Arab refugee problem on a purely humanitarian basis, and at the same time he demanded that the JDC allocate funds for the refugees. He also addressed meetings of the friends of the university. A week before his death, at one of these gatherings Magnes presented an account of the preliminary report on the discovery and significance of the Dead Sea Scrolls prepared by Sukenik.[106]

The last two letters Magnes wrote were addressed to Dr. E. R. Bluestone, chairman of the planning committee for the Hadassah-sponsored university medical school, and to Sukenik. In the first he presented his arguments for the site he preferred for the school. In his letter of congratulations to Sukenik on the appearance of the report he noted that Sukenik had dedicated the publication to his son, Matti, who had fallen in the war. "I recall," he wrote, "how Matti accompanied you that dark night amidst the shelling when you brought the scrolls in your faithful hands to our home."[107]

Magnes died the morning of October 27. Despite his stroke in June his activities during the summer and fall of 1948 belied his condition. Death came as a new era opened for his people. He who had feared its most singular feature — Jewish statehood — entered it planning for the new challenges and opportunities it presented to be directed toward humane and peaceful ends. The message he sent to the opening of the academic year of the Hebrew University read in part: "The people of Israel now confronts such problems as subjects and not merely as objects. In the eyes of many among us the chief value of an independent state is, that we our-

105. JLM to Robert McClintock, June 14, 1948, document 132; JLM to Count Folke Bernadotte, July 14, 1948, JMP, and August 10, 1948, document 134; JLM to Hannah Arendt, July 20, August 31, 1948, documents 133 and 136; JLM, Comments on Eban's Comments of July 10, 1948, n.d., and JLM to Aubrey Eban, August 25, 1948, Archives of the State of Israel Foreign Office Papers, Box 129; JLM, "For Jewish-Arab Confederation," October 1948, document 138.

106. JLM to David Ben-Gurion, August 19, 1948, document 135; JLM to Edward M. M. Warburg, September 2 and 29, 1948, JMP; JLM, stenographic report of meeting, American Friends fo the Hebrew University, October 20, 1948, MP, 2529.

107. Bentwich, *For Zion's Sake*, p. 305; JLM to E. L. Sukenik, October 24, 1948, MP, 384.

selves bear the responsibility for our own decisions and that we do not just have to accept the consequences of decisions made for us by others."[108]

Magnes's critics disparaged and censured his political activity. They saw him as a noble but dogmatic innocent who, never doubting his rightness, acted as though possessed of a higher authority. There is a measure of truth in these charges. Who indeed had given him a mandate in May 1948 to urge the Secretary of State and the President to stop the process leading to the proclamation of the Jewish State? The final months of his life, however, pointed to another truth as well. Victory on the battlefield had not resolved fundamental issues. While others celebrated the beginning of a new epoch in Jewish history, Magnes entered it no less cognizant of its possibilities but filled with trepidation. Thus his continued preoccupation with the Arab-Jewish question was not merely the behavior of an obstinate and contentious opponent of Zionist policy. For Magnes the establishment of the Jewish state made a political accommodation with the Arabs even more imperative. At stake was the security and moral well-being of the State of Israel, which, now that it existed, had to be guarded and nurtured. A sovereign Israel, Magnes believed, must become not only the instrument for the ingathering of the exiles but the vessel for the flowering of Hebrew culture and values, Zion redeemed in justice. The moment of victory was the occasion for largesse, extending the hand of conciliation, discouraging the spirit of revanche, which would bring only more bloodshed and turn the Jewish state into a besieged fortress. This was as much Realpolitik as moral politics. And as in the past Magnes placed the moral burden most heavily on the shoulders of his own people, demanding perhaps more than the unfolding events of the years allowed.

He was obstinate and single-minded, a preacher turned political man who refused to accept the dichotomy between the moral and the real worlds. Therein lay the source of his influence and his appeal. However, he was no absolutist or innocent in dealing with political reality. Indeed, he deftly used his reputation for integrity and candor to advance his political goals. Failing, he tried again. Yet his failures also frustrated and baffled him. He had few collaborators, though he believed he had many well-wishers. Thus his main influence remained that of a dissenter in Zion, the agitator and troubler in Israel, a role that he chose for himself while still in America and that he played out in Jerusalem.

108. JLM to Simcha Assaf, September 7, 1948, MP, 1985.

1
Rebel Rabbi:
Judaism, Zionism,
and
American Life
1900–1910

M AGNES WAS ORDAINED a rabbi at Hebrew Union College in June 1900 and arrived in Berlin in October to begin his graduate studies at the university. His nearly two years in Berlin and his half year at Heidelberg, where he took his degree in December 1902, proved to be the most influential period in his life, one he later called "those days of a great Jewish awakening." This awakening expressed itself in an intense emotional and intellectual immersion in Jewish matters: from academic studies at the Hochschule to agitating for the establishment of a nationalist society of Jewish students to attending services at Orthodox synagogues. On one occasion, after visiting an immigrant congregation in Berlin, he wrote home, "I took so much interest and felt so much pride. It was as noisy as any Orthodox service. The worshippers were of the same stripe that compose other Orthodox congregations. It was I who was different, who saw it all with different eyes."[1] The ideological expression of his "Jewish awakening" was Zionism, which for Magnes meant much more than a political or cultural program (documents 1 and 2).

His letters from Berlin, as well as those he wrote soon after his return to the United States, reflect family tensions and misunderstandings that developed as a result of his Zionist ardor. His mother in particular feared that his "idealism" would hamper his career in the rabbinate or divert him altogether from the calling. Magnes was torn. He recognized the financial benefits and the prestige that went with a wealthy pulpit as well as its usefulness in serving the broader goals in which he was interested. He was no less conscious of the moral obligations he had incurred to those who had enabled him to study in Europe. However, he also harbored serious reservations about being a "practical theologian." Indeed, he questioned whether he possessed the inner faith to be a rabbi. An academic career appealed to him; on the other hand so did a public one. Offered a short-term appointment to teach Bible at Hebrew Union College in

1. Norman Bentwich, *For Zion's Sake: A Biography of Judah L. Magnes* (Philadelphia, 1954), pp. 27–29.

February 1903, he accepted it with alacrity as a convenient way station, where he remained until June 1904.[2]

In January 1904 Temple Israel, the wealthiest Reform congregation in Brooklyn, invited him to be its rabbi. In a long, introspective note that he wrote while en route to Oakland, where he had been summoned to the bedside of his dying mother, Magnes set down the considerations that led him to accept the call. The account also provides insight into the world of Reform Judaism, as does his personal chronicle, written several years later, of his experience as rabbi of Temple Emanu-El (documents 3 and 6). Magnes served the Brooklyn congregation from September 1904 until May 1906, when he accepted Emanu-El's call.

During his tenure at Emanu-El, where he remained until May 1910, he eloquently called for a "counter-reformation."[3] Only the return to a more traditional form of Judaism, he exhorted the congregation, could reverse the tide of assimilation engulfing the native-born generation. In his religious outlook he was close to Solomon Schechter's notion of historic Judaism as the will of universal Israel: veneration for the religious tradition but also respect for modern scholarship and the demands of time and place. In a farewell sermon delivered at Passover in 1910 Magnes summarized his ideas and offered a program for the reconstruction of Reform (document 10). He briefly held one more pulpit, beginning in the spring of 1911, at B'nai Jeshurun in New York, which he intended turning into a model Conservative synagogue (document 13).

Magnes's dissatisfaction with the synagogue touched more than religious practices; he felt that its institutional form required change. When he wrote to his family explaining his resignation from Temple Israel and later from Emanu-El, he mentioned his interest in organizing a "People's Synagogue" that would in time develop into a "movement" appealing to thousands (documents 4 and 12). The idea appeared in his personal account of Emanu-El, in which he described the "platform downtown" he hoped to establish, and in his plans for B'nai Jeshurun, where he saw the congregation developing into a "Jewish Center — a *bet ha'am*, a House of the Jewish People." Others were groping in the same direction. Mordecai M. Kaplan, with an Orthodox background, was endeavoring to create such a model center, and Stephen S. Wise was experimenting with a branch of the Reform Free Synagogue on the Lower East Side.

Zionism, with its emphasis on the totality of Jewish needs and its call for the democratic mobilization of the community to meet those needs, broadened Magnes's communal vision. Elected secretary of the Federation of American Zionists in June 1905, he in fact directed the day-to-day

2. Sophie Magnes to JLM, October 23, 1901, MPWJHC; JLM to family, February 12, 1903, MP, 10c; JLM to Sophie Magnes, February 13, 1903, MP, 10c.

3. JLM, "The Counter-Reformation in Judaism," March 13, 1909, MP, 447.

affairs of the organization, as Harry Friedenwald, the president, resided in Baltimore. To win greater support for the federation Magnes urged it to emphasize "practical work" in Palestine, a policy at odds with the declared stand of the world movement (document 5). He supported too the creation of a fraternal arm for the federation, which would provide the social welfare services immigrants found so attractive in the existing fraternal orders. In 1908 he presided over the formation of the Order Sons of Zion, believing that it would bring thousands into the fold.[4] His Zionism also predisposed him to support other causes. He explained his work for the Jewish Defense Association as an outgrowth of his Zionism: the association was an expression of "Jewish manhood" and the activation of the democratic spirit among the Jewish masses.[5]

In September 1908 New York Police Commissioner Theodore A. Bingham asserted that 50 percent of the city's criminals were Jewish. The Bingham affair, as it came to be called, aroused New York Jewry to a frenzy of protest. Magnes acted quickly and called for a democratic community organization (document 7). He portrayed the formation of the New York Kehillah as a further expression of group pride and communal democracy (document 8). Thus it was his Zionist duty to fight for its success.

Magnes's belief in Jewish group survival in America led him to a theory of American democracy that sanctioned ethnic pluralism. America did not "demand the sacrifice of national individuality," he declared in a Lincoln's birthday sermon in 1909. America in fact thrived on ethnic diversity; Magnes utterly rejected the melting pot image (document 9). His thinking paralleled that of Israel Friedlaender and anticipated Horace Kallen's better-known and more elaborately argued interpretation.

4. JLM to Beatrice Lowenstein, April 26, 1908, MP, 767.
5. *Stenographic Report of Proceedings of a Mass Meeting of Jewish Citizens held on Wednesday evening, January 17, 1906 . . . Cincinnati, Ohio. To Organize a Local Branch of the Jewish Defense Association of the United States* (Cincinnati, n.d.), pp. 22–27, MP, 457.

1

To Family
Oakland, California

My dear Folks:

As I had written you from the Harz Mountains, we came into Berlin Thursday evening. I enjoyed the trip very much, perhaps better than my other trip. Besides, it was very inexpensive. Upon coming home that night I found letters awaiting me. In one respect, it was very funny to get these letters all at one time. Besides Mamma's letter to Ilse[1] about my Zionism and Papa's dictated letter about my Zionism and Izzie's[2] letter about my Zionism, I read a letter from Regina Wise[3] who roasted me for not writing, and a letter from Mrs. Herzog[4] who did likewise, although my friend Birdie had no real cause for doing so. You see I received a very warm welcome home. I was glad they all came together; for had any one of them come alone, I should have thought too much about this one, and that would have made me feel too bad for my comfort. Still Izzie's letter had one good effect. I wrote to Dr. Voorsanger as I had intended to for some time. Still, funny as it appeared to me that all these letters should have come in a bunch, I assure you they have given me much food for thought and many serious moments.

I am afraid, my dear people, that we do not understand each other well enough. You seem to think that my Zionism has nothing to do with my studies, or at least that it has but very little to do therewith. Izzie thinks that it is merely a pastime of mine, and Papa thinks that it interferes too much with my University and Hochschule[5] work, and Mama thinks that it interferes with my writing home. Now, my dear folks, you must not think that I am provoked because you give me your candid opinions. I thank you rather. You must not, then, object if I give you also my candid opinion. Mama ("as usual," as Roseltosel[6] would say) is nearer right than any of you: my Zionism does interfere to a certain degree with my writing home. But do you know why? Not because I am writing Zionist dramas, which I mentioned in a spirit of fun, and not because I am spending my days and nights in helping downtrodden brothers, and not because I am gathering people together in order to take them along to Palestine with me, but, rather, because my Zionism has made me more eager than ever to study and to study hard, because it has filled me more than ever with the desire to get my Ph.D. and to come home in order that I may work as I see fit to work.

You imagine that I can leave Zionism alone in a corner until I have a large enough congregation and salary to enable me without fear to busy myself with such an unpopular doctrine. This shows that you misunderstand altogether what Zionism means for me. The fact that I am a Zionist has, in the first place, changed the course of my studies here. I came here with the idea of getting a degree in philosophy and of doing but little or no work at the Hochschule. Instead of carrying out my original plan, I am working to take a degree in Semitics and am working along Jewish lines, i.e., along lines dealt with at the Hochschule — and this because of my Zionism. Furthermore, Zionism, besides making my intellectual, my spiritual interest different, has worked a change in my mode of life. I seek to live now more like a Jew, i.e., you would call it, more like an Orthodox Jew. Furthermore, my Zionism has given me a definite point of view in the search after which I came to Europe rather than in the search after a Ph.D. While a Ph.D. is very fine and I shall not come home, I hope, without one, were it simply for the Ph.D. I should never have come here, but should have stayed in America. This is what Zionism has already done for me.

What it is doing constantly, all the time, I can simply describe by saying that it is now my whole philosophy. It is my "Lebensprogramm", and to stick it into a corner would be the same as sticking myself into a corner. Since I have become a Zionist, my view of life has changed; my view as to my calling has changed; my view as to my future has changed; my hopes, my prayers have changed. The questions concerning the Jewish people — and the Jewish religion is but one of these questions — are the questions that are consuming my days and my nights. I no longer picture myself a liberal preacher whose chief duty it is to preach goodness and to minister tenderly to a congregation of wealthy Jews. Do not from this infer that I love goodness any the less; or that I intend giving up the preaching of goodness; or that I should be less pleased if I had a wealthy congregation. For on the contrary, since I have become a Zionist, I have learned better to value wealth and to wish for some of it myself.

My Zionism, however, makes me more than a mere preacher or community leader. It makes me a worker for the preservation of the Jewish people as a whole and for their greater glory and better life in their own land. It makes me a politician, if you please, who has in his charge great interests, interests which have come to him from the centuries that have past and which are more sacred than the interests of any individual, be it myself, be it my family. Zionism is a very unpopular thing, I know, and how am I to work with it in America, I myself do not as yet clearly see. One thing, however, is certain: if I can preach my Zionism to, and work for Zionism with, a large wealthy congregation, I shall be only too pleased, for I am not aching to pose as a martyr, and, as I said, I am also desirous now of attaining to some degree of wealth. If, however, I can not preach Zionism to such a congregation, it will have to be to another kind of congregation; and if I can find no congregation, I shall earn my bread in another way; and if I cannot have riches, I shall work without riches; and if it be not in America, it will be in some other land—Palestine, if you will. At any rate, I hope I have made clear to you that I am in earnest in the matter, that my Zionism is more to me than anything else in the world.

I should like to live a happy life, a life, too, in which I could be of service, first of all, to my family—to my parents, to my brother, to my sisters. But, unfortunately, the chances for such a life are not so bright for those who wish to be leaders of men, moulders of the lives of men. A businessman, a physician, an ease-loving rabbi—in short, any other class of men can work and become rich and perhaps happy no matter what opinions they may happen to hold as to the make-up of things. But I happen to be in the position where my opinions as to the make-up of things are all that I have. If my opinions happen to be correct and I have enough energy and mind to carry them through, happy me. But if my opinions happen to be despised—even though they be not incorrect—and I do not succeed in pushing them through, woe is me.

My dear ones, let me be even franker with you, for you are my best friends, and to you I can open my heart. If I want simply a good, respectable position as rabbi of a large congregation—a position in which I shall receive much honor and a large salary, and in which I shall be able also to satisfy myself as regards study, and in which I shall be able to do much good—I am sure that after taking my degree here I could come back to America and in the course of time get such a position. Everyone is not given such an opportunity to serve himself well, to serve his family well, and also to do his little share of good in the world. Perhaps it is foolish of me not to embrace such an opportunity, and perhaps it is a pity that I do not embrace it. The Germans have a saying something like this: "Wenn es dem Esel zu gut geht, will er auf's Eis treten."[7] I hope that this is not the case with me in so far as I have joined myself heart and soul with the Zionist idea. Whether my Zionism will stand in the way of my getting an influential position, I do not know. As I said, I am as yet uncertain as to how I shall apply my Zionism in America. One thing, however, I am quite sure of, that in order to get a comfortable, paying, influential position, one in which I could also do honest work, I shall not sacrifice my Zionism which has given rise within me to some of the best thoughts and noblest feelings I have yet had. I am not a Zionist for revenue only, as I am afraid some of our American Zionists are. I am a Zionist who will draw all necessary conclusions from his Zionism and who will not shirk in the carrying out of what he holds to be his duty.

I have talked enough for today—perhaps too much. Still I hope that we understand each other somewhat better than before.

Much love and kisses,

from, Leon

1. Ilse Mühlendorf, a cousin of Sophie Magnes, who lived in Berlin.
2. Isaac Magnes (1880–1969), JLM's younger brother.
3. Regina Wise, daughter of Rabbi Isaac Mayer Wise of Cincinnati.
4. Birdie Herzog, close friend of the family who resided in Cleveland.
5. The popular name for the Lehranstalt fuer die Wissenschaft des Judentums, the eminent liberal rabbinical seminary.
6. Pet name of JLM's younger sister, Rosalind Magnes (b. 1891), who married Eugene Blumenthal.
7. "When life is too good for the donkey, he wants to tread on ice."

2

To Family
Oakland, California

Berlin, December 26, 1901

My dear Folks:

Today is the second day *yomtov* [holiday], i.e. the second day of Christmas. Some people celebrate tomorrow also, and since Saturday is only one day before Sunday, they will celebrate Saturday and Sunday also. The Dutchies do their Christmas celebrating in fine style. The streets are packed, jammed two weeks in advance with people bringing Christmas presents. Every one has to give every one else a present, else, to the winds with such a friendship! The stores have official permission to remain open until 10, and the two Sundays before Christmas they are open all day long until 10 at night. The last Sunday is known as "der Goldene Sonntag." because that is the chief business day for the small shop-keepers. Every family with children has a Christmas tree, i.e., every German family, and you can rest assured that our dear Jews here as well as elsewhere can not resist the temptation of adopting this pretty custom. Christmas eve, Dr. Schloessinger and I took a long walk, and in almost every story of the rows on rows of high dwelling buildings, a Christmas tree with its dozens of lights and sparkling draperies could be seen. It is a custom here to put the Christmas tree near the window so that the passers-by can see them, just as with our Hanuka lights. The Christmas tree, indeed the whole Christmas season with its purported message of peace and goodwill, is a beautiful institution, and we, as Jews, should be glad that the *goyim* also have a few seasons that are worth the while.

But we Jews are apt to forget that any single one of our own numerous festivals has had and has a meaning as significant, and surely some of our festivals have a much deeper meaning than the Christmastide. And it is my principle — and that is National Judaism — that even though all of our festivals put together in a lump were not as beautiful as the one Christmas festival, that even then, aye just then, it would be our duty as Jews to celebrate our own inferior(?) festivals with zeal and enthusiasm, just as it is our duty to hold ourselves aloof from all influences, however noble they may be, that tend to rob the Jews of their own peculiar, Jewish characteristics. We cannot afford to make a single concession. We are in duty bound to preserve all that we have, and equally in duty bound to resist all temptation to make ourselves as the others are.

We Jews shall be able to accomplish something only when we have left off imitating the rest of the world. Why can we not live our own lives? Why must we ever be on the lookout lest we offend the sensibilities of this one or of that? Why do we make it our first business to wipe out everything that marks us out as Jews? Why should not a Jewish nose be as beautiful to us, aye more beautiful than another nose? Who laid down the laws of beauty? No one; and we have as much right to our peculiar type as any one else has to his. It is too sad. In our hearts, in the midst of our families, we feel ourselves other than our neighbors. Outwardly we want to appear just as they do. It is an ignoble struggle, and the sooner we get out of it one way or the other, the better for us. The one way is to give up everything, i.e., call ourselves Christians, Americans or whatever you will. The other way is the way that Zionism proposes.

You see, there I am again at my Zionism, I can't leave it out, i.e., "cut it out", as Eva's[1] slang will have it. This reminds me to tell Papa how pleased I was to hear from him that the Zionism that has for its object the relief of our oppressed brothers in Eastern Europe, etc., meets with his hearty approval. Of course it does. How could it be otherwise? Everyone who feels himself in any way a Jew must welcome the opportunity to settle this terrible question of life and death with our poor Jews once and for all. The Zionistic plan is, in this respect, gigantic. The Alliance Israélite,[2] Jewish Colonization Association,[3] and all the other institutions that have attempted to solve this problem, have done so on a small scale and through private means, e.g., Baron de Hirsch and Rothschild. The Zionistic plan is to solve the problem along political lines, and through a Bank[4] to which the Jews of all the world are to contribute. This is self-help. The shares cost at present $5 per. It is expected, of course, that when the Bank has more capital, the shares will increase in value, and that in time they will pay dividends. At present the capital is small money, about $1,250,000. Ten millions are asked for in order to make the first deals with the Sultan. In what way this money is to come, only the future will show. The poorer Jews of the world are doing their share. Whether the rich Jews of Germany, France, England, America, etc., will come to the assistance of this plan depends, among other things, upon what the Bank accomplishes without their help and upon the conditions, political and social, in which the Jews will find themselves in the years to come. One thing is certain, the Christian world will soon be helping us, and out of business reasons. Palestine is in the center of the world's commerce. To have this sleeping land cultivated by Jews will be a commercial gain. Israel Zangwill spoke recently before the principal industrial club of London on the business prospects of the resettlement of Palestine by the Jews. But in whatever way the money is to come, come it will, because the movement is genuine, because it has youth, enthusiasm, love, and the will to live behind it. Of course, I believe I can do more for the movement by working in America. America is destined to be first in line to see the great value of it all.

But, my dear father, Zionism has more sides to it than simply the helping, along political lines, of our oppressed brethren in Europe, America, or wherever. That is the so-called negative side of the matter. We must think a little farther. First, suppose that our plan fails. What will become not alone of our oppressed Jews, but of the Jews of the rest of the world? Second, granted that our plan succeeds, what will become of the five millions of Jews who are supposedly not oppressed? Zionism has an answer: not alone must we relieve our oppressed; we must again put all our energies to work, *as a people*, in order to create a Jewish culture. This scattering of our forces all over the world is a loss, not only to ourselves, but also to the world. What could we not accomplish if we Jews were all together! So great is my faith in the Jewish people that I believe that from this people, working together as a people, a new and great culture will emanate. The center of this culture must be the old historical land where our fathers produced so glorious a civilization whose classic expression is the Bible. Here in this land, the greater number of the Jews of the world must live. Here we shall have Jewish standards for everything: Jewish learning, Jewish goodness, Jewish beauty, Jewish forms of state, Jewish music, art, sculpture. In America we cannot produce Jewish forms of life. In Germany we cannot have Jewish standards. No one can sit down and say: I am now going to write Jewish literature. Jewish literature is possible only when it is the product of a Jewish mind in a Jewish atmosphere, where it is the natural run of things to produce things Jewish just as it is the natural run of things to produce that which is German in Germany.

All the Jews of the world will not, cannot live in Palestine and in the surrounding country. What does Zionism say to the others who cannot, who do not want to, who will not live in Palestine? This is a very serious and uncertain problem, and to get its answer will require decades of development and the best thoughts of our best minds. In the first place, Zionism says to those who do not want to take part in the reestablishment of a new Jewish culture in Palestine: you have the right, of course, to stay where you are; we do not want you.

To those who want to contribute their lives to the reestablishment of the new Jewish culture, but who for hundreds of reasons cannot go to Palestine, Zionism says: every land has foreigners. When the Jewish state comes into existence, are you ready to regard yourself as a citizen of the Jewish state, and a foreigner, a Jew, in the land in which you live? Will you be zealous in spreading Jewish standards of life, not alone of religion, in your present home, just as, for example, the German brings German standards of life into his new home in America? Are you ready *now* to keep intact all the time-honored Jewish customs and traditions that constitute at present our standard of culture? Are you ready *now* to work for the reestablishment of the Jewish state? To him who answers 'yes' to these questions, I believe that Zionism will say: you are a true Jew. If Zionism were *only* the helping of our oppressed brothers, and the rehabilitation of Palestine in a commercial sense, Christians as well as Jews could be considered good Zionists. But only a Jew can be a real Zionist, insofar as he is ready to work with his whole strength for the higher ideals that Zionism preaches.

I have preached so long that I forgot to use this side of the paper, and if I use more sheets, I'll have to pay extra postage, and that would never do for a poor man. I hope I haven't disturbed your equanimity again by my Zionistic speech. You see, it isn't such a devilish monster after all.

I shall read some Syriac now and then wander about a bit. The weather is clear, wintry weather, for a change. I am well; I hope you all are.

Much love and many kisses,

Leon

1. Eva Magnes (1881–1962). JLM's sister, married Chester J. Teller.

2. Founded in 1860 in Paris to secure Jewish rights in countries where they were discriminated against; extended aid to Jewish immigrants and established network of educational institutions for Jews in Middle Eastern countries.

3. Also known as ICA; established by Baron Maurice De Hirsch (1831–1896), a German financier and philanthropist, to assist in large-scale resettlement of East European Jewish immigrants, particularly in agriculture.

4. The World Zionist Organization had announced the formation of a colonizing bank, the Jewish Colonial Trust.

3

Journal: A Call to the Ministry

En route to California, January 14, 1904

I shall now attempt to note on paper those incidents and conversations that took place during my Brooklyn stay. It is at a sad time that I am writing this. I am on the way home to California. The telegram announcing dear Mamma's serious illness came last night. I had expected her to be the main reader of my report. God grant that she may be spared. I do so much want to give her pleasure.

I had heard much of Mr. Abraham,[1] the President, from Nelson.[2] Everything that Nelson said of him is, as far as I can judge, true. He is a middle-sized man with a thin face and a gray, pointed chin-beard and moustache. His nose is prominent, being long and pointed. He must be about 60 years of age. He is quiet of manner, has a kindly look and a soft voice. He is evidently a man well posted in Jewish affairs. He seems to have many general interests and is not backward in using his vast wealth to the advantage of worthy institutions. He is, in short, a gentleman of refinement and culture and one with whom work is pleasant to contemplate.

The Thursday evening of my arrival he had arranged a supper in my honor. But my train was late, and I preferred staying with Schloessinger that night. So Nelson and I visited him at his private office in his magnificent department store which, by the way, so Nelson tells me, employs 4000 people all told. The main points of our conversation that morning were the following: he asked if I was conservative or radical in my views. The very fact that he, as president of a supposedly radical congregation, could ask such a question is proof enough of his openness of mind. I answered that in my views, i.e. theoretically, I was radically inclined much more than, e.g. Nelson. Practically, however, there were many phases in Jewish life which appealed to me and many which did not. He summed it up by saying that I was an eclectic, as he declared himself to be; he admired the old Friday eve, for example. Further, I said that one of the reasons why I wanted to come to New York was in order to be able to interest myself in the Brownsville community. Brownsville is the "East Side" of Brooklyn. I asked whether or not the congregation would regard my work there as part of my communal activity. I furthermore said that the Brownsville people for the most part would interest me more than many

71

members of my own congregation because there was in them more material to work with. He answered that it would be a matter of course that my first interest should be my own congregation, its members, and its upbuilding. For, as he rightly remarked, the greater the influence of my own congregation, the greater my own influence outside of it. He then added that there would naturally be no hindrance put in the way of my working for, with, or at Brownsville as much as I pleased to. As a matter of fact, his son-in-law, Mr. Rothschild,[3] type of quiet, forceful, successful businessman I admire, is president of the Hebrew Educational Society of Brownsville, a society similar to the Educational Alliance in New York. As a matter of course I recognize that my first duty is toward my own congregation. Indeed, it is one of my thoughts in wishing to have charge of a large and wealthy institution that I may not alone help it, but by helping it be enabled to help other institutions in which I may be interested. I heard e.g., of three young Russians who were conducting a school *ivrit b'ivrit*.[4] Now if I can bring it about that men of my congregation interest themselves in such a school, my work will not have been in vain. He then asked as to my Zionism, whether I was an active or a passive Zionist. Upon receiving the reply that I am an active Zionist, he asked whether I expected to see a general exodus of Jews from America to Palestine. I told him I did not expect to see it; nor was such an exodus a necessity. He said of Brooklyn what Nelson had told me, that the Jewish community is growing at a phenomenal rate and that there was great room for building up a good congregation. After talking of personal matters — age, college, Europe, etc. — Nelson and I were taken to lunch by Mr. A's other son-in-law and other member of the firm, Mr. Blum.[5] He, too, is a pleasant gentleman. At the club we saw all the big politicians of Brooklyn.

Then Nelson took me to see the synagogue. It is a pretty place. It can hold about 600 people. It has a large dome above the auditorium which is arranged in a semi-circle and is occupied by open chairs. The whole has neither a lecture hall nor a church aspect, but is a modern synagogue. The school building which was erected at the rear over a year ago is a solid and useful structure. The large hall downstairs and the rooms upstairs make an ideal place for a school and for other congregational activities.

Upon returning to Nelson's house, we found Schloessinger waiting for us. I went to Nelson's study to learn my sermon. This took me about an hour and a half, but the fact that I learned it so quickly rather hampered me in the evening. The service passed off well; the cantor is a straightforward young man with a fair voice. The sermon was well received; the people came up afterward and were rather enthusiastic in their expressions of satisfaction. The people seemed to be intelligent and young. Mr. Abraham made the remark that I might have wanted him to make: the sermon was along new lines of thought; it was not hackneyed. This pleased me because I really did write the sermon out of my own experience for the most part. Henrietta [Szold], with her usual penetration, told me that the position was mine.

Friday, January 15, 1904, En route past Omaha

Since yesterday I have known of my mother's death. I do not understand what it means. I can not believe it; and yet I know it is true. I am afraid to think of it. I must reserve my strength for the sadness at home. My dear Mama will not hear what I have to say; still it was chiefly for her that I wished to write.

In the morning before the service, Mr. A. asked me to hand in a formal application for the position. I told him that I did not want to do this as it did not appeal to my sense of the dignity of the position, but that if it be a matter of necessity I should do so. Immediately after the service he said to me, "You were right; it is better that you should not hand in an application."

I talked that morning on Jewish individuality. The evening before I had preached on spiritual freedom, i.e. on the human personality. The evening's sermon had not contained the word 'Jew.' It was a purely religious, even theological discourse, if you will. In the morning, however, I spoke of my views of Jewish culture. I did not mention the word 'Zionism' or 'nationalism,' but anyone with eyes to see knew the logical conclusion. Indeed, afterwards I said to Mr. A., "This is my Zionism." He said, "I understand it. The more one looks into the matter the more one realizes there is something to it." My remarks must have impressed them more strongly than on the previous evening, as their enthusiasm was very marked. Mr. A. asked me for my manuscript so that he might publish it in the papers and distribute it to all the members. I was amused at his astonishment at my saying that I had not written it out but had spoken freely. He then wanted me to write it out and send it to him. I objected for several reasons: that I had written an academic treatment of the same (Wednesday club paper) which I expected to print, and that I objected to publishing things in the daily press, and that I should not be held accountable for the members' absence. With a laugh he declared my points well taken.

He then took me aside and said that it would be best to make arrangements now instead of by correspondence. He proposed to present my name at the board meeting the following Monday. He could assure me unofficially, of course, of my being chosen. Would I accept if it were tendered me—to which I replied yes. He then asked if a contract for three years, the first year at $2500, the next two at $3000 would be satisfactory to me. I answered, 'yes.' I added, "I have, as you have noticed, without hesitation answered yes, and I mean this. But I think it only fair to remark that I am earning about $2400 at Cincinnati. There I have no communal obligations which necessitate an extra expense. It would cost more for any man to live in Brooklyn than in Cincinnati, but more especially for one like myself who would now enter into a public position." I did not want to haggle about the salary. I had said 'yes' to his proposition, but I had thought it fair to say what I did. He said I was right to say it and that I should leave it to them; they would do the very best they could by me. He thought they would give me $3000 from the start. The larger the congregation grew, he said, the more I should get. He thought, too, that I had a good idea when I mentioned to his son-in-law, Mr. Blum, the day before, the organization of a Wednesday Club in Brooklyn. I said also that I should like as many children as possible to come to the services on Saturday morning. This he agreed with, too.

He then put the question: "Do I intend staying a rabbi?" He justified this by citing the examples of Geismar [6] and Nelson, both of whom retired to enter the law. I said that I could just as little foretell what would happen to me after six years, after one year, as could Nelson. "What was my present intention?", he asked. My present intention was to go into it for all I was worth. I could do no more than try my best. Were I to shovel snow in the street, I should do my best at it. "Then you are frank enough, that if you did not want the position you would say, 'I do not want it.'" "Certainly." But, I added, "I wish to be perfectly frank. There are certain things in the ministry with which I have but very little sympathy. For example, I do not understand how it is possible for a man to preach twice a week and give forth from his own experience and his own knowledge something which is not hackneyed, to use your own term." He then comforted me, "You are inexperienced; you will grow." I answered, "I hope to grow in experience and in knowledge, and the fact that some men can preach honestly and in a way worthwhile gives me hope. But in case I find that I can not do this, there would be but one thing for me to do." But he did not seem to feel uneasiness upon this point. I then said, "Were I a merchant, or physician or lawyer or someone who had an intense interest in some pursuit, a service like the one that morning would not be sufficient to attract me." He looked at me in surprise and said, "I am not attracted by it either." I continued, "In Cincinnati where I have no official position as reader or preacher, I attend services rather seldom. Sometimes I do go. I think this is because of a religious feeling, but I am not sure. But I much prefer to go to an Orthodox service. There, I, as a student of Hebrew literature, find something to interest me: a Hebrew prayer book with ancient prayers, customs of great age, etc. All of these attract me from a romantic and historical point of view. I will not claim that it is religious. But my religious feelings are, to say the least, expressed as well as at a Reform service. Of course, it would be absurd to wish for an Orthodox service here. But I must confess that I do not know what to offer that will make the present service appeal to a man's intellect and emotions sufficiently to take him away from his life's predominant interests. The service as it is, has at best (except of course for the too few who come out of religious need), only an aesthetic interest. One hears good music, is in a pretty building, finds himself surrounded by congenial people, feels a certain hush, but this interest is not powerful enough to draw men away from more engrossing things." "What then do you expect to do?," was his proper question. "In the first place, I shall try to study the needs of men and thereby to contribute to the production of a service that may have some power over them. And in the second place, it is unfortunately the case, but it is the case nevertheless, that people are nowadays attracted chiefly by the personality before them. Now I do not know whether I have strong enough personality. If I find that my personality is not powerful enough, there will, again be only one thing for me to do."

This being the case, it was necessary to speak about the freedom of my platform. I said that my whole Jewish point of view was Jewish-national; that while I did not have to reiterate this constantly, all my thoughts on Jewish matters were colored by it. He said that he did not expect in his life-time to see a general exodus of Jews to Palestine. I said that this was a different question, a practical question; that we might differ as to the practical side of the matter; that this did not militate against the correctness of the Jewish national theory. He then made a remark which shows his deep insight. He admitted the correctness of my stand and added that many great movements have sprung out of philosphic ideas — 1848, e.g. — and, I added, the French Revolution. I said that in case I came I should expect to have an absolutely free platform; that I was to be bound by no congregational dogmas. He thought that might be regarded as a matter of course; indeed, they wished to be informed and to hear various sides of a question. It was not necessary, to be sure, that they always agree. Nelson and Mr. Blum and the Vice President, Mr. Goodstein,[7] heard parts of our conversation. I think we understood one another. At any rate, I did not know how to make my side of the case plainer.

It is a remarkable incident; not because I was party to it, but because it shows after all the strength and the weakness of American conditions. It shows their weakness in that it reveals the utter anarchy and helplessness and anchorlessness of our Jewish life. We do not know what we are, what we stand for, if the future is to see us alive or dead; our present is without a point of view; we are drifting, and we do not seem to care much whither. It shows our strength in that a man with ideas such as I have as to Jewish nationalism, the ministry, and the Reform service can be favorably considered as head of a congregation with opposite views, if it has any. This is strength inasmuch as it shows freedom, liberty. It is but another indication to me of the correctness of my belief that because we American Jews are free, we shall therefore work out our salvation as Jews (salvation meaning for me, of course, our national salvation).

There are several motives that have led me to want to leave Cincinnati and go to Brooklyn as a rabbi. I wish to enumerate them. First let me say why I should like to stay in Cincinnati: (1) I should have more opportunity to engage in scientific work. I acquired a scientific ideal in Germany. It would be a great satisfaction to me to be able to do some productive work along Jewish scientific lines. I regard the ability to do this as of transcendent importance. I do not know whether or not I have this ability. I may, at least, have the ideal. (2) The Cincinnati authorities and people have placed confidence in me and have treated me well. My life there had fallen in pleasant places. I could not wish for pleasanter associations. (3) I have a deep aversion to a purely theological profession. Theology as an academic science has not the terrors it formerly held for me. But it is something else to be a practical theologian. (a) He presumes to be on speaking terms with God, whereas my whole bent of mind leads me to a negative attitude to God's attributes and the lessons of His manifestations of Himself in nature and to men. The preacher ought to feel an inner "call" for him to lead others to regard life from a religious point of view. I have not this call. I do not rise in my wrath when I know men are atheists. My view of God does not go farther than my conviction that He is and that I therefore need not fear. (b) The preacher should be a man with confidence in his own moral and spiritual life. I am not ashamed of my moral and spiritual life, but I can not say that I am burning to impose my standards of right and of wrong living upon my fellows. (c) There are aspects of the rabbi's vocation that do not appeal to me. I have treated some of them at length above. He must be a well-oiled talking machine; he must reveal his most sacred thoughts and feelings; he must officiate at marriages and funerals; he must be the representative of the community in its service before God. (d) My Jewish national point of view makes the Jewish theologian distasteful to me. Modern Jewish theologians have attempted to make of the Jews and their history, as Zunz[8] says, only *Kirchen* [church] *material*. They interpret Jewish history as anti-national, i.e. theological. They see in us only a sect. They would have us be only *ḥasidim* [righteous ones] and *anavim* [humble ones]. All of this runs counter to my deepest feelings and convictions. I believe we are more than *Kirchenmaterial*, more than a mere theological sect; I would not have our people all *ḥasidim* and *anavim*, i.e. all Jewish Salvation Armyists. In becoming a professional Jewish theologian I am placed in a difficult position as regards a Jewish national-political life. But in spite of all this I have consented to leave Cincinnati and go to Brooklyn because (1) I am not sure whether I shall be able to accomplish much in a scientific way. At any rate I have felt that mere professorial activity without constant contact with a larger audience through the spoken word does not give full expression to my energies. I have felt the need of addressing audiences on Jewish topics, i.e. on Zionism. This open activity has incurred the displeasure — quite justifiably I sometimes think — of the College authorities. Dr. Kohler[9] "warned" me against it as it did not represent the College's point of view. His word "warn," by the way, was a translation of the German *"warnen"* [warn] and not of *"drohen"* [threaten], as I was willing to make myself believe, at least. I have, therefore, felt that it would come to a clash sooner or later. I do not know whether I should have engaged in extensive propaganda by word of mouth. I am inclined to think I should not. Nevertheless, the feeling that I might not, the feeling that I was in an incongruous position, that my activity there was conditional upon good behavior, could not have resulted in good for me or for the institution. By going to Brooklyn, I insure myself, so it would seem, perfect freedom. Furthermore, I shall try to arrange my time so that I shall be able to devote my mornings at least to study and to work. (2) I hope to form pleasant associations in Brooklyn, too. (3) The understanding with Mr. A. that I have described above makes my Brooklyn prospects rather attractive even from a theological point of view. The call as theologian and preacher that I said was missing, I never expect to receive. Still, this will not keep me from modestly expressing myself in religious and other spiritual matters. I expect to work hard along these lines and to see whether in the development of my point of view I shall not be able to [A page of approximately eighteen lines is missing.] . . . and may be argued only by one who wishes to deceive himself. For there is no *voraussetzingslose Wissenschaft* [objective science]; and one of the reasons that attract me to the school is the very fact that my influencing the teachers of the people could be of greater service to my ideas than my influencing only my own community. (4) Taking the position of rabbi means fulfilling the year-long dreams of my family. Now my poor mother is no longer here to share in the pleasure that my occupancy of a pulpit will afford my family. I shall not forget how I hurt her when I accepted the College position in preference to a rabbinical position that had been offered me. Nor shall I cease being thankful that she knew of my intention to go to Brooklyn. Unfortunately, she could not know of the successful outcome of it. The deepest, sincerest feeling I had was to please her. What would I not have done to make her happy! What beautiful plans I had to bring her to me to Brooklyn after we had been separated for so many long years! But the fact that my going to Brooklyn was partly under her auspices gives it now a certain sacredness that it might otherwise not have had. (5) The position of rabbi has, despite its inherent drawbacks and the disregard of the majority of Jews for it, certain social and communal advantages of such a nature as to make its occupant *eo ipso* of some influence in the shaping of a communal policy. In this way, I hope to be able to further the interests of many Jewish institutions, projects and individuals that might otherwise be denied such support. (6) The establishment of a Jewish school in connection with my congregation and not merely a mamby-pamby Sunday school is an object of worthy endeavor. If it only starts with a few children, I shall be satisfied. It will be of some good to have taken the children of Jewish indifferentists or amalgamationists and have given them some Jewish consciousness by teaching them Hebrew and Jewish history and love of all Jews and hopes for a Jewish future. This will not be easy, but it will be grateful work. (7) I shall be in New York, the great center of Jewish population. This means much to me. On the one hand, it gives me an opportunity of coming into first-hand contact with the problems of Jewish immigration and the Jewish immigrant. On the other hand, it brings me into conflict with a non-anti-national and for the most part ecclesiastically inclined rabbinate. There is room in New York, above all places, for men. Besides, New York offers many incentives for one of my temperament for work. I am surrounded by *Gesinnungsgenossen* [spiritual companions], there are plenty of *maskilim* [intellectuals], there are great libraries; there is, in short, some evidence and some remnant of a Jewish life. I would be of that new generation of young nationalists mentioned by Waldstein in *Hashiloaḥ* for September, "Me'amerika"[10] — a generation made up of American born and reared, and of Europeans raised under Jewish national influences. (8) I shall be able to earn a greater salary. This reason could not be decisive with me, but it is one that appeals to me strongly in a consideration of the situation as it now is. I have many obligations that I shall the better be able to fulfill on this account; and I am not at all insensible to what money stands for: for work and for ability sometimes, and for most of the things of life. While on this point, I want to add something that I told Mr. A. I said that I should never have come to Brooklyn to preach a trial sermon were it not for two reasons: first, because I knew Nelson so well and the circumstances under which he was retiring, but second, because I was occupying no pulpit so that the congregation could get no line on my abilities. Should I ever wish to leave for another pulpit, the congregation wanting me would have to send a committee to hear me and to consult with me. I told Nelson something more—I did not tell it to Mr. A. for fear he would think I was trying to coerce him—namely, that should they have any one else preach in Brooklyn, I should withdraw my name as I would under no circumstances enter into a competition with someone else. I ridiculed to Mr. A. Temple Emanu-El's [N.Y.] present intention of inviting a dozen men to preach there every other Saturday. I characterized it as exhibiting the spiritual poverty of both the temple and the rabbis: of the temple that it would consent to having rabbis come to engage in a continuous performance on the theatrical order; of the rabbis that they would so forget their own dignity and that of their calling as to accept an invitation to fight one another. Mr. A. thought my attitude the proper one.

I have heard nothing as yet from Brooklyn although today is Friday, and I have asked Lowenstein to telegraph me any results. I hope nothing has hitched. The only thing I can think of is that some would like to hear some more for their money. I trust this is not the case as by that very act I am out of it. At any rate I have put down my experiences and my feelings as they occur to me almost a week afterwards, and at a time when my heart is heavy with thoughts of the calamity that has befallen me. But let me express the one hope in closing, that my mother's spirit will never forsake me, and that I shall never be afraid.

The following telegram has come from Lowenstein:

Cin. Jan. 15. c/o Comdr. Overland Limited I, Kearney, Nebr.
Elected Brooklyn three thousand three years. Have forwarded letters. Wired Nelson. Wrote Abraham.

S. C. Lowenstein

1. Abraham Abraham (1843-1911). Merchant and philanthropist; born in New York City. With Nathan and Isidor Straus and Simon F. Rothschild established Abraham and Straus Department Store of Brooklyn; president of Hebrew Orphan Asylum of Brooklyn.
2. Leon A. Nelson (1876-1941). Rabbi, lawyer. Served Temple Israel of Brooklyn, 1896-1904; practiced law in Richmond, Virginia.
3. Simon F. Rothschild (1861-1936). Merchant and philanthropist. Married a daughter of Abraham Abraham; president of Abraham and Straus, Inc.; treasurer of Bardon de Hirsch Fund.
4. Teaching "Hebrew in Hebrew," modern method of Hebrew language instruction.
5. Edward Charles Blum (1863-1946). Merchant and philanthropist. Chairman of board of directors of Abraham and Straus, Inc., and president of Federated Department Stores; director and president of Jewish Hospital of Brooklyn.
6. Alexander H. Geismar (1869-1939). Rabbi, lawyer, jurist. After serving as rabbi of Temple Israel, studied law; justice of the New York City court from 1927.
7. Samuel Goodstein (1849-1909). Merchant and Jewish community leader. Vice president of the Brookly Orphan Asylum and a founder of the Hebrew Benevolent Society.
8. Leopold Zunz (1794-1886). German-Jewish historian and one of the founders of the Wissenschaft des Judentums (the Science of Judaism).
9. Kaufmann Kohler (1843-1926). Rabbi and theologian; born in Fürth, Germany, and came to the United States in 1869. Served congregations in Detroit, Chicago, and New York before being elected president of HUC in 1903.
10. *Hashiloaḥ* 12 (September 1904), 264.

4

To Family
Oakland, California

Dear Folks:

I have not written to you for some time because I have been rushed with meetings night and day. I am feeling very well, for which I am very thankful.

This letter will perhaps contain some news concerning myself which may not seem very pleasant to you but which leaves me rather indifferent. I am writing you these words in the hope that you will have enough confidence in me not to censure me.

At a meeting of the trustees of the congregation yesterday I felt that the only manly and honest thing for me to do was to resign my position as rabbi of Temple Israel. I trust that you will not feel that this is a great calamity, because it is not. I suppose I should have had to leave sooner or later, and it is perhaps better that it should have been now rather than in a few years. I have many other things to do. Should I want to go into another congregation I could get ten. I have several plans, and I shall tell you about them later on after I tell you something of the details of my resignation. The resignation has not, by the way, been accepted as yet; but it will be next week, very likely. Nor is it decided when I shall leave. That will very likely depend on the congregation. Many of the members have already expressed their sorrow to me.

Yesterday I was invited to a meeting of the board at Mr. Abraham's office. Without much notice Mr. Abraham delivered a tirade against me, the upshot of which was that I was too active in Zionism, that I was too conservative in my Judaism, and that I associated too much with revolutionists. This latter statement was brought about by the fact, which you may know of, that I am chairman of the Jewish Defense Association, which has as its object the sending of money to Russia for the sake of the arming of Jews to defend themselves. He claimed that I always irritated them when I spoke, and our views were incompatible. He expressed great admiration for my character and for my ability, but he believed that I was harming the congregation because of my views rather than benefiting it. I answered to the effect that I was not in the habit of defending myself and would not do it now. I was sorry that they felt that way. I had worked hard and had large plans. I did not believe that the sentiments which Mr. Abraham expressed were the sentiments of the congregation.

The congregation was now in better shape than it ever had been. The services were better attended, the school was larger, the influence of the congregation larger. But the only honorable thing for me to do when such things were said to me was to resign. They were hardly prepared for this, and it was quite a stunner to them. Several expressed their regret at my action while others agreed with me. There will be a meeting of the board this week when everything will be decided.

I am not at all worried over the matter. I feel as though it were a release from a certain kind of bondage. I never felt altogether at ease there. I have the plan of organizing a people's synagogue either here or in New York. The membership fee will be $5 per year to everyone, man or woman. We shall also have to depend on donations. I know from my experience here and from the friends I have made that I can get probably a thousand young men and women to join me in such a movement. I believe that such a movement can develop into the most powerful in America.

I shall consult with many people in the matter — with Judge [Mayer] Sulzberger, with Dr. Schechter, with Miss Szold and with others. Miss Szold said to me not long ago that my duty was to be on the East Side of New York, and Judge Sulzberger expressed the same opinion last June. My one year of experience here has taught me that I have a great deal of strength and power within me. I have created a position for myself in the community — an honorable and an influential one, and that, almost despite the fact that I was associated with Temple Israel. If I did not feel that I had the power to do big things and that the opportunity for big things was there, I should feel more aggrieved than I do. What I am interested in now is to see what the members of the congregation have to say to it all.

I trust that you will not feel sad about it. Eva[1] and I have considered the matter, and we are each of us glad in a certain sense. I am somewhat sorry because I was commencing to feel a little better satisfied. How long that would have lasted is another question. The whole thing is not pleasant, but it is one of those things which sometimes must happen for the good of all.

I have a splendid appetite and last night I slept like a peaceful child, and I shall do the same tonight. I know that at a distance you will imagine all sorts of things. But the whole situation is just as simple as I have pictured it to you so that there is no need for any excitement or any bitterness or any sorrow. It is a situation which I have created, and I must be the one to make the most of it. This is a crisis in my life. It will mean either my advancement to very great power or to mediocrity. I trust it will mean the former. With calm judgment, with complete honesty, with love of the Jewish people in my heart, I am sure that it will mean power to me to do the good in a larger way than I have been doing at present. You must help me by preserving your calm, and your confidence in me and in the future.

My love to all of you.

Leon

1. Magnes's sister, who kept house for him at the time.

5

To David Wolffsohn
Cologne

New York, June 19, 1906

Dear Mr. Wolffsohn:

Permit me to thank you, in behalf of the Executive Committee, for your kind words of greeting to our convention[1] and for your statement as to the general policy of our movement. At the convention, which is to be held at Tannersville, we shall pass a resolution along the lines of your letter, namely: first, emphasizing the fact that our movement has been and must remain a political movement in the full sense of the term; and, second, that we are in favor of immediate and intense activity in Palestine.

I am sorry that my letter to you seemed to have a tone not warranted by the circumstances. You will, however, understand that we are preparing for a very active campaign in behalf of Zionism, and we believe it to be altogether necessary to have a statement from the chairman of the Small Actions Committee. We were careful to state that we did not want the impossible; but we did feel that if we could have the assurance that our movement, while not losing its thorough political character, would still sanction—if not officially, at least morally—immediate and intense active work in Palestine, we should be able to come to the American Jews with some sanction of our own plans in this direction. It is true that the Zionist movement in this country has not amounted to much as yet. We are far away from the center of things; we use a language which the organs of the movement do not use. We have also suffered, and are still suffering from the awful blunders that have been made in the past. For the past six months—indeed, ever since the massacres[2]—we have been practically at a stand-still as far as the increase of our active work is concerned. These months, however, have not passed without some profits to us. We feel that we can now go about our work for the next year with increased energy and with renewed hopes. Our convention will take very definite action in many matters; and we shall transmit to you a copy of our proceedings as soon after the adjournment of our convention as possible. Whereas we feel the importance and the need of political action, that is, of the safe-guarding of our interests from the point of view of the development of politics in Europe, we feel that all we can do in the matter is to talk about such things; so that the political movement, in so far as no suggestion comes to us from headquarters, is not a matter of our concern. There is, therefore, left to us the strengthening of the Zionist institutions: Shekel, National Fund, Bank and so forth. This strengthening of such institutions we expect to take actively in hand. We do feel, however, the great need of emphasizing that all our strength lies in practical work in Palestine. We are of the opinion that such a thing would find an echo in the Jewish masses of this country. We have not moved "vom Fleck" [a bit] for the past six months. Now we feel that we must make a move, even though it be an erroneous one. We do not think, however, that a move in the direction of practical work in Palestine will be an error.

We have also communicated with Dr. Nossing,[3] Chairman of the Propaganda Commission, in the matter of having sent here two or three speakers from Russia for the sake of making propaganda for our movement in the fall.

Permit me to thank you for your kind words of congratulations to me upon my election to the position of Rabbi of Temple Emanu-El; and allow me to express the hope that my activity there will prove of some benefit to the Zionist movement. I am sorry that it will not be possible for me to attend the Jahresconferenz in Cologne in August. Mr. Lewin-Epstein[4] will, however, in all likelihood, represent our Federation at that time.

With kindest regards and Zion's greetings to Mrs. Wolffsohn and yourself, I am,

With Zion's greetings,

Yours very truly, JLM, Secretary, Federation of American Zionists

1. The Ninth Convention of the Federation of American Zionists was held at Tannersville, N.Y., June 29 to July 4, 1906.
2. In November and December 1905 a wave of pogroms swept through Russia.
3. Dr. Alfred Nossig (1865–1943). East European writer, publicist, and sculptor.
4. Elias W. Lewin-Eptstein (1863–1932). Early East European Zionist, administrator of Rehovot settlement, and founder of Carmel Wine Co.; came to the United States representing the company in 1900; served as treasurer of Federation of American Zionists.

6

Journal: Temple Emanu-El

New York, Saturday night, September 8, 1906

The long black coat, the black tie, the new hat — even these after the careless, light dress of the mountain months did not awaken me to the reality of the new duties at Emanu-El. I soon forgot everything at the half-way station between Brooklyn and Emanu-El — i.e., the Astor Library reading room. But all too soon I found myself seated in one of the red leather chairs of the trustees' room, and it seemed at first as though I had been there many years, and nothing were new to me. But the strangeness of it all began to dawn upon me as soon as I came into contact with one of the persons of the institution. And so it has been since: the new faces, the unaccustomed voices, the foreign outlook upon the world and upon the Jews. These have caused me to straighten up and my cheeks to burn a little and my heart to flutter and my resolution to conquer, to become stronger. After all, in the midst of the waking hours, in the constant thought of my new work in the shadow of Temple Emanu-El, my summer was a dream and hardly a realtiy, but a dream from which I have drawn nourishment, as it were from a clear brook coming down a mountain's side.

Mr. Pollack, the clerk, (they say he earns $10,000 a year as funeral director, marriage factotum, and secretary of the board), was the first hard substance against which I bumped, and then Mr. Holzinger.[1] It was as though his "Bayerisch" accent were something entirely new to me and his dickering with the clerk for seats for the holidays was another something of which, in the midst of the sun and the mountain freshness, I had not dreamed. Mr. Holzinger informed me, too, that I had reached "the high water mark," that I could get no further; and in my distraction, I answered foolishly enough, "I hope so." "Much luck to you" — kind of him to say it, but it was as though I were about to enter a game of tennis, or speculate on the market, or sing a song, instead of going into what, for me, pretty much means my life. Yet it may be well that I should not exaggerate the importance of my work; a lack of proportion, of humor, is fatal to any work.

And then Silverman[2] himself. I had a little bibelot there (some poems of an American parson), and the *Shilton hasekhel*[3] of Ahad Ha'am. I have made up my mind to take him into my confidence as far as my reading and studying and thinking go, in order that, perchance, he may become more like me than he now is. But, I could not give him these two things. They represented, on the one hand, some latterday English, the delicate attunement of a modern man to this shaky world, and on the other hand, Ahad Ha'am. What a world separates the two of them! I suppose Silverman cannot read the Hebrew, and what is worse, is not interested in this phase of modern Judaism which Ahad Ha'am represents. And Silverman says, "You was" and "old veteran." I would that I could have so honest a conviction as he has as to the value of the spoken word, of the "fine people" composing the Temple, and of the "ministerial" work in general. But I must be careful not to begin with a sneer. If I am to be fair to him and true to myself, I must undertake to extract the best of him and use it and help develop it. The work is too big, and the stake of too much importance, for me to lose any time in making our personal relations other than the most harmonious. Still, the politics which Silverman and Pollack discussed — including as it did "Stevie" Wise[4] and myself and Mr. Marshall[5] did not edify me, and contributed its share to my awakening to the fact that I was out of my dreamland and in the enemy's country.

The Temple is a beautiful structure. I think I shall never tire of looking into its lofty spaces; the mysterious power of cathedral and church of the medieval architecture was upon me. To be sure, the *niggun* [melody] at Jacobson's dance hall in Tannersville,[6] or in the little room for *minyan* [quorom of ten adult males required for services], the close contact with the shaking, praying Jew in a small, stuffy *"shtiebel"* [room] has its own charm and spiritual influence. But the freedom, the expansion of spirit, the loftiness of emotion that the magnificent sweep of the buildings, walls and ceilings and open spaces give; and the quiet play, too, of the shadows of many a nook and little turret and cranny. But if the building itself can give you a glimpse into heaven, the music that pours through it is like the singing of a chorus of angels. Every tone of the organ and every chorus swell streamed forth rays of light, rained down showers of melody.

We do not stand at *barakhu*,[7] but we do at the *sh'ma*,[8] although I should rather do just the reverse in accordance with the custom of the "shul" [Orthodox synagogue]. I wonder that the Reform service did not add the ten commandments to the service. The parallel to the antinominians of the Talmudic times, who emphasized the *sh'ma* as a battle cry, would be more complete then. The cantor reads as much English as possible; it is the choir at *barakhu* that sings the Hebrew! The melodies of the *ahava rabba* [with an everlasting love] from Mr. Bernstein through Tannersville floated through my head; and I read and hummed the Hebrew to drown the English out, I suppose. The cantor's English is not as good as I had thought. With some one to coach him for six months, he might improve. And I think he is an *am ha'aretz* [unlearned] too, albeit a very respectable gentleman and a good singer. It was a *kaddish*[9] audience; at least seven-tenths of it stood up. There may have been 150 persons present. What a neurotic, back-bone-less, simpering, ecclesiastical abomination the mournful, grave-digging *kaddish* reading is. What manhood or womanhood is there in the endeavour to bring tears? That is always easy. Tears count for something when they come despite our efforts to restrain them. Poor Judaism, that it must be dependent upon its dead for life; or rather, poor synagogue, if death be its only sustainer. The crisis of death is to be sure, an important one in the lives of those left behind. It is but natural that at this time the human mind should be turned to thoughts of "religion"; but is that all of "religion," and is that the way of death to make us sickeningly weak? I delivered the benediction; I had not expected to. I was somewhat nervous. I wish Silverman would do the "benedicting."

I said: *v'atta b'rov hasd'kha avo vetekha eshtahave el hekhal kodsh'kha v'yir'atekha.*

In the greatness of thy mercy, Lord, do we come into thy house; in the fear of thee do we bow down in the temple of thy holiness. May the words of our mouth and the meditation of our hearts have been acceptable before thee. Lord, give thy people strength, bless thy people with Sabbath peace, Amen. —

In the morning I came late by two minutes. They had already begun. Not a very good beginning for me, although it would not have hurt them to have waited a couple of minutes for me. The morning service has always disgusted me more than the evening service; this is due, I suppose, to the mockery of the reading of the Torah. But the service is fearfully monotonous. I wonder if a Hebrew service would be so tedious to a person not understanding it. I wonder what young Lubarsky,[10] who was there with his father, thought of the first goyish service he has attended in this country. Perhaps he thinks it is better than what he would call "antiquated forms"; and yet what is the use of the service at all? If you must have a service, then the old service. A modern man does not need any at all. If you *believe*, then does *such* a service satisfy you? If not, then why compromise with your God? We can compromise with everything in life; we ought not to compromise with our God. And if he should say this, I should probably know how to answer him, but would I be convinced entirely as to the truth of my answer?

In the *k'dusha* [sanctification] we stand only at *kadosh* [holy]. We dare not tire ourselves, you know. On the whole, the congregation is singularly inactive in the service. The service about the Torah is probably impressive because of the distances we have to walk to and from the ark.

The small reading from the scroll might mean something, if only some one understood it. Indeed, it may be a good principle to judge everything not from present conditions, but from the way it would be under better conditions. It is our duty to bring about the better conditions, and to mould our service, therefore, not so much in accordance with present ignorance and dullness, as with future knowledge and high spiritedness.

I read the *haftara* [prophetic portion]; it was from Job. Frisch[11] of Pine Bluff, who was seated in the very back, told me he could not hear all of it, although I had thought that my voice was pitched properly. It was better with the "prayer" after the reading of the scroll. It could be heard. I said: *tora tsivva lanu moshe morasha kehillat ya'akov, bet ya'acov lekhu v'nelkha b'or adonai.*[12]

> The Torah which God gave through Moses is the heritage of the house of Israel. It is the authority according to which the lives of our fathers were guided. House of Israel, come ye and let us walk in the light of this law. Lord, give us strength to obey the authority of this law and of this land. Amen —

or some such thing, in some such division. And then, after the service, Mrs. Schafer and Mrs. Kowalsky and daughter of J. F. and Mrs. Wolf and Mrs. Basch and others. It is a new world into which I am entering. How much of the old world, of *my* world, of the world I love, will I be able to bring into the new? In the words of the weekly portion: *hashkifa min hashamayim uvarekh et amkha yisrael v'et ha'adama.*[13]

Rosh hashana eve, 5667, September 19, 1906

In the midst of my sermon for tomorrow. I am writing here, chiefly because I seem to need some legitimate excuse to stop thinking and writing. It is an alarming matter to see how slowly I write. One should never stop writing a single day of one's life, if writing is ever to be a chief occupation.

I wanted to record my impressions of Silverman's first sermon last Saturday. It is now almost rosh hashana, although you would not think so, seeing me here in pyjamas, trying to get a few thoughts squeezed out of this poor head of mine, so that I can not say many bad things about the sermon. There was one very effective part, where he said that religion meant getting an entirely "new life," new strength, new hope. That is true, if one is a real believer. In this event, nothing can sap the strength. But is Silverman of that kind, or is it only a conventional preacher's phrase? He spoke as though he knew what he meant. The sermon was on the text, *v'ko-ye adonai yahalifu khoah,*[14] and he proceeded to discuss, "The Relative Merits of Physical and Spiritual Strength," as he announced the evening before. I thought the sermon as a whole rather poor — poor in conception and in execution, both from a literary and from an oratorical point of view. My criticism might be severer, too, were I not about equally as weak at times. If that is a sample of his style, I do not blame the congregation for having tired of him. He put me to sleep in a couple of places. I wonder whether I shall hiss and cut and chop my words as he does, after I have been in the Emanu-El building for some time. Well, a Happy New Year to you, Book. I trust that you will not be the receptacle of too much woe and weeping.

Friday, November 23, 1906

Today the old yearning and the old discontent are upon me for the first time in a long spell. The cause is the newest evidence of *avdut* [servility] which our rich Jews have given. Shmaryahu Levin is here, but they have virtually taken no notice of him. When Maxim Gorki came, Oscar J. Straus called on him, and was told that Gorki was busy and could not be seen. Our Jews have no appreciation of their own great men, no appreciation of themselves. They have money and a deal of good character, but what they lack is some courage as Jews. They will hardly admit that we have any problems as Jews; or if admitting these problems, they think they can be answered, overcome by a $500,000 gift here or there. They do not understand that it is they whom the Jewish people wants, their hearts and minds, not their money so much. Money comes by itself if the heart and the mind be there. It is heartburning at times to be their servant, to be paid by them, to have to do their bidding in the various minor matters of congregational life. I hate many of them, and yet as a good pastor I must call on them. At times, I would speak words of fire about their sins, but I am threading my way through the mazes carefully and I must be cautious. Can I serve two masters? the plain people, the young men and women, mostly of Russian descent, in whom some Jewish life is still left, and on the other hand the rich Jews, who would buy the soul of their servants for coin? Time alone can tell. Perhaps the "common people" may best be served by drawing pay from other sources than themselves. Perhaps it would be better to work *there* and among them exclusively, become a preacher among them, and eat *lehem etsev* [the bread of toil], as I am willing, in case of necessity, to do. I still dream of a platform downtown where I may speak out my whole heart without the necessity of "threading my way." But should that platform be created by myself or by means of the money of others? Would this serve my purpose: an endowment fund to be raised by those who will, the interest of it to revert to the contributors upon my withdrawing from its benefits; I to have full and complete freedom to preach and do where and as I please? Or must I earn my living at something else, writing or what not, and take up my work in my leisure hours? This latter plan is, I think, impossible of fulfilment. It would have to be an endowment, if anything at all. I do not want to be paid by means of monthly or yearly dues. The rich Jews are men to be admired and some of them are men to be liked. Furthermore, I should want to get from them always what I could. What I am asking now is: can I not get more from them if I am not their paid servant than if I am? On the other hand, can I not get from the "common people,'" i.e., serve them best and stir them to best results by getting no living from them? And then beyond all of this comes the vision of Palestine. I stand ready to go there or to stay here, as necessity may decree. Boris Schatz[15] created a place for himself there; can I do as much, or must I wait until "necessity may decree"?

Sunday-Monday, May 12–13, 1907, 1:30 A.M.

It's a long time since I've come to you, my book.

Yesterday I preached on the text, lo tih'ye aharai l'ra'ot.[16] I spoke of the Jews being a minority, that they suffered in order to keep themselves such; that nevertheless they were great imitators; that it was but natural that men seek to adapt themselves to their surroundings. There was a time when we were original — when the people were on their own soil. I mentioned the Bible. But especially in the 19th century have we been imitators, not constructive. For example, in theology, wherein we boast we are supreme, there have been new movements, e.g., "new theology," but we were not touched by these. We have been in the rear-guard of spiritual movements. The same with the national movements of the 19th century. We Jews were the last to discover our national manhood. So it has been in every phase of life, except perhaps in social movements where Jews have been original, as in socialism, whatever we may think of this doctrine.

Jews have been laggards in religion in particular. But we boast that we are the teachers of the world in this. We say we have a particular call to teach justice and righteousness. But do we teach this in our lives? Are we any different from our neighbors from the point of view of morals? Or is it in our doctrine that we are the great "missionaries"? Do we make propaganda like other minority communities like Mormons, Ethical Culture, Christian Science? Our boast of our "mission" to the gentiles is only an idle phrase, for if we believed in it, we should go out and teach. My opinion is that we are a national community with universal ideals, namely of human brotherhood and divine fatherhood. But there are others who claim we are only a universal church, and not a national community. If this be true, why Sukkot instead of Thanksgiving, why marriage only

89

among our own? Why not, if we are the universal church, go to the world saying, "We stand upon our principles and believe in them. Our church is open where you can pray. No ancient tongue disturbs your meditations," etc. etc.

To show the inconsistency of our lives, I cited the incident of Hebrew Union College. I quote: "Three of the teachers of that school have been deposed from their chairs because they happened to hold such beliefs as I have been preaching to you this morning."[17] I showed that [Isaac Mayer] Wise did not intend the school to be one of a petty Jewish sect, but rather a Jewish University for Jewish learning and investigation. It was, to be sure, the school of "Reform Judaism." But what is that? Is it only a petty sect? Then I will have none of it.

But I believe that Reform Judaism is broader. That it represents the principle of development in Judaism. Now no synod has ever fixed the lines of this development. It is the very principle of "Reform" to give everyone the freedom of development and of living. No breath of suspicion against deposed men, and yet we confront the humiliating spectacle of a kind of heresy trial in Reform Judaism. What a mockery! A college founded on the principle of tolerance, becoming sectarian. Is this your view of Reform?

Jewish nationalists have not relinquished hope of Messianic times. But we are not willing to say that we are no national community when we are, and that we are teachers when we are only pupils. We wish Jewish life to be enriched from all sides, that Jews become more Jewish instead of less Jewish, in order in this way to contribute to the world's culture. Our idea is that we should establish centers all over the world, with the chief center in the land of our fathers, and use literature, art, painting, sculpture, music, religion, language for our purposes.

If the Jew is to mean something to himself and to the world, he must first find himself, and not merely repeat lip phrases that have no meaning for himself or his children. If those who believe Judaism to be a universal church would only go out into the world and *teach*, perhaps even from this our life might be bettered. I protest against proclaiming one thing with our lips and in our life being something else. Shall this go on? Shall we not rather take our bearings and begin our life anew?

Thus far my sermon.

When I seated myself Silverman crossed the platform and sat next to me. He asked me what I meant and I answered, "What I said." "But you ought to retract." "I have nothing to retract." "You said those men were deposed, whereas they resigned." "That they were forced to resign everybody knows, and my interpretation of that is that they were deposed." "That is not correct and you should retract it." "I have nothing to retract." "Then I shall retract it." "That would be very bad, Dr. Silverman."

"Perhaps, that's what you want, that I should do something like that."
"That would be very bad, Dr. Silverman." With that he went to his seat.

After the *kaddish*, he went to the pulpit and began to announce the closing exercises of the school which were to be held on the morrow. He said that the school was an important part of our religious work and that all interested in it should show their encouragement of the work by coming to the exercises which were to begin at 10:30. He then announced the confirmation exercises of the school for *shavu'ot*, May 19, at 10 A.M. The exercises were to be held at 10 and not at 10:30, and for this reason everyone should inform his friend to be on hand at the first named hour in order to avoid any confusion. Then, finding himself in the midst of a stream of words (alas, the bane of the preacher), he could not stop, and he made the additonal remarks, "I would like to add a little note to what has been said this morning. I have consulted with my honored colleague, and I wish to say that what he said about the three professors being deposed was only his interpretation of their resignations, which were altogether voluntary." Being a member of the Board of Governors, and being intimately acquainted with the facts, he wished to state that one professor resigned because of his dissatisfaction with his salary, another because he did not believe in Reform Judaism, and the other because he had had differences with the president, Dr. K. Kohler. The men were not deposed, but resigned.

This statement naturally caused a great stir in the congregation. At the close of the service, a great many persons shook my hand and offered words of thanks and appreciation for what I had said. Never before had so many come up to me. Whether that was because of resentment at Silverman's action, or because my sermon had been exceptional is hard to say. I think both elements entered into it. Indeed I felt afterwards, and I feel now, as though I had known that it was a moment when inspiration was needed. I lost myself and was carried beyond myself. Usually the congregation disperses quickly, but they did not on that day. They remained in many excited groups, and it was all I could do to keep many of them calm. Everyone, without exception, seemed to condemn Silverman's action. There was really no excuse for it. As I told him in threshing the matter out with him, even had every statement that I made been wrong, he had no business to do what he did. But the statements were all true, and his hiding behind "resignation" instead of "being deposed" is a piece of Jesuitry concocted in Cincinnati in the brain of the arch-Jesuit, B. Bettman.[18] The upshot of my conversation with Silverman was that he was to understand that I could not be interfered with either in or out of the pulpit, that I was to say what my heart dictated and when it dictated it, and that I would do my duty as I saw it, and as no one else saw it.

I do not care to go into details either of the conversation with Mr. Pollack to whose house I went for dinner, or with Mr. Moses[19] and Mr. Marshall, both of whom I saw in the afternoon, or with the Schechters, Gottheils,[20] and Lubarsky,[21] and Mania Wilbuschewitsch,[22] both of whom happened to be there. This morning at the closing exercises of the school, Silverman pleaded with me to make his cause mine and to make light of the whole matter at the meeting of the Board of Trustees that was called for this evening.

I am writing this after coming from the Board meeting. Every member was there. I sat between Mr. Seligman[23] and Mr. Marshall, and Silverman between Mr. Seligman and Mr. Schafer.[24] I can not give exact details of this meeting because what was said was not altogether in sequence. First there was a discussion as to what was before the house. Judge Dittenhoefer[25] thought that I ought to tell what I had said. But Silverman interrupted, as indeed he kept doing constantly, and said that the matter ought not be made more serious than it was.

While on what he said, I may as well record some of the many things he said at different times. It was a very embarrassing position. He hardly knew what to say. Among other things he gave a psychological explanation of the matter. He told the history of the College matter in a few words, then described my attitude, my I. M. Wise sermon, my alumni letter, our differences of opinion in our conversation on the matter, his sermon on Universal Judaism — which he had the audacity to say, at first, that I was answering — his position on the Board of Governors, my attitude toward Reform Judaism which I called ossified; and then to hear my sermon Saturday (which, by the way, he said was a very powerful one!) he could not contain himself. It was, he said, just like the Prophets. They could not contain themselves, and sometimes spoke quickly and from their hearts. Mr. Marshall said to this that the Prophets had been used for so many things during the past twenty-five years that they ought to be left out of this, and Mr. Spiegelberg[26] (I didn't know Willie could do it) said it was rather a deliberate prophecy. When Silverman said it wouldn't happen again, Spiegelberg suggested that the prophetic fervor might again overtake him.

Silverman also said that the Temple had enemies, that spies were there every Sabbath, that the Trustees should take no action but leave all matters to the rabbis who would adjust the matter. He also said that if he was to be humiliated it would appear as though the pulpit were indeed muzzled. (Personally, I can't figure this out, because it was my statement that he wanted to muzzle).

At length, I was requested to state the facts. I stated them as given above from the time when I took my seat till when Silverman finished his reply to me. I had a badly reported stenographic copy of my sermon there, which I left for reference, if necessary. At another time I added that I did not conceive that I was present to defend myself for anything, and the other remark that I made was a statement at the very end that I believed the matter could be amicably adjusted between Silverman and myself; that we each understood the situation and that we knew that no interference in the work of the other was possible in the future, upon lines of my talk to Silverman above.

My feelings during the whole proceedings were of extreme shame and pain. Almost every one of Silverman's statements contained a faux pas, and I literally writhed in humiliation. He stirred within me a deep sense of pity because of his own shame and helplessness.

We were then asked to retire. Silverman insisted upon waiting. I sent Pollack down with the statement that we were waiting to hear the outcome in person. The meeting lasted about an hour after we left, being over at about 10:45. When it was over they sent up word that they would communicate in writing with both of us. (I wanted to go home long before in order to avoid any such statement from them.) We, i.e. Silverman, Pollack and I, went to the Manhattan for something to drink. Rosenberg told us that four reporters had held up the Board on its way out, but I suppose they got nothing. A *Tribune* reporter stopped us, but he got nothing.

I am almost afraid to write here what I think of the whole thing. Among other things, I am sorry to say that I am now very suspicious of Silverman. Unfortunately, I shall not be able to have implicit confidence in his frankness and square dealing. As for the rest, I feel that the congregation is too small for two men with equal positions. It is large enough for two assistant rabbis who shall be subject to the direction of the senior. The present situation — two men of different views, with equal authority and freedom — appears to me to be intolerable. Silverman is a man of large family; I have none. Furthermore, he is happier here than ever I could be, and his point of view is more likely to be theirs than is mine. Furthermore, I have dreams of my *bet hak'neset hal'umi* [nationalistic synagogue]. Is not this the opportune time for it? But there must be no cowardice shown, and perhaps leaving at this time would smack of it.

1. Julius Holzinger (1835–?). Merchant, born in Feuchtwang, Bavaria, was a longstanding member of the congregation.

2. Joseph Silverman (1860–1930). Rabbi, ordained Hebrew Union College; junior rabbi, Temple Emanu-El, 1888, and senior rabbi 1903–1922.

3. "The "The Supremacy of Reason." In his essay Ahad Ha'am discussed Moses Maimonides's *The Guide to the Perplexed* and the "supremacy of reason over religion."

4. Rabbi Stephen S. Wise (see glossary of names). Wise gained nationwide attention when he broke off negotiations to accept the Emanu-El pulpit when he claimed the trustees refused to assure him complete freedom of expression in preaching.

5. Louis Marshall (see glossary of names), the secretary of the congregation.

6. The traditional chant of the Orthodox services, which Magnes recalls from the synagogue services in Tannersville, New York, and from the Hassidic synagogue.

7. "Praise the Lord," the call to worship in the prayer service.

8. "Here, O Israel," the prayer of affirmation of the oneness of God.

9. "Holy," a prayer recited by mourners and by those commemorating the anniversary of the death of a parent.

10. Son of Abraham E. Lubarsky (see note 27).

11. Ephraim Frisch (1880–1957). Rabbi of Congregation Anshe Emet, Pine Bluff, Arkansas, 1904–1912.

12. "The Torah bequeathed to us by Moses is the heritage of the congregation of Jacob; House of Jacob, come let us walk in the light of the Lord."

13. "Look down from the heavens and bless thy people Israel and the land." Deut. 26:15.

14. "But they that wait for the Lord shall renew their strength" Isa. 40:31.

15. Boris Schatz (1867–1932). Painter and sculptor; founder of Bezalel School of Art in Jerusalem.

16. "Thou shall not follow a multitude to do evil" Exod. 23:2.

17. Magnes referred to the resignations of Max L. Margolis, Henry Malter, and Max Schloessinger. The resignations created considerable controversy. Magnes, among others, believed the three teachers were forced to resign because of their Zionist views.

18. Bernhard Bettman (1834–1915). Prominent Cincinnati merchant; president of the board of governors of the Hebrew Union College.

19. Moses M. Moses (1841–1919). Merchant and philanthropist; a trustee of Emanu-El since 1868.

20. Richard Gottheil (1862–1936). Professor of Semitic langues, Columbia University; president of Federation of American Zionists, 1898–1904.

21. Abraham J. Lubarsky (1856–1920). Businessman, Zionist, and Hebraist. He was a close associate of Ahad Ha'am in Odessa. In 1903 he emigrated to the United States and was active in the Hebrew movement founding the Histadrut Ivrit.

22. Mania Wilbuschewitsch; see Shochet in glossary of names.

23. James Seligman (1824–1916). Banker, philanthropist, partner of J. and W. Seligman and Company; a founder and the president of Emanu-El.

24. Samuel M. Schafer (1840–1918). Banker, senior member of the New York Stock Exchange; treasurer of Emanu-El.

25. Abram Jesse Dittenhoefer (1836–1919). Appointed justice of New York City court, 1857.

26. William I. Spiegelberg (1862–1932). Textile manufacturer and philanthropist; vice president of Emanu-El.

7

To the Editor of the Yiddishes Tageblat
New York, September 29, 1909

A CENTRAL NEW YORK JEWISH ORGANIZATION

Mr. Louis Marshall's admirable letter to you in connection with Commissioner [Theodore A.] Bingham's[1] retraction seems to overlook the real "cancer which is gnawing at our vitals."[2]

Mr. Marshall seems to hold mass-meetings, etc., as ineffective in comparison with the dignified and effective work of a few of the more prominent of our Jews. I make bold to say, however, that mass-meetings, etc. are at times necessary, both in order to stir the more influential into activity and (votes being votes) in order, upon occasion, to whip anti-Semitic officials into submission. I am proud, and I am sure Mr. Marshall, in the last resort, also is proud, of the indignation of our Jews and of their readiness at their mass-meetings, etc., to resent insult. This is the way every healthy and manly people gives expression to its elemental emotions. Is it not then the part of wisdom to try to organize the Jews so that their mass-meetings and their power in all ways may be turned to the general good?

You, on the other hand, Mr. Editor, are often guilty of error in the opposite direction. You seem to think that no good can come from our *gedolim* [notables], our *mayofesnicks* [sycophants], as you are pleased to call them. But you forget that they have assumed the leadership of the Jewish community only out of a sense of duty and because our masses are themselves utterly unorganized.

When shall we understand that the two sections of our community need each other? Mr. Marshall represents, in some measure, that section of the community with leadership and wealth. You, Mr. Editor, represent, in some measure, that section of the community with our masses and our hopes. An army without leaders is almost as absurd as leaders without an army. The opportunity is now at hand for leaders and soldiers to recognize the need they have of each other and to join ranks.

The task of the Jew of New York is now to develop a real Jewish community. We have no organized community; no Jewish public opinion; no conscious scheme of activity.

The American Jewish Committee is the first attempt of the Jews of this city at real organization. It must, however, be restricted in its usefulness because it has no mandate from the people. Permit me in this connection to recall to you Mr. Mashall's ill-fated plan of democratic organization for the American Jewish Committee to show how he, too, has felt the need of the principle of democracy in our activities.

The next step in the formation of a New York Jewish Community is the organization of the "Great East Side." A conference looking toward such an organization is to be held at Clinton Hall on Sunday evening, October 11, and Monday evening, October 12, 1908, at 8 o'clock. This conference is the outcome of the Clinton Hall Conference called to consider the statements of Commissioner Bingham, and all of the Jewish organizations of New York are invited to send delegates to this conference.

Will the New York section of the American Jewish Committee be alive to its great duty of leadership, and will it take advantage of this opportunity of coming into direct touch with the Jewish masses? I feel confident in assuring the gentlemen of the Committee that they will be fully as happy to have a united Jewry at their back, as the Jewish masses will be to elect many of them as their leaders. The Protectory,[3] and all other worthy institutions and movements will then have access to the people at large; and once a good cause reaches our masses, there are no men and women in all the world readier to respond. It is time that our institutions be of our masses, and not above them. It is time that we work with the people rather than for the people.

Very truly, JLM

1. General Theodore A. Bingham (1858–1920). Police commissioner of New York City, 1906–1909.
2. Marshall, who negotiated Bingham's retraction of his statement of a high Jewish crime rate, criticized the immigrant community in a letter to the *Tageblat* (September 18, 1908, p. 6) for evincing little gratitude for the discreet intervention by the "so-called Jewish magnates" in securing a "dignified solution" of the episode, and for ignoring "the existing evils . . . which have led to juvenile delinquency."
3. The Jewish Protectory and Aid Society was founded in 1902 to meet the need for prison work and rehabilitation among Jewish prisoners and delinquents.

8

Address, Opening of the Constituent Convention of the Jewish Community of New York City
February 27, 1909

This meeting has been called as the result of·many meetings which had as their aim the formation of a Jewish Community of New York City. When Police Commissioner Bingham made the statement, which he afterwards retracted, that the Jews contribute 50 percent of the criminals of New York City, many meetings were held by Jewish organizations and indignant protests were made. Any number of plans for redress were proposed. Many of these plans bordered on the absurd. Some suggested that we march to the City Hall in overwhelming numbers and demand of the Mayor the head of his police commissioner. Others proposed that a political organization be formed for the one purpose of supporting that political party which would demand the removal of the commissioner. Many a speech was delivered, and many kinds of conferences in various parts of the city were held. The whole movement of indignation seems to have been crystallized in those conferences held at

Clinton Hall on October 11th and 12th, 1908, and now known as the Clinton Hall Conference. The discussion at that conference was long and earnest and interesting. It was shown that the Jews were capable of righteous indignation and that this indignation might be followed by decisive action on their part. It was the sense of the Clinton Hall Conference that an attempt be made to form a central organization of the Jews of New York City. A Committee of Twenty-five was appointed with authority to consult with other organizations looking to the creation of what might be known as the Jewish Community of New York City. The proceedings of the Clinton Hall Conference were followed with eagerness by large sections of the Jewish population, and the result of its deliberations were hailed with general satisfaction.

The Committee of Twenty-five, after several sessions, found it to be its duty to consult with the American Jewish Committee. The reasons for this determination were these: first, the American Jewish Committee was in existence and had been organized for similar purposes. Second, the Clinton Hall Conference was representative particularly of "downtown," whereas the American Jewish Committee, while it contained many "downtown" Jews, also contained a very good representation of the "uptown" Jews. Third, the American Jewish Committee was not only a local organization but also a national organization with a constituency throughout the United States. Relationship with the American Jewish Committee might therefore give the Jews of New York City some voice in shaping not only local Jewish policies, but also the policy of Jews throughout the land; and, by reason of the international connections of the American Jewish Committee, some voice also in fashioning the policy of international Jewry.

A short sketch of the democratic movement that led to the organization of the American Jewish Committee would now seem to be in place, especially because this convention is, I think, but the last phase of this democratic movement in Jewry. In the year 1905, as a result of the Russian massacres, two organizations were formed in this country. The one, the Committee for the Relief of Sufferers by Russian Massacres, was effective in raising over a million dollars for the relief of our persecuted brethren in Russia. The other organization, the Jewish Defense Association, succeeded in raising a considerable sum to be used by our brethren in Russia for their own defence. The Jewish Defense Association began an agitation also on behalf of what was then characterized as an American Jewish Congress. The leaders of the Relief Committee too had begun to feel the necessity of an organization to take the place of individual effort and to relieve the individual of too much responsibility. The prime movers in the creation of an American Jewish Congress accordingly believed it to be their duty to give up their own plan and to labor for the creation of a general organization. This eventually became the American Jewish Committee.

The American Jewish Committee was constituted in this Hebrew Charities Building. A plan of organization along completely democratic lines was discussed, but after earnest consideration, rejected as, for the present, unfeasible. It has been held by many that the American Jewish Committee does not represent the Jews whom it pretended to represent, because it had no mandate from the people. Those who passed this criticism on the Committee were willing to admit that were a plebiscite to be had, the mass of the Jewish people would approve the selection of perhaps most of the men now constituting the American Jewish Committee. It was granted also by the critics of the Committee that the men constituting that Committee had taken upon themselves the burden of its work not for any personal aggrandizement, but because the work had to be done and it seemed there was no organization to do it. Nevertheless, the fact remained that the Committee was self-constituted, and no one was more alive to the justice of this charge than the members of the American Jewish Committee themselves. An attempt was therefore made by the American Jewish Committee to democratize itself by creating large Advisory Councils which were to elect the members of the general Committee.

While the plan of the Advisory Councils was being put into effect, the Bingham incident occurred, the Clinton Hall Conference was held, and the Committee of Twenty-five was appointed. This Committee of Twenty-five and the New York City members of the American Jewish Committee met frequently in conference. The result of their conferences was the call which was signed jointly by the members of the Committee of Twenty-five and the New York members of the American Jewish Committee. And this call has brought you here for the purpose of forming the Jewish Community of New York City.

The question that now remains to be answered is what the Jewish Community of New York City should be organized for. The Jews of New York City have a twofold problem. We have what might be called our external problem and our internal problem. Our external problem concerns our relationship with the outside community of which we form a part. Not long ago, there was a great uproar about the singing of Christmas songs in the public schools.[1] That is but an instance of the many problems which concern us as a community in our relations with our non-Jewish fellow citizens, and to solve which, it is necessary that there be among the Jews some properly constituted authority. At the present time, however, there is no representative, authoritative, permanent organization that dare speak for the Jewish people. Any individual or any organization can claim to be the spokesman of the Jews and as a result there is confusion worse confounded. If, however, a representative, well-organized community were in existence, the Jews would know whom to regard as their spokesman and the non-Jewish world would know to whom to listen. But for such an organization to possess the authority to deal with external problems, it must receive its mandate from the Jewish people at large.

We have, furthermore, our internal problem. This is, to my mind, the more important, for it concerns the development of our inner life as Jews. Nothing Jewish should be foreign to a Jewish Community of New York City. There are, for example, hundreds of synagogues of various shades of observance and belief. Whereas the Jewish Community should have no right to interfere with the autonomy of any of these synagogues or of any other organization, it ought to be able to suggest to the orthodox synagogues that they organize themselves into a union for the purpose of furthering the cause of Judaism, and to the reformed synagogues that they form a union for the same purpose. There are also questions of *sh'hita* [ritual slaughter], of *mila* [circumcision], of marriage and divorce, of the mushroom synagogues that spring up at the time of the high holidays. The Jewish Community should endeavor to have boards created for the regulation of all such questions and for the proper conduct of all these and similar activities. On these boards, only such men should sit as have rabbinic authority, and as will be recognized by the mass of the people as possessing such authority. Any difficulties, moreover, that synagogues may encounter, might be brought before the proper board for adjustment, and when new synagogues are to be established, advice and help in many directions might be secured from the Community.

We have, furthermore, the question of Jewish education. Thousands of dollars and boundless energy and affection are expended each year on the education of the Jewish child, but it may be said that we have no Jewish educational system. Some schools are good, some are not. What the Community might do is, for example, to help such a movement as is now beginning to develop, that of forming a board of Jewish education and of employing a superintendent of instruction.[2] This would be instrumental in introducing something like a uniform system into the various Jewish schools of this city, and of improving their teaching methods. It would help to correct many abuses practiced by unlicensed and incompetent private schools and teachers. It would also show the necessity for additional schools for thousands of Jewish children who now are willing to go to a Jewish school but who find no schools to receive them.

We have also charitable and social problems which an effective community might help to solve. In this building, for instance, the United Hebrew Charities is housed. Each year, this institution complains that it is not supported as it ought to be. It is thus with other worthy institutions.

This lack of support is, in some measure, due to the absence of a way to reach the masses of the people themselves. The Jewish masses are perhaps the most charitable of people. Their many independent benevolent societies might be induced by the Community to form a union of benevolent societies. Furthermore, if the Community is really representative of the whole people it could reach the people on behalf of a worthy cause more quickly than any other agency might. Perhaps, also we may eventually devise some means of collecting a per capita tax from the whole Jewish population in order to meet the needs of our charitable organizations. It may also be possible to create sentiment in favor of the creation of an employment bureau, a committee on conciliation between employer and employee, and other such agencies. This beautiful building, moreover, or some other such building, might be made into a *bet am*, the Jewish Communal House, and here Jewish communal activities might find a center. Communal organizations might have their offices here, and this auditorium might be used for occasions of interest to the Community or its constituent parts.

All of this is dependent upon the creation of a Jewish public opinion. There is no such thing at present, and a central organization like that of the Jewish Community of New York City is necessary to create a Jewish public opinion. Here the various tendencies within New York Judaism may find a meeting ground and an organ through which to express themselves. And it may be that by means of a Jewish public opinion, Jewish institutions will adopt a policy in conformity with the expressed wishes of the Community.

Much of this work has as its prerequisite the gathering of Jewish statistics. Who are we and what are we? How many and of what nature are our synagogues, our schools, our charitable institutions, our lodges and our societies? Who are our criminals, what our communal needs? We seem to be a community of over a million souls, the largest Jewish community in the world, but we are hardly cognizant of what we possess or what we require.

If we organize this Community together with the American Jewish Committee, we shall be able so to influence the American Jewish Committee as to make it entirely democratic. Communities similar to ours will be formed in Chicago, Baltimore, Philadelphia, Boston, Cleveland and other large cities. Then, not only the local community but the national organization of which it is a part will be democratic, representative, authoritative. As a result, as I said before, each local community will have a voice in shaping not alone its own policy but that also of Jewry and Judaism throughout the land, and perhaps, throughout the world.

But one word more. If we organize the Jewish Community of New

York City, it will in some measure be a realization of the words we are inclined so often to use: *haverim kol yisrael*, "all Israel are brothers." It will wipe out invidious distinctions between East European and West European, foreigner and native, "uptown" Jew and "downtown" Jew, rich and poor, and it will make us realize that the Jews are one people with a common history and with common hopes.

1. During December 1906 Orthodox rabbis, with the support of the *Morgen Zhurnal*, led a school strike in the Jewish neighborhoods of New York over the issue of Christmas celebrations in the public schools. *New York Times*, December 25, 1906, p. 8.

2. Several of the *talmud toras*, afternoon religious schools, planned the establishment of a central board of Jewish education.

9

Sermon Delivered at Temple Emanuel
New York, October 9, 1909

THE MELTING POT

I wish this morning to take a look with you into the Melting Pot. I do this not for the sake of being quoted in an advertisement of Mr. Zangwill's play, but because the play has the merit of presenting a thought that should be of deep concern to us.[1]

At the outset let me say that from the point of view of a Jew interested in the preservation of Judaism, the play is a pernicious one. It has, to be sure, a powerful and artistic indictment of Russia's barbaric treatment of her Jewish subjects. It puts a problem also which many have been grappling with, but which few have had the courage to face as logically and as poetically as Mr. Zangwill has. For clarifying the atmosphere about us Mr. Zangwill deserves our thanks. But we cannot be thankful to any one for preaching suicide to us. For that is what the play means for all the nationalities in this great republic.

The play purports to describe to us the melting process through which the children of every nationality are becoming Americans. Here are the fires of God, says the author, the fires of love. The fires of hate have not been able to melt your stoniness of heart and make you at one with your neighbors. It is left for young America to be God's crucible of love in which all men will give up the particular traditions of their own history and be formed into a new people of freedom.

101

This description of the process now going on is, I believe, only partly true, and the work which the artist has fashioned is but a molten image, an idol, a golden calf. Yet who will deny the boldness and the majesty of this conception of America? In this view of it, Americanism has almost the force of a religion. Put away the past, all ye children of oppression. Come ye unto me, and I will open unto you a new heaven and a new earth. History is being made. It is as though each man throwing himself into the Melting Pot were a creator of a new species. The best blood of all the nations is, according to this idea of the future in America, to be fused into the making of the perfect man.

There is no denying that under the influence of this enthusiasm for America, the disintegrating process of the Melting Pot is taking place in large measure. That it is not, fortunately, taking place altogether is the point that vitiates the author's argument. Yet how familiar the cry of Americanization is to us Jews, and how frequent. Americanization means just what Mr. Zangwill has the courage to say it means: dejudaization. This dejudaizing process is conducted also under the shield and inspiration of other lofty ideas. The Jew is asked to give up his identity in the name of brotherhood and progress. Now it is a fact that in this country, as throughout the world, men are ready to understand one another and to give up many of the hatreds and jealousies of the past. Men are willing to recognize the things that unite them as well as those that separate them. In this country it is not strange to hear the call to unity among the differing Christian denominations. The historical dogmas that divided them are losing their meaning. Now, in this disintegrating movement of the times, many Jews, too, have found their place. Give up the past, they say to their people, in the name of the future. Give up your distinctions, your peculiarities, your race, your individual outlook upon life, and become like neighbors — Americans in the complete sense of the word. Many Jews have been among the first, for example, to set the seal of their approval upon the new religion of the twentieth-century American, as expounded lately by President Eliot of Harvard.[2] Reformed Judaism, many say, may accept this new religion without much protest, for its basic principle is service to man, and it rejects as worthless the distinctions that have historically and authoritatively held men apart. As to the little difference of a name, call it Judaism, Unitarianism, New Religion, Americanism — that can make no essential difference. In the course of time, such little historical vanities will go the way of all flesh, and this country in particular will be the birthplace of the new man.

It is this very process that Mr. Zangwill is describing. He is not concerned with religions, to be sure, so much as he is with races and nationalities. It is evident, however, that for the Jew, this is but a superficial distinction. For once a Jew gives up his people, he gives up his religion.

He may give up his religion and not give up his people, but the reverse process never takes place. There may be Jews without Judaism, but there can be no Judaism without Jews.

I do not regard it as my fucntion today to enter into polemics with Mr. Zangwill. I have, on the contrary, tried to see what of beauty and grandeur his view of America may contain. Nor can I deny that the process he describes is very largely going on. I see children who are less Jewish than their parents, synagogues intended for the gentile and not for the Jew, an ignorance and contempt of such spiritual possessions as our people have always held sacred. And in view of it all, I wonder how our leaders can be blind, how they can believe that a few lip-phrases about a Jewish mission, about Jewish religion (however correct these phrases be as abstract propositions) can suffice to stem the tide that is carrying a goodly number of our children away from the old anchors.

What I wish now to emphasize is, that Mr. Zangwill's description of the melting process by no means covers the whole situation, and that his view of Americanism is the old Know-Nothing[3] view and is, in large part, outworn even in America.

For, side by side with this process of Jewish decay, there is the process of Jewish awakening. Many a radical and intellectual Jew who for years has had no contact with his people, is now claiming his Jewish heritage. Some have become Jewish nationalists, advocates of the continued existence of Jewish nationality. Some of the nationalists, furthermore, are reaching out for the strength and consolations the Jewish religion offers. Many a religious Jew, on the other hand, who formerly would hear nothing of nationality, now begins to understand the riches of Jewish national culture, and the need of a national Jewish life for the expression of the Jewish religion. I think I can point to a considerable part of the membership of this synagogue to show that Reformed synagogues without previous attachment to Jewish ceremonials are beginning to feel the warmth and the beauty with which many of our traditions and customs can fill their hollowness of spirit. The need of organization is constantly creating new elements of Jewish strength. Earnest Jews and Jewesses are devoting thought and wealth to the problem of Jewish education. Our national language and literature are winning new devotees. And above all, there are the thousands who are striving to create for the Jewish people and the Jewish spirit their natural center in the ancestral land of the Jews.

Lo alman yisrael—"Israel is not yet widowed." It is not a fact that the melting process is the only one that can be remarked in Jewish life. Alongside of it is another movement working in the opposite direction. The melting process is centrifugal, the Jewish process is centripetal. The melting process glorifies disloyalty to one's inheritance. The Jewish process is expressed in the words of Joseph: *et ahai anokhi m'vakkesh*: "I seek my brethren."

But just as the melting process describes only a part of the actual state of affairs, so is the theory of America as the Melting Pot, as the Moloch through whose fires the children of all nationalities must pass, but one of the ideal pictures of the America of the future, and by no means the finest picture.

It seems to be generally admitted at present that a man may be a good American no matter to what religious body he belongs. It was not always thus. It has taken a long struggle with the Know-Nothing and the A.P.A.[4] spirit to bring Americans to an understanding of the fundamental truth that loyalty to an historical religion portends no disloyalty to the state. But this exalted conception of freedom in America is being extended by the influx of large masses of those very nationalities whose presence here has given rise to the whole problem. They are making Americans realize that the America of the future is to be not a republic of individuals and religions alone, but a republic of nationalities as well. The Melting Pot is not the highest ideal of America. America is rather the refining pot. Here, indeed, men have the opportunity of losing their old-world hatreds, their petty spites and jealousies. Here, indeed, the faiths and practices of the ages are being tested and measured in accordance with new and wholesome and young standards. Everything that cannot endure the breath of fresh life upon it must perish. In the refining process the dross will be lost. But "surely there is here a mine for silver and a place for gold where it may be refined." Each man as he strikes root here is no more obliged to yield his individuality, his race, his speech, his culture, his ideals, than he is obliged to yield his religion. To become a citizen he must forswear allegiance to every foreign state. To prosper and have peaceful intercourse with his neighbors he must learn the language of the land and adapt himself to its general customs. But here too under the starry banner of freedom he may develop himself and save his own soul as he will. What a great ideal for America this is, and what a lofty mission America has in the economy of nations. Here at last the world is to be shown how men of varied religions and nationalities can learn to understand one another, and to work together in peace and in concord. In this refining process the Jew is to lose all cringing and servility. His bent back is being straightened in his new-found freedom. He looks into the world's face without fear or favor. But that does not mean that he is to give himself over to destruction. On the contrary, here if anywhere he has the chance of clinging to all of his Jewish ways and aspirations. To be regarded as a man he need not cease being a Jew. Nay, the more of a Jew he is, the more of a man he is likely to be.

It is said that the author does not intend his work to be regarded as dealing with Jews alone, but with America and all its peoples. If so, it is unfortunate that the Jew is chosen as the vehicle of expression. For is not the position of the Jew different from that of others? I have already said that when he gives up his race he gives up his religion. This does not hold good with other nationalities. Furthermore, if indeed all of the races are here to be merged, that will not mean their extinction from the earth, for they are all indigenous in some fatherland of their own. The Jew, however, has his fatherland only in history and in his hopes, and until that fatherland be secured to him, America spells his great hope for the preservation of Judaism.

Indeed, it may appear strange to many that Mr. Zangwill, a Zionist, believing in the creation of a national home for the Jewish nation, advocates with such brutal frankness the destruction of Judaism in America. That is, however, one form, if rather a backward form, of Zionism. Its thesis is that anti-Semitism or the fires of hate on the one hand, and America or the fires of love on the other, make it impossible for Judaism to exist in the Diaspora, that is, outside of a Jewish land. In a spoken aside, not in the printed edition, the young hero puts the alternative: America or Zion. This alternative, however, is by no means necessary. For myself I would say: America and Zion — America for the thousands who can live as Jews here, Zion for the thousands who must live as Jews there. Anti-Semitism would, it is true, be of itself sufficient reason for the creation of a Jewish fatherland, the existence of which would remove one of the chief causes of anti-Semitism. Pessimism as to the outlook here would also be sufficient reason for the fatherland. But while these two powerful elements are not to be overlooked, they are not the higher motives of Zionism. Zionism is the desire not so much for the mere preservation of Jewish religion and Jewish nationality. These can and will be preserved here. Zionism is rather the desire for the live and unhampered and harmonious further development of Jewish nationality and Jewish religion. Zion is the complement to, the fullfillment of America, not its alternative. Zion is the foundation stone and the capstone of the whole structure. It is our duty and our privilege to preserve and develop Judaism in America to the utmost of our powers. The difficulties are great. That does not excuse our ceasing to try. What we cannot do here, Zion will help us do — revive and develop our national life and make it fuller and finer than it ever was.

If Mr. Zangwill were describing but one phase of Jewish life in America no criticism would be offered. What we now resent, however, is the preachment he delivers himself of. He exhorts us to absorption and destruction, and he does it boisterously, joyously, without so much as a suggestion of the great tragedy that may be involved. I have no quarrel with such Jews who have become so far removed from Jewish life as to find in Mr. Zangwill's play a text justifying their own attitude. But there are the thousands who still feel themselves living members of a living people, who still love Judaism, for whom Judaism is an actual help in reaching answers to the questions of life. We object to being urged that we give up our Jewish identity, that we and our children prove disloyal to our Jewish heritage and our Jewish religion. For Judaism is a religion to us. It is the finest and most important part of our lives. It brings us strength in our life's battle, and through it we can express much of what is deepest in us.

If the play, finally, be merely a prophecy, there are those of us who do not hesitate to say that the author is a false prophet in whose prophecy we do not believe.

The hero of the play is writing the great American symphony. If his symphony were really written, it would be a vast monotone. Its music, if any, would be that produced by one sound. The harmony of a symphony, however, is produced by a variety of distinct sounds blending into music under the artist's hand. The symphony of America must be written by the various nationalities which keep their individual and characteristic note, and which sound this note in harmony with their sister nationalities. Then it will be a symphony of color, of picturesqueness, of character, of distinction — not the harmony of the Melting Pot, but rather the harmony of sturdiness and loyalty and joyous struggle.

> Surely there is a mine for silver
> And a place for gold where it may
> be refined

1. Israel Zangwill's play *The Melting Pot* opened in Washington, D.C., on October 5, 1908, in the presence of President Theodore Roosevelt. On September 9, 1909, it opened in New York. The play, which was published in 1909, was extensively reviewed, and its message of assimilation aroused widespread controversy.

2. Charles Wiliam Eliot (1834–1926), president of Harvard University from 1869 to 1909, discussed the "new religion" in an essay, "The Religion of the Future," *Harvard Theological Review*, 2 (October 1909), 391–407, which was based on a lecture delivered the previous July. Eliot described a broad, humane, "natural religion . . . consistent with the nineteenth century revelations concerning man and nature."

3. Anti-immigrant and anti-Catholic party of the 1850s.

4. American Protective Association; anti-Catholic organization of the 1890s.

10

Sermon Delivered at Temple Emanuel
New York, April 24, 1910

REFORMED JUDAISM: PLANS FOR RECONSTRUCTION

"For, lo, the winter is past, the rain is over and gone; the flowers appear on the earth; the time of the singing of birds has come, and the voice of the turtledove is heard in our land."[1]

For two generations and more the bleakness of winter has been resting upon Judaism, and destruction has been threatening it; and there has been dread in the heart lest Judaism perish. But, lo, the winter of despair is past, the rain is over and gone, and the springtime of Judaism is come again. Now the hearts of countless young Jews know no fear. For them the green shoots of renewed Jewish life are beginning to show above the ground. Flowers are appearing on their earth. The time of the singing of birds is come and the voice of the turtledove is heard in their land. Wondrous revival, the old man among the peoples become young again! Judaism the mother of religions, decked and garlanded with new strength! The poet, the artist, the singer, the workingman, the farmer, the statesman, the scholar, the preacher, the parent, the child, are here and there filled with the spirit of hope for Judaism and love of its power and beauty.

But as I contemplate this congregation Emanuel-El, it is the autumn season that I see. The old tree that brought forth many beauteous blossoms is almost stripped of its foliage, and one by one the golden autumn leaves are falling as the older men and women of the congregation pass to their rest. There is no springtime here. It is the winter that is before us. For we have no youth, no young Jews and Jewesses, to take the places of the elders. Let each family of the congregation ask itself where the young are, and the answer will be, not within the congregation but outside of it, indifferent to it; and faithless and disloyal to Judaism.

It is concerning the problem of your future that I would talk to you today. I shall speak to you without reserve. I realize that searching and simple truths can always be dismissed in a word by the caricaturists and flippant cynics among you. Yet there are the earnest among you who will recognize the importance of the problem that confronts us.

I have been with you three years and more, and the fact that I had come to a childless congregation has more and more been borne in upon me. I came here, thinking perhaps that the tidings of the springtime might hearten you and give you new life. I came to you, so I believe, as a messenger from the Jewish people, sent to my brothers and sisters who had strayed far away from the ancestral home. I came to you with many misgivings. Your Judaism is not altogether my Judaism. Your Jewish ideals are not altogether my Jewish ideals. And yet, there are among you men and women with true Jewish hearts and of high Jewish aspiration. You have might, wealth and honorable traditions, and a power within you to be of vast service to Judaism. I have, therefore, fortified myself in the thought that it was a duty to bring such as you back into the arms of the ancient mother.

I recognize the justification for all degrees of Reformed Judaism, even up to that degree on the periphery of Jewish life as expressed in the Society for Ethical Culture.[2] The justification for these kinds of Reformed Judaism lies in this, that they have met some of the spiritual needs of many Jews and Jewesses, and have kept them more or less within the limits of the Jewish community. But it has always been clear to me that Reformed Judaism of whatever degree is but an offshoot of the main branch, is but a small stream deflected from the great river of Judaism. Insofar as it is Reformed, your Judaism and mine has something of a parasitic nature. Such Judaism draws its sustenance from the central organism; and just as the parasite may at times have more outward beauty than the parent tree, so have the richer Reformed congregations an outward appeal in the beauty of their buildings, their glorious music and their perfect decorum. But these outward trappings have not been able to hide from me the emptiness and the shallowness of your Jewish life. Whenever I have spoken to you it has been with the purpose of announcing the glad tidings of the springtime, of calling you back to the sources of living Judaism, of bidding you participate in the creative life of the bulk and body of the plain Jewish people.

To what extent my words have found an echo in your hearts, I shall not undertake to say. But whether they have found an echo or not, the fact remains that the youth is estranged from this congregation, that there are no younger men and women to assume the responsibility of this Jewish institution. Our young men and women are completely ignorant of Judaism. How, then, can they be loyal to it? In Judaism, the *am ha'aretz*, the ignoramus, is regarded with contempt. Judaism is a religion that depends upon study, knowledge, upon mind, upon history, just as much as upon imagination and the emotions. Our young men and women experience nothing of the joy of Judaism. When they think of it, it is only with a sense of the burden that it imposes upon them. It is for them a misfortune because it restricts their social activity. If they apply a test to Judaism or Jewish institutions, it is the unmanly and cringing test of *ma yomru hagoyim?*, 'what will the goyim, the gentiles say?' I shall tell you what the gentiles say. They say, and with truth, that our younger Jews and Jewesses are ignorant of Judaism, that they have cheapened themselves insofar as their religion is concerned, that they have lost their moral tone, that they have no self-respect, no pride of birth, no traditions, no hopes for their people. Look among you. Your sons and your daughters, many of them, are marrying outside of their people. They are rearing their children with all modern accomplishments, but with no religion. Their homes are bare of piety and of the spirit of prayer. Some of them perhaps are engaged in charitable work, but the work of charity is a negative work at the best, and with our young men and women it is very seldom carried on in the spirit of Jewish brotherhood, but rather in a spirit of remote pity mingled with disdain. Are you satisfied with this result of your reform Judaism?

I do not make these charges in a spirit of bitterness. Neither you nor your children nor this congregation are at fault. It is only the past one hundred years of Jewish history that can explain the depths to which the Judaism of this congregation and of similar Reformed Congregations has sunk. Why should we expect that our young men and women have a knowledge and a love of Judaism? They do not get it in the schools they go to day by day, though many of these schools are "ghetto" schools in that they are attended only by Jewish children. They do not get Judaism in the universities or in the market-places. They see no signs of Judaism in their homes. Nor can they acquire the spirit of Judaism from attendance once a week for a few months in the year at a Jewish Sunday school. The school of this congregation is, to be sure, conducted as well as any Reformed Jewish Sunday school. It has received praise, particularly from our Christian neighbors (who have no conception of our problem). Our children are as beautiful and as sweet and as keen as only Jewish children can be. They are diligent in learning the names and the dates their devoted teachers place before them, and it may be that they receive a hurried glance at our classic book, the Bible. But when they have left our school it is inevitable that they are ignorant of the Bible itself and of the vast literature of the Jews beyond the Bible; it is inevitable that Judaism should mean nothing to them, for they are not brought into contact with actual Jewish things, with actual Jewish life, with Jewish ideas of life, with Jewish symbols, ceremonies, observances, traditions. They do not observe the Sabbath and the holidays, and their Judaism receives slight encouragement in their homes. Our boys and our girls imbibe no Jewish view of life itself. They do not look upon the world through Jewish eyes. You fathers and mothers of the congregation who, in your early days were trained in Jewish books and in Jewish surroundings, almost unconsciously meet the problems of life as Jews. The new generation, however, by reason of its training, looks out upon life through Christian eyes and regards Judaism from un-Jewish points of view. The Jewish people has always had the power, upon the basis of its Judaism, to assimilate or reject the vital elements of the numberless philosophies with which it has come into contact. Our present generation, however, has no Judaism which may serve as a basis for comparison with non-Jewish or anti-Jewish teachings.

You may tell me that this disloyalty is due to the religious unrest that has seized hold upon men and women of all peoples and denominations. Much of the disloyalty to Judaism is doubtless to be traced to this cause. Yet, just as there are hundreds of thousands of young non-Jewish men and women devoted to their peoples and faiths, so there are tens of thousands of young Jewish men and women who are enthusiastic about their Judaism, who have absorbed the wisdom and culture of all the schools, and yet are intense and active and militant Jews and Jewesses. Why is it that in so large and so powerful a congregation as is this, we do not find a goodly proportion of such young Jews and Jewesses? Fathers and mothers of an older generation, you will bear me out when I answer, that our children do not go into the world from a Jewish environment. You fathers and mothers of an older generation were children in Jewish homes. You have recollections of Jewish prayers, of the sweetness and warmth of Jewish piety. You have sat at the Seder table with your father and your mother, and you have memories of the family reunion and of the songs and of the gracious warmth of it all. You men were doubtless bar mitzvah. You were shown the inside of a Jewish book. You were taught to respect Jewish learning, and I have heard some of you, in crises in your lives and upon other occasions, cite verses from our ancient literature as the best expression of your feelings of joy or of sorrow. On the Sabbath eve, you saw your mother bless the Sabbath lights, and your father placed his hand upon your head, and the father's blessing was upon his lips. Yet, when it is proposed to yield to the desires of several members of our congregation who wish to have their boys bar mitzvah, you throw up your hands in horror, and pronounce the awful word, "Orthodoxy." But the bar mitzvah means only this: that your boys should receive a special Jewish training at the hands of your rabbis in the hope that at least some of them may become cultivated and masterful leaders of Judaism. Is it true that your Reformed Judaism has become so petrified that it is impervious to new life? You yourselves, I repeat, have come from a Jewish atmosphere, but you do not seem to be willing to give your children the same chance. You are eager to buy for them all the outward graces your money can secure. But how unwilling and undesirous you are that they secure for themselves the inward grace of Judaism. And, knowing all this, you sit back, resting on your laurels, and you are unmindful of the disaster that is threatening you and your descendants. In moments of doubt it occurs to me that you are not at all anxious to avert the calamity. If you are anxious and have the remedy, bring it forward, and let us argue together. But if you have no remedy, give ear to what I say to you. Give it your deepest attention, your most earnest thought. Then, either reject the remedy I offer you, or apply it with heart and with mind. You cannot remain as you are. The retention of the status quo means a gradual sinking into decay. You must be moved by a new spirit if you wish to live. Unless it is your desire to become less Jewish rather than more Jewish, the one direction this or any other Reformed Congregation can take is that leading towards the living Jewish people where living Judaism is to be found.

I intend to give you a picture of the goal which a congregation such as this must strive to reach. Whether or not it will be capable of reaching this goal depends upon the degree of its Jewish education and its good will. But the life of such a congregation will be measured, not by its attainment of the objective point, but by its endeavor to reach this point. The struggle to achieve the aim will in itself be a sufficient reward. What I shall now have to say, therefore, is not to be understood as a plan for immediate adoption by Congregation Emanu-El. It is to be regarded rather as the ideal towards which it must strive. It is, in fine, part of a plan for a reconstruction of Reformed Judaism that I would bring before you; and I am of the firm belief that it is in this direction alone that Reformed Judaism, in order to be saved, must make its way.

It is difficult to determine just what is meant by the terms "Orthodox Judaism" and "Reformed Judaism." There is an orthodoxy that is in principle fixed and immovable. Such orthodoxy does not admit the possibility of change and development in Judaism. But there is another kind of orthodoxy which, holding fast to Jewish tradition, admits the possibility of change and development, of accommodation to new surroundings. Such an orthodoxy is that of a Zecharias Frankel[3] or a Solomon Schechter.

There is, on the other hand, an official Reformed Judaism. This Reformed Judaism is expressed and closely approaches petrifaction in the Union Prayer Book and in some conferences of Reformed Rabbis. But there is also an unofficial Reformed Judaism which, while not as yet organized, is, I venture to believe, the Judaism of the large majority of the Jews. These unofficial Reformed Jews, and I count myself as one of them, are less observant of Jewish religious practices than are the Orthodox, but they are in far greater sympathy with Jewish traditions than are the officially Reformed.

What I ask of this congregation and of others like it is that they cease to be officially Reformed. The principle which Reformed Judaism has established once and for all is that of change and development, of the possibility of adaptation to new surroundings. What I ask of this congregation and of similar congregations is that they be true to this principle, that they develop, that they change, that they open themselves to new influences, that they become increasingly Jewish. What I ask of this congregation and of similar congregations is that their synagogues be based upon this cardinal principle: intimate contact with and affection for the sources of Judaism.

What are the sources of Judaism? They are, first, the living Jewish people; second, the Torah (that is, the literature) of this people, its history, its language, its land; third, its living traditions, customs, observances, its aspirations.

Who are the living Jewish people? They are the bulk and body of the Jewish masses, the poor as well as the rich, the lowly as well as the learned, the immigrants as well as the native. They are the Jews, whether they be in this congregation or elsewhere, who have been trained in Jewish schools, through Jewish books, in the Jewish spirit; who find in Judaism a source of strength and of light; for whom Judaism is a religion, that is, their most sacred possession. The living Jewish people are those who live Judaism, and in whom the power to create Jewish values in religion, in philosophy, in social service, in literature, in art, has not been diminished. It becomes the duty of a congregation such as this to have a share in the life of the living Jewish people, to share not alone its burdens but also its hopes and joys. In order to do this, the religious service of such a congregation should be thrown open to all who wish to come. On a day such as this Passover when some of our front pews are empty, they should be placed at the disposal of some of the living Jewish people, many of whom I now see standing in the rear. Membership fees in this congregation should be reduced to so low a figure that any Jew might participate in our congregational activity. Brotherhood in the living Jewish people, furthermore, signifies that the religious service of such a synagogue must be, in the first place, of a nature to satisfy the particular religious needs of its immediate congregation and, in the second place, to give no offence to any Jew who is intimate with the sources of Judaism. Brotherhood in the Jewish people, in other words, consists not alone in calling ourselves brothers with our lips, but also in enabling us to share with our brothers common ideals and forms of worship. Much is said in these days of the relation of workingmen or the poor to synagogues such as this. In a synagogue, the only possible basis for common Jewish activity is not common economic theories, but common religious forms and ideals.

To establish such a synagogal service as will be neither Orthodox nor officially Reformed, but as will retain the essence of our old service and be acceptable to almost all Jews, it will be necessary to abandon the

Union Prayer Book. Far be it from me to underestimate the struggles endured in the creation of this book of prayer and the benefits that a modernized, uniform service has conferred upon numerous congregations. But I cannot be blind to the fact that the Union Prayer Book, as at present constituted, has done its work and has lived out its day. The one prayer book that can ever be the Book of Common Prayer for the Jewish people is the traditional Jewish prayer book, hallowed by the sufferings and the hopes and the religious yearnings of countless generations of our ancestors. Yet I do not mean to say that for a synagogue such as this the old prayer book, in its entirety, must serve as the customary ritual. My plan would be the following: that the prayer book of this congregation contain two parts. The first part is to be the traditional prayer book word for word, so that any Jew desiring to *"daven"* [East European way of praying] may do so. There would also be an English translation. The second part is to contain an abridged service in Hebrew and English for congregations such as this, that are less observant. An arrangement of the traditional prayer book can be made for the less observant and yet the service can retain its vital Jewish character, its manly strength, and its tender piety. Matters of dogma should be changed as little as is possible for modern men and women. The amount of English translation to be used in the public ritual would be determined by the degree of Hebrew culture of the congregation.

The forms and ceremonies of such a Congregation would be determined upon the principle: has a given form inherent strength or beauty and a vital message, and is it necessary in order that the service may be characterized immediately as Jewish? Unfortunately, at the present day, our forms and ceremonies are determined upon the principle: will a given form look well to the goyim, the gentiles, who may happen to drop in upon us? A prominent Christian lawyer of another city has told how he entered this building at the beginning of a service on a Sunday morning and did not discover that he was in a Synagogue until a chance remark of the preacher betrayed it. The consequences of the adoption of the positive principle I have just mentioned would, to be sure, change the aspect of our service considerably and would give it a Jewish hue and some of the virile vigor of traditional Judaism. It would be necessary for us to review all of the traditional observances and ceremonies, and to determine, in conjunction with Jewish authorities, which of them had meaning for us upon the principle I have just enunciated, namely: has a given form inherent strength or beauty and a vital message, and is it necessary in order that the services be characterized immediately as Jewish?

In a cosmopolitan city like New York, the pulpits of such congregations should be open not alone to Jewish preachers who speak the English language, but also upon occasion and if necessity demands, to such distinguished foreign visitors as can address Jewish audiences in the Hebrew and other languages.

The development of the educational system would have to be the most important activity of such a synagogue. There must be education for both young and old. The children's school of the congregation would have more than one session a week, and would regard the study of Hebrew as one of its chief disciplines. The bar mitzvah of boys as well as the confirmation of girls would be parts of this educational system. For the adults of the congregation it would be necessary to institute classes, not so much for the study of Jewish literature or of Jewish history as for the study of Jewish religion itself. By this I mean that it is necessary in our day that the riches of the Jewish religion be placed at the disposal of our individual Jews and Jewesses, in helping them to arrive at answers to their individual spiritual problems. What is the attitude of Judaism as to sin and suffering and death? What is the attitude of Judaism as to mind and work and joy? What does Judaism teach us as to man, the world and God? What of this life — what of the next? Do not for a moment think that there are none among the younger men and women of this congregation who have natural religious feelings, who have intense religious aspirations. I see many of them — and not by any means the worst — turning to other religions or desiring to do so, that they may fill the aching void in their souls. This points to an alternative: either Judaism itself is not capable of satisfying the religious needs of modern men and women, or it is we who are faulty in our methods of interpreting and presenting it. Believe me, dear friends, it is we, not Judaism who are deficient. The religious ideas of Judaism are as potent today as ever they were to dominate the Jewish being. But we have made these ideas words and phrases, topics for sermons alone, instead of teaching them by means of the concrete Jewish vessels and symbols in which great Jewish religious ideas are contained and expressed. Upon the basis of traditional forms and ceremonies, how inspiriting and thankful a task it would be to give instruction to young and old in the religious ideas of Judaism.

Such institutions, finally, should endeavor to include in their large structures all kinds of Jewish activity. The building must become for the congregation the center of its Jewish life. It must become a center for all activities of the Jewish spirit, a miniature Jewish world reflecting the whole life of Jewry as in a mirror.

"For, lo, the winter is past, the rain is over and gone; the flowers appear on the earth; the time of the singing of birds is come, and the voice of the turtledove is heard in our land." Will you share in the renewed hopes of the Jewish springtime? Will you celebrate this z'man herutenu, this season of Jewish freedom,' by an indication to me and to the Jewish people of your willingness to take the road that has been pointed out to you? Will you, as the prophet of old, see the dead bones rise in the valley and stir with the breath of life? Will you have the courage to attempt the long journey? Will you have the vigor to cover the long distance should you attempt it? Will the blessing of God rest upon this congregation, or is it doomed to inanition? Look into your hearts and ask yourselves, do you or do you not wish to remain Jews? The way of life and the way of death is before you. Choose.

1. Song of Songs, 2:11–12.
2. The society was founded by Felix Adler (1851–1933), whose father, Samuel Adler, occupied Emanu-El's pulpit from 1857 to 1874. The father had expected his son to succeed him to the pulpit.
3. Zacharias Frankel (1801–1875). Rabbi and scholar, born in Prague. He was the founder of the Juedisch-Theologisches Seminar at Breslau and was the most influential European spokesman of the historical school of Judaism, which stressed the importance of maintaining traditional forms but admitted the desirability of gradual change in response to contemporary needs.

11

To the President and Board of Trustees of Temple Emanu-El
New York

New York, May 16, 1910

Gentlemen,

I have learned from the committee appointed by you to discuss the matter with me, that my views as to Judaism and as to the situation in Temple Emanu-El, as stated by me in a sermon on the first day of Passover, have encountered the hostility of a majority of your honorable body. Your committee assumes that this hostility expresses the attitude of the membership of the congregation also.

When I accepted the position of Rabbi of Temple Emanu-El in 1906, it was with the explicit understanding that I was to be free to give unhindered expression to whatever convictions I might hold; and that, should the congregation at any time indicate to me unmistakably its hostility to my views or activities, one such indication would be sufficient for me.

If I should remain with Temple Emanu-El, I would expect to amplify my views as stated in my Passover sermon, and I would expect you to assist me in carrying out my plans, or other plans of like tendency, for a reconstruction of Reformed Judaism.

In case you are not ready for this, I beg leave herewith to tender my resignation as rabbi, the resignation to take effect on October 1, 1910.

Thanking you for your many acts of courtesy to me, and hoping for Temple Emanu-El an increased influence for good in Judaism, I am,

Very truly yours, JLM

12

To David Magnes
New York

New York, May 24, 1910

Dear Daddy,

This afternoon telegrams came from you and from New Orleans.[1] They were, I presume, in answer to mine sent this morning telling you of the result of the Board meeting last night. Tess[2] is, no doubt, supplying you with newspaper clippings. You will see from them what I wrote to the Board. This letter was drawn up with Mr. Marshall's assistance. Mr. Schiff wanted to postpone the decision, thinking that perhaps a compromise might be reached. But a compromise was an impossibility from the beginning. The result was not, of course, a surprise to me. Now that it is over I can hardly describe to you the feeling of comfort and of peace that has taken hold of me. It seems to me that I have come back to life, that I am a citizen of a new state, that I am at last, where after many wanderings, I belong. It is a wondrous sensation to realize that I am now fully, officially as well as unofficially, a Jew. Beatrice and I are agreed that I have nothing to regret, but that on the contrary we have much to be thankful for. Indeed, I had hardly imagined that so much kindness could be shown me by both friends and strangers. I constantly think of Jacob's words, *katonti mikol hahasadim* ["I am not worthy of all the mercies"].[3] It is quite uncanny and yet an inspiring thought to feel that I am being used by some greater Power for some good purpose.

Our plans are the same as they were. We expect to leave on June 14. It is possible that we shall be back a few days later. We had planned to be back by Oct. 1, in time for Rosh Hashana. Now that it is likely that I shall not have a position for the holidays, we may take a different steamer bringing us in Oct. 3. As to my plans for the future, all that I can say in this letter is that I have received several offers of help from rich men and poor men, and that I believe it possible to establish a great People's Synagogue here. I have several ideas as to how that should be worked out. Among other things I would say that I don't plan to have one building for the present, but rather an office and several centers in different parts of the city, each center to begin with a school and a small place of worship. The principles of the movement as well as the practical details will require careful working out; and I expect to enlist the support of several men of means to make it all of benefit to Judaism.

Tess and Bill[4] are to be here this evening for a little while. On Saturday night we we are to take them to the Schechter dinner at the Hotel Majestic. I am to speak there on "Regeneration of Judaism and Jews." David yells with laughter these days and he is just beginning to find his toes.

I almost forgot the *Hauptsache* [main point], from Daddy's telegram which pleased us most and about which we have been talking ever since — Zuie's[5] arrival in California. Well, we can just imagine the *simcha.* [joy]. We received letters from him from Chicago and along the road, and now he is home again. What a delighted Tate [Daddy] you must have been. I hope he is well and that the Wooltex Geschäft is good.

Much love to all of you.

Enon[6]

How are you, Ebie?[7] Wouldn't you like to be here now? Knocks Brooklyn all to spots.

1. Magnes's sister, Eva, and her husband, Chester Teller, were living in New Orleans.
2. Tess Magnes Popper (1883–1942), Magnes's sister, was then living in New York.
3. Gen. 32:11.
4. William Popper (1874–1963). Magnes's brother-in-law. An Orientalist and biblical scholar, born in St. Louis, Popper was professor of Semitic languages at the University of California at Berkeley.
5. Isaac Magnes's nickname.
6. JLM's nickname.
7. Eva Popper's nickname.

2

COMMUNITY
BUILDER
AND
MEDIATOR
1911–1916

I N 1912, THREE YEARS after the founding convention of the Kehillah, Magnes could report a number of achievements. Promising steps had been taken to help the Orthodox community meet some of its formidable problems. Magnes's successful mediation of a long and brutal strike in the fur industry had brought the Kehillah into the field of labor relations. He also had acted energetically in the aftermath of the Rosenthal murder, when exposés of collusion between organized crime and the police implicated numbers of Jews. Magnes established a Kehillah bureau to collaborate with the authorities in ridding the Jewish quarter of criminals. Most impressive, however, was the progress made in the area of Jewish religious education. With the financial aid given mostly by Jacob Schiff and Felix Warburg the Kehillah's Bureau of Education had taken a major step forward in creating a modern education system (document 14). Striving to broaden the Kehillah's base, Magnes approached leaders of the Jewish labor movement to join the organization. "It will be an element of great strength to the whole community," he wrote to Meyer London in 1913, "if the radical element will take up the problem of Jewish communal organization together with the rest of the community. We are, after all, one people — whether we wish it or not."[1] But socialist principles and the assimilationist ideology of Jewish radicals like London outweighed the cordial ties that existed between them and Magnes.

To Magnes's mind one of the chief obstacles to community building was the destructive role of the Yiddish press: power-hungry and corrupt, it presented to its readers a distorted image of American society, vilified the responsible leadership of the community, and singled out the Kehillah for its most vicious assaults. Magnes appealed to his wealthy uptown friends to finance a Yiddish newspaper that would "uphold everything high and good among the Jews" (document 15). The appearance of the *Tog* in 1914, was, in large measure, due to this initiative.

1. Arthur A. Goren, *New York Jews and the Quest for Community* (New York, 1970), p. 206.

Though no longer active in the daily administration of the Federation of American Zionists, Magnes continued to be one of the dominant influences in the organization. He served as its vice-president, spoke extensively from Zionist platforms, and in the spring of 1912 made his second trip to Palestine with his wife and the philanthropist Nathan Straus and his wife. Magnes's ties with Arthur Ruppin, director of the Palestine office of the World Zionist Organization, and his staff, and with Aaron Aaronson, the agronomist, and other veteran settlers established Magnes as the best informed of the American Zionists on Palestinian affairs. (At Ruppin's request, Magnes allocated money to the Palestine office to be used to improve Arab-Jewish relations, an intimation of his later concerns.)[2] In the aftermath of the Balkan war, he raised once again the possibility of reaching an accommodation with Turkey as the best hope for facilitating Jewish colonization in Palestine, a position he maintained as late as 1916 (document 16).

From September 1914 to July 1916 Magnes took a leading role in the organized efforts of the American Jewish community to aid European Jewry. His outstanding ability to move audiences made him the most effective fund raiser for the Joint Distribution Committee. At the height of his influence Magnes tried to resolve the conflict that raged over the issue of establishing a representative central body for American Jewry. An early advocate of the idea of a Jewish congress, he agreed with those who claimed that the outbreak of war made such a body more necessary than ever. Throughout the winter and spring of 1915 he warned the American Jewish Committee leaders that unless they responded to the groundswell of feeling for a congress, they would lose their preeminent position in Jewish life. The committee remained impervious to his pleas and later to his compromise proposals (document 19). Nor did Magnes succeed with the Zionists. His call to the Zionist convention in June 1915 not to align itself with the congress movement and thus leave a door open for further negotiations wiht the American Jewish Committee was rejected by a convention dominated by Louis D. Brandeis. Faced with a polarization of positions, Magnes threw his support to the American Jewish Committee. In an open letter published in the Yiddish press he declared that though he continued to believe in the principle of a congress, he felt that to establish one when no consensus existed was self-defeating; it would deepen the rift rather than unite the community.[3]

Magnes resigned from the Provisional Executive Committee for General Zionist Affairs criticizing Brandeis for deviating from accepted Zionist policy, which he declared to be the exclusive concern with building

2. JLM to Arthur Ruppin, July 24, 1912, MP, 784.
3. To the Delegates to the Conference of the Congress Organization Committee, March 26, 1916, MP, 1594.

the national center in Palestine (documents 20, 22). His estrangement from the Zionist organization carried personal overtones. At its heart was the rise of a new, aggressive leadership personified by Brandeis and Stephen Wise. Brandeis and Wise had supplanted Magnes as the democratic leaders and spokesmen of the masses. They rejected Magnes's pleas for accommodation rather than confrontation between the establishment and its challengers. In July 1916, on the eve of Magnes's departure on a four-month mission in Europe on behalf of the Joint Distribution Committee, the break with the Zionist movment became nearly irreparable. Magnes's letter of apology to Brandeis for his attack on the newly appointed Supreme Court Justice hardly placated his foes (document 24).

His warm relationship with Chaim Weizmann, which grew out of their common endeavors on behalf of a university in Jerusalem (document 17), suffered as well. When the Turkish government's policy of Zionist repression threatened the physical survival of the *yishuv* in December 1914, Magnes placed a share of the blame on Weizmann. His diplomatic activities in England on behalf of Zionist political aspirations in Palestine had violated the organization's decision to remain neutral and had angered Turkey (document 23). Magnes now stood opposed to Brandeis, Wise, and Weizmann, who had risen to commanding positions in the world Jewish scene.

13

To Solomon Schechter
New York

New York, February 5, 1911

Dear Doctor Schechter,

You will understand, I am sure, why I have not written to you all these months. I have been torn between conflicting thoughts as to what work I was to do, and I have wanted to spare you any of the uncertainty of it. More than that, I have imagined that each week might bring something definite to write to you; but as week followed week and I was still uncertain, I determined to continue my silence until I had some positive news for you.

To show you how much you are in our thoughts, I want to say that it was only today that a definite plan has been decided upon; and almost the first thing that Mrs. Magnes said was, "Now you will write to Dr. Schechter."

The B'nai Jeshurun Congregation[1] has agreed to all of the conditions that I have made. I am enclosing a copy of the conditions as accepted unanimously at a meeting of the members today. I am enclosing also a copy of a statement to the press which I am issuing tonight. I have already a sufficient number of new members to outvote the old ones if ever that becomes necessary. But I have no fear of this. They have been very tractable, and I can get anything I want. There is to be no organ during service, and there are to be *sheva k'ru'im*.[1] I did not ask for a separation of the sexes. That is a question I should like to have take care of itself. Mr. Marshall and Felix Warburg are particularly pleased, as are Mr. Schiff, the Judge,[2] and a whole host of our *ba'ale batim* [prosperous] friends of the "Russian" community. At the meeting in March, your letter will be read.[3] I hope for good results. We can now, I hope, form a union of congregations in New York City so that a meeting like that of the "American" union[4] may not again pass without a strong counter-demonstration.

I have several plans which I shall not bore you with now. This is being written in haste. David has four teeth, and can say a few words, and can walk by holding on to some support. Mrs. Magnes and I are exceptionally well. We enjoyed Frank's[5] visit here. I shall write you more at length at another time. Remember us kindly to Mrs. Schechter and Amy.[6] We are anxious to see you here again.

Affectionately, JLM

Enclosure

The Congregation B'nai Jeshurun, at its annual meeting today, has done me the honor of asking me to become its leader.

Many Jews have proposed to me the formation of a new Society for the Advancement of Judaism.[7] I have, however, taken no steps in this direction, and I have chosen to do my work upon the basis of an existing organization because my general idea is, to endeavor to preserve what is best in Judaism rather than to create unnecessary institutions. The B'nai Jeshurun Congregation has offered to become the Society for the Advancement of Judaism, and says in effect:

We have an organization established since 1825, with a building of our own, and with a desire to serve the cause of Judaism. Take us and make of us what you will. I highly appreciate this mark of confidence, and the opportunity thus given to me and to all the Jews of New York City.

My work with the organization will begin on April 1. Before that time, however, it is my intention to convene a preliminary meeting at which I shall outline my views, and invite the Jews of the city to join the movement. Meanwhile, I wish to quote some of the clauses, which the congregation, at my request, has incorporated into its by-laws:

> The Congregation is to further Judaism as it has been handed down to us by the Jewish People, and which, though capable of modifications to suit time and place, is always and everywhere essentially the same.
>
> The organization shall strive to become not only a house of prayer, but also a place for study and for other Jewish activities; in other words, the organization shall strive to become a Jewish Center — a *bet ha'am*, a 'house of the Jewish people.'
>
> The organization shall pledge itself to further the cause of Judaism not only among its own members, but in the community at large; and to this end the rabbi shall be left free to do such Jewish work as he feels called upon to do. In case of necessity, an assistant shall be appointed.

It will be seen that, in addition to strengthening the central organization, we shall look forward to carrying our work beyond the four walls of our building. The organization has agreed to fix the membership fee at so moderate a rate, that young Jews and Jewesss at present without affiliation in a synagogue and yet desirous of maintaining a living, positive Judaism, will be enabled to become members. We shall make our appeal to all Jews who believe in a society where the aristocracy of Jewish tradition may be cherished and where the masses of the Jewish people may find a genuine spiritual center.

J. L. Magnes

1. B'nai Jeshurun, the second oldest congregation in New York City, moved increasingly from Conservative to Reform practice in the early 1900s in an effort to stem a dwindling of the membership. The congregation invited Magnes to be its rabbi, despite his traditionalist views, in the expectation that his leadership would revitalize the institution. Individual members of the congregation were important supporters of the Jewish Theological Seminary.

2. Mayer Sulzberger.

3. Magnes was installed as rabbi on March 30, 1911. Letters from Solomon Schechter and Mayer Sulzberger were read, and Cyrus Adler addressed the meeting.

4. Union of American Hebrew Congregations.

5. Schechter's son.

6. Schechter's daughter.

7. An organization by that name, not to be confused with the one established by Mordecai Kaplan in the 1920s, was formed in January 1912, when Magnes resigned from B'nai Jeshurun in order to devote himself "to those problems of Jewish religious organization and Jewish education without being attached to any particular synagogue" (*New York Times*, January 31, 1912, p. 1).

14

To the Executive Committee of the American Jewish Committee
New York

New York, November 6, 1912

Gentlemen:

On the occasion of your Sixth Annual Convention, we beg to present you herewith a brief summary of the more recent activities of the Jewish Community (Kehillah) of New York City.

Since reporting to you last, the Kehillah successfully held its Third Annual Convention, on April 27 and 28 of the present year, and copies of the reports presented and of the proceedings of this Convention were sent to all of the members of the American Jewish Committee.

Some of our activities brought up to date may be described as follows:

Religious Organization: The organization of our Va'ad Harabbanim, or Board of Rabbis, has, after many difficulties been perfected. It now has thirty-one authoritative rabbis. In accordance with the plans previously outlined, the Board has begun its work of regulating kashrut by the establishment of a number of Boards of Kashrut throughout the city. Each Board, presided over by a rabbi living in the district, employs a number of inspectors to supervise the sale of kosher meat in the different butcher shops in the district. In this way the fraudulent sale of *tref* meat as kosher, with its accompanying scandal of fraud being perpetrated in the name of religion, will in the future be eliminated. To those acquainted with the Jewish conditions in our large cities, there can be no question that many of our most serious difficulties are due to the chaos in this phase of Jewish life.

As part of the work of the Board of Rabbis, dayyanim [rabbinical judges] have been appointed, who will answer all questions of Jewish Law and settle disputes in different localities of the city.

Continuing our work of synagogue extension, we have endeavored to combat the evil of "mushroom synagogues" and to provide places of worship for the poor on the High Holidays. We conducted seven provisional synagogues and distributed several hundred tickets which we purchased at reduced rates from regular synagogues of the downtown district.

We have also made investigations of all the temporary synagogues conducted in different halls by private speculators throughout the city. The investigation has confirmed our own observation that the temporary synagogues are decreasing in number. The total number of temporary synagogues for the different sections of the city is 286. These were divided for the different sections of the city as follows: Lower East Side below Houston Street, 50; Lower East Side between Houston and 21st Streets, 47; Yorkville, 13; Harlem, 95; Washington Heights, 2; Bronx, 29; Brooklyn, 31, Brownsville, 15; Borough Park, 4.

It will be noted that the largest number of temporary synagogues were found in Harlem, the section of the city which has been more recently settled by a large number of our people and which, consequently, has fewer permanent synagogues than the Lower East Side.

Having before us now information as to the needs of the different sections of the city and as to the location of suitable auditoriums, we have decided to take options on some of the large halls for the next year and, with the aid in some instances of permanent synagogues of the neighborhood and in other instances of local committees which we expect to organize, we plan to conduct these synagogues next year on a large scale and on a self-supporting basis.

Education: The Bureau of Education has, during the second year of its existence, fully kept up the remarkable pace which it set from the very beginning of its activity. The initial fund of $50,000 per annum, referred to in the last report, having been secured, the Bureau immediately set out to carry out the plans which careful investigation had indicated as the most effective means of grappling with the tremendous problem of Jewish education. An important step in the direction of bringing harmony into the hitherto prevailing educational chaos was taken through affiliation with the bureau of four out of the eight largest talmud torahs [communal religious schools] of Greater New York.

By granting annual financial assistance on condition that these institutions comply with certain standards calculated to bring about a more uniform system and greater efficiency in the Jewish schools of New York, the Bureau has succeeded in raising very considerably both the educational and economic level of these institutions and of forming the nucleus of a Jewish educational system in the largest Jewish community of the world.

The Department of Investigation, Collection and Attendance has in some cases resulted in raising the revenue from the parents of the children of the talmud torahs thirty-five to fifty per cent. It has systematically followed up all the children visiting these institutions, thus stopping the leakage which has been a source of great weakness in all these schools.

The Bureau has also established a third model school of its own and has helped to establish other schools to which it gave either financial or moral assistance. The Bureau is now cooperating with twenty-five educational establishments both in New York and outside of it. The number of children in the New York schools cooperating with the Bureau is about twelve thousand.

The question of teachers, which is the cornerstone of the whole educational problem, has received close attention. Training courses for English or pedagogy were established for those teachers — forming the bulk of Hebrew teachers — who are adequately equipped in Hebrew but are deficient in their secular education. The courses are in a flourishing condition and have helped to raise considerably both the educational efficiency and morale of the teachers. The Bureau has further succeeded in interesting a considerable number of college men who are anxious to devote themselves to Jewish education. The Teachers' Institute of the Jewish Theological Seminary of America has now taken charge of the training of these men, who will no doubt, prove of the utmost assistance in solving this difficult problem.

The Bureau has, by means of literature and parents' meetings, endeavored to acquaint the Jews with the problem of Jewish education and with the means for solving it. The unusual interest which is everywhere evinced in the problem of Jewish education is, no doubt, due in large degree to the efforts of the Bureau.

The Bureau has made considerable progress in the preparation of proper textbooks, the lack of which has been keenly felt by all Jewish pedagogues. A number of publications are out, others are in the course of preparation.

The Bureau has from the very beginning been keenly interested in the problem of the overwhelming numbers of our children who, because of lack of accommodation, remain outside a Jewish school, deprived of all Jewish instruction or influence, and are all too ready victims of the destructive effects of the street. In the course of the last year the Bureau has made a most steady and successful attempt to solve this problem by means of extension teaching given on Sunday mornings in one of the large theatres downtown. While systematic instruction is out of the question, the children are made acquainted with Jewish history by lectures and lantern slides and are taught the most important Hebrew prayers and responses. A number of Jewish public school teachers have been interested in this extension work as volunteers. The results achieved thus far have clearly shown both the necessity and the possibility of getting hold of many thousands of Jewish children in this city and of acquainting them with the essentials of Judaism.

It is impossible to go into detail here, nor can the minor yet important activities of the Bureau be pointed out. The elaborate reports presented to the last annual convention of the Kehillah by Dr. Samson Benderly, the director of the Bureau, and Professor Israel Friedlaender, Chairman of the Board of Trustees, give full information about the many-sided endeavors of the Bureau and have been sent to the members of the American Jewish Committee.

One thing is certain, the work of the Bureau has grown to such an extent that expansion is a natural and unavoidable process. The Bureau cannot pointedly disregard the urgent requests for affiliation which come to it from the various educational institutions, this affiliation being just as important for raising the status of these institutions as it is for working out the system of Jewish education in general.

Nor can the Bureau leave unheeded the tremendous problem of the thousands of children whose parents would be only too happy to bear the cost of instruction but who are not in a position to put up the necessary school buildings. The Bureau will also be called upon to greatly increase its facilities and expenditures in connection with the extension work indicated above, for the benefit of the children, no less numerous, who, on account of lack of room, must perforce remain outside the Jewish school. This expansion is absolutely indispensable if the Bueau is to continue its normal and healthy development and is not to be checked and dwarfed in its growth. But it is to be expected that the Jews of New York will realize the vital importance of Jewish education for the preservation and perpetuation of Judaism, and that the appeal for larger funds which will make this expansion possible will find the same ready and generous response with which the first appeal met.

Social and Philanthropic Work: Our Employment Bureau for handicapped Jews, conducted in cooperation with the United Hebrew Charities and with the Jewish Protectory and Aid Society, has continued to do its good work by finding employment for persons who experience the greatest difficulty in securing work and who, without positions, would either become charges of our charitable institutions or would be a menace to the welfare and the good name of our people.

We have also carried on considerable correspondence with firms who are more and more frequently inserting the word "Christian," when advertising for help in the "Want Columns" of the newspapers. These advertisements indicate the alarming growth of the evil of discrimination, and it is remarkable that many concerns which cater to the trade of our people display this form of bigotry.

The work of naturalization, which we had taken up at the suggestion of the American Jewish Committee, has already been reported on in our last annual report. The distribution of circulars and booklets on naturalization among the Jewish organizations of New York might be profitably continued, if we had the means wherewith to carry on this propaganda. We have cooperated with the Department of Public Lectures of the Board of Education of New York City in furnishing them Yiddish lecturers on citizenship.

In connection with our naturalization work, we have, during the year, made an investigation of the number of Jewish voters in Greater

New York. This study, which was made under the direction of Dr. Abraham Lipsky,[1] showed that there were 113,000 Jewish voters in Greater New York.

The *Jewish Communal Directory*, which we issued last January, containing information about 3,500 Jewish organizations of Greater New York, has served as an index and guide to the multitude of public Jewish activities in our city. The book has been found to be of value to all those who are interested and who have occasion to get in touch with Jewish organizations. In this directory was also published an important statistical study of the Jewish population of New York by Dr. Joseph Jacobs.[2]

In this connection we are still considering the plan of establishing a Bureau of Jewish Statistics, and since our last convention, a committee of our organization has been working out a plan for the formation of such a statistical bureau.

Pursuant to a resolution of the last convention, we have also appointed a committee which is to make a thorough and impartial study of the question of the federation of Jewish charities and which is to report its findings at our next convention.

The Committee on the Caricaturing of the Jew on the Stage has carried on an extensive correspondence with theatrical managers and agencies of this city, and the Committee is now making further plans for the elimination of the misrepresentation of the Jew on the stage.

We have continued to give our attention to the matter of dependent Jewish children who for a number of reasons are placed with non-Jewish institutions and whom we endeavor, as soon as room is found for them, to have transferred to Jewish child-care institutions. The great difficulty in this matter is that there is not sufficient room for all the Jewish children who become homeless and that we have no institutions at all for certain classes of crippled and diseased children who must be let to the care of non-Jews.

Welfare Work: The activities of Jewish gangsters and the development of other forms of delinquency in the congested districts had previously been called to our attention, and when the case of the Rosenthal murder which occurred last July, revealed conditions of vice and crime which besmirched the Jewish name, we thought it our duty to take action. The Bureaus of Information and Investigation were established and are now operating with some success.

These are, in brief, some of the leading activities in which we have more recently been engaged. We have, in addition, been called upon to take up various other matters pertaining to the welfare of our people. Individuals as well as organizations which found themselves in difficulties, and were either discriminated against racially or otherwise subjected to unnecessary hardships, appealed to us for our aid, and we have in every instance endeavored to help those who were in trouble and to protect the rights of those who were in need of such protection.

We have been asked to settle several disputes, and the settlement of the Furriers' Strike, which lasted many months and which brought a great deal of hardship to many thousands of Jewish workingmen, was one of the achievements of our work of conciliation.

I have the honor to remain

Yours respectfully, JLM, Chairman

1. Abraham Lipsky (1873–1946). Author and educator; brought to the United States from Russia in 1875. He received his Ph.D. from Columbia University and taught German in the New York City high schools.

2. Joseph Jacobs (1854–1916). Author, historian, editor. Born in Sidney, Australia, studied at St. John's College, Cambridge. Jacobs was called to the United States in 1900 to edit the *Jewish Encyclopedia*. He was the editor of the *American Hebrew* from 1906 to his death and from 1914 was the director of the Bureau of Jewish Statistics.

15

Memorandum: A Yiddish Morning Daily

New York, circa January 1913

There are four daily Yiddish papers in this city, one morning and three afternoon papers. There are, in addition, four Yiddish weeklies and two Yiddish monthlies. Of the Yiddish dailies, the *Varhayt*, cleared above all expenses, $30,000 last year; the *Morgen Zhurnal*, $40,000; the *Tageblat*, $60,000, and the *Forverts*, $75,000. The *Forverts* has a daily circulation of over 120,000; the *Tageblat* has the smallest circulation, somewhat over 60,000 daily.

It is needless for me to explain what a power, for good or ill, the press in general is. With a clean, intelligent press, the citizenship of a community is helped. With a corrupt press, the citizenship of a community is corrupted. This holds true particularly among the Jewish immigrant population reading Yiddish. America appears to the immigrant as it is pictured to him day after day, year in and year out by his Jewish press. It is no wonder that the immigrant is cynical and contemptuous concerning the political, moral, intellectual, aesthetic and religious standards of America. The readers of the Yiddish papers know, to their own shame, that all of the Yiddish papers are in some manner or other corrupt and venal. But they shrug their shoulders, and ask with a bitter smile, as I have so often heard, and as is reflected throughout the literature produced in America, "What do you expect of America? A curse upon Columbus!" All of the Yiddish papers have private axes to grind, either political or personal. The *Forverts*, which is the only paper supposedly conducted for idealistic purposes and not for personal gain, is wildly socialistic, and is not free from definite and specific charges of money corruption. The other papers are conducted frankly for personal gain, and have no sense of their public duty. They can be bought for every purpose. They sell themselves to the highest bidder. Politically, they are in one campaign Democratic, in the other campaign Republican; and it has happened that on one day, two editions of the same paper were issued, one edition in behalf of one party, the other edition on behalf of the other party. In this campaign, the editor of the *Morgen Zhurnal* has received at least three autograph letters from the President of the United States, who saw fit to lick the boots of a corrupt Jewish editor for the sake of the political gain he thought he could secure. The President of the United States issued a luncheon invitation on White House stationery in honor of the nephew of this editor.[1] Secretary of Commerce and Labor [Charles] Nagel made a special trip from Washington to take dinner with this man who would not be welcomed at the table of any poor, self-respecting Jew. This is but one instance in one campaign of the political power which a Yiddish paper exercises and of the way this power is sought and prostituted. Can this help our Jewish honor in the eyes of those of our neighbors whose good opinion of us it is most worth our while to keep; and is it not inevitable that this cynical indifference to decency on the part of the molders of Jewish public opinion must reflect itself in everything that they undertake?

As far as the Jewish side of these papers is concerned, not a one of them stands for the great idea which I know is uppermost in the minds and hearts of most of us, namely, the unification of the vast and growing Jewish community in this city and in this country. Not a one of them will, for example, support the Kehillah idea with heart and soul, because they realize that with a strong Kehillah creating Jewish public opinion, their hegemony would be interfered with. They delight in setting "uptown" against "downtown," the German over against the Russian. They do not scruple to attack Jewish institutions in this city, such as the United Hebrew Charities, the Protectory, the orphan asylums. Is it any wonder that the Jewish Theological Seminary has practically no supporters among the masses of our people, when the Yiddish newspapers either pass it by in silence, or, when they mention it, condemn it by innuendo and untruthful insinuations of all kinds. Not even the venerable person of the President of the Jewish Theological Seminary, Prof. Schechter, has been spared from the meanest and vilest attacks.[2]

The whole nasty campaign against the Bureau of Education of the Kehillah was instigated and conducted by a single newspaper. Without this newspaper, this campaign was unthinkable. It is only a man of courage and of steel such as Dr. Benderly, who could have withstood the merciless attacks made upon him, his family, his integrity.[3] It is only through the efforts of the same Yiddish morning newspaper that another Russian rabbi has been brought to this city from Boston in order to create additional disturbance in the community in the name of a so-called Adath Israel, an organization which had its inception in frauds connected with the purchase of cemetery plots, which has its existence through charges of malfeasance and misappropriation of funds.[4] This rabbi was brought here, also, in order to bring about meat scandals such as have but recently led to proceedings in the courts of Philadelphia, and which were of so shocking a character that the Christian judge referred the matter to a Jewish committee of three, of which Judge Sulzberger and Dr. Krauskopf[5] were members. The importance of the kosher meat situation can hardly be overestimated. The foreign rabbis in this city are dependent almost entirely for their income and their standing in the community upon the kosher meat situation. I wish to fortify this statement by a remark of Dr. Cyrus Adler in a recent letter. He says that in his opinion the degradation and the corruption of the Russian rabbis in this country are due in large measure to the chaos prevailing in the kosher meat situation.[6] This Yiddish morning newspaper knows these things — what a grip upon the community it would secure if the recently imported rabbi could get control of the kosher meat situation, or bring confusion into it! In general, what is the use of our condemning our foreign Orthodox rabbis whose very existence is jeopardized by a single word in one of the Yiddish papers, if we do not come to their rescue and stand behind them with a paper which will afford them some refuge and which will spur them on to higher and better things?

Commercially, the existing newspapers sell themselves to patent medicine fakers, fortune tellers and other illegitimate enterprises. They are the particular friends of the Yiddish theatres and vaudeville houses and low variety shows. They do not dare to pass an unfavorable criticism upon plays which even go so far as to portray to the Jewish public a Jewish house of ill fame conducted by a man who displays a Torah scroll.

From the point of view of news-gathering itself, they do not seem to have any sense of proportion in knowing what is important Jewish news and what is unimportant. If an item of Jewish interest appears in the morning *Times*, a miserably translated reproduction is placed in the Yiddish afternoon paper. In the very passport question, the *Morgen Zhurnal* was at first opposed to pressing the President,[7] because it was hand in glove with Mr. Henry Goldfogel[8] in his weak endeavors to disturb the passport movement.

What is perhaps of most serious consequence is that these papers cannot be secured for high-minded, energetic agitation on behalf of Jewish ideas. They prefer to be silent about evil conditions among the Jews, attacking us at the present moment because we are pressing the Police Department to clean out affairs.

A Yiddish newspaper is needed that knows no fear or favor, that will uphold everything high and good among the Jews, whether it be known as Zionism, or Orthodox Judaism or Reform Judaism or what not; that will advocate all decent policies of civic betterment under whatever name they be known; that will condemn everything low and corrupting among the Jews, whether among the Zionists or Reform Jews or Orthodox Jews, or what not. We need a paper that will not hesitate to lay bare our wounds to the Jews, in order that once and for all, a gigantic effort be made to throw off the poison that has these many years polluted our body. We need an organ that will in season and out of season preach the unification of the Jews of this city and of this country and of all the world. The blessings that such a paper, well managed, commercially profitable, and morally clean and aggressive, could bring to the Jews of this city and of all the world, are incalculable.[9]

1. Jacob Saphirstein (1853–1923). Founder and publisher of the *Morgen Zhurnal*, supported the Republican Party. His nephew Israel Friedkin (1890–1939) joined the paper in 1905 and became its publisher in 1916.

2. The *Morgen Zhurnal* claimed that the institutions supported by the German-Jewish philanthropists, including the Jewish Theological Seminary, subverted the Orthodox beliefs of the immigrants.

3. The *Morgen Zhurnal* accused Benderly of being a "free thinker" who was using the Kehillah's Bureau of Education to gain control of the Orthodox talmud toras. These attacks became especially strident in the summer and fall of 1912. See, for example, *Morgen Zhurnal*, December 13, 1912, p.4.

4. Adath Israel (United Hebrew Community of New York) provided burial and death benefits for its members. The society also attempted unsuccessfully to centralize the supervision of kashrut. In September 1911, Adath Israel, with Saphirstein's encouragement, invited Rabbi Gabriel Zev Margolis (1847–1935) to serve as its spiritual leader. The *Morgen Zhurnal* supported Margolis's denunciations of the Kehillah's Board of Rabbis and his efforts to organize a federation of Orthodox organizations in opposition to the Kehillah.

5. Joseph Krauskopf (1853–1923). Rabbi of Reform Congregation Knesseth Israel in Philadelphia.

6. Adler headed the newly-established Jewish Community of Philadelphia, which was modeled after the New York Kehillah.

7. The American Jewish Committee urged President Taft to abrogate the Russo-American Commercial Treaty of 1832 on the grounds that the Russian government discriminated against American citizens of Jewish birth who desired to visit Russia. In December 1911 the President abrogated the treaty.

8. Henry Goldfogle (1856–1929). New York City Democratic Party politician; municipal judge; member of Congress representing the Ninth District (the Lower East Side) from 1901–1915, 1919–1921. Goldfogle sponsored congressional resolutions condemning Russia's discriminatory practices. The American Jewish Committee considered these efforts to be ineffective and damaging to its own strategy.

9. Magnes's uptown supporters provided only minor financial help in launching *Der Tog* (November 1914), and the paper's policies disappointed them. For the next two years

Magnes tried to win financial control of the paper. He wrote to Schiff, Marshall, Warburg, Samuel Strauss, and Irving Lehman on December 18, 1916: "Unless such a paper is in the hands of the present leaders of the community, much of the work now being done will have been in vain, and the position of the present leaders will before long become an impossibility . . . If they wish to continue to exercise Jewish leadership in these critical days, when world-Jewry turns to America, particularly to New York, for leadership, they will not be able to bear the responsibility to do their full duty and to hope for positive achievement unless they have an organ of their own through which they can talk to the masses of the Jews in this country and throughout the world" (MP, 1592).

16

To Oscar S. Straus
New York

New York, January 2, 1913

Dear Mr. Straus:

Enclosed please find a translation of a letter which I have just received from the Palestine Office in Jaffa.[1] I am sure that you will be interested in this, and that you will be the more convinced of the wisdom of Jewish colonization in Palestine and in the Ottoman Empire, a movement with which you have repeatedly shown yourself in sympathy. What a part we Jews could now play in shaping the destinies of a great empire and in re-making the map of Europe, had we a strong Jewish element in Palestine and in the Ottoman Empire! The present moment shows us how powerless our unorganized Jewish power is. With all of our millions of money and of souls, we cannot command anything like the hearing which Montenegro commands, despite the fact that her whole population is less than one-half of the number of Jews of New York City alone. You probably have read that the Zionist organization, by means of a letter in the London *Times* from Dr. Max Nordau, has brought to the attention of the peace conference and of the ambassadors of the Powers the desirability of securing for the Jews the opportunity of helping the Ottoman Empire in its coming struggle for rehabilitation and orderly development.[2] Unfortunately, heretofore the Turks have been as blind as the Jews. Had the Turks been willing fifteen or twenty years ago to make a compact with the Jews of the world to the end that Jewish capital and labor and energy and devotion might be applied to the development of the Ottoman Empire, I am convinced that Turkey would still be in Europe, and that the Ottoman Empire would have shared in the progress of the nations.

Now, it seems to me, is the time for the Jews to be active. The Zionist Organization is pressing the claims of Jewish migration to the whole Ottoman Empire, including thereby Palestine. The Jewish organizations of Europe are endeavoring to extra-territorialize Salonica and its district.[3] This would mean a preponderance of Jewish influence; at any rate, the ousting of the anti-semitic Greeks, who have shown their colors by the excesses committed upon the Jews in Salonica and by compelling the Chacham Bashi [chief rabbi] of Salonica to declare falsely that no outrages had taken place. I think that the American Jewish Committee also is prepared to take some kind of action.

With regards, I am,

Very truly yours, JLM

1. Dr. Jacob Thon, assistant director of the Palestine Office, urged mobilizing international support for Zionist colonization in Palestine as a way of strengthening the Ottoman Empire (Thon to JLM, December 5, 1912, CZA).

2. Max Nordau (1849–1923). Physician, writer, Zionist leader, friend and collaborator of Theordore Herzl; critical of the cultural and practical Zionists. Born in Pest, Hungary, he lived for most of his life in Paris. Nordau's letter appeared in *The Times* (London), December 30, 1912, p. 3, and was reported in the *New York Times*, December 30, 1912, p. 3.

3. During mediations concerning the boundary dispute between Greece and Bulgaria a proposal was made to turn Salonika into a free port. The Jews formed a slight majority of the population.

17

To Chaim Weizmann
Manchester, England

New York, May 25, 1913

Dear Chaimchik:

I thank you for your interesting letter of April 19, and I wish to say that I envy you the privilege of presenting to the next [Zionist] Congress the idea of a Jewish university in Jerusalem. Together with many other persons, I have thought very much about a Jewish university in Jerusalem, and I am of the opinion that such an institution, properly founded and conducted, can be of inestimable service to the Jews of all the world.

You ask me several questions, among those, that I discuss the questions outlined in your letter with Sokolow. In the hope that I might have been able to get an interview with him, I postponed answering you. But, unfortunately, he has been so extremely busy lecturing and speaking in all kinds of possible and impossible places, that it has been next to impossible to get even a glimpse of him.[1] His present plans, I think, bring him back here at the beginning of June, and I hope at that time to have the opportunity of talking to him.

You ask me for a statement of my views on the subject of a Jewish university. It would, I think, be possible to write quite an extensive treatise on the subject. You do not want that. A Jewish university in Jerusalem may, in brief, be considered from several points of view: first, as the natural capstone of the educational system in Palestine; second, a place of refuge for such European students as are unable to secure a university training in other places; third, — and what appears to me to be the most important — as the heart of that spiritual center which we have been constantly talking of establishing in Palestine. To my notion, all of these aspects of the situation ought to be taken into account; and, if we had the means, all should be given some concrete form at once. If our means are limited — and I know they are — it will all depend upon the personal predilection of each individual, as to which phase of the whole should be most emphasized.

I agree with you that a medical school and a school of law would be good institutions to begin with, and I can well appreciate how deeply interested you would be in the establishment of departments for chemistry, physics, and anatomy. I question very much, however, if the idea of working together with the German institute, is a proper one.

My chief interest in the whole matter lies in the hope that a Jewish university would give to Judaism, as much as to the Jews, new and fresh values. For example, if a school of law be established, it would have a genuine Jewish value, in addition to what an ordinary law school might have, if questions of law were taken up from a Jewish point of view, and on the basis of Jewish legal literature and experience. The same thing is true of all other branches of the *Geisteswissenschaften* [humanities], particularly history, literature and philosophy. If the various schools of the university are to be nothing else than Palestinian replicas of European and American schools, they will, of course, have their immediate practical value, but they will not be serving Judaism as much as they might.

In line with this idea, it has always seemed to me that a beginning ought to be made with what might appear to be the least practical thing of the whole subject, but which, in reality, might prove to be the most practical of all, namely, with a Jewish school of archaeology, which should be developed as our means permit, into a school of *Geisteswissenschaften* treated from the Jewish point of view. This is, of course, different from a school established for *jüdische Wissenschaft* [scholarship]. A school for *jüdische Wissenschaft* takes up the body of Jewish literature or history or philosophy as a branch of literature, history, or philosophy in general. A Jewish school for *Geisteswissenschaften* would take up history, literature and philosophy in general, and use Jewish material primarily, but by no means exclusively, as the basis of instruction.

This phase of the whole subject has, of course, the disadvantage of seeming to be removed from more practical things, such as medicine and law. We have all too many of the spiritual proletariat, *batlonim*, in other words. Yet I feel that such a school will strike a responsive chord throughout the whole Diaspora. Jewish teachers of all kinds would come to such a school for a year or more in preparation for their Jewish work in the Diaspora. Moreover, the Catholics and English Protestants and German Protestants have schools for biblical archeology in Palestine. This would commend our school to many of our assimilated Jews. There are other considerations which make such a school particularly attractive to me. I shall not go into these at the present time. I have written only in hints as it is, in the hope that it will not be necessary to go into detail for you who have given so much time and thought to the whole problem.

You will perhaps be interested to know that Mr. Nathan Straus has purchased a considerable tract of land just outside of Jerusalem on the Bethlehem Road, to be used when the time came for a Jewish college or university. This has not been made known generally. If you would like to make use of this, kindly let me know, and I shall talk the matter over with Mr. Straus.

Nothing much can be done here on behalf of this plan before the Congress. In case the plan takes definite shape, I think you would be just the man to come here and make propaganda for it. We can consider this later. I shall try to lay hold of some of the reports of the Beirut institution and send them to you.

I regret to say that, in all likelihood, it will not be possible for me to attend the Congress.

With affectionate greetings to you and Wertschka,[2] I am,

Very truly yours, JLM

P.S. This letter was written before your note of reminder came this morning. How is your boy? We have two of them.

1. Nahum Sokolow, a member of the executive of the World Zionist Organization, arrived in the United States in April 1913 (see glossary of names).
2. Vera Weizmann (1882–1966). Married Chaim Weizmann in 1906.

138

18

To Walter Lippman
Weggis, Switzerland

New York, September 26, 1913

Dear Mr. Lippman:

I was very glad to have had your letter from Weggis [Switzerland]. I remember Weggis with a great deal of sentimental interest.

As to Zionist books from the sociological side, I would suggest the *Jews of Today*, the English translation of *Die Juden der Gegenwart* by Dr. Arthur Ruppin. It is published in England by John Lane, I think. I would suggest also that you subscribe to *Die Welt*, the official weekly of the Zionist Organization. The address is Sächsischestr. 8, Berlin W. 15, Germany. You would also be interested in a number of books published by the Jüdischer Verlag, a publishing concern conducted by the Zionist Organization. Their address is the same as that of *Die Welt*. Write them for some of their catalogs.

I hope to see something of you during the coming winter. With regards, I am

Very truly yours, JLM

19

Memorandum for the President and Members
of the Executive Committee of the American Jewish Committee
May 9, 1915

The responsibilities resting upon the leaders of the American Jews at the present time cannot be overestimated. The whole Jewish world looks to American Jewry for material help, for political and moral help during the war and at its conclusion, and for help in receiving the thousands of new immigrants who will come to us after the war. If America is not drawn into the war, there can be no question that the center of Jewish gravity for the next decade, at least, will be in America.

Can the American Jewish Committee in its present form accomplish any of the large tasks thus placed upon the American Jews? To my mind, it cannot.

Because it was not a really representative and democratic institution, it was compelled to form the American Jewish Relief Committee. Its organization should have been of such a nature as to have enabled it to appeal to a united American Israel for relief funds in the great calamity. It is true, the American Jewish Committee might have gone right ahead and collected funds on its own account, without regard to the claims of the "democracy." While this would have saved time, it is doubtful if as much money could have been raised, seeing that a number of additional funds would then have continued to exist. The moral side of having but one fund under the auspices of the American Jewish Relief Committee more than justified the delay in submitting the appeal for funds to the public. The American Jewish Committee should be so organized that it will be able at any time to appeal to a constituency that includes every city and town in the United States having any sort of Jewish population. Great sums are needed now for the relief of suffering and for the building up of waste places. If the Jews of America are permitted to elect their representatives and to assume the responsibility of collection and distribution, large sums can still be raised.

Can the American Jewish Committee in its present form exercise the political and moral leadership expected of the Jews of America during and upon the conclusion of the war?

To my mind, it cannot, First, because in formulating its policies, it is not in close enough touch with (a) the Jewish masses of America, and (b) the aspirations of the different kinds of Jews in the belligerent lands; and, second, because it has not, in its present form, what it absolutely needs in carrying out whatever policies it determines upon — the united support of large sections of the Jewish people of this country.

What is the policy of the American Jewish Committee? As far as I am aware, the attempt has not yet been made to formulate it. Yet I assume the policy to be (1) neutrality; (2) aid in securing freedom and liberty for all Jews. If that be a proper statement of our policy, have we the right to assume the responsibility for even this policy without endeavoring to learn the sentiments and thoughts of the Jews of this country and the Jews of the world? Is neutrality to be underrated as making us oblivious, for example, to the treatment Jews have received and are receiving at the hands of Russia? Is a neutrality possible that will be anti-Russian, i.e. in so far as pogroms are concerned, and at the same time not be pro-German? Does neutrality mean that we are to be absolutely silent as to what is happening to the Jews, as to what the Jews want, or is neutrality compatible with a methodic attempt to educate the public opinion of the Jews and the non-Jews of this country? Does neutrality require us to disregard the views of the Jews of Russia, for example, if they should want us to enlighten the world as to what is transpiring in Russia? I personally have definite views as to these and other questions presented by the idea of neutrality. Yet the procedure and the make-up of the American Jewish Committee do not give the members the chance of bringing out their views systematically, and, what is of real importance, of securing expression of sentiment and opinion from the representatives of the Jewish people in America and in other lands. Strong as my own views are in these grave matters, I should not be willing alone, or even with the American Jewish Committee as at present constituted, to bear the awful responsibility for any policy unless I had had also an opportunity of placing a share of this responsibility upon all the Jews of this country; and, as far as possible, of other countries.

We all want, of course, to help if we can, the Jews secure freedom and human and Jewish rights. But what kind of rights do the Jews themselves want? What of the rights of the Jewish minority in Poland? Do the Polish Jews want rights that, in addition to securing their lives and property and freedom of worship, will also safeguard their Jewish culture? What of Palestine? In how far does the Jewish people want to secure freedom of immigration and of movement there? Eager as many Jews may be to secure a Jewish settlement in Palestine, are they willing to secure it at the cost of the freedom and happiness of the Jews of Poland and of Russia? What of the whole question of free immigration, its regulation, the financial instruments necessary to help the Jewish people rehabilitate itself after the war? I contend that the American Jewish Committee in its present fom is not in a position to formulate adequate policies on these subjects, and that even if it were, it would not have the right to assume the moral responsibility for a policy on such matters without having consulted with various leaders and groups, and having placed a portion of the responsibility upon all the Jews of the country; and, if possible, of other lands.

Above all things, we should try to become clear as to what the Jews of this country and of the world want; and we can then determine in what way, and when, and before whom, these desires or demands for rights are to be placed and secured.

If this holds true of the formulation of policies, how much truer is it that in carrying out any policy determined upon, it is essential to have behind you the actual support of at least a large portion of American Jewry.

Let us assume, for example, that it be decided that our best policy is to keep silent. How do you expect this to be carried out unless you give a chance to the leaders and representatives of the people to work this policy out with you, and to make them equally responsibile with you in carrying it out? The people will then understand that their silence is not due to a command or to their own dumbness, but to the fact that their own leaders, chosen by them, have so concluded; and the responsibility will then be borne by everyoone and silence will be secured. So, too, with every step taken to carry out any policy thus determined upon.

It may be that the American government will have to be consulted, or enlightened, as to what is happening to the Jews, or be asked to be of some specific service. Is it not clear that even the best and greatest among you will be given a more respectful hearing by the President, or the State Department, or the Congress, if it be known that you really represent the most numerous and perhaps most influential portion of the 3,000,000 Jews of this country? Do not interpose the technical objection that dealing with governments is delicate and cannot be done in open meeting. Everyone knows that; and the only way that the proper technique of dealing with governments can be worked out is by securing a united backing that will have reason to believe that everything possible is being done in the circumstances.

I personally believe that now, when the issue of the conflict is not decided, more documentary promises concerning the Jews can be secured from all governments than at any other time. Assuming that, after deliberation, this became our policy, will it not give us some standing if one man or two, or whoever will be our representatives, can say they represent the careful thought of the representatives of the Jews of America? And if American Jews are not able to take any steps themselves, will it not help the Jews of other lands, in their private negotiations with their own governments, to be able to point to a formulation of the wishes of the great and powerful Jewry of America?

And if it be our policy that nothing can be done now, how can we secure the backing of the American Jews for this unless their chosen leaders be the very men who have concluded that nothing is possible now?

And if peace is concluded tomorrow, do we know, or do the Jews know, what we want or what we shall do? And if there be a peace conference, do we know and do the Jews know, what they will want to do? Is it all to be left to chance, to personal communications, to the caprice of the moment, or of this or that individual? Or are we to be prepared in advance with ideas, men, money, public opinion — all of us together, systematically, with a full sense of our responsibility; and then, if nothing can be achieved by us — which is also possible — we can face Jewish history and say we failed because we were weak, but we did what we could.

It is necessary that a plan be devised whereby all of the Jews of the country will be given the opportunity, through their chosen representatives, of expressing their views and sentiments, and of sharing the great responsibility that rests upon all of us.

Objection is made on the ground that intemperate words will be uttered. They are being uttered now, every day in all quarters, and the one possibility of checking such utterances is by convening the representatives of the people, to place more responsibility upon them for their utterances and their actions. It would be a sign of demoralization and low vitality if the Jews of the country, and the great majority of whom are directly affected by the war, were not excited and alarmed and eager to help by word and deed. We must take advantage of the righteous and natural excitement and eagerness, and, while being stimulated and influenced by it, convert it into real strength and dynamic power.

In addition to the immediate problems arising from the war, we must begin to prepare American Jewry to meet the great problems which now confront it and which will be intensified manyfold by the enormous immigration which we will receive after the way. The one hope of our coping with these problems, of doing justice to the Jews and to this country, is to set in motion a democratic, nation-wide Jewish movement that will place upon every Jew in the land a portion of the responsibility for the future. There are in this country 100 cities in which the Jewish population is over 1,000, and there are 282 cities and towns where the Jewish population is less than 1,000. The local problems of these communities, and the national problems before all of us, have a chance of being solved only if we now take advantage of the historic responsibility placed upon us and endeavor to create a genuinely democratic representation of the Jews of the country.

We Jews are not a government, yet we have governmental problems. With a population of 3,000,000, over one half of whom are in one city, with a population that will soon be much greater by additions from other lands, with the other questions of the war before us for consideration, we shall be guilty of criminal negligence if we do not take hold of the question of our organization, heroically, determinedly placing it above every other interest, lef it be public or private.

To everything there is a reason, and a time to every purpose under heaven. This is a time to plant, to build up.

20

To Louis D. Brandeis
Boston, Mass.

New York, June 30, 1915

Dear Mr. Brandeis:

I present herewith my resignation as a member of the Provisional Executive Committee for General Zionist Affairs.

I do this with the more regret because my conviction of the great need for the Jewish people of a Jewish center in Palestine is stronger now than it ever was.

I feel it necessary to resign because through the resolution of the Provisional Committee to call a congress of American Jews to discuss all phases of the Jewish problem, the Zionist Organization is, so it seems to me, departing from the object for which it was created.[1] The Zionist organization was created for Zion.

The action of the Zionist Organization in calling a congress is bound to create a split in American Jewry. I need hardly say that I am a believer in Zionism. But I have always realized that the Zionist Organization cannot create that platform upon which all the Jews of America, or the Jews of any land in the Diaspora, can come together on behalf of the Jewish cause. The Zionist Organization requires — and rightly so — the test of allegiance to Zionism. Congregational organizations require — and rightly so — the test of congregational allegiance; and so with the other large Jewish organizations of the country which have been established for specific purposes. The only kind of organization that can hope to bring about a united Jewish front is one which will require of each of its members but one thing — interest in the Jewish cause from whatever point of view.

The American Jewish Committee, through its call for a conference to be constituted of representatives of every possible kind of large Jewish organization in this country, has given evidence of its good will and its sincere desire to bring about the creation of a common platform for all the Jews. The Zionist Organization has seen fit to refuse the invitation to participate in this general Jewish conference. It has seen fit to reject a plea for unity — heretofore a cardinal Zionist principle. It has seen fit to engage in party politics. It has seen fit to seek party advantage through the calling of a congress of its own, which, in the nature of things, must exclude large sections of the Jews of this country.

I am not willing to sin against my people in being a partisan of any kind in this crisis in Jewish history. If anything is to be accomplished for

:he solution of the Jewish problem, including the Palestinian problem, it must be through a unity of Jewish forces. I want no part in bringing about disunity. If the representatives of the American Zionist Organization force me to choose between being a partisan and being a Jew, I choose at this juncture to be a Jew.

I need hardly tell you that anything that I can do, as one of the rank and file of the Zionist Organization, to further the cause of Palestine, I shall be glad to do.

With Zion's greetings, I am

Very truly yours, JLM

1. The Provisional Zionist Committee met the end of June 1915 during the convention of the Federation of Amrican Zionists in Boston. It rejected by a vote of 66 to 11 Magnes's plea to accept the American Jewish Committee's invitation to attend a national conference of major Jewish organizations. It then voted to join those groups calling for the formation of an American Jewish congress.

21

To Israel Friedlaender
New York

New York, August 31, 1915

Dear Dr. Friedlaender:

I am writing you this letter not because I want to, but because I have gathered from your embarrassed manner and hesitating remarks that you think it worth my while to take notice of some of the remarks that have been made about me personally by some of our Zionist friends.[1] You know how absolutely indifferent I am to what is said about me personally. You have characterized it as a fault of mine that I have never regarded it as worth the effort to defend myself. I still hold the same opinion, but I shall yield to your judgment at the present time and mention here a couple of the matters you have brought to my attention, in order that you, at least, may know the truth.

1. Zionist meeting in Boston, March 14, 1915

I went to Boston and delivered an address at the Temple Mishkan Tefila, the synagogue of Rabbi Rubenovitz,[2] on Sunday evening, March 14. I did this at the urgent request of Mr. Brandeis. It was a great sacrifice for me to go to Boston at that time. A committee met me at the station and took me directly to the synagogue. We arrived there considerably ahead of time, so that I had an opportunity of looking over the side rooms of the synagogue, where any "ice cream and cake reception," of the kind you mentioned to me as having been planned, might have taken place. There was no sign of such a "reception." The meeting was not well attended, and I am sure that my address was not a good one despite the fact that as you told me, Mr. Brandeis and Mr. De Haas[3] assured you that I had spoken very well. My judgment is probably better than theirs, inasmuch as they were not in Boston at the time. At the close of the meeting I stepped down from the platform and shook hands with a number of men and women. Nothing was mentioned about a "reception." I had not of course expected any. I stayed in the synagogue to the very last, with Rabbi Rubenovitz, Mr. and Mrs. Bromberg,[4] and Mr. Julius Mayer. It so happened that the janitor had locked all doors, with the exception of one, so that when we attempted to leave by one exit we found it locked, and had to leave by another. Mr. and Mrs. Bromberg, Rabbi Rubenovitz, Mr. Mayer and I walked a couple of blocks together, whereupon we bade good-night to Mr. and Mrs. Bromberg, and Rabbi Rubenovitz, Mr. Mayer and I walked to the subway station. I proposed that we walk the whole distance to the railroad station but the other gentlemen claimed that I walked too quickly for them. We rode to the station together and sat down for a bit to eat at the Hotel Essex, opposite the station. The gentlemen were kind enough to accompany me to the entrance gate to the sleeping cars. I took the midnight train back to New York.

This, it seems to me, ought to dispose once and for all of the stories that you told me, that I had angered the people of Boston by leaving the synagogue immediately after my address, and refusing to accept their hospitality through the "ice cream reception" which they had gone to much trouble to prepare for me.

2. Invitation to speak at Mass Meeting of Zionist Convention

On May 26 I received the following telegram from Mr. De Haas: "Please wire whether you can accept invitation of Convention Mass Meeting Committee to speak Sunday evening, June 27."

On May 27 I replied as follows:
"Provided I can come to Convention, shall accept your invitation to Mass Meeting."

Under date of June 4, I received the following letter from Isidor Neiditch, secretary of the Mass Meeting Committee, written on stationery of the Zionist Bureau for New England.

"Dear Dr. Magnes:
    The Mass Meeting Committee begs to acknowledge receipt of your telegram advising your conditional acceptance of their invitation to speak

at the Mass Meeting on Sunday, June 27, at Mechanics Building, Boston, Mass.

In view of the fact that the list of speakers must be completed, and the program printed, and other arrangements have to be made at this time, the Committee finds itself forced to advise you, that sorry as it is, it will have to make definite arrangements to have someone else substitute for you at this meeting.

We assure you that we are indeed sorry that you could not give us a definite answer, and regret very much the step that we were forced to take.

With Zion's greetings, I am

Very truly yours,"

I accepted this letter at its face value without further comment. I had forgotten the whole question and, as far as I remember, did not mention it to anyone until our talk on the train to Boston, on the night of June 26. You will recall that I mentioned the fact that I had been invited, only by the way. It was you who made me feel for the first time that perhaps my being omitted from the list of speakers was not as simple a proceeding as I had imagined. From recent developments, and from what you told me, I can see, much to my regret, that a deliberate snub was intended. This leaves me, of course, perfectly calm.

3. *Change of name of American Jewish Relief Committee*

Mr. Brandeis seems to make quite a point of the fact that the name of the American Jewish Relief Committee was not changed at his suggestion to the National Jewish Relief Committee, and he seems to hold me responsible for this. When the American Jewish Relief Committee was being formed in November, 1914, an organizing committee was created. This committee consisted of Mr. Brandeis, Mr. Oscar S. Straus, Judge Mack, Mr. Meyer London,[5] and Mr. Harry Fischel.[6] I was not a member of the committee. Despite that fact, I foolishly allowed myself to be drawn into the deliberations of the committee and to do a considerable part of its mechanical work. The question of the name of the whole committee occupied the attention of the organizing committee for some time. It was finally agreed that the name should be the American Jewish Relief Committee. Mr. Brandeis was in favor of changing the name to the National Jewish Relief Committee, in order that there should be no confusion with the American Jewish Committee. I was in favor of this suggestion. Mr. Oscar Straus, however, was quite insistent that the name be the American Jewish Relief Committee, and I have in his own handwriting, although I cannot at the moment lay my hand upon the paper, the name of the committee as American Jewish Relief Committee. Despite that fact, I communicated with Mr. Louis Marshall, Chairman of the Executive Committee, both by word of mouth and in writing, the desire of Mr. Brandeis to have the name of the whole committee changed from the American Jewish Relief Committee to the National Jewish Relief Committee. Certainly my function in the matter could not be interpreted to extend further than this.

What pains me is that a man like Mr. Brandeis, who I had thought was above all manner of pettiness and of personalities, should have harbored a grudge against me for a matter of that sort, and should have made mention of it to a number of persons as a count in a supposed indictment against me, without ever having told me of it until July 12, 1915. I did not even at that time think it worthwhile to answer Mr. Brandeis, because even then the fairness was not shown me of at least asking about my connection with the name of the American Jewish Relief Committee and the fact that it was not changed to the National Jewish Relief Committee.

I think I have never before written a letter of this nature. I feel it a great pity to have wasted time consulting the records and composing the letter. But as I said at the beginning, you seem to have been the butt of a number of diatribes against me, and I appreciate the friendliness that prompts you to want to know my side. In order that the whole record may be clear to you, at least, I shall appreciate it if you will let me know some of the other matters about which you should like to have information.

Very truly yours, JLM

1. Friedlaender, "deeply pained" by the treatment accorded to Magnes at the Zionist convention in June 1915, discussed the causes of the estrangement between Magnes and the Zionist leadership with Brandeis and Jacob de Haas. Hoping to conciliate the two sides, Friedlaender informed Magnes of his conversation with Brandeis and de Haas. Magnes replied to their charges, and Friedlaender forwarded Magnes's explanation to Brandeis. In his covering letter, Friedlaender wrote: "You will see from the content that the letter was not meant to be shown to you, and I should not be suprised if Dr. Magnes who is a very proud man were to look upon my action as a breach of confidence. But I am taking a chance, believing that the very frankness of the letter may have a salutary effect" (Friedlaender to Brandeis, September 2, 1915, Israel Friedlaender Papers).

2. Herman H. Rubenovitz (1883–1966). Rabbi of Temple Mishkan Tefila, Boston, from 1910 to 1946.

3. Jacob de Haas (1872–1937). Zionist leader and journalist; migrated from England to the United States in 1902. He was secretary of the Federation of American Zionists from 1902 to 1905; editor of the *Boston Jewish Advocate* from 1908 to 1918, when he interested Brandeis in Zionism; secretary of the Provisional Executive Committee for General Zionist Affairs from 1916 to 1921.

4. Edward J. Bromberg, a prominent Boston lawyer. A founder of the New Century Club, he served as secretary of the congregation.

5. Meyer London (1871–1926). Lawyer, socialist leader, and Yiddish publicist; emigrated to the United States from Russia in 1888. London represented the garment workers' unions. He was elected to Congress from the Lower East Side of New York in 1914 and was reelected in 1916 and 1920.

6. Harry Fischel (1865–1948). Businessman and philanthropist; emigrated to the United States in 1885, settling in New York City, where he entered the construction and real estate business. He became involved in Jewish community affairs, showing special interest in Orthodox Jewish institutions.

22

To Louis D. Brandeis
New York

New York, September 2, 1915

Dear Mr. Brandeis:

In the course of our talk on July 12, you asked me to write you more at length the reasons that prompted me to resign from the Provisional Executive Committee for General Zionist Affairs. I have waited thus long before complying with your request in order to give the matter further consideration, as also to observe the further progress of events. To my regret, I feel now more than ever that I must persist in having my resignation acted upon at once.

This is due not only to differences in the question of a "congress" and a "conference," but more especially to the attitude towards Palestine itself on the part of the Zionist Organization in America, and of the "Congress" organization, for which in many senses the Zionist Organization stands sponsor.

The Congress program of the Zionist Organization is: equal rights for the Jews throughout the world and a secure homeland for the Jewish People in Palestine. In my opinion, persistence in this formula at the present time, without constant and official interpretation by the Zionist Organization, is fraught with grave consequences to the Jews of Palestine, the Zionist Organization and the Jewish People.

Have you made clear to yourselves, to the Zionists, to the Jewish People, to the American nation, to the Ottoman Government, what you mean by a "secure homeland"? As far as I am aware, you have not. It seems to have been overlooked that Palestine is a part of the Ottoman State, and that the Ottoman State is at war. Can the Ottoman government, then, be blamed for viewing us with suspicion if, in formulating a political program for the Jewish People, we make an exception of Palestine and say that while we want equal rights for the Jews of the world, we want more than equal rights in Palestine? I want equal rights for the Jews, no more and no less, in all lands, including Palestine. I do not want it said, as it has been said, that the Jews of Russia, for example, should be denied equal rights in that country in view of the more than equal rights they are supposed to receive in Palestine at the end of the war at the expense of the Ottoman State. I want the Jews of Russia to be on a level with the other peoples of that Empire, and I expect the same equality for the Jewish People in Palestine—no more and no less. Equal rights for the

Jewish People in Palestine must mean that the Jews have the same rights as other peoples of the Ottoman Empire. Just as the Turkish, the Arabic, the Armenian and other groups of the Ottoman Empire have full political rights and full freedom to develop their specific culture, that is, their religion, their language, their school system, so too should the Jewish group in Palestine have the same political rights and the same cultural freedom. In this the Jewish People in Palestine would be on the same level as the Moslem, the Christian, as the Turkish, the Arabic, the Armenian, and other groups of that empire. All that we have a right to ask is that the Jews be permitted to migrate to, and settle in and develop their Jewish economic and cultural life in Palestine freely, just as other peoples of the Empire have the same right. To ask more than this, to withhold this commentary upon the phrase "secure homeland for the Jewish People," is to make an exception of Palestine in the formulation of a political program for the Jewish People, is to impute to the Turkish Government a degree of stupidity for which it has not hitherto been noted.

Then, what about Zionism, you may ask. Zionism must mean now, as it has in the past for most of us, the building up of a Jewish cultural center in Palestine through the inner cultural strength of the free Jewish People in Palestine, an Ottoman province. As Zionists, also, we may hope and believe and work to the end that Palestine and its environs, in addition to becoming the cultural center of the Jewish People, may ultimately also become the numerical center of the Jewish People. In the Zionist sense, then, the war cannot give Palestine to the Jews; the Turkish government cannot give Palestine to the Jews. All that the war can give to the Jews, all that the Turkish government can give to the Jews, is free ingress into Palestine and equal rights as I have described them above. It is only the organic development of Jewish life in Palestine in full view of, and with loyalty to the State in times of war and of peace, that can give such a Palestine to the Jewish People. It is our Zionist conviction, springing from our faith in the creative powers of the Jewish people, that with free immigration, with equal rights, the cultural and perhaps the numerical center of the Jewish People will be established in Palestine. As Zionists, we believe that the "air of Palestine maketh wise"; that Jewish cultural values, Jewish religion, the Jewish outlook upon life, will in the Holy Land have a natural growth that can fructify Jewish life throughout the world. The war cannot give this to us. All that we can ask of others is, free immigration and equal rights. If, with free immigration and equal rights, we cannot develop a Jewish cultural center, our faith in the creative powers of the Jewish People will have disappointed us. The Jewish People will then have shown that the hundreds of years of wandering and persecution have robbed it of its creative spirit. But I believe, as I know you believe, that, given a fair chance, given equal opportunities, the Jewish People will be able to develop their Jewish cultural center in the Land of the Fathers.

I was astonished to note, in consulting the record of the Zionist convention in Boston, that though many expressions were used about "small nationalities," "embattled states," "issues of the war," not one syllable was uttered manifesting the Zionist loyalty to the government which is sovereign in Palestine, not one syllable tending to show that what we expect of the sovereign government is not exceptional consideration, but equal consideration with all the other peoples of the Ottoman Empire.

Moreover, I am pained to observe that the presentation and interpretation of the Palestine ideal seems to have been taken out of the hands of the American Zionist Organization by other more "radical" elements who have come to be associated with the Zionists in the so-called "Congress." Many of these "radicals," for whom personally I have much regard, are among those who during the Russian Revolution were not content with securing political emancipation, but who insisted upon bringing about at the same time the great "Social Revolution."[1] As a result, Russia secured neither political emancipation nor the social revolution. Some of these extra-organization Zionists are now, by the intemperance of their utterances, the "radicalism" of their demands for the "secure homeland" in Palestine, endangering the Jewish inhabitants of Palestine and the international Zionist organization, to say nothing of the danger to the hopes of the Jewish People for an eventual Jewish cultural center in the Land of Israel.

I am convinced that all of this is due primarily to the fact that the energies of the Zionist Organization in America, the thoughts of its leaders, have been diverted from Zionism to questions of the so-called "Congress," with all of the controversy incident to it. Instead of being single-minded about Zionism and Palestine, as was the case for almost a year from the time that you began to devote your splendid powers to the Zionist Organization, instead of having the single purpose of winning — as I think might have been done — all the Jews of America, the American people and the Ottoman government for the simple program of free immigration to Palestine and equal rights for the Jewish People there, the Zionist Organization has unfortunately helped to confuse the issues arising from the war, and to inject into American Jewish life a spirit of discord. Instead of enlightening the world as to what a "secure home" in the Zionist sense might mean, the Zionist Organization has undertaken, under the guise of the term "Jewish question as a whole," to bring up the entire question of Jewish organization, of Jewish development, of Jewish authority in America. As though the Palestine problem were not large and complicated enough, as though the Jewish question as it affects the Jews of belligerent lands were not critical enough, the Zion-

151

ist Organization is undertaking through the "Congress" and a doctrinaire emphasis upon the phrase "the Jewish problem as a whole," to give rise to a fruitless debate as to who is who in American Judaism, who has the power, who shouldn't have it, and who covets it, what should and what should not be done here—a fatuous, romantic endeavor to anticipate the organic development of Jewish life in America, and to bring about completely centralized Jewish authority in this country with a suddenness similar to that with which it is hoped that the war may establish the "secure home for the Jewish People in Palestine." This is the way of error, of danger here—of catastrophe in Palestine.

Holding these views, I might still remain a member of the Provisional Committee and be in the opposition there; or I might, after withdrawing from the Committee, create opposition within the Zionist Organization itself. I have neither the desire nor the talent nor the time for this. This does not mean—I say this in order to avoid any possible misunderstanding—that I cease to be a Zionist. As I wrote you in my letter of June 30, "my conviction of the great need of the Jewish People of a Jewish center in Palestine is stronger now than it ever was." I wish also to repeat the assurance I gave you in that letter that I am at your service whenever I can be of help. But I cannot, much as I should like to, continue to share the responsibility for a course which, I am convinced, is dangerous to Jewish development both in Palestine and in America, not to mention the belligerent lands of Europe.

May I not urge you, in the light of what I have written, to set these matters straight before it is too late; and may I not express the sincere hope that the time is not far distant when the Zionist Organization will permit me, in good conscience, to cooperate with it again.

With Zion's greeting, I am

Very truly yours, JLM

1. Magnes is probably referring to Pinkhas Rutenberg, Hayim Zhitlovsky, and Ber Borokhov, who had been active in Russian radical politics and after coming to the United States supported the congress movement.

23

To Chaim Weizmann
New York

New York, January 28, 1916

Dear Weizmann:

I have just sent you the following telegram:

> Alarming Alexandria reports concerning Palestine considered here conse-
> quence your negotiations. Jehiel Nahum must come immediately. Wire.[1]

We have received here long and alarming reports about the dangerous
situation in Palestine from the Alexandria committee, of which Gluskin,[2]
Levontin,[3] Dr. Weitz[4] and others are members. We are bending every
effort to secure some authentic confirmation of these reports. We all hope
that they are greatly exaggerated, or that if hardships are being suffered
in Palestine it is due only to the necessities of the military situation and
not to any change in policy in the government or lawlessnes among the
surrounding population.

It is clear to us here that the Zionist Organization as an organization
must pursue an absolutely loyal policy over against Turkey, whatever be
our sympathies in the war. Palestine is a possession of Turkey. Turkey
has been friendly to the Jewish people for many centuries. It will not do
for the officials of the Zionist Organization, acting in their official capacity, to arouse the slightest suspicion of hostility towards Turkey. The
reasons for this ought to be clear. If Turkey remains in the possssion of
Palestine and the Zionist Organization has not been loyal, we shall have
absolutely no claim upon the friendship of Turkey. If the Allies are victorious, no one can take it amiss that the Zionist Organization remained
loyal. For, just as the Zionist Organization must be loyal to the Turkish
government, so are the Jews of every land loyal to their respective governments. And, just as the Zionist Organization is loyal to Turkey as
long as Turkey is in possession of Palestine, so, too, must we be loyal to
whatever other government may, by the fortunes of war, come into possession of that unhappy land.

It was all of this that I had in mind when I sent you the telegram asking you not to take any further steps, and when I wrote you my letter of
January 24. I did not think that it was necessary or prudent then to go
into details of your activity or of the activity of Jehiel and Nahum to pass
judgment upon it. Nor do we know sufficiently of what is transpiring in
Palestine, or what has caused a change of heart on the part of the govern-

ment, if there be a change of heart. I have merely wanted to indicate in this letter and in the telegram I sent today a possible interpretation of the present changed attitude of the Turkish government. The newspapers here have been full of reports and despatches to the effect that the English Government is making promises to the Jews about a Jewish settlement in Palestine under English suzerainty. If the English Jews, as Englishmen, wish to carry on this propaganda, it is their right; but no officers of the Zionist Organization ought to be engaged therein. This is the course adopted, I understand, by Dr. Bodenheimer[5] who, when he became a member of a German Jewish committee, retired from the chairmanship of the National Fund.

With best regards, I am,

Very truly yours, JLM

1. Reports reached the United States that the Ottoman government was continuing the mass expulsion of non-Ottoman subjects, a policy directed against Zionist settlers. Yechiel Tschlenow (1863–1918) and Nahum Sokolow were members of the executive of the World Zionist Organization who were in England at the time. Shmaryahu Levin, who was also a member of the executive and was then in the United States, urged Tschlenow and Sokolow to come to America to clarify the international political position of the Zionist movement.

2. Ze'ev Gluskin (1859–1949). Russian Zionist. Early settler in Palestine; director of G'ula land purchase society and founder of Carmel Mizrahi Wine Company; during First World War active in relief work for Palestine Jewish refugees.

3. Zalman D. Levontin (1856–1940). Russian Zionist. Early settler in Palestine; founder of Anglo-Palestine Bank in Jaffa; during First World War established branch of bank in Alexandria and aided Palestinian Jewish refugees.

4. Naphtali Weitz (1866–1935). Physician; early Zionist leader; born in Odessa, Russia; migrated to Palestine in 1898. He practiced medicine in the Jewish settlements of the Galilee before moving to Jerusalem, where he was active in the cultural life of the city. He was deported to Egypt during the First World War; he served on the Refugee Aid Committee.

5. Max Isidor Bodenheimer (1865–1940). Early Zionist leader; a founder and first president of the Zionist organization of Germany; resigned as president of the Jewish National Fund in 1914. He was instrumental in organizing German-Jewish relief work for East European Jewry.

24

To Louis D. Brandeis
Boston, Mass.

New York, July 25, 1916

Dear Mr. Justice Brandeis:

I have a letter from Judge Mack under date of July 24, in which he expresses his opinion that the words and manner of my address at the Conference of Jewish National Organizations on the afternoon and evening of July 16 were a downright insult to you.[1]

If that be true, I wish to apologize to you for this in this way, as I did publicly during the meeting.

I have never, as far as I am aware, intentionally insulted any man. I could therefore not intentionally have insulted you, the value of whose services to the Jewish People, my people, I have always recognized.

It may well be that in my surprise and chagrin over your second statement that peace could be had in American Jewry only if all the resolutions and technical details of the Philadelphia Conference were accepted, and in my amazement at Judge Mack's declaration in the evening presumably coming from you that peace might be had in other conditions, I overstepped the bounds of propriety.

I feel that in view of what Judge Mack, whose friendship I value highly — as I know you do — tells me, I should make this statement to you before I leave for Europe.

Very truly yours, JLM

1. The American Jewish Committee, which convened the conference, invited Brandeis, as head of the Jewish Congress Organization Committee, to attend the meeting in the hope of reaching a compromise over ways of establishing a representative body of American Jews. Brandeis insisted that he was bound by the decisions of the preliminary conference of organizations favoring the Jewish congress that had taken place in Philadelphia on March 26 and 27, 1916. That conference bound the Congress Committee to all decisions adopted by the delegates unless changed by a three-fourth vote. When Brandeis rejected a number of American Jewish Committee proposals at the July 16 conference as conflicting with his mandate, the American Jewish Committee leaders saw Brandeis's declarations as an ultimatum that peace was possible only on terms set by the congress movement. Magnes charged Brandeis with autocratic behavior. An editorial in the *New York Times* criticizing the propriety of a Supreme Court Justice becoming embroiled in affairs "of such controversial nature" appeared on July 18, 1916. Three days later Brandeis resigned all offices he held in Jewish organizations. Mack wrote to Magnes, who was about to leave on a relief mission on behalf of the Joint Distribution Committee, "If you sail for Europe as chairman of a committee representing the united American Jewry without an expression of regret for your actions, the deep and bitter feeling produced thereby and against you will inevitably impair the value of anything you may be able to do in the name of American Jewry in Europe" (Mack to JLM, July 24, 1916, MP, 1594).

3

DISSENTER: PACIFIST AND RADICAL

1917–1922

MAGNES EMERGED SIMULTANEOUSLY as a public dissenter in Jewish affairs and in American politics. When in the fall of 1916 he returned from surveying relief operations in Poland, many criticized his praise for the work of the Jewish relief organizations in Germany as the biased view of a member of the American German-Jewish establishment. This internal Jewish quarrel took an ominous turn months later when Magnes embraced the pacifist cause as America moved toward war. His relief mission through German-occupied Poland while Russia had refused him entry to the areas it held and his insistence since the outbreak of the war in 1914 that the Zionist organization remain politically neutral were offered by his opponents as evidence of his pro-German sympathies. The war hysteria pervaded Jewish community life no less than it did American life. Stephen Wise, a pacifist until America declared war, chided Magnes for his antiwar activities, accusing him of "aiding the cause of peace for the sake of Pax Germanica."[1] In the fall of 1917 Brandeis proposed postponing the convening of the American Jewish Congress lest it be "captured by the pacifists under the leadership of Magnes."[2] When Israel Friedlaender was nominated by the Joint Distribution Committee to serve as the Jewish representative on a Red Cross mission to the Middle East, he was forced to withdraw because of spurious stories stigmatizing him as pro-German (document 28). Magnes admitted that his radical pacifism had drastically impaired his effectiveness as a Jewish community leader. Privately he expressed his estrangement from those circles that had admired and supported his work. "I do not fit in there as I used to," he wrote. "I cannot approach as many persons as formerly. They have not the same desire to see me, and I have not the same desire to see them" (documents 28, 34, 35). While his radical views

1. Stephen S. Wise, "What We Are Fighting For," *Free Synagogue Pulpit*, 4 (1917–1918), 159 (delivered September 23, 1917).
2. Stephen S. Wise to Horace Kallen, September 24, 1917, Stephen S. Wise Papers, American Jewish Historical Society, Waltham, Mass.

were an embarrassment to many Jews, his eminence in Jewish life still carried weight and made him especially welcome in pacifist and radical circles. Although he failed to persuade Jacob Schiff, for example, to aid the peace movement (document 25), he did raise substantial sums for the People's Council—money that came from his Jewish contacts. Moreover, as a rabbi—a moral teacher of the Jews—he held a special place among those non-Jews influenced by religious radicalism.

For Magnes Judaism was the source of his pacifism. The prophetic tradition required placing moral imperatives above institutional and group interests. Proof that this tradition still had a powerful hold on the Jewish masses was their "anti-militarist outburst" and "their elemental passion for peace" despite the danger of playing into the hands of anti-Semites.[3] Paradoxically it was these Eastern European Jews—from the strictly pious and observant to the freethinkers and radicals—who exemplified Reform Judaism's notion of Israel's mission to the nations by being in the vanguard of the movements for peace and social justice while "the preachers of the 'mission' were either silent or had become high priests of the patriotic cult" (document 26).

The universal ethic of prophetic Judaism led Magnes almost immediately from pacifism to social radicalism. His rhetoric drew upon socialist theory and analysis and was directed at concrete economic and political issues; yet it remained firmly rooted in his Jewish ethos (documents 27, 31). Incongruities nevertheless existed and troubled him: he sympathized with the Russian Revolution yet rejected force; he wanted to visit Soviet Russia ("to see the new life that is developing in the Old World") but also wished to spend a year or so in Palestine; he endeavored to be a universal man and to be a whole Jew (documents 34, 35, 37). Thus he spoke from radical platforms, worked for radical causes, and published articles and a book justifying Soviet policy; yet at the same time he continued to give thought and time to Jewish affairs. Jewish education—how to assure group continuity and enrich Jewish life—was his main concern. Circumscribed as he was in his ability to lead, he remained the key figure in the attempts to give new life to the movement for Jewish educational reform that he had initiated a decade before (documents 35, 38). However, the intellectual confusion that marked the early postwar years posed philosophical questions for Judaism. For over a year, beginning in 1920, Magnes corresponded and met with a number of Jewish intellectuals, hoping to establish a forum for "creative Jewish life in the broadest sense." Mordecai Kaplan collaborated in the effort, and when he established his Society of the Jewish Renascence—the precursor of the Society for the Advancement of Judaism—Magnes responded sympathetically but critically to his program (document 36).

3. JLM to Mayer Sulzberger, October 10, 1917, MP, 1348.

For the Jew and the humanist Zionism remained the great challenge. Magnes viewed the physical act of building the homeland as suffused with universal significance. Would the return to Zion be guided by biblical ideals or by ordinary political norms? Like Martin Buber in Germany Magnes insisted that a politics of morality guide the operational choices before the Zionist movement. In the euphoric atmosphere that followed the San Remo Conference in May 1920 Magnes wrote his bitter critique of political Zionism (document 33). This letter to a friend, together with his earlier letter to Brandeis explaining his resignation from the Zionist leadership (document 22), contained the core of his Zionist thinking. Ten years later, when he published his booklet *Like All the Nations?*, he incorporated large parts of both letters in his programmatic essay.

His pacifism placed a great burden on his personal and family life. Twice the family moved during these years as a consequence of the intolerance they encountered. He held no regular position, aside from the nominal one of chairman of the Kehillah. There were those who avoided him or maligned him. It was a transitional time, he wrote, not only in world affairs but in his personal life. In diaries and in stray notes he repeatedly analyzed his situation. He was in his middle forties and had reached, at least for the moment, a dead end in his Jewish community career. Radical politics was no vocation; speechmaking fatigued him now, and he eschewed the factionalism endemic to the left. He was not an organization man, he admitted to a socialist audience: "Organization requires a certain kind of sacrifice of intellectual and spiritual integrity which I for one like to preserve as long as I can."[4] He was groping for a way. The war had upset all the old canons. As early as 1919 Magnes discused the notion of a year abroad with his wife: a leave of absence from America and exposure to the new Old World would give him renewed strength and perhaps a clear direction in life (documents 29, 30, 35, 37, 38). At last in May 1922 the family sailed for Europe en route to Palestine. His plans to visit the Soviet Union proved unfeasible. For six months Magnes surveyed the cultural institutions of the Jewish communities in Europe for the JDC. Then on November 2 the family arrived in Jerusalem.

4. JLM, "Remarks," May 15, 1919, MP, 1259.

25

To Jacob H. Schiff
New York

New York, March 26, 1917

Dear Mr. Schiff,

The Emergency Peace Federation[1] believes that there is a last chance to avert war between this country and Germany. They plan to have thousands and thousands of letters and telegrams sent from all over the country to Congress and the President urging them to find some way out of the difficulty other than war. They plan also to ask thousands of people to go to Washington and be there on April 2 and 3 when the "War Congress" opens. They want to get prominent labor leaders there, representatives of the Farmers' Granges, etc. The Middle West and West are opposed to war, and it is expected to bring the peace sentiment out in this way. If $50,000 (fifty thousand) can be secured it will be possible to do all of this on a gigantic scale. It may, who knows, be possible in this way to influence the House of Representatives which, after all, is part of the machinery to declare war. I admit, this seems to be a kind of final gasp. But maybe it will carry this time. Compared to the cost of one day's war, this sum is insignificant. Would you be one of five men to give $10,000 apiece? Will you please wire your answer. Heaven grant that this great land of ours may be spared the crime and the calamity and the woe of war.

Yours truly, JLM

1. The Emergency Peace Federation was formed in Washington in February 1917 and ceased to function in May. It included representatives of leading peace organizations.

26

Journal: Jews and Pacifism

New York, October 2, 1917

I want to note some of the thoughts that come to me in relation to the war.

I am charged by many with misrepresenting the attitude of the Jews of America towards the war. It is said that, as a consequence of my own attitude, there will be a great wave of Anti-Semitism here. Pogroms against the Jews are predicted.

I am convinced that I have not misrepresented the attitude of the Jews. On the contrary, I am sustained constantly by the knowledge that what I have said and done has been out of the very heart and soul of the Jewish people.

One of the most remarkable phenomena of the war is the spontaneous, elemental outburst on the part of the Jewish masses against the war. To me this outburst is a vindication of the Jewish tradition, as well as striking evidence of the vitality of this tradition. Christianity as a whole and occidental Judaism have shown themselves to be bankrupt religions. It is only the Jewish tradition of Eastern Europe that has kept itself alive and powerful. This utter abhorrence of war, this elemental repugnance to bloodshed, to murder, this absolute pursuit of peace — what else can it be due to but the living tradition of the Jewish people still active in the East-European Jewish masses of America? It is nothing but short-sightedness that can claim than any man or act of men could have started this conflagration. This Jewish explosion against the war came from all classes of East-European Jews — from the strictly pious and observant, from the freethinking and the radical, from workingman and business man, from young and old, from man and woman, from the illiterate and the intellectual. It accorded with the philosophy and the reasoned theories of many; but for the most part this hatred of militarism, this passion for peace broke forth without philosophies and theories out of the depth of Jewish life and experience. It might even be called a primitive, subconscious, unreasoning outburst. It lay bare the innermost being of the Jew; it revealed the very essence of his tradition. It was incautious; at the time it reached its fullest expression, it was not even bold; in its practical consequences it may be proven unwise. But it was real, genuine, sincere — such welling-up of emotion as could have come only from deep sources. The Jewish experience of centuries seemed to find a voice. It is as though through the Jewish masses, that mystic thing called "race" was coursing and speaking. The Jewish masses seemed to be wise with the wisdom of many centuries, and of many countries and of many wars. They showed that the Jewish People was an ancient people. How many empires have we not seen destroyed, how many cities laid waste; how many battle cries have we not heard, the iron of how many armies pierced our flesh, how many religions and philosophies and ideals and patriotisms have we not seen justifying the slaughter of men! We look upon the madness, the lust after blood horrified, yet detached, with wisdom, shaking our heads over the folly of it, sated with it through our

163

long experience. We are sick, God knows, of the strife between Jacob and Esau, between Israel and Edom, between Judea and Rome. We have been taught from our earliest days that "the blood is the life," that even the sacrifice of animals for food was a sacramental act. Our literature, our rabbinic tradition has its being in a glorification of the spirit of Jacob and in a condemnation of Esau the hairy, Edom the red, the bloody. "Not by might and not by power but by my spirit, saith the Lord."[1] We have called ourselves a kingdom of priests and holy people—the priests were to guard the truth and to pursue peace.

As for myself, I am more devoted than I ever was to the Jewish People and the Jewish religion. The Jewish masses have shown themselves worthy of the Jewish religion, and the Jewish religion has once again given evidence of its vitality and its eternity. We can now see how right we were when we contended that the Jewish People was worth saving because we believed in the Jewish People—in its spiritual power. The Jewish masses have not been found wanting at this crises in human history when most peoples and most of the spiritual forces and organizations have given themselves over to this orgy of blood-letting and destruction.

Of course, there are many who say that the outcry of the Jews against the war was in large measure due to physical cowardice and the fear of death. I have no doubt that this has to do with much of the Jews' attitude. But where is the shame of fearing such a death? Is not our whole Jewish instinct towards life? This is, in fact, a result of that very experience in which we are so rich; we have been drafted into too many armies and we have been subject to too many governments to have forgotten what armies and governments in wartime are.

What the consequences of this Jewish attitude in America will be, it is hard to say. Whatever be the consequences, I pray the Jewish masses will have the strength to bear them with the same dignity and powerful resistance and self-confidence as has been theirs in other and infinitely worse crises. Everything is, of course, possible—pogroms and what not. But I can not get myself to believe, even yet, that America will tolerate pogroms.

That anti-Semitism will increase in certain circles I have no doubt. In every country at war anti-Semitism has increased on two scores: the lukewarmness of the Jews towards fighting in the trenches, and the number of Jewish profiteers. This lukewarmness is manifested in America not only in the spontaneous revulsion of the Jewish masses, but also in the desire of many "high-class" Jews to keep out of the trenches by serving the country in administrative capacities of one kind and another. Nor should we forget that before the war, anti-Semitism of various kinds had reached an intensity in America unequaled elsewhere.

164

But the anti-Semitism which is threatened today is that which will arise, or has arisen, specifically from the anti-war impulses of the Jewish masses. What will be the consequences of this anti-Semitism?

The immediate consequences must soon be apparent. They will probably amount to nothing more than an intensification of the anti-Semitism already abundantly in existence. This will be counterbalanced in some measure by the many manifestations of loyalty which prominent Jews have shown, and by the effectiveness and heroism in the trenches of Jewish soldiers such as their brothers in all other armies have evinced. But our view of the larger and less immediate consequences of this intensified anti-Semitism will depend upon our view of anti-Semitism in general. If we regard anti-semitism as an historic phenomenon having to do with the Jewish Problem as a whole, it is mere superficiality to hold that more or less of so-called "patriotism" can tip the scales for or against the Jews. As long as the Jews remain a distinctive people; as long as they give evidence of original independent thought; as long as they achieve conquests of the spirit and in material ways among populations numerically and physically their masters; as long as the status of the Jew among the nations is abnormal; so long, among other reasons, will there be anti-Semitism. There will never be a complete disappearance of anti-Semitism, any more than that any other people that is active, creative, can produce spiritual values without stirring up enmities.

But the disappearance of disgraceful anti-semitism, of common Jew-hatred and Jew-baiting is dependent first, upon the manner in which the Jewish Problem, i.e. the Jewish status among men, is determined; and in the second place, upon who achieves mastery in the world at large — the imperialists and militarists and capitalists, or the democrats and workers of the world. If the organization of the Jewish People as a people both in the Diaspora and in Palestine is recognized by men, and if plain peoples of the world led by workers and democrats secure the political and industrial power that is theirs by right, the aid of the Jews in the building up of the new world will be welcomed instead of dreaded. They will be urged to give their full energies, to rise to their complete spiritual stature, instead of as now looked upon as minority interlopers. It is only upon such conditions that anti-semitism will disappear for lack of material to feed upon.

But if the Jewish Problem remain indeterminate and mysterious, and if the now dominant forces of reaction retain control of the political and industrial machinery of the world, anti-Semitism will unfortunately grow. It will grow despite Jewish heroism and Jewish manifestations of loyalty; it will grow where there are no Jewish masses instinct with the Jewish tradition; and it will grow in America with added virulence because, in seeking justification, there is to hand this wonderful outburst of

Jewish anti-militarism and pacifism. Alas for the world, if after the holocaust through which it is now passing, the common peoples should go back to their work silently and not take power into their own hands! Alas for the Jews in such a world of reaction and darkness and slavery! If in such a world, American anti-Semitism should commit excesses, I am ready to bear them together with my fellow Jews, confident that I have spoken out of their hearts and souls, confident that they will regard me as one of their own more firmly than if I had held my peace.

The spiritual "mission" of the Jews to the nations, as formulated by the early 19th century Reform Jewish scholars and teachers, is a revolutionary doctrine: Israel, the international people retaining its identity in order to aid the world in achieving justice and peace.

But this revolutionary doctrine was in the hands of petty, bourgeois priests and merchants who used it in order to make Israel safe and sane among the nations.

Whatever of the revolutionary mission has been carried out by Jews has been in the hands of those religionists who know nothing of a "mission"; or in the hands of those masses who were outside of the "church" and who slaved and toiled for a living; in the hands of those for whom political and industrial progress was of more consequence than formal political emancipation or the attainment of a competence.

What a mockery of the "mission" that in a crisis, in a time of war and of death, the preachers of the "mission" should either be silent or become high priests of the patriotic cult! What a hopeless feeling as to the future, had there been no Jews to give voice to the dictates of the Jewish spirit!

1. Zech. 3:6.

27

To Scott Nearing
New York

New York, January 24, 1918

Dear Dr. Nearing:

I thank you cordially for your letter of January 23,[1] and for the frankness of your remarks.

I think I need hardly tell you how greatly I have admired and appreciated the self-sacrificing work which you have done. I must confess to a light bit of disappointment on my own part in finding that, in your opinion, I have not given you cordial and adequate support. It was my impression that I had, and it was certainly my intention to do so. The holding of mass meetings for the Council, especially when these mass meetings were few and far between did not, so it seems to me, constitute the real significance of the People's Council during these difficult and dangerous months, nor is that, in my opinion, the real importance of your own work. You will recall that after the President's message I was rather warm for a real mass meeting which might have meant something. Furthermore, I attended the dinner given in honor of Mr. Angell.[2] I do not recall that I was ever asked to speak at a dinner. Please do not think I expected to be asked, because I thought your policy of getting persons in some degree outsiders to speak at these dinners a good one. My unwillingness to address meetings may or may not have been based upon a proper understanding of the situation, but my unwillingness to do that was not a decision lightly made. It was rather due to my conviction that mass meetings of the kind held, and at the times and places they were held, did not strengthen our cause. I think that this conviction of mine is at least debatable. Aside from this, I have been under the impression that I have stood by the People's Council and by you through thick and thin.

I need hardly recount the ways in which I have done this or the difficulties involved.

Whatever differences of opinion there may be between us in this cannot in the slightest degree detract from my wholehearted respect for your own efficient and noble work carried on under circumstances of the greatest danger. You will let me say, will you not, that I account my getting to know you as one of the best things I have had in the past year; and I want to express the sincere hope that I may be able to cooperate with you in the future in behalf of a people's peace, and after that, of a people's world.

As to the People's Council, the more I think of it, the more I think that the People's Council should by all means maintain its identity as the People's Council. Its struggle with the government has been valuable, and, as you know, I have felt right along that one of its greatest assets is that it is impossible to attack it more violently than it has been attacked. But maintaining the People's Council is not necessarily synonymous with having the People's Council take the lead at the present moment in mass meetings, conferences, or other public activities. I do not say that the time has come, but this is subject to conditions over which we have no control and which are changing from hour to hour. Wise "statesmanship" on our part would be to maintain and strengthen the People's Council as much as possible. and at the same time to recognize the People's Council as much as possible as a kind of extreme left, and to recognize, and if need be, to encourage other forces that are not quite so far on the Left, and also if need be, such forces as are even further to the Left than we are. I know your obvious retort will be that the person who makes suggestions of this sort should come in and take hold and do it. That I am not fitted to do this I thought had been made clear to you. If this is not clear, I shall be glad for the first opportunity you give me to try to make it clear.

Very truly yours, JLM

Copy sent to Mr. Morris Hillquit.[3]

1. In his letter, written jointly to Magnes and Morris Hillquit, Nearing stated that he had accepted the chairmanship of the People's Council primarily because of their urging. He had expected both "to take a public stand for the Council," but both had refused to speak at public meetings.
2. Sir Norman Angell (1874–1967). Economist, journalist; member of the Council of the Royal Institute of International Affairs, 1928–1942; knighted 1931.
3. Morris Hillquit (1869–1933). Labor lawyer and socialist leader. Born in Riga, Latvia; settled in New York City in 1886. He was a key figure in the American Socialist Party and opposed the United States' entry into the First World War.

28

To the Members of the Joint Distribution Committee
New York

New York, March 11, 1918

This is the statement I had intended reading at the meeting of the Joint Distribution Committee on March 11, 1918, but upon the earnest solicitation of Mr. Marshall, Mr. Warburg, Dr. Frankel,[1] and Dr. Bogen,[2] I refrained from doing it.   JLM[3]

Gentlemen:

In connection with the appointment of Prof. Friedlaender by the Red Cross, Dr. Stephen S. Wise issued on March 8 in the *New York Times* a statement which contains false statements and unfounded charges, to some of which I wish to refer:

I. Dr. Wise says that he "earnestly urged the members of the committee, including Mr. Warburg, not to designate Prof. Friedlaender on the ground that he was widely suspected of pro-German sympathies prior to our advent into the war, and that, moreover, it has been reported that a protest would be lodged against Prof. Friedlaender's designation if it should be made."

I leave it to Dr. Wise's colleagues on the committee that chose and recommended Prof. Friedlaender to the Red Cross, namely, Dr. Bogen, Dr. Frankel, Judge Mack, and Mr. Warburg, to inform the Joint Distribution Committee of just what transpired in the committee. I leave to them, also, a characterization of Dr. Wise's action as a member of the committee in repudiating publicly the decision to which the committee had unanimously come.

What it is impossible for me to pass by is the public denunciation of Prof. Friedlaender by Dr. Wise. Dr. Wise has no hesitation in saying in these critical times that Prof. Friedlaender was "widely suspected of pro-German sympathies prior to our advent into the war." Can Dr. Wise point to a single public utterance or to a single line written by Prof. Friedlaender to justify this public charge? Personally, although knowing Prof. Friedlaender closely, I have not heard anything from him that would indicate his attitude either pro- or anti-Ally, or pro- or anti-German. Have we come to such a stage when possible private conversations are distorted and made the basis of public accusations? It is incumbent upon the Joint Distribution Committee to tell Dr. Wise what it thinks of a Jewish leader who publicly spreads abroad "suspicions" concerning a man of Prof. Friedlaender's character and learning and lifelong devotion to the Jewish cause.

II. Dr. Wise says that "the Joint Distribution Committee undertook to send as its representative to Russia a man whom the Russian government found it necessary to deny admittance to Russia on the ground of reputed pro-German and anti-British sympathies." As a matter of fact, the State Department has declared that the reason for my exclusion from Russia by the government of the then Czar was because of an address I had delivered in Chicago the previous May when, upon substantial authority, I declared that the Russian Government was preparing pogroms, and that a revolution might take place in Russia. As to my "reputed pro-German and anti-British sympathies," I would say that if pro-German means wishing Germany to win the war, I am not now and I have never been pro-German. It is not true that my sympathies are anti-British. It is true that my sympathies are opposed to the settlement of international questions through any form of militarism.

Statements of this nature, made in public and in effect to governmental agencies by Jews against Jews, are not unknown in Jewish history. For such statements the Jews have the term m'sira [betrayal] and for the persons making such statements the Jews have the term mosrim [informers]. Jewish history is replete with tragedies that have come over the Jewish people because of the activity of Jewish mosrim.

1. Lee K Frankel (1867–1931). Social service administrator and business executive; born in Philadelphia. He was manager of the United Hebrew Charities of New York, 1899–1909); president of the National Conference of Jewish Charities, 1912–1913; vice president of Metropolitan Life Insurance, 1924–1931; and a member of the non-Zionist committee that negotiated the formation of the Jewish Agency.

2. Boris Bogen (1869–1929). Social worker; born in Moscow and emigrated to the United States in 1888. He was director, United Jewish Charities, Cincinnati, 1904–1910; European representative of JDC, 1917–1924; superintendent, Federation of Jewish Welfare Organizations, 1924–1925; executive secretary, B'nai B'rith, 1928–1929.

3. When the American Red Cross proposed including a representative Jew on a commission to be sent to British-occupied Palestine, the JDC recommended Israel Friedlaender. As soon as his appointment was announced, Professor Richard Gottheil attacked Friedlaender for having been pro-German prior to the entry of the United States into the war. On March 8, 1918, Stephen Wise, chairman of the Provisional Zionist Committee, supported Gottheil's charges in a statement to the *New York Times*, adding that the Zionist movement shared no responsibility for the nomination and remarking that it was an embarrassment to the American and British governments and to the Red Cross and American Jewry. Friedlaender vehemently denied the charges and demanded that Gottheil and Wise be called to account, but to no avail. On March 13 Friedlaender announced his resignation.

29

Journal: Europe or Palestine

New York, June 29, [1919?]

I would regard my going to Europe at the present time as educational and transitory, and not as something absolutely essential and a field of permanent work. I do not expect to devote my energies to Europe. I expect to devote my energies to either New York or Palestine, and perhaps in the course of things, to both. Europe as containing the bulk of the Jewish people and the most active of the revolutionary movements must of course always appeal to me and call me. But I have never, or perhaps only once or twice in moments of great uncertainty, thought of myself as staying there and working there for years, and of being willing to grow old and die there. I have, however, pictured myself as doing all of this either in New York or in Palestine.

For either the New York or the Palestine task, going to Europe *now* has appeared to me of advantage.

Now is a transitional time not in my own life alone. The whole world is struggling to pass from war into peace. Men's minds are still unsettled here and there. It has seemed to me that at just such a time an educational and transitory European trip could be undertaken with least disturbance to myself and things in which I may be interested. People are still talking of doing this or that, hardly as yet doing. Education in New York is still in the talking stage. Palestine is still in the talking stage. In a year's time both situations will become clearer, and I should be able to judge them both more clearly from the vantage point of a European year. Certainly I should be better fitted to take up New York work after a year away from the strife and strain of Jewish organization work here. I should have more heart and freshness for the work, and I think after my return I should be the more valuable and welcome in the work.

Staying here during the coming year will almost inevitably commit me to certain pieces of work, to certain persons, to certain organizations with their politics, etc. I am, of course, not afraid of this. I had only thought that it would be better all around to get away *now* while I was still detached and free to do it. The lure and the possibility (perhaps also the need) of a European year will, after I am again committed here, be that much less. In other words, I am not holding up the trip to Europe as a permanent ideal for some future time as I do with Palestine, but as a present need. Next year or two years from now it may be altogether different — or it may not be.

It is therefore somewhat hard to put off the European trip. Its urgency *now* was part of the need for it. If it is put off, it is not at all with the thought that it may be made next year or the year after. It is not that kind of ideal nor, as far as I can see at this moment, that kind of necessity. But though it be hard, if not impossible, to make a European trip now less urgent, it is easier than would be the giving up of a trip to Palestine under similar circumstances. It so happens that I do not feel the present and immediate urgency of a trip there — though I should dearly love to go and live there. The sooner the better. But the absence of the immediate necessity does not make the difference that it makes in the whole idea of a European stay. The Palestine stay has the nature of a permanent ideal, and a present European stay the transitory nature of an educational venture, which because of the problems I would confront would fit me the better to meet the similar problems in New York.

Certainly, if the children's health is such that leaving Dr. Terckney's treatment now might be bad for them, there is nothing more to be said. I shall have to consult him upon that.

Staying here, the question is where to live. Disregarding other questions for the moment such as health and expense — we should discuss them later — and looking at it solely from the point of view of my Jewish activities, I should say this: if I am to throw myself wholeheartedly and with energy into Jewish activity, the city would be the place to live. If, however, I am to continue to have a detached attitude, living out of town would be an aid. Which it is to be will depend chiefly upon Beatrice's decision.

30

Journal: My Personal Problem

New York, c. November 1919

My Personal Problem

1. The Kehillah

2. The Young People

3. Education

4. Making a Living

1. *The Kehillah*

Under any circumstances, whether I go to Europe or not, I believe it advisable that I withdraw from the Chairmanship of the Kehillah.

Either the Kehillah is to be a Kehillah of the bourgeois — the *ba'ale battim*, in which case it must be adequately financed, or it must be a Kehillah of the many and the young, in which case it must have a different type of organization, different men, and must make a different appeal.

As to a *baalebattisch* [respectable] Kehillah, it is clear from Dr. Benderly's recent attempt to get funds, that funds can be gotten (with difficulty) but that this involves giving my whole self to the work of the Kehillah and "behaving." The funds are not adequate enough to justify the one or the other. It would be worthwhile devoting all one's energies to the Kehillah and even "behaving" (in a measure) if the real funds and real men were forthcoming. At the moment funds are not adequate and the men are the same gang.

Moreover, in the Kehillah, as in any democratic organization, a permanent chairmanship is an absurdity, and it is about time that I made room for someone else.

2. *The Young People:*

I want to do Jewish work among the young people of New York. I want to win them for Judaism and for freedom. If I knew just how, there would be no problem. Not knowing just how, the steps would have to be taken gradually. The first step might be to have a committee consisting of a number of men and women of light and leading interest in Judaism and in freedom from different points of view, and take up with them the whole problem. With them, a first activity might be the establishment of a platform from which, from week to week during the winter, Jewish problems (in the widest sense of this term) may be discussed freely by different persons from differing points of view. A club of the Jewish "intelligenz" might also be considered. Negatively, this should not be an effort that will require large funds. Whatever funds are needed will have to be supplied out of the thing itself.

Can I leave New York when the new day is beginning to break?

3. Jewish Education:

That is something I want to work for. Large plans are talked about. Perhaps I can help them into fruition.

The "group," moreover, of young men and women about the Bureau may need me here, and may not understand my going at this time.

4. Making a Living:

Ben kakh v'khakh, 'one way or the other', it is necessary for me to make a living.

I do not want to be on the pay roll of any Jewish organization, least of all the Relief Committee.[1] I have broken with the thought of making my living out of Jewish organizations, and I do not want to go back to it. I have broken inwardly with those who run and support Jewish organizations, and I do not see why I should not do the same thing outwardly.

Beatrice tells me that all I need to earn is sufficient to pay Daddy and my office expenses and insurance — a minimum of $3,000 a year. Surely I can earn this much writing and lecturing. The necessity of writing and lecturing in order to make a living will keep me studying, and, who can tell, maybe I shall produce something upon occasion that will not be without value.

Advantages in Going Abroad

(a) If I should go abroad with the family, I could doubtless arrange to earn sufficient through writing for publications here.

Moreover, the Bureau of Education still owes Beatrice and me $5,000, and provision ought to be made to have this paid me through the contributions of a number of men.

(b) By going abroad I shall be able to get a deeper knowledge of Jewish life and of international affairs. This deeper knowledge can be of benefit not only to the Jews and others, but also to myself as an aid in making my living when I return.

(c) Soviet Russia will probably open up soon, and I want greatly to go there for the Relief Committee.

(d) I shall be able to do some concrete good in any event.

(e) I shall have a perspective on New York and time for contemplation, and perhaps clearer ideas as to what is needed when I come back.

Tentative Conclusion

I might be willing to consider going under the following conditions:

1. That the date be fixed so that I may do justly by the Kehillah, the educational work, and the young people's idea. The date should probably be March or April.

2. That either a commission (with Dr. Goldman as chairman)[2] and on which I shall have a voice and a vote, shall be in charge of affairs in Europe, in which case my own functions shall be determined by the Commission, and I shall be responsible to it; or, if there is to be a director general, I shall be charged with defining my own function, and I shall be amenable to the director; veto only on matters that affect the general standing of the whole committee's work and that have to do with bringing about proper coordination among the various commissioners.

3. That some assurance be given that the committee in America will measure up to its responsibilities.

4. That I be paid the $5,000 which Beatrice and I loaned the Bureau of Education and that I be privileged to arrange for the placing of articles written abroad for American publications.

1. Magnes was considering Warburg's offer to join the staff of the Joint Distribution Committee.
2. Julius Goldman (1853–1938). Lawyer and communal worker; born in Philadelphia. He was a founder of the New York Federation for the Support of Jewish Philanthropic Societies and chairman of its budget committee; was first European director of the Joint Distribution Committee, serving from the end of 1919 to the end of 1920.

31

Address Delivered in Chicago
February 8, 1920

THE OLD AMERICA AND THE NEW

I hope that I may speak a word for the old America and for the new. The old America which we were brought up to love has been, during the last three years, almost done to death. But in the death struggle of the old America, the new America is being born; and not all the reactionaries with their violence and bloodshed and not all the anarchy of our government authorities can keep the free thought of America from joining the free thought of all the free peoples everywhere.

The old and glorious America made its first utterance to the world in the Declaration of Independence. It maintained "the right of the people to alter or abolish a government, and to institute a new government, laying its foundations on such principles and organizing its power in such form as to them shall seem most likely to affect their safety and happiness."

It has become treasonable to give utterance to such thoughts in the America of today. We are told that "America has had her revolution," and that further fundamental changes are not necessary and are not to be permitted. We answer that fundamental changes are needed in the world today fully as much as when the Declaration of Independence was written. For example, political dictatorship must be taken out of the hands of the minority, of the privileged few, and political power placed in the hands of the great masses of the people. Further, economic dictatorship must be taken out of the hands of the small oligarchy of big business and the imperialists and their satellites of lawyers, teachers, clergymen and journalists, and economic power put in the hands of those to whom rightfully it belongs — the masses of the people who work and produce with hand and brain. Finally, the schools, universities, churches, the organs of public opinion, must be made free of the dictatorship of the small minorities who now own these institutions and the bodies and souls of their ill-paid servants, and placed under the control of intellectual and spiritual forces in close touch with the real life of all the people. Indeed, we question the whole conception of the modern state with its unlimited powers over life and human personality, and those who in smug complacency announce that "America has had her revolution" and that the last word has been spoken, are little aware of the great forces astir in the world and of the intense yearning of the common people to establish justice, brotherhood and peace in place of the injustice, the ignorance, the hatred that characterize our present-day social systems. America requires, together with the rest of the world, a new birth of freedom — political, economic, spiritual.

But it is being made a crime to mention these things. We want to discuss these questions, but they say we may not. We want to form political parties to give ideas effect, but they send their police to break these organizations up. We want the American workers to understand, as the British and Italian and German and Russian workers now understand, that economic power can and must be used to achieve political ends. But they make this sedition and treason.

The old America understood the meaning of freedom better. In the days of the Declaration of Independence "the sacredness of the right of revolution" was a current political maxim. It was based upon the theories of natural right and social contract, and had come to America primarily from England through the treatises of John Locke, whose very phrases Jefferson often used and whose political philosophy had its root in a "substratum of the Old Testament teaching derived through the Puritan revolution."*

But it was not only the classic Declaration of Independence that gave utterance to the natural right of men to be independent as they themselves understood independence. This doctrine was current also in the political theory, although not always in the practice, of another representative of the old America—Abraham Lincoln. He says in his first inaugural that "Whenever the people grow weary of their existing government, they can exercise their Constitutional right of amending it, or their revolutionary right to dismember or overthrow it."

We have grown weary of our government and of the brutality underlying the whole concept of the modern state. We have grown weary of its terrorism, of its "abuses, injuries and unsurpations," and we wish to consider and talk over freely here and with like-minded men and women abroad how and if and to what degree we shall exercise our constitutional and revolutionary right.

We are told by some that we have a right to discuss and advocate fundamental changes, provided they are not brought about by force or violence. There is a great deal of talk—particularly by presidential candidates—about the overthrow of the government by force and violence. We are so much influenced by what we read in the reptile press that we are apt to accept these suggestions without question. But where is the clear and unmistakable evidence proving the existence of organizations or conspiracies for the overthrow of the government by force and violence? The Communist platforms and manifestos are not clear and unmistakable evidence, as must be manifest to anyone at all familiar with the traditional Socialist and Communist terminology. On this very issue Federal District Attorney Kane of Philadelphia sent in his resignation as a protest against the attitude of the Department of Justice; and it was only last Friday that Mr. Kane declared before the House Judiciary Committee that "reports that conspiracies are on foot to capture the government by force and violence as ridiculous."[2] There are, doubtless, individuals who believe in force and violence, and a very, very few of them have committed bomb outrages. Why does not the Department of Justice employ its time to better advantage and hunt them down? But where is the clear and unmistakable evidence implicating organized groups in open advocacy of, or secret plotting for, the use of force and violence?

* See Chapter IX, *The Declaration of Independence*, by Herbert Friedenwald; Macmillian, 1904.

176

We may be sure that if there were such evidence it would long ago have been held high for our chastisement and for the edification of a gullible public.

But if we would discuss this question frankly we must go a step further, and assume that this or that group may be found which openly advocates in speech or writing the overthrow of government by force or violence. And our answer must be: — let them advocate it — so long as they advocate this in speech or writing, as ideas or as a program and no overt acts of force and violence are committed.

May I interject a personal word? I abhor bloodshed. I believe that human life and the human personality are sacred, and that human life may not be taken at any time. I do not believe in war between one people and another, and I did not believe in this past war, and I do not believe in the next. I recount these personal items because, as a pacifist, I may differ greatly from this or that radical group. I stand nevertheless for the right of every man and every group to advocate any and every governmental, political, economic, spiritual change, no matter what be the doctrines they preach and no matter what be the methods they talk and write about. I am as much opposed to the use of machine guns and bombs and hand grenades and poison gas by the workers, by the proletariat, as to the use of these instruments of hatred and murder by organized governments. But I believe that every man and every political and economic organization have the right to formulate their doctrines in speech and in writing freely. Only when speech and writing are left in the background and actual overt acts of physical violence and bloodshed are committed has a people's government the right to intervene. Under all circumstances we must maintain the right of free speech, without qualification and without let or hindrance.

Government has no right to interfere with ideas, with programs, with opinions formulated in speech or in writing, no matter what these ideas and opinions may be. If men wish to advocate the use of force and violence in the change and overthrow of government, let them advocate it openly, above ground, frankly. Then let you and me meet them by reason if we can, by argument, by free discussion. Prove them wrong, if we can, by trying to remove the underlying causes of their impatience and their skepticism. It is injustice, cruelty, terrorization of the weak by the strong, spiritual and physical slavery which they wish to force out of existence. Can we show by precept and by example that these age-long iniquities can be removed from the lives of men in other ways than through force and violence? If even then men wish to take upon themselves the burden and the odium of writing or talking in advocacy of force and violence, let them. It is old American doctrine that freedom of discussion, the conflict of ideas, debate, argument, will bring out the true

177

and will suppress the false. It is old American faith that the masses of the people are sound at heart and in mind, and that it is possible to reason with them, to convince them through information, through candor, through mental integrity. It is an old American idea that government is based upon free consent, and that it is perpetuated or changed through an informed and honest public opinion.

Many of our so-called liberals are, I have no doubt, perfectly sincere in professing readiness to submit to fundamental changes, however distasteful to them, provided that these be brought about by time-honored and constitutional methods. But I venture to say that there is also a great deal of cant in these protestations that it is only the methods to which they object. Why deceive ourselves? At the basis of this whole struggle, at the bottom of this great war after the war, there lies a fundamental difference of opinion, of outlook and of desire. This can be summed up in a phrase — Private Property. It is a basic struggle between those who believe in the sacred right of the individual to acquire and to use private property freely and those who believe that there is no sacred right to private property and that property is to be used collectively, not for private profit but for service to the entire population.

I am afraid that it is here where we shall find the real enemy of free speech. It is the substance of social change that hurts, not so much the methods. If by some chance the sacredness of private property were to be questioned at an American election, be quite sure that under existing conditions some excellent private property lawyers, judges and statesmen would find a good excuse for declaring that election illegal. The talk about methods is in large measure a smoke-screen to hide the fundamental and bitter struggle over the substance of social change. That is the all-sufficient reason why we are forbidden to write, to meet, to form political parties, to formulate in speech and in writing such ideas as the various groups among us may have at heart.

The chief answer that I know of to all of this is that the great working masses of America begin to realize their solidarity and exercise their power intelligently. It is they who can establish freedom in America. They are beginning to understand that the difference between what is called political and what is called economic is often very slight and nebulous. They are therefore increasingly turning their backs upon the tweedle-dee and tweedle-dum differences between the old reactionary political parites and they are commencing to work out conceptions of the state and political programs of their own. They are more and more alive to the fact that there is such a thing as the political strike, that is, economic action for political ends. The economic strike for better economic conditions is now universally recognized. The logic of the situation will soon bring well nigh universal recognition of the political strike as well.

This is the more important because it shows that the workers do not live by bread alone, but that they are concerned and are thinking hard about the basic problems of mankind. In England and in Italy economic mass action, the threat of the political strike, has forced the British and Italian governments to seek peace with the Communist Soviet Republic of Russia. It is high time that the workers of America should at last understand what their power for good to all peoples might be.

But some of our liberals are horrified at the very words, economic mass action for political purposes. Some seem really to believe that the effective remedy for all our political ills is to be found in the American ballot box alone. What does the political ballot-box of the present-day America mean? It means that after certain issues have been formulated by political parties and after ostensible public discussion, the voters go to the polls and elect servants to govern them. But how are these issues formulated and under what auspices is this ostensible political discussion conducted? How is public opinion manufactured? Who controls the organs of public opinion? Is it not that small minority which we know by the varying names of "big business," or "the capitalists" or "imperialists"? Who owns the newspapers which publish their lies and spread their poisonous propaganda day after day? Who controls the public school system and the teachers and the subject material to be taught, and to whom belong the universities and the colleges with their fearsome and trembling professors, anxious for their small pittance for the daily bread of their children? Who owns the churches and the synagogues and their smug and complacent preachers — men supposed to be set apart and dedicated to teaching the Word of the Living God — but O! how many of them spitting forth malice and ignorance and hatred? Who controls the moving picture theaters with their constant and powerful propaganda, the billboards with their appeal to the passer-by? Who owns the meeting halls which, for the most part, are rented only to those who come with police passports? Who owns the street corners and public squares where men are no longer permitted to congregate for discussion? And who controls the means of communication — the express companies, the railroads, the telegraphs, the telephones, by means of which information and something of the truth might be exchanged and spread abroad? Under such conditions is it not absurd to maintain that there is such a thing in the America of today as free political discussion?

The whole atmosphere about us, the phrases we use, the information we have, the opinions we form, the prejudices we cherish — everything comes from this ceaseless mill which is turned by the hirelings of capitalism, and which grinds out day after day and year after year the grist of our undoing. We are blind, uninformed and confused because, by the nature of the social order, truth and the facts are salable commodities doled

179

out to us in portions which are regarded as harmless and innocuous for us by our betters. Every political election under present conditions, therefore, means just this: that our economic masters make full use of their economic power to secure political dominance; and it ill becomes them to object to the use by the organized workers of the only kind of economic power which the organized workers possess in order to achieve the political ends thought desirable by labor. Of one thing we may be sure, that power in the hands of labor could not be used more blunderingly or malevolently, than during the past five years by our all-wise statesmen and business men and our far-seeing imperialists.

But when mass action is talked of, let the organized workers of America be beforehand and at once take the wind out of the sails of their opponents by defining mass action to mean mass action that abhors guns, that despises bombs, that suffers revulsion at bloodshed and that is convinced of the sanctity of human life. The organized workers at Seattle pointed the way, and the organized workers in Winnipeg followed that path, and had the coal strike continued it gave every evidence of becoming another example of economic mass action without brute violence and bloodshed. It is true that this organized non-resistance, this revolutionary pacifism, may upon occasion be accompanied by brute violence and bloodshed, due primarily to provocation by the agents of the forces of a fictitious law and order. But this need not be so. There is no inherent necessity for bloodshed in this mass action method of achieving fundamental changes. It is essentially different from the military method. There, in the military method, violence and bloodshed are part of the very nature of the case. Only one use can be found for guns and bombs, and that is to kill. But let the workers of America understand their organized strength, and, through discussion and interchange of opinion and education and the use of science and of art and the development of real leadership, assert their economic brotherhood without brute violence and bloodshed; and the time will come — and perhaps the time is not at all too distant — when in a grave political crisis engineered by our masters such as, for example, the impending threat of a Mexican war — when the word would go forth to the organized workers of America and to the organized workers of Mexico, "Lay down your tools!" And with proper provision for the sick, the young, the weak, the processes that lead to war would be halted and our imperialist masters taught the limitations of their power.

The world has just passed through a war, the consequences of which cannot be foreseen, but which even now has torn apart the world's social structure. Transportation, exchange, the supply of coal and fuel and of raw materials, everything is broken down; and literally millions of human beings are now suffering hunger and are being ravaged by disease, by pogroms and by the anarchy which our wise masters have created and which they seem not to be able to control. Peace treaties have been made which for savagery, hypocrisy, ineffectiveness know no equal in history. The western world is falling apart. Throughout the belligerent lands, with the possible exception of America and Japan, the masses of the people are asking themselves what has been the meaning of this catastrophe. They want to know who has led them into it, and what fundamental causes are responsible for it, and how the world can be made newer and better and cleaner, more just and more loving. Soviet Russia stands as a beacon on the hilltops, cheering on the agonzied peoples with light in the darkness, with new hopes and philosophies, with wonderous longings.

The agonized peoples have turned, too, to America to help give them an answer to their vital, bitter questionings, just as so many of them turned to America to help them during the war. During the war Americans were welcomed most everywhere because the plain peoples of Europe had in mind the old America, the America of freedom, of liberty, of independence; the America that had given shelter to political refugees and to the tens of thousands of families that had come here seeking work, and education, and happiness. But now, when the peoples of Europe are freeing themselves of their tyrannous masters and of the old systems that wore them down, what a disillusionment in the answer that comes to them across the seas from America! Deportations of political prisoners, the torture of conscientious objectors in dark and damp prisons, the suppression of political parties, the invasion of private homes without warrant, the clubbing of innocent men and women, the proscription of newspapers and other publications, the breaking up of economic organizations, and all the while the land flows with milk and honey and our population is bidden to rest easy under the official declaration that America has had her revolution and has achieved finality in political, economic and spiritual ideals. Finality? When even the most liberal of the interpreters of the Constitution, Mr. Justice Holmes, stands by the decision that keeps Eugene V. Debs and Kate O'Hare in jail?[3] Finality? When we are summoned to bow down before the counterfeit liberalism of A. Mitchell Palmer and his political and spiritual chief, Woodrow Wilson? What a tragic disappointment, when all the world needs the healing of America — and not of our money alone, so much as the healing to be had through the spirit of sturdy, generous American freedom, that once spoke to mankind through the Declaration of Independence and Jefferson and Lincoln and Emerson, Whittier, Lowell and Thoreau. The humiliation of it, the crime against humanity — that our America should have become the chief center of the world's reaction, the greatest of reactionary lands! America needs to be re-Americanized, and through whom can we look for this re-Americanization, if not through those very immigrants and aliens, who are despised and rejected of men but who have the light of human freedom in their eyes?

My fellow countrymen! Let us not fear the reaction that is upon us. Let us have confidence that the American people has not been spoiled by its wealth and that it is still fair and open-minded. Let us aid, as best we can, in organizing the political, economic, spiritual forces of labor. Let us throw in our lot with the lot of free and liberty-loving men everywhere. Let us uphold the ideals of internationalism in the name of the old America that was free and is now dead, and in the name of that new America which is now being born!

1. Magnes delivered this address before a mass meeting protesting restrictions on freedom of speech. The rally was sponsored by the American Freedom Foundation, a Chicago-based radical organization. He shared the platform with Sidney Hillman, Scott Nearing, and Duncan McDonald.

2. Francis Fisher Kane submitted his resignation as United States District Attorney on January 12, 1920 in protest over the raids, arrests, and deportation of aliens that were directed against radical elements by the Attorney General, A. Mitchel Palermer, in November 1919 and January 1920.

3. The socialist leaders Eugene V. Debs and Kate R. O'Hare were sentenced to long prison terms under the Espionage Act for antiwar speeches. Debs's appeal to the Supreme Court was rejected.

32

Journal: On the Staff of the Joint Distribution Committee

New York, March 25, 1920

My few weeks' experience at the JDC office have been the straw to break the camel's back.[1] It is now as clear as day to me that it is forever impossible for me to accept a commission, paid or volunteer, direct or indirect, from the bankers, the bourgeois group in Jewish affairs. It is surprising that I needed this additional lesson after the experiences during the war when I had, in effect, broken with all of them insofar as responsibility to them in Jewish affairs was concerned. It was very naïve of me to have been attracted even by the "emergency" task in the office of the JDC. Never again. I can work *with* them, or *against* them, or *over* them, but not *under* them. Our conceptions of things, our ideals, and our methods of work are fundamentally different. The realization of this makes it imperative that I hand over the "foreign correspondence," and the "committee meetings" immediately after the next meeting of the executive.

After the staff meeting yesterday, young Mr. Menachem came in with questions written all over his face. "Shall I stay, what shall I do?" was the burden of his talk. I suggested that there was a piece of work to do and that he was doing a good thing by turning that piece of work out. "But," he cried out, "there will be no soul in the work here. For three weeks I have been working because I felt that with you here there was a soul in the work."

Is that not it? Where the "golden touch" is to be found, the soul is usually missing. How can it be otherwise? F.M.W. [Felix M. Warburg] and his family are among the finest and noblest of human beings. They are inherently good and have a real sense of service to others. But just because they are rare among their kind they are called upon to assume burdens which they cannot carry. No human being can carry these burdens and do justice to the "soul." The JDC, the Federation of Jewish Philanthropies, the Henry Street Settlement, the United Hebrew Charities, the YMHA, the Jewish Theological Seminary, the Institute of Musical Art, the Educational Alliance, and I do not know how many others — how is it possible for one family, or the small group revolving about that family to breathe "soul" into these institutions, each one of which requires deep understanding, and constant personal attention? All they can do is to give money and secure "efficiency," and become convinced that whatever of "soul" is to be found in these institutions is not "offensive" and lacking in "good taste." A superficial, ostensible "efficiency" keeps things together and enables these institutions to turn out a certain standardized product. In reality, not even their "efficiency" is deep and genuine, because it is based for the most part upon lines of least resistance and lacks real information and tends to crush the "soul," which is the life of all spiritual movements.

1. On February 1, 1920, at the request of Warburg, chairman of the JDC, Magnes undertook to reorganize the JDC administration. On March 17, in response to Warburg's criticism of his work, Magnes replied, "In the hope that I might give you relief from the increasing burden that the poor organization of the JDC was placing upon you, I consented to take up this emergency work."

33

To Dear Friend

New York, May, 1920

Dear Friend,[1]

You now have your mandate for Palestine, and you seem very happy with it, and you ask me, who you know to be a Zionist, why I am not able to share your rejoicing.[2]

I wish I might, for though I have grown quite accustomed to the position of outsider, it would be pleasant to be able to give a lusty *hedad* [hurrah!] together with those with whom for many years I had the privilege of working within the Zionist Organization.

Unfortunately, the war has sobered me all too much. Not that I have lost my faith or my hope that Zion will welcome back her children, as the Comforters of our People have always predicted. But the war has given me a horror and a mistrust of all governments, quite in line with the traditional Jewish suspicion and loathing of the: *al titvadda larashut* "become not too intimate with government." You know this saying and how it speaks truly out of the experience of the Jewish People throughout its long and checkered history. I mistrust the mandate, the government that is to exercise it, the peace conference that gave it, and the League of Nations that is to sanction it. I mistrust the motives that prompted the giving of it, and I do not want this gift to blind my eyes or to bribe me.

I do not know the terms of the mandate, or what the Balfour Declaration really means, and as a consequence I cannot judge for myself the ability of the Jewish People to carry out its terms. But whatever the conditions, the present state of the world, the dominance of economic imperialism, the precarious condition of the Jews of Eastern and Central Europe, the bewildering problems of the Eastern and the Mohammedan worlds — all make me fear that the mandate has no reality to it, that Palestine and the Jews are a kind of plaything in the hands of dark, unscrupulous forces, and it is rather pathetic to see the Jews — those great sufferers and mourners of the centuries — rejoicing and parading over the gift of the San Remo Conference. One telegram of congratulations from Jerusalem was dated: "The First Year of the Redemption." The day before, when the conference at San Remo was in doubt as to the status of the Balfour Declaration, there was desolation among the Zionists and the Exile had not yet come to an end. But on the day when Messrs. Lloyd George, Mitterand, and Nitti decided to incorporate the Balfour Declaration into the Turkish treaty, the Deliverance from Exile had come.

Is it in truth the Deliverance from Exile for which Jews have prayed and struggled these centuries gone? Is that the way Deliverance comes? Suppose Lloyd George and Mitterand and Nitti had said that thing instead of this, would we still be counting the days of our Exile? I am afraid the exile of a people does not end by political fiat and that redemption does not begin with political favoritism. It is only the exiled people itself that can put an end to its exile through its inner freedom and inexorable will, and it is only through its own hard day by day labor and unchanging faith that a people can be redeemed. Certainly the Jewish People with its complex "Jewish Problem" and its scattered and precarious status in the world cannot be redeemed by a vague political decree.

The growing imperialism and militarism of the world, which will probably lead to future and more devastating wars, can change the meaning of that decree in a twinkling and just as casually as it was granted. And where is the Redemption then?

For those of us who believed in Zion even under the Turks, the need of the Redemption is always clear, regardless of the political circumstances. But it is clear, too, that the constant factor in the Redemption is the will, the faith, and the work of the Jewish People itself, and that the political circumstances are the accidents which are of more or less importance in accordance as the Jewish People is convinced of its own destiny. Indeed this rejoicing over an equivocal political accident would seem to be evidence that the Zionists were not at all sure of the hold of their idea upon the inner convictions of the Jewish People, and that it was hoped through hurrah and the usual political claptrap to suggest to the Jewish People what it ought to want. I hope that the future is smooth. Otherwise the Hurrah of Mandate Zionists of today may become the deserters of tomorrow. Naturally those of us who were not frightened by the Turk will surely not be frightened by the British; and a mandate with the Balfour Declaration, whatever its nature and by whomsoever exercised, gives the Jews a better chance for Zion than a Zion closed to the Jews by enmity and political restrictions. But I am talking about the hurrah and the "Deliverance from Exile" and the swollen expectations which Mandated Zionism has called forth, and I am trying to answer the question why I cannot participate in the holiday. I understand that the Zionist Organization having asked for a British mandate for Palestine on the basis of the Balfour Declaration, naturally rejoices that it has gotten what it presumably asked for. It has achieved the goal of the organization.

But that is one thing; and another is to make this appear to be the same as the goal of the Jewish People, as the end of Exile, as the beginning of Redemption. It is not that. It is conceivable that under certain political conditions in the British Empire and in the Near and Middle East even the Balfour Declaration would not give the Jews many more opportunities than they had under the Turks. For this reason in particular it seems to me that the Balfour Declaration is of much less importance than the conditions under which it was canonized by the San Remo Conference and under which it is to be interpreted. Political declarations and treaties are mere scraps of paper when made by imperialist powers for imperialist ends no matter who these forces may be.

The rejoicing, therefore, seems to me to lose sight of two fundamental factors; the one, that the inner strength and freedom and the work of the Jewish People is of vastly more importance than any political decree or mandate even under the best of circumstances; and the second, that the present circumstances are not of the best, and that the economic imperialism of the British Empire is by no means to be relied upon for a favorable interpretation of the Balfour Declaration. Doubtless, people in the Zionist Organization see these things very clearly, but they are estopped from expressing them for fear of offending their political benefactors. All the more reason, therefore, for others among us who are organization outsiders to warn the Jewish People against trusting any economic imperialism and to convince the Jewish People that its Redemption and Deliverance, either in Zion or elsewhere, can come only through its own hard, day by day work and its making common cause with the day by day workers of all other peoples.

When I think that Palestine was conquered by force of arms and that it is made "Jewish" by the iniquitous Peace Conference, I am reminded of the well-known Jewish description: "Conceived and born in uncleanness."

You know that I am "absolutist" in so far as anti-militarism is concerned. The war has confirmed me in this fundamental belief. Nothing that has come out of the way, not even the Russian Revolution, can make up for the war's destruction of life and of hope; and the victory of the Allies and the way it has been exploited make it clear that the way to best your rival and to achieve greater power is the way of arms. Even the defeated nations know this and lament their military weakness. Certainly the Russian Revolution shows this. It is only the Soviet bayonets, not their ideas or the aspirations for a new society, that are forcing other governments to recognize them. This renewed confidence in the power of arms will eat at the vitals of men for long years to come.

That Jerusalem the Holy City of three great religions should have been conquered by force of arms is a paradox worthy of a smile of derision. As for the Jews, I am convinced that they have never gained anything from militarism; and as to Zion, I should rather have seen it remain under the heel of the Turks until — until such time as not only the Jewish People but all the common [?] peoples might be made to understand that chiefly through their own labor and their union as laboring peoples can they and the world find "Redemption."

But Allenby entered, and I remember your rejoicing.[3] I suppose Zangwill knows when he says that the only way to hold a country conquered by arms is by arms. As to Zion, he is a genuine *Realpolitiker* and militarist. Not only should it be held by arms but the arms should be in the hands of Jewish soldiers. Perfectly logical and straightforward. Of course he had something quite different in mind than your tiny "Jewish Legion." I remembered with a certain sadness your rejoicing when Allenby deigned in a military communique to mention the "Jewish troops" fighting about Es-Salt. This was the only time they were as far as I recall mentioned, but you were sure that a new and glorious period in Jewish history had begun—perhaps a new Maccabean era. Since then the "Jewish Legion" has disbanded. But Allenby is still there; and the San Remo Conference naturally reckoned with that fact.

San Remo is the legitimate heir to Versailles. Just as the Versailles Treaty is a denial of almost every principle of democracy, of self-determination, of reconciliation, so is San Remo. As to Palestine, the principle of self-determination was disregarded. If self-determination is a just answer to other disputed problems, why not for Palestine and for the Jews? The fact is that Palestine has five or six times as many Arab inhabitants as Jews. You speak of the "historic rights" of the Jews to offset the claim of the present-day Arab majority. I am aware of the way in which historic rights and strategic rights and economic rights have made short shrift of the principle of self-determination whenever this suited the needs of the conquerors. Yet I, too, believe in the "historic right" of the Jewish people to the Land of Israel, meaning thereby the right to make their historic land their own not by major force but, if they can, by labor, by work of brain and hand, by collaboration with and education of the present majority. Historic right means that the Jews should be given the free and unimpeded opportunity to come into the land, to bring there their workers, their peasants, their wealth of money, of brain, of human material; and to become in the course of time, if they can, the preponderant element of the population. In other words, "historic right" means for me: equal opportunities for Jews, Arabs, Syrians, Moslems, Christians to live their lives freely and in proportion to their labor of hand and brain, to achieve power and the direction of affairs. Such a determination would have permitted me to rejoice somewhat with you. It seems to be much less than what you asked for and apparently got. But it would have been based upon a just principle with which neither Arab nor Syrian nor Moslem nor Christian could have cavilled, and it would have rested not upon hypothetical political power granted as a favor from without, but upon the ability of the Jewish People through labor to achieve its desired end.

As it is, I believe you will find that you have gotten no more than this, no more than in justice the Jewish People has deserved. What the "Jewish National Home" of the Balfour Declaration means has never been made clear. It can be made to mean anything which British imperialism finds it to its advantage to mean. What is the Palestine problem of British imperialism? It is, first, under all circumstances to hold Palestine as a "military bastion" for the protection of the Suez Canal. Arab or Jew, this bulwark the British were bound to possess. Any other political solution—Palestine under an international condominium or as part of an Arab federation—was therefore ruled out from the beginning. Palestine once theirs, the second consideration for the British imperials is to harmonize as far as possible the "Jewish and Arab interests" in Palestine. This will tax the patience and ingenuity of all concerned, but is probably not beyond the ability of those genial British colonial administrators. During the war, promises were made to both Jews and Arabs. The Jews were promised "a national home," and the Arabs were promised the lands they should conquer and an administration drawn from the "indigenous population." The Jews of the world are a power and faith must be kept with them — on paper at least. The Moslems of the British Empire — the greatest present-day Moslem empire — are a power, and faith must be kept with them. Faith will doubtless be kept with both by means of the famous British knack of compromise, or, if necessary, in the traditional way of all economic imperialism — *divide et impera* — playing off one element against the other, making political declarations and promises that are intended to mean all things to all men.

Political favoritism is not be be depended upon for long. The one practical way and the one decent way towards permanence is through labor, through sound economic development, and through inner spiritual freedom and not through political patronage. What the Balfour Declaration means or does not mean is really secondary. The important thing is that Jews and Arabs, Moslems and Christians have a free and unhindered opportunity to develop Palestine through honest labor of hand and brain. Whoever does it — his will be the glory. But in all your rejoicings now do you not make it appear that the Jewish hegemony is once and for all settled by political decree regardless of self-determination and future labor?

That is the kind of gift that places a handicap upon the Jews from the start. You think it an advantage to be the darling of the ruling power. The bayonets are on your side. I grant you that is the way of all imperialism — also of Jewish imperialism, if we are to be blessed with this new contribution to the world's culture. But is it the way for the Jewish People which wishes to people the ancient land in behalf of a new civilization? And is it the practical and neighborly way? This gift of political primacy to the Jews in Palestine rather than political equality contains the seed of resentment and future conflict. Unfortunately the functions of political governments everywhere seem to be to confer privilege upon a class that has not earned it through work. Under the Balfour Declaration the Jews are that privileged class in Palestine — the recipients of political favor from Great Britain. It may appear on the surface to give the Jews a good headstart in their race for control in Palestine. But underneath it lays up for them the hatred and mistrust of their neighbors and of liberal forces everywhere. You say that the Jews have had such a raw deal politically throughout the world and for so many centuries that their being favored in Palestine ought not to count against them. But I answer that the Jewish People cannot suffer injustice to be done to others even as a compensation for injustice done to them. What the Jews can claim, and all they have a right to claim, is equal opportunity with others to live their Jewish life freely and to secure themselves in the land through labor, through sacrifice. This is an attitude which will enable them to face bravely British imperialism and Arabic imperialism, and to say: "Let your political machinations and decrees be what they will. What we want is the opportunity to work and build like free men." Your Balfour Declaration — if it be interpreted as you expect — decrees into existence a Jewish ruling class from the outset. The one way of escape from the dilemma, the one justification to our neighbors is to make our labor more important than our political preferment. When I speak of labor it is the labor of free men, free Arabs, free Jews that I have in mind. Labor in Palestine must be neither an exploitation of the Arabs by the Jewish ruling class, nor an exploitation of workers by employers.

What a pity that Palestine comes into the forefront of Jewish life during these days of political cataclysms and industrial revolution! How cozy and comforting the thought of that Palestine to which many of us looked as a land of refuge from the impossibility of Western industrial civilization! Even now, as far as I personally am concerned, I should like nothing better than to till a piece of its sacred soil, to spend my idle days on horseback traversing the length and breadth of the Holy Land, awakening echoes of a wondrous past and piercing the mists that come from Mt. Hermon for a glimpse of the blessed future. I should love to have time each day for the study of the Torah, and to teach my children the wisdom of our People in the sacred tongue of our tradition. And what joy it would be to help search out some of the archaeological treasures that might illumine many dark places in our history from the days before the Bible down to our own! But all this was possible under the Turk and with no abatement of the Oriental and no intrusion of Western "civilization." And I presume it will be possible for a long time under the British — for the politically circumspect. Perhaps you will use your influence with the British authorities and the Zionist Organization to permit me to live in Palestine for a while at least and thus carry out the longing of the greater part of my adult life. But unfortunately, I know that if Palestine is to be peopled by Jews from the rest of the world, not even the strictest British-Zionist immigration laws can keep proscribed ideas and dangerous Jewish persons from entering. For after all, we live in new days when the world is growing smaller, when hidden continents are revealing themselves, when the "inferior races" are stirring into a sense of dignity and power, when the lowliest of workers are actually beginning to touch the rim of a new social order.

1. Internal evidence indicates that the "dear friend" Magnes had in mind was Norman Bentwich. Magnes published parts of the letter in an article in the *London Jewish Chronicle* (August 26, 1921, pp. 17-18) and again in his *Like All the Nations?*, pp. 50-56.

2. At the San Remo Conference, April 26, 1920, the Alied Powers incorporated the Balfour Declaration in the mandate for Palestine, which was assigned to Great Britain.

3. On December 8, 1917, General Edmund Allenby, Commander of British Forces in Palestine, entered Jerusalem unopposed.

34

To Members of the Executive Committee of the Kehillah
New York

New York, June 3, 1920

Gentlemen:

I wish herewith to present to you my resignation as Chairman of the Executive Committee of the Kehillah. This is merely carrying out formally a step that I have discussed with the members of the Executive Committee and with delegates to the Kehillah for some time past. May I suggest that a small committee be appointed which should be given authority to determine, with me, the exact date upon which my resignation is to take effect.

For purposes of the record, I wish to repeat some of the reasons that prompt me to take this step.

(1) You are aware of the opinion that I have held for a long time, that in a democratic organization such as the Kehillah, it is inadvisable, under any circumstances, for one man to be the Chairman for too long a time.

(2) The work of the Kehillah has gotten into a rut out of which it must be taken. This requires new blood, and in order to secure this new blood and new enthusiasm, I am convinced that there should be a new Chairman of the Executive Committee. As long as I remain Chairman of the Executive Committee, the members of the Committee and the delegates at large will continue to have the attitude, which is very complimentary to me personally but which is bad for the organization, that the responsibility for the Kehillah is concentrated in me and that therefore they need not worry.

The current expenses of the Kehilla are being met, and its sole financial obligation is an indebtedness to a few friends which can with very little effort be made up. I should have preferred, naturally, to have turned over to my successor more activities, but it was necessary to cut our coat in accordance with out cloth. The recent special Conferences of Delegates must have convinced everyone attending them that the Kehillah spirit is strong, and that the Kehillah idea has taken deep root. I am sure that if the additional $25,000 proposed by those conferences is raised — and in view of the pledges made, this would not seem to be too difficult — the activities of the Kehillah during the coming year can be made very much alive and very fruitful.

(3) The need of rotation in office and of securing new blood was clear enough three years ago to have prompted me to present my resignation at that time. But with the entrance of America into the war and my own attitude towards the war and problems arising out of it, it seemed to me and others of the Committee to be the part of wisdom that I remain Chairman of the Executive Committee. It is known to the Committee that I was ready to resign at any time since the entrance of America into the war, but that it was not regarded as advisable that I do this. Whether or not this was best for the Kehillah, I am not competent to say. But if my resignation during the war might have raised public issues which it was deemed advisable not to raise, this situation does not prevail at the present time, the war being, in effect, over, and the public attitude somewhat changed.

(4) In addition, there is the personal reason that I desire to have, if this is any way possible, a year without the responsibility for the conduct of any organization. It is my firm belief that a new era in human history is beginning as a result of the war. New forms of life are developing. In this change, it is the Old World which is becoming the New. For this reason, I am anxious to come into direct contact, if this be possible, with the new life that is developing in the Old World. Moreover, the Jews, in their great majority, are at the center of the Old World and new life. And I hope that, by contact with them after these years of their suffering and struggle, I may have a deeper understanding than at present of the Jewish destiny. I hope that after the experience and added knowledge thus gained, I may be better able than ever to devote myself to the developing life of the living Jewish people.

Very truly yours, JLM

35
Draft of Letter

New York, c. 1921

Dear Friend,[1]

You ask me why I am planning to go away from here for a year or so, and why I am anxious to go to Russia, to Germany, to Eastern and Central Europe. You tell me, rightly, that there is work to do here in New York, in America. You recall to me the endless number of times that I myself have urged the organization of Jewish forces here for work and progress here, and you call my attention to the fact that only the other day I declared that the time was now ripe, the psychological moment had come for the integration of the community forces on behalf of Jewish education.

I owe you an answer to your questions, and I shall give you the answer I have given myself.

I really am convinced that the time has at last come when a large organization on behalf of Jewish education can be created. The problem is here. The thousands of Jewish children are here, but what is more, the men to create the organization are here, and the money, and the readiness.

That the men are here is primarily the result of the past ten years' work. A few men had been educated to an understanding of the problem, and to the determination to devote their energies to a solution of the problem. If that were not so, it would be a sad reflection upon our labors for a number of years past. Moreover, the war and the relief drives have taught men to think in large figures, and to give of themselves and of their substance more generously than ever before. I think it may be said that the question of Jewish education will, accordingly, be faced no matter which of us drops out. No man is ever indispensable. Yet my leaving a few years ago could have been much more serious than it is now. Dr. Benderly's leaving a few years ago could have been almost irreparable. The fact that he gives only part of his time now is the most serious of drawbacks. Yet even if he were to drop out, the question will be faced, much as his information and devotion and coordinating ability would be missed.

But he is not to drop out, and no one else is, except myself — and that only for the moment. The men are here who are about to take the problem up seriously.

How could I help now? Not nearly to the extent that you seem to think. The first year of organization will be the time of small conferences, of getting initial subscriptions, of negotiations with the Charity Federation, the schools, groups and individuals. I have no doubt I could be of help here. But I do not fit in there as I used to. I can not approach as many persons as formerly. They have not the same desire to see me, and I have not the same desire to see them. I think I have earned — at least I need — a respite from organization work and administrative work. I am no longer handy at it, and my heart is in other types of work.

But I hope I can be of help in an entirely different direction. The problem has its two aspects — that of organization, money, and that of the spirit. It is with the spirit of Jewish education, religion and life that I am in hopes I can be of greatest help.

A new period in human history is beginning, a new period also in the history of the Jews. If the future is clear to you, it is not clear to me. What is the content of Jewish education, of Jewish religion, of Jewish life? What is its relation to the new society now developing? These are questions upon whose answer the "spirit" of Jewish education will in part depend. Who will communicate this to the teachers, the preachers, the directors, the children, the young men and women? Only those who are willing to face the new day with open minds.

I can best face the new day by seeking a replenishment of knowledge and inspiration away from here and at the center of suffering and aspiration. I want to go to Russia and to Central and Eastern Europe because I need first-hand knowledge of the new forces operating there. The bulk of the Jewish people have had much to do with setting these new forces in motion. They live in the midst of them. I want to observe how Jewish life is affected and to listen for signs of a new springtime for the Jews and the world. It may be I shall be disillusioned. So much the worse, and not only for me alone. At any rate, if I am to give the next twenty years—I hope I may have them—to Jewish life, it is necessary that I see and hear and experience what little there may be of those fresh, new forces, speaking and acting in the name of a new world and a better society. If I find them I shall be able the better to enrich Jewish life with them. If I do not find them it will have been at least another step towards the attainment of the unattainable ideal. Whatever be the outcome, do you not agree now that in the way I see it I can make my best contribution to the very cause which you yourself have at heart?

1. No indication of the identity of the addressee was found.

36

To Mordecai M. Kaplan
New York

New York, January. 14, 1921

Dear Dr. Kaplan:

You know how long I have hesitated to write to you on the Society of the Jewish Renascence.[1] I hesitate all the more now since I hear that you are under fire. I would not say a word that might in any way weaken your strength or help your opponents. I know who you are, and I know who they are.

You seem, however, to want my views. As I have told you often, whenever I sit down to write them out, I see a book looming up. I shall therefore write only *rashe p'rakim* [main points], the elaboration of which must be left to a more propitious time.

I. Your movement is purely synagogal. You seem to leave out of account the large Jewish life and the important Jewish forces, spiritual and material, outside of the synagogue.[2]

II. It is, of course, perfectly proper and within reason for you and other rabbis to concentrate upon a synagogue movement. The synagogue has been the great source of inspiration in the past, and certainly ought to be now and in the future.

III. As a synagogue movement, however, I do not find that the Society of the Jewish Renascence is a "religious" movement in the synagogue sense of the term. Paragraph 2 of your Platform reaffirming faith in God is interesting from a sociological point of view, but is hardly a religious apperception of God.[3]

IV. Your theological or philosophical theories have nothing in them inconsistent with thoroughgoing "Orthodox" practice and conformity.

V. Your quarrel, therefore, is based upon "reform" in certain practices, namely, Sabbath observance, second-day holidays, dietary laws, and ritual.

VI. This is but a repetition of the old Reform struggle and can lead to no better results.

VII. The difference between your Society and the Reform movement is that your Society is expressedly Zionistic, and that you take your stand in the Halakha [Jewish traditional law].

VIII. Zionism, in the sense in which it may distinguish your organization from the official declaration of the Central Conference of American Rabbis, is a political movement, and therefore necessarily within the synagogue.

IX. As to the Halakha and practical adaptations of it to changed conditions, you disregard the traditional sanctions which lie only with a consensus of recognized and authoritative rabbis and communities.[4]

X. In effect, you are using energy and an apparatus, leaving aside your splendid personality and powers, worthy of a revolutionary movement. But your movement is not revolutionary. It resolves itself into a quarrel over minor Sabbath, and holiday, and food and ritual observances.

XI. Nor does your movement carry a great social message. Account is taken of the overwhelming social needs of this day and generation only in the non-committal Paragraph 5 of the fundamental duties of members.[5]

XII. From all of this, I conclude that you might, with great benefit to everyone, give utterance in speech and in writing, without let or hindrance, to your fundamental intellectual conceptions as to Revelation, the

Bible, the Halakha, Jewish life, etc., etc., but that you are making a mistake in tinkering, upon your own authority and without regard to traditional sanctions and the Jewish religious psychology, with such really inconsequential minutiae as your practical program seems to contain.

Very truly yours, JLM

1. Kaplan sent Magnes his pamphlet "The Society of the Jewish Renascence" (reprinted from the *Maccabaean*, November 1920) soliciting his comments. "The Society," Kaplan wrote, "is an organization that has been recently formed for the advancement of Judaism in an historic, progressive and Zionist spirit. The Society represents an organized effort to introduce into the spiritual life of our people conscious direction in place of aimlessness and drift." The Society was short lived, and in 1922 Kaplan established the Society for the Advancement of Judaism.

2. "For a long time to come, the Society will have to consist only of those who have that degree of stability in things Jewish which one gets from being affiliated with synagogue life. Only men and women of that type can bring with them the kind of constructive discontent whereupon we base all our hopes for a Jewish future" (Kaplan, p. 13).

3. "We reaffirm the abiding need for humanity of faith in God, because we hold that, whatever else belief in God means, it denotes the belief in the dignity and sacredness of human life, in the reality and worth of human progress, and in the ultimate establishment of freedom, justice and truth" (Kaplan, p. 10).

4. "We accept the Halakha, which is rooted in the Tora and developed in the Talmud, as the norm of Jewish life, availing ourselves, at the same time, of the method implicit therein to interpret and develop the body of Jewish Law in accordance with the actual conditions and spiritual needs of modern life" (Kaplan, p. 11).

5. "To devote some time during each week to the study and consideration of social, civic and economic problems" (Kaplan, p. 12).

37

Notes: "The Jews Are the Revolutionaries of Western Civilization"

Sheffield, Mass., May 31, 1921

The Jews are the "revolutionaries" of western civilization. They should endeavor to maintain that role. Their earliest tradition is revolutionary — Mt. Sinai, the Prophets, and their history during two thousand years past has forced them into this role. They have seen most Western lands, they have suffered in all of them. Their conception of the Messiah and his coming has a "revolutionary" basis: it is the way of the new heaven and a new earth, a better world of men than that in which we live now. Their conception of *kiddush hashem* [martyrdom] is a "revolutionary" one, insofar as it means that this people is ready to sacrifice life itself rather than yield certain fundamental beliefs. They gave Christianity to the Western world with its "revolutionary" figure of Jesus, and the whole conception of the coming of the Kingdom of God. Try as they will to escape it, this "Christian" conception which came from the Jews is "revolutionary." Over and over again, the Jews have given the Western world individuals whose personality has left its deep impress—Spinoza, Marx, the Russian revolutionaries of today. (They have not given the Eastern world its impress—Buddha, Confucius . . .)

Why should they give up their identity? Whom would it avail? It would be merely the physical fact of a little more blood admixture. But the maintenance of their identity is and can continue to be a *spiritual* fact of real importance. If they continue to exist (as they will), their tradition and their international position will continue to *force* them (much against the will of many of them) to be the great disturbers of the world, the wakers of the sleepers, the yeast in the dough, the preachers of justice and brotherhood.

This does not mean that each individual Jew is a "revolutionary" or is conscious of any such role. He is more likely than not an ordinary human being who wants what other human beings want. But his position as part of the Jewish people is something that he can hardly determine; and it is that position that determines his "revolutionary" character and drives the Jews as individuals. They have all the stuff of the revolutionary: temperament, imagination, vitality, individualism, critical faculties, the power of sacrifice (illustrations of these and other traits from his daily life would be interesting), and his political, economic and social position helps all of this along.

Will Zionism carry him away from this position?

(a) Hope of those for whom Zionism means "normalizing" of Jewish life, taking Jews away from Bolshevist surroundings.

(b) Fear of those who see Jews thus divided in their struggles for new world and new Zion. This means dividing their energies.

For me Zionism means helping the Jewish people to preserve its identity and deepen its spirit. With its identity preserved it will continue its historic mission; with its spirit deepened it will be the more effective in carrying this mission out. Zionism means enabling the Jewish people the better to set its creative energies free in literature, art, etc. For "revolution" does not mean social, political, economic alone; it means also . . .[1]

1. The text breaks off here; the remainder could not be located.

38

To Beatrice Magnes
New York

New York, January 17, 1922

Dear Beatie,

The Jewish education work towards which I have been giving most of my time for the past two years is now on the right road. Dr. Pool[1] has, I am glad to say, taken hold in the Jewish Education Association in a vigorous and intelligent way; and today Dr. Dushkin has been installed as Assistant Director of the Bureau of Education. Within the next two months the working progress of both organizations will be clear enough to indicate to everyone just what both are after singly and together.

I feel very much pleasure and relief in this. As you know, since the fall of 1918 I have been having a struggle with Dr. Benderly to get the Bureau down to simple terms, both financially and spiritually. It is fortunate for all of us that I have been firm and perhaps ruthless in my insistence that the Bureau deflate both its swollen budget and its swollen pretensions. The process has been somewhat harder than anyone knows. It has meant for me the strain of a near break with Dr. Benderly (and the same for him, I have no doubt). It has meant his withdrawal from full-time work in the Bureau and his preoccupation first with business and then with Palestine work. It has meant for him (and for others of the Bureau, including myself) the strain of cutting down on cherished work, of permitting valuable men and plans to be dropped. It has meant for us a deep change in the outlook for Jewish education.

Then in July 1920 came the death of Professor Friedlaender.[2] This took place while Dr. Benderly was on his first business mission to Palestine. At this time, also you will recall I was desirous of going abroad with you and the children. I felt that under the circumstances it would not do for me to leave and that it was my duty to stay with the educational work, not for the educational services I could render (which were very few), but because the work had been deprived of its two main workers, and my going away would be a symbol of dissolution. You and I talked everything over, and as a result I promised myself, and a few others, that I was prepared to give the next two years to Jewish education. It was on this account, too, that we moved into the city and felt justified in spending so much money for our apartment which was to be paid for by the $3,500 a year which I had persuaded myself I should take from my *Baalebattish* education friends.

The two years have not yet passed, and I am glad to say that the Jewish Education Association is now established, our deficit in the Bureau of Education paid off, and the beginning made of additional and more systematic work. All signs point to cooperation between the various educators concerned, and a feeling of renewed hopefulness is beginning to manifest itself. It is questionable if this would have been accomplished had I not been here.

But now that the organization side of the work has made this amount of progress, it is necessary for me to turn my attention more and more to that aspect of Jewish education where I can be of greatest help and where I am probably most needed. I refer to the more "spiritual" side rather than to that of organization. During these years I have come to greater clarity with myself, and I am more interested than ever in Jewish education in the larger sense, as a way of living and thinking in these great days of world change. What I want to be able increasingly to do is to become a Jewish teacher through preaching and writing and interesting people in Jewish education in its important bearing upon the life of the present day.

As I told you, I am gradually releasing myself from such matters as do not bear upon my main task.

Towards carrying out this task, I have been thinking over a series of addresses. I have a great deal to say, but as I approach it, I realize keenly how ill prepared I am to handle such weighty themes as I have in mind. I need to study ever so much.

I should like to get out a volume of my wartime addresses, and perhaps a volume of Jewish addresses of the past.

I should like also to get out the material on the Russian Secret Treaties which Mr. Greenberg and I have been working at.

I should like to undertake a mission abroad for the Culture Committee of the Relief organization.[3] I have in mind a whole plan whereby Jewish learning and Jewish education in the broadest sense can be helped. If I were to do this, I should want you and the boys to go abroad with me about May. This would mean that from that time we should try to sublet our apartment until the Fall.

As you know, I should want also to go to Palestine. If I can go as a member of that Holy Places Commission it will be just right. But failing that, I am not certain as to what should be done. At least, I should want to be prepared to go with you and the boys from Europe to Palestine, if this should be possible with advantage to all of us.

I am writing this to you as a record, and because you will have more time to think it all over before we get into a conversation about it.

As I see it, it is no small thing to want really to do things in life as genuinely as I want to do these things. I am sure you will bear that in mind even though what I want to do does not altogether appeal to you.

In any event, I rejoice that I can write and talk to you freely of what is in my heart and mind.

January 18, 1922

More about the trip to Europe.

I presume that the Relief Committee would be willing to have me go for it on the Culture mission if I offered my services in return for the R.R. and other living expenses I incurred for myself in connection with the work.

The work would be cultural reconstruction, not an attempt to give "relief" to needy schools. Just as the Committee is now interested in "constructive relief" on the material side, rather than the continuation of mere palliative charity, so the funds for cultural purposes would not be spent for the mere support of needy institutions, but for such enterprises as have a central value and an important bearing upon the strengthening of Jewish spiritual life. We must save from the ruins as much of cultural value as possible, and we must strengthen that which will strengthen Judaism. With limited funds, care will have to be exercised in choosing the points at which we want to concentrate.

The first point is *higher Jewish learning*. Dr. Heller's "super-yeshiva"[4] is a case in point. Without the development of higher Jewish learning, some of the chief sources of Jewish life will be cut off, and the soil for the growth of Judaism made that much poorer — theological seminaries, libraries, academies of Jewish science.

The second point is those institutes which are in strategic positions for the development of secondary and primary Jewish education of various kinds.

The third point is the encouragement of the investigation and collection of original material of consequence to Jewish life: documents, Kehillah registers, MSS, Jewish art objects — in brief, saving for the Jewish people those visible remains of the old Jewish life that can be made valuable for Jewish culture.

The fourth point is publications (Gesellschaft für die Wissen des Judentumus, private scholars . . .)

(The point must be considered as to whether trade and technical education come within the scope of our work).

This work would be of value to me personally. It would give me a deeper insight into the cultural life of the Jews, throw me into contact with men and institutions worth knowing. It would mean my better education for the work of Jewish education. Moreover, it would give me the opportunity I crave of getting first-hand contact with Europe after the war. I should want among other things to go to Russia for the purpose of considering what are the possibilities there for advancing Jewish culture.

In any preaching that I do, there are two sides of life that concern me — the one that has to do with the individual soul, the soul of man, and the other as it has to do with present-day society. The first requires constant study and deepening of the self, and cultivation of the mind and the heart; and the second requires actual contact with postwar European society.

Do you not think I could be helped by carrying out such a plan?

Of course I want to talk to you about how it will affect the children — and you.

But I hesitate on this score until we have grown clear on what I have written above.

1. David de Sola Pool (1885–1970). Rabbi, Zionist leader, educator. Rabbi of Shearith Israel Congregation of New York from 1907 to his retirement in 1956; member of the Zionist Commission to Palestine, 1919–1921; founder and director of Jewish Education Committee of New York, 1922.

2. Israel Friedlaender was murdered in the Ukraine while on a mission on behalf of the JDC.

3. The JDC's relief activities in Europe was being expanded to include the cultural reconstruction of Jewish life.

4. Hayim Heller (1879–1960). Biblical and Talmudic scholar; born in Bialystok, Poland. After serving as rabbi at Lomza, Poland, he moved to Berlin and founded the Bet ha'midrash ha'elyon in 1922, a modern yeshiva. He joined the faculty of the Isaac Elhanan Theological Seminary in New York in 1929.

4

JERUSALEM: CHANCELLOR OF THE HEBREW UNIVERSITY 1922–1935

Several times in the course of their first year and a half in Jerusalem Magnes and his wife reached the decision to return to the United States. However the uncertainty of what awaited him in America and the beauty and tranquillity they found in Jerusalem led each time to second thoughts about leaving. The children had adjusted well, and Jerusalem offered opportunities for the intellectual growth and personal fulfillment that Beatrice Magnes craved. But what would Magnes do in Jerusalem? The country had no need for functionaries or organizers of his kind. Furthermore, he gave his best, as he wrote later in his journal, "only when the cause calls, only when I have the conviction (or illusion) that I am really needed" (documents 40, 42, 43, 58).

Felix Warburg's munificent gift in 1924 assured the opening of the Hebrew University and made possible the "call." However, it was a call that spoke with two voices: Warburg's, which insisted that Magnes head the university in order to assure its independence, and Weizmann's, vexed over losing control of so central an instrument of nation building. Other interests complicated matters. Professorial advisers — Albert Einstein preeminent among them — residing in Europe and ignorant of the realities in Jerusalem prescribed their own academic formulas and standards (documents 46, 50, 51). Research institute or teaching university? Piority for the sciences or humanities, for the pure or applied sciences? Preferment for scholars already settled in Palestine or better-known scholars from abroad? Locating the supervisory and policy-making bodies in Jerusalem or removing them to London, with the possibility of co-opting men of means and experience? These were the issues over which legitimate differences of opinion arose and occupied the meetings of the board of governors from 1925 to 1930. But they were suffused with personal rivalries and politics that spilled over from the wider world of Jewish affairs.

To contain the conflicting interests scattered across three continents, a complex, cumbersome governing structure evolved to direct the stripling university, possessed of a great vision and meager resources (document

52). The result was frequently a stand-off betwen contending parties, conflicts in which vast energies were expended in the maneuverings of headstrong men. In this situation Magnes, with Warburg's wavering support, faced Weizmann, who leaned on the prestige of a fickle Einstein (document 74). Magnes staved off repeated efforts to dislodge him. From 1926 to 1935 Einstein periodically resigned or threatened to resign as chairman of the university's academic council unless Magnes was stripped of all academic functions. The chancellor, Einstein charged, was academically unfit to direct a great scientific institution. However, Magnes continued to "rule," as his critics put it. Much about the university was improvised, they claimed; some academic appointments provoked bitter criticism; advancement was ponderously slow. All this Magnes readily admitted to the committee of inquiry that investigated conditions at the university in the fall and winter of 1933. "I am the person who is responsible in the last analysis for that which is bad here and that which is good here," he told the committee in an angry interview. "I have been responsible because there has been no one else upon whom responsibility all these years could be fastened" (documents 69, 72, 73, 74, 75). The report resulted in a reorganization of the university, and Magnes was "kicked upstairs," as he put it, to the honorary position of president. Nevertheless, in the years of his presidency, from 1935 to his death, his presence was felt. To the public he remained the titular head of the university, speaking in the name of the intellectual center of world Jewry.

In the fall of 1929 Weizmann's apprehensions were realized: Magnes returned to the political arena, a dissenter once again but now bearing the prestige of his university office and the backing of the American non-Zionists. With the death of Louis Marshall in September Warburg became the key non-Zionist in the newly established, enlarged Jewish Agency. He had hoped that Magnes would serve with him as cochairman of the agency. Though Magnes refused, his long and intimate friendship with Warburg made him a person to be reckoned with (documents 55, 63, 65).

Magnes had restated his concept of spiritual Zionism—which would become the basis of his political program in 1929—soon after his arrival in Jerusalem. In a controversial lecture entitled "Eretz Israel and Galut" he assigned equal place to both in the unfolding of Jewish history. In a statement that for his listeners bordered on heresy he rejected the notion that the national home was the sole hope for Jewish survival. The dispersion in fact was providential, for "Jews were participating in the world's redemption even against their will" (document 41). There is no record of further addresses on ideological or political issues until 1929. Magnes's notebooks, however, bear witness to his political concerns. The question of reaching an understanding with the Arabs increasingly agitated him. He viewed the invitation to Lord Balfour to attend the opening of the Hebrew University in 1925 as a provocative act that would aggravate relations with the Arab world (documents 48, 49). In an outline for a talk he developed his thesis that Palestine was "a land *sui generis*" belonging to neither people. He questioned too B'rit Shalom's moral stance: seeking peace, he insisted, was more than a tactical necessity (documents 61, 62).

Religious questions were inevitably linked in Magnes's mind to the political. Repeatedly he returned to the theme of the universal and the national. "After you have rooted yourself in your nation you can overcome nationalism—not before," he wrote (documents 45, 57, 76). He sought an ethical universalism—hence his interest in the *g'dud ha'avoda* (the legion of labor), the most militant of the communitarian groups (document 53). The same line of thought led him, in 1928, to begin discussing with friends the creation of a religious fellowship committed to social activism. Thus his plea in 1929 for a reordering of Zionist goals combined the themes of Arab-Jewish rapprochement, cultural Zionism, and prophetic Judaism. Magnes clothed a nonpolitical vision with political form, to the approval of non-Zionsts and American liberals and to the irritation of the majority of Zionists (documents 64, 65, 66, 67, 68). Weizmann's response to Magnes's 1929 speech appeared under the *New York Times* banner "Jews Want Homeland Not Cultural Museum." On the other hand, John Haynes Holmes wrote in a private letter, "Magnes is the greatest prophetic spirit in the world of Jewry today."[1]

Living in Zion confirmed for Magnes his long-held views of Judaism and Zionism. It also stirred in him a religious sensitivity, a painful, introspective groping for personal faith. He had experienced moments of self-doubt as a young rabbi. But now in Jerusalem he hungered for the perfect faith of the true believer. The experience of estrangement in his last years in America and the search for roots in the new land—Zion with its demands and its promises—surely explain, at least in part, the turning inward. He first gave written expression to these feelings in a long entry in his diary in September 1923, the first Rosh Hashanah following his arrival in Jerusalem. Ten trying months had passed, and the season of reflection and taking stock had come. He began by describing the events of the day, the attempt of a score of English and American Jews to organize a "Western" prayer service. Then the account turned into a religious confession of anguish and uncertainty (documents 44, 59). The theme would reappear in his most personal writings to the end of his life, a side of the private man that few, if any, knew.

1. *New York Times*, December 31, 1929, p. 6; John Haynes Holmes (see glossary of names) to Jacob Billikopf, December 3, 1929, MP, 384.

39

Note: Palestine — A Country of Extremes

Jerusalem, February 13, 1923

Palestine — a country of extremes: the contact of old and new civilizations; frontier life and dress-suit life; people on camels, asses, on foot and in roaring autos and airplanes. Veiled women, and low shoes and high heels. Difficult to get a bath, yet dress suit required. Some few have telephones and others have to hoof it to get things sent and done, yet the telephone tempo is the standard.

Palestine — a *hard* country full of stone and rock, irrigation and dry farming, extremes of altitude and depth. People hard, struggling each one for his living. Whatever idealistic impulses may have brought them here, they are immersed in the daily struggle to maintain themselves, their work, or their organization. Not much mercy. People permitted to go their own way. Not much easy social life, except formal Society. A small country, Jerusalem a small city. Yet one organization distinct from another with little coordination and cooperation. Institutions receiving money from same funds, so engrossed in their own work, they do not think of what the others are doing. Blinkers, blinders. Feverish, one-tracked as though this were indeed the "center of the universe," and salvation depended upon this piece of work at this time. But little perspective. Hard to make an appointment because hard to break it. No telephones. Before you get a messenger, you take the message yourself. No meeting place. Rain and mud and rocks in winter. Sun and heat and malaria in summer. Letters "by hand." In California, you keep the rains and water away from the house. Here you gather each drop of rain water through pipes into cisterns. Water troubles generally: washing, drinking (boiling), gardens, courtyard, leaks, drains, barrels.

40

Journal: If I Went Back to New York

Jerusalem, May 3, 1923

If I went back to New York

(a) A house with a room. Invite weekly this or that group to meet this or that kind of person with something to say, or read, or sing, or show. If a playwright wanted a critical audience of his peers; a scholar, a musician, a politician, an economist, a distinguished guest, a painter; if young and budding talent wanted the judgment of their betters (elders, more successful); if finance or industry or Society were to be brought into touch with personality or ideas or movements—do you not think that I know (or could easily get to know) sufficient persons of all kinds and conditions to bring this constant contact about? With Beatie's everpresent help, of course. (There ought also to be a few persons with whom I could advise—and the ethical, i.e. the public opinion side, the forward-looking side of pressing questions is not to be omitted.)

(b) A school. To begin with, a limited number of pupils if they can be found. It shall be a modern institution and at the same time include the Jewish core of things—Torah. A combination of radical outlook, Jewish reverence and beauty, and piety. Something like the Friends School. Non-Jews could come if they wanted to, though they probably would not. The beginnings must be made of training a new generation in this spirit of freedom and tradition and a newer and better world.

(c) The pretentious name of the Kehillah should be changed to Jewish Communal Council (or some such name). It should be representative only of organizations with no elections by districts or groups of individuals. Perhaps it should be only a council of central organizations. One of its purposes should be to help create a Kehillah corresponding with needs of American life. The idea of Kehillah is too valuable to lose. Ways and means of helping create a Kehillah and furthering the cause of Judaism are establishment of bureaus, open discussion of Jewish problems, bringing all groups of Jews together. Bureaus of Education, Industry, Discrimination, Religious Affairs.

(d) Some publication and opportunities for public speaking to propagate ideas.

41

Address delivered in Jerusalem
May 22, 1923

ERETZ ISRAEL AND THE GALUT[1]

In preparing this address I find myself saying much more of the Galut than I had intended. I have caught myself arguing against that attitude which one sometimes finds in Palestine and elsewhere that the Galut is of but little real and permanent value for Judaism. If I seem to have overemphasized the Galut, I hope it will not be ascribed to any lack of interest in the meaning and function of Eretz Israel. It is perhaps not unnatural for one who believes in the unity, the wholeness of the Jewish People to direct attention to the spiritual significance of the Galut while in Eretz Israel and to point out the meaning of Eretz Israel while in the Galut.

Last summer I had an interesting talk with Maxim Gorki in the course of which we came to speak about Zionism. He said he recognized the spiritual power of Zionism but that he did not favor it because it intended taking Jews away from the large world where, particularly in these days of stress, they had so important a part to play. I answered that my conception of Zionism did not at all provide for the Jews being taken out of their place in the struggling world. If it were physically possible to bring all Jews here — which of course, it is not — the world would be a poorer place and the Jewish people would deprive itself of a large part of its opportunity to be of service to mankind. Zionism, Palestine, in my opinion was not an end in itself. It was a means of strengthening the Jewish people. The Jewish people of flesh and blood wherever they lived were the chief consideration, and Palestine was one of the means, perhaps a chief means, but not the only means of making the Jewish people cleaner, better, truer. The creation of a Jewish community here would thus make the Jews everywhere fitter to perform their historic task in the great world. Gorki acknowledged that it was possible for a good European to agree with such a conception of Zionism.

I do not wish to stir up the old controversy between those who believe in and those who deny the Galut. I was brought to the selection of my theme by a remark made recently by a splendid and enthusiastic teacher in Galilee who said: "Why does not the Galut send us more funds for our work? Are we not their only hope? Are we not creating cultural values? Will not Judaism perish without us?" With all my admiration for his fine personality and self-sacrificing work, I was compelled to give what must have been to him a disappointing answer. For the Galut is more than a source of funds; it has great spiritual significance beyond this. Eretz Israel is indeed holding out great hope to the Jewish people. But it is not the only hope, and it would be fatal to blind our eyes to the spiritual and intellectual activities of the Jews in the Galut. Take Poland, for example. I was delighted and greatly encouraged last summer to find an immense stirring and awakening among all sections and classes of the Jews there. In America there is a slow but sure deepening of Jewish thinking and feeling and living. Much of this is taking place under the inspiration of the Eretz Israel ideal. But this is not the only factor. There is also operative the inner need of the spiritual values of Judaism; and there is the force of the new anti-Semitism which in its own turn is largely due to the Jews' irrepressible spiritual activity.

As to the continued existence of the Jewish people, my own belief in its eternal quality is so profound that I do not fear for the continuance of the people even though our present hopes for Palestine be not realized. One should not be too hasty to prophesy evil about so complex and amazing a phenomenon as the Jewish people. They used to prove mathematically and scientifically in Germany that with the rate of conversions to Christianity then going on, German Judaism would soon be at an end. But see what has happened. German Judaism is today one of the most vigorous branches of the ancient tree. I need not go into the causes for this. It merely suffices as an example of the vitality of the Jewish people, and it is a symbol of the larger forces in the world which bear upon the development and destiny of the Jewish people.

Why set Eretz Israel and the Galut over against one another at all? It is true that in actual life it is difficult because of geography to work on behalf of both Galut and Eretz Israel at the same time. But making the distinction between them too sharp is to break up that historic unity which has been part of the secret of Israel's persistence and strength. Jewish life requires the harmony of Eretz Israel and Galut. The complex Jewish people can not be explained by a simple formula. Both Eretz Israel and the Galut are manifestations of the life of this people. It is the people which is larger and more important than either Galut or Eretz Israel. We are one people, a k'lal yisrael, despite all our diversities. The struggle and achievement of the Galut, on the one hand, and this magnificent experiment in Eretz Israel, on the other hand, are expressions of the life and creative energy of the living people. Whatever is produced either in the Galut or in Eretz Israel — be it language or literature, philosophy or art, or social ideals — all this is by and for the living organism of the people wherever situated. Eretz Israel is beautiful and interesting and worth loving if we are convinced that it will aid the Jewish people — help strengthen it and make it fitter for its service in the world of men.

The people will live, therefore, and it will continue its creative and benevolent work, even without present-day Eretz Israel. But with Eretz Israel it is that much richer and because of Eretz Israel it has the prospect of becoming that much stronger, more secure, and useful at a time in the world's history when men need a strong, useful, idealistic Jewish people.

Galut is more than a geographic term. Galut means the bulk and body of the Jewish people. I do not know to what extent the view now obtains, but not so long ago there were Zionists whose affection for Eretz Israel was so great that they could view with comparative indifference what was happening to the people in Galut. This is a false idea, because even though we despair of the Galut and all it stands for, our guiding principle must be love of the Jewish people. As things are in the world, Galut stands for the people in its great majority.

Galut also means the wide world of men beyond the Jewish people. It means the suffering and striving and achievement of the Jewish people and their place in the great world. Galut means considering the function of the Jewish people in the history of the last two thousand years, and trying to determine the part the Jewish people can play in the troubled life of the present day. Eretz Israel will have to be judged by whether or not it can help the Jewish people to do its work and determine its function in this larger world.

I do not want to talk in terms that are too vague, but when I think of the present position of the Jewish people I am overcome by the mystery of it all. After creating the Bible in this tiny land of Israel, and giving birth to religions that have subdued empires; after having developed a glorious Torah both in word and in ways of life; after having given the world some of its great figures and ideas, and after having through misery and struggle and wandering accumulated experience through centuries and over half of the globe, there is Israel again at the very heart of the world's life, engaged as mighty protagonist in today's gigantic social and political and spiritual struggles. There we find the Jews massed chiefly in the centers of a brutal, vigorous industrial civilization that threatens to destroy itself on account of its greed and arrogance, and lack of intelligence and true religion. By their enemies the Jews are absurdly accused of being responsible for the world war and for the treaties of peace — two of the greatest iniquities in the history of man. Despite its absurdity the charge shows what a large part the Jews play in the imagination of this declining age. They are chief actors in all phases and in all parties of the Russian Revolution — one of the greatest of all historic phenomena. They are among the most important factors on both sides of the industrial struggle. They are among the great theoreticians of a new social order, and among the chief sacrifices in the attempt to bring it about. Out of the fecundity of the Jewish people, what a large number of men of spirit and of wisdom and of achievement have been given the world in our own day; and all the while there is preserved among thousands of this people the forms and the essence of a traditional religion that is one of the main sources of this amazing, mysterious power.

Throughout the Roman Empire the Jews were, so the historian Mommsen tells us, a ferment; and whether we like it or not the Jews are a ferment in our present civilization, both destroying and building up, both in the conservative and in the radical ranks, but always penetrating reality with their minds and spirits, and unfolding a creative activity that is astounding in its complexity and significance.

For me all of this has a meaning, a purpose. It means that even against their will the Jews are participating in the world's redemption, that above and independent of their will they are in the grip of major, mysterious sources that give them no rest and that are constantly using them as the media of creation and change, and as instruments for the expression of the world-soul.

This exercise of spiritual power, this throwing up out of the Jewish people of so many men of mind and spirit is not primarily a conscious act. It does not occur because of any resolution passed by a Jewish organization, or because the Jews are involved in some stupid conspiracy to get hold of the world's sources of power. This productivity is first of all the result of the traditional Jewish way of life, of Jewish struggle, of the influence upon the Jewish people of generations of interpreters of the Torah. It is the unplanned for, natural outcome of the discipline and heritage and training and environment of the people.

Nor is this flooding of the world with Jewish talent due to the fact that Jews are different from other human beings. I need not tell a Jewish audience what a great abundance we have of stupid, petty, vulgar, brutal men and women; how much there is among us of sinfulness as well as saintliness; how much poverty and misery, and selfishness and greed and impurity. No, we are nothing but flesh and blood, just as all other humans, and in some ways worse than others. But a people is in many respects like the individual. Just as a great genius is very often exactly like other men and sometimes worse, except that there is within him some strange spark that lights him up on occasion and illumines the darkness about him, so the Jewish people is *menschlich allzu menschlich* [human, all too human], but upon occasion throws out of itself men and ideas and forces that make a great difference in the life and destiny of the world. From even the black corners of our life there suddenly bursts forth from time to time the spark of the *sh'khina* [Divine Presence].

This creative, spiritual function of the Jewish people is going on irrespective of present-day Eretz Israel, and the eternal quality of the Jewish people is an earnest that it will continue to be a spiritual force in the world even without present-day Eretz Israel. But our hope for Eretz Israel has always been that there might develop here a natural and complete Jewish life under the extraordinary social and spiritual circumstances which this historic, beautiful, yet hard, stubborn land affords; that out of this Return from Exile there might be produced men of spirit, ideas of truth and beauty, eternal forces that might help mankind along its painful way to salvation.

Now, to all of these subconscious processes of the people's life here and in Galut, we must add conscious motives. It is in our nature to philosophize and find reasons for our existence. The Prophet Isaiah, for example, spoke of the people as the Servant of the Lord. Although, in accordance with the old saying, the Torah was imposed upon us from above as we stood under Sinai, nevertheless from generation to generation interpreters and philosophers and men of action have wished fo find or read into the Jewish life and tradition their own highest ideals of duty, of happiness, of truth.

All of us have such ideals; and there are some which I should like to feel proceed from our Torah, our tradition, our life; or, if they are not inherent therein, that they be consciously wrought into the substance of Jewish life now and for the future. For example, I should like to see the Jewish people determine consciously and deliberately that it would oppose every species of organized warfare. There is no greater sin and crime than organized war. I want to see the Jewish people, or large parts of it, say when the next war comes: "We will not go, and we will not let our sons and daughters go." This is no platonic love of peace or academic opposition to war. It is a burning hatred of the misery, hypocrisy, lies, disaster of every war, it is a passion for the sanctity of human life and the spiritual possessions of humanity. The world is now being done to death by the hatreds of the past war and the preparations for the next. The Jewish people glorify life. The Jewish people believe that humanity is capable of being saved. We must refuse to serve as cannon fodder for any group of men, however small, who are the governors of the world by virtue of the brute power in their hands. The Jews ought to use their brains and help expose the lies and shams of the last war and of the next and of every war. We must resist the domination of life by brute force. We must exalt the spirit, the power of mind and of soul. "Not by might and not by power but by my spirit." The religious Jew should proclaim this in the name of his religion, the liberal Jew as a fundamental of his philosophy, the radical Jew as the only basis of a new structure of society. It is the belief in the kindgom of heaven and the rule of the Torah as against the power laid up in rulers of the world. I do not know if society and government are at all possible without bayonets and the support of brute force. But I do know that if brute force continues to rule, the world is surely doomed to destruction. Into this dilemma the Jew must enter and he must reaffirm his belief in the capacity of mankind to save and redeem itself with mind and spirit, and without the devil's instrument of organized warfare. He must live his life as a group in the conviction that it may be his example and the achievements of his life that may tip the scales which decide if the world is to live or be destroyed.

Alas, I have not much confidence that the official Jewish communities of the Galut will seize this unparalleled opportunity to make Judaism a vital, decisive, spiritual force at this critical period of history. The persecution of the Jews almost everywhere forces all too many to show an exaggerated allegiance to various and rapidly changing patriotisms and nationalisms, and many are thus prevented from following their true bent to become citizens of the world. Nevertheless, there are, happily, throughout the Galut Jewish groups (most of them strangely enough outside of the synagogue) who have been loyal and who will continue to prove their loyalty to this truly religious ideal.

And Eretz Israel? Here the Jew expects to develop a nationalism of his own. Of what kind will it be? Will the Jews here in their efforts to create a political organism become devotees of brute force and militarism as were some of the later Hasmoneans, and will they, like the Edomite Herod, become the obedient servants of economic and militaristic imperialism? Is it among the possibilities that some day it may become political treason for someone sincerely to repeat in the streets of Jerusalem Isaiah's teaching that swords are to be beaten into ploughshares and men are to learn war no more? Or will the Jews of Eretz Israel be true to the teaching of the Prophets of Israel and attempt to work out their ideal society so that Jerusalem may be restored and Zion redeemed through righteousness and peace?

Is not the Jew fitted for such a task? Not only the prophets of Eretz Israel, but the accumulation of suffering and experience of the long Galut have taught him how low an ideal is that of soldiery. It has often been remarked that in the woodcuts of the old Pesach Hagadahs, the *rasha* [wicked son] is pictured as a soldier. Esau, Edom, Rome, are the type of the *Goyim*, while the *bet hamidrash* [house of study] and works of the spirit represent the tradition of Israel. There was a time when I used to think that this Galut ideal was a sign of cowardice and weakness. Since the great war I think it the essence of bravery and strength and wisdom. I remember reading Ahad Ha'am's review of [Max] Nordau's play, "Dr. Kohn", and condemning Ahad Ha'am as having the Galut psychology because he saw no virtue of heroism in Dr. Kohn's accepting a challenge to a duel on the score of some injury to his honor.[2] The whole conception of honor, said Ahad Ha'am, was gentile and not Jewish. I am glad to think he was right. This miserable, insulted "honor" of the nations, this vanity of vanities — how often has it not driven nations into slaughtering one another and how it prevents understanding and reconciliation among nations! If hatred of wars and of brute force, if the despising of soldiery is Galut psychology then I think the Jews and the world should be grateful for something the Galut has given. This Jewish attitude toward barbarism can be made use of, and if ever a Jewish religion here or in the Galut was in search of cardinal doctrines, here is one at hand that corresponds with Jewish ideals, with Jewish experience, with Jewish psychology, and which is at the same time a crying need for the world if mankind is not to be drowned in blood and poison gas and hatred.

Everyone who lives here in Eretz Israel and works is helping the Jewish people create spiritual values and is thus aiding the Jewish people to carry out its work in the world. The same is true of those who live and work in the Galut. Where a man can do best for his people is an individual and private matter. But whatever happens to the individual, may Eretz Israel give the Jewish people new forms of beauty and of speech, and may it see created ways of life and a society based upon human freedom and filled with knowledge as the waters cover the sea.

1. Magnes delivered the address in Hebrew. It was published in *Hapoel Hatzair*, June 8, 1923. He wrote the address in English before translating it. The English version is used here.

2. Ahad Ha'am, "Ha'musar ha'leumi," *Hashiloaḥ*, vol. 5 (Tevet 5659 [1899]).

42

New York or Jerusalem?

Jerusalem, June 16–18, 1923

If I went back to New York–June 16, 1923

(a) Bureau of Conciliation as private venture with Abelson. Attempt to make living out of it (?) Rather develop Bureau of Industry. $1,500.[1]

(b) Bureau of Education. Become its chairman again. Increase its support. Make it not only local, but national, and not only for children's education. Develop its printing department — textbooks, etc. Preach education as Jewish culture and Jewish spirituality: Jewish centers (including Palestine) and Jewish Mission. $1,500.

The Palestine University

(c) Lectures on International Political Situation; also on origins of war. Twenty lectures = \$1,000.

I shall not want to take paying position with the JDC cultural machine. I don't want to be so exclusively in the Warburg-Marshall pay; I can't quite visualize the whole scheme except as bombastic "campaigns and drives" and I am not for that; to be shouting for the Hebrew Union College would be a joke. And besides, the "education" wanted by some of these rich gentlemen is not the "education" I am after. I should be willing to help in this, but only if my independence were maintained, and not on full time.[2]

Why stay in Palestine? There is but little *real* work for *me* to do here. I could, of course, potter about with Hadassah, *Kupat Milveh* [charitable loan society], some cultural institutions, as representative of the JDC. On the other hand, there are these considerations:

1. Staying another year might result in my leaving something worthwhile behind here.

2. I could be helping a little.

3. People here want me to stay.

4. I might get clearer as to what I ought to do in America.

5. I might get the opportunity for study.

6. Beatrice's health has been good on the whole, and another year here might still improve it.

7. The children's Hebrew education would be permanently grounded in another year.

8. The Haifa School seems particularly good for David.

On the other hand, I sometimes feel that the only thing that will relieve Beatrice and help her out of the helpless and hopeless feeling that so often overtakes her is once and for all to try to establish a home in which she will have a permanent interest. I think this can only be in America, and perhaps the sooner we get to it the better for all of us.

Is it not clear after what was said and what transpired tonight that we must come to a decision quickly? And can the decision be anything else than America? It is impossible for Beatrice to endure any further indecision, and staying here another year means postponing decisions again. We must get back and try to find a home and settle down finally in life to some definite, income-producing work.

We must try to avoid precipitancy and hysteria. Tonight I feel as though I want to sell myself to the highest bidder. But that's the way I felt when I went to B'nai Jeshurun, and what good did it do to anyone? I must try to get work that is as congenial as possible, and that will pay as much as possible. If it is not all congenial, or does not pay as much as I should like, I shall have to put up with this as so many myriads of others do.

Where shall we send David to school? That will be among our hardest problems. And where shall we live when we get there? And, finally, should we be in the city or outside of town? If it is the latter, I am afraid we shall have to settle in some Jewish section like Far Rockaway or Arverne, because a non-Jewish community will never be able to give Beatrice a place in its life — or the children or myself. We ought to wait until David's term is over. Pity he cannot stay at the school in Haifa.

June 18

Last night I wrote letters to Sol and Linda [Lowenstein], Rosalind [Blumenthal], Marshall, Mrs. [Bertha] Weyl, Dr. Benderly, David and Dr. Biram[3] telling them that we have decided to leave here the middle of August and return to America. I said that much would hold us here, but that the controlling impulse was to get settled once and for all — a sign of advancing age.

I hope this getting settled — i.e. getting a home and my getting work and an income — may help Beatrice out of her present despondency. She despairs of herself — and of me. As to herself, she says she has not developed in mind, that her health is uncertain, and what seems to distress her greatly, that she and I are not interested in the same things. All these years, since the Kehillah and the War, she has loathed the publicity stunts that I have been engaged in, but she has been cherishing the hope that I would do some writing. That is to her taste, and that she considers a worthy occupation. But I have told her, I am more of a talker than a writer, and that I cannot promise to do writing. I hope to do writing, but there are difficulties. I am no scholar in any branch of Jewish learning. I know enough to talk, but writing is different. As to my experiences in Jewish life, I may be able to put them down in some worthy written form, and I should like to, and I shall try, but I can give no promises about it. Beatrice made the interesting remark that my name is never in any list of written works. I have often felt the same thing.

This is, as far as I remember, the first time that Beatrice has said so definitely what *she* would *want* of me. Surely, something that I want too.

Now, what to do? Where can I write best? Not where shall I have most *leisure*, but where shall I get most impulse? I have often thought

216

that this might be Germany. There there are men, schools, movements that go deep. But I am afraid that this is just another pipe dream, and that the difficulty is in myself. I suppose I am lazy, but I know also that I have too high a standard in relation to writing, and that I am not able to reach this standard. Perhaps that, too, is but another form of vanity and selfishness. If I had to earn my daily bread, I have no doubt I should not have these very refined discussions with myself, but would go ahead and *do* (but hardly write for a living). In brief, I am not a writer, and Beatrice would like me to be one. Well, then, try, and maybe you will suprise yourself. Where? Anywhere, as long as you determine to keep some time for yourself each day and burn the midnight oil each night.

1. Paul Abelson (1878-1953). Labor arbitrator and educator; born in Kovno, Lithuania, and brought to the United States in 1892. He received his Ph.D. in history from Columbia University in 1906. He was founder of Madison House Settlement in New York City; a member of conciliation staff of the New York cloak and suit industry; a director of the Kehillah's Bureau of Industry; an impartial chairman for fur, men's caps, and other industries.
2. Warburg and others suggested to Magnes that he return to New York and head a Jewish education fund that would support all phases of Jewish education.
3. Arthur Biram (1878-1967). Hebrew educator; born in Bischofswerda, Germany; studied at University of Berlin and Lehranstalt fuer die Wissenschaft des Judentums in Berlin. He emigrated to Palestine in 1914; was appointed by Zionist Organization to be principal of Reali High School in Haifa.

43

Journal Entry

August 1, 1923
Under the tree, Abu Ghosh — El Kubeibe road[1]

Beaten, physically and morally. Physically, both Beatrice and I have malaria, mine in an aggravated form. The doctors say that leaving the country, for a time at least, is desirable, and if an attack recurs, necessary. Beatrice has lost her 14 lbs. of which we have been so proud for a year now. No free choice. We had wanted to leave the country — if we left — because we had chosen freely to do it. But we leave now under a kind of physical compulsion. Morally, we have not arrived at the peace of mind we had been looking forward to. It has come at times and has stayed at times. Nerves have not been calmed. A vision and a task beyond self have not been achieved. No joy in making any choice — everything seeming indifferent. Not much greater community of interests than a year ago. The common interest in the land is something, but we are leaving it. It has been an interesting time, but it is not ending triumphantly. Perhaps I am unduly depressed after the malaria. I hope that is it.

Monday, August 6, 1923

These few days of rest have made all the difference — days of understanding, of closer approach. The decision is again in our hands. We are again free to choose, again masters of the situation. Whichever way we decide it will be because we want it thus, because thus we think it better, not because we must. For Jerusalem and for New York, there are ways of cooperation, objects of common interests. We have explored a couple of them and they seem possible and good. For Jerusalem: common interest in archaeology and history, and religions and churches and libraries — and culture. Work together. As to Hadassah and *Kuppat Milveh* and the rest with their unending line of *shamashim* and documents, they will have only my spare time of an afternoon now and again. They will become completely secondary. Our primary consideration will be the other — Jerusalem with its cultural riches, the land with its history and places and peoples of interest. More details of the cooperative settlements among the Jews, more knowledge of all the schools — Jew and non-Jew. Invite Jewish and non-Jewish scholars. What scholarly work of all kinds is being done in the country?

For New York: invite individuals and groups to interest themselves in creative work or ideas, or plans of individuals — the significant and those who want to be significant or should be encouraged to be. A writer's new play or story, a young artist's first contact with connoisseurs or patrons of art, a musician's theory of Jewish music, a distinguished guest's intimate views and aspirations. Bringing various types of Jewish intellectuals together. Bringing together of creative with acquisitive (money and influence). Jewish intellectuals and non-Jewish. Eventually a kind of center for Jewish creative effort.

1. The Magneses vacationed on occasion at the German hospice in the Arab village of El Kubeibe near Jerusalem.

44

Journal: Reflections on the High Holy Days

Jerusalem, September 11, 1923
Rosh Hashannah

Jonna[1] wakes up with bad stomach. Vomit shows tons of food swallowed without chewing. Ben[2] also has a bit of temperature, so only David and I go to shul. Moss Levy[3] early *hazzan l'shaharit* [cantor for morning service]. Kesselman[4] chief *hazzan l'shaharit*. I read *tora* (the *niggun* [melody] went off well). Bentwich *haftara* [reading from the prophets] and two semi-professionals, *musaf* [additional morning service] and *shofar* [ram's horn]. The *shofarblasser* was phenomenal—not one hitch. Services lively. Bentwich announces that we expect to hold regular Sabbath services after *sukkot* at Zichron Moshe Shul. "Dr. Magnes has promised his assistance." I suppose the way to begin is to begin, but I thought more preparations and conferences necessary. During services I was thinking of term "Western" Jews used in invitation to participate in the services. All the time I have fought to be identified with "Eastern" Jews. But here in Jerusalem the term "Western" does take on a meaning that it would not have in Poland. It is further away from Europe here than Poland is. Moreover, in Zion a Jew ought to be himself, whatever he is—so I used to think. Zion is the place for differentiation—so I used to think, and so it is in theory. In practice it is a different thing, and "Western" in relation to the synagogue is about as abhorrent to the Jerusalemites as Reform is to the Orthodox. The eternal question of where the women will sit is bothering the new congregation. Miss Landau[5] has her followers, and the question is, who of the Westerners, if not the women-separationists, will be interested. They are not satisfied with having the women on one side and men on the other: there has to be complete separation. I was wondering if in some such manner the Western and the Eastern Synagogues (churches) might not have had their rise; and if some earnest Easterners now will not begin the "Western" tendency in this way. The Western Synagogue must be in the tradition, and in Hebrew, but it must above all things seek to accommodate itself in *thought* to the best Western mind. Forms, ceremonies, customs, traditions—all may remain Eastern or whatever they now are and have become. Nor should convenience be the criterion, although Westerners do keep different hours and have not the same impassive *sitzfleisch* [patience] as our Easterners when it comes to devotions. Throughout, *ideas* must be the first consideration. E.g., the *musaf* is a substitute for the sacrifices. But Westerners do not really believe in the restoration of sacrifices. So why pray for them? Something, ancient or modern in its wording, on sacrifice can be substituted.

But the main question here, as so often and almost everywhere, is that of God. The service is full of the divinity (not so much of humanity), and there is a definite air and fullness about it that leaves no room for any questioning. Ah, the divinity, if only I knew as much, a thousandth part as much about Him as about man. Books and life are full of man. War, politics, man's greed and brutality, his capacity for nobility, the motives that guide him and his hopes, ambitions, his ugliness and beauty – a person can get a very fair notion of man, and his knowledge of man increases with the years. The essence of man's soul remains a mystery and can never be probed to its very depths, but it is possible from history, from literature, and our own experience to gain a working-picture of him.

But the Divinity: the older I get, the less I seem to know and understand about it – Him. Oh, I have the deepest of emotions. I am moved (as are but very few of the people I know, so I think) by the mystery of life, by its depth, by simple loves and friendships, by the bravery of weak persons, by sacrifice, by beauty and music, by sincere worship, public and private, or when persons kneel in a church, particularly uneducated and simple people. In a ḥassidic *klausel* [small synagogue] I am caught up in the rhythm of worship and sometimes the dark and ancient beginnings of being seem to come nearer. But God, the Father, the Comforter, the Quickener of the Dead, the Creator of the World and the soul of man, the Redeemer of mankind? Oh, how I understand all of this, and feel most of it from time to time, and how I want (and need) it all! But there is never abandon, there is always mental reservation (sometimes more, sometimes less, sometimes bordering upon disbelief, at others merging comfortably with belief). Yes, I can even (at times) come to philosophic conclusions or to the logical necessity of the God-head (as they call it), on the need in life for absolutes, for *the* Absolute. But I am never free of doubt, and at times doubt is the major force (at times belief is). I have no doubt that many a preacher and "religious" person is in a similar quandary, and it is no wonder that so many throw themselves into social work and make that the substitute for "religion". Of course, it's part of religion – everything in life is. But that is not *belief*, belief in God, a living force, be He near or far, an active force in individual life and in the redemption of mankind.

It might not be so hard to have a polite belief in divinity, as the Theists (Deists) have, but that is no active *religious* force. Also, for those whom doubt crushes, what a blessing and comfort is authoritarian religion – Christian and Jewish. Perhaps that is the kind I need. But that's the kind I can't (my mind can't, my makeup can't) accept. My religion has to be free and voluntary and flowing and capable of abandon if it is to mean sincere and creative prayer. I can sing with abandon, and I can sometimes *davven* with abandon (what a great thing *davvening* is), but that is not belief grounded in mind, in the whole being.

I presume it is only for such as I am that the "Western" Synagogue would have to meddle with prayer book versions, etc. For the true believer (and for the simple, as for the shallow, of whom there are considerable numbers), what difference, essentially, does it, can it make if a passage here or there is crude and "oriental" in its fulsomeness and imagery; what difference if there be sacrifices restored in the prayers? He has the main fact, the supreme fact — God. There is nothing that can compare with this. Everything else must fade into insignificance. For some it may mean quietism — calm, serenity despite the ills of humanity, of life. For others it is a message to do, to battle for the Lord, to save men, to redeem life in justice and truth and mercy and beauty and brotherhood and fellowship. Sometimes I feel this call to action, to help redeem. But is that from "Divinity"? Divinity has never appeared to me to tell me. May it not be sheer humanity, great human pity and love? "To justify the ways of God to man" — what a noble undertaking — difficult, painful, but when done by eager, honest souls and minds, how glorious, and pathetic, and encouraging!

I often talk this way to myself. But I have never thought to commit the "*sin*" of putting it into writing. Writing is for other eyes, as well, and I do not convey in a few stray notes, all that I think and feel on this side, and on that. If I went to Europe after Hebrew Union College and came back refusing to be a preacher; if I have wandered from Brooklyn to Emanu-El and through Jeshurun, and if I have done administration and organizing and social-political work; if I have not dared to create my public platform, to be a "great preacher pointing the way," and if I am still here in Zion (at ease), and apprehensive of each "sermon" I am asked to give and of the "sermons" I would be giving in America — there, there is the chief source of it all: I am a deeply "religious" man, but Divinity is hazy and vague to me, not always active in me. I may be a religious man, but I am not a religious leader. An understanding of God is what is lacking within me. I doubt Him and question Him — His ways, His aloofness, the sufferings He causes man, the uncertainty of life, the blackness of death. When I read a statement like that of Bertrand Russell in the booklet I picked up yesterday: "I hope that every kind of religious belief will die out . . . I regard it as belonging to the infancy of human reason, and to a stage of development which we are now outgrowing," I have greatly mixed feelings. I do not at all hope religious belief will die out. I hope we shall learn more of God — if there is God; more of the soul, of the creative power in life and in the universe. We *are* in the infancy of human reason, and maybe for that reason we know so little of God, of that Great Fact outside the self, outside of, beyond man—be that Fact, that Power (or those Powers) evil, or good, or just non-moral.

Yet on the other hand, all the rest of our knowledge is outgrowing our "religious" knowledge, i.e. knowledge—*real* not merely abstruse knowledge—of "God." The passion to make a better, cleaner, more beautiful world is, so it would appear, deeper and more real—i.e. giving rise to action—in those who are not "religious" than in the confessedly "religious." We are learning more about the material side of life, more about astronomy and abstract sciences than about philosophy and theology. The philosophy and theology we learn seem to revolve in the same radius. Where are the extensions of our knowledge, that is, our living knowledge of Divinity? Certainly, if measured only by the "pure light" of cold "reason," Divinity, to say the least, can be (and has been) as easily disproved as proved. Does it then all come down to our desires? Oh, I desire God, with all my heart. But does that make Him real, does that give Him existence, actuality outside of me? Or, does He exist only in the desire, in the human heart? Do we, then, worship a desire, pray to the human heart? Most of our philosophic conclusions, as indeed most of our conclusions in life, have their final basis in our desires, our natures, our wills. Oh, but I desire God. I will God. Yet my reason has never, never genuinely, wholly accepted Him as a conclusion. Perhaps I have not read enough or thought enough. I must read and read, and search and search. But ought I not to have heard of that book or that man who had found God with his reason and his soul and his life—who had found Him for such as me? That's why I have wanted to go to Germany. They write and search and philosophize and dig so much and so deep. Perhaps the book, the man, the saving word, the light is there, or somewhere else. But would I not have heard of it?

"It is not in Heaven or across the sea, but nigh unto you, in your heart, to do it." That was about the *mitsva*—something to do. How simple that is, how easy to *do*. Duty is real. Your desires to do, to make things better, to assuage suffering, to create new life are real. You can accept their decision frankly, even though the materialist philosophers tell you they are but desires, self-deception with no validity in anything absolute or eternal. With divinity as sanction, your duty takes on additional fervor, and it assumes permanence. But even without divinity your duty, your desire for new heavens and a new earth for man can be (and is, for many, many) genuine. If divinity were something to *do* then 10 times the 613 *mitsvot*—provided you knew that was divinity—would not be near enough. *Yissurim shel ahava* [the sufferings of love]—if you *knew* or felt that these sufferings were from divinity — with or without purpose, with or without hope — then why not? Flagellation and the infliction of greater pain upon yourself would be pleasing.

God is to be recognized by his works? Which of his works? A composite picture of Him taken from the beauty and ugliness of nature and of man would hardly be flattering to omnipotence and omniscience. God is the suffering, not omnipotent, not omniscient Being of William James, H. G. Wells, and Richard Roberts — requiring the help of man in order to save the world of man which He has made? I held this theory once, too, thinking it fitted in best as a working hypothesis with the realities of life. But do you pray to an hypothesis? How do they know such a half-God exists? Has he appeared to them? There is no reason to accept this being as more *real* than the God of the Fathers, simply because on that hypothesis some of the imperfections of life are better explained away.

It is, so it seems to me, a more reasonable assumption to lay down the dogma: man is capable of salvation, of saving himself; pitch in and help. Your work, your life may tip the scales. Why bring in the hypothetical half-God here? If you ask how we know that man is essentially capable of salvation, we would answer that we do not *know*, but that we *think* so, we feel so, we desire it so, we see that man has great qualities, as well as petty ones, and we hope, we are sure his great qualities can overcome the others. At any rate, we shall act and live and suffer and die and rejoice and create on that assumption, act and live as though it were true. Our experience of man gives us the right to this assumption, although we are aware that the contrary assumption can be held validly. We are ready to take our chances, on our *conviction*, our *belief* in man's redeeming qualities. We have seen some of them, we know how they work, we hold them to be "right" and "true" and "good." We can act in this way wholeheartedly. We are not sure that we shall win, but it is worth everything, worth life itself, to try. We can accept such a working hypothesis — knowing it to be hypothesis — because it has to do with man. Man and hypothesis — that is an inner contradiction. But suppose we brought God in? God — hypothesis! What hollowness, what a contradiction in the heart that yearns for God in order that there might be certainty. What need of God if there be only an hypothesis? On the basis of hypotheses we can work out a very cogent, acceptable working-program in life.

This half-God is but the half-answer of those who are in the same position as I am — who yearn for God with their hearts, yet who need grasp Him, and perceive Him, and naturally yearn to have Him with reason as well. *Their* life needs him, but life and reason do not reveal Him convincingly, wholly. Perhaps we are all waiting for the appearance of a great personality (or many of them), who will show us the presence of God, who will guide and convince our reason, and who will give wings to the yearnings of our heart; a great personality who will be a master of science and philosophies, and who will be a great reader of the heart and a lover of mankind, and who will lead the way in the struggle (the final struggle?) towards the new world.

How futile it is for Christians to talk of Jesus as having said the last word. *Love!* Of course. That is *doing* something, that is what we want to do with or without his inspiration. Because a man gives inspiration to thousands, that does not mean he has said the last word or the necessary word. We can get the inspiration to *do* from a thousand sources. Surely we Jews have sources. But the Christian *theology? That* is what talks of Divinity. They say that Jesus was the Son of God, that he came as a revelation, as a sacrifice, as messiah. Happy they who can believe such as this! But how does that appeal to our *reason?* Is not the revelation on Sinai simpler, more reasonable, more "progressive" (in fact, if not in point of time) than the Christian dispensation? But the revelation on Sinai, is *it* the final test for the reason of man? Of course it is not. But some of those early Jews and Christians were right about one thing: they wanted not a political messiah (King of the Jews) alone, they wanted the religious, the spiritual messiah as well. And if we were to get our just social order, and its abolition of poverty (which is a far way off), we would still be *m'vakshe adonai* [seekers after God]; we would still be in need of conquering human suffering and death; we would still be in need of approaching closer and closer to the sources of creation, of creative power.

God as creative power, not only as life, but as the fashioner and the shaper of life and the creative interpreter of its meaning — that is the beginning, the *bereshit*, and that is the ultimate end towards which great men strive. The moral values of good and of evil, the mind values of true and false, the esthetic values of beautiful and ugly, the creation of these more and more in individuals and in society — that is the beginning of the end.

No wonder men could worship the sun, throw their arms out to it, the great creator of warmth and growth; or the water, which slakes the thirst of the parched soil and helps create food and shade. To throw your arms out to God, the creator; to ask for creative power more and more, to create the good and make the bad serve as so much raw material for the good; to deepen and broaden and enlighten the truth of things, to make man see and understand *every thing*, to make the world and life and man stronger and stronger and more healthful and more sensitive to beauty of all kinds; to increase man's moral stature, to strike the shackles from his mind; to give him access to the springs of creation; to pray for such with devotion and enthusiasm and abandon — what a release for the pent-up emotions, what an increase of warmth and power — *if, if* it were to a Being with objective existence and validity outside ourselves.

Such a person as I have pictured myself to be has no business tinkering with a Prayer Book, be it Western or Eastern. But what is more serious: what of my becoming that "Preacher" when I return to New York? Could I establish a platform which, besides standing for the new moral and social world, I should be bold enough to call "religious"? For I *am* religious in that I want God, yet my platform would not be "religious" in that I have not found Him; "religious" in that I am searching for Him, want Him brought nearer by those who think they know Him and understand Him, yet not "religious" in that He should also be discussed, and questioned, perhaps demolished, by those who think they have not proven Him? Can *I* say as much as this publicly, I who have been a preacher of religion; I who feel myself to be "religious"; I who am willing to subscribe to the doctrine: "God above the State, God above Everything"; I who believe that leadership should be in the hands only of those who are certain and feel they know the way? And yet could I say less than this? Could I, knowing myself as I am, preach the sanctity of life and the search for justice, for truth, for beauty, for the new City of God, and yet conceal my religious uncertainties? Or is it perhaps the function of a "religious" teacher in these uncertain days, to lay his soul bare before the admiring and scoffing gaze of the multitude, in order that the racked and storm tossed of the times may serve as so much clay in the hands of a master potter of tomorrow?

That spirit that is working in man, moving him to seek greater right, and truth, and beauty, driving him to work for a better society, for clearer thoughts, for deeper insight — is *that* God? Oh, I hope it may be. But do we *know* that it is? It is at least of the stuff that we should want God to be created. Certainly this spirit — may we, in reason, call it divine? If so by what reason? — works its way wondrously, deviously, and in the most unsuspected of places. [It works] through the wise and the ignorant, in and out of churches (mostly out?), through individuals and groups, through history and at the moment — sometimes with disastrous effects for the individual, often without leaving a trace in the sands, but at times with benefit to men. The spirit that makes men yearn for freedom for a fuller expression of life morally (socially), in reason and in beauty, the spirit that impels men to pursue the ideal, to pursue the spirit — is that God?

1. Jonathan Magnes.
2. Benedict Magnes.
3. Moss Levy (1892–1967). British Zionist and businessman; settled in Jerusalem in 1920.
4. Robert Kesselman (1881–1942). Accountant and active Zionist. Born in Russia; migrated to the United States in 1901; settled in Palestine in 1919, serving as auditor for the Zionist Commission; was employed by the Mandatory government; in 1926 established his own accounting firm.

5. Ann Landau (1873–1945). Jewish educator; born in London. In 1899 she was chosen by the Anglo-Jewish Association to be principal of the Evelina de Rothschild School for Girls in Jerusalem, which she headed until her death. During the First World War she interceded on behalf of Jews persecuted by the Turkish governor of Jerusalem until she herself was deported.

45

Journal: Universalism and Nationalism

Jerusalem, March, 1924

After you have rooted yourself in your nation you can overcome nationalism—not before. Everyone belongs to some people—even the most universalistic and denationalized amongst us. Tolstoi was certainly a Russian of Russians. Every man speaks the language of his mother and loves his home, has a given physique, and is influenced in a thousand ways by his heredity and his history. There are some of the healthy-minded, normal peoples who are so well established that they need not give much thought to the national aspects of existence. This was so much more before than since the war. A man like Scott Nearing, for example, is American—speaks English, belongs to a dominant race, has none of the self-consciousness of a minority, yet he can talk universalism without in any way dreaming that in the process *he* will become assimilated to some other people. He can overcome his nationalism almost from birth, as it were. There is no danger, no chance of his ever becoming basically anything else than he is, or of any one asking him to, so universalism means for him growing up out of his roots normally like a firmly rooted tree. It is like the musician who has his technique so perfect that he need no longer bother much about it; it is the spirit, the higher things with which he is concerned.

With a Jew this is different. Many things predispose him to universalism—his prophets, his wanderings, his experiences—but he has a much harder job overcoming his nationalism. The only Jew who can really overcome it is the Jew who feels himself firmly rooted in the Jewish nation, for whom there is not the slightest possibility that he can be anything else than a Jew. Such a Jew can become a genuinely tolerant universalist. He cannot give himself up, and he can therefore forget himself in higher things. Klausner writes in Hebrew, lives in Jerusalem, and is in general deeply rooted in the Jewish soil. Just such a man can write an objective study of Jesus and Christianity.

The doctrine of the Reform Jews was universalism. Who can quarrel with the doctrine? It is the doctrine of the prophets, of human brotherhood, of the merging of nations and races and peoples into a spiritual synthesis. But while preaching this doctrine they were all the while trying to escape from their Judaism, their Jewish fundamental selves. They made this doctrine an excuse for abandoning their selves, instead of growing into this doctrine with their feet firmly planted on the Jewish earth. The result? They uprooted much of their wholesome, vital *Volkstum* [nationality] and proved themselves false to the very doctrine of universalism they preached. For the most part they remained part-Jews, and in every country became chauvinistic and superpatriotic. Universalism as a mere excuse to become something your comfort or your social standing demands is a spurious universalism.

Two kinds of Jews can become universalists: the Jew who knows and thinks so little of himself as a Jew that he can in very truth say he is no Jew but an internationalist, universalist (e.g. Trotsky), and the Jew who has so thoroughly grounded himself in his Judaism that his universalism becomes the development and crown of his Judaism.

Many a Jew of the latter type is himself predisposed to this higher attitude, but he is afraid that his people is not strong enough nationally to bear this development. The question is really fundamental, and my answer is that the Jews are a strong, vital people and not a weak one — and this despite pogroms and wanderings. They are mighty and vital physically. They seem incapable of being annihilated, and give Jewish children a chance in fresh air and with good food and see how they blossom. His spiritual forces are equally great. See how he maintains himself and grows with the Diaspora, and how he is embedding himself in Eretz Israel. This very experiment must give every one of us courage. It shows that the Jew can and will live apart and at the same time render homage to the highest of human ideals — witness his communistic settlements.

General rule: so to act as though the Jews were strong and not weaklings. So to act as though Zion were already rebuilt and were sending her messengers out into the world of man. Zion will be rebuilt; she is already rebuilt in our minds and souls. Therefore with our feet in the soil of our Judaism let us seek our brethren of all peoples. Fear for the Jews or fear of others cannot be our guiding force, only confidence in Jewish strength and belief in great human ideals.

46

To Felix M. Warburg
Paris

Jerusalem, April 11, 1924

Dear Mr. Warburg,

Your letter of March 29 from Vienna came today, and I am glad you found Gerry[1] and his wife well.

You will be interested to know that Mr. Jacobus Kann,[2] who is one of the Trustees of the Wolfssohn Foundation, has definitely come to the conclusion that the £15,000 in his possession for a library building is to be expended in connection with the University buildings. We were there the other day. The Jewish National Fund is ready to donate the land, which is in front of the present structure and which is the highest spot facing Jerusalem. We feel that the Jewish Department should be housed in the same structure. This will, of course, require more than the £15,000, but this amount is a good beginning. Mr. Kann has asked me to serve with him as a committee of two to work out details.

I am absolutely in accord with you that in the administration of the University's affairs "an absentee committee would spell a failure." The London Committee wants headquarters to be in London, and the Paris Committee in Paris, whereas the only possible headquarters for a Jerusalem University is Jerusalem. In my opinion they ought to appoint a general board with representatives from various countries of the world, and also an adequate number from Palestine. The Palestine members should be the administrative committee and should render its reports to the general board, monthly or quarterly, or however often it may be determined. The general board should meet annually in Jerusalem, if possible (this would help bring some of the members here occasionally), or, if not possible, in such other place as the majority of members desire. The same would hold good with special meetings of the general board, if such meetings really are necessary.

I proposed to the London Committee a meeting of representatives of the various groups, and I would be ready to go to Europe (perhaps on the way to America) to attend such a meeting, which could also discuss all outstanding questions. For some reason that is not quite comprehensible to me, they have not as yet agreed to such a meeting. But I do hope that before they face us with faits accomplis — they have suggested they might — they will see the wisdom of beginning only after questions of organization have been thoroughly threshed out by all concerned. I have written them about your proposed gift and about your readiness to place its administration in my hands and in the hands of such colleagues as I might select. Perhaps they will now be readier to move forward on a united front.

On the other had it is, in my opinion, equally a mistake on your part to make as a condition my participation in a "leading position." I want, of course, to be on the general board, and, if I am in Palestine, on the administration committee. But to go beyond this, as I am afraid in your friendship for me you are tempted to do, would not be right. You are ready to make your handsome gift for the University, not for any individual. It should be administered by good men, and I should like to help find them. But that need not mean that I must necessarily be the chief administrator. Moreover, I am also thinking of other things—going to America, for example; the time may be ripe for that General Culture Fund. Also, I should not want to have it seem as though I had tried to interest you in the University with myself in mind. In addition to being on it myself, I should be glad to represent you on the board, or any other givers. Let it rest at that, and let the whole thing develop organically and objectively with as little reference to persons as possible, and I am sure you will be satisfied and a great idea will be helped forward.

When you get to see the Baron,[3] I hope you may be able to persuade him to have his representative, Grand Rabbin Levi[4] look upon the whole project with a wider vision, and with less prejudice to things Palestinian than he has shown in years gone by.

And if you get to see Dr. Weizmann, I am sure you will be able easily to persuade him to try for a general agreement all around. The London Committee also has in mind three old or sick men as the first professors. Whereas they are very good scholars, and it is all very well to have pity on them, that is not the way to start this important undertaking. What we need is men in the full vigor of life.

As to America, I should like to get there in the not too distant future in order to look over the general situation and specifically to see if I can be of help in getting that Fund for Jewish Idealism going. It ought to be made to call out every form of idealism among the Jews, religious, educational, social. The Jerusalem University would be one of its high spots. If Beatrice were to come along, I should be wanting to leave soon. But she does not think she should leave the children now, so I may put off the trip until the children's summer vacation begins, which is at the end of July.

For the Passover week we are to take the children north. We shall celebrate the Seder with Miss Berger[5] and her orphans at Balfouria, and we shall go to Safed via Beisan and the Jordan Valley, which you saw only from a distance. Then we are going to the northernmost colonies—

Metullah and Kefar Giladi. We had a picnic yesterday and the day before with the Bentwiches, and we talked of you.

Give our love to all the children.

Yours truly, JLM

1. Gerald F. Warburg (1901–1971). Son of Felix Warburg. He made his debut as a cellist with the New York Philharmonic, 1925; member of Stradivarius Quartet, 1930–1936.

2. Jacobus Kann (1872–1945). Dutch Jewish banker and Zionist leader; helped establish the Jewish National Library on Mount Scopus.

3. Baron Edmond James de Rothschild.

4. Israel Levi (1856–1939). Rabbi, scholar, and French communal leader. He served as chief rabbi of France from 1919 to 1939. He was a member of the governing board of the Hebrew University's Institute for Jewish Studies.

5. Sophia Berger (1882–1958). A founder and first treasurer of Hadassah. Born in La-Crosse, Wisconsin, she emigrated to Palestine in 1918 to take charge of orphans for the JDC. Married Emanuel N. Mohl.

47

To Roger Baldwin
New York

Jerusalem, January 30, 1925

Dear Roger Baldwin,

I am very glad that Scott Nearing has been elected President of the American Fund for Public Service.[1] Much as I appreciated the honor of being even the nominal President, it made me feel uncomfortable. I am particularly glad to know that the differences that existed last year (I do not even know what their nature was) are now out of the way. Even though I am no longer a member of the board, I should greatly appreciate receiving the minutes, or in some other way being kept in touch with the Fund's problems and activities. I have always read whatever was sent me with the greatest interest, and I am really sorry not to be able to participate in the work.

Heaven knows when, if ever, we shall be back. I am thick in this very fascinating task of helping create a center of Jewish learning in this ancient (and new) center of the Jewish people. Compared with the political and industrial problems that face you in New York, one is really at ease here in Zion. But the moral problems are the same, though not nearly so intense. For one who is interested in history and philosophy and religion, this is a glorious place. I wonder if I could ever again get up steam to make my way through an American task. Absence from America does not seem to make the heart grow fonder. [Written in margin here: It does for many of the people there.] I feel myself very much one of the Jewish people, and that seems to give one freer play to be an internationalist than any other way I have yet discovered. Very often I wish I might have it out with you and Scott Nearing and Norman Thomas.

I cannot get over thinking of Albert DeSilver.[2] What a horrible end for one of the sweetest, most dependable of men.

Please give my best regards to the members of the Board of Directors of the Fund, and to my friends of the Civil Liberties Union.

Mrs. Magnes and I hope Miss Doty is well. With kindest greetings, I am

Yours truly, JLM

1. The Fund was established in 1921 by Charles Garland to support liberal and radical causes. Roger Baldwin was the most active figure in administering the fund.
2. Albert DeSilver (1888–1924). Lawyer and associate director of the American Civil Liberties Union. He was killed in a train accident in December 1924.

48

Journal: The University "Opening"

Jerusalem, March 22, 1925

1. The falsehood of "opening" what does not exist. Warburg: "Ein jüdische Bluff." Adler[1]: wants to go to Petach Tikvah for work. Will create false impression, and lose confidence of universities and scholarly world. For sake of big impression, making of University a propaganda instrument. Eder[2]: "Want to advertise Palestine."

2. Balfour: making University into political instrument. If Balfour brought here by English to open legislative assembly, or on change of High Commissioners, in order to confirm *English* determination to uphold Balfour Declaration, that is different from having Jews bring him here.

Relations with Arabs, Muslim world, whole Near East exacerbated. Horovitz[3] reports Egyptian scholars as now definitely hostile. University has political aspect in their eyes now. Only help for this is over a number of years to do useful scholarly work, particularly in language, literature, culture of East. The Jews the tool of imperialism.

3. The worst aspect: that of opening under shadow of guns, *sub auspiciis regis*. Our high spiritual enterprise defiled by desire of Zionist leaders for "advertisement of Palestine" consequent on Balfour's coming. Any other person in the world might have been invited—not the author of the Balfour Declaration. A red rag to a bull, and of course 100 extra British gendarmerie in Russian barracks, and police prohibition of school children's parades, etc. If "Opening" had inner meaning, should have been Palestine Jewish folk festival. All of the spontaneity robbed, and the military on guard.

As I write, Jonathan has just come back from Danzigers:[4]

"Did you hear that singing and parading, father? It was a great crowd up by the training college. Peter Danziger said, '*Atta rotse l'kabbel makkot? Im ken lekh alehem*'[Do you want a beating? If you do, go to them]. They wanted to hit Dr. Danziger, and all because Balfour is coming. They are singing their national song. I went down the wall into the training school grounds and so didn't have to go by them."

Abdul's brother said: Balfour *mush tayib* [Balfour is no good].

March 28, 1925

The excitement and the exaltation of the Balfour visit very great. As Jacobs said today: "It was taking a great risk having Balfour here; but now that nothing has happened, it's just like getting the Balfour Declaration over again. Great political gain." Weizmann said the other night: "It's taking a great risk, but it's worth it." The reception at Tel Aviv praised by everyone. Balfour declared that the Declaration is unchangeable. Whole world listening and looking on. Even Manya [Shochat] said: "Great thing that so many Goyim are coming and getting interested in Palestine." (I answered: 'They would have come here for the University and other occasions without Balfour and bluff.' Mistake to think that they have come only because of Balfour and the exaggerated picture of what University is.)

But to my mind, politically (leaving morally alone) it is a real loss. It means that it will take that much longer to get over the handicap of the Balfour Declaration. The beginnings of getting over it had been made in the last two years. Now we shall have to begin all over again. Balfour will be leaving soon. The excitement will be over. What will be left? In the mind of the outside world—the fact that the Jews rejoiced and the Arabs struck. In the Arab-Moslem mind, increased bitterness and determination. In the Jewish mind outside of Palestine, increased inflation. Among the Jews of Palestine, increased difficulties with their neighbors.

H.E.[5] had said: Arabs oppose so violently because they know that

Balfour's coming means once and for all ratification of Declaration. How? Will Balfour give official interpretation?

It is very kind to have given Balfour the opportunity of seeing the land of the Bible, and it is fine of the Jews here to show gratitude. But surely they cannot justify the arousing of increased bitterness and determination on part of Arabs?

This is all taking place at same time as renewed tensions in Egypt. It makes Palestine but part and parcel of the general scheme and tactics of British imperialism. The strike was an impressive demonstration of Arab unity and discipline — Jerusalem, Haifa, everything closed, no violence. Beginning to learn passive resistance. Much more powerful than their stupid outbursts of violence.

This visit is the logical conclusion of the Balfour Declaration. Those who welcomed and who talk of Balfour Declaration must not complain about this visit and its consequences, except that they see that the Declaration itself is not all it was thought to be.

There can be no other such demonstration. One might say that this is the last of the war-"victories" of the Zionists.

The problem now is practical work. The University will suffer, but it must get beyond all this, just as the country itself must.

As to policy for the future, a mandatory power that will maintain the peace, the open door, cultural and economic freedom for Jew and non-Jew.

1. Saul Adler (1895–1966). Physician and parasitologist; born in Russia and brought to England in 1900. He studied at Leeds and Liverpool Universities; joined staff of Hebrew University in 1924, becoming professor and director of its Parasitological Institute in 1928; fellow of the Royal Society; received Israel Prize for Medicine, 1957.

2. Montague David Eder (1865–1936). British psychoanalyst and Zionist leader. Medical officer of the Zionist Commission for Palestine following First World War; close collaborator with Weizmann; member of executive board of the Zionist Organization.

3. Joseph Horovitz (1874–1931). Orientalist, University of Frankfurt am Main; advised Magnes in establishing the School of Oriental Studies at the Hebrew University.

4. Dr. Felix Danziger (1888–1948). He and his family were close friends of the Magnes family. Danziger was a German Zionist and surgeon; emigrated to Palestine with his family in 1923.

5. His Excellency, the High Commissioner, Lord Herbert Samuel (see glossary of names).

49

To A[had] H[a'am][1]
Tel Aviv

Jerusalem, April 1925

Now that the storm connected with the University inauguration is beginning to subside, I feel the need of writing to you, one of the moral guides of our generation.

As you are aware, I have not been enthusiastic about two phases of the "opening." First because we have, unfortunately, very little to open, and I was fearful lest we create the false impression that we already had a University when really we have not; and second because with the coming of Lord Balfour the University inauguration would be converted into a political demonstration which in the long run would do us no good.

I continued to do what I could, nevertheless, as chairman of the Arrangements Committee to make the inauguration as true and as worthy as possible, because I feel, as I have felt for many years, that the idea of the University is of the utmost importance in the development of Judaism.

What has the presence of Lord Balfour meant? To me it has been the discovery of a rare personality.

We have had the privilege of meeting an Englishman of the very finest traditional stripe — a man of the utmost charm, a man who in an extraordinary way combines statesmanship with philosophy and letters, a lover of the Bible and the Holy Land, a man without the faintest prejudice against any race or religion. His stately figure and the joy with which he has seen the progress made by our pioneers in the land will ever be memorable; and one cannot help but be glad that this distinguished and venerable statesman and scholar has had this happiness, and that the Jews of the land acclaimed him with such genuine expression of gratitude and esteem.

But could not the University have been inaugurated without stirring up the Moslem world against us? And must it not have been clear from the outset that the coming of Lord Balfour would do just that thing?

It is difficult for me to write this because the noble Lord conferred so much distinguished grace and beauty by his wholehearted and generous participation in the proceedings. But would not the memorable scene in the open theater on the first day; the dignified presentation addresses by the learned representatives of universities and academies on the second

234

day; and the great interest of the Jewish people both here and in the diaspora have been possible (perhaps in not so large, but nevertheless in very large measure) without making the coming of the author of the Balfour Declaration of at least equal importance with the opening of the University itself?

I shall not go into the merits of the Balfour Declaration. I have printed my views on that subject. I have given expression to that view in print, and that is sufficient. And I grant you that this celebration is really a logical conclusion to the Balfour Declaration period of the war.

But why push doubtful political expedients to their logical conclusion particularly in connection with our University? Under the wise guidance of H.E. the High Commissioner and the interpretation he has given the Balfour Declaration, the country was being brought to settle down to a period of peaceful work; and the improvement in the relations between Jew and Arab was becoming more manifest day by day. It was to have been expected that the University of all enterprises would be that agency which upon the high plane of pure scholarship, would in the course of time, bring about a spiritual reconciliation between the two most gifted races of Semitic stock. But the University has become the instrument of the very reverse. It may take us long years of hard work to overcome this disadvantage.

There are some who think that because fortunately no excesses were committed in connection with Lord Balfour's presence here that therefore the Arab demonstration had no meaning. I must confess that the very absence of any violence deeply moved me. I should like to think that this was due not to the shadow of government bayonets, but the conviction that is growing in the Moslem world as elsewhere that understanding and reconciliation between peoples can come only through pacifist and nonviolent methods. It is a good augury for the future.

All that we Jews here have a right to ask is peace, and the open door for our immigrants, and the opportunity without let or hindrance to live our spiritual and cultural life. This is all the Arabs have a right to ask for themselves, or any other people in this international land. Thus the country can be developed and forms of life created upon the basis of a free field and no favors. Our University should be the highest of our spiritual endeavors, preaching peace and practicing it, devoted to the passionate pursuit of truth, to the ideals of righteousness and brotherhood.

I am writing you in order to solicit an answer from you as our great ethical teacher. The inauguration of the University is, I hope and believe, one of the great moments of our history, and we should be unworthy of this great hour were we not to seek out its deeper spiritual meaning.

1. The handwritten original was a draft of a letter Magnes apparently planned to translate into Hebrew and send to Ahad Ha'am.

235

50

Journal: President Eliot[1]

Cambridge, Mass., May 28, 1925

Problem that chiefly interested him was: how will it be possible to get Jewish student from America to go there (to the Hebrew University).

"Now let me ask you a question: Are you not concerned with the fact that the young Jews of America have fallen away from the ways of their forefathers? They have forsaken their own religion, and they have no religion in its place. What can be done to help them here? Will the Jerusalem University be able to do anything to help them? If they could go to Jerusalem to study that could be a great thing. But can you get them to go?"

I answered that we must in the first instance get their leaders and teachers, their rabbis and leading minds to go for graduate research work. They would influence their communities upon their return. Then by means of publications. Then by interesting (or perhaps inspiring) visitors and tourists. The University would widen the perspective of Judaism for the Jewish intellectual.

"Do you know Mr. Mortimer Schiff?"[2] He had had this experience: last summer Mr. Schiff had rented a very expensive place out at N.E. Harbor, Maine, and had brought his whole family there. He wanted to get into the tennis club, the swimming club, etc. But the bigoted neighbors would not let him in. Then M.L.S. came to C.W.E. and the latter tried, but without success. So M.L.S. stayed most of the summer in N.Y. A servant who worked there and for the Eliots had told him that on the card tray in the hall was just one visiting card. That's the way with men of M.L.S.'s type: they want to get into Christian society by way of sports. When I told him (Eliot) I was afraid that M.L.S. would not give anything, he said he was not surprised. He agreed with me that the spiritual state of such a man was very sad, and he broke into a broad smile when I said that such men almost get what they deserve. He often spoke in high terms of Felix Warburg and Jacob Schiff.

"Do the young American Jews really *study*?" They enter college and university, and Jews give money to these. But does not the majority of these students enter because that is a rather easy way to a higher social position and a career?

Using the Institute of Physics and Mathematics as an example, I drew the conclusion that all of knowledge was one, and that our theology and philosophy and the basis of our ethics had to take into account the results of scientific research; that just as Maimonides had codified the sources and the tradition, and had at the same time written his *Guide to the Perplexed*, so would the University apply the same method.

He said that this was very good reasoning, and that it would attract Europeans. But Americans — could they be attracted by any such high ideals?

I told him of those Americans who had been there, of the requests for information I had received from students and teachers, and this pleased him exceedingly.

He was interested to hear how the University was of use to the settlers — extension courses, chemistry, medicine, pedagogy.

"Are most of the settlers capable of doing manual labor?" The rush of Jewish students in Dentistry Dept. suggested that they be put in clinics, and as a matter of fact, many weeded out because could not show manual skill, the result of long persecutions. He was happy to hear of the various manual pursuits engaged in in Palestine, particularly farming and quarrying.

"Confidentially, can you tell me how far Judaism is a religion for my very good friend Judge Mack?"

"He has a deep sentimental attachment to the tradition."

"A deep sentimental attachment to the tradition?"

"But I do not know how far that takes him into the realm of belief."

"That is just what I meant. He seems to have given up most of the practices of Judaism, such as the dietary laws."

"But his morality is greatly influenced by the traditional Jewish morality."

"Oh, undoubtedly. He is in many ways a very bold judge. But I sometimes do not understand why he should be timid in Jewish affairs. He himself admits his timidity. He is not always the fighter. But I must say that it was due to him more than to any other man that the Overseers — our second board — refused to exclude Jews from Harvard."

"I congratulate you upon the opportunity for doing real service."

"I am very happy over the outlook."

"I had expected to find a man of about 67."

"I am about 48. That seems time to be old enough."

A chuckle. "Oh, that is just in the prime of life, is it not?"

1. On his first visit to the United States on behalf of the Hebrew University Magnes called on Charles W. Eliot (1834–1926), the retired president of Harvard University.

2. Mortimer L. Schiff (1877–1931). Son of Jacob Schiff; member of Kuhn, Loeb and Co.

51

To Felix Warburg
New York

Bucharest, October 1, 1925

Dear Mr. Warburg,

We are sailing for Palestine from Constanza tomorrow, and I want to write you before leaving Europe about the meetings at Basel and Munich. Judge Mack attended both meetings, and he will give you and the American Committee extended accounts of them. I would suggest that you call a meeting of the Committee soon after his arrival.

The Basel meeting, despite its many difficulties, was very satisfactory, insofar as it marked a great step in advance of the meeting last year and in London in June. Had the meeting in Munich begun in the same spirit of understanding with which it was ended, it might have been a more valuable gathering than it was. I shall not begin to tell you of the influences—I do not even know all of them—that poisoned the atmosphere and brought about a provisional form of organization about which I am skeptical. But I am ready to try it out, and I hope the American and the Palestinian Committees will also be ready. Perhaps many of my misapprehensions are ill-founded.

I do not have here the formulation which was adopted. In short it was this:

(1) A Committee on final constitution is appointed to draft a constitution. This draft is to be submitted to the following groups: The Board of Governors, the Academic Council, the teaching staff at Jerusalem, recognized University committees (I am thinking primarily of America and Palestine) and the Jewish Agency (the Zionist Organization). The attempt is to be made to harmonize all views. Dr. Weizmann (who was not present) offered to have the first draft made. I assume that when the draft is presented to your Committee, you will submit it first to a subcommittee, consisting, among others, of Abraham Flexner[1] and Cyrus Adler. Until the first draft of the constitution is adopted, the form of organization agreed upon is to remain in force.

(2) The Board of Governors (Kuratorium) is to have two presidents, a presidium (Prof. Einstein and Dr. Weizmann). This Presidium is to have a secretary, Mr. Leo Kohn.[2] (Mr. Ginzburg[3] remains Secretary of the Board of Governors and Registrar of the University.) Although no headquarters is fixed for the Presidium, it will, to all intents and purposes, be London and probably at the Zionist office. As you know, I opposed such

a plan, as did the other Palestinians; and you and Dr. Libman[4] were good enough to send your proxies to Judge Mack and myself. Had we wished to be formal and use the proxies, we could easily have carried the matter our way. For me the main consideration against such an attitude was Prof. Einstein. I regard him as far and away the most important asset the University has at present, and he was for a European Presidium. Why, he did not make clear. If he will take an active interest, as he promises and intends, it will be of great help. I believe that he and the others present learned something of conditions in the course of the meeting. The functions of the Presidium are strictly limited: (a) to represent the University outside of Palestine; (b) to aid the University authorities of Palestine in preparing the agenda for the meetings of the Board of Governors; (c) to be responsible for the deficit, if any, in the budget adopted by the Board. The proposed budget, a copy of which I expect to send you, ends up with a deficit of £2,000 to £6,000, depending largely upon the way the Zionist University funds jump. When I get to Palestine (October 6) we shall go over the budget thoroughly again. I am determined that, as far as the Palestine end of the University is concerned, there shall be no deficit. Judge Mack will, I think, tell you how inflexible we have determined to be on this point. Any deficit, however, that may arise from any source, will have to be met by the Presidium. The whole question as to who was to be responsible for the systematic raising of funds was left in abeyance. Certainly a Kuratorium of professors won't do it.

(3) There is to be a Provisional Academic Council, Prof. Einstein, Chairman, which is to act as a Senate until a Senate is established in Jerusalem. I think this is a very good idea. This Council will propose nominations on the academic staff to the Board of Governors. In this way we shall be able to get the help of many a Jewish scholar in various parts of the world. I am eager that American scholarship be well represented on the Academic Council, and I hope that steps will be taken to secure the aid of eminent and interested scholars. The professors of the University are *eo ipso* members of the Academic Council.

(4) I have been asked to be Chancellor of the University and Mr. Bentwich to be Vice Chancellor. The complete administration of the University in Palestine is to be in our hands. You know how little I care for titles. But I shall not let my personal preferences or prejudices stand in the way. I said that before accepting I would seek the advice of the American and Palestine Committees. I would ask that your committee consider the whole question and let me hear its frank opinion.

(5) New members were elected to the Board so that, as far as I can remember, the Board of Governors now consists of the following:

America:	F. M. Warburg	Emanuel Libman
	J. W. Mack	N. S. Ratnoff[5]
	Cyrus Adler	

Holland:	Prof. Ornstein[6]	Palestine:	Ahad Ha'am
	Dr. Max Schloessinger		Ch. Bialik
Germany:	Prof. Einstein		Harry Sacher[10]
	Prof. Landau,[7]		N. Bentwich
	Goettingen		J. L. Magnes
	Prof. Ehrmann,[8]	Austria:	Prof. Freud[11]
	Berlin		Dr. Chajes[12]
	Prof. Horovitz,	England:	Dr. Weizmann
	Frankfurt		Sir A. Mond
	Prof. Taeubler,[9]		Mr. Sokolow
	Heidelberg		Dr. Hertz[13]
	Dr. Buber,		James de Rothschild[14]
	Frankfurt		Sir Herbert Samuel

The American Committee is asked to add three more members to the Board, and I would say that in view of the size and character of the Board, and the size and character of the American participation in the University, more members from America might well be added.

As far as the work of the University is concerned, the following was decided:

(1) Institute of Jewish Studies: Basel appointments ratified. I shall write more at length on this.

(2) School of Oriental Studies: Prof. Horovitz to work out plans on enclosed basis. Not open until Spring. More about this later.

(3) Courses in Pedagogy: (Mrs. Isabella Freedman was interested in this.) Adopted in principle, but not to begin before a year.

(4) Institute of Chemistry: As proposed by Prof. Fodor.[15]

(5) Institute of Microbiology: Dr. Kligler appointed as proposed.

(6) Institute of Palestine Natural History: Small allowance for Botany, Geology, and Zoology, building on the already existing Agricultural Experiment Station.

(7) The Library: To receive every possible support. The Library building to be proceeded with. Architects Geddes, Mears, and Chaikin (Palestinian). Possible contribution of University funds in two years: £10,000.

(8) Mathematics: To be begun when funds available.

(9) Physics: Too expensive for the present.

The Einstein Institute building, the money of which is given by Mr. Wattenberg (he ought to be on the American Committee) to be proceeded with. Architects: Geddes, Mears, and a Palestinian.

I am enclosing a list of contributions from America which I think can be counted on. I said that America would send $100,000 this year. I would propose that funds be sent in half-yearly installments, beginning October 1.

If I am not seasick, I shall write you more from the steamer; otherwise from Palestine. We are anxious to get back and settle down after our long wanderings. We are well and happy.

This is a funny place — a mixture of Poland and Italy.

Our love to everyone.

Yours, JLM

1. Abraham Flexner (1866–1959). American educator, expert in higher education. His 1910 survey of medical schools in the United States resulted in fundamental reform in medical education; founded and from 1930 to 1939 directed the Institute for Advanced Studies at Princeton.

2. Leo Kohn (1884–1961). Zionist leader. He was a close associate of Weizmann, representing him in Hebrew University affairs; member, political department of Jewish Agency; political adviser to Weizmann, 1948–1952; appointed to the chair of international relations at the Hebrew University, 1953.

3. Shlomo Ginzberg (later Ginossar) (1880–1969). Born in Odessa, son of Ahad Ha'am. He studied in Paris, Manchester, Geneva, Zurich; was secretary of Department of Hebrew University Affairs, Central Zionist Office, London, 1920–1921. He served on preparatory committee of Hebrew University; as inspector, Department of Education, Government of Palestine, 1922–1925; registrar and later administrator, Hebrew University, 1925–1937; adviser to the administration, 1937–1949, 1951–1953; minister to Rome, 1949–1951.

4. Emanuel Libman (1872–1946). Physician and medical researcher. He was professor of clinical medicine at College of Physicians and Surgeons, Columbia University, from 1909; chairman of American committee for the development of the medical department of the Hebrew University.

5. Nathan Ratnoff (1875–1948). Physician and community worker born in Poland; emigrated to the United States in 1891. He founded the American Jewish Physicians' Committee in 1921 and was a member of the board of governors of the Hebrew University and a key organizer of the medical faculty of the university.

6. Leonard S. Ornstein (1880–1941). Dutch Zionist and physicist; professor of mathematical and experimental physics at the University of Utrecht and director of the Utrecht Physical Laboratory.

7. Edmund Landau (1877–1938). Professor of mathematics at University of Goettingen until he was forced to resign in 1933. As visiting professor at the Hebrew University, 1927–1928, he played a major role in developing the Institute of Mathematics.

8. Rudolf Ehrmann (1879–1963). Professor of internal medicine, University of Berlin, from 1916 to 1939; professor at New York University Medical School from 1939 to 1944; was Einstein's personal physician in Berlin and again after his migration to the United States.

9. Eugen Taeubler (1879–1953). Professor of Jewish history at the Lehranstalt fuer die Wissenschaft des Judentums, 1910–1918; professor of ancient history at the University of Berlin and at Heidelberg until 1933 and at Hebrew Union College until 1951.

10. Harry Sacher (1881–1971). British lawyer and Zionist leader; member of executive of Zionist Organization, 1927–1931, when he resided in Palestine; close collaborator with Weizmann.

11. Sigmund Freud (1856–1939). Founder of psychoanalysis; born in Freiburg, Moravia; lived in Vienna from age of four until 1938, when he moved to London following the annexation of Austria by Nazi Germany. A member of board of governors of the Hebrew University, 1925–1926, he maintained a continuous interest in the university.

12. Zvi Chajes (1876–1927). Rabbi, scholar, Zionist leader; chief rabbi of Vienna Jewish community, 1918–1927.

13. Joseph Hertz (1872–1946). Elected chief rabbi of Great Britain in 1913; religious Zionist and supporter of Hebrew University.

14. James de Rothschild (1878–1957). British Jewish communal leader; born in Paris, son of Edmond de Rothschild; became British subject; was Member of Parliament. He continued his father's interest in Jewish settlement in Palestine, serving as president of the Jewish Colonization Association.

15. Andor Fodor (1884–1968). Biochemist; born in Budapest, Hungary. He was professor at University of Halle, Germany; invited by Weizmann to establish an institute of chemistry at the Hebrew University in 1923; first professor appointed at Hebrew University.

52

To Julian W. Mack
Chicago

Jerusalem, November 4, 1925

Dear Judge Mack,

Enclosed please find some notes on the famous Munich meeting. I would ask you to use your own judgment as to whether these notes should be shown to anyone. I must confess that I have not a proper perspective on the whole thing, and I dread doing anything that may seem petty or personal. If you think these notes will help clarify a *situation*, please show them.

I have written a long letter to Mr. Warburg, enclosing revised budget and notes. I hope a meeting of the University Committee will be called to consider these and other questions. I am much distressed by the reports of discord between the JDC and the Zionists. I wish I had at least the facts based on documents and that I might do something to help. I believe in both the Russian and the Palestinian proposals, and I am sure that most people do.[1]

We are well. Remember us to Mrs. Mack.

Yours truly, JLM

NOTES ON THE MEETING OF THE BOARD OF GOVERNORS
OF THE HEBREW UNIVERSITY MUNICH, SEPT. 23RD AND 24TH, 1925

I am writing these notes for the purpose of recalling what I can of the Munich meeting, and I shall send a copy to Mack and Schloessinger with the request that they supplement or correct them from their point of view. I shall ask Mack to show these notes to Warburg, Marshall and such others of the American University Committee as ought to be informed. I dislike confining petty things to paper but perhaps it is necessary.

Munich was selected as the place of the meetings, so I was informed by Dr. Eder, because Mr. James de Rothschild had said that Munich was the farthest place east that he would be prepared to come. Mr. Rothschild did not attend the meeting because he was sick. The date — September 23rd — was selected, so Dr. Eder said, so that Dr. Weizman could attend after resting up from his exertions at the Congress which was the end of August. Dr. Weizmann did not attend despite my best efforts and those of Judge Mack to secure his presence. Nor did Dr. Eder attend, despite personal requests, letters and telegrams.

The only members of the original Board of Governors present were Professor Einstein, Mr. Sokolow and myself. Messrs. Warburg and Libman sent Judge Mack and myself their proxies and Messrs. Ahad Ha'am and Bialik sent me their proxies. Had we desired to use those proxies we could have voted the meeting in accordance with our views. To me this seemed inadvisable because it seemed worthwhile to have the whole discussion out with some of the eminent scientists in whose name ever so many changes in the structure of the University organization were being proposed. Indeed I am informed that at the Congress the resolution to have the seat of the Board of Governors of the University outside of Palestine was passed owing to the insistence of Dr. O. Thon[2] of Lemberg that this was the desire of Prof. Einstein.

The presence of Prof. Fodor at the meeting was a surprise to me. He informed me that he had received an invitation from Dr. Eder through Mr. Selig Weizmann.[3] Inasmuch as so much of the meeting was taken up with Prof. Fodor's grievances I was glad that he had come.

After greeting those who had come I explained that all of the gentlemen who were present had been invited in an advisory capacity, each one to advise us in his particular field. I had asked Mr. Leo Kohn more than once in what capacity Messrs. Ornstein and Landau and Ehrmann had been invited and he assured me that it was as experts. It was in this capacity also that I had invited Prof. Horovitz (Oriental Studies), Prof. Warburg (Palestine Natural History),[4] Dr. Buber (*Landesvolkshochshule*) [adult education college], and Dr. Schloessinger for the Wolffsohn Foundation (with which we had come to an agreement) and as having served in the Institute of Jewish Studies for two months during my absence.

Professors Ornstein and Landau immediately declared that they had received two letters, one inviting them as members of the Board of Governors and the other inviting them as experts, and they said that if they could not remain as members of the Board of Governors, their time was too valuable and they would go home. I replied that it was only in the competence of the Board of Governors to elect new members, that so far as I was concerned they could be members of the Board, but that no one had the right to elect them without a decision of the Board, and such a decision could be taken at the proper moment in the proceedings. Upon being asked whether they could participate in the proceedings with the right to vote, I said that I had no objections and if Professor Einstein and Mr. Sokolow and Judge Mack had no objections, they might participate with the right to vote.

I had prepared two documents for the meeting. The one a tentative budget for the coming year and the second, organization proposals upon the basis of the understanding that had been arrived at between Dr. Weizmann, Mr. Marshall, and myself at Geneva. I proposed that we take up the budget first and questions of organization second because, upon the basis of the budget, it would be possible for me to present a statement on the present status of the University's work and to explain proposals for the work of the coming year. Then upon the basis of the information thus acquired, we might proceed intelligently to the discussion of questions of organization.

This met with the decided opposition of the scientists who wanted to discuss the organization questions involved. I consented to this procedure but in the course of the sittings it became apparent to them, and since the meeting I had a letter from Prof. Ornstein to the effect that it would have been better had my suggestion as to procedure been followed.

The meeting lasted two days and I should say that two-thirds of the time was taken up with the discussion of problems of organization involving personalities and politics and ambitions; and that the time left over for a discussion of the real work of the University was altogether inadequate, indeed, so inadequate that had I put forward entirely different proposals for the budget and the work of the coming years, they would have been adopted with as little understanding of the real situation as were the proposals actually made.

The difficulties arising out of questions of organization can, so I think, be traced back to two sources. The one — a desire, perhaps natural — on the part of many members of the Zionist Organization not to permit the ultimate control of the University to pass out of the hands of the Zionist Organization, and second, to the difficulties between persons arising out of personal ambitions and other causes. With many of the chief actors there was doubtless an admixture of both the Zionist and the personal motives. Indeed this admixture created the real difficulty of the situation.

244

The first speaker was Prof. Ornstein and it became apparent at once from his words and from those of Prof. Landau and Prof. Einstein that these gentlemen had come to the meeting laden with prejudice and wrong information. I do not know how much of this prejudice was directed against me personally, although a remark made by Prof. Einstein to Prof. Horovitz and later repeated by the latter is characteristic. Prof. Einstein, after the close of the second sitting, said to Prof. Horovitz: "I did not know that Dr. Magnes was the kind of man I found him to be"—meaning this as an expression of approval. At any rate, the atmosphere had been poisoned against everyone and everything Palestinian, and it was evident very quickly that the chief source of this was Prof. Fodor who, so it appeared in the course of the discussion, had been writing letters of complaint and condemnation to various parts of Europe, and who at the meeting himself said that the atmosphere of Palestine was entirely unsuited to the prosecution of scientific work; that those connected with the University had absolutely no appreciation of what scientific work meant; that the position of professor was one of an inferior grade; and that in general it was difficult, if not impossible, to work with those who had been in charge of the University's administration.

Along the lines of the proposals made by the Zionist Executive when they repudiated the agreement arrived at in Tel Aviv, it was proposed that the seat of administration be outside of Palestine. The administration in Palestine would report once a month to this extra-Palestinian Executive and the teaching staff was to regard the Executive as a court of appeal in case any differences of opinion arose between members of the teaching staff and the Palestinian administration. On the other hand, so it was proposed, there should be at the head of the administration in Jerusalem one who enjoyed the confidence of the Board and of the scientific and Jewish world, a man who would have great authority, and who would, in fact, be known as the Chancellor of the University to indicate that his authority was great. It was not, however, explained how the idea of an extra-Palestinian Executive with the functions desired for it could be reconciled with a Chancellor in Jerusalem with great authority. I think it only fair at once to mention that Prof. Ornstein, who was most vigorous in his advocacy of having the center of the University's administration and development outside of Palestine, declared to me towards the close of the meeting that he had been thoroughly convinced that this would have been a fatal blunder and he was almost in favor of having decisions of the meeting taken up again and revised in the light of what I had wanted.

Indeed towards the end of the meeting Prof. Einstein, after realizing some of the realities of the situation, turned to me and said, "How would you really want to have it organized?" I repeated what I had said at the beginning of the sittings—that until the final constitution was adopted, we regard the organization as provisional, that we make as few changes as possible in this provisional organization, creating no new posts with the exception of the provisional Academic Council of which I was heartily in favor. In this way, we should leave the Committee on Constitution unembarrassed and we should be having another year of experience in accordance with which to guide ourselves. I also said that I had never heard Palestine vilified and blackened even by its worst enemies as it had been at the meeting under the influence of Prof. Fodor and that I was of the unshaken opinion that the center of the development and administration of the Jerusalem University had under all circumstances to be in Jerusalem. Not only was Jerusalem a symbol but it would prove practically unworkable to have the center of operations elsewhere. Moreover, I was personally very much impressed by the high moral quality of large elements of the Palestinian population and I should be willing to trust it to the full. It pained me to hear eminent men repeating innocently such slanders.

Despite the increasing knowledge of the situation that was secured by all those present as the sittings progressed, Prof. Einstein maintained his view to the last that there ought to be an extra-Palestinian Presidium. All of his objections to having the center of gravity in Palestine disappeared with the creation of the Academic Council. He had been under the impression that we in Palestine wanted to have full say as to who should be appointed to the teaching staff. He heartily welcomed the creation of the Academic Council and was glad to be its chairman, but that without being able to give reasons for it, he maintained that there ought to be outside of Palestine a Presidium for purposes of representation. Had it been anyone else but Prof. Einstein who desired this Presidium, I should have felt called upon to oppose it to the end, but I regard Prof. Einstein as far and away the greatest asset which the University possesses and I was reconciled to the idea in view of his willingness to become a member of the Presidium. He was willing at one time to be the sole president. Judge Mack, with a great deal of logic, opposed Prof. Einstein as sole president, but I think it would have been better to have been illogical under the circumstances.

Prof. Einstein declared himself to be "der grosste Strohmann den es jemals gegeben hat,"[5] but I have the conviction that he will give considerable time and attention to some of our problems. At any rate, in parting he shook my hand for a long time, and said that he understood the situation much better than before and that he would be "auf der Wache" [on guard] and that he was particularly happy to see how firmly determined we in Jerusalem were to have in every way "eine saubere wirtschaft" [a tidy administration].

246

I have the conviction also that Prof. Ehrmann, who seems to be a cool-headed, reasonable man, would be of assistance to Prof. Einstein in Berlin, and Prof. Ehrmann told me that they regarded Prof. Fodor on the basis of some of his statements at the meeting as "ein pathologischevfall, ein Neurastheniker" [a pathological case, a neurasthenic person] and I found myself in the peculiar position of telling them of his many undoubted good qualities.

As to the question of the Executive in Palestine, the proposal was first made that there be an Executive consisting of myself, Mr. Bentwich, and some "natur-wissenschaftler" [natural scientist] whom we would nominate and whom the Board of Governors outside must confirm. This "natur-wissenschaftler" was to be there because they had been informed that we in Jerusalem were interested only in the humanities of the University, and not on the side of exact sciences; and, moreover, the "natur-wissenschaftler" would be a kind of guarantee that Prof. Fodor and his friends would have proper personal treatment.

In the desire to have things move along without undue friction and controversies over titles and forms of organization, I was at first inclined to accept this suggestion which was, after all, rather humiliating for the people in Jerusalem. But in the course of the meeting the proponents of this suggestion themselves saw its meaning. It was, as Dr. Schloessinger aptly put it, to build up the whole system of organization of the University upon the supposed grievances of a few men. They then urged upon me the chancellorship and I told them that titles were an odious thing to me, that I would be perfectly satisfied with a modest title or none at all, provided the functions of the office I was to fill were very clear and that this office would not mean that between meetings of the Board of Governors, we in Jerusalem would have to accept orders from an office outside of Jerusalem or be confronted with faits accomplis or obligations of which we had no prior knowledge and which we had no voice in determining.

I wanted the Board of Governors to be supreme, to receive as many and as detailed reports as might be required, to meet as often during the year as it chose, but it must be understood that the Board of Governors and no office outside was to be the authority to which we in Jerusalem were to be responsible. This being clearly understood, I said that it would be necessary to have someone act as Deputy-Chancellor and I proposed Mr. Bentwich, who was immediately accepted. For my part, I said that I would accept the title and position of Chancellor only provisionally and that I would make my definite acceptance depend upon the conversation that I would have with the Committees in Palestine and in America as whose representative I regarded myself.

I endeavoured to discuss the question of Dr. Weizmann in a frank and friendly way. I said that I opposed Dr. Weizmann as head of the Board of Governors because he was head of the political Zionist Organization, and I did not believe that the University ought to be controlled by any political organization. If Dr. Weizmann wished to become the head of the University or of the Board of Governors, I believed that his services on behalf of the University entitled him to this post, but I thought that it would be necessary for him first to relinquish his position as head of the political organization. Zionist control would make of the University something partisan and sectarian, whereas it ought to be the University of all sections of the Jewish people. Moreover, the enormous practical difficulties of Dr. Weizmann's position as head of the Zionist Organization had already caused the University considerable embarrassment. We were, in the first place, confronted with a debt of £E15,000. which, Dr. Weizmann had been told while in Palestine last April was £E3,000. Some of those responsible for this large indebtedness are said to have replied that Dr. Weizmann was capable of collecting large sums of money, why not also large sums for the University indebtedness? He had also made certain promises which were embarrassing to us — promises of positions to men whom we could not employ and of money which he did not secure. I was not blaming him for this because I know how difficult his task was in view of all of the requests made to him, but it was impossible that such things continue in connection with the University.

The device of a double-headed presidency of the Board of Governors is, so it seems to me, rather questionable. I do not know how it can work out. I noticed in the public statement issued by Mr. Kohn that London had been decided upon by the meeting as the seat of the Presidium and that the Presidium was to serve as a Court of Appeal in matters of dispute. Just the contrary, it was decided not to mention a seat of the Board of Governors in view of the fact that the two presidents were in two places; and the whole idea of a Court of Appeal to an outside body was given up when the idea of an inferior kind of Executive Committee was given up in favor of responsible and authoritative heads like a Chancellor and Deputy-Chancellor. There are other misstatements in this public announcement and I mention this in this connection merely in order to indicate that with the office of the Presidium at the Zionist Headquarters in London, a great deal is apt to be done not entirely corresponding with the facts. I hope I am wrong and no one will be happier to have these apprehensions removed.

A very large amount of the time of the sittings was taken up by Prof. Landau in his endeavour to secure for his pupil Mr. Amira[6] what he regarded as a righting of the wrong done to him. I do not want to go into the question of Mr. Amira now. It involves unfulfilled promises by Dr. Weizmann, a lack of clarity as to the functions of Mr. Amira, etc. Prof.

Landau also made vigorous attempts to secure considerable sums for mathematics, and it was all I could do to show that our limited resources would not permit us to engage upon extensive preparations for the Institute of Mathematics at the present time.

I am afraid that I did not make myself particularly popular with Dr. Buber who after explaining his ideas of a *Landesvolkshochshule* with which I am in general accord said that it would require £E300 for him to make the trip to Palestine. I said that there was not the money for that purpose now and that there was no money for any purpose except such as were absolutely indispensable.

I requested the meeting to vote on general principles for the creation of courses in pedagogy, first because they would be of great advantage in relation to the whole educational problem in Palestine and second, because an American donor, Mrs. Freedman, had expressed an interest in that phase of the University's work. I cited the Teachers College of Columbia University as containing eminent philosophers, psychologists, and scholars in other fields; and I said that in general the side of the humanities of the University would have to be taken into account. In view of the financial stringency, I would propose that these courses be not begun until a year hence. There was a most peculiar discussion on this proposal. Pedagogy was called by one of the distinguished exact scientists "der hohere dreck" [superior muck] and the same distinguished gentleman went on to praise the work of Madame Montessori. Judge Mack made it clear how unintelligible such an attitude towards pedagogy would appear in America. In general, Judge Mack was exceedingly helpful in bringing out some of the positive sides of American university organization.

An incident occurred with Dr. Isaac Straus[7] that ought to be recorded. It was on the second day. Mr. Sokolow had asked me for an account of the subscriptions to the University which had been promised in America. I was in the course of giving this account when Dr. Isaac Straus, who is the brother of Dr. Eli Straus, in whose home we were meeting, came into the room. After shaking hands all around (he seemed to be well acquainted with Einstein and the other scientists), he took his seat at the table. I remarked that we were now discussing the University budget and that this could hardly be of interest to him. He arose and said that he would leave if he was not wanted, but putting his hand to his pocket he said that he had received a telegram signed by Weizmann, Sokolow, and Einstein inviting him to attend the meeting. Both Einstein and Sokolow declared that they knew of no such telegram. Dr. Straus then explained that he had been in Italy and had received a telegram from his wife in Basle informing him of the telegram which she had received and as a consequence he did not know from which place the original telegram was sent off. No further remarks being made, Dr. Straus sat down at the table, for a time acting as secretary of the meeting, and participating in general in the discussion. A rather strange incident of which I have my own interpretation.

I neglected to say that during the discussion as to where the seat of the Board of Governors ought to be, Mr. Sokolow declared that both Dr. Weizmann and Sir Alfred Mond had instructed him to say that they believed the seat of the Board of Governors should be in London. It was politically of importance.

In the discussion of Dr. Kligler's name, Prof. Fodor distinguished himself particularly. I presented the proposal for the creation of a Department of Public Health, or as the American Jewish Physicians' Committee wish to term it — Preventive Medicine. The proposal met with everyone's approval except that of Prof. Fodor who declared that Dr. Kligler was a man of eminent practical attainments but was not a scientist. I interrupted to ask if Prof. Fodor knew this to be a fact. He said that he was not, to be sure, an expert in this field but he had been so informed. I thereupon drew out from among my papers a list of Dr. Kligler's scientific publications — 54 in number, covering four long sheets — and I handed this to Prof. Ehrmann and the others who declared that they did not know the quality of the work, but the publications were certainly on scientific themes.

On the question of a committee on the drafting of the constitution, Mr. Sokolow said that Dr. Weizmann had declared that he wanted to have the privilege of working out the original draft. There was someone whom he would like to entrust with this task.

In connection with the budget of the proposed Institute of Natural History, Prof. Warburg showed that as a Palestinian he knew some of the realitites of the situation. He declared that he was ready to give up a number of his plans until the University had more adequate funds.

By the time we had reached the question of the establishment of a School of Oriental Studies, so much time and energy had been taken up with the discussion of mathematics and physics and some of the other matters mentioned above that Prof. Horovitz, who had come to the meeting for the purpose of reporting on the School of Oriental Studies, was greeted with the remark that everything that he would propose would be satisfactory and, therefore, it would not be necessary for him to proceed. Prof. Horovitz, however, properly said that he had been listening to long and wearying discussions on other matters, and that he requested patient hearing for what he had to say because he did not want someone someday to stand up and say that, "Oh, I did not know that you were going to propose that." The School of Oriental Studies was a far-reaching idea, and it was better that it be understood now rather than later. He thereupon unfolded his suggestions in his own lucid way.

Prof. Ornstein said that he would be prepared to come to Palestine as head of the Institute of Physics within two or three years provided the Institute was built in accordance with his ideas, provided it was properly equipped, and provided that there were adequate funds to run it. This would be a sacrifice on his part because he was now in charge of one of the largest and newest physics institutes on the Continent, but he was a Zionist and he and his wife wished to bring their children up in Palestine. He did not, however, wish his name to be mentioned permanently in this connection as yet.*

Prof. Landau said that in view of all he had learnt at the meeting, he was ready to withdraw his definite refusal to be considered as a candidate for the Mathematical Institute, and that he would hold the matter under advisement again. He declared mathematics to be "die billigste und Judischste Wissenschaft" [the cheapest and most Jewish of the sciences].

Geddes's first sketches for the library and physics' institute were on hand. I made it clear that the Board of Governors would have to raise £E10,000 in addition to the £E20,000 in the hands of the Wolfssohn Foundation for the library building. Naturally, the professors present voted "Aye" at once. One might have proposed £E100,000 with the same result because none of the eminent gentlemen themselves will have to be responsible for raising any of the funds. No one seemed to have given much thought to the question whose *function* it was to raise funds.

I hope I have not been too cynical in these notes and that I have not given the impression of possessing more virtue than the others who were present. But I did happen to have more detailed information than anyone else, and I think I can say with certainty and honesty that what I am after is not at all titles or anything of the sort, but merely the privilege of working on behalf of the University in a position that I think by reason of my experience and temperament I may be able to fulfill.

* Prof. Ornstein declared that in April he had received a telegram signed by Weizmann and Fodor which he interpreted as a definite call to become professor in charge of Physics at the University.

1. See JLM to Weizmann, October 5, 1926, document 55.

2. Osias Thon (1870–1936). Philosopher, early follower of Herzl. He represented the West Galician Jewish National Council on the Comite des Delegations Juives at Versailles Peace Conference; elected to the first Polish parliament, 1919.

3. Moshe ("Selig") Weizmann (1897–1957). Brother of Chaim Weizmann. Studied at Kiev Polytechnic Institute, then studied chemistry at Geneva and Grenoble. He settled in Palestine, 1924; became head of Organic Chemistry Laboratory at Hebrew University with rank of professor in 1947.

4. Otto Warburg (1859–1938). Born in Hamburg; botanist; Zionist adviser of Herzl. In 1921 he became director of agricultural research in Rehovot and in 1925 was appointed head of the department of botany at Hebrew University.

5. "The biggest scarecrow that ever existed."

6. Binyanin Amira (1896–1968). Mathematician; studied at universities of Geneva and Goettingen; taught at Herzlia High School, Tel Aviv, from 1919 to 1921. He joined the faculty of Hebrew University in 1925 and became an associate professor in 1949; retired in 1960.

7. Isaac Straus (1881–1933). Merchant, industrialist; aided Weizmann in 1913–1914 in planning for Hebrew University; lived in Basel from 1924.

8. Sir Patrick Geddes (1854–1932). British biologist, sociologist, and city planner; drew up first plan for Hebrew University on Mount Scopus in 1919.

9. Weizmann, informed about the meeting of the board of governors by Einstein and Kohn, took exception to Magnes's interpretation of the decisions reached. Weizmann understood that the presidium (Weizmann and Einstein) was to direct the affairs of the university between meetings of the governors and the chancellor was to act as chief administrative officer in Jerusalem. Weizmann in fact objected to the titles of chancellor and vice chancellor as inappropriate since they implied more authority than was intended. He also criticized Magnes for agreeing to inflated expansion of the board of governors, accepting funds earmarked for applied sciences and thus neglecting the basic sciences and for objecting to an active role for the Zionist Organization in shaping university policy. See Weizmann to Magnes, October 12, 1925, and December 15, 1925, *The Letters and Papers of Chaim Weizmann*, ed. Joshua Freundlich, vol. 12 (New Brunswick, N.J., 1900), pp. 418–423, 454–457.

53

Journal: The *G'dud* and Soviet Russia

Jerusalem, February 16, 1926

Manya [Shochat]: The *G'dud*[1] wants to establish contact with Russia because they can find in Russia, and only there, the human material, the help in ideas, the technical aid without which the efforts in Palestine to establish the communist society must languish. They came to Palestine twenty-two years ago to carry out the high ideals of the Russian Revolution (without revolution), i.e. to make actual in life the communist ideal which for them is also the highest ideal of Judaism. They felt they could achieve this synthesis between their social and national-spiritual (religious?) ideals in Palestine, and in large measure they have achieved it.

But in order to grow, to deepen and expand their movement, they greatly require the refreshment in persons, in technique, and in "ideology" which they could receive if the way were open and free for them to have legal contact with Russian Jewry. This would also afford the possibility of saving Russian Judaism which is at present in a perilous state. Even the JDC-Rosen colonization[2] is not based upon a deep ethical impulse. Shor[3] says that Rosen "weeps" over this phase of it. (Rosen should come here *now* and make use of results in Palestine for his work there.) But with the contact the *G'dud* could establish in Russia, Judaism there could be put upon the same Communist-Jewish basis as in Palestine, and one could help the other immeasurably. For two years they have been trying to have their position explained to the present Russian Government. They have refused to do this through the *Frakzie*[4] because of their unwillingness to be bound to or even associated with the *Frakzie*.

Two months ago they received an "official invitation." (Manya was not sure if it was from the Comintern or the Government.) And they are now considering sending two of their men from here — Israel Shochat[5] and Elkind[6] — to Russia (a third will join them in Berlin) to try and secure an open road for Palestine. They want to write to Henrietta Szold about money — £150 — and they want me to add a few words. I said I was in entire accord with the main idea.

There was, however, one great danger: that they might give the impression in Russia or, what was more precarious, some of them might themselves be tempted to think, that they would be instruments of the present Russian government's Oriental politics. They must continue to be absolutely independent of this, otherwise what was the essential difference between them and the *Frakzie*? Both they and the *Frakzie* were Communists. But the *Frakzie* says that constructive, creative work here and now is impossible, that this is possible only after the revolution which will drive out both Britain and the exploiting class. Whereas the *G'dud* says, let the political position be what it may in Turkey, Germany, England, they not only can but must try with all their strength to build and create here and now, despite all difficulties. This makes them the servant neither of British nor of Russian politics; it leaves them independent. This must be emphasized in Russia and here. The sole question in Russia ought to be: are they interested in the spread and deepening of Communism as an idea and ideal movement in the Orient and elsewhere? If so, let them open the doors to the Palestine-creative movment. If they want only aid in their present day politics, they should say so, and the *G'dud* would have to leave them severely alone. Manya said that they had recently expelled *Frakzie* members from the *G'dud* from just that point of view, and that Israel Shochat, who was the instigator of that expulsion, was *davke* [in fact] to be one of the men to go to Russia.

If indeed they can open up Russia to their purposes, it will be a great thing fo them, for Palestine, for non-bloody Communism, for Russian Jewry. One of the reasons why I have welcomed the JDC Russian move is because it seemed to me to promise a strengthening of the Communist-Jewish basis of life, which is at the bottom of the *G'dud* labors here. Is it indeed not a great thing to be able to say quietly: we are making the synthesis between our Communism and our Judaism because we believe them in Palestine to be one and the same thing? That is *the* great achievement of the new Palestine. The other great achievement is the Hebrew language and the study of the Bible—the language of the Bible and Mishna, and a great tradition. But this second achievement concerns the form, whereas the first has to do with the essence of Judaism and life.

Yesterday passed through an open field on way from Gymnasia to University. Saw two young men in caps, open shirts, sitting on a rock, and one saying to the other slowly in Hebrew, "*Tsarikh lomar patah v'lo kamats*".[7] Spending their spare time studying grammar!

On Sunday met the young nurse at Hadassah station in the city. She is doing work of humanity, which should give her soul full satisfaction, but she has learned Hebrew besides and is doing it in Hebrew. When I see the likes of her, or hear working men and women on *shabbat* [the Sabbath] or after work or in a *kvutsa* [collective settlement] talking Hebrew —vocabulary limited, hard as *k'riat yam suf* [parting the Red Sea]—I ask myself, why do they do this? Have they not enough hardships to overcome? Then I think each time that this is *ham'haddesh b'khol yom ma'ase v'reshit*.[8]

Brainin[9] and Shor here yesterday. Shor has saved many a Zionist from hanging, shooting, Siberia. He said that Mme. Kanienoff had mentioned my name.[10] Brainin says of Weizmann, "*Hahashad ala b'libbo shehu m'kabbel shohad mehamemshala habritit. Eneni yodea im ze nakhon, aval dai shehahashad ole b'libbi. Ze haya i efshar b'nogea l'hertsel o l'mek o l'varburg.*"[11] His idea is that Mack take over the political work. Only an American to cope with the British, and that there be a committee in charge of the *hanhala* [executive] like in the "days of Warburg."

1. *G'dud* (Hebrew) "legion"; short name for *G'dud ha'avoda*, founded in 1920 by followers of Joseph Trumpeldor. The group believed that a disciplined Jewish work force organized in a countrywide commune could best meet the pioneering needs of the yishuv while building a socialist Zionist society. The G'dud split in 1926 over the issue of expelling the left-wing faction that was strongly influenced by Communist Party elements.

2. Joseph A. Rosen (1877–1948). Agronomist and administrator; was sent by the JDC to Russia in 1924 to organize land settlement projects in the Ukraine and Crimea as part of an economic rehabilitation program for Soviet Jews.

3. David Shor (1867–1924). Eminent pianist and educator; born in Crimea, Russia; appointed professor of music at the Moscow Conservatory by the Soviet government. Shor interceded with Soviet leaders on behalf of Zionists exiled to Siberia, succeeding in many instances in having their sentences commuted to expulsion from Russia. He migrated to Palestine in 1927, where he continued his professional career.

4. *Frakzia ha'poalim* ("workers faction"), established by the Palestine Communist party when it was outlawed by the Mandatory government: virulently anti-Zionist. The General Federation of Jewish Workers expelled the *Frakzia* from its ranks in 1924. However, it continued its activities within the G'dud and elsewhere.

5. Israel Shochat (1886–1961). Founder of the *Hashomer* (first self-defense organiza-

tion in the Zionist settlement); a leader of the G'dud and the Jewish labor movement. In 1925 he entered secret talks with Soviet officials.

6. Menahem Elkind (1900–1937?). Emigrated to Palestine from Russia in 1920; leader of the left-wing faction of the G'dud; returned to the Soviet Union with a small number of followers and established a communal farm in Crimea, which was liquidated in time by the Soviets.

7. "One has to say [the vowels] *patakh* and not *kamats*."

8. An abbreviation of the phrase from the morning service, "who renews [in his goodness] every day the work of creation."

9. Reuben Brainin (1862–1939). Eminent Hebrew literary figure and Zionist who migrated from Russia to the United States in 1909. In the 1920s he supported the JDC's campaigns to raise funds on behalf of Jewish colonization in the Crimea.

10. The reference is apparently to Kamenev, in which case Magnes is referring to Olga, the youngest sister of Leon Trotsky and the wife of Lev Kamenev, a leader of the Communist Party in the 1920s. Olga Kamenev headed a Soviet commission that dealt with foreign relief organizations.

11. "I began to suspect that he received bribes from the British government. I don't know if it is true, but it is enough that one harbors such suspicions. It would be impossible to imagine having such thoughts in connection with Herzl or Mack or Warburg."

54

Journal: The Caste System of the English

Jerusalem, February 18, 1926

My mother's birthday. She would have been 74.

Beatie was telling me of the meeting at Sophia [Berger's] house yesterday, and what interested me most was her account of Bowman.[1] This worthy gentleman who is head of the Department of Education — a High Government Official! — got up when the agenda was being discussed, and, reading from a paper, said: "In my opinion the agenda should be as follows . . ." Mrs. Hyamson[2] afterwards said that this agenda had been prepared by the Agenda Committee and was supposed to be presented in their name. This is a characteristic instance of feeling that seems to pervade the whole place, that the Government official of highest rank must upon all occasions show that he is a man of authority and of highest rank. Bentwich is, I think, afflicted with this the least of all, but nevertheless afflicted.

The question of precedence in processions, seating, performances, and at table, is very important. It is amusing to see how this is transferred to some of our Jewish brethren. Our friend Kisch, for example, talks of himself and regards himself, and is largely regarded as the Leader of the Jewish Community (although Yellin[3] and Ussishkin also claim this honor). Kisch would not think of taking a back seat at a lecture or performance. This is below his station. His bald head must be among the bald ones in the first row. At Sachs's tuberculosis meeting he attended, and having to go early, very formally (and somewhat pompously) blessed the meeting. At the show of the Town Planning Commission, it was quite interesting. I happened to be next to Storrs[4] and Lady Storrs as the procession about the room to view the maps started. Suddenly Kisch was found edging his way in, and of course I made a dash for a place in the rear; but our friend stuck to the highest officials the whole time. When the time came to sit down and have the large map explained, there was Kisch in the front row of chairs, exactly in the middle chair (the High Commissioner's?), flanked by Mohl[5] on one side. Who was it who was on the other? I had been looking at the map showing educational institutions and took my seat near it — it happened to be the end seat of the second row. Dr. Thon[6] sat in the middle of the second row, and was among those who asked questions. Then at the end of an answer to one of his questions, while he was still standing, he thanked the Governor in the name of the assembled guests. Consternation in the front row. Kisch had been preparing to do the honors and shifted uneasily, and nodded his head. This evidently was meant to confer approval upon Thon's boldness.

This characteristic of the English amazes me. I knew that this was true of "Continentals" (Germans, etc.) But I did not realize how strong the caste system of the English was. They have, after all, a King and Court, and House of Lords, and Birthday Honors. The democratic element of it is, I suppose, this: that you are not estopped by birth or social station from reaching a high post in the hierarchy. But once you are in the hierarcy, you play the game as though your past were yours by special dispensation of heaven, or heaven's representative, the King. The whole community is ablaze with rules of precedence for consuls, church dignitaries.

1. Humphrey Ernest Bowman (1879–1965). Director of education and member of advisory council, Palestine government, 1920 to 1936.

2. Mrs. Albert Hyamson, wife of the head of the Department of Immigration of the mandatory government.

3. David Yellin (1864–1941). Teacher, writer, scholar; leader of the yishuv. From 1920 to 1928 he was chairman of the Va'ad Le'umi; was founder of the Hebrew Teachers Seminary in Jerusalem; professor of medieval Hebrew poetry at the Hebrew University, 1926.

4. Sir Ronald Henry Storrs (1881–1955). Senior British official in the Middle East; military governor of Jerusalem, 1917–1920; civil governor of Jerusalem and Judea, 1920–1926.

5. Emanuel Nehemiah Mohl (1883–1956). Engineer and economist; representative in Palestine of American group of investors headed by Julian Mack and Brandeis; active in the Palestine Economic Corporation, 1921–1934.

6. Jacob J. Thon (1880–1950). Zionist administrator and leader of the yishuv; born in

Galicia. He served as Ruppin's assistant in the Palestine Office from 1908 to 1916 and as director from 1916 to 1920; was on the presidium of the Va'ad Le'umi from 1920 to 1925 and vice chairman from 1925 to 1929. He was managing director of the Palestine Land Development Company from 1921 to 1950.

55

To Chaim Weizmann
London

Jerusalem, October 5, 1926

Dear Dr. Weizmann,

The course outlined in your cable to me, after I had sent you a copy of Mr. Marshall's, is, it seems to me, altogether sound.[1] I am convinced that you and Mr. Marshall, dealing directly with one another, without a third person by, will come to a satisfactory understanding. Should you, however, need me, I am ready.

I shall try to write to you in somewhat the same strain, as if I had been going to America with you.

Your Zionist Organization has a permanent, alert machinery (disadvantage: retinue of bureaucrats and politicians). The JDC is essentially an emergency organization, and the American Jewish Committee — practically a one-man organization (disadvantage: catastrophes are necessary for the one, and sometimes attacks for the other, before they move). The emergency character of Jewish life will probably last a long time, and the present fight with the Zionists has been just the thing needed to galvanize the JDC into a more or less permanent, alert machine (doubtless with its own bureaucrats and politicians). You and Mr. Marshall are the chief protagonists, and I am sure that both of you are more than satisfied with the laurels gained by each organization as a fighting machine, and I am sure that you both want peace without victory. At any rate, the problem seems to be to recognize the fact that there are now two more or less permanent machines in the field, and nevertheless, to arrange for cooperation between them.

My own view is that your ultimate objective must be to have the JDC organization or those connected with it do ever so much more for and in Palestine than they are now doing. To say that they have created a Palestine Economic Corporation[2] is not enough. This is a most useful undertaking. But it is slow in getting under way. It has taken over old assets

257

(thereby decreasing the JDC contribution of new money); it is altogether an investment corporation, as it should be; and if that is all the JDC or the JDC group will be, they are not giving to Palestine the benefit of their constructive endeavours and of the experimentation they are putting into Poland and Russia and other places. Heaven bless them, say I, for what they are doing for Jews everywhere. My point is that they should be gotten to do more for the Palestine experiment than at present. It will require the united efforts—not only money, but also men and mind and spirit—of the whole Jewish people to give the Palestine enterprise a fair chance.

Just how far you can get at present with the united Jewish Agency there, I have no means of knowing. Everyone knows how you have struggled and suffered in order to carry through this most essential idea. If through the Jewish Agency, the forces of America Jewry could be mobilized for Palestine materially and spiritually, that is what you have been after, and I think you must be convinced that that is what Mr. Marshall has been after. Indeed, I think it no exaggeration to say that not so very long ago there was hardly a single anti-Zionist, certainly no anti-Palestinian in any position of authority in the JDC. What the situation now is I do not know. But I do know, and I think it of the essence of succes to your mission that you be convinced that men like Messrs. Marshall and Warburg and Adler and Flexner[3] and Herbert Lehman are altogether pro-Palestine, no matter what may have become of others.

But if, in spite of this, it is difficult, impossible for the present, to come to a working understanding of the Agency, that should not spell failure to your mission. I think the touchstone should be this: will they increase their aid to the upbuilding of the Jewish Community in Palestine, i.e. will they put into this all-Jewish enterprise more money, more thought, more men than at present? That is their all-Jewish duty, and if you cannot agree as to the Agency for the moment, and if they don't like the Zionists or Zionist methods, let them come into Palestine in force—they have made good beginnings—by themselves; or let them join with the PICA[4] or find other combinations. Perhaps in agriculture they could settle a number of families as they are doing in Russia. (Joseph Rosen might be sent here to work out their plan.) Or in industry they might arrange for credits, as they do in Russia, Poland, and Rumania. Or in education, trade schools as in Poland; and charity organization, as everywhere. I think this is of more importance for the moment than any forced, artificial understanding as to the Jewish Agency that may be distasteful to both sides. The Agency will come of itself, and quickly, the more forces are thrown into Palestine for its upbuilding. Despite the present economic crisis here, you are dealing not with today alone, but with developments over a long period of years to come.

But in their turn, the JDC people have a right to demand that the Zionists at least understand the JDC Jewish point of view. This is an all-Jewish point of view. Wherever Jews live they are our brothers, and all of us together make up the one Jewish People. Zionists are those who place greatest emphasis upon Palestine, and if there had not been Zionist fanatics at all times, the sacrifices for Zion would not have been so astounding and heartening as they have been. But though fanaticism has its uses, that does not justify the virulence with which everyone with a good word for Crimea[5] or other Jewish things is attacked. I know you do not share this virulence of attitude, but you are being severely criticized for not exercising your authority as President of the Organization and as a distinguished Jew concerned for his brethren everywhere, in calling a halt to all of this heartbreaking mud-slinging which is going on in the name of the "priority of Palestine." The mud-slingers are certainly not all on the Zionist side, nor is virtue all on the other side. But it seems to me that before the other side can now come in wholeheartedly for Palestine, the Zionist side must somehow recognize the complete legitimacy of an all-Jewish point of view which includes within its purview and sphere of activity Jews wherever they may be. When Palestine is discriminated against, Zionist must protest, and it is their great task, too, to put forward the claims of Palestine, not from the easy, conventional point of view of numbers of Jews and of costs, but from the point of view of its historical and spiritual implications, in fact its effect upon Judaism.

Inasmuch as I seem to be writing you rather fully, I should like to add a few words about the Russian colonization. I think I want it to succeed even more than any man in the JDC not so much because the Russian Jews are my "poor brethren" or because the JDC has not been able to help them sufficiently up to the present — that is important enough, and would be a complete justification for the JDC. Rather, I am interested in Russia itself, perhaps as much as anyone in the JDC. Whatever one thinks of the Soviets, etc., a special experiment is going on there such as the world has never seen. Just as Jews were among the destroyers of the Czarist tyranny and among the chief actors of the Revolution, so are they now a large community in the new Russia, and they will be there for a long time. A Jewish community of such magnitude has never been subjected to similar ideas and influences, and who can foretell the result? It may be of transcendent importance — Russia, a land going through all this social, political, religious, artistic ferment.

More than this, there is a genuine spiritual relationship between our Palestine *halutsim* [pioneers] and the *halutsim* of Russia. Russia is in large measure their spiritual background and Russia will continue to influence them. But it is interesting to note how in Palestine certain ideas take on a different hue. For example, Russian Communism is chiefly militaristic, and dependent upon the "social revolution," while Palestine communism is chiefly pacifistic and the sacrifices for the new society are being made here and now, whether or not the "social revolution" comes about. Sooner or later there will be free intercourse between Palestine and Russia. Palestine will recruit its *halutsim* from among the Russian youth. Tel Hai in Palestine[6] and Tel Hai in the Crimea will be nearer to one another both geographically and spiritually, and not the least of the tasks of the Palestine Jewish center will be the sending of its missionaries to the new Russian Jewish community.

Indeed, you who have visualized the destiny of the Jewish People in terms of grandeur will not let your view be deflected from the totality of the Jews' fate by the exigencies of a bitter family quarrel.

And as to the personalities involved in the quarrel, I know that that is always where the shoe pinches most. I wish I could help you in this regard. I am afraid you may have a harder time with certain personalities among the Zionists than with the JDC. I know, too, that you are a past master in meeting such situations. But there is one thing I feel I must say, and that is that I wish you good health and your nerves a deep calm so that you personally will be able to rise above personalities. Your example in this regard can, I think, save the situation.

In thinking over what I have been writing, I find that while I have been writing to you—at perhaps too great a length—I have also been thinking of Mr. Marshall and Mr. Warburg. I shall therefore have this letter copied, and send each of them a copy, despite the fact that I might have put things somewhat differently had I been writing to them direct. Both they and you will, I am sure, understand the spirit in which I have ventured to talk about all of you.

Please keep me informed as to the progress of things.

With many greetings and with the blessing from all of Eretz Israel I am

Yours truly, JLM

I neglected to tell you that I had a telegram from Wise[8]-Lipsky[9]-Neumann[10] asking me to come for two months for the United Palestine Appeal. I answered that after prolonged telegraphic correspondence with you, Marshall, and Warburg I had decided to stay here, and that I was writing them.

1. Long and difficult negotiations between Marshall, the outstanding American non-Zionist, and Weizmann over non-Zionist support for Zionist settlement work in Palestine through the medium of an enlarged Jewish Agency reached a crisis in the fall of 1926. Weizmann cabled Magnes to join the negotiations with Marshall. Marshall cabled Magnes, "Your presence [in the United States] inadvisable. Peace depends entirely [upon] action Zionist leaders here who alone have been warring, and Weizmann's firm authority."
2. Founded by American Jews in 1925 to provide financial aid to commercial, banking,

industrial, and agricultural enterprises in Palestine. It took over the assets of the Palestine Cooperative Co., founded in 1922, and the Reconstruction Committee of the JDC. Bernard Flexner was the first president, and it was supported by Louis Brandeis.

3. Bernard Flexner (1863–1946). Lawyer, administrator, social reformer; born in Louisville, Kentucky. He was a member and counsel of Zionist delegation to the Paris Peace Conference; first president of Palestine Economic Corporation; active in the JDC and Jewish Agency.

4. Palestine Jewish Colonization Association, founded in 1924 by Baron Edmond de Rothschild, who placed his son, James, at the head of the association; aided agricultural and industrial development in Palestine and supported the Hebrew University.

5. After the JDC reached an agreement with the Soviet government in 1924 to sponsor Jewish agricultural settlement in the Crimea, it launched a major campaign for funds. The Zionists criticized the Crimea scheme for diverting support from Jewish colonization in Palestine. They condemned the JDC leaders, who were either non-Zionists or anti-Zionists, for collaborating with a Soviet government hostile to Jewish group life in Russia. The acrimonious debate between American Zionist leaders and the leaders of the JDC and American Jewish Committee jeopardized negotiations to establish a joint fund-raising campaign to support Jewish settlement work in Palestine and to create an enlarged Jewish Agency.

6. Tel Hai, a settlement in the Galilee, gained fame for its stand against Arab attackers in March 1920.

7. Tel Hai in the Crimea served as an agricultural training center from 1922 to 1928 for Russian Zionists preparing to be pioneers in Palestine.

8. Stephen S. Wise (see glossary of names).

9. Louis Lipsky (1876–1963). Zionist leader and writer. Born in Rochester, New York. Founder and editor of *The Maccabaean* (1901–1918), the organ of the Federation of American Zionists; co-editor of the *American Hebrew*, 1899–1914; chairman, executive committee of the Federation of American Zionists, 1911–1918; president of the Zionist Organization of America, 1925–1930; member of the executive of the World Zionist Organization, 1923–1931; representative of the Jewish Agency in the United States, 1933–1946.

10. Emanuel Neumann (1893–1980). Zionist leader; born in Latvia and brought to the United States as a child. Educational director of the Zionist Organization of America, 1918–1920; first national director of the Keren Hayesod, 1921, and chairman of the executive committee of the United Palestine Appeal, 1925; member of Jewish Agency executive in Jerusalem, 1931–1939; political representative of Jewish Agency in Washington, D.C., 1940–1946, and to the United Nations in 1947; president of the Zionist Organization of America, 1947–1949 and 1956–1958; chairman of the executive of the Jewish Agency and World Zionist Organization, 1953–1971.

56

Journal: The Jewish Messianic Approach

Jerusalem, May 21, 1927

Neither Bolshevism or Marxism on the one hand, nor Capitalism or Nationalism on the other correspond to the Jewish messianic conception of right and equality and the new order. They are both founded on force and violence. Far be it from the pillars of present-day capitalist and nationalist society to chide Bolshevism with the use of force and violence. They are all based upon bayonets and blood-letting, prisons and terror

But there is a difference in their avowed purposes. Bolshevism holds out the ideal, the end of a social commonwealth based upon justice. Capitalism is almost, if not quite, content with things as they are in the best of all worlds. If one *must* choose between the two can there be any doubt that one must sympathize more with the bearer of a great ideal?

But a Jew's approach (that is, the Jewish messianic approach) to either or both must be skeptical in the extreme. His Jewish idealism is in method quite the opposite of force and violence. It is, rather, a belief in spirit and the efficacy of mind and soul. How far his ideal is practical and will work in the natural course of things is questionable. But that is what keeps him apart. Perhaps, by being true to this ideal even unto death, the miracle of a new heaven and a new earth may be realized. If there is only as much hope as *perhaps*, that is sufficient to keep us alive and drive us on.

The Jewish "socialist" idea cannot be so thoroughly absorbed in materialist things and thoughts as is the materialist socialism of the day. It cannot be so concerned with absolute equality of possessions. Rather, it is in the Jewish nature to say: neither riches nor poverty; enough for life and education (perhaps the middle-class attitude towards riches).

57

Journal: Judaism and Universalism

Jerusalem, August 7, 1927

Tish'a B'av,[1] 5787

The irony of life: the Reform Rabbis wanted to make tish'a b'av a day of rejoicing—a sign of the Jew's emancipation from Zion and Jerusalem, his being freed from the fetters of narrow nationalism. Here *in* Palestine tish'a b'av is largely a *yom tov* [holiday] and hardly a day of mourning and desolation. What the Reform Rabbis could not do in practice, the nationalist life in Palestine achieves in a measure by itself. The Returned (in contradistinction to the Reformed) Jew has again the substratum of that which tish'a b'av mourns the loss of — his land, his nationality. Having it, even in small measure, he is freer to forget the woes and defeats of the past, and to look into the future. This is but another illustration of the thesis that in order to grow beyond nationalism it is necessary first to be done with the constant preoccupation with it. Before the tree can blossom and look up into the sun and give its shade, it must first strike deep root in nature.

There are two aspects to each process:
I. Striking national root can produce:
    (a) the freedom to look beyond nationalism. In Palestine the first "universal" institution = the University, or
    (b) its opposite: a deeper more racial, protect-the-home-and-hearth-and-soil patriotism.
II. Universalism can be and is achieved by Jews:
    (a) through first getting a deep and complete Jewish background — soil under the feet and raw-material (from Jewish literature and life and education) for the mind, or
    (b) through the attempt to forget or make your children and the succeeding generations forget or neglect their Jewish heritage.
Of the latter case (b) there are also two aspects:
1. The Jew becomes a humanitarian or an internationalist with an American or a Russian or other background in language, manners, ideas of political and even social organization, or
2. He becomes a landless, backgroundless cosmopolite. This is the most difficult of types, for a man must have a language, manners, etc. But these things, whatever be the chance national or racial coloring of them, are of genuine importance.

From the point of view of *Judaism*, I *a* and *b* and II *a* are of course more fruitful than II *b*. From the point of view of *Judaism* there might be a dispute as to which was more fertile, fruitful, I *a* (II *a*) or I *b*.

From the point of view of humanitarianism, universalism, internationalism, I *a* and II *a* and *b* are more fruitful than I *b*. From this point of view there might be a dispute between I *a* (II *a*) and II *b* as to which is more fruitful for humanity.

I *b* therefore, is most objectionable from the viewpoint of universalism and II *b* most objectionable from the viewpoint of Judaism. There are left I *a* and II *a* which are in the main identical as being useful, fertile from both points of view.

The question now is: what are the differences between I *a* and II *a*.

That is, how does one best "strike national root" from the point of view of Judaism and Universalism? Is it through concentration in Palestine, or through Judaism abroad?

There can be no absolute answer. It differs with individuals. I *b* can be harmful to Universalism, and II *b* to Judaism. If this harmony be sought, there is a problem both here and there. It becomes a problem of emphasis, and the final answer must be that both forms, Palestine and Golah [exile], are suitable and necessarily complementary to the complete and diversified nationalist-universalist Jewish People.

That there can be no absolutes about the *forms* of Jewish life (but only about its ethical and spiritual *content*) is shown by the recurring controversy now raging over the merits of a Congress-Delegations meeting in Zurich. The American Jewish Committee and Alliance and Board of Deputies people deprecate it. They fear irresponsible talky-talky. *They* will care for things, for the Jews, for minorities. They are in many ways absolutely right. Yet on the other hand the (spuriously) "Democratic" forces have two arguments on their side: (1) That unless they make a noise the Committee forces will not move, and the offending governments (Roumania, Hungary) will not heed the still, small voice of the more diplomatic Committees. Public opinion loudly proclaimed is necessary. (2) That for the sake of the Jewish People itself, there ought to be a wider distribution of responsibility, more active participation in the discussion and possible solutions of these problems than the Committee form of Jewish leadership affords.

In other words, they are both necessary, due to the scattering of Jewish life and force. No need to complain about this. A great and wonderful phenomenon. Would not have it otherwise. Could not be better or righter for a people with a world-mission. Not Palestine, not a Jewish World Congress, and not even the most powerful Committee organization can make it otherwise. That is the structure of the Jewish people, and it would be the part of wise and informed leadership to recognize it. There cannot be and there need not be but *one* organization of the Jews. In the very nature of things there must be more than one form.

One might, however, ask that the American Jewish Committee and the American Jewish Congress be more modest about its name. Neither one speaks for all of American Jewry, and most certainly the Congress is no congress.

1. The ninth day of the Hebrew month of Av is a fast day commemorating the destruction of the first temple by the Babylonians in 586 B.C. and the second temple by the Romans in A.D. 70.

2. In August 1927 representatives of forty-three organizations from thirteen countries met in Zurich to establish a world Jewish congress to defend the civil and political rights of Jews. Conservative organizations such as the American Jewish Committee, Alliance Is-

raelite Universelle, British Board of Deputies, and the Hilfsverein der Deutschen Juden did not attend. Nine years later the World Jewish Congress was established.

58

Journal: Weizmann and the University

Jerusalem, February 13, 1928

Yesterday I wrote a letter to Dr. Weizmann in answer to his and that of Professor Einstein (Jan. 17, Jan 8).[1] It concerned the proposal for an Academic Head for the University, and it accordingly concerned my own place in the University structure.

My letter was not altogether frank because it did not deal with my relationship to Weizmann. Down deep in me I have a mistrust of him that I am sorry for. He has many high qualities — mind, knowledge of science and of men, courage, vision and often in crises a suprising moral dignity. But it is his moral quality that is questionable. He is through and through the politician. He is constantly playing a game, very cleverly, and one does not know what he is after. His statement to me recently that he would resign if Einstein did, is part of some game calculated to bring him advantage — just what I do not know. At the same time the little paragraph appeared in the *Jewish World*: "It is intimated that Dr. Weizmann will become Chancellor of the University, etc." Ballon d'essai. He probably is not altogether sorry that there are certain difficulties here — Fodor, as the best example. He doubtless explains, with a sigh, that he may have to take the matter in hand some day.

If I had been perfectly frank in my letter, I should have said something like this: for me, if I am to be part of the University structure, there seem to be the following possibilities:

(a) To be head of the University in Jerusalem as I am today having final responsibility for both the lay and the academic administration. I have always insisted that there be deans of faculties to carry on the actual academic administration with final authority resting in the head. This I believe to be the best form of administration for a young university with all of the difficulties of administration and organization that, in the nature of things, the University at Jerusalem must encounter. This form of administration seems to me best quite aside fom whether or not I am the head. If an academic head can be secured who could also take over the full administration satisfactorily, I should be the first to be for him.

(b) Or to be lay head of the University. But the lay head of the University is and should be the President of the Board of Governors. That is Weizmann. But Weizmann is not in Jerusalem; nor has he the time to devote to building up the University. Therefore I am to be the lay head. There are thus two lay heads, and the President of the Board is the lay head with the greater authority if it comes right down to a question of authority. He is always in the background "eine andere, eine hohere Instanz" [another, a higher court], as someone suggested when demurring to me against my decisions. When Weizmann was here in October he held a kind of hearing with Selig Weizmann as chief adviser in Selig's house. Nothing wrong, nothing bad, but nevertheless the lay head in the last analysis. If I did not mistrust him, I do not think I should care. If I did not mistrust him, I should welcome his exercising authority or his taking my place and more in two years' time or so when he decides he wants to live in Palestine for part of the year as head of the University. I have no objection to creating a place for a successor as long as *during the period of my own tenancy* – however long or short – I can bend all my energies to the task without feeling that there is a sinister figure in the background with his own game to play and his own axe to grind. All I want is to have the privilege, over however short a time, of making a real contribution to the creation of the University. This is that much more difficult, particularly for a person of my temperament, if my position is equivocal. Lay head no. 1 or lay head no. 2 – let it be no. 2 or 3 – but it must be clear, and though I only referred to this problem in my letter to Brodetsky[2] of September 29, it is a problem that has to be clarified at the meeting of the Board at the end of May. The question is, how this can be done. I do not want to say or do anything now that will harm Weizmann's position as "presiding genius," as Bentwich calls him, "over the whole Palestine enterprise." I have always been most scrupulous in pointing out his finer sides when he was being attacked in my presence. Nor do I believe that one can be perfectly frank with him and have him understand and not be resentful. But the clarification will have to come. Perhaps its form is, as suggested by Bentwich: the President of the Board has definitely no responsibility for the University's conduct any more than the ceremonious chancellor of an English university. He is there as a figure head, if this is possible.

In any event, in order not to be unfair to the University I shall have to keep strict watch over myself, over my weaknesses, if you will. I am so constructed that I can give my best to a cause only when I have the inner conviction that I am the "called" man for the work. I work best only when the cause calls, only when I have the conviction (or illusion) that I am really needed, that my whole being, perhaps life itself, is required. I can work only when I feel I am driving ahead. I have thought up till now that the University needed a dynamic force behind it.

In view of the doubts and scruples of Brodestsky and Einstein, I have begun to slow down, to relax my hold. Instead of driving ahead, I am now dropping gradually into the waiting attitude. Who will be the academic head? Will the functions of the lay head be laid down clearly and satisfactorily? Will the new Academic Council, the new Academic Committee, the Board of Governors help or hinder? Maybe they are right and I am wrong. Let's wait and see.

This may be the very best thing for the University. Perhaps it should go along for a time on its own momentum. Perhaps I have been driving too hard. But I doubt if it is good for me, that is, for that which I can give to the University. With relaxation comes a certain measure of indifference as to whether the decision will fall this way or that. With relaxation comes deterioration, the line of least resistance, moving along in the groove without the feeling and joy of creativeness.

I do want to guard against all this, because I am interested in the University and believe in its great functions.

1. Einstein wrote to Weizmann on January 8, 1928, that it was pointless to participate in the university's governing institutions since Magnes continued to retain control over academic affairs, a task for which he was unqualified. Einstein insisted that an academic head responsible directly to the board of governors be appointed. Weizmann enclosed a copy of Einstein's letter with his own letter to Magnes of January 17, 1928, and supported Einstein's views. He asked Magnes "to give the matter your careful consideration . . . in the same frank spirit in which you wrote me before and in which I am writing you this note."
2. Selig Brodetsky (1888–1954). Mathematician and English Zionist leader; born in the Ukraine and brought to London in 1893. He received his Ph.D. in Leipzig in 1913; was a professor at University of Leeds, 1920–1949. In 1928 he became a member of the executive committee of the Zionist Organization in England and head of its political department in London. He was a member of the board of governors and academic council of Hebrew University; was supported by Einstein and Weizmann as candidate for academic head of the university; from 1949 to his death was president of the Hebrew University.

59
Journal: Reading Karl Barth

Jerusalem, March 7, 1928

I evidently slapped my knees while finishing an article on the theology of Karl Barth. Beatie asked me why, and I said I could not tell her. "Was it because of the past?" No. "Because of questions like that of peace?" "Hardly. It is because of present agonies of which I hardly speak." "But I must know of them." "It is because I am sometimes tortured with the need of an infinite God." "You sleep well. Perhaps you could stay up all the night and tell me about it." "That's it. I don't know how to tell about it. Strange that I should be such a thing as a university administrator." "But if you were not that, then what?" "If I were altogether free and honest, and were to follow the glimmer of the gleam that I sometimes have, I would be a Voice, perhaps in the wilderness. My father's father, and my mother's grandfather talk to me and I do not listen enough."

There is no way to God. But there is a way from God to us. Man needs God, seeks him, but the search is futile. If man thinks he has found Him it is a Dead Sea apple in his hands — nothingness, farther and farther away. But let a man open himself to receive God's influence upon him. That seems to be the essence of the article I was reading. The first part is true. The second has a glimmering of truth for me.

"The paradox, once more, is our refuge: let a man realize at once his infinite need for finding God, and the infinite futility of his search, and in the clash of these two infinities within his soul, the God of the infinity will be adumbrated, but only adumbrated." Author of the article in *Christian Century*.[1]

Paradox ethical: "To seek God's will zealously, with the foregone conclusion that God's will cannot be found — to join the contemporary crusades for righteousness with the conviction that they will one day be proved, like the great crusades, to have been ill-advised and wrong. This is not *discovering* God's will, but it is, after all, *acknowledging* it."

To whom, to what, our highest loyalties? The State, the family, the nation, the Land — all of this important but all of it imperfect. Loyalty to the spirit — if we only dared say 'God' — the only really worthy loyalty.

This loyalty of Zionism to the Empire, to political forms, to the narrow side of nationalism — it is impossible that that should be the thing that stuffs our mouths and holds our tongues from speaking and our hearts from expanding.

What gives the more perfect freedom — retaining American citizenship or sharing the lot of those with Palestinian? And sharing this lot, trying to rise above it, while being a pawn in the hands of neither British imperialism nor Arab nationalism, but a pawn, if that it be, of Jewish religion — the higher loyalty. The war has shown the hollowness of Church, School and State. Real loyalty can only be rendered the Spirit. But Spirit is vague. If one only had a real God!

The Zionist paradox (after Barth): to seek the fullness of Judaism zealously, with the conclusion foregone that this cannot be found; to join the Palestine movement, to live in Palestine with the conviction that one day (now!) this will have been proved to be illusory and almost barren. This is not discovering Judaism, but it is, after all, acknowledging it.

1. Douglas Horton, "God Lets Loose Karl Barth," *Christian Century*, February 16, 1928, 206.

60

Journal: Psychology of Palestine Jewish Community

Jerusalem, March 25, 1928

1. *E-ne yisrael n'su'ot elenu* [the eyes of Israel are upon us]. The success or failure of this individual or that enterprise does not end there. Both Palestine and Galut draw conclusions from it. The individual not private, and the enterprise not individual.

2. The letter of the Students Organization, threatening use of all "pressure direct and indirect" (strike, etc.) if more studies — rounded course, certificates — not given them. Was ever a strike heard of before because of lack of studies? The desire for this is legitimate, but surrounded with so many queer expressions in letter and resolutions that one begins to feel that one is too old to learn and to change his mentality.

3. The varieties of language, of costume, of custom, of mental outlook. In a large city each group can live unto itself. In Jerusalem an infinite variety, yet place so small that these differences become noticed, bump against one another. Each group as it goes down to and stands before the *kotel ma'aravi* [Western Wall] — autonomous, independent, tiny, stubborn. Ever so many of them, each conscious of his minutiae of differences, each self-contained, economically independent (supported from without), no desire for larger organization or community. Purpose of life here is the living out of individual spiritual aspiration. No other small place with so many Chief Rabbis and scholars. No other place where large proportion of population composed of *p'kidim* [officials] supported mostly out of funds from without.

4. Hebrew: Hear forms, words, expressions, rhetoric, rather than content. Other languages give better living, other languages more modern philosophy, literature, history, sociology, science, politics . . . Not the same necessity to learn Hebrew here as to learn English in America. As a consequence, many of best minds and most influential personages incapable of free, full, vigorous, varied expression in Jewish

269

public, official, or even private life. Consequently, rough, brusque snatches of speech, no real communication or communion.

5. Social Station. The immigrant who went to America was, for the most part, of lower social station. Went, for the most part, to better his economic position and usually rose in the economic, social (intellectual) scale. The immigrant to Palestine, in large part, of higher social position. Usually a more or less important man in his community. A Zionist worker, a *klal tuer* [community leader], a professional man, a pious man, a student, an idealist. Coming to Palestine, he finds others of his kind gathered in one community, and he is not of as much importance as at home. (Often important town men who came as visitors are disappointed at the reception they receive as *tayyarim* [tourists]. There are other *tayyarim* of as much importance).

Life is strange, difficult. Often a lowering in the social and economic scale. Where in America the *am ha'arets* [ignoramus] rose and became important, the few intellectuals socially high from the old home sneered. But there were so many other ignoramuses aspiring to rise that the majority felt no indignation. In Palestine when an *am ha'arets* rises, he does so among a population which Jewishly speaking is in its great majority his superior. Life becomes hard. The socially superior man finds it hard to compete. Or if he does, he thinks he is losing his idealism and he actually does begin to lose it. There is a process of deterioration discernible in many a man. The difficulties of life seem to bring out the worst in many a man. He becomes less generous. When a teacher loses a job, where has he to go? It is not as in a larger country where there may be other schools. Here no other opportunities; or, over the border is Europe, America. If he has to leave here it is a more difficult uprooting. He is giving up that for which he has striven his whole life. When he gets away, life has lost much of its meaning. The teacher holds on to his job because there is no other. His children's food is dependent upon it.

61

Journal: The Arab Question

Jerusalem, July 4, 1928

"The Arab Question"
Involves many others: Judaism, Zionism
                      Nationalism, Internationalism
                      Imperialism, Pacifism

1. Begin with the thesis that Palestine is *sui generis*. No spot in history has so many memories for so many peoples and faiths. Land of Bible — Old and New. Home of at least three major faiths, and subsidiary faiths (Bahais). Never lived unto itself. Was always a bridge. Fauna and flora. Life understood only in relation to others. While this true of many, most nations, lands, especially so of Palestine. The Holy Land, the Holy City, the Holy Places. The monasteries, convents, the consuls, the interest of the nations. The sects of Christendom — the tourists.

2. Thus Palestine does not "belong" to anyone in particular in the spiritual sense. *Ki li kol ha'arets* [for the land belongs unto Me].[1]Palestine belongs in a very real sense to all the nations that have come under the influence of Judaism. Christianity and Islam. It is historically, spiritually (geographically) of too great importance to say that it "belongs" to its inhabitants for the time being. These inhabitants are privileged, trustees (and must so act).

3. One of the inferences from this exceptional status is, therefore, the "internationalism of Palestine." The League of Nations is therefore the proper form of final sovereignty and control. The interest of the League in Palestine must be increased. The Mandatory must be brought to feel more and more his international position as trustee for an international land. The land should serve as little as possible the political or economic imperialism of the Mandatory power. No favored nation, no tariff preferences. An international obligation never to maintain imperial armies but only police forces; never under any circumstances to conscript the inhabitants in behalf of any war whatsoever, offensive or defensive. A Free State similar to a Free City, with harbor open to all comers, with governor of another nationality — perhaps governors of various nationalities over given periods.

4. One of the first inferences from this international status is "Open Door" — that gates to land are open to all peoples. He who wants to come as a tourist or settler may, whatever his nationality or religion. A free

immigration policy — but always, of course, with due regard to the land's economic power of absorption. There shall never be immigration restrictions due to race or religion or political or social views. This must be part of the fundamental law, and it is the obligation of international society to maintain this principle. In fact, it is likely, though by no means certain (cf. the influx of Greeks, or possibly of Italians) that for the immediate future this would mean a larger access of Jews than any other people. But the international policy outlined is not to be condemned because its operation would favor Jews. The Jews must accept both its favorable and its unfavorable aspects.

(Other Jewish Desiderata and Rights):
Land purchase
Cultural life
No majorization (whether Jewish or Arabic)

1. Exod. 19:5.

62

Journal: B'rit Shalom

Jerusalem, September 14, 1928

Erev Rosh Hashannah [The Eve of the New Year]

When the B'rit Shalom was started, I would not join despite the fact that I thought some of its practical objects good and essential. I advised Kohn[1] and Bergman[2] to join with me in organizing a B'rit Shalom that would have a genuine pacifist basis, and that would seek peace with the Arabs (and with everybody else) not because such a peace was a tactical, practical necessity, but because such a peace was a direct outcome and necessary and logical deduction from the pacifist and Jewish position generally.

I tried to illustrate the difference by citing Dr. Ruppin, who was taking an active part in the formation of the B'rit Shalom. His common sense had led him to see that a theory of proper relations with the Arabs had to be worked out, and he had come to the Two Peoples Theory, and this was all to the good. But he was not a pacifist in the spiritual sense of that term, i.e. he would be ready, if the possibility and the means were present, to get rid of the Arabs in a non-peaceful way. It was at about this time that I heard Selig Weizmann say at Ussishkin's, with the assent of Ussishkin and Dr. Mohilever,[3] that if he could, he would drive every Arab out of the country by foul means or by fair. He knew this was impossible, therefore it was necessary to work out a modus vivendi. What wonderful times those were in Haifa, he declared, just after the occupation! The British soldiers were in charge. They and the Jews fraternized, and you should have seen the beaten look on the Arab there.

In other words, living at peace with the Arabs here has to be the outcome, not only of the practical considerations which are apparent to everyone, but also of the basic theory of a Jewish pacifism, that has applicability not only here, but throughout the world, and that is valid not only for Jews and Arabs, but for human relationships generally.

There is no hope for the Jewish Community of Palestine, either materially or spiritually, unless their life be the outflow of a deep theory of pacifism. For that reason, the working out of this theory in its roots and in its details is a matter of urgency.

1. Hans Kohn (see glossary of names).
2. Shmuel Hugo Bergman (see glossary of names).
3. Joseph Mohilever (1872–1943). Educator and Zionist; born in Radom, Poland, and emigrated to Palestine in 1920, where he became the principal of the Hebrew High School in Jerusalem.

63

To Felix Warburg[1]

Jerusalem, April 28, 1929

Dear Friend,

I have been struggling hard with the Agency-University, Weizmann-Magnes problem you have presented, and it would be less than fair to have you leave without telling you that my whole "reaction" is negative. This is the more distressing to me because you have set your heart upon this combination of things and men, and you and Frieda are so sincere and large-minded in your relationship towards Palestine that I should like in every possible way to make your work here full of nothing but joy. Moreover, I am distressed because it would seem that my own deepest prejudices are involved, and I do really try literally each day to lift myself above them. Nevertheless, my answer is negative. I shall, of course, keep on trying to have an open mind, to purge myself of prejudice, to listen to the advice of my associates here in the University and of my friends in America.

If you were to ask me my honest answer to the problem you have set, it would be: keep me where I am and keep Weizmann where he is. Keep me out of the Agency, and keep Weizmann out of the University.

I think this the right answer for both personal and objective reasons.

Personal: I can do the University job and Weizmann can do the Agency job. I cannot do the Agency job, and I doubt if Weizmann can do the University job. Moreover, for all his great qualities, I do not trust Weizmann, and I doubt if Weizmann trusts me. I do not want to spend my time warding off intrigue. The human relationships in the University are difficult enough without having them added to by Weizmann's presence and without piling on my head the human relationships of the Agency.

Objective: The leader of the political machinery, here or anywhere else, should not be the head of the University, and the leader of the University should not head the political machinery. One of the great evils of the present day is, in my opinion, the authority which the State exercises over religion and education. The modern State presumes to be higher than a man's conscience and the modern state has destroyed the old res publica of learning. Everything is subservient to the State. The command of the State is higher than the command of God or the light of learning. Coming to Palestine: one of the evils of the educational system is its absolute dependence, financially and spiritually, upon the Zionist political machinery. The fact that the University is, fortunately, independent of this is helping us create a true University. Why drag it into politics by putting Weizmann into it, and by putting me out of it, wholly or in part? I am not charging Weizmann with anything in this instance. I am sure I would be no better or no different. It lies in the nature of the case: occupation with the State's political machinery leads to bargaining, manipulation, unworthy compromise, nepotism, the sacrifice of the ideas of learning to political advantage, and finally the desire, particularly in moments of crisis, (and when do we Jews not live in moments of crisis particularly in Palestine) to regiment the mind and the conscience — always, of course, from the highest of motives.

This difference between Weizmann and myself is the scarlet cord running through the whole thing from the beginning — from the very moment you gave your $100,000 for Jewish studies to this day. The details might be instructive at some other time. I would only say here that this difference finds some slight expression in the minutes of the first meeting of the Board at Tel Aviv, and it was from this point of view that I was opposed to Weizmann's election as chairman of the Board at the Munich meeting in September 1925, and this is also the meaning of the Zionist charge that the University was taken away from them and of the Zionist reluctance to turn property over finally to the Board of Governors. If I were a member of the political machinery I should probably feel the same way about it as they do.

I realize that "keeping Weizmann out" of the University is not as simple as it sounds, but keeping me out of the Agency, as long as I am in the University, seems to me the only sound way. Sometimes men having to do with universities go into politics during moments of stress. But they leave their university posts for this purpose. If you and others for whom I have regard thought this was my duty, I should be ready to consider leaving the University, although I think myself much better fitted for the University job. But to do both—University and Agency—is, I think, impossible and undesirable.

Weizmann and the University: If any man has a claim to be in and not be kept out of the University it is Weizmann. He has preached the idea longer (though not so much longer) than I, and he has kept the idea alive within the Zionist Organization. Yet I am convinced (this being probably one of my deep-felt prejudices) that Weizmann's entry into the University will mean its entrance into the whirlpool of politics and intrigue. I am that much attached to the University and its great idea to say that I want to protect the University against this. I owe too much to the men who have come here, some of them because I asked them to, to shirk this issue. No plan of Weizmann's participation in the University work here could therefore be acceptable to me unless it was clearly and formally and officially understood that between meetings of the Board of Governors, final authority in both academic and administrative matters rested in the Chancellor. Under these circumstances I should be willing to try cooperation with Weizmann, knowing full well that he would not rest until final authority was reposed in him. But I am ready to go through with this, and if I lose (which I think in this instance means the University losing), then we lose.

1. Magnes drafted this letter in long hand. There is no indication that he actually sent the letter to Warburg. Until the final negotiations leading up to the formation of the enlarged Jewish Agency in August 1929, Warburg hoped that Magnes would serve as associate chairman of the agency.

64

To Chaim Weizmann
London

Zurich, September 7, 1929

Dear Dr. Weizmann,

You asked me over the telephone last night to write you my views on the present situation. I wanted to have a long talk with you, and for that reason had been trying to get in touch with you for several days. Writing is a poor substitute for an oral exchange of opinions, and I shall try to be brief.

I think that the time has come when the Jewish policy as to Palestine must be very clear, and that now only one of two policies is possible. Either the logical policy outlined by Jabotinsky[1] in a letter in the *Times* which came today, basing our Jewish life in Palestine on militarism and imperialism;[2] or a pacific policy that treats as entirely secondary such things as a "Jewish State" or a Jewish majority, or even "The Jewish National Home," and as primary the development of a Jewish spiritual, educational, moral and religious center in Palestine. The first policy has to deal primarily with politics, governments, declarations, propaganda and bayonets, and only secondarily with the Jews, and last of all with the Arabs; whereas the pacific policy has to deal first of all with the Jews, and then with the Arabs, and only incidentally with governments and all the rest.

The imperialist, military and political policy is based upon mass immigration of Jews and the creation (forcible if necessary) of a Jewish majority, no matter how much this oppresses the Arabs meanwhile, or deprives them of their rights. In this kind of policy the end always justifies the means. The policy, on the other hand, of developing a Jewish spiritual Center does not depend upon mass immigration, a Jewish majority, a Jewish State, or upon depriving the Arabs (or the Jews) of their political rights for a generation or a day; but on the contrary, is desirous of having Palestine become a country of two nations and three religions, all of them having equal rights and none of them having special privileges; a country where nationalism is but the basis of internationalism, where the population is pacifistic and disarmed — in short, the Holy Land.

The one policy may be termed that of militarist, imperialist, political Zionism; the other that of pacific, international, spiritual Zionism; and if some authorities will not choose to call the latter idea Zionism, then let it be called the Love of Zion, or the Return to Zion, or any other name that you will.

We have been toying with the words 'Jewish State,' 'majority,' 'Jewish Palestine,' 'politics,' 'Balfour Declaration,' etc., long enough. It is time that we came down to realities. We have passed resolutions concerning cooperation with the Arabs, but we have done very little seriously to carry them out.

I do not say that this is easy of achievement nor do I absolutely know that it is possible. The Palestine Arabs are unhappily still half savage, and their leaders are almost all small men. But this policy of cooperation is certainly more possible and more hopeful of achievement than building up a Jewish Home (National or otherwise) on bayonets and oppression. Moreover, a Jewish Home in Palestine built up on bayonets and oppression is not worth having, even though it succeed, whereas the very attempt to build it up peacefully, cooperatively, with understanding, education, and good will, is worth a great deal, even though the attempt should fail.

The question is, do we want to conquer Palestine now as Joshua did in his day—with fire and sword? Or do we want to take cognizance of Jewish religious development since Joshua—our Prophets, Psalmists and Rabbis, and repeat the words: "Not by might, and not by violence, but by my spirit, saith the Lord." The question is, can any country be entered, colonized, and built up pacifistically, and can we Jews do that in the Holy Land? If we can not (and I do not say that we can rise to these heights), I for my part have lost half my interest in the enterprise. If we can not even attempt this, I should much rather see this eternal people without such a "National Home," with the wanderer's staff in hand and forming new ghettos among the peoples of the world.

As you know, these are not new views on my part. I was read out of the Zionist Organization of America in 1915 because among other things, I contended that the Jews should ask for no special privileges in Palestine, but should be content with equal rights. When the Balfour Declaration was issued and the Mandate signed, I did not rejoice. I wrote two modest newspaper articles and delivered a speech (which is printed) in the sense of the views as given above. When you and Felix Warburg and I were discussing matters in Palestine, you with your usual keenness referred to me as believing Zionist policy was altogether too political. I have, as you also know, done what little I could to help bring about a united front for Palestine ever since the beginning, and I must confess that I had hoped that the non-Zionist members of the Agency might give the whole movement a non-political, non-imperialist turn. But your great persuasiveness has carried them with you on the political issues also, and it was mainly on this account that I could not accept the invitation to participate in the Agency. It is also for this reason that I have resolutely tried to keep the University entirely distinct from the political organization.

All these years I have kept silent, not wishing to obtrude what appeared to me my minority views, and I had thought that by devoting myself wholly and without deflection to the University, I could make a contribution to my kind of Zionism. But I cannot keep silent for Zion's sake in these tragic days, and I want to do what little I can to give voice to the views to which I have been trying hitherto to give expression through work alone.

You said you would want to convey my views to the meeting of the Actions Committee, and you are at liberty to read them this letter if you think it worthwhile.

I am sending a copy of this letter to Felix Warburg.

I sympathize with you in the fearful burden you now have to bear, and I can only pray that you may be led to walk in the right path.

Yours truly, JLM

1. Vladimir Ze'ev Jabotinsky (1880–1949). Zionist leader, writer, and orator; born in Odessa. He founded the Jewish Legion during the First World War; was founder and head of the Betar movement and World Union of Zionist Revisionists which demanded a more activist program and declared the political goal of the Zionist movement to be the establishment of a Jewish state.

2. *The Times* of London, September 6, 1929, p. 8.

65

To Felix Warburg
New York

Paris, September 13, 1929

Dear Felix,

I am enclosing a copy of a letter I wrote to Doctor Weizmann on September 7th. I have had no answer as yet. From this you will get my general point of view. You will see from this probably more clearly than I could make clear to you before, why I could not join with you in the Agency. You may have thought that there was too much of the personal element in it. There is, of course, in everything. But my attitude is based on something much deeper, as you have doubtless felt, but as I doubtless have been unsuccessful in conveying to you.

I have, I regret to say, no confidence whatever that Doctor Weizmann and his associates understand the situation today any better than they have before. They may pass peace resolutions and agree to White Papers and lots of other things out of political necessity, but not out of inner conviction. Unless the whole aim of Zionism is changed, there will never be peace. Maybe there can be no peace anyway, but in that event the Jewish People would have added a glorious instead of a disgraceful page to its history.

Palestine does not belong to the Jews and it does not belong to the Arabs, nor to Judaism or Christianity or Islam. It belongs to all of them together; it is the Holy Land. If the Arabs want an Arab national state in Palestine, it is as much or as little to be defended as if the Jews want a Jewish national state there. We must once and for all give up the idea of a "Jewish Palestine" in the sense that a Jewish Palestine is to exclude and do away with an Arab Palestine. This is the historic fact, and Palestine is nothing if it is not history. If a Jewish national home in Palestine is compatible with an Arab national home there, well and good, but if it is not, the name makes very little difference. The fact is that nothing there is possible unless Jews and Arabs work together in peace for the benefit of their common Holy Land. It must be our endeavor first to convince ourselves and then to convince others that Jews and Arabs, Moslems, Christians, and Jews have each as much right there, no more and no less, than the other: equal rights and equal privileges and equal duties. That is practically quite sufficient for all purposes of the Jewish religion, and it is the sole ethical basis of our claims there. Judaism did not begin with Zionism, and if Zionism is ethically not in accord with Judaism, so much the worse for Zionism.

I must say that I have been amazed that not one official Jewish voice has been lifted in sympathy with such slain and injured Moslems or Christians who may have been innocent; that no money was earmarked for their injured. Of course, the Arabs were the aggressors and the most bloodthirsty. Do I also have to be shouting that? But do you not know that we, too, have had our preachers of hate and disseminators of lies, our armed youth, our provocative processions, our unforgivable stupidity in our handling of the Western Wall incidents since last Yom Kippur, making out of what should have been a police incident an international political issue?[1] Politics, statesmanship, hobnobbing with the masters of empire, using high-sounding phrases instead of disciplining and purifying our community and trying to understand and make terms with our neighbors.

Is it conceivable that responsible men should at this moment of all moments make additional demands for increased immigration, etc., a "blue-white book" instead of the White Book which they signed with more than Jesuitical reservations? Is it conceivable that among all the official Zionist demands and proposals there is not the faintest hint that a Jewish-Arab understanding, a peace conference if you will, is more important than anything else? Of course life must be protected by the Mandatory Power—that is the most elemental of considerations. Of course the bureaucracies of Jerusalem (British and Jewish) have not done their simplest duty and should be investigated without flinching. Of course the guilty—Arabs, British, Jews—should be punished. But he who takes it all out in this and in making chauvinistic demands is no better than were the war mongers in 1914 and 1917. The situation is essentially the same; each side talks of the other's *Alleinschuld* [sole blame] and of war *a la victoire integrale* [for total victory], whereas they should be thinking also of their own sins and of ways of stopping the war and of living at peace. And if the Arabs are not capable of this, we Jews must be, else we are false to our spiritual heritage and give the lie to our much-vaunted higher civilization. If I were as religious a man as I should like to be, I should say that this was God's testing of His People. Can we be humble and courageous and intelligent enough to make this testing into a source of blessing?

You may ask me for a practical program. There are practical programs long since worked out on paper. But what is the good of them if the whole spirit and aim of those officially charged with carrying them out are such as to make these programs only a necessary evil for them or a burden or a lie?

I hope you will bear with me for writing with such violence. But I am in agony about it all, and I am taking myself to task for having kept silent for so long. After my "political" activities in Jewish New York with the Kehillah and other things, and then particularly during the war, I felt I had enough and that I wanted to do quiet, constructive work, and that nothing again could rouse me after what I had been through during the war. And now that I am roused again the thought that I may be playing into Jewish Zionist politics is a burden I can hardly bear. But what is one to do when he sees sacred things laid hold upon by unclean hands?

Do you remember that in Jerusalem I said to you that I could not become Co-chairman with you because at the very first meeting my views would be such that a fruitful working together with the Committee would be impossible? Now perhaps you know better what I meant. Cyrus Adler knew something of what I meant, and perhaps you will show him this letter. And I can hardly keep from asking you to show it to Louis Marshall, too.

I had succeeded these many years in putting many of these thoughts into the background, and of trying, despite many difficulties, to keep the University in the foreground and to give myself to it wholly. I had become happy, too happy, in this, in the thought that others could fight around about politics, while I might have the privilege of helping build a basic institution in Judaism. But I see again what I knew before and tried to forget, that politics means lives, safety, and the determination of moral and religious attitudes, and I ask myself the question where my duty lies. I have heretofore done everything possible to keep the University divorced from politics, and the Zionist leaders have secretly or openly resented this and worked against me. But that was something quite possible to bear. But now, while keeping the University as such out of politics, I, who am so closely connected with it, can no longer hold my peace, and, speaking, I shall say what I believe, that the University is *the* place where Arab-Jewish relations can and must be worked out. That is, I am, after all, to bring the University into politics in *my* sense and on behalf of my views. Is that fair? right? good for the University? Certainly, without speaking my mind and acting as I thought best I could not attempt to collect another dollar for the University or to persuade any new men to come to Jerusalem or to be responsible for the University's administration and the spirit of it.

This is one of the reasons why I must go back now and meanwhile I shall ask of you to think these questions over by yourself and with others. Perhaps you will also let Sol Lowenstein read this letter.[2]

Yours, Judah

1. Disputes between Arabs and Jews over Jewish rights to pray at the Western ("Wailing") Wall led to the disruption of Yom Kippur services and the desecration of Jewish holy objects in September 1928. In August 1929 tensions reached a new peak as a result of Arab construction work adjacent to the Western Wall. The Revisionist youth group held a protest march. Arab counterdemonstrations grew in intensity and on August 23, 1929, crowds of Arabs attacked Jews in various parts of Jerusalem. The killing and looting spread to other settlements in the days that followed.

2. Warburg cabled Magnes on September 24, 1929: "Stirred by your letter. My views have always been absolutely yours that is why I wanted you as associate chairman. We must strive for these peaceful ideas. My steamer statement weekend cable Weizmann speech Town Hall all dwelled on this. Laid Marshall to rest simply with extraordinary expressions from everybody. Missed you. Felix."

66

From the New York Times
November 24, 1929

AN INTERNATIONAL ENCLAVE

I am glad of the opportunity of commenting on Mr. Philby's[1] statement, and I should say with all emphasis that I am speaking for myself
alone, and not for any organization.

The statement of Mr. Philby is a great advance upon what is usually
put forward as the Arab case in Palestine. If one were to compare this
statement with the intransigent nationalistic attitude of the Arab Delegation as expressed in the Churchill-Samuel White Paper of June, 1922, it is
apparent that much has been learned, fortunately, since that time.

Whereas then it was said that the "Balfour Declaration can not be accepted as a basis for discussion," now Mr. Philby sensibly declares that
"no solution can be regarded as practical which postulates the abrogation
of the Balfour Declaration." Whereas then the mandatory idea, with its
great international background, was reduced to making the Mandatory
merely an "Assisting Power" for the immediate creation of an Arab independent government, Mr. Philby says that no practical solution can en-
visage the abandonment of her mandatory position by Great Britain."
Finally, as far as the Jewish position is concerned, Mr. Philby grants,
what the Arab Delegation of 1922 refused to admit, that in any constitutional and legislative scheme, the High Commissioner, representing the
League of Nations and the Mandatory, is to have wide powers, including
the responsibility for the maintenance of security, something which the
Jewish community, especially after the recent riots, must be fully guaranteed, and the right of veto, in order that international obligations may be
met and the rights of minorities safeguarded; and he grants what has
heretofore been resolutely contested, that "freedom of immigration subject to the capacity of the country to absorb immigrants might be stipulated as a condition precedent to the establishment of such a government;
and the Arabs would certainly raise no objection even to the continuance
of the present Jewish Agency to watch over and protect the interests of
the Jews."

Men of good will should be grateful to Mr. Philby for thus formulating so much of the case. For, it ought to be clear that it is impossible for Great Britain, the principal Allied and Associated Powers and the
League of Nations to abandon international declarations which they

have made so often and with so much solemnity. Even those who felt, like myself, that the form of the Balfour Declaration was a handicap rather than a help, because of its lack of clarity and more especially because it emphasized unduly the Jewish relationship to Palestine, rather than emphasizing the nature of Palestine itself as an international Holy Land, can not wish to see international good faith discredited as it would be should this Declaration be nullified. From the point of view of international decency, if for no other reason, this is undesirable, "unthinkable", to quote Mr. Philby. It is necessary, of course, to strip the Balfour Declaration of the extravagant meaning which the British Government permitted to be given it when it was issued; and the Declaration was thus stripped in a series of interpretations, most notably in the Churchill-Samuel White Paper of June, 1922, which was accepted formally and officially by the Zionist Organization as the basis of its policy. Unfortunately that organization has done all too little to carry this policy into effect or to educate the Jewish public as to its implications. Many good Jews are still under the impression that Palestine was "awarded" to the Jews. But this interpretation of 1922 put an end practically to what Mr. Philby calls "the political Zionist dream of ultimate domination of the Holy Land." What the Balfour Declaration gives the Jews after being thus whittled down is nothing more and nothing less than, in the words of the White Paper, that "the Jewish People is in Palestine as of right and not on sufferance." This is a great thing — basing the historical connection of the Jewish People with Palestine upon a generally accepted international dictum; and this is, to my mind, no more than the Jews need have in order to enable them to make a home in Palestine of the kind that Ahad Ha'am pictured, a spiritual and intellectual Center for Judaism and the Jewish people, rooted in agriculture, industry and all kinds of labor.

Mr. Philby continues to the other side of the picture — the Arab. He says that "no solution is really feasible which ignores the unquestionable moral and legal rights of the Arabs." Here again he is right, and the only question is what these moral and legal rights of the Arabs are.

Mr. Philby cites the promises made to the Arabs through Sir Henry MacMahon in 1915 as the legal ground for the Arab demand for the "cancellation of the Balfour Declaration, the relinquishment of the Mandate, and the establishment of an independent national government in Palestine." In the White Paper of 1922 the British Government has declared that "it is not the case, that during the War His Majesty's Government gave an undertaking that an independent national government should be at once established in Palestine." It is not unthinkable that governments in wartime should, unfortunately, make contradictory promises and declarations, and it is high time that this controversy be cleared up. This could perhaps be done through the appointment of a committee of historians — an Englishman, an Arab, a Jew — to go through the Arab Archives at the Foreign Office, and to publish authenticated and annotated texts of the fundamental documents, in some such way as is being done with other diplomatic archives in various countries, including England.

But the crux of Mr. Philby's argument, as is the Arab contention from the beginning, lies in what is called an independent national government. Mr. Philby himself qualifies the term "independent" by saying that "the Mandate cannot simply be abandoned." Indeed, I should add that from the international point of view, from the fact that Palestine is a land sui generis sacred to three great religions, it should always be under international control through a mandatory. This is probably the only way of safeguarding international obligations here, and of guaranteeing to all elements of the population — the majority as well as the minorities — their equal rights and privileges, including immigration, settlement on the land, and the living of a free cultural life.

On this account too it seems to me that the High Commissioner, who is to be clothed with such great powers, should, to be sure, be nominated by the Mandatory, but he should be confirmed by the League of Nations in order to emphasize his position not as Administrator so much as the symbol and guarantor of international obligations, rights and duties. Moreover, the Palestinian Government should have much more contact with the League of Nations generally.

But what is meant by the term "national government"? If it means Arab national or if it means Jewish national I am opposed to it. If, however, it means a bi-national government, a Palestine Government, in which the word Palestine includes all three religions equally, a Palestine government, moreover, that is more than a petty autonomous Balkan thing, and that has its great international function to fulfill, i.e. to keep Palestine as the Holy Land, and to help make it into a Home for Jew, Christian and Moslem alike, then I am for it.

I am not unmindful of the risks of such an experiment particularly because of the political immaturity of large parts of the country, and the low state of morals and of education. But if Jew and Arab are to live together in Palestine, it must be as an act of faith — of faith that they are brother peoples, and that they can rise above their weaknesses and their passions, however difficult this may now seem. And if it is only through an act of faith that living together under such complex conditions is at all thinkable, then the more generous and openhearted Jew and Arab are to one another right now during these times of hatred and distress, the longer they will remember each other in gratitude and friendship. If political concessions are to be made let them be made now with an open hand and ungrudgingly. The Jew must say to the Arab, "We want no political domination by any one," and the Arab must say to the Jew, "We recognize the Jew's full right to be here." Jew and Arab should sit down together and then submit their joint proposals to the Mandatory Power. I should like the Palestinian nationality to mean that Palestine is no place for an Arab state or a Jewish state or a British state, but that Palestine is a place where all together will create an international enclave, an interreligious and an interracial home. If a constitution and a legislative machinery can be worked out with this in view it is everything that I, personally, should desire as far as the Jewish cultural and spiritual center was concerned. Palestine should not be a place of political "domination" at all on anyone's part. It is of much more importance to mankind than that. It does not "belong" to Jew, Christian, or Moslem but to all of them together, to humanity. It does not belong, even in the narrower sense of that term, to its actual inhabitants, but to Jews and Christians and Moslems everywhere, for whom their brothers in the Holy Land have the privilege of acting as trustees. This making of Palestine the football of politics — Jewish, Arab, European — ought to be brought to an end. Unless Palestine can be built up upon a high ethical basis it is not worth anyone's having. Let the political issue be settled so that the work of real cooperation along economic, cultural and social lines can begin in earnest. It is one of the high privileges of the present Labor Government in England to bring all its international idealism and all of its political ingenuity to bear in order to make the Holy Land sacred not only to religious bodies, but also to all those whose aim is peace on earth and good will to men.

The Joshua method is not the way for us of entering the Promised Land. The retention of bayonets in the land against the will of the majority of the population is repugnant to men of good will, and the Eternal People should rather continue its long wait than attempt to establish a Home in the Holy Land, except on terms of understanding and peace.

1. Harry St. John Philby (1885–1960). British diplomat, Arabist, and author. He served in Mesopotamia from 1915 to 1921; was British representative to Trans-Jordan from 1921 to 1924, when he left the Colonial Service. He was adviser to King Ibn Saud of Saudi Arabia, converting to Islam in 1930.

67

To Stephen S. Wise
New York

Dear Dr. Wise:

Professor Klausner was good enough to show me your interesting letter.[1]

I am afraid that your chronology is wrong. It is not I who have disturbed liberal opinion, but rather the events in Palestine. I began speaking in the middle of November, whereas if you will consult your *Nation* or *New Republic* or *Survey* or *Manchester Guardian*, to name but a few, you will find that they began to speak their mind immediately after the August events. Indeed the Zionist office in London issued a lengthy communication in September to Action Committee members and others containing extracts from such publications and acknowledging frankly that the liberal opinion that had heretofore supported Zionism had turned against it.

I am told from many sources that what I and others have said, has enabled many a liberal Jew, as well as non-Jew, to retain his faith in Zionism. This is but natural, because my attitude is due to the same causes as prompted the unfavorable liberal attitude — the fact that, whether we willed this consciously or not, we are keeping down many of the justified political aspirations of the Arabs, instead of, as liberals, taking the initiative in working out political forms and institutions that should attempt to be just to both of us. As it is, we are hated and feared, perhaps also despised, not only in Palestine but throughout the East. A pretty pass for the "intermediaries between East and West," about which we so often talk, to have gotten into. We have done everything we could to encourage the extremists among the Arabs, and nothing to encourage or to work together with moderates, of whom there are many. We seem bent upon using our influence at court in keeping down all Arab aspirations, thus making the Arab revolution, of which the August events were only a presage, that much more inevitable and, for us, tragic. Can you therefore blame liberal opinion?

For me this is not so much the Arab question as it is the Jewish question. What is the nature and essence of Jewish nationalism? Is it like the nationalism of all the nations? The answer is given by our attitude towards the Arabs, so that the Arab question is not only of the utmost practical importance; it is also the touchstone and test of our Judaism.

Those who have not as yet comprehended this may well wonder why, at a critical time, all of us did not do, as you did, "join the organization," and create the "united front" (blessed war-time memories). But those who understand that this is a testing-time for Judaism, and not the time to fall prostrate before the idol with clay feet named Organization, will do everything they can to take advantage of this exceptional moment and to try to mould the Jewish mind and heart in the image of its higher and better self. All questions of organization are now of but minor importance, and all our present victories or defeats with the Colonial Office and the rest can mean but very little. The main question is, what is *our* attitude to be, and resulting from this will come organization forms and practical activity that will either make us or break us here over a long period of years.

I have written you thus at length, despite the names you call me and my friends, because your request that Prof. Klausner show me your letter seems to me an indication that you are struggling with the problem.

The University has emerged from the crisis strengthened, so I think, and am hopeful that when I come to America next we can more than make up for lost time.

I am sending a copy of this letter to Felix Warburg, whom you mentioned in your letter.

With regards, I am,

Yours truly, JLM

I am sending copies also to Prof. Klausner and to Mrs. Lindheim.[2]

1. Commenting on the public reaction to the 1929 riots in Palestine Wise wrote: "Those who ought to be our leaders have risen up and seem to justify the worst things that have been said and done against us . . . I have no desire to criticize Dr. Magnes and his associates of the B'rit Shalom, but they have done Israel and Eretz Israel an irremediable injury by speaking and acting as if we had burned their [Arab] homes and injured and wounded them in every way . . . You will never know, my dear Dr. Klausner, of the injury that has been done in America by reason of the B'rit Shalom attitude. It has done most to turn the whole current of liberal opinion in America against us." Stephen S. Wise to Joseph Klausner, January 3, 1930, Stephen S. Wise Papers, American Jewish Historical Society, Waltham, Mass.

2. Irma L. Lindheim (1886–1978). American Zionist and social worker. Born in New York City; a founder of Hadassah and president, 1926–1928; settled in Palestine in 1933.

68

To Chaim Weizmann
London

Jerusalem, June 3, 1930

Dear Dr. Weizmann:

Now that the situation has become so serious I shall try again to offer my help despite the fate of similar attempts on my part in the past.

At your request I wrote you a letter from Zurich on September 7th, 1929, of which the enclosed is a copy,[1] and I had a talk with you the same month in London. The burden of that letter and talk, and of other utterances on my part was, that our position in Palestine is impossible without an Arab-Jewish understanding. This is the most important thing before us today, and the longer it is put off the more difficult it becomes. I do not refer to an understanding expressed merely in the resolution of a meeting, but to an actual understanding.

Such an understanding is still possible if courage and wisdom are shown. Doubtless you would have to disregard the well-meant, but, as the event has shown, erroneous advice of many of your present advisers.

I am appending the basis of an understanding with the Arabs. It may be possible to lull oneself and others to sleep a little longer, and even to persuade Britain to keep on putting more and more bayonets into the country. But you will not thus arrive at an Arab-Jewish understanding; and without this a Jewish National Home is not possible.

Or do you still think it can be done against the Arab will? Alas, then, for you and the rest of us! But I hope that the present situation has had its sobering effects upon all of us, and that you will apply your great qualities of leadership to meeting the new situation through new and wise and courageous methods. There is no need to despair if only we face realities.

I shall be glad to help in this direction in every possible way.

Yours truly, JLM

I am sending Felix Warburg and a few others copies of this letter.

ARAB-JEWISH-BRITISH UNDERSTANDING

I. *Economic and Social*

1. The general economic and social development of Palestine through the cooperation of Jewish, Arab and British capital, and in all other ways.

a. Jewish colonization and land purchase on basis of retention by present cultivators of land necessary for their sustenance.

b. Help to fellahin by Arabs, British and Jews to enable the transition to intensive agriculture through irrigation, methods of cultivation, sanitation, cheap credits — the tempo of Jewish immigration to correspond to the success achieved during this transitional process.

c. All questions under "a" and "b" to be regulated by a neutral, impartial commission.

d. Cooperation in industry and in the exploitation of natural resources and public utilities.

e. Education and health.

2. The economic and social development of other Arab lands through Arab, Jewish and British capital, and also through Jewish settlement.

II. Political

3. A democratic Legislative Assembly based upon a constitution which recognizes the Mandatory position of Great Britain and the Jewish National Home and which provides safeguards for minorities generally.

4. The furtherance of political, economic and social cooperation between different Arab lands, always providing that the special position of Palestine be safeguarded.

1. See document 64.

69

Journal: The Trip to America

Kubeibe, March 23, 1932

I have been here for nine days, and of these Beatie has been here the last four with me.

I am grateful for the peacefulness of this home in these hills, for the quiet of soul it is possible to achieve here, for the renewed understanding, deeper than ever, which Beatie and I have found here.

I am so arrogant and proud that I would not for the world reveal much of my true self to anyone. Yet Beatie finds it out, and I reveal it all to her. How strange, wonderful, cleansing!

I know why I am tired, exhausted.

Not because of bothering with too many details or because for years I have not been away from University documents, etc., but because my last trip to America exhausted me spiritually. That is, I went through so many spiritual and mental contortions to meet the mind and personality of so many different people, that I almost feel myself to have been a spiritual prostitute. Not surely for my own profit, but for the University. I think I was like a thief in the night watching for the right opening, the propitious moment, to find money. Through an accommodation of my argument to the other man's temper and prejudices and views, it was as though I was trying to chloroform him in order to get his money. The thought of getting other people's money was never, never out of the back of my head. How many people I attacked and in countless ways—dear friends and persons whose souls I know, others whom I despise or am indifferent to or hardly know at all—trying to get money or its equivalent from each and all of them; meeting their moods; on the alert for hints as to their views and prejudices so as to make use of or avoid these; public speaking; dinners; lunches; talks in parlors, in offices . . .

I ask myself if the wound would be so deep—it is now a year since we got to America last year—if I had gotten more money, had "succeeded" better in this sense. Though they all told me the "spiritual" success was magnificent, the "seed was planted"—for the next time. And I would like to think, or I think I am persuaded that if, if I had "succeeded" I could not bring it upon myself to go to America again and ask for funds at such a time and in such a way. I can picture a situation after the elapse of years when I might go and present a case simply basing the case upon its own merits or demerits—but not upon my "charm," or my "personality," or my "eloquence," or my "sacrifices," or my power of reading the other man's soul and then using it for getting money. Oh yes, I believe in the virtue and legitimacy of persuasion, but not under circumstances when, if I came away from a person or a group without money, I had failed of the *real* object of my talking to them, however much it might have another setting or appearance. When I talked so "successfully" to the luncheon in Philadelphia, for example, it was a real joy to have had academic men there and to have talked to their minds; but the real *motive* behind the talk was to persuade Fels[1] and this Jew or that who had money, and even Billikopf who arranged the luncheon, and Cyrus Adler, a member of the Board of Governors, to give or to get *money*. So I could recount person after person, occasion after occasion, somewhat like standing on my head sometimes in order finally to get the *money*—which I didn't for the most part get. But suppose I had! The strain is too great to be repeated. I have spent too much, a very large part of my life in just such endeavors, and I am tired, tired, spiritually weary, mentally exhausted, inwardly sick of it.

It might be illuminating but rather mournful to give a list and description of the persons, places, occasions when I underwent the exhausting process of spiritual acrobatics. One's spiritual limbs really need to be younger and more supple than mine now are.

Under the circumstances I am constantly putting to myself the question: should we not make a systematic, friendly search for someone else to assume responsibility for the University's development? My money-raising powers are obviously restricted — and not only because of the spiritual exhaustion I have mentioned above, but also because my friends from whom I have gotten money and help before are either dead or dying, or if they be alive and vigorous — heaven keep them for many years — both they and their children belong to the pre-war world, my world also. They are not as rich or as powerful as they used to be. On the other hand, there are the new rich. All such crises as the one we are living through produce their newly poor and newly rich. I am not agile enough to be after the newly rich of today and tomorrow. Yet the University should grow and develop. It has proceeded along sound lines thus far — the attempt to maintain an equilibrium between the humanities and the sciences. It is the turn of the agricultural college now. I wrote to Felix [Warburg] about it the other day. Perhaps he will let us have the £2,000 profit yearly from his *pardess* [orchard] that I have asked him for. But it is always and only Felix. I have no one else now. Is there not someone who can tap new sources? Can we not search for someone and perhaps find him? At any rate, this is the problem I should want to place in the center of the discussion at the next meeting of the Board of Governors. I can, for a time yet, maintain the spiritual unity and integrity of the University. But it is its financial integrity and soundness that I feel someone else must be responsible for. And if that someone is the kind of person who will want also to be the spiritual head, in justice I must let him be that, too.

It is interesting and encouraging to me to see how completely I am at the moment the spiritual prop of the various parts of the University in Jerusalem. I have not had to do any contortions or acrobatics here. At first I was, for most (not all), primarily the provider of bread. But gradually and particularly latterly when the bread is the harder to provide, I seem to have become for professors and assistants, academic staff and workers, the *ruhende Pol* [axis] spiritually both in large problems and in small. In many ways this is the greatest satisfaction of my life because it has come from long and steady contact, from day by day relationships, out of the necessities of taking decisions and trying to be just and fair to human beings, and at the same time understanding of their scientific and scholarly problems and characters and aspirations.

I think sometimes that perhaps Weizmann ought now to take the University over. He has probably made his way into the confidence of some of the newly rich in England, South Africa, Germany, and other places: But I know that there would be intense mistrust *within* the University, particularly among the genuine scholars and scientists. They would fear his character—his making use of them and then discarding them for other than University purposes. Yet I could try to help. I am sure that even though I were no longer the head, my presence would be a strength and comfort to many. Or perhaps there is another man. We must look for him.

1. Mary Fels (1863–1953). Widow of Joseph Fels, Philadelphia philanthropist and supporter of the single-tax movement.

70

Journal: Change without Violence

Jerusalem, July 30, 1932

The Jews are not a cruel people. They call themselves *raḥmanim b'nei raḥmanim* [the compassionate of the compassionate]. There are, of course, cruel Jews. But Jewish tradition is one of pity, of charity, of human kindness. The Jew's sense of charity is well known. He supports many charity institutions. The wills of rich Jews almost invariably contain provisions for charity. Their family sense is also well known. They have a deep sense of family responsibility—loyalty. Their family life is as a rule full of affection and warmth. Many of the family ceremonies and celebrations of the Jewish religion—as e.g. the family gathering on the Sabbath eve, the Seder at the Passover—are not without influence and are continued even by Jews who are no longer "religious." This sense of pity, of affection, of loyalty is doubtless due to historical causes. A persecuted people can either become brutalized or be made full of pity. As a general rule the latter has happened to the Jews. It has become so much a Jewish characteristic that the historical causes are forgotten and Jews who have known no persecution are nevertheless among the kindest and fullest of pity.

This is probably the reason why today Jews have had such an aversion to war and militarism, to the cruelties and excesses of the Soviet revolution, even when they were sympathetic with the Communist idea;

why they shrink from the primitive blood-letting ways of the backward Arabs; why they are revolted by the excesses of anti-Semitism, even though they themselves be immune from attack; why crude, violent nationalisms are espoused by them in cases of necessity with no enthusiasm or conviction.

If one can generalize at all, if one may be permitted to generalize about the Jew — despite all his varieties — it should be possible to say that the problem before the Jew is here and now, as almost everywhere for two thousand years: how to live, how to develop society, how to produce change without recourse to cruelty, to torture, to bloodletting, to killing — in a word, to physical violence.

If applied to a newer order of society, the Jewish communist has before him the problem: how to bring about the communist society without cruelty and torture. The best theoreticians of revolution, the best students of history say that revolution cannot be produced without physical violence. Vested interests — material, moral and religious — are usually so strong, convinced of their usefulness, of their essential rightness, so determined to protect themselves and their ideals, that in order to overcome them in the name of other (presumably higher) ideals through revolution requires, historically, the use of arms, espionage, cruelty, etc. This is probably true. The dilemma for the Jewish communist, or revolutionary, or colonizer, or nationalist is therefore: either to give up the idea of revolution and of sudden mass change entirely and depend solely on education, persuasion, religious conversion — or to work out theory and practice (that is the thing) of bloodless revolution. I do not know how the latter can be done. I have thought of it much but find no answer.

On the other hand, depending solely on education and conversion is a devilishly slow process. Of course we must lay stress on them — what would we have or be good for otherwise? But the process is not only tantalizingly slow, it seems entirely ineffective. No wonder we burst our bonds and want to make the world over through force! This is the same problem raised eternally by the defeat of the righteous and the victory of the wicked. "Use the ballot box, my boy," say the smug. "Use education. Use moral suasion." This sounds in their mouths too much like a sneer. Who am I to have my daily bread, and my brother to have none? Am I virtuous and he a sinner? By no means. See the bloated sinner with all that he needs and much more. See the wasted, angel mother bending over the sick bed of her rickety, starving child. Can we be patient and smug under the sting of this? Can we so lightly talk of evolution and progress and legal means and law and order when the whole thing is illogical and cruel and without order?

I am free to say I do not know the practical answer. It almost comes down to a quietism that through helplessness and hopelessness finds a way of life for the individual and leaves to the ruthless, the violent, the swollen the reign of government and the machinery of protection and the means of satisfying our elementary wants.

Yet I do not want to be condemned to quietism. More, I *will* not be. I want to engage upon work of education and conversion. But I want also to continue thinking of the basic problem, and to work it out practically. How also to bring about mighty changes in our time but without cruelty, without bayonets, without the rack and screw of a physical and moral inquisition? How be a communist without violence, how be a nationalist without hatred, how colonize in Palestine with the consent and not against the will of the Arab? These are problems of prime importance, and it is not a disgrace to say that the answers are not easy or available, but that the attempt to find actual, day by day, sincere answers can give life content and meaning and enthusiasm, even if disapointment at the results be our lot.

71

Note: Growing Estrangement Between Jews and Arabs

Jerusalem, October 29, 1932

— Estrangement between Jews and Arabs growing wider and wider.

— Arabs will not sit on any committee with Jews.

— Want less and less to meet Jews personally and privately — not only commercial but spiritual boycott, passive resistance.

— Teachers (whose chief source of inspiration is the Arab newspaper) teach children more and more Jew-hatred.

— Arabs less active politically — commercial, industrial enterprises beginning increasingly to absorb their attention.

But are relying on time; on the independence of all other Arab countries of mandatory powers; of their chance again to take the political initiative.

— The only key to relations with the Jews is the political.

— Now that Arabs more quiescent, should take advantage of opportunity and make Arabs political offer.

These might, of course, be misinterpreted, and might fail. Would depend on what they were, and who made them, and how they were made.

72

To Chaim Weizmann
London

Jerusalem, June 29, 1933

Dear Mr. Weizmann,

I am in receipt of a letter from Professor Brodetsky dated June 23rd. enclosing copy of a minute of a meeting at Sir Philip Hartog's house on June 18th, at which Prof. Einstein was also present. I am sending you a copy of Prof. Brodetsky's letter and of the minute.[1]

I am ready to have an inquiry on one condition — that Professor Einstein also agrees to abide by its results. If the result of the inquiry is favorable to the University — it could not be otherwise — Professor Einstein would seem to reserve to himself the right to continue his attacks. This is hardly acceptable.

Moreover, I should like to warn against the term, "Committee of Inquiry." If an inquiry could be made by an impartial man, say Sir Philip Hartog or Dr. Abraham Flexner, both of whom have large experience of different universities and university organization, there would be everything to gain. I have, as you may recall, on more than one occasion made such a suggestion. But if a "Committee" comes and expects to set up a judicial inquiry and to summon witnesses, etc., the excitement and the humiliation both within the University and the Palestine community and beyond would not be worth even having Professor Einstein back.

A great deal could be done in advance, even before an inquiry is made in Palestine. The names of all the scientific workers might be listed, their publications gone into, inquiries made concerning them from experts in their respective fields. An inquiry might also be made in advance as to the work the students are doing and other preliminary inquiries could come to mind. The inquirer or adviser would then be prepared the better to come to Palestine and look into the organization of the University, the lecture and laboratory system, the academic standards, and the spirit of the place.

I have no doubt that Professor Einstein's chief objection is to myself. This has been an "idee fixe" with him since even before the first meeting of the Board of Governors in 1925. Perhaps time and expense might be saved everyone through the following: if the Board of Governors thinks that through Professor Einstein's return to active service on behalf of the University there will be an accession of new men both in the Board itself and at the University, new chairs, new forces generally, that will give greater assurance of the University's permanence and expansion, I shall be ready to retire without further ado. All that I want is the welfare of the University, and I shall be satisfied that I was privileged to serve the University in its beginnings.

But bearing the responsibility I do towards the University at the moment, I cannot well withdraw until it becomes clear to the Board that my withdrawal and Professor Einstein's coming in will result in giving the University new and better possibilities of expansion.

As you are aware, I have written you proposing that a committee be appointed before which Prof. Einstein and I and anyone else he chooses to invite should appear. I have also written to Prof. Einstein asking that he join with me in this proposal. I have not had a reply from either you or him. I still think that this would be advisable without in any way prejudicing the inquiry. It might aid in formulating the tasks and methods of such an inquiry.

I am sending copies of this letter to Professor Brodetsky and to the others present at the meeting at Sir Philip Hartog's house.

I am, Yours sincerely, JLM

1. At the June 18, 1933, meeting Einstein declared that he still took a warm interest in the Hebrew University and that he much regretted not being able to take an active part in the administration of the university, due to his distrust of the present administration. He would, however, be prepared to do so provided the board of governors resolved to set on foot an unbiased inquiry into the present state of affairs and to remedy the shortcomings of the present administration. He welcomed the proposal to send an independent committee of inquiry to Jerusalem, and declared that he would refrain from any further public criticism until the board of governors had had an opportunity of deciding on this proposal. Should the board decide to send out such a committee, he would not embark publicly upon criticism of the university until the committee had returned and submitted its report. In case the committee would then submit such proposals as aimed at a reform of the university, that satisfied him as being a safeguard for the proper amelioration of conditions at the university; and should the board of governors at a meeting, which might perhaps be called at Christmastime, approve such proposals and decide to give them effect, he would then again become an active member of the board and endeavor to promote the interests of the university in every way, including his participation in a financial campaign. In this event, he would also be prepared in principle to accept the directorship of mathematics and physics.

73

To Sir Philip Hartog
Jerusalem

Jerusalem, December 21, 1933

Dear Sir Philip Hartog,

I would herewith repeat in writing my verbal request that you furnish me with a copy of the charges made against the University or individual members of the University by Professor Einstein, Professor Yahuda,[1] and Dr. Felix.[2]

I must confess to my surprise that a request on my part of these charges is necessary.

I have been responsible for the conduct of the University's affairs since its beginning, and I have had to bear the burden of public and private attack and criticism, particularly on the part of Professor Einstein, for many years. Despite my efforts to secure them, Professor Einstein has never specified his charges. In view of the harm to the University of these unsubstantiated criticisms, the idea of a committee to investigate those charges arose, and I accepted this committee in good faith.

I consented to its appointment in the conviction that at long last we would have a straightforward, clear-cut formulation of charges and an opportunity before fair-minded men of answering them. The University Council in Jerusalem, the conference at Utrecht, the meeting of the Council of Jewish Studies at Geneva, all placed on record their agreement to an inquiry on the expressed condition that Professor Einstein's charges be formulated. The conversations and correspondence with Dr. Weizmann all bear this out. This committee would not have been appointed on any other assumption.

I must insist that every charge made against the University or its members by persons outside the University be formulated and handed to me so that we may know its sources and so that we may have the opportunity, which is elemental and a matter of course, of knowing what is said and who has said it. This will give the opportunity for adequate defense before you and for the formulation of counter-charges, if these be necessary.

It is not sufficient for you to assure us of your fair-mindedness. We have no doubt of that. But we want to be confronted with specific charges so that after our answer, and it would be possible only then, you may be in a position to say in your report that this or that charge of Professor Einstein or of anyone else has or has not been proven. The reader of this report could then form an opinion not only about the University, but also about the sense of responsibility of some of its critics.

You yourself have used the term, "judicial inquiry." We expect that you, as a judge, will not be content to investigate charges by indirection. We expect direct and definite confrontation.

I shall be grateful to you for an answer before you leave on your trip for Haifa.[3]

I am, Yours sincerely, JLM

1. Abraham Shalom Yahuda (1877–1951). Semitist; born in Jerusalem. He was educated at the universities of Heidelberg and Strausbourg; lectured at the Hochschule in Berlin, 1904–1914, and at the University of Madrid, 1914–1922. Weizmann wrote to Ornstein that Yahuda was supplying Einstein with false information concerning affairs at the university with the intention of creating a crisis that would enable Yahuda to become the head of the university.

2. Arthur Felix (1887–1956). Distinguished bacteriologist, who served with the Hadassah medical organization in Palestine, 1922–1927. He failed to be appointed to the university; was on the staff of the Lister Institute in London, 1927–1945, and was a fellow of the Royal Society.

3. On December 28, 1933, Hartog wrote to Magnes: "When I last saw Professor Einstein he said that he had obtained his information about maladministration at the University from numerous sources. The impression he had gained was that good men were kept away, or even intrigued away from the University; furthermore, that certain men who did practically no scientific work of importance obtained high salaries, while exploiting their assistants . . . Dr. Magnes possessed, in his opinion, neither the capacity to understand his task nor the ability to judge the level of scholars. He did not think that an inquiry would discover any criminal misdeeds, but there was certainly enough intrigue and maladministration to justify a searching inquiry. No man would, he thought, go out to Jerusalem as long as the present regime prevailed" (*Reply to the Survey Committee,* pp. 157–158).

74

Excerpts from Interview of the Survey Committee with Judah L. Magnes

Jerusalem, January 1, 1934

Magnes: You [Sir Philip Hartog] wrote me under date of December 29th as follows: "I am afraid I have no information to add to that contained in my letter of 28th December." I should like to permit myself to ask you some questions. Do I understand that you have no information concerning maladministration of the University, or that you don't care to divulge it? . . .

Hartog: Professor Einstein mentioned to me certain names in confidence. It has affected our judgment in no wise. Our report will only deal with information we have had at first hand . . .

Magnes: Professor Einstein wrote a letter to the University here in which he said that from four independent sources he had heard that the University was a *"verwanztes Haus"* [bug-ridden house]. Do I understand that you do not know the source of this information? . . .

Hartog: I have not placed before this Committee any information given by Professor Einstein not obtained direct from witnesses . . .

Magnes: In other words, I understand your answer to me to be this: that you have the information but that you do not think it necessary to divulge it . . . I venture to say that unless Professor Einstein had been in back of the charges, accusations and insults, there would be no Committee investigating things at the Hebrew University today . . . I am responsible in Jerusalem more than any other one person. I am the person who is responsible in the last analysis for that which is bad here and that which is good here. If the financial administration is good, I am responsible. If the academic administration is good, I am responsible for it; if bad, I am responsible and have been throughout the whole life of the University, which was being built up during these years primarily by myself. Now, I do not know whether the Committee had addressed itself to its task with that in mind. If there be human relations here that are pleasant, I am responsible; if there are human relations not pleasant I am responsible. I am responsible also in large measure whether there is money or not. I am responsible in large measure whether or not the Board of Governors functions properly, which it has not. I am responsible whether or not the Academic Council has functioned properly; it has not. I have been responsible because there has been no one else upon whom responsibility all these years could be fastened. When, therefore, you put questions to my associates here from the top to the bottom, you are in the last analysis putting these questions to me, yet I do not know what these questions are . . .

Hartog: We have found some things that are good, other things that are not satisfactory . . . On the whole, the Department of Jewish Studies and the Department of Humanities . . . are satisfactory . . . With exceptions, the departments of science are working well from the scientific point of view; but the human relations . . . between the senior staff and the other teachers are unsatisfactory . . . I have never come across a state of affairs so unsatisfactory as the state of affairs that exists in the scientific departments of this University. Do you believe that their condition is satisfactory?

Magnes: No. I would agree that it is unsatisfactory from the point that we have not had enough money; that due to lack of money we have not been able to make promotions. On the other hand, I believe that the scientific work that is being done is scientific work of high quality; that the teaching is teaching of a high quality. That there should be difficult relations between heads of different departments and some of their assistants is due, I should say, at least 90 percent to the fact that we have not money for promotions, for adequate salaries, for adequate working budgets. I venture to say that with adequate new money in hand these human relations could be adjusted within two weeks' time, despite all the bitterness that exists here and there within the University.

Hartog: Have you been accessible to its members? . . . We have information from a very large number of the staff saying that they found it impossible to see you — a month's delay has been mentioned as a minimum.

Magnes: There is a great deal of truth in that. Whether a month is a minimum or not I would not undertake to say. But there is truth in the fact that I have hesitated to meet with the assistants upon every and all occasions that they requested, and it has been a very conscious attitude on my part, and the reason is this: whenever an assistant would want to meet with me I would endeavor to find out in the first place what it was that he required. We are a small place, and if the head of the University is available always, or too readily, I think that his life would probably become unbearable. Moreover, I have asked that a statement be made as to what was required, because knowing our poverty it was hardly necessary to meet with this and that man to have to tell him, "No, it is impossible to promote you now; it is impossible to give you additional funds."

Hartog: You really think that these are the only grievances?

Magnes: No, but I think, this is my genuine opinion, that the large majority, 90 percent, of the grievances are due to that.

Ginsberg[1]: Our impression was that in certain departments the relations were perfect and in others bad. How would you explain that very strange fact? The economic situation in all faculties of science is the same.

Magnes: Difference in human beings . . . It cannot be explained entirely by economics. I venture to say that if certain promotions could be made, certain salaries raised, it would mean defining a certain status in the scientific department, then most of these difficulties, not all, would disappear. I do not know if there is any place where there are not difficult human relations at different times; that is necessarily so, since as a matter of human temperament, one man is easier than another. For example — publications . . . In Germany — it is true also in England, America and France — a head of an institute puts his name to a publication together with his young assistant. Sometimes, I understand, even though he has had nothing to do with the working out of the problem, but may have suggested the theme, his name is added. The thing goes further. When in Germany the head of a department wants to have a lecture given by someone in his section who is not of the official standing of lecturer, he permits the lecture to be given by that person in his name . . .

There are different men and traditions here. We are in the process of creating a tradition which we are fond of saying will some day be composed of the good aspects of various traditions. For that reason I have always been in favor of trying to allow the head of the department to work out his tradition as best he could and not introduce a uniformity of tradition. In the matter, therefore, of publications you find one man is more generous than another. One will say, "Yes, you publish that, my young assistant; it will give you a good name. Leave my name out" . . .

Hartog: Do you think it satisfactory that there should be most bitter discontent and that persons feel the Chancellor is not accessible? . . .

Magnes: There is nobody in the University who does not get seen if he really wants to be seen.

Hartog: The general impression from not less than 30 people, and from professors as well as students, is that you have been extraordinarily inaccessible.

Magnes: It is not a surprise to me to hear that members in the scientific staff have found it difficult to see me and I told you I have made it difficult in part, and I told you the reason why . . . I can only repeat what I have said before, that in spite of these intolerable relations, in my opinion — I may be all wrong — the root of the difficulty is money.

———————

Hartog: Our reference is: to inquire generally into the affairs of the Hebrew University . . . The Department of Chemistry, for instance, absolutely needs professors of inorganic and physical chemistry . . . You have no chair of physics.

Magnes: Take bio-chemistry for an example. The bio-chemist was appointed at the very beginning of the University. That may have been a mistake in the first place. At meetings of the Board of Governors that question has been discussed without cessation. There are resolutions by the Academic Council. Several years ago, for example, Dr. Weizmann, always our person of reference as far as chemistry is concerned, was authorized to get in touch with Professor Ephraim.[2] There has been a resolution about additional chemistry every year. There was a resolution last time about chemistry but nothing has been done . . .

Hartog: Would it not have been better not to start biology and to concentrate all your money on mathematics, physics and chemistry?

Magnes: We have been building this University up. In the process of creation one does not always do things logically. I think that may be a very legitimate point of criticism. We have not acted logically, but we have acted in accordance with possibilities. Creation consists of taking advantage of something that lies around that you yourself have not put there. In botany for example, what was lying around was Professor Warburg, whom we took advantage of. He was head of the Agricultural Station. The first question I asked was, "How can we make use of Professor Warburg, who is here part of the time, in botany, an important subject for the research of the country?" Thus we created what was called an Institute of the Natural History of Palestine which was to have a botanical section, a zoological section, and geological section. That is the way botany arose. That is the way, in large measure, that zoology arose. Bodenheimer[3] was at the same experimental station. Picard[4] was lying around loose, and that is how geology arose. For a long time we gave him £P5 or £P7 a month, just in order that he might feel he was in the University and had a background. He got to know the country because then nothing was required of him at the University. Then Blankenhorn offered to Professor Warburg his geological collection. We made a contract to buy it; and thus many of the things at the University have arisen — haphazard, without any logical plan in advance. There is much in the University that is not logical at all. Absence of chemistry and physics is the most illogical of all things we have. Therefore, we have been hoping in connection with German funds that something could be done.

Hartog: It has been suggested to us that you were all-powerful in the University because of your financial powers . . . I want to get it from you that it was not because of your desire to take over the duties of Treasurer.

Magnes: They were my duties, unfortunately, from the beginning. I have always in fact acted as Treasurer. Nobody, for one reason or another, would do it . . . I believe that in the formative years of this University's life it appeared to be necessary that large powers—excessive powers—be vested in one man. It was necessary because the Board of Governors was hardly capable of action. An international board is a difficult thing in any case. Our Board has been particularly difficult for a number of reasons, and it was absolutely essential that a certain authority be vested in someone here, and that happened to be myself. Whatever be the situation in the future, I venture to say that authority must be vested here in the largest measure, whether in one, two, or three bodies, depending on the discussion of the situation. But a University cannot be run if questions must be referred to a body abroad. That was one of the difficulties at the very beginning and one of the chief elements in the background of discontent, in the background of Professor Einstein's mind, although he may not know that. It was the struggle that went on between the Zionist Organization in London on the one hand, and myself and my American friends on the other hand. It was the desire of the Zionist Organization to have the center of authority of the University in London within the Zionist Organization. I do not know that I should have been selected by the Zionist Organization, but I was told that the Zionist Organization wished me to act here in the same capacity with regard to University affairs that Colonel Kisch acted, first for the Zionist Organization and then for the Jewish Agency in other affairs; that the center of authority for the University would be in London, with an executive agent named Magnes in Jerusalem. From the beginning I said that was absolutely impossible as far as I was concerned. I could not work that way . . .

Einstein's mind was poisoned against me even before he met me, as I happened to know from at least three sources. One source was my brother-in-law, Louis Marshall, who warned me in Geneva in 1925 before we had the Board meeting in Munich. He said Einstein had been told by the Zionists that I was gonig to make the University in Jerusalem a *Bauren-Universitaet* [plebeian university] and that I was going to run the University in accordance with the lowest of American standards, and he had also been told that I was also merely the agent of the *haute finance* of America. And as a matter of fact when Einstein entered the meeting in Munich, he said, "I find myself here among many financiers from America." They were myself, Judge Mack and Dr. Scholessinger. It was on this account that difficulties were created with me at the beginning. Professor Landau and Professor Horovitz of Frankfurt and Professor Ornstein are other sources of my information. All have told me of certain conversations and messages bearing upon that. That was the problem at that particular time. Since then, at the 1929 meeting of the Board of Governors, before the riots here, the question of the position of the Chancellor was brought up by myself. I said it is an unbearable thing now. The University has gotten along. We must define all this, and I propose to make the Chancellor, formally and officially, a person of very considerable powers, because there was no other way. That was recognized by the Board by a resolution formulated so as to make the Executive here merely advisory, at the discretion of the Chancellor.

1. Louis Ginzberg (1872–1953). Leading scholar of Talmud and Midrash; Born in Lithuania and came to the United States in 1899. In 1903 he became professor of Talmud at the Jewish Theological Seminary; in 1934 was appointed to the Hartog Commission to inquire into the operations of the Hebrew University.

2. Fritz B. Ephraim (1876–1935). Professor of chemistry at Berne. In August 1928, Weizmann wrote to Warburg that he was negotiating with Ephraim to replace Fodor. That October he informed Magnes that he had failed to secure Ephraim's services.

3. Fritz S. Bodenheimer (1897–1959). Zoologist. On completing his studies in Germany he joined the new agricultural experimental station near Tel Aviv in 1922, and with the opening of the Hebrew University was appointed to head the Institute of Zoology and Entomology.

4. Leo Picard (b. 1900). Geologist; born in Germany and emigrated to Palestine in 1924, joining the staff of the Hebrew University in 1925. After completing his studies in Europe, he became the head of the new department of geology in 1936.

75

Journal: On Being Salaried

Jerusalem, April 6, 1934

I have not taken any salary for my work not because of any excess of virtue on my part and not because I am insensible to the security and fine things money can buy, but rather because we, Beatrice and I (particularly Beatrice), have had an income from securities sufficient to enable us to live comfortably, if modestly. We thus did not need the salary and the University did. Neither she nor I created the capital with which these securities were bought. She inherited hers, and "mine" were the result of savings out of her income. That is, both her income and mine represented an unearned increment. To set this off, I have accepted no salary, i.e. I have regarded our "unearned increment" as the equivalent of the salary which I really earned. Had I accepted a salary I would have regarded the unearned income from the securities as just so much "graft."

Now that our "unearned increment" from the securities has fallen off by at least two-thirds and it is becoming difficult to get along (or so we seem to think) on that reduced amount, there is no reason why I should not accept that much of a salary which, added to the "unearned increment," would enable us to "get along."

Of course there has been an enormous satisfaction in the freedom which taking no salary confers. One is more independent of bosses and one's work depends on love of the work and not on the need of keeping a job. There is always the possibility of throwing up the job more readily than one's duty allows. But I think I have resisted this temptation and have carried my responsibility towards my job and towards others fully as seriously as if I had been paid a direct salary for it.

76

Note: "There is no Party I Can Join"

Jerusalem, June 1934

Are you a Communist or a Socialist?

I am not a communist, nor am I even a socialist. The reason is that I fear the totalitarian state. This communist, socialist, fascist Hitlerist totalitarian state is like the god Moloch. It demands the sacrifice of our dearest possessions: our children for war, our individual consciences, our liberties.

What are you then?

I am what might be called a radical liberal. I am opposed economically to the dominance of the motive of private profit. I believe in the coexistence of other powers alongside of the state and independent of the state: the church, the university, the family, the individual conscience. I am also a pacifist.

There is in Palestine a considerable body of young men and women opposed to the private profit motive. These are to be found chiefly in the k'vutsot [collective settlements]. But aside from this I am afraid that the views I have expressed are very unpopular here. Not being a national chauvinist, or a militarist, or a racialist, or a socialist, or a communist I find that there is no party that I can join.

There are two problems of prime importance here to my way of thinking: the relations of the Jews and the Arabs, and the problem of Judaism as a religion.

There is not overmuch concern here with either of these fundamental questions.

77

To Musa al-Alami
Sharafat

Jerusalem, August 1, 1934

Dear Mr. Alami,

I sent the book I spoke about to your office.

Today I had a brief talk with Mr. Ben-Gurion. I was glad to see that he felt as I did that everything was to be gained for both the Jews and the Arabs if large-minded and influential men were to be permitted to live here. In that way the whole Palestine question would find its proper place and perspective within the larger question.

Mr. B-G asked me to ask you if you cared to have a thoroughgoing discussion with him on the Palestine question in relation to the whole Arab question. Could you send me an answer by bearer? I am taking this exceptional means of reaching you because I am sailing tomorrow morning early.[1]

My address abroad is care of the Central Hanover Bank, 20 Place Vendome, Paris.

Remember me kindly to the Emir[2] and your father-in-law,[3] and with all good wishes for your health, I am,

Sincerely yours, JLM

1. The meetings that ensued are described in David Ben-Gurion, *My Talks with Arab Leaders* (Jerusalem, 1972), pp. 24–35. They led to talks between Ben-Gurion and Arsland and Jabri in Geneva in September.

2. Shekib Arslan (1869–1947). Syrian Druze pan-Arab leader. During the First World War he held various military commands in the Turkish army. In 1922 he settled in Geneva. He participated in all of the important pan-Arab conferences over the next twenty years. In 1930, together with Ihsan al-Jabri, he opened an Arab information office in Geneva and began publishing *La Nation Arab*. He supported Mussolini and in 1939 called on the Arabs to support Germany.

3. Ihsan al-Jabri. Syrian pan-Arab leader who collaborated with Shekib Arslan in establishing the Arab information office in Geneva. Together with Arslan he headed the Syrian delegation that negotiated Syrian independence.

The Oakland High School baseball team, 1892. Magnes is at right in the third row.

Magnes during his student days in Berlin, c. 1901.

Magnes in 1907.

The Magnes family, c. 1917. Front row, left to right: Benedict, David, Judah Magnes. Back row, left to right: Beatrice and Jonathan.

Magnes visiting a German military hospital in Poland during his mission for the JDC, September 1916.

Magnes speaking at the opening of the academic year of the Hebrew University, November 5, 1933. Seated in center row from left to right: Max Schloessinger, Chayim Nachman Bialik, Menahem Ussishkin, Shmaryahu Levin.

Magnes with members of Kibbutz Ein Gev on the shores of the Sea of Galilee, c. 1940. Left to right: Magnes, Yaacov Shteinberger, Teddy Kollek.

Magnes visiting Kibbutz Bet Ha'shita, c. 1940. Seated on bed from left to right: Magnes, unidentified person, Henrietta Szold.

Magnes at a conference of British Army medical officers, 1941.

Representatives of the Ihud Association appearing before the Anglo-American Committee of Inquiry, Jerusalem, March 14, 1946. Left to right: Martin Buber, Magnes, Shmaryahu Levin.

Magnes with American students in his office on Mount Scopus, 1946.

5

The Pursuit
of
Compromise:
Arabs and Jews
1935–1939

In the spring of 1935 the university celebrated its tenth anniversary. That fall Magnes announced the reorganization that made him president. "The time had come," he remarked, "when it was no longer just either to the University or its Chancellor that the full burden of the University should rest upon any one man regardless of who he was."[1] The way was open to devote even more of his energies to the Arab-Jewish question.

During the previous five years he had endeavored to win support for a program of political development leading to self-government. He had projected the increasing participation of Arabs and Jews in government. The first stage would be the election of local councils; then an Arab and a Jew would head government departments. Over the course of a number of years a legislative council would be transformed from an appointed to an elected body. Finally, Palestinians (Arabs and Jews) would head all departments of government, and an independent Arab-Jewish state would be declared. In 1931, on his way to visit America, Magnes discussed his plans with the British colonial secretary, Lord Passfield, and at frequent intervals with the high commissioner, Sir Arthur Wauchope.

Magnes's support for a legislative council — the chief Arab demand at the time — and his criticism of official Zionist policy won favorable notice in Arab circles. The Arab press regularly reported his pronouncements. Magnes met occasionally with young Arab intellectuals and established ties with a number of Arab lawyers and government functionaries. When Ben-Gurion entered the executive of the Jewish Agency in 1933, becoming its chairman in 1935, Magnes served him as an important channel to the Arabs (documents 77, 86).

The outbreak of the "Arab rebellion" in April 1936 confirmed for Magnes his most pessimistic predictions: unless Zionists entered into direct negotiations with the Arabs rather than maintaining their British ori-

1. Judah L. Magnes, *Addresses by the Chancellor of the Hebrew University* (Jerusalem, 1936), p. 286.

entation — depending on the British to honor their obligation to support a Jewish national home — conditions would deteriorate drastically. Such direct negotiations required compromise: an agreement for ten or fifteen years, without prejudicing either side's ultimate goals, during which time Jews would agree to a limitation on immigration and to minority status. Magnes encountered skepticism and then uncompromising opposition from Ben-Gurion, Moshe Sharett, and Weizmann, who felt that Magnes's formula for agreeing even temporarily to minority status imperiled the entire Zionist undertaking. The yishuv had become at last the main asylum for the Jews; moreover, at the time, the rate of immigration held out the prospect of attaining a majority in the near future. In the light of Magnes's known position, going back beyond 1929, that the magnitude of Jewish immigration and the attainment of a Jewish majority were not the essential goals of Zionism, they suspected his disclaimers that he had not agreed to a permanent minority status for the Jews. What would happen, his critics asked, at the conclusion of the interim agreement? "If one agrees," Weizmann wrote in 1938, "that for ten years Jews should accept a certain minority position, and after that further Jewish immigration should be regulated in agreement with the Arabs, this clearly means to anyone who can read between the lines that you concede to the Arabs after the ten-year period the right to interfere in all important questions of Jewish immigration."[2]

The Zionist leadership was wary of Magnes for an additional reason: they feared that Magnes would rally the non-Zionists, particularly his American followers, in an attempt to impose his views on the Jewish Agency by threatening to split away from the agency. Magnes in fact was urging his American friends to act in concert, but whether he intended to lead them out of the agency is questionable (documents 80, 85).

The Peel Commission's proposals to partition the country into Jewish and Arab states, announced in July 1937, kindled a vehement and frequently tumultuous debate within the Zionist movement and in the Jewish world. The imminent possibility that a state would be established alarmed Jews who, like Felix Warburg, had supported the Zionist endeavor out of philanthropic motives. Magnes won the support of this group, and at the August 1937 meeting of the Jewish Agency's council in Zurich he fought partition and proposed a bi-national solution as an alternative (documents 83, 84).

In the fall of 1937, when Magnes received a detailed set of proposals purportedly approved by highly-placed Arab leaders, he considered the development a major opportunity for direct Arab-Jewish negotiations. The intermediaries were Albert M. Hyamson, a former official in the Pal-

2. Weizmann to Sol Stroock, April 19, 1938, *Letters and Papers of Chaim Weizmann*, ed. Aaron Klieman, vol. 18 (New Brunswick, N.J., TK), pp. 365–367.

estine administration, and Colonel Stewart F. Newcombe, an Englishman and founder of the Arab Information Office in London. Ben-Gurion and Sharett were highly skeptical that important Arabs had in fact endorsed the proposals. (Their skepticism proved correct.) They considered the move to be at best a ploy to sidetrack partition, which Ben-Gurion favored, by entangling the Jewish Agency in barren negotiations and implying that agreement between Arabs and Jews was possible. A wary Zionist leadership encountered an impatient Magnes, who was convinced that diplomatic flexibility could open an avenue to direct talks (documents 88, 89, 90, 91, 92).

Events moved rapidly: the renewal of Arab violence; the Munich agreement in September 1938; Kristallnacht in November, when hundreds of Jewish institutions in Germany were destroyed; and the British White Paper of May 1939. At this time of national gloom and despondency Magnes drafted an open letter to the yishuv, which he never published, offering some ray of hope. He opened the letter by paraphrasing chapter 32 of Jeremiah, in which at the very moment Jerusalem is delivered into the hands of the King of Babylon, the prophet, imprisoned because he had prophesied the event, buys the property of his kinsman as a symbolic act of faith. Ever since the Balfour Declaration the Zionists had counted on British imperialism to achieve their ends, Magnes wrote. Now, in issuing the White Paper, British imperialism had abandoned the Zionists for a preferred client. Having played the game of imperialism and lost, the Jews had little to complain about. Unbalanced and unfair as the White Paper was, it nevertheless provided some possibility for pursuing a policy of accommodation with the Arabs. Magnes outlined what he believed to be a plausible program, one that in the final analysis depended on reasonableness and good will. "Who knows," he wrote, "it may even come to be realistic politics again to permit a sense of justice and decency to get the upper hand, so that the destinies of the Holy Land may be determined not from the point of view of imperialist interests, but from that of the welfare of the Holy Land and its peoples and religions." Despair, he concluded, "may be justified for the moment, but despair is not a wise counselor in the formulation of a positive policy for a vigorous, far-seeing people."[3] Five months later, and two months after the outbreak of war, he stood before the university community at the opening of the academic year. The man for whom pacifism was virtually a religion had become an advocate of war: "Satan is abroad. The incarnation of the devil sits on the German throne. It is the principle of evil made flesh" (document 111).

3. Draft of unpublished letter, May 1939, MP, 400.

78

To Arthur Ruppin[1]
Jerusalem

Jerusalem, April 18, 1936

Dear Dr. Ruppin,

What you said about B'rit Shalom in your letter to Dr. Weltsch I will not even touch upon.[2] You know the members and the organization better than I do. It is daring on your part to state that B'rit Shalom entered into negotiations with the Arabs. They were incapable of such action. Furthermore, B'rit Shalom was lacking in will and courage to interfere in day to day political activities. In that respect too, they remained loyal to you, their spiritual founder. B'rit Shalom remained a discussion circle and therefore was condemned to die.[3] Why don't you help to reestablish it since you emphasize its right to exist? B'rit Shalom has contributed much toward the clarification of the problem. Many of its leading members, in my opinion, have taken essential steps in the direction indicated in your letter.

Someone like you who has lost the belief in an agreement with the Arabs, at least for the next ten years, and therefore has also lost the desire to search for it, should in my opinion leave the political leadership.[4] The least he can do is to hurry out to where the shooting and fighting is and man the front line. After all it is not possible to present the Agreement [*verstaendingung*] with the Arabs as an eternal topic of discussion and quietly come to a negative conclusion. As long as there is no agreement there will be many dead and wounded. The leaders who are not able to bring about such an agreement and who view even the attempt at it as hopeless should leave the task to others who believe more firmly in it. If they are unable or unwilling to do so, they certainly should not demand a martyr's death of others while they themselves are sitting in their offices and backrooms. They should accept the consequences of the "impossibility of an agreement" for themselves. After all, the others don't know that their leaders gave up the attempt and unsuspectingly pursue their activities — unless these leaders are Revisionists. They state openly what you say in a private letter. The Jewish people and the Arab people know that the Revisionists harbor no hope for an agreement until the Jews are a majority. Then — we would behave like good people. Exactly as you state, only just with the difference that you, presumably for tactical reasons, are not as candid about it.

You are willing to make agricultural concessions. There is no logic here as the ceding of land to the Arabs measurably hinders or at least, slows the creation of a Jewish majority. If it has no logic it must be meant for our own conscience and for world opinion ("conscience", "world" and "League of Nations" you mention twice). Why our own conscience and world opinion should be satisfied with agricultural concessions only, and no political ones, deserves more elucidation on your part. It is a well known fact that we Jews or you in the PLDC [Palestine Land Development Co.] did not transfer the Hula areas to the Arabs but it was a *conditio sine qua non* of the Mandate Administration without which the Jews would have lost all concessions.[5] That has little to do with "conscience" but seems more like propaganda for "world opinion."

I do not want to prolong this letter too much and therefore do not touch upon the many particulars of your letter. It is rather unnecessary as whatever you state is based on and can only be understood in the light of your main theme that an agreement with the Arabs is not possible and not to be desired, rather, on the contrary, that it threatens Jewish interests — at least for the next ten years.

"Docile subjects in an Arab state," "National minority"[6] — what happened to the bi-national state?

"Compromise with the Arabs" would "kill the enthusiasm for Zionism."[7] Only the propaganda is sacred.

"Parties to an agreement," "a less extreme party," "an ultra extreme party."[8] We do not find this among Jews? or among Englishmen? Therefore no treaties are made in the world?

"Legislative Council,"[9] "Democracy and the good of the people," "Political maturity."[10] The ideology of dictatorship. Similar things were said when the United States was founded by "conservative" Englishmen against "progressive" Englishmen. And what became of our enthusiasm for "smaller nationalities"?

"Arab interests."[11] Go easy.

"Incorruptible officials of the Mandate Government." The country reeks with rumors to the contrary.

"I do not share the opinion that the Legislative Council will act as a safety valve for the Arabs and deter them from violence against the Jews." Why not? The "moderates" among the Arabs as for instance Khalidi[12] were for the Legislative Council and the "extremists" were against it. The latter fought explicitly under the slogan: The Legislative Council exists to divert us from our straight, revolutionary, nationalistic path. I believe this is true.

"Seventeen percent," "28 percent,"[13] "numbers and strength," "to stay in balance with the Arabs"[14] — what does this really mean? Against Arab opposition we certainly can bring in Jews up to a point — a point not to be determined by us, but by British imperialistic considerations. If this will take you five or ten years is questionable. I am of the opinion that we can bring in at least as many Jews with Arab cooperation — to be sure, at a slower pace. I am ready to sacrifice tempo if it will change the hatred and animosity of the Arab Moslem world into brotherhood. We understand what anti-Semitism means, intellectually as well as physically, but in our own National Home we virtually burden ourselves daily with such an anti-Semitism that makes the Polish and German ones look like child's play. It is doubtful that such a powerful intellectual challenge can be met by the pretty slogan "Be shot or commit suicide."[15]

The lines are drawn quickly, so it seems. There are those who no longer are capable of or willing to pursue an agreement with the Arabs, and those who actively and with the best intentions feel compelled to search for an agreement either for ethical or political reasons or both, will the latter succeed? Who knows? But I am convinced that the possibility exists even at this time. That it becomes increasingly difficult with every passing day, and not least for lack of willingness on our part, I know. If we permit ourselves to talk about conscience, it can only be, in my opinion, by saying that in spite of all difficulties and even hopelessness one *has* to strive and persist towards a given goal. There is no alternative.

As you know I replied to your letter at your request. If I used a careless expression you will, I hope, forgive me.

May I ask you to kindly send me a copy of your letter. Also please have my letter copied (with all the mistakes in the German) and let me have a copy as well.

Sincerely yours, JLM

1. Translated from the German by Miriam Rochlin.
2. In a congratulatory article Robert Weltsch published in the *Jüdische Rundschau* on the occasion of Ruppin's sixtieth birthday he expressed his regret that Ruppin concerned himself so little with the Arab question. Ruppin replied on March 18, 1936, in a detailed letter explaining why in his view an understanding with the Arabs was impossible at the time.
3. Ruppin opposed B'rit Shalom's radical element, which called on the organization to take political action, particularly in support of the British government's policy in favor of a legislative council. The differences of opinion came to a head in 1929, when Ruppin resigned as chairman of B'rit Shalom. Magnes sympathized with the position of the political activists.
4. Ruppin was at the time a member of the executive of the Jewish Agency.
5. The Hula area of the Upper Galilee became a major colonization project for the Zionist movement at this time. In purchasing the area, largely swamp land, the Arab inhabitants were assured their continued domicile.
6. Ruppin wrote: "We can come to an understanding with the Arabs at the present only if we are ready to integrate ourselves as docile subjects in a Palestine which is an Arab state."
7. Ruppin wrote: "The fate of the Jewish minority in Palestine would always depend on the goodwill of the Arab majority holding the reins of power. For the East European Jews, who constitute the vast majority of all Zionists, such a settlement would be totally unacceptable. It would kill all enthusiasm for the Zionist cause. A Zionism ready to accept such a compromise with the Arabs would lose all support among the East European Jews."

8. Ruppin wrote: "On the Arab side there are no parties to an agreement. The Arabs are split into various parties, all with a negative attitude towards Zionism, but there are nuances from less extreme to ultra-extreme."

9. Ruppin wrote: "Another point on which I differed from the other members [of B'rit Shalom] was their attitude to the Legislative Council. Democracy was the mainstay of their political thinking. One should not regard democracy and the good of the people as identical concepts. One might say that as far as the Legislative Council in Palestine was concerned, it was not a question of a parliament elected by universal suffrage but only a first step towards the people's participation in the government . . . Should we welcome this step when we know with certainty that the Arabs will make every possible use of the Legislative Council to fight against the Jews and Zionism?"

10. Ruppin wrote: "Democracy can be judged the best possible form of government only in countries where the population has reached a certain political maturity. The experiences in . . . Syria, Trans-Jordan, Iraq, and Egypt shows clearly that the Arabs do not possess this political maturity."

11. Ruppin wrote: "If one asks oneself whether the interests of the Arabs are in better hands with the well-intentioned, administratively experienced and incorruptible officials of the mandatory government, or with an Arab government constituted by a parliament, everyone who knows the local conditions must prefer the first alternative."

12. Dr. Ḥusayn al-Khalidi (1894–1962). Physician, political leader. Born in Jerusalem of prominent Muslim family; studied medicine at American University in Beirut; founded the Reform party in 1935, which supported the British proposal for a legislative council. Served as mayor of Jerusalem 1934–1937; member of Arab Higher Committee, 1936–1937; and secretary of reorganized committee, 1946. Khalidi held various ministerial posts in the Jordanian government after 1948, serving as Prime Minister in 1957.

13. Ruppin wrote: "The correctness of this tactic (the effort to postpone the establishment of the Legislative Council) is proven to my mind by the fact that had the Council been established in 1931 our share [of the representation] would have been seventeen per cent, whereas today it would be twenty-eight per cent."

14. Ruppin wrote: "The existence of the Zionist movement depends upon our ability to increase our strength and numbers during the next five or ten years under the protection of the mandatory government, so that we can more or less stay in balance with the Arabs."

15. Ruppin wrote: "I do not consider it possible that we would commit suicide out of fear that we might possibly be killed." Ruppin refers to the possibility that Jewish resistance to the establishment of the Legislative Council would result in Arab riots and the loss of Jewish life.

79

To Reginald Coupland
Jerusalem

Jerusalem, January 7, 1937

Dear Professor Coupland,

I am herewith sending a few remarks, supplementing my pamphlet *Like All the Nations?*

My reluctance to testify has been due to my fear lest by some word of mine I might add to the deep suffering of my people here and elsewhere.

Yet I regard it as necessary to record the fact that within both the Jewish and Arab communities there are those who are convinced that the only way of living together in peace is through concession and compromise. I do not know how large the number of those is, but I think it larger than is usually supposed. You might be interested to meet some of them if ever you were here for a longer time and with more leisure.

You know, I think, that I do not write in the name of any institution and that I am not the representative of any organized political group.

Sincerely yours, JLM

Enclosure: Memorandum

I

There does not seem to be much hope unfortunately of securing a permanent political agreement between Jews and Arabs at the present time. Aside from the excitements of the moment, this is due primarily to the cardinal question of majority and minority. Arab spokesmen declare their unalterable opposition to the Jews becoming a majority at any time; and Jewish spokesmen declare their unalterable opposition to remaining a statutory minority. The Arabs believe that they would be deprived of the natural rights attaching to domicile over many centuries, and the Jews look upon Palestine not only as their historical national home but in the present tragic circumstances as a sanctuary also for thousands of their oppressed brothers.

A truce, therefore, over a limited period, say of ten years, should be sought in the hope that it might be renewed over further periods. The basis of such a truce was worked out unofficially by some Jews and Arabs in May and June, 1936, i.e. after the disorders had begun.[1]

It contained the following main points, each of which was elaborated in the text:

(a) Fixing a satisfactory maximum of Jewish immigration over that period;

(b) Adequate safeguards for the fellah and the tenant farmer in land sales;

(c) Equitable distribution of labor and other employment among both communities;

(d) Greater participation by both Jews and Arabs in Government, in the Executive Council and with a Legislative Council under well-defined conditions.

A political truce is a prerequisite for understanding and cooperation in intellectual and other spheres. Without some such temporary political agreement, the cleavage between the two peoples threatens to grow greater and greater.

II

I would urge as strongly as I can that before the findings of the Royal Commission are made into policy, representative Jews and Arabs, both official and non-official, be called together to meet representatives of the British Government to discuss the general findings of the Report, and more particularly to fill in the necessary figures and details arising out of the Report's general principles. A similar procedure was, I believe, adopted at some stage in connection with the findings of the last Royal Commission to India. However hopeless it may appear at this moment to bring Jews and Arabs together, the opportunity here proposed could not lightly be brushed aside. Round tables have been rejected thus far because there never has been, as far as I am aware, a realistic basis for discussion.

It is of the utmost importance that any policy to be adopted be not only just and fair in itself, but that everyone be made to feel that the British Government is giving additional evidence of its traditional fairness and goodwill by granting both peoples the chance of participating in the final making of policy. This would help to restore that confidence in Government which is greatly needed. Should this offer, however, be rejected, the British Government would then be in a better position to superimpose its policy and public opinion everywhere would doubtless uphold this action.

Whatever be the policy adopted, it ought to be unequivocal. The knowledge that pressure in its various forms could be exercised on Government here and in London is one of the reasons why Jews and Arabs in Palestine have not tried harder to come to an understanding among themselves. If there cannot be a voluntary agreement between the two peoples, the knowledge that a definite, unmistakable policy is to be carried out over a considerable period may conceivably create conditions in which the two peoples will be more inclined than at present to find ways of living together in peace.*

III

Not nearly enough stress has been laid upon the fact that Palestine is a Holy Land for three great religions.

No one should expect to have his maximalist aspirations fulfilled in such a land. The presence here of so many differing sects and peoples requires moderation, concession, compromise, so that they may live together in peace witout at the same time giving up their peculiarities and the differentiae to safeguard which they may have come here.

Palestine is no place for the satisfaction of the maximum of Britih aspirations. In a recent number of *Great Britain and the East* one finds the

---

* Note: In what form the Permanent Mandates Commission of the League of Nations might participate in this discussion before a final policy has been adopted is also a question which I think should be given serious consideration.

statement that Britain is in Palestine primarily for strategic reasons. There are those who would have Britain rule in Palestine with the Arabs against the Jews, or with the Jews against the Arabs. However much the adoption of either of these policies might simplify the problem from the point of view of British imperialism, that is, from the point of view of the political, economic and strategic interests of the British Empire, it should nevertheless be the primary duty, so it seems to me, of Great Britain unselfishly to maintain Palestine as the Holy Land of three religions and to help create here a bi-national, a biracial state. If Britain shows the way of unselfishness, the Jews and Arabs can be expected the more readily to follow the same path.

Palestine is no place for maximalist Jewish aspirations. That this is so, is also part of the Jewish tragedy. There are those who speak of a Jewish National Home containing many millions of Jews—present-day Palestine, Transjordan, the Hauran, and Sinai as far as the Suez Canal. Such aspirations are due in large measure to the pressure of Jewish life, the persecution to which Jews are being subjected in all too many parts of the world. When Israel Zangwill said: "Give the land without a people to the people without a land," neither he nor many other Jews realized that there was a people here. The Jews are justified in seeking the active support of Government for settlement possibilities for as large a number of Jews as is in any way possible; but this must always be compatible with the natural rights of the Arabs. If the Jews could come to a political understanding with the Arabs as to Palestine, there would doubtless be an opportunity for the settlement of large number of oppressed Jews in other Arab lands. These would not, to be sure, be part of the Jewish National Home, but they would be contiguous and helpful to it.

Palestine is no place for maximalist Arab aspirations. The whole world knows that Palestine is not just an Arab land. It belongs in the spiritual sense to millions of peoples scattered throughout the world; and in a real sense not only to the Arabs but also to those Jews and Christians who, coming here and living here, are trying through their devotion to make of it a land worthy of being called holy. Palestine may some day become a member of an Arab federation and/or of the League of Nations, but not just as an Arab land. Rather as a bi-national land, entrusted to the two peoples who are the sole actual descendants of the Semites of antiquity; a Holy Land, entrusted to these two peoples, from whom these religions are derived, and entrusted also to the League of Nations and to Great Britain, the representatives of the European mind and the Christian conscience.**

** Note: The neutralization of Palestine in case of war is, so I think, a logical consequence of the recognition of Palestine as the Holy Land of three religions. It is in this regard much like Vatican City. This is a complicated question that requires a large amount of careful thinking-through.

The mandatory form of government, if taken seriously, is most appropriate for such a country. It emphasises its international background. Great Britain should be the most appropriate among mandatories because of the mighty influence of the Bible upon the British peoples and because the idea of gratuitous trusteeship implicit in the Mandate is not strange to British policy.

IV

By reason of the vacillating policy of Government during the past eighteen years British officials have probably not really known why they are here. Officials have been at liberty to interpret the Balfour Declaration and the Mandate practically as they chose, and they have been known to give the most contradictory of interpretations. The difficulties of the situation are probably so great that it may have required these eighteen years to find out at long last what clear and definite policy ought to be adopted.

Would it not be advisable that officials be trained for a career in Palestine, that there be a Palestine Civil Service in the same sense as there is a Sudan Civil Service? The education of these civil servants would begin with the idea of trusteeship. Britain is the trustee of a precious charge just as are the Jews and the Arabs. It is of importance that every official be imbued with the idea that one of his chief functions is to help as best he can to throw a bridge between Jews and Arabs. At the present time this is not within the instructions of British officials. Acting as a bridge is a very hard task at best, and one does not know if it will succeed. But it must be tried for the Holy Land as part of the official duty of everyone participating in Government. To this end officials of the Palestine Civil Service should get to know the intellectual and spiritual life of the peoples here, their institutions, their languages, their ideals.

V

It is possible to say that the Jews are right and that the Arabs are right. Such a situation has within it the elements of tragedy. The whole history of Palestine has been one of tragedy. But the question is, must the tragedy again march to its appointed end? Is there perhaps no solution to the problem?

Yet those of us who are not willing to accept fate without an effort to influence it, must make our choice. There are those on all sides who say that there is no way out of the impasse except through sword and blood, because that is the history of conquest and that the history of Palestine. Yet there is another way that must be tried: through a moderation of ambitions, through concession and compromise, to find the way of life.

1. Magnes was one of five Jewish notables who conducted unofficial talks with Arab leaders in an effort to bring representatives of both sides to the negotiating table.

80

To Felix Warburg
New York

Jerusalem, January 11, 1937

Dear Felix,

I am enclosing a statement I have sent the Royal Commission.[1] I was asked to testify, and the covering letter to Prof. Coupland explains my reluctance.

I am glad to know that several people to whom I have shown this statement are in accord with it.

Perhaps you have been able to imagine some of my feelings since last April. What is becoming very hard for me is just to sit still and do nothing because of the terror exercised by most parties here.

It is possible to form a group here that is ready to fight for the ideas that you and I hold. I am ready to devote a great deal of time and strength to forming an organization provided there is adequate backing.

This organization must have a fund out of which it can establish a press — English, Arabic and Hebrew. This would begin modestly.

I think it possible to collect about £2000 here towards a fund of £20,000 = $100,000. Without some such backing it would be dangerous to begin. This fund will probably not be needed in its entirety. But it should be there.

I do not know how much you are really concerned with all of this. If you, I, and a few others would put our backs into it, disagreeable and hard as it may be, we could make a real difference in the situation.

If anything is to be done, it should be prepared now, so that public work might commence immediately the Royal Commission's report is published.

Yours, Judah

P.S. Active support can be expected from such men as Novomeysky,[2] Schloessinger, Rutenberg, Pollack,[3] Smilansky. Hexter and Julius Simon are in accord. There would be a considerable following from among the University people, merchants, and some of the labor organizations who have no fair chance at present of expressing themselves.

1. See document 79.
2. Moshe Novomeyski (1873–1961). Mining engineer and industrial pioneer; born in Siberia; immigrated to Palestine in 1920. He was founder and director of the Palestine Potash Co., established near the Dead Sea. He employed Arabs as well as Jews and devoted himself to improving Arab-Jewish relations.

3. James H. Pollack (b. 1893). Palestine government official; district commissioner of Galilee, 1942–1943; member of advisory council, 1939–1948, and executive council, 1945–1948.

4. Moshe Smilansky (1874–1953). Hebrew writer and agriculturist; born near Kiev, Russia. He emigrated to Palestine in 1891, settling in Rehovot, where he cultivated orange groves and vineyards and headed the farmers association. His short stories won critical acclaim. He maintained close ties with Arab circles and supported various efforts for Jewish-Arab reconciliation.

81

To Felix Warburg
New York

Jerusalem, February 10, 1937

Dear Felix,

You mentioned in your last letter the proposal of the Jewish Theological Seminary to confer an honorary doctor's degree upon me in connection with its semi-centennial celebration. Enclosed you will find a copy of my answer to their very kind offer.

I suppose it is just another form of vanity, but I have never been able to bear the thought of medals and honorary titles — at least, as far as I myself am concerned. This feeling has grown stronger the longer I live in an environment influenced, as ours is here, by the flunkeyism of British royalty. When I hear on the British radio or read about some really distinguished man having been given an honorary title or an order with some initials, I ask myself how he could really consent to such a thing.

It is taking hold of the Jews here, too. Ever so many of our public men and women, too, are after these ribbons. It is, of course, human nature to seek recognition of some sort, and governments that give these medals and titles reckon with that. I am far from blaming anybody else or wanting anybody else to refuse such honors; but as far as I myself am concerned, I want none of them.

Perhaps it is because I was born in the far West. I recall how my first teachers used to talk of the glories of the real America — no badges, no titles, no special uniforms, etc. I know that it is somewhat different at the present time in America, but I am sure that the true America still feels the same way.

Beatrice and I are considering our summer plans, and with two boys in America, we are naturally looking in that direction.[1] But we are held away because it may mean for me another campaign on behalf of the University, for which I am not ready.

321

It is too bad that Mr. Schocken cannot go to America.[2] He and his wife have been making all preparations for this, and I have done everything to encourage them to do it. Mrs. Schocken may have to undergo an operation, and it is not known at the moment whether or not this will be serious.

Dr. Bergman you know. He is a very attractive man and a good thinker, and he has worked hard and successfully as the first Rector of the University. You are aware that, in accordance with the rules of the University, the Rectorate changes hands every one or at the most two years, so that he is now at the close of his Rectorate. It will, I am sure, be very helpful to the University to have a man like him appear before the academic and non-academic public in America, and it will be a good thing for him in that it will enlarge his experience. It will, in general, be of value to the University and to our men here if there could be more contact between them and America.

Things here are by no means quiet, politically or economically.

Much love to all of you.

Judah

1. Jonathan Magnes was pursuing graduate studies at the University of Pennsylvania; Benedict Magnes was studying at the Juillard School of Music.
2. Salman Schocken (1877–1959). German Zionist, publisher, and book collector. Settled in Jerusalem, 1934; chairman of executive committee, Hebrew University, 1935–1945.

82
Journal Entry

Jerusalem, February 22, 1937

I find myself saying for the first time in my life. "I do not know how long yet I have, but . . . (I should like to do something toward the solution of the political problem.)"

That is what a number can do to me. I am sure the thought as to how long would not occur were it not for the warning of the number. I was always poor at arithmetic. Now arithmetic is taking revenge.

It is really the sign of *zikna* [old age] to be talking in such terms. Perhaps at seventy one does not say it—one is used to it by that time. But the coming of "sixty" is like striking a bell or putting up a red flag: stop, look and listen.

One of the advantages of being young and healthy at sixty is that one does not take the warning all too seriously. Certainly there is nothing to mope about. But there it is: "Figures do not lie." Therefore, my son—.

The doctor who said that at sixty one should make way for younger men was right. Not that at sixty your force has weakened or your judgment become dim. On the contrary, you may have more judgment and better than ever. But there is a lot of wisdom and good judgment lying around—age is everywhere. But the imagination of youth, its enthusiasm and hopes, its faith in itself and its ability to do good and "make a difference" in the world—that is the precious substance that has oozed out a bit at sixty.

Moreover, if you have been an administrator and gatherer of funds, as I have been, you are really weary of it at sixty. You would like to drink deeper of scholarship and science, of the sources. But the pity of it is that you are too late to begin again at sixty. You have reached *zikna*. It is here where you realize that sixty means something. Your memory is weaker. You fall asleep over a book. Your attention wanders; the *schwarze gevire* [the demonic] has let you down; your passion, if not spirit, no longer drives you.

If you can afford it financially, it is well to take stock at sixty and ask if you are to continue doing what you have been doing up to the present. I had said for a number of years that "at sixty" I thought the University would be established sufficiently to let me go. I was promoted (kicked upstairs) to the Presidency two years before. I ask myself if I would have found that my notion of retiring from the active and responsible administration "at sixty" would still have appealed to me.

I think I can say frankly, yes. Whereas "at sixty," as far as the University is concerned, was just an arbitrary figure, there seems to have been some proper calculation behind it. The University *is* here, and here to stay. All the others had to do was to take it over and run it as it was run. Peace was reestablished, to be sure, and that's important. But that was due to giving the intrigants what they wanted—position and *kavod* [honor] and also by increasing salaries generally. But the organization was so securely built and the process of education for self-government had gone so far that Bergman could take over without changing anything, and Schocken without friction. This shows that with another two years—"at sixty"—it would really have been possible for me to transfer responsibility and authority as I had planned.

Well, now "at sixty" I have a sense of freedom. I encourage the University, its workers and supporters morally. I am no longer responsible for its finances. Beatie is well, generaly speaking. Jonathan and Benedict will not be long in earning their own living. I hope that the oranges will enable David and Norah to pull through without too much more investment on my (Beatie's) part.[1] I am full of vigor. Perhaps I can enter the political battle without having to give up the University. It is a pleasant position here and the salary (£750) that I am now drawing for the third year helps greatly at this stage.

Do I not talk like a contented, well-fed Philistine?

But I am not that. Below my placid surface I am racked by religious doubt; by pessimism as to the world and Palestine; by skepticism as to the efficacy of the pacifict point of view; by loathing of German heathenism; by pity for the suffering of Spain and other millions; by disillusionment as to Russia as evidenced by the recent trials, by —, by —.

And yet I am happy. — What a confusion!

I do not even envy those whose lives are less confusing. "At sixty" the battle is still attractive. But the pain, deep down, is sometimes unbearable.

1. David Magnes and his wife, Norah, were living in Netanya, where David was a citrus fruit grower.

83

To the Editor of the *New York Times*
July 18, 1937

PALESTINE PEACE SEEN IN ARAB-JEWISH AGREEMENTS

The Report of the Palestine Royal Commission is a great State paper. It is incomparably the most thoroughgoing and most penetrating analysis of the Palestine situation that has ever been made.

It is a pitiless document. That is one of its great merits. It exhibits in all its nakedness our miserable failure — the failure of each of us, Jew, Arab and Englishman. An extraordinary work of building up a wasteland has been achieved. But we have failed. We have not known how to make peace. It is the well-documented story of two fierce nationalisms at war with one another, a document that would have commended much more confidence had it exposed equally to the light of day the failure also of mandatory imperialism to rise to its unparalleled opportunities.

The failure of my own people is hardest to become reconciled to. We have been returning to a small, already populated, even if not over-populated, land and despite all "rights" conferred on us by the States which won the war, these rights are a thousand times less important than the consent, if it is at all to be obtained, of the Arabs who live in the land and of the Arab peoples who will continue to be our neighbors even after British imperialism may have passed. Moreover, my people has a long and high ethical tradition. We have been the incomparable witnesses to the ideals of justice for ourselves and for others, and we have suffered as perhaps no other people from the brute force and selfishness of nations. Our duty in Palestine to make peace was and remains our primary practical duty as well as the duty of noblesse oblige.

The commission's report should once and for all clear the atmosphere of cant that has surrounded the whole of the Palestine enterprise. We should all of us hang our heads in shame that we have not been worthy of the historical task placed upon us.

The question must, however, be considered from a purely practical point of view: What are the practical alternatives before us?

There is one final test to any proposed answer: Will it help to secure freely and openly negotiated agreements between Jews and Arabs? Every other question, however important in theory or result, is secondary.

The commission says that any kind of political agreement between Jew and Arab is impossible under the present system and that such agreement may be possible in the future after the partition of the country.

My reply is: I agree that the present system must go. It has proved its inefficiency. But is partition the most practical alternative? I do not think so, although I admit that the commission has made out a strong case for partition. I do not think so drastic a step should be taken now, with all the passionate dissatisfaction it is bound to create, before the policy has been seriously and sincerely tried of creating conditions leading to freely and openly negotiated agreements between Jews and Arabs.

It may be asked if that is not what has been tried and failed. By no manner of means. Thus far there has been government by see-saw. First one people, then the other, would be favored or punished. There has never even been formulated, much less worked out or put into effect, a conscious day-by-day policy that would have the one great basic object in view: freely and openly negotiated agreements between Jews and Arabs.

His Excellency the High Commissioner, in announcing the results of the commission's inquiry, says that every effort has been made to "encourage cooperation between Arabs and Jews." Anyone living in Palestine is in a position to challenge that statement. The High Commissioner or some official might occasionally out of sheer good will have done this or that to try to bring the Jews and Arabs nearer one another. But has there been a clearly worked-out and persistent and methodically pursued policy to that end? Have government officials been trained and instructed in what should be the basic policy, the primary duty and chief justification for the existence of the mandate, namely, to try to create the conditions in an atmosphere in which Jews and Arabs would be enabled, should they so desire, to negotiate an agreement freely and openly with one another? We know that the answer is in the negative.

The Royal Commission admits as much. Indeed, each official, high or low, has had his own policy, his own interpretation of the mandate. Many have frankly said that rapprochement between Jews and Arabs was none of their official business. Indeed, some officials have gone further in their opposition to Arab-Jewish rapprochement, perhaps on the theory that it was patriotic to apply the ancient formula of divide and rule.

The Royal Commission itself seems to contend that the mandate as drafted precluded the mandatory from taking the necessary steps towards this Jewish-Arab entente. If this be so, then the mandate should be changed, the more quickly the better. A new mandate should have two basic points. First, both Jews and Arabs are in Palestine as of right and not on sufferance; second, the chief reason for the mandatory's presence in Palestine is to endeavor to create conditions favorable to free and open negotiations of agreements between Jews and Arabs, such agreements to be incorporated progressively into the basic law of the land.

To such a suggestion the commission might reply that without partition such a policy could not succeed. My reply is twofold: first, this policy has never been tried, and until it is, the prophecy as to its success is as legitimate as the prophecy of failure; second, when I mention freely and openly negotiated agreements I mean such as in the first instance will be for limited periods of time.

This limitation of time is of the utmost importance. Political agreements are in their nature neither abstract nor eternal. Thucydides tells of the most sacred treaty that was made for sixty years and lasted fifteen. There are many examples nearer home. The commission contends that Jews and Arabs will "never be united unless there first be partition of this union." Never is a long time for the historian. The commission is right in saying that a majority of the Jews will "never — that is, today — agree to become a statutory minority." The situation becomes different if such an agreement is made for a limited period.

The commission says that the Arabs will "never — that is, today — make a political agreement with Jews unless the Jews agree to remain a minority." But if you leave out agreements that are presumably made forever — abstractions — and negotiate agreements for limited periods, there is the possibility of advance. And who knows better than the statesmen of the British Commonwealth that many an apparently insoluble problem is met not by dealing with absolutes but empirically step by step?

Even during last year's rebellion — it is the proper term — some Arabs and some Jews were able to work out the outlines of a program for the next ten years. The commission was informed of the existence of such a program. The commission did not ask to know more about it. Such an agreement must necessarily contain many elements of vital interest to both peoples. In addition to immigration, land and employment, it would contain points on agricultural, economic and cultural development in common, self-governing institutions, and Arab federation with the League of Nations.

With Arab consent we could settle many hundreds of thousands of persecuted Jews in various Arab lands. That is worth a real price. Without Arab consent, even our four hundred thousand in Palestine remain in jeopardy despite the momentary protection of British bayonets.

With Jewish help Arab lands would have the chance of rising to their former economic, political and cultural glory. I believe that there are Arab statesmen both in Palestine and elsewhere, of sufficient stature to know that that is worth a real price. Without Jewish help the destiny of these Arab lands will in all likelihood remain unfulfilled.

If a meeting of minds was possible even during the rebellion for a few Jews and a few Arabs by no means the least among their people, this should be possible today, the more so in view of the hostility which partition arouses among both peoples. In the negotiations which the mandatory must enter with the League and the United States Government, and above all with Jews and Arabs of Palestine and with Arabs of Trans-Jordan (which holds one of the chief keys to the riddle), there should be many opportunities for proposing freely and openly negotiated agreements for limited periods between Jews and Arabs, between Jews of the world and Arabs of the world. If a first period of comparative peace from five to ten years could be established, as I firmly believe it can, there would be a necessary breathing space during which to prepare for the next five or ten years. Is this not in the true British political tradition of making haste slowly, of dealing practically with the political questions of today and tomorrow rather than those of the next generation?

It may well be that all these efforts would result in failure. But as in every effort to end a war, it is our duty to make the attempt, certainly to make this attempt before partition is carried through as a counsel of despair.

If, unhappily, for whatever reasons of State such proposals are thrown out without even a hearing, I hesitate as to the course which, in my opinion, would best lead to the possibility of agreements freely and openly negotiated between Jews and Arabs. With or without partition, the question of Jew and Arab remains the most important of all Palestine questions, a number of which has been so splendidly met by Jews in the work of upbuilding. Without a solution of the Arab-Jewish question all work of upbuilding will be on shaky foundations.

Partition has many attractions and advantages as well as many drawbacks. For the Jews it means a State — essentially a Zionist solution. Its two chief advantages seem to me to be: First, that the responsibility for peace is placed where it belongs, upon us and not upon an outside body, and, secondly, that the government of the enlarged Arab State including Trans-Jordan must become willing in its own interest to negotiate agreements one by one, step by step, with the Jewish government.

The chief disadvantages are, in my opinion, the terrible irredenta on both sides of the new frontiers, the new Balkans with their fierce comitadjis winked at by governments; and then the tiny size of the narrow Jewish State deprived of the South, of the Negev. Shall we be able to breathe spiritually in such an atmosphere any more freely than today, and shall we be able to make a living in what looks like a toy State?

I should like to say a word about Jerusalem. A Jewish State without Jerusalem has been called Zionism without Zion. Not only Jewish history and Jewish prayers throughout the centuries, but Jewish messianic hopes as well make Jerusalem the center of our being, "If I forget thee, O Jerusalem." But Jerusalem is not Jewish alone. It is Christian, it is Moslem. The Christian Redeemer was crucified there and Mohammed's mystic flight began there. Jerusalem is an interreligious sanctuary and an international city, and it should remain this, Jewish State or no Jewish State. Its function is to be the center of religions of the world, at least of the Western world. It should be internationalized, neutralized; its constitution should give municipal citizenship to all its bona fide inhabitants regardless of their political allegiance, and it should provide that the head of the municipality be in turn Jew, Christian and Moslem.

Such remarks at this stage seem not to be superfluous. Despite the Jewish majority in the Holy City, its municipality has thus far been permitted to be predominantly Arab. Now, if I understand aright the terms of the commission's recommendations, it is in future to be predominantly Christian and British. "My house shall be called a house of prayer for all peoples," and the government of this Holy City should be equally in the hands of Jew, Christian, Moslem; Jew, Arab and European.

To my Jewish brothers I would say that such a destiny for Jerusalem, if finally planned and generously carried through, is of importance to all the world, and it would redound more to the honor and glory of the Jew than if Jerusalem were just the capital of the Jewish State.

The Jewish people is faced with a threefold destiny in its return to Zion. First, the forming of a living creative center for Jewish people and for Judaism. Second, helping to maturity the slumbering spiritual and intellectual forces of the whole Semitic world. Third, helping Jerusalem to become the true sanctuary of three great Semitic religions.

These are tasks worthy of the people of the Book. They are within the realm of practical possibility on one condition — understanding between Jew, Arab and British.

Paris, July 12, 1937

84

Address to the Council of the Jewish Agency

Zurich, August 18, 1937

Mr. Chairman, Ladies and Gentlemen: I know that at a meeting of this sort there is not much chance of impressing the members with the point of view that I expect to present here. Nevertheless, I feel it to be a duty to give expression to certain opinions which I believe are of some importance. I have been asked by a group of my friends to present a resolution for the attention of this meeting, which I should like to read to you:

> That the Jewish Agency, in view of its recognition by the Mandate for Palestine as the proper body to negotiate with regard to Palestine, shall appoint a Committee of members, one half of whom shall be Zionists and one half non-Zionists, to enter into negotiations with Great Britain, with the Arabs, with the League of Nations and with the United States of America, for the purpose of considering how best a bi-national state can be established in an undivided Palestine, the Holy Land.

We present this resolution to you, in the first place because we think that, before you take any steps to bring about the establishment of the Jewish State it is incumbent upon the Jews to endeavor to come to terms with the Arabs and to endeavor to come to terms with them, if in any way possible, with the consent and good will of Great Britain, of the League of Nations and of the United States of America, which has certain treaty relations in connection with the Mandate.

I have not understood the logic of the Zionist Congress resolution[1] or the logic of one of the speakers today, who said that there is no valid reason why the Mandate should not be carried forward. From such a premise, which is the premise of the Congress resolution, the logical conclusion would be: inasmuch as the Mandate ought to be carried forward, therefore let us endeavor, let us take every step, in the first place to persuade Great Britain and all other elements involved to help us carry the Mandate through, as one presupposes it can be carried through. The resolution that we present is not just that, but it is a resolution anterior to that which seems to meet with the favor of the great majority of this Meeting. The resolution that we propose is, that before any other step of whatever nature be taken, we charge our committee with the task, if I may use the term, the sacred task of endeavoring to persuade all of the factors that have been enumerated, to sit down together to reason with one another, to try to bring about a peaceful settlement, in accordance with which Palestine, an undivided Palestine, shall not be an Arab state, shall not be a Jewish state, but shall be a Jewish-Arab or an Arab-Jewish state which will try to find itself in the course of the years, under the tutelage of the greatest of educating powers, Great Britain.

Why should that not be done? We are told that we are confronted with a fait accompli, that Great Britain has decided once and for all, and that is the end of it. Gentlemen, I do not happen to be in the secret councils of Great Britain. But I do not believe for one moment that the British government has decided absolutely, once and for all, on this or on any other question. It is part of the great political wisdom of Great Britain to adapt its decisions day by day, and not abstractly, to conditions as they arise. Assume, for a moment, that the Arabs are going to set up a united opposition to this proposal of the division of Palestine and of the creation of two states. Do you mean to tell me that the British Empire or the British government will endeavor, against that opposition, to superimpose an Arab state upon the Arabs? By no means. If the Jews were to come and to say: "We oppose that, too," Great Britain would hesitate before endeavoring to compel the Jews to accept a decision which was distasteful to them.

But you are not proposing to do that; you are proposing to say to Great Britain: "Well, you are giving us something very unpleasant, something that we do not want. We cannot help taking what you are forcing down our throats." I may say I admired the speech today of Mr. Simon Marks,[2] not only because of its quality and the earnestness with which he endeavored to meet one objection after another, but also because of its sincerity, and by that I mean that Mr. Marks did not pretend that for him this solution was distasteful. He spoke of it with pleasure; he welcomed it; he asked the question: "Has there been such an opportunity in centuries for our people? Let us accept it with joy and make the best of it." That attitude I understand, although I may not agree with it. But those who say, as I understand the Congress resolution to say and others here who seem to agree with that attitude, that, "Whereas we do not like what is being done," to them I say the British government does not act that way. Mr. Warburg pointed out today that after the Passfield White Paper, an official declaration of government policy, there came the Mac-Donald-Weizmann letter.[3] The British government upon many an occasion laid down a variety of policies for India. Finally, there was a Royal Commission and then select committees and the round tables and then one declaration of policy after another, until, after many years, they finally reached a conclusion that will have more or less the consent of the majority of the people of India. If you follow the political history of Great Britain almost from time immemorial to this last minute, you will find that Great Britain reckons with—and that is its great distinction—that it reckons with the sentiments of the people over whom it is supposed to have authority or influence. We, therefore, say to you, do not first take this step of the State, if it be distasteful to you; and if it be not distasteful to you, say so clearly, without endeavoring to arouse an impression that may not be entirely correct.

What is the Jewish State that is being offered? It is a Jewish State which, in my opinion, will lead to war, to war with the Arabs. [Laughter] Perhaps the man who laughed has not been through what happened last year. I was. My sons were. The sons and the daughters of my friends were. I see some of my comrades from Palestine here who were. It is not a laughing matter for them. My friend Ussishkin and I differ on almost every political question and yet I have been rejoiced to find that, on this particular thing, he and I see eye to eye. What is it that connects us in this? It is his fear, it is my fear, and I have no hesitation in telling you that I am afraid, of the consequences of this State in the relations between the Jews and the Arabs. I happen to have been born in a country where people are raised without fear, and, if I may utter another personal remark, I think that I, personally, have not very much fear. Yet I am afraid for my people, afraid for those tender plants in my country, in that Eretz Israel. I do not want to see the Jewish State conceived and born in warfare.

Why will it lead to war? In the first place because the Jewish State as it is offered to us contains lands about three quarters of which are in the hands of the Arabs. I want to read you what the Royal Commission quote on page 40—Mr. Chairman, you are calling me to time. I have not had the great pleasure of appearing at a meeting of this sort for many years. You have heard most of the speeches here in favor of the Congress resolution. If you want me to stop I will stop. [Further discussion that ended in Dr. Magnes's being given additional time] I would like to read to you the passage from the statement of President Wilson, which the Royal Commission quote on page 40 of their report. The Royal Commission there state that the mandatory system had arisen out of the conception of President Wilson that had been accepted by the nations of the world, namely, "that peoples and provinces are not to be bartered about from sovereignty to sovereignty as if they were chattels and pawns in a game." Now if your Jewish State has three quarters of its lands in Arab hands; if there are 225,000 rural Arabs in this State, more rural Arabs than there are rural Jews; if in the four cities which are to be under temporary British Mandate there are many thousands of Arabs — in the city of Acre, for example, I believe hardly a Jew — and you accept this gift from the nation that conquered that country, for it is only by the right of conquest by the sword that that country would dare to try to present you or me with these lands; if you accept them you are transferring in these words "peoples and provinces from sovereignty to sovereignty as if they were chattels and pawns in a game." If you can get the consent of the Arabs, it would be different. But you do not even think of asking them for their consent. [Interruptions from all sides]

By the Treaty of Versailles peoples and provinces were transferred from sovereignty to sovereignty, against the will of those peoples, and the world today is suffering from that action.

The Royal Commission understood what it was doing. The Royal Commission tried to find an answer to that grave problem. It said, in the first place, we must transfer those Arabs, otherwise you will not have any room in which to settle your people. If three quarters of the lands are in the hands of the Arabs who live there and they are even to cede the lands in their possession, there will still, I fear, be no room for those millions of immigrants who, it is claimed, can be absorbed into this tiny State. But they give a second answer. They state that because you have not owned these lands, because you have not worked them, because they do not belong to you, and because we are transferring these lands to your sovereignty, you shall, therefore, pay to the new Arab state a subsidy in money. You shall pay in money for these Arabs and these Arab lands that you receive from us.

Mr. Asch,[4] in his beautiful speech this afternoon, turned to me and said — and I do not know why, though I feel complimented that he did — "Do you not realize that your young men and women went into a wasteland?" I do, I went into that wasteland with them. "Do you not realize," he said, "that they have watered that land with their tears and their blood and that they have tilled it with their strength and their life?" I realize that, because I have seen them and I love them for it. For every foot of land they have tilled, we have paid. It has been the money of the Jewish People that has paid for it, your money, mine, the money of the poor and of the rich. They have earned this land through labor and through love.

But what will happen tomorrow when you are given the sovereignty over this conquered land as a gift? You have not paid for it in money. You have not sent your young men and women into it to till it with their tears and with their love — you have not had the opportunity. You are getting something that does not belong to us.

Under the Mandate, as it existed up to the present time, we have had twenty years in which to try to procure what belongs to us, paying for it, working for it, loving it, yearning for it. But to take sovereignty that is given to us in this way, as it looks in my view of it, is not worthy of our Jewish history and of the ideals that have brought us to this Holy Land.

Moreover, the irridenta — the irridenta that is being created in the Jewish State will be a problem that we cannot deal with. You say that you want to transfer the Arabs to Trans-Jordan voluntarily, although the Royal Commission state that if they would not go voluntarily, they should be taken by force. They will not go, and if they wanted to go they would not be permitted to go by their brothers in the Arab state, because every man there is valuable to them for their irridenta. And then those beautiful schools which Dr. Ruppin spoke of, which we are going to establish for the Arabs. [Interruption by Mr. Ben-Gurion]

I would like to answer Mr. Ben-Gurion. His question is a legitimate one. He asks did I go to Palestine with Arab consent. No, I did not, but I did not have a Jewish State there in the first instance, and I was not trying to get a Jewish State in the second place, and everything I have said and done in my life, as far as Palestine is concerned, from the beginning up to this day, has been based upon the fundamental thought that in what we do and what we plan, we should endeavor to get Arab consent. And that is the purport of this resolution that we are presenting. This resolution provides for a bi-national state, if it can be secured with the consent of the Arabs and the Jews and of the British government. [Further interruptions]

I should like to talk for a moment in connection with the problem that is engaging the attention of every one of us here, the Jewish misery in Poland, in Germany and in other places. We are told that with the establishment of this state, the Jewish problem in those lands there will be met. Well, Mr. Asch pointed out this afternoon that it cannot be met, even in the undivided Palestine. How much less can it be met in a divided Palestine. It was said here today that, as long as there is a Jew outside of Palestine who wants to enter and work there, he ought to be allowed to enter and to work. I imagine that one of the first things which the Jewish State will have to do is to pass its own immigration laws, in order that the tens of thousands who are prepared to go may not bring the country to catastrophe through over-running it. One of the most deplorable aspects of this whole thing is the false messianism that is being engendered.

333

We know what happened when Sabbatai Zevi called upon the Jewish communities of the world to pack their belongings and be prepared to proceed to the Promised Land. When the call of the false Messiah proved to be a delusion, we all know of the catastrophe that followed. What I fear is that these tens and hundreds of thousands of our brothers and sisters who are in the lands of oppression and who have heard this message from here have believed that in the course of a short time the Jewish State will open its arms, as Rachel opened her arms to her returning children, and they will find that there is room but for few and not for many.

If, however, there be a bi-national state, if there be the possibility of Jew and Arab coming to an understanding in Palestine, then there are these vast possibilities in Trans-Jordan and in other Arab countries where you will be able to settle many thousands of these suffering Jews, in whose name you are now trying to establish a state that has but little help and but few opportunities for them. If you will come to this understanding first of all with the Arabs of Palestine, I do not say it is certain, but then, upon that basis, you can tell these young men and young women that there are tens and tens of thousands of dunams for settlement, instead of the pitiful thing you would otherwise have to offer.

You start out on the assumption that this cannot be done. It can be done. I tell you that last year during this rebellion of the Arabs, there were some Jews and some Arabs who came to the basis of an understanding. It must be tried; it is the one thing that is worthy of us Jews. Find shelter for the people — that is agreed, but not by strength and not by force, but by the spirit. That is the Jewish stronghold.

1. The Zionist Congress convened on August 3, 1937. A vague resolution was passed that rejected the Peel Commission's conclusions that the mandate was unworkable and Jewish and Arab nationalist aspirations were irreconcilable. It instructed the Zionist executive to negotiate with the British for the establishment of a Jewish state.

2. Simon Marks (1888–1964). Merchant and English philanthropist; chairman of Marks and Spencer, Ltd. He supported Weizmann and was a member of administrative committe of Jewish Agency, 1929–1935.

3. Ramsay MacDonald's statement reaffirming the government's obligation to fulfill the terms of the mandate was issued in response to Zionist criticsm of the Passfield White Paper, which had implied that Britain had fulfilled its commitment to supporting the Jewish national home.

4. Sholem Asch (1880–1957). Noted Yiddish novelist, born in Kutno, Poland; lived in the United States during the First World War, when he was active in the People's Relief Committee. He later lived in France, returning to the United States in 1938. He was a member of the council of the Jewish Agency.

85

To Gladys Guggenheim Straus
New York

Jerusalem, October 14, 1937

Dear Gladys,

Your letter of September 26th came here from Caux and I opened it after I had written a letter to Mr. Backer[1] who, because of this coincidence, would not object, I am sure, to my enclosing a copy of it herewith.

The reason I am sending you this copy is because it gives me the opportunity of writing to you and asking if you can undertake to organize some help for the idea of Jewish-Arab understanding. I told Beatrice "in co" [in confidence] that I had composed a letter to you and, of course, had not sent it. I said to her that you seemed to me courageous, intelligent and genuinely concerned, and you have also shown capacity for organization.

We should have been carrying on this work of education and organization all these years instead of leaving it to a few individuals who, singlehanded, have had to brave the storm. These individuals will, I am sure, keep on with their efforts, even though they be alone. It stands to reason, however, that their efforts would mean that much more if they had some organized backing.

What I have been thinking of is something like the following: That in America a committee be gotten together (it need not be large) of people who are *genuinely* resolved to do what they can to bring about this understanding. The purpose of such a committee would be twofold. In the first place, it would itself keep informed as closely as possible of what is going on and do whatever it thinks may be necessary to educate public opinion in America in favor of this Arab-Jewish understanding. The second purpose of the committee would be to give moral and material help to those in Palestine who are ready to undertake the work here.

I need not tell you that under the best of circumstances this would not be easy. The moral aid of such a committee to those here undertaking this work is not to be underestimated. There are times when one's spirits get very low. I need not say that without material help the work would be less effective.

I do not know how much money we ought to have. When I was in Geneva with Mr. Warburg in April, I told him that I thought we ought to have a fund of $100,000 — not at once, but in the background for use if necessary over a considerable period. At that time he did not think this sum excessive. I do not feel at liberty, however, to turn to him because I have had the impression, unfortunately — and I sincerely hope I am wrong — that whereas he is wholeheartedly in favor of this Arab-Jewish entente, there are ever so many influences which are capable of swaying him in different directions. Perhaps you could do better with him than I.

Dr. Lowenstein at the Federation of Charities, is as wholeheartedly in favor of this general objective as I am, and as I believe you are. I think Maurice Wertheim[2] and James Marshall would be willing to help, and I am sure that a number of others could be found.

There ought to be a very modest English publication here, perhaps gotten out once a week or once in two weeks. There ought also to be Hebrew and Arabic publications — all done modestly and unpretentiously.

There ought to be means of encouraging, morally and financially, some of the Labor groups here in favor of this entente. They are within the General Labor Federation, but they are the poorer and less numerous groups there. There ought also to be the possibility of doing a little social work among Arabs in order to establish friendly relations between them and the Jews in their neighborhoods.

As to this latter point, I am not thinking of a large undertaking, because if this is done properly, considerable sums would be required. What I am thinking of is, for example, a little loan fund in certain Arab villages in order to free some Arab land workers from the clutches of usurers. You would hardly believe how much a loan of £1 at a very low rate of interest means to such a person. At times, in order to get it, he has to pay 50 percent and more in interest. If we could establish a tiny first aid hut in several places, it would be a work of humanity and at the same time a work of conciliation and peace.

But I would not, under any circumstances, want to try to do more than our limited forces here permitted us to do. I think there are a few of us who, through the bitter experiences through which we have gone, would be very well content to do a modest thing here and there.

I wonder if, in the midst of your other preoccupations, you are ready to take such an undertaking in hand.

We arrived in Jerusalem four days ago. Beatrice has made a very fine recovery from the unfortunate accident that kept her in the hospital in Paris for so long a time. We spent two days with our son David and his wife at Netanya and were rejoiced to see how beautiful everything there was. If you were to meet our son Jonathan, who is to be in Philadelphia for a year, and his young wife, you would I am sure find her most charming.

The University year is to open in a week's time.

Remember us, please, to Roger,[3] Iphigene and Arthur,[4] and with greetings to you, I am

Affectionately, Judah

1. George Backer (1903-1974). Born in New York City; publisher, writer, philanthropist. He was president, Jewish Telegraphic Agency, 1935-1956; president and publisher, *New York Post*, 1939-1942; active in New York Democratic party politics; member, JDC board of directors from 1937 and vice chairman, 1937-1944. With several other American Jewish leaders he conducted talks with Arab leaders in the summer of 1937.

2. Maurice Wertheim (1886-1950). Investment banker, philanthropist, patron of the arts, active in civic and Jewish community affairs; born in New York City. He joined the banking house of Hallgarten and Co. in 1915 and established his own firm, Wertheim and Co., in 1927. Publisher of *The Nation*, 1935 to 1937; president of the American Jewish Committee, 1941-1943; during Second World War served on War Production Board.

3. Roger Straus, Gladys Straus's husband.

4. Iphigene and Arthur Hays Sulzberger.

86

Journal: Shabbat Veyehi[1]

Jerusalem, December 18, 1937

9:30-11:30 A.M. Heinz Kappes[2] (who arranged it), Miss Liesveld and Wadi Tarazi.[3] BLM [Beatrice Lowenstein Magnes] was present part of the time and suggests that I write it up in detail — as far as I can remember it. Miss Liesveld is a Dutch Quaker who was in America on a scholarship. Four years at girls school, Ramallah, and now at the National Arab High School at Bir Zay. Sole European there. Miss Nabiha Naar is the head mistress. Kappes and Liesveld visit Jewish settlements and persons (Givat Brenner, Tel Aviv, Ben Shemen) and then communicate their experiences to these Arabs, this being their only source of information other than the newspapers. Wadi Tarazi is 29. Born at Gaza, old family there, Christian. (1400 Christians at Gaza among 40,000 Moslems.) From Boys School at Ramallah to Haverford — two years and B.A. Has written a novel about the younger Arab generation in Palestine. *He said he had never met a Jewish young man in Palestine*. While in America he met some Palestinian Jewish young men at International House. He teaches history. Their school prepares for matriculation.

I said I wondered if he wrote a simple style of the type Taha Ḥuseyn[4] employed when he wrote his novel. He said he was striving for the utmost simplicity. I had met Taha Ḥuseyn in Paris. He said that T.H. had had great difficulties in Cairo University because he was advanced in his views. I said he was greatly under the influence of French ideas — his wife was French. I admired his courage and good humor. Kappes had read part of his autobiography. We talked of Baladhuri,[5] and I regretted that students of the Arab college no longer visited our library as in former years. They, at least, had gotten to know the names of some of the books of their own literature they otherwise might not have heard of. He said many Arabs would like to enroll at the Hebrew University but the political situation would have to be settled first. I told them of our Moslem student who had to stop and who bemoaned the fact that now he could not do his thesis on the archeological material in Tagribirdi. He had told me that "we" had the printed material, but "we" did not have the manuscript, for which he would have to go to Cairo. They were all amused and impressed by that "we." He had heard of the great scholarship of Dr. Baneth[6] in "mysticism." I said it was not mysticism but rather the regular Moslem philosophy. Baneth had not wanted to teach, but since Billig[7] he had thought it his duty to do so, and I believe he was happy at it. He and she and others whom they would like to bring must visit the University soon. I should be glad to show them around.

I shall not endeavor now to give in order the points of the conversation, or the give and take of it, only the main headings and main points, primarily what I said.

Moral courage: I thought the great drawback on the Arab side was the lack of moral courage. If only one man would step out now and brave his people and plead that his leaders should sit down with Jewish leaders, the situation would be saved. I had asked in a public speech in 1929 that only one Arab stand up and it would be accounted to him for righteousness. How often the finger of scorn had been pointed at me because not even one Arab stood up. Many had spoken to me, and I had even had something in writing. But that was as far as they would go. In May-June 1936, five responsible Jews — of whom I was one — had appended their names to a document looking towards an Arab-Jewish understanding. This was after several important Arabs had agreed on the general lines laid down. But no Arabs would put their names down, and that was one of the reasons for the breakdown of that attempt. I realized there was a great deal of terror and that people were made afraid.

Five young Arabs: If the one man could not be found perhaps five could or maybe fifty, seeing that there was safety in numbers. Why should not some young Arabs and some young Jews (I could get young Jews — lawyers, teachers, doctors, workers — two to every one Arab, or even more) sign a common declaration to their leaders, or at least separate declarations of similar purport? He asked what the document should

338

contain. I said merely this: we the undersigned, thinking of the future, appeal to our leaders to sit down with the Jewish (Arab) leaders to discuss the Palestine situation and to try to find a solution. Miss Liesveld said that that's what had not been done, the sitting down together.

I suggested at the end of the conversation that I meet "five young Arabs" and five young Jews together. He had said the Arabs would respond to my invitation. But they thought I should meet the young Arabs first, and I agreed. He thought of Dr. Husayni (Dept. of Education),[8] Sa'id Taji,[9] Khulusi al-Khayri,[10] Abd el-Hamid Yasin[11] and himself. He couldn't arrange it just now — examinations, Christmas vacation, etc. In January — *Buqrah*! [tomorrow, not now].

Violence: The Arabs had to use violence. There was no other way. First the large waves of immigration; second, the promise of Government to have a Legislative Council no matter who objected; and then the Jewish victory in the House of Commons showed that Government was under Jewish influence. Miss Liesveld wanted to make a distinction between "peaceful violence" (strikes, demonstrations, etc.) and other violence such as murder. Kappes said there was a front trench of violence and then a second line. The front line was occupied by many: the British Government in maintaining an imperialist policy, the Arabs in their murder campaign (I do not remember him saying anything about the Jews here). But it was time to withdraw to the second line and give up violence all around, and try to work out the problem reasonably and peacefully.

The Mufti: As an example of the lengths to which this unwillingness, to cooperate went, I cited the effort of the Angelican Bishop to have the heads of the religious organizations issue a common prayer for the peace of the Royal Commission when it came, and the success of its labors. The Chief Rabbis' consent was secured, but the Mufti, after he had presumably agreed, had telephoned that it was after all impossible. Tarazi said it was because he was a political leader also, and possibly felt himself wronged. I said that that was a great pity. A religious leader is just the man to lift himself above such feelings of being wronged and to stretch out the hand of brotherhood. Moreover, I did not see why the Mufti should feel so wronged, seeing that he had been having such a fine time watching Jews being killed.

Race: He did not think it was a racial problem at all. Were we not Semites together? I said that we were surely of one race, insofar as there were races in the world. What a great work we could do together in these days of hatred!

Christian Arabs: I agreed that it was at present primarily a political problem, but that the religious question was of importance in the whole complex. Islam seemed to be a religion of the sword. He said Islam was very tolerant, and I said Islam was the most democratic of religions. Nevertheless it was not so long ago that the Moslems called Christians, "You Christian dogs." If he himself had not heard it, his father undoubtedly had. He said there were no animosities between Moslems and Christians in Gaza. I said that if the Christians were 20,000 out of 40,000 inhabitants instead of being 1400, I wonder what the situation would be. The position of the Christians here was psychologically much the same as the Jewish minorities in various countries. It was necessary for the minority to show that it was 101 percent patriotic. The German Jews were — Kappes added, still are — 101 percent German. So with the Arabs here. At the beginning of the troubles here last year Dr. Canaan[12] had issued a 101 percent Arab brochure. No Moslem could have written so extreme a statement. It was just this minority position of the Jews that lay at the basis of Zionism which held that since the Jews were a minority, had the minority psychology everywhere, there was one place, namely Palestine their ancient homeland, where they should be a majority, have the majority psychology.

Numbers: He asked if the Jews could not agree to a stoppage of immigration for a few years. I said they would not. I said they would agree to remain a minority for a period of years provided they could be given a satisfactory rate of immigration. He asked how much, and when I said that there were Arabs who were ready to talk about a Jewish 40 percent of the population at the end of 10 years, i.e. an average Jewish immigration of about 30,000 a year, he seemed greatly troubled. He wanted Palestine to remain Arab, and how could it if such large numbers of Jews came into the country? I said that it was no use dealing in absolutes. We were both Semites, and as such we talked of religious absolutes that may have been part of our strength. But talking in absolute terms is a great political weakness. We must be content with making progress step by step. We must try to achieve a period of calm when we can work together, get to know one another, have common tasks and ideals. Did he believe in an Arab Federation? He did. Well, then, on the day the Federation comes into being and Palestine becomes a member, on that day I think the Jews should be granted numerical equality in Palestine. What difference did it then make to him? The whole background would be Arab. But meanwhile before this Federation came into being — who knows how long it would take? — the Jews must be content with less than 50 percent. He seemed to be moved by the argument, but he said that nevertheless Palestine should remain Arab.

Bi-nationality: One of the reasons I gave why Palestine should not be an Arab state or a Jewish state was this: it would not give either Jews or Arabs here the opportunity of exercising their nationality to the full. When I saw what the free exercise of nationality did these days to great peoples such as the Germans, what it did to the Arabs, what it did to the Jews, I felt that Palestine could again become a holy land by exercising restraint upon the nationalism of both Jews and Arabs here. It would be good for both of us that we should have to think of each other and not of ourselves alone, and that might be of great influence in the Arab Federation, and perhaps beyond. He seemed impressed with this.

Histadrut: "But," he said, "the Jews would be ruled by the Histadruth, and they would be wanting to secure labor for Jews." I said: "Is that not a good thing, trying to get labor for people?"

1. The Sabbath, "And Jacob Lived"; the Sabbath when the Torah reading begins with Gen. 47:28.

2. Heinz Kappes (b. 1894). German Protestant minister and Christian socialist. An anti-Nazi, he visited Palestine in 1934 and returned in 1936 to work with the Quaker school in Ramallah. He was interned in 1940 and released on Magnes's personal bond. He returned to Germany in 1948.

3. Wadi Tarazi (1911–1979). Palestinian Arab educator and writer. Son of a prominent Christian family from Gaza, he studied at Haverford College from 1929 to 1932, taught at the Arab National School in Bir Zayt, Palestine, and later headed the school. He was a founder and principal of the Arab college in Gaza. From 1945 to 1946 he served in the Arab information bureau in Jerusalem established by Musa al-Alami.

4. Taha Huseyn (1889–1973). Egyptian novelist, educator, and intellectual leader, considered the doyen of modern Arabic literature. He was rector of the University of Alexandria and minister of education.

5. Ahmad ibn Yahay al-Baladhuri (d. 892). Early Arab historian and best authority for the period of the formation of the Arab empire. The Hebrew University's School of Oriental Studies undertook to publish his *Ansab al-Ashraf*.

6. David Z. Baneth (1893–1973). Semitic scholar; born in Germany and educated at the University of Berlin. He was assistant librarian, Hebrew University, 1924 to 1937; senior lecturer in Arabic language and literature, 1936; professor, 1946.

7. Levi Billig (1897–1936). Semitic scholar. Born in London and educated at London University and Trinity College. In 1926 he was appointed lecturer in Arabic literature at the newly formed School of Oriental Studies of the Hebrew University. He was shot dead by an Arab assailant.

8. Ishaq Musa al-Husayni (b. 1903). Palestinian Arab publicist and Semitic scholar. Born in Jerusalem; he studied at the American University in Cairo and received his Ph.D. from the University of London. He served in the Palestine government's department of education from 1937 to 1943; was principal of Rawdah School from 1943 to 1946; and professor of Arabic literature, American University in Cairo from 1955 to 1967.

9. Sa'id al-Faruqi (Taji) (b. 1914). Agronomist; born in Ramle, Palestine.

10. Khulusi al-Khayri (b. 1908). Palestinian Arab leader. He studied at the American University in Beirut and at the London School of Economics; served in the mandatory government as press officer and district commissioner from 1934 to 1945, when he resigned to join the Arab information office in Washington. From 1949 he served in various Jordanian cabinets and in parliament.

11. Yasin Abd-al-Hamid (1908–1975). Palestinian Arab publicist, educator, and political leader. Born in Lod, Palestine; studied at the American University in Beirut. After holding various administrative positions in the mandatory government, he resigned in 1946 to join the Arab information office in Jerusalem. From 1948 to 1953 he taught at and then was dean of the American University in Cairo. After 1953 he held various university posts in Jordan and served as adviser on education to the Jordanian government, UNESCO, and UNRRA.

12. Tewfik Canaan (1882–1964). Physician and publicist. Born in Beit Jalah, Palestine, to a Christian family, he was educated at the American University in Beirut; practiced medicine in Jerusalem, maintaining close ties to the German Lutheran Hospital. He was editor of *Palestine Medical Journal* and wrote extensively in support of the Arab nationalist position.

87

To John Nevin Sayre
New York

Jerusalem, January 12, 1938

Dear Dr. Sayre,

I am enclosing a letter from the Reverend Dr. Wilhelm,[1] who is a Jewish refugee from Germany and who has established a congregation in Jerusalem with a very interesting membership.

From this letter you will see that he proposes that help be secured for a German pastor, Mr. Heinz Kappes,[2] who has been in this country since the outbreak of the Hitler terror.

He is one of the "spiritual refugees" from Germany, in the sense that he would not have had to leave had he been willing to submit his conscience and his activities to that regime. He could go back today, but he refuses to do so, and he is even ready for the enormous sacrifice of leaving his wife and four children in order that they may have their bread and butter, while he remains here, carrying out what he conceives to be his mission in life — doing as much as his forces allow him to for the peace of the Holy Land.

I have known him ever since he has been here, and I can testify to his high, clean character and to his unusual abilities. He has gathered about him a group of younger men and women, some of them teachers and writers, and is engaged upon a task which — as far as I am aware — no one else in this harassed land is attempting to carry through. He has a regular program of visiting both Jewish and Arab settlements, urban and rural, and in all he has made a number of admiring friends. When visiting Jews, he tells them of what he finds among Arabs; when visiting Arabs, what he finds among Jews.

Only the other day he and a Dutch Quaker lady who is doing work at a village about twenty miles from Jerusalem, came to see me with a young Arab. He is a teacher and writer. He received his university education in America. He told me — and I could hardly believe what he said, but I know that it is so — that since his return to his home here from America several years ago, he has never met or conversed with a single Jew. While living at International House, he and some Palestinian Jewish students used to meet and discuss common problems, but not here. What a tragic commentary this is upon our life here, and how the burden of it should weigh upon every one of us having the privilege of living here in this holy land!

Do you think that it would be possible to secure from the American Friends a kind of scholarship or fellowship or subvention—whatever it be —in order to maintain Mr. Kappas and his family? It would have to amount to about £10 ($50) a month. If this could be secured, I am sure that the second £10 which this family of six souls requires could be raised here, primarily through the teaching which Mr. Kappes is doing. I think that if a fund could be guaranteed for about three years, it might be possible for him in that time to have established himself on a self-supporting basis. I know that he is trying to do this in any event, and I should like to add that he has never once broached to me even a suggestion that he is in need of help, nor does he know that I am writing about him.

I do not know the addresses of some of our old "Friends" like Hollingsworth Wood[3] or of Mrs. Leach[4] and others, whom I hold in a most cherished place in my memory. I know there are multitudes of problems before all of you, and I am wondering if this appeal, coming from me for a righteous worker in the vineyard, may not bring some help to him.

I thank you with all my heart for anything you may be able to do, and with kindest regards, I am

Yours sincerely, JLM

1. Kurt Wilhelm (1900–1965). Rabbi in Germany from 1925 to 1933, when he emigrated to Palestine. He founded the Reform congregation in Jerusalem, Emet v'emunah, in 1936; was a member of Ihud. He accepted the position of Chief Rabbi of Sweden in 1948.

2. See document 86.

3. L. Hollingworth Wood (1873–1956). Prominent New York lawyer active in peace movement and interracial betterment cause. He was a founder of American Friends Service Committee, first chairman of National Civil Liberties Bureau, prominent member of Fellowship of Reconciliation and New York Society of Friends; trustee of Fisk University and Haverford College; president, National Urban League.

4. Agnes Brown Leach. Supporter of pacifist and civil libertarian causes. She was treasurer of the New York State branch of the Woman's Peace Party; a member of the executive committee of the American Union Against Militarism and the national committee of the American Civil Liberties Union.

88

Journal: Nuri Pasha al-Sa'id

NURI PASHA

Beirut, February 6, 1938

British government wanted to be done with Palestine annoyance. Both sides criticized English. They now have more important imperial interests, and Palestine problem must be disposed of. Do not favor temporary solution or armistice. Hyamson[1]-Newcombe[2] document was handed them, but they turned it down. They will go through with partition if found feasible by technical commission, or if no better solution put forward by Arabs and Jews.

Nuri thinks partition will be bad for both Arabs and Jews. It will make Arabs poorer, besides taking away some of their territory. It will create hardships for Jews in Baghdad and other Arab lands. Same thing will happen here as happens to Jews in Poland. Moreover, life will be made unbearable and they will be forced out and told to go to the Jewish State.

But he must confess to his discouragement as to Arab-Jewish understanding, and he thinks it better for partition to go through than to keep present unsettled position.

We work out new immigration paragraph. He thinks main thing is to get sides together and give them chance to explain things to one another, therefore favors keeping in Hyamson-Newcombe text as many of the words and phrases as possible even though not agreeing to all.

Does not think that technical commission will find partition feasible, and that therefore British Government will be forced to come to some such text as Hyamson-Newcombe.

Said in England, if British Government would insist upon Jewish minority position, Jews could come to understanding with Arabs quickly enough.

He and Weizmann had had two talks in London in May 1936, one at a house near Asde Park with another man along, and one in Iraqi Legation. Nuri had agreed to Weizmann's proposals that a portion of Palestine be set aside and the Jews be permitted to buy up to one-third and regulate the immigration to this section the way they chose. Immigration would also be stopped for a few weeks. Weizmann had required consent of his associates. Could not get it. Nuri had telegraphed Iraqi Minister to urge Weizmann but he said his colleagues objected. Nuri gave me permission to tell this. I ask to see copy of Weizmann's proposals to which Nuri agreed.

Thought that in eventual solution country would have to be divided up into different administrative districts because Jews and Arabs on different levels, and the Jewish and Arab districts would have to have different regulations.

Always made a large point of Arab Federation idea ever since he and Feisal met first Zionists in Istanbul in 1913. Jews must look at question in large way, and their success with Arabs would be ever so much greater than they anticipate.

Weizmann very pleasant and intelligent. But not a real President. More of a French than an American President. Shertok seemed to be all-powerful.

Would be glad to see coming into Palestine as many American and English Jews as possible (the Bishop called them the Anglo-Saxon Jews). They had the wisdom, science and wealth. But not the Eastern European Jews. I said he overestimated one and underestimated the other.

He could not intervene in local matters, such as the percentages. The Palestine Arabs would have to be the authority in those things. All he could try to do was to bring both sides together, and he could sit in the back and try to be helpful. I said I should like to sit next to him.

Baghdad would be best place of meeting for Jews and Arabs, or Egypt, or Syria, or Lebanon—not Beirut. Not Cyprus because Mufti wouldn't go there. Afraid of Ḥuseyn's fate.[3]

1. Albert M. Hyamson (1875–1954). British civil servant, historian, and Jewish communal worker. Assistant director of Immigration Department of the Palestine administration, 1921–1926, and director, 1926–1934; became an advocate of binational state in Palestine.
2. Stewart F. Newcombe (1878–1956). British army officer, engineer, and adviser to Arab leaders. Served in the Middle East during First World War, retiring with rank of Colonel; represented Hashamite family in London; founded the Arab Information Office in London.
3. Nuri is probably referring to Ḥusayn ibn Ali (1856–1931), the self-proclaimed king of Hejaz until he was defeated by Ibn Saud in 1924 and was exiled to Cyprus.

89

To Nuri Pasha al-Sa'id
Baghdad

Jerusalem, February 23, 1938

Dear Nuri Pasha,

It is said here that you sent a statement to the Foreign Office in London about our conversation in Beirut on February 6th, 1938, together with Dr. Graham-Browne[1] and Dr. Izzat Tannous.[2]

Your statement is said to have declared that:

(a) I favor a settlement of the Palestine difficulties upon the basis of a *permanent* minority status for the Jews here, and

(b) I would try to isolate the Zionists from such Jews in America, England and other places as also favor such a *permanent* minority status.

I am sure that you could have sent in no such statement.

In our long and interesting talk, the chief topic of argument was that very question of *permanent* or *provisional* minority status.

I tried to make it very clear that the only practical solution that I saw was one based upon a term of years.

I proposed ten years.

This is more than many Jews want, and is less than many Arabs want.

I also proposed that at the end of ten years the Jewish population be no more than 40 percent of the total population.

I am enclosing a table giving figures on that basis which, I hope, will be of interest to you.

You were good enough to make what seemed to me valuable suggestions for the proposed *basis of discussion*.

I am enclosing a statement of the three formulations thus far made of this proposed basis of discussion.

Although in our argument you thought that a *permanent* solution was required, you nevertheless proposed a formula for paragraph 6 that envisaged a first period of agreement, and then a second between the two peoples.[3]

I do not think this formula good enough yet, but I think it decidedly a step in the right direction.

What we need is an armistice of long duration that may, with hard work and good will, lead to peace.

As to the Jews of America, etc. I stated that if a proposal for an armistice based upon ten years and 40 percent could be made, there was a fighting chance of overcoming Jewish opposition through the aid of such American, English, Palestinian and other Jews as were opposed to partition.

I expressed the opinion also that such a proposal would carry among the Arabs as well.

I am writing to you in order that my attitude may be made perfectly clear.

Could you perhaps throw some light on how such a statement as above was attributed to you?

Thanking you and in the hope of being able to collaborate with you in bringing about the armistice we all so deeply desire,

I am, Sincerely yours, JLM

1. Rt. Rev. George Francis Graham-Browne (1891–1942). British cleric. He received his Doctor of Divinity from Lambeth. Ordained in 1922, he was principal of Wycliff Hall, Oxford, from 1925 to 1932 and Anglican Bishop of Jerusalem, 1934 to 1942.

2. Izzat Tannous (b. 1895). Palestine Arab leader and physician. Born in Nablus, he studied in Beirut and London and made his home in Jerusalem; one of the leading Christian Arab supporters of the Ḥusayni family. He headed the Arab Information Office in London in the 1930s.

3. Paragraph six of the Hyamson-Newcombe proposals for opening negotiations between the Jewish Agency and the Arab leaders read, "The maximum Jewish population of Palestine and later of Trans-Jordan shall not exceed an agreed figure which shall be less than 50 percent of the total population." The final paragraph read, "This agreement shall hold for a term of . . . years from . . . and shall be renewable." Nuri Sa'id suggested, "The maximum Jewish population shall be X percent until there be a further agreement between the two peoples." The precise percentage was to be negotiated.

90

To Sir Arthur Wauchope

Jerusalem, February 25, 1938

Dear Sir Arthur Wauchope,

I have given much consideration to your suggestion to send you a statement on the present status of the conversations I have been having, as you are aware, on Jewish-Arab relations.

I would prefer that this statement, which I am glad herewith to give, be for you personally, and not, as you were good enough to suggest, for transmission to the Secretary of State or to the incoming High Commissioner.

From our talks you know my attitude, and I know yours, and I am sure that your great desire for the peace of the Holy Land will continue to influence the course of affairs.

The Jewish Agency authorized me on December 6, 1937, to try to bring about a secret, unofficial, preliminary meeting with representative Arabs. The purpose of this meeting was to be, to find out if formal negotiations between Jewish representatives and Arab representatives could be entered into. It had been proposed by me to the Agency that the *basis of discussion* at this first preliminary meeting be a text that had been drawn up in London by Colonel Newcombe and Mr. Hyamson.

The Jewish Agency did not agree with all the points in this text. But they were ready to meet with it as the basis for discussion, provided the Arab representatives were also ready to do this.

You will find the text in the attached Appendix: Text No. 1.[1]

As you are aware, Dr. Graham-Browne, Dr. I. Tannous and I had a number of meetings. Dr. Graham-Browne and Dr. Tannous also visited Beirut.

The upshot of this was the preparation of another text (Text 2 in the Appendix) which gives the views of the Palestine Arabs in Beirut.[2] These Arabs were ready to meet with the Jewish Agency, but only with this amended text as the basis of discussion.

The Jewish Agency refused to meet with this amended text as the basis of discussion, because the amendments had radically changed many important points, as a comparison of the two texts will show.

The Jewish Agency declared that in view of the attitude of the Arabs in Beirut, this document could no longer be considered by the Jewish Agency in any form.

Nevertheless, in my personal capacity I met with Dr. Graham-Browne, Dr. Tanous and Nuri Pasha in Beirut on February 6, 1938.

As a result of this long conversation, Nuri Pasha declared his willingness to be of every possible service.

He thought the original Hyamson-Newcombe text suitable as a *basis for discussion*. He proposed text No. 3[3] in the attached appendix.

I told Nuri Pasha that his suggestions in his paragraph 6 were an advance in the right direction, but that they were not yet good enough.

The chief difference of opinion between Nuri Pasha and myself was as follows:

Nuri Pasha thought any agreement between Jews and Arabs must be permanent. He was opposed to a provisional agreement, which I called an armistice. In his opinion, the Jews should accept permanent minority status in Palestine. That would not only give them peace here, but also the open door for the settlement of many Jews in other Arab lands.

My contention was that the Jews could not accept permanent minority status. If a proposal could be made whereby at the end of ten years the Jews could form 40 percent of the whole population, there was a chance of putting that through with the aid of those Jews in America, England, Palestine and elsewhere who were opposed to Partition.

I expressed the opinion also that this would carry among the Arabs as well.

You will notice that the Arabs in Beirut seem to be looking for some kind of outside "authorization" before they can budge on immigration figures or land sales.

The question therefore is: how can that authorization be secured, how can it be made of such a nature that the Jews also will fall in with it?

In my opinion this means: how can the neighboring Arab states or kings be influenced to propose to the Palestine Arab leadership an armistice between themselves and the Jews upon the basis of a ten-year agreement at the end of which the Jews could be no more than 40 percent of the population?

With my very best wishes for the complete restoration of your health, I am,

Sincerely yours, JLM

1. For the text and a detailed account of the negotiations see Herbert Parzen, "A Chapter in Arab-Jewish Relations During the Mandate Era, *Jewish Social Studies*, 29 (October 1967), 203–233. Text no. 1 is the Hyamson-Newcombe Document, dated October 9, 1937.

2. For the Arab counterproposals (text no. 2, dated January 12, 1938), see Parzen, *Jewish Social Studies*, pp. 232–233. The paragraph on immigration stated that "the Jewish population of Palestine should be the present population."

3. See Parzen, *Jewish Social Studies*, pp. 232–233.

91

To David Ben-Gurion
Jerusalem

Kallia, March 3, 1938

Dear Mr. Ben-Gurion,

I received your letter of February 24th this moment,[1] it having been sent to me at the Dead Sea, and I am now telephoning my answer, which I hope will reach you in due course.

Permit me to say the following:

(1) I did not agree, when I met with Nuri Pasha in Beirut, nor have I agreed at any other time privately or publicly, to the idea that the Jews

should remain one-third of the population of Palestine or any permanent minority in Palestine.

(2) I did not meet the Mufti or Jamal Husayni[2] in Beirut. I met Nuri Pasha with the Anglican Bishop of Jerusalem and with Dr. Tannous. There is a minute drawn up by the Anglican Bishop concerning this conversation, which will confirm what I am saying to you.

(3) I did not undertake to convince the Agency or any other group of Jews to accept permanent minority status, whether it be at the figure of one-third or any other figure. I did say, and I say now, that if the Arabs would agree to a proposal for ten years at the end of which the Jews would form about 40 percent of the population, there are Jews in America, England, Palestine and elsewhere, who would endeavor to get this proposal through with the Jewish Agency.

(4) As to the Hyamson-Newcombe document and all that you say about it, you have doubtless received my letter which was sent to all members of the Jewish Agency Executive last week.[3]

(5) I do not believe that Nuri Pasha made this statement to H.M.G. which is imputed to him. The whole conversation between us, which lasted a long time, was a debate in which I took the position that the Jews would not accept permanent minority status.

(6) I am glad that you say that as a private individual I may have full freedom to think as I please. As to the activity of the kind you impute to me, you will gather from the above that there has not been anything of the kind.

(7) I proposed to the Executive that they invite me to meet in order to clarify the situation. I have not yet heard from them with regard to this proposal.

Sincerely yours, JLM

1. Ben-Gurion, writing from London, informed Magnes of the information he had received concerning Magnes's meeting with Nuri Sa'id: that on the basis of the talks Nuri Sa'id had informed the British government that influential Jews had agreed to the Jews remaining a permanent minority in Palestine. Magnes had thus allowed himself to be used in the Arab diplomatic attempt to influence Britain to withdraw its support from a Jewish national home. He was instructing the Jewish Agency executive to summon Magnes and demand an explanation for activities "jeopardizing our entire future." David Ben-Gurion, *My Talks with Arab Leaders*, (Jerusalem, 1972), pp. 184–186.

2. Jamal al-Husayni (b. 1892). Palestinian Arab leader. Cousin and chief aide of the Mufti, he served as secretary of the Palestine Arab Executive from 1920 to 1934, founded the Palestine Arab Party in 1934 (the Husayni party), and was instrumental in organizing the Arab Higher Committee in 1936. He headed the bureau of Arab national propaganda and led Palestinian Arab delegations to London in 1929, 1936 , 1937, and 1939. During the Second World War he was interned by the British in Rhodesia. When he returned to Palestine he was appointed by the Arab League as acting president of the new Arab Higher Committee.

3. For the text of the letter see Ben-Gurion, *My Talks with Arab Leaders*, pp. 167–182. It contained forty-two numbered topics presenting Magnes's account of his negotiations with the Jewish Agency and the Arab mediators.

92

To Sol Stroock
New York

Dear Mr. Stroock:

Many thanks for your letter of May 18 which came three days ago. As to Dr. Weizmann's letter to you of April 19,[1] permit me to say:

(1) You will find an account of my talk with Nuri Pasha on pp. 12 and 13, paragraphs 38 and 39 of my letter to the Executive of the Jewish Agency, Feb. 21, 1938. This talk took place on Feb. 6, 1938 at Beirut. It lasted four hours and was conducted in the presence of the Anglican Bishop of Jerusalem and Dr. I.T. [Tannous], an Arab physician of Jerusalem.

(2) It was not necessary for me to inform Mr. Shertok beforehand of this visit inasmuch as on Jan. 25, 1938 Mr. Shertok wrote me:

> I regard the matter under consideration between us during recent weeks concerning the possibilities of negotiating between us and the Arabs as liquidated.

I was therefore no longer accredited by the Agency, and when I met Nuri Pasha it was in my individual capacity, and I was careful so to inform him. It has never been my practice, nor do I intend beginning now, to ask the Agency with whom I may or may not meet in my private capacity.

(3) I thought the conversation important enough to communicate it to the Agency on Feb. 21, 1938. I asked for a meeting with the Executive to discuss the whole question with them. This meeting took place *two months* later, April 24, 1938. But the meeting did not discuss the Nuri Pasha proposals or any other proposals I had to make. The Chairman said another meeting would be called soon for this purpose. It is now June 6, and no such meeting has been called.

(4) Dr. Weizmann says of the Anglican Bishop in Jerusalem that he "is very far from being a friend of ours." I do not know if Dr. Weizmann has ever talked with the Bishop. I have had many conversations with him and I have seen him in action. I have the greatest admiration for him. He is the best type of religious Englishman, high-minded, intelligent, courageous and filled with a burning desire to help bring about peace in the Holy Land. He is both "a friend of ours" and a friend of the Arabs. Doubtless there are people who cannot conceive that being a friend of both Jews and Arabs is possible.

(5) Despite what Dr. Weizmann says, you can take it from me that I did *not* "agree that the Jews would accept a permanent minority status in Palestine." Indeed almost all the four hours of my talk with Nuri Pasha were taken up by trying to persuade him to accept the idea of an agreement for 10 years at the end of which the Jews would be 40 percent of the total population. This is an attitude it is well known that I hold. I have given expression to this on more than one occasion, among others in the *New York Times* on July 18, 1937. Nuri Pasha categorically denies ever having reported anything to the contrary to anyone. He declares it to be a mystery to him how the Zionists can spread abroad such false reports.

(6) The proposals of Nuri Pasha, which Dr. Weizmann discusses, are Nuri Pasha's proposals, not mine. He proposed them as a *basis for discussion,* and I felt it to be my duty to transmit them to the Jewish Agency as *his* proposals, not mine. The Agency has never thought it worthwhile to discuss these proposals. In my letter to the Agency, Feb. 21, 1938, I said (paragraph 39, p. 13),

> I am aware of many objections to these further proposals as thus formulated. A better formulation can, I am convinced, be found through a direct exchange of views or through intermediaries, if there be the will. The important point is, that the above formulation indicates a serious attempt on the part of one important factor to bring the discussion another step forward.

(7) Dr. Weizmann says: "The new High Commissioner complained about negotiations which unauthorized persons carry on with the Mufti." The attempts I made with the authorization of the Agency to find a basis for discussion between Jews and Arabs, as well as my personal talk with Nuri Pasha, were carried on when Sir Arthur Wauchope was High Commissioner. He was fully aware of what was going on. He asked me for information as to the status of this action, and he wished it success.

(8) I do not think it necessary to answer Dr. Weizmann's personal remarks.

(9) May I emphasize one thing to you or any others who may be in earnest in their opposition to partition? Those who are in control of the Agency and its Executive are very eager for partition, almost any kind of partition, and they are not eager for an understanding with the Arabs.

(10) Messrs. Hexter and Julius Simon who are in America and Mrs. Jacobs who will be there shortly, can give you further information on all these points.

Remember me kindly to Mrs. Stroock, and with kind regards, I am

Sincerely yours, JLM

I am sorry I have no stenographer available and that you must read my handwriting. Can you send me a copy of this, and give a copy also to Dr. Lowenstein and Mrs. Warburg?

1. For Weizmann's letter see *Letters and Papers of Chaim Weizmann*, vol. 18, pp. 365–367. Inter alia he wrote: "Dr. Magnes rendered a very poor service to his people when he undertook these negotiations behind the back of the Jewish Agency . . . His methods certainly are of the worst and I think it is the duty of responsible men in America to urge him to stop his dilettantish interferences in the conduct of our political affairs . . . The only effect on the Arabs of these so-called negotiations is to keep alive the hope in their more extreme sections that by keeping up the pretence of readiness to negotiate with some Jews they may split our ranks and induce the American non-Zionists to break away from the political leadership of the Jewish Agency."

93

To Benjamin V. Cohen
London

Jerusalem, September 1, 1938

Dear Mr. Cohen,

After Julius Simon received your telegram about your arrival in London next Monday, he and I talked the situation over and as a result I have dictated the enclosed memorandum and letters at his office.

The memorandum is strictly for *you alone*. I have mentioned names which I otherwise would not have mentioned. You are at liberty to use any part of it without indicating the source, or mentioning the names I have mentioned.

The letters that are enclosed are for your use or not, just as you choose. Mr. Waterfield of the Partition Commission,[1] who is mentioned in my memorandum, is an official of the Treasury in London. In addition to being a financial expert he is a man of scholarly interests. He is a classical scholar and seems to know a great deal about Greek and Latin sources of Christianity.

The Arab, Musa Effendi Ḥusayni, is a young man of the Ḥusayni Family and a cousin of the Mufti. He is the assistant of Dr. Izzat Tannous who is at the head of the Arab Information Center but who is now in this part of the world. If Dr. Tannous comes to Jerusalem, as I hope, it may be that I shall see him and in that event it may be that I shall communicate with you further.

I am also sending you a copy of a letter which I have written to the Anglican Bishop of Jerusalem who is now in London.

With best regards, I am

Sincerely yours, JLM

Memorandum

About six weeks ago while the Partition Commission was still in Jerusalem, the High Commissioner made a statement concerning the political situation which was then communicated to me by the person to whom the statement was made. This was, in brief, that the Jewish State proposed by the Peel Plan could not be administered or defended. Moreover, the enclaves such as Nazareth and Tiberias made the whole scheme impossible. Any Jewish State that might be proposed would have to be capable of being administered and defended. The only possible Jewish State from that point of view was one extending between Athlit and Tel Aviv on the coast and eastwards up to the foothills, this eastern line excluding Tulkarm from the Jewish State. The British would have to defend this state with their own troops. The Jews would have the opportunity over a long period of years of showing what they could do. As to the rest of Palestine, there would be no Arab State and no special British Mandate for Jerusalem. There would be a new and revised British Mandate over all the territory outside of the Jewish State. The Arabs were not capable of self-government as yet. They required British tutelage for at least the next twenty to thirty years. He thought that the reduced size of the Jewish State might help appease the Arabs.

Subsequently, the High Commissioner repeated the substance of this statement to a newspaper man. This could have been, I imagine, only for the purpose of giving newspaper publicity to this idea without, of course, mentioning the source of the information. The *New York Times* and the *Evening Journal* carried, so I believe, dispatches from their correspondents to the above effect.

The substance of these dispatches was at first vehemently denied by the Jewish Agency here. Subsequently, so I was told, Mr. Shertok delivered a speech before the journalists of Palestine in which, after first denying this information, he later more or less confirmed it. Yesterday I was told that a letter signed by Mr. Ben-Gurion to members of the Zionist Organization prepared them for disappointments. The substance of the above information concerning the reduced Jewish State is confirmed and the letter adds, so it is said, that the only consolation to be derived from this is that there is to be no Arab State.

In a long conversation with Mr. Waterfield, a member of the Partition Commission, a day before the Commission left Jerusalem, the statement was made to me that the alternatives to partition would have their day and become of great importance. If I were H.M.G. what would I propose? My answer was a new Mandate with two main points:

1. Great Britain is in Palestine for the protection of the holy places.

2. Great Britain is in Palestine for the purpose of facilitating the creation of a bi-national state containing two equal nationalities—the Arabs and the Jews. It might not be possible to create such a state overnight but if that were the declared object of British policy it could, in my opinion, be achieved. In any event these two main purposes of the new Mandate would, so I thought, secure for Great Britain the applause of all the world.

Mr. Waterfield asked a large number of questions upon the basis of the memorandum I submitted to the Partition Commission. You may not have seen it and a copy is being enclosed.[2] The idea of the bi-national state appealed to him. He said that the memorandum had been very helpful. He added that most of the memoranda submitted by Jews had not been helpful. He thought that the idea of neutrality mentioned in the memorandum very attractive on paper but he did not see how, if the British Empire were pressed to the wall in the Eastern Mediterranean and were fighting for its life, the British Empire could relinquish Haifa and all that that might mean for the defense of the Empire.

In talks with other persons more or less close to Government circles, the statement has been made that if partition is not carried through, a scheme of cantons might offer the way out. The scheme of cantons had not been, as far as I could gather, worked out in any detail. The discussion would seem to range from the idea of two cantons—a Jewish and an Arab—all the way to twenty-one cantons, this latter being a plan which Nuri Pasha, the former Iraqi Premier, had worked out in Baghdad a year ago. As far as I recall, the number of Jewish cantons in the Nuri scheme was seven. Another view is that the cantons be called "counties." Some of them are to be Arab, some Jewish, some mixed, and there is even a thought of two British counties, namely, Jerusalem and Haifa.

It is emphasized by everyone that the decision to be taken will be more or less dependent upon the international situation at the time.

The neighboring Arab states are naturally greatly interested in the Palestine problem. It is being used in connection with party politics in each of these Arab states. In Egypt, for example, the *Wafd*[3] which, when in power would have nothing to do with the whole problem, is now using Palestine as one of the points with which to rehabilitate itself. But despite this and the generally weak political position of the Arab states, their interest in Palestine is real and they are in any event being compelled by Arab public opinion to do what they can to prevent partition. The Saudi Arabian Crown Prince and the Foreign Minister of Iraq are either in London or to be there and they are in accordance with all reports bringing up the Palestine question. At the meeting of the League of Nations the representatives of Iraq, Egypt and Iran will, so it is said, bring up the question of Palestine.

The one chance of securing a moderating influence on the Palestine Arab leadership is through the representatives of the neighboring Arab states. In my opinion these states can be won to the idea of a bi-national state in Palestine containing two equal nationalities — the Jews and the Arabs. By "equal" is meant, at least for the present, equal political rights but not equality in population. As to population I am convinced from the various conversations I have had with different kinds of Arabs during the past two years, that an agreement could be secured with the Arabs of the neighboring States and subsequently with the Arab Palestine leadership, looking to a Jewish population in Palestine of 40 percent of the total population by the end of ten years. In round numbers this would mean about 800,000 Jews and 1,200,000 Arabs. It would not be easy to achieve this but as I have said, I am convinced it is possible.

What would happen at the end of ten years is, of course, a very important matter. If the idea of an Arab Federation could be supported by the Jews, the question of what would happen at the end of ten years would be easier of solution. The Idea of the Arab Federation is at the present time no part of the policy of England or of France. The action in the Sanjak [province] of Alexlandretta is evidence of this. All the more would the adhesion of the Jews to this idea bring the Jews political benefits at the present time.[4]

1. Arthur Charles Waterfield (1866–1943). Professional soldier, scholar, and civil servant. He was a member of the Woodhead Commission, which investigated ways of implementing the partition plan recommended by the Peel Commission. The Woodhead Commission toured Palestine in the summer of 1938. In November it published its conclusions that partition was impossible to implement.

2. See document 79.

3. Egyptian political party formed in 1918. The Wafd espoused independence from Great Britain, parliamentary government, and social and economic reforms. In 1928 it won a majority in the elections and its new leader, Nahas Pasha, became Prime Minister but was soon dismissed by the king. The Wafd held power from 1936 to 1937, 1942 to 1944, and 1950 to 1952.

4. Cohen criticized Magnes's proposals on several counts: it was unnecessary to mention a specified percentage of the population which the Jews would form at the end of ten years; settlement of Jews in Trans-Jordan should be mentioned. The greater difficulty, Cohen stressed, was the necessity of having the Jewish Agency endorse any statement to be used as a basis of negotiations. (Benjamin V. Cohen to JLM, October 25, 1938, MP, 2462).

94

To Musa Effendi Ḥusayni
London

Jerusalem, September 1, 1938

Dear Musa Effendi:

I think it of importance that you meet with Mr. B. V. Cohen[1] of Washington, D.C. He is to arrive in London on Monday, September 5th on a strictly personal visit and he can be reached through the American Embassy. I hope that you will be able to do this because it will, I am sure, be well worth your while to familiarize yourself with the views of a man of such great importance in America as Mr. Cohen is.

If Mr. Cohen could be persuaded to meet with the Saudi Arabian Crown Prince, the Egyptian Prime Minister, and the Foreign Minister of Iraq it would, I think, be helpful all around.

Your mother seems to be keeping well and I am wondering when you will return to Jerusalem.

With kind regards, I am

Sincerely yours, JLM

1. See document 93.

95

Opening Address of the Academic Year of the Hebrew University
October 29, 1939

WAR AND THE REMNANT OF ISRAEL

As we open this term, students are still in Europe, caught by the war while visiting their parents, and many of you who sit here have been waiting for weeks, thus far in vain, for word of your families and their fate. Nor do we know how many of you may have to leave the University to take up arms or some other service. The funds of the University are low and it is not clear what economies may be forced upon the University in its work of research and instruction. Nor is it simple to go on studying and teaching and investigating when the world is in an uproar.

But the work of the University must go on. Many of the great centers of Jewish learning in Central and Eastern Europe have been destroyed within the past few years, and as we meet here the ruins of some but recently destroyed may still be smouldering. Moreover, thousands of Jews have been driven from the halls of various universities and colleges, and thousands from professions which require university training.

This is all the more reason why the Hebrew University must be maintained and, if possible, strengthened.

Let us try as far as possible to keep our balance, our perspective. We shall, if we consult Jewish history. This is by no means the first time that the Jewish people is in the center of a world at war. So grave have been the threats to our existence throughout the centuries that the escape of the Remnant of Israel is one of the most familiar conceptions of our literature and liturgy.

When this war is over the Remnant of Israel must find that the Jewish tradition of learning has been continued at all costs and hazards—particularly in this epoch when honest intellectual work is increasingly subordinated to the irrational. The Jewish people cannot live without its Torah, and Torah means deep study as well as a way of life. The Hebrew University has established a great center of Torah in Jerusalem. During war the study of Torah and the humanities generally is apt to be regarded as superfluous, as not making scientific contributions to the winning of the war. We cannot accept this view. The Jewish people have continued the tradition of learning throughout every year and through every degree of degradation and poverty between wars; and we are resolved to do the same.

Let me give a translation of two passages from books that were begun during the last war.

In the Introduction to their edition of the Poems of Solomon ibn Gabirol, Bialik and Ravnitzky say:

> In days of war and revolution, when mankind rose up utterly to destroy every stronghold, two men escaped and hid themselves in an ancient ruin, which they undertook to restore. They did their work, lacking everything—without tools, without helpers and often without a candle for light. But they worked with love. An aperture however small, a tiny fissure which could be made whole, brought them joy and comfort. For they knew they were at work in one of the ruins of their own people, and their hand was one with those who "established the border of the widow."

Israel Davidson, whose death the Jewish world mourns, says in the Introduction to his monumental Thesaurus of Medieval Hebrew Poetry:

> At a time when all the world was shaken by the din of war, and every town and city resounded with the noise of armies, I withdrew from the

clamour of life and entered a large hall — our past. Without, the sword was bereaving parents of their children, and on all sides was heard the voice of them that shout for mastery, and the voice of them that shout for being overcome, while I kept walking up and down the length and breadth of this hall, scrutinizing every turn and corner, and examining every room and niche. While myriads of men were girding their loins with swords for combat with one another, I kept setting up memorials to our heroes of bygone days.

But in addition to his studies here, every student should try at this juncture to give time and energy to some kind of social service. I have for a long time thought that the student body of the Hebrew University were not making themselves felt sufficiently in the various tasks of education and of mercy known as social service. The war is making the poor poorer, the helpless more helpless, and it will leave the backward more backward; and I would ask you to give earnest attention to the question, how you can in these trying days not only continue your studies, but also come to the aid of the community. There is only one settlement house in Jerusalem — there ought to be more. More children are now without schooling, and the work of teaching them is being organized. I mention these two activities merely as illustrations of what I have in mind.

In what I am about to say, you will pardon me if I strike a more personal note than is usual in these opening addresses. These are, I am sure, days for clear, simple words, especially when speaking to the young. We old men of the passing generation, who have set ourselves up as teachers and leaders, have made a ghastly failure. I keep asking myself if we have any right to speak to the young. For a second time in our generation the world is at war. We have not had the wisdom, the courage, the humanity to prevent it. High ideals have been handed down to us. But here we are, having to confess again, as so often in the tortuous, bleeding history of mankind, that although we know of better ways than war, yet we have not the spiritual, the intellectual, the physical power to meet our problems except through war.

Although the war confronts each one of us with a difficult spiritual problem, yet I shall ask you to bear with me if I discuss the problem of those radical pacifists and conscientious objectors, of whom I was one during the last war, and who now regard it as their duty to give their support to this war.

This may seem but a slight change to some, just a change in tactics. But it is in fact a very deep change, I might say an agonizing change. It is virtually a change in religion. For pacifism was (can I say, still is?) a fundamental tenet of the religion of these men. But the matter is even more complicated. For, when a man changes his religion, it is usually in order to accept what he thinks is a higher belief. The change of which I speak is of the opposite nature. It is, with one's eyes open, accepting a lower be-lief, the belief that the taking up of arms, though never righteous, is in-evitable at this juncture, now that the war has been unleashed. This is apostasy from the pacifist faith. One may still hold this faith, but with-out having the strength to carry it through at this moment in practice.

This is something like a tragedy for many. It is contrary to all their public professions hitherto. There is a small volume of mine in the Li-brary, called *Wartime Addresses*, which will tell anyone interested what this may mean to me. Men who were threatened with imprisonment, death, the torture of their families on account of their pacifism then, are now no longer pacifists in action. They know that war settles nothing, despite the killing of millions. They know, too, that until millions of men in all the nations refuse war service there will continue to be wars. Yet, now that the war is on, they cannot remain impartial and say to the Ger-man Satan: Keep on conquering. Come in. We shall not use arms to op-pose you.

I have just said that no war is righteous. Let me try to explain what I mean.

In the first place, no war is righteous in the sense that blame attaches to only one of the combatants. There may be an assessment of the rela-tive amount of blame on either side. But who is the righteous judge among men capable of a just judgment on this? All sides have prepared the ground for the war, politically and spiritually. I do not know that any side tried to avert this war through contrition for the last war, through renunciation of conquered possessions, through justice at home and abroad, through real sacrifice. How then can this war, which arises largely out of such a background, be called righteous?

In the second place, a righteous war may be one which you believe ac-ceptable to God, a holy war. But how can any man know that it is ac-ceptable? Have not the wars of religion been at least as pernicious as other wars? Do you know that God has sent *you* and *your* armies to ac-complish His will? Isaiah tells us that He sent not Israel against Assyria, but Assyria against Israel: "Oh Assyria, the rod of mine anger . . . against a hypocritical nation." And who knows if He is not sending this modern Assyria as the rod of His chastisement against the nations?

Let us say anything we will about a war, but not call it righteous. The very most that we can say is that it has seemed necessary to many, that because of our own weakness and wickedness we know no other way of putting down the great evil that is afflicting mankind.

Only recently our whole community solemnly and sincerely repeated the commandment, "Thou shalt not kill", when a few of the hotter-headed broke this commandment in retaliation for wrongs committed upon their people. Yet now we are all of us in full pursuit with the cry,

"Kill, kill", upon our lips. Wherein lies the authority of the Commandment, "Thou shalt not kill", if yesterday killing was wrong, and today it is regarded as inevitable?

I shall say something which it is hard to say. When I support this war, as unhappily I do, I know that thus I am in conscious rebellion against the divine command, "Thou shalt not kill." I have not the steadfastness, as once I thought I had, to fulfill this divine command under any and all circumstances. It is a terrible thing to realise that what one thought was part of one's religion is subject to change because of what a single man can do. Citizenship can be changed, the place of a man's home, his friends, his interests, his social and political ideals. But when a man speaks of his religion, he speaks of his God, of that Absolute which gives life substance and meaning. It is for our sins that we are thus punished. God has hidden His face from us. We must throw ourselves into the dust and try to find forgiveness. We are transgressing His word knowingly, consciously. We do not know what else to do.

What has happened?

Satan is abroad. The incarnation of the devil sits on the German throne. It is the principle of evil made flesh. The devil has unleashed his war, and who can sit back and not take sides, with the devil or against him? I shrink from the blasphemy that ours is the side of God, and that we are His chosen. But what I say is: there, the devil is for all men to see, his voice for all men to hear, his deeds for all men to abhor, his plans for all men to frustrate. It is the idol in the Temple, the abomination of desolation, and it is ours to bring it down. Perhaps we may be brought down in the effort, for who knows the ways of God's wrath and punishments? But we must make the effort.

To Judaism the incarnation of divinity is basically alien. But there is an ancient and continuous Jewish tradition of the incarnation of evil in human history again and again. This is the origin of the Christian tradition of the Anti-Christ, the Anti-Messiah. Certain differences have arisen in the development of these two traditions. One of the chief differences is, that in the Jewish tradition the devil is almost always identified with an historical personage in an actual political situation, whereas the Christian tradition, while often connected with historical events and personages, deals principally with a superhuman, more abstract Satan, in whom can be explained the mystery of wickedness, the end of the world, and the final contest between God and the devil. The Jews' long experience and sense of reality kept them, for the most part, from claiming that any given situation, no matter how terrible, was a precursor of the end of days. Pharaoh of Egypt and Amalek, Sennacherib and Haman, Antiochus Epiphanes, Pompey and Herod, Caligula and Nero are names in the Jewish tradition of very definite historical personalities. These are figures of tyrants who persecuted both the Jewish people and other nations, and all are regarded as various manifestations of Satan, the archpersecutor who is compared to the Angel of Death. The prophets of Israel were all of them completely preoccupied with the political situation of their day or of days to come, so that in them one can hardly differentiate between what we today call by two different names, religion and politics. The later apocalyptic literature of the Jews is in this regard in the true prophetic tradition. The Satan of Jewish history and of the Christian tradition is called by many names and appears at different periods of history, but in both traditions he is always the persecutor. Thus with the German reincarnation. He sets himself up as a messianic figure, a demi-god, and his method is the same as that of each former incarna-- tion, described by a Jewish apocalypse: "And he shall say 'I will first war upon their God, and after that kill them.' "

How do we know that there sits Satan?

I have already answered this question. There is one criterion: persecution. It is through persecution that Satan expresses his "unconquerable will and study of revenge, immortal hate."

Persecution — that is, the deliberate and systematic torment of men, women and children because of their religion, or political and social beliefs, or race, or color. It is the torture of old and young, the sick and the strong. It is the degradation of individual souls and of groups who differ from the persecutor in one way or another. It is this impulse to inflict never-ending pain and cruelty upon those in the persecutor's power — imprisoning them, stamping them down, putting them to tasks beyond their strength so that they fall helpless in their tracks, driving them from their homes, separating parents and children, depriving them of the right to be free, to study and to work.

This, I am convinced, is the deep, underlying cause of this war. There are doubtless other causes of varying degrees of importance, particularly to the governments involved. But it is persecution that has aroused you and me and the man in the street in the Western countries, whether or not we are always conscious of this — this grinding, ceaseless infliction of pain and torment upon human beings because of their beliefs — Jews, pacifists, socialists, communists, members of the Glaubensgemeinde, Catholics, this raging lust to bring misery upon men whose religion or race or politics Satan does not fancy or whom he fears or for whom he has contempt. These are the sure signs that Satan is abroad, and when he lets his war loose, men must band together to restrain him and if possible to destroy him.

No one can pretend that the democracies are without sin. They are crowded with cruel plutocrats and cynical oligarchs, and one sees in them an abundance of the evils and injustices inherent in capitalism, in imperialism, in militarism. Avoidable poverty is rampant, the fatness and callousness of those that have, and the misery of the poor and the economically enslaved. Then the cruelty of the nationalisms of some of the states in behalf of whom we are at war—how merciless they have often been to some of their minorities, and I am not speaking of the Jewish minority alone. The passion for power and for dominating other men and peoples, the so-called white man's burden with its racial arrogance and its contempt of the black and brown and yellow man—the skirts of the democracies are by no means clean of this filth and blood.

The slogans of the democracies—freedom for nations and individuals, the rights of the human personality, the creation of a new world based upon justice and mercy—how plain, simple men and women throughout the world long for these things! But are these not suspiciously like slogans of the last war? And what a sorry mess was made of the world at the peace and after! No, that is not the way—war is not the way. If democracy, freedom, goodness may happen to result, it is not because of the war but in spite of it. It is of course the duty of each of us, however insignificant we may be, to do whatever we can, so that the foundations of the new world are laid in fact, and not just dangled before our eyes. But however much we may work and pray for such a world at the end of this war, it cannot be promised, and we should try not to deceive ourselves. The primary and direct reason for our helping to prosecute this war is only a negative reason: war is not for something good, but against the greater evil—to help put down the devil. That is an end in itself, whatever else may be the consequences.

For, no matter how strongly and bitterly we may condemn the democracies for their weaknesses and their villainies, there is in them no substance at all to compare with this savage, demonic, bestial persecution which is embodied in one man and which has seized hold of all the organs of government and society, and which keeps poisoning and blunting the humanity of multitudes within Germany, and beyond her borders. This willing, eager, joyous persecution, this official, judicial, calm infliction of pain and suffering, this systematic, scientific martyrization has been exalted into a creative political principle and into a passionate religious doctrine.

What a debasing thing it is to be at the mercy of a few men! Think of those thousands of young idealists from different lands who laid down their lives recently in Spain fighting in the Communist ranks for what they believed a better world; and now with a stroke of the pen the leader of the Communist State puts their memory to shame and forsakes the millions of adherents who have clung to this ideal as to a religion. Think of what can happen to the millions of democratic idealists going into war now for democracy and freedom, if a few of the old men by a stroke of their pen leave the democratic idealists to their fate.

When the devil offers peace, can it be anything but a devil's peace — faithless, cynical, cruel? Nevertheless, no possible chance should be lost to save the millions of lives on both sides. Peace at almost any price is better than war. But what is the price? For myself, I would answer in a word: that the devil be bereft of the power of persecuting. Can the devil cease persecuting? Persecution is the very breath of his nostrils, the very law of his being. Persecution for religious, political, social, racial or other reasons — if the breaking of such persecution were made the express object of this war, multitudes of plain men and women everywhere would understand it. Other war aims and peace aims are of the utmost significance and should be given concrete expression at the earliest possible moment; and we must all be on guard that these aims be worthy of the high hope of humanity for a better, cleaner, juster world. But this world will not come unless the power of the arch-persecutor is first shattered.

I ask myself constantly: do we feel this so deeply merely because we are Jews? I sincerely hope that this is not the case. The bitterest of indignation and the noblest of protests have found true expression among men of all states, peoples and religions. In this struggle against Satan the Jew happens to be merely the first, and perhaps he will be the last, as he has so often been in history, to experience the full measure of such a calamity. Much of the world instinctively feels that what can happen to the Jew, can happen — has already happened — to other men, and they fear the spread of this deadly plague. The Jew is an exposed signal-station, flashing a warning to other men of religion and good will. Perhaps that is part of his destiny — a destiny he constantly rebels against — to give this warning, to suffer at the hands of persecutors, and sometimes, too, to suffer at the hands of those to whom he has given this warning of the wandering to and fro of Satan upon the earth. Heaven protect us from this at the end of this war.

Before our eyes the great center of Judaism is being destroyed, the Judaism of Poland. Some historians assert that Polish Judaism had been given a Bill of Religious and National Rights in the year 905. For more than a thousand years the Judaism of Poland has been creative, now in times of great trials and sufferings, now in times of freedom. From it have come some of those deep spiritual values which sustain us to this day. It is beyond our power of imagination to picture our Judaism without this creative original force. All that we can do at this moment is to repeat the Prophet's words, "And they shall weep for thee with bitterness of heart and bitter mourning."

In a few days it will be November 10. On that day a year ago 600 synagogues were burnt down in Germany. Let us rise, and remain silent for a moment in memory of the killed, the wounded, the imprisoned, and for the torn and burnt and bespattered scrolls of our imperishable Torah.

Guardian of Israel, guard the Remnant of Israel.

6

WAR
AND THE
POLITICS
OF
DISSENT
1940–1947

T HE WAR BROUGHT NO ABATEMENT in the conflict between the Palestinian Jewish community and the mandatory government. An embittered yishuv watched the ships laden with refugees turned back from the country's shores, from the *Patria* in 1940 to the *Exodus* in 1947. The small number of immigrant certificates allowed under the White Paper were doled out with a parsimonious hand. Soon after the outbreak of the war 138,000 Jews voluntarily registered for army service, yet relatively few were called up, and these were directed to noncombatant duties until late in the war. For a time the German army driving through North Africa posed a threat to the Suez Canal and Palestine. Only in November 1942, when the Germans were stopped at El-Alamein, seventy miles from Alexandria, was the danger lifted. Within the yishuv extremist elements split away from the Hagana, the main underground defense organization. The Irgun Zeva'i Le'umi (Etsel or IZL: National Military Organization) and Lohame Herut Yisrael (Lehi: Freedom Fighters of Israel)[1] adopted a policy of reprisals and political assassination against the British. British forces raided Jewish settlements in search of arms, disregarding the legitimate defense needs of the settlements. Mass arrests took place, and scores were exiled, provoking further violence. Magnes spoke out against terrorism and the use of coercion: violence had become an instrument of policy, and, tragically, an idealistic and self-sacrificing youth was being indoctrinated to believe there was no other way.

Magnes did not evade the hard issues. The discussions he held with the new commanding general of British forces in Palestine, General Sir George Giffard, are a striking instance. In May 1940 the general delivered an ultimatum to a meeting of representative figures of the yishuv, including Magnes, demanding that the Hagana surrender its arms. Prior to the meeting Magnes met with the general then with Moshe Sharett, the agency's chief negotiator, and in the weeks that followed again with the

1. The foreign press referred to the Lehi as the Stern Gang. Abraham Stern was the founder of the group.

general, seeking through these informal talks to prevent what appeared to be a fateful confrontation between the British and the Hagana (document 96).

His integrity, recognized by all, enabled him to undertake a number of sensitive tasks. As chairman of the JDC's Middle East Advisory Committee he used his reputation to break through bureaucratic barriers (documents 105, 107). In July 1944 he went to Turkey in the name of the organizations involved in rescue work to mediate between feuding officials and to evaluate the operations conducted from this key base. The trip to Turkey was also a searing personal experience. While in Istanbul he met a shipload of survivors of the death camps disembarking for the overland journey to Palestine. When he opened the academic year of the university in November 1944, the experience and the stream of reports documenting the methodical destruction of European Jewry compelled him to speak out publicly on the religious question that tormented him: Was there a living God for whom all this has meaning? (documents 106, 110).

In the summer of 1942 Magnes moved to build a political base from which to press his program. The adoption of the Biltmore Platform the previous May persuaded him and his coworkers—Martin Buber, Ernst Simon, Chaim Kalvarisky, Moshe Smilansky, Henrietta Szold, and Gavriel Stern—to establish the Ihud Association. To succeed Ihud required financial and political support from America. In October 1942 Magnes approached his American friends, the moderate Zionists and the non-Zionists. He hoped that his article in Foreign Affairs, "Toward Peace in Palestine," published in January 1943, would win like-minded Americans to his cause. However, by spring 1943 he faced an American Jewish community overwhelmingly aligned behind the maximalist program of the Zionist organization (documents 100, 101, 102, 104).

With the war's end the Palestine question acquired a new urgency. Magnes reformulated his position to meet the exigencies of the postwar world as he saw them: the ascendency of the United States to the leadership of the free world and the major role he expected the United Nations to play (document 108). In January 1945 he traveled to Cairo and met with Mahmoud Fawzi Bey, the Egyptian diplomat who had served as consul general in Jerusalem and was being reassigned to Washington. Back in Jerusalem he joined other Ihud leaders in talks with Weizmann, hoping to win Weizmann's support for a moderate, alternative program to the Jewish commonwealth formula.[2] In March 1946 Magnes appeared before the Anglo-American Committee of Inquiry, and in May he met Azzam Pasha, secretary of the newly formed Arab League, in Cairo (document 112).

2. Minutes of the Ihud Council, April 22, 1945, MP, 2547.

Later that month he and Beatrice flew to the United States. It was his first visit in twelve years, and for Beatrice the first in fifteen years—a homecoming and respite from the tensions and dangers of Jerusalem but a political mission as well (document 113). He met with State Department officials and wrung promises of financial and organizational support from his American friends. The political fruits of the trip were meager. In a plaintive note to Dean Acheson, written in December 1946 on his return to Jerusalem, he reminded the Acting Secretary of State of their earlier meeting: "You were good enough to say that perhaps the time for consideration of the binational proposals might come 'tomorrow or the day after.' I wonder if this time has come yet."[3] The supporting body for Ihud, the American Association for Union in Palestine, he complained to his American correspondents, "has been in the process of gestation since last August" (documents 114, 115, 116, 117).

In February 1947, on the eve of his departure for London for talks with the Colonial Secretary, Magnes fell ill and was forced to cancel the trip. "I think it might have made a difference," he wrote to Nelson Glueck, who had left Jerusalem to accept the presidency of the Hebrew Union College. "I think this was the one real frustration of my life."[4] His illness, bronchial pneumonia, kept him bedridden for months and placed an added strain on his heart. He never fully recovered his vigor.

In the fall of 1947 he took up the fight against the majority report of the United Nations Special Committee on Palestine (UNSCOP), which had recommended partition (document 118). As the United Nations moved toward a decision his long-time colleague and loyal coworker, Ernst Simon, writing from America, questioned Magnes's tactics, indeed the whole program of Ihud. "How shall we act after our defeat," he asked, "simply as though nothing happened?" (document 119). In the spring of 1948 the vagaries of United States foreign policy presented Magnes with one final opportunity to press his formula for peace.

3. JLM to Dean Acheson, December 12, 1946, Department of State Papers, 867N.01/12-1246.
4. JLM to Nelson Glueck, April 24, 1947, MP, 2564.

96

Journal: Notes of Meeting with General Sir George Giffard

Jerusalem, June 15, 1940

Interview with General Giffard,[1] 3–4 P.M.

This morning I called up Cumming Bruce for an interview with the G.O.C. [General Officer Commanding]. Subject: The G.O.C. to address the whole University body on the present situation before the summer vacation in three weeks. 3 P.M. was fixed.

The G.O.C. said that he knew of the general nature of my request — what did it mean specifically?

I said I thought it would be a good thing all around if he would meet the University community and if they could see and hear him. With students, teachers, and other workers it was a community of well over a thousand, and if we included the doctors and nurses, etc. of the hospital it would be at least 1500. This was as intelligent a community as the country had, and it exerted considerable influence. It was a critical community and it was anxious to be of service. I would ask that he come and tell them how they could be of service in these critical days. Of course the doctors and the nurses and such had their tasks. There were many others interested in one form or another of communal service. Some of our students and staff would, I had no doubt, join the force, which so I understood, was being enlisted — an enlarged police or Civic Guard. The question which above all others interested us at the moment was that of possible combatant units. Whether he was free to talk about this he would know. But whether or not, his presence and his words would be appreciated and would bring an important group of the public, particularly the youth, into closer contact with the authorities, and that was, I thought, all to the good these days.

He said his inclination would be to accept. It was an attractive invitation. But he would like to think it over for a day or two and he would let me know.

As to the combatant units — that was not in anyone's hands here, but in the hands of London and they had decided against this for their own reasons, at least for the present. Aside from political considerations, one reason had doubtless been lack of equipment. Every last rifle was needed in France. The evacuation from Dunkirk was nothing short of a miracle, that was the only term he could use, but as Mr. Churchill had said, the loss of material was enormous.

I said that up till recently, as far as I was aware, this shortage of equipment had not been known as a reason for failing to organize the combatant units. But it seemed to be generally known now, and it would be all the more helpful if he could nevertheless say how the youth could be of service. It would be well to hold out possibilities of service.

He would think it over, and if he could, he would accept. He had before him the manuscript of what he was to say on the radio, and he had not corrected it carefully as yet. He was not a speaker, but if he came he would do his best.

I prepared to go when he said that inasmuch as I was here he had decided to talk to me about the question of hidden arms. He was greatly disappointed with the outcome of his efforts — they had resulted in nothing. He assumed that I was more or less acquainted with what had transpired since the meeting at which he had read his statement.

I said that Mr. Shertok had made it a point to keep me informed, and he had let me know that he was to be in Tel Aviv today and maybe tomorrow, but that upon his return he would inform me as to the meeting yesterday. I had also been invited to a discussion. I hoped that although he was disappointed with the results, he would not give up trying to come to some understanding with the Jewish Community on such basic matters — that was of the utmost importance.

He said he was afraid he had said some rather sharp things. But when he saw that there was no inclination to cooperate with him he felt that he must say how he felt. People can go a long way in finding a basis of understanding if only there is the will, and he doubted if this was present.

I said I was sorry to hear him say that because I could assure him that his fair and frank attitude had been greatly appreciated. There had been real searching of heart, and there was a sincere conflict within many persons between the genuine desire on the part of the Agency and the Va'ad Le'umi to cooperate, and the fear of the settlements that declaring their arms would mean a lessening of their security. After all, the arms were not under the direct control of the Agency.

He did not mean to say that the Agency had definitely imported arms, or that they controlled the use of these arms. But they did know of their existence, and where they were, and their numbers. The leaders of the Jewish Community had prided themselves that during the years of rebellion they had been able to persuade the Jews to use arms only for defense and that was something of which they might be proud. But now when they are asked to help him at a very grave crisis they say they have no authority.

I said it was one thing to use moral pressure to prevent the use of these arms for attack and another to persuade people to deliver them up. There was sincere doubt if some of the settlements would do this. Rightly or wrongly they were convinced that these arms were necessary to their security.

That was just where they were wrong, he answered, and where they will not understand that as the person responsible for the country's security he *must* know about these arms. In these days of the fifth column, it is dangerous to have hidden arms. The settlements do not seem to realize the danger to them. With tens of thousands of Jews here from various countries and many of them recently arrived, we must take every possible precaution against the activities of some Jews as fifth columnists. One must assume that not all of these tens of thousands are 100 percent perfect. There may be many motives actuating them. There are fifth columnists here from among all communities. Such agents have been sent and planted here. In the stress and confusion of war, the first thing these fifth columnists will get are these arms which will be turned against those who now rely upon them for protection. He wanted to give the settlers *legal* arms, and he would see to it that they had sufficient together with the settlement police. He could then make his disposition without having to worry about the unfortunate uses which fifth columnists would make of these hidden arms.

He had no doubt that among the population generally there was a surge of readiness to be helpful. But it was the leaders who were not helpful. Mr. Shertok had said that a government was only as strong as its following would let it be. The G.O.C. had answered that his view of a government was that it led. Leaders were there to lead, not just to follow.

He had said at the meeting yesterday that if one took up any day's paper one would imagine that the Jewish leaders were really anxious to cooperate. They were constantly saying they were. But the record was different. They opposed the pioneer corps.[2] They opposed the recruitment of Czech and Polish volunteers.[3] They maintained a secret radio till last Monday which the Germans were using against the Allies.[4] They refuse cooperation in the matter of secret arms. People who refused cooperation to this extent were not helping to win the war. They might think they were helping their own narrow Zionist interests. He would have to draw his own conclusions. He would probably have to go after these arms in view of this unhelpful attitude.

The H.C. had agreed not to reduce the number of the settlement police and he and the H.C. agreed that it was not sound in a country like this that there be any arms in anyone's hands except the Government's. But in view of what had happened during the [Arab] rebellion and in view of the nervousness of those who had recently come from lands of oppression, they were willing to make the concessions he had read out; and he had gone further and had suggested that they tell him how many arms there were, and he would judge as to whether they were too few or too many. He would guarantee to let the settlements retain a reasonable proportion, and he would see to it that each settlement would have an adequate supply.

As to arms in the hands of citizens, I said, that depended upon the country and upon circumstances. In Switzerland every man was a member of the state militia and had a gun which he kept at home. I remember my father telling me of the vigilante riots in California when he carried a rifle, and I remember some of the anti-Chinese riots in San Francisco during my youth. The citizens were armed by the authorities.

But might I ask him a question? Did he tell the committee that came to see him how many hidden arms he thinks the Jews have? He said he had not mentioned any figure. Might I ask if he would tell me? His officers tell him that there were from 4,000 to 5,000. Without having any definite information in the matter, this is a number that I had heard also. General Barker[5] had said there were "30,000 rifles in Jewish orange groves along the coast." I had told him that his information had been grossly exaggerated. One very responsible person had said to me recently that if the G.O.C. knew how few the number was he would not believe it. He would accuse the Jews either of lying or being fools.

Would he be willing that I tell Mr. Shertok of this conversation and ask Mr. Shertok if the figures 4,000–5,000 was approximately right, with a view to informing the G.O.C.?

How was he to be sure, he asked, that the answer I got was truthful?

I could assure him, I answered, that if I got an answer it would be truthful. I might not get an answer; or I might get a different figure with permission to tell him; or I might get a different figure without permission to tell him, in which case, of course, I could not. But the answer I got would be truthful.

He then said I might do as I proposed.

I then asked, "Do you think 4,000–5,000 arms too many?"

He answered, "I must not permit myself to answer that question because I do not know. I would want to take into account each settlement's locality, general position, numbers, the number of settlement police, the proximity of the army, and other points." From his general impression he thought about 3,000 arms would suffice but that was a mere guess and the matter would have to be gone into.

I asked, "Would you give each locality the opportunity of sitting down with you and arguing the case? After all, it is their lives that are at stake."

G.O.C.: He would not be doing the investigation on the spot himself, he would delegate it to his officers. He would instruct them to hear the arguments of each settlement. But the army's decision would have to be

375

final. One thing he could definitely not allow: machine guns and bombs. The settlement police had Lewis guns.

I told him the settlements believe machine guns and bombs in their hands to be defensive weapons. I said the settlements could cite case after case which would seem to show that machine guns and bombs used defensively had saved these settlements.

He said he knew that argument but it was false. It was entirely inadvisable that such weapons be hidden or that they be in anyone's hands but that of Government. That was the most dangerous kind of irresponsibility.

I asked would he instruct his officers to put a liberal interpretation upon his expression that he would permit the settlements to retain a "reasonable proportion"? He said he could not answer that question. I said that there were many who said that if they could be sure the army was always to be here they would deliver their arms without question. But armies were mobile, here today and there tomorrow. He said that was right but there were police forces also.

I said there were those also who said that it would be all right if General Giffard were always here. But there might arise a king who knew not Joseph. In 1921 the Jewish Legion was at Sarefend an hour away when rioting against the Jews broke out in Jerusalem, and the Legion was not sent for. In 1929 the sealed armories were sometimes not adequate or expeditiously used.

He said, "Poor organization."

I said, "That is just it. The very organization may be good today, and tomorrow of such a nature that some Arab sergeant would know of the sealed armory and would forbid the settlement the use of it."

The G.O.C.: "But I have never mentioned sealed armories. I want to give the arms to the settlers for such use as they wish to make of the arms to act with the settlement police."

I asked, "Will they be allowed to carry these arms?"

He answered, "Yes."

I asked if he had explained all these details.

He said that he had not.

I said that if he were to reallocate the arms, could he say that although he might give one settlement more and the other less than at present, he would permit the total number to remain the same?

He said he could not give such an undertaking.

I told him that I was asking these questions in order to become clear and in order to be able to find a way out if possible. A last question: if he were to reallocate arms, he would have to know the localities where they were and not merely numbers.

He answered that "eventually that would be so."

I said I would meet with Mr. Shertok and let him know the result. The authorities and the Jews should make every effort to come to an understanding.

He said in the conversation that people did not seem to realize that the war had not begun here. He pointed to the map and said that we might expect hostilities to develop over this whole region. There might be a great shortage — surely no luxuries, and maybe a shortage of essentials, and great suffering, and the country would therefore have to be organized as a disciplined community.

I referred to this as I was leaving and suggested that he might speak along these lines to the University. Our young men and women were not afraid of hardships. The young were inspired if told they would have to bring sacrifices. He said he would think the University invitation over and let me know.

I asked when the Italian professors of the University could be released.

He said the matter was really not in his hands but in those of the police and the Chief Secretary. He had been warned at home against the mistake made there at the beginning of the war. They had attempted to sift the alien enemy population and sequester only those of whom they were suspicious. They realized the mistake. The method now was to gather everyone in, and then to sift each case, and to release those who were not suspect.

I said I had no doubt that was the right method, only it worked hardship on elderly and weaker persons.

I forgot to note an important point.

Among the reasons why hidden arms were dangerous he cited the animosity between the Histadrut and Revisionists in labor matters. When quarrels broke out it was bad enough if they used any kind of arms, but if they got hold of machine guns and bombs the consequences were not to be foreseen.

I asked if a composition of these quarrels for the duration would make any difference in his attitude.

He said it was hard for contending parties to make such promises, and if made, to implement them. We know what took place in a country like England at the end of the war. This country was not nearly so orderly. There would be shortages (etc. as above) and unemployment, and there would be a fierce struggle for bread. Under such circumstances it would be more than human if people did not fight one another.

1. General Sir George James Giffard (1886–1964). Commanding general of British forces in Palestine, February–June 1940.
2. The Jewish Agency policy was to demand the establishment of large Jewish combat

units to serve, in the first instance, in the defense of Palestine. It therefore did not cooperate in recruiting for the Auxiliary Military Pioneer Corps, which was being dispatched to France.

3. The Czech and Polish consulates were recruiting Jews with Czech or Polish citizenship for service in the free armies of their governments-in-exile.

4. The Jewish underground radio was supporting the Jewish Agency's recruitment policies.

5. General Michael George Henry Barker (1884–1960). Commanding general of British forces in Palestine, 1939–1940.

97

To Felix Frankfurter
Washington, D.C.

Jerusalem, November 12, 1941

Dear Justice Frankfurter,

Your kind letter of August 30 concerning my end-of-term letter to the University last June reached me today.

I am sending you herewith a copy of the address I gave at the opening of the University last week. I tried to make it much briefer, but unfortunately did not succeed. There is altogether too much to say in these days, and yet how little saying them seems to help.

Some time ago I sent you three articles on Palestine and Arab Union.

I come more and more to the conclusion that there should be the smallest possible number of small states with independent armies and independent foreign policies. Armies and foreign relations should be in the hands of unions or federations.

Of course to work out "the national genius," a state ought to be absolutely and completely sovereign and independent. But the ills resulting from this are so massive that it is better that the "national genius" suffer than that these states and peoples plunge the world into misery through their exaggerated national egos.

Remember me kindly to Mrs. Frankfurter, and with best regards, I am
Sincerely yours, JLM

98

Journal: The Constituents That Make Up My Being

Jerusalem, December 17, 1941

If I try to examine the constituents that go to make up my being, I find that they are greatly mixed up, but that it may nevertheless be possible to analyze them somewhat:

(a) I am *religiously* a Jew. That means that the religious tradition of Judaism has had a great influence upon me — the Bible, the Prayer Book, the Sabbath and the Festivals, Jewish home and family life; the marking of turning points in the individual's life — birth, circumcision, bar mitzvah, marriage, death; the moral instruction of our children — benevolence, respect for parents, regard for the poor, and the great ideals of justice and righteousness and mercy for all men, particularly the afflicted and the oppressed; and beyond all of this the ultimate sanction of morals and the ultimate life of grace and salvation for man in the God of Israel.

(b) I am *politically* an American. I feel this the more deeply since the outbreak of this war. I have felt it keenly in recent years, more especially because of the distance that seems to yawn between my political views and those of the Zionist leaders in Palestine and abroad. By "politically" I mean that the American (and English) tradition of democracy has had a great influence upon me — the political institutions of voting and parliamentary government; free speech, and a free press; freedom of religious conviction and worship; the idea of the equality of all men, black and white, great and small; the possibility of men of all races and origins and creeds living together cooperatively; the feeling of individual responsibility for the welfare of the community, for the proper and honest working of the democracy; the opportunity for criticism and the duty to criticize (for me, particularly) the failure of the American democracy thus far to distribute its wealth and products so that every man may have work and a modest living in just the same way that every family has the right and the duty to send its children to the schools.

When I use the words "religiously" and "politically" as above, I do not mean to say that religion and politics are divorced from or confined to separate compartments of being or of living. I have learned from the Hebrew prophets how absolutely the religion of Israel meant for them their intervention in the political affairs of the nation; and by "political affairs" (a term they never used) they meant the foreign relations of Israel on the one hand, and on the other, social justice within Israel and beyond Israel, for other peoples. The Puritan democracy of England was based upon the same idea, and this influenced the American democracy basically. This is primarily due to the Old Testament which is therefore my heritage "religiously" and "politically."

If I am asked which of these two influences is the greater, the deeper in my life, I can only answer that that depends upon the moment the question is asked. To take the present moment — it is in every way beyond the ordinary — both my feeling of being a Jew and my feeling of being an American is unusually alive within me. How overwhelmingly the Jew within me is stirred not only by the bestiality shown the Jews by our enemy, but also by his anti-Judaism, his subversion of Jewish morals and spiritual values, his onslaught against our most precious heritage. Moreover, the place of America in this world conflict is so decisive, the difference between America and Germany, symbolized by the difference between Roosevelt and Hitler, is so deep and fateful that I want to make any and every sacrifice to be of help to America which at this moment I regard as "my country." It is the proof of the inner harmony between my Judaism and my Americanism that at this moment they are so completely and irrevocably on the same side of this gigantic struggle. I can conceive of a situation where America would be opposed to Jews and Judaism. Should that unhappy event occur, then there is no doubt that my Jewish self would become dominant. Is it possible to conceive of a situation where the Jews would be against America? If so, then I am certain that my American self would be the more potent.

There is at least one fundamental, perhaps decisive difference between a man's religion and his political allegiance. He can and does change his political allegiance almost at will. The Jews driven from Germany despite their great love for Germany do become, and should become citizens of more hospitable lands. There are many reasons leading men to change their political allegiance, and no dishonor is attached to this. But it is different with a man's religion. For this he endures martyrdom. He may, of course, change his religion out of inner conviction. But that, in an honest man, is a long, difficult, painful process. It is infinitely more soul-searching and harder than the political change. Apostasy is a term used of religious change. There is hardly political apostasy in the same profound sense of the term. In religion the 44th Psalm is a most moving expression of the inescapable, unswerving steadfastness of the "believer" (also a term hardly appropriate in the political sphere). Despite the Psalmist's complaint, almost his charges against God for having delivered Israel into the hands of the enemy, he cries out: "All this has come upon us; yet have we not forgotten thee and dealt falsely with Thy covenant."

In all of this I have not mentioned Palestine and Zionism.

Palestine, Zion, Jerusalem and the other dear and familiar names of the places and persons of the Bible and our later history are also part of the Jewish religious heritage. Palestine *is* the Holy Land of Judaism, Jerusalem the Holy City.

Zionism is based on this, but it adds also the political element, and this to such an extent that the religious origin of it all is lost, and the political aspect has usurped its place.

I said above that I am politically an American. This means that I am not a Palestinian politically. Yet I am keenly concerned with the political life of this country, where I live, and with political developments, and it is, so I think, perfectly legitimate that I, as an American citizen, devote my thought and energies to the political problem here. American citizens of all kinds have on innumerable occasions expressed their interest in the Holy Land, their sympathy with a Jewish return to the Holy Land, their interest in cultural, social and political developments here, and their readiness to be of help in one way or another. An American citizen is (or was) chief adviser to Chiang Kai-shek, and I have no doubt that there are American citizens who are Chinese and who are aiding the establishment of Chinese political institutions in China to the great satisfaction of the Americans acquainted with their activities. Of course one assumes that their activities are colored by the best they have received from America. How much the more could similar activity of American Jews meet with the approval of the "best" Americans!

The problem assumes a somewhat different aspect when we talk of a Jewish State. I think I could, as an American, work for the establishment of that State, or of the conditions leading to its creation. But once the State was created, I would be placed before the choice of remaining an American citizen or becoming a Palestinian, a Jewish citizen. Thus far no scheme of double citizenship has been worked out in the world, although the English proposal to France in May 1940 approached this.

Even before the establishment of the Jewish State there are some American citizens (e.g. Agronsky)[1] who have given up their American citizenship and have become Palestinians. But all of those who have retained their American citizenship, though continuing to live in Palestine, are legitimate, bona fide American citizens, "Americans politically."

There are other constituents in a man's make-up besides the religious and the political.

(c) I am *culturally* an American (English), a Jew, a German . . . The languages a man speaks, the schools where he has been educated, the work he does, the friends and interests he has, his travels, all influence him culturally.

I speak English, and English and American literature and history are somewhat familiar to me and have influenced me.

I speak German. I heard German spoken in my youth by my mother and her mother, and I went to German universities for two years.

I speak Hebrew and I have learned something of Hebrew literature and history in Cincinnati and Germany, in New York and in Jerusalem.

There is such a thing as the international republic of letters and of science. I have come together with the citizens of many nations and with the Jews of many citizenships on such matters.

1. Gerson (Agronsky) Agron (1894–1959). Brought to the United States from the Ukraine as a child. In the First World War served with the Jewish Legion in Palestine; was editor of the Jewish Telegraphic Agency, 1921–1924; founder of the English-language daily, *Palestine Post* (the *Jerusalem Post* after 1950); mayor of Jerusalem, 1955–1959.

99

Journal: America Must Impose a Compromise

Jerusalem, August 30, 1942

The slogan "Jewish State" (or Commonwealth) is equivalent, in effect, to a declaration of war by the Jews on the Arabs.

This slogan is mobilizing the Jews for a diplomatic onslaught upon the Arabs, and at the same time preparing them for an onslaught of another kind, in case this be necessary. Speeches and articles here and elsewhere are an indication of this. In responsible quarters here the words "Fiume" and "Vilna" are used as a symbol of what the Jewish stormtroops may be called upon to do.

The agitation for the Jewish army—legitimate enough perhaps in itself—is partly vitiated by the *arrière pensée* [mental reservation] as to its use at the proper time as a conquering force in the tradition of Joshua.

The Jewish State (or Commonwealth) slogan is also mobilizing the Arabs. A Jewish Agency account recently declared that the quantity of hidden arms in the hands of both peoples was about equal. There are many Arab deserters from the Army—deserters with their arms. The whole Arab world is in touch with these developments which lose nothing of their excitement in the telling.

This agitation is having a most serious effect upon the moral position of the Allies in this part of the world. It adds fuel to the fire of Axis propaganda. It wins more and more sympathy for the Axis advance.

An Arab for whose honesty and judgment I have learned, through the years, to have much respect said to me recently: "The Jews want England to win and they will get what they want (a State, a Commonwealth), so they think. The Arabs, with some exceptions (my friend is one of these), want the Axis to win, and they will get what they want (Arab independence), so they think. But on the day that the Jews get their State, their real war with the Arabs will begin."

I am convinced that one of the few hopes of comparative peace for the Holy Land is for America, more especiallly President Roosevelt, to have a decisive voice in the settlement. The authority of Britain is, unfortunately, at a low ebb. For this reason I keep using the formula "Anglo-American" in order to indicate that these two great powers — they are Bible powers, too — will have to be associated in any settlement that is made here, now or later.

But America will be able to exercise her great moral and political influence only if she fights shy of the maximalists on both sides, the maximalist Jews and the maximalist Arabs. America must come in and help impose a compromise. But this compromise, though imposed as almost every compromise is, must be of such a nature as not to lead to armed rebellion.

Can such a compromise be found? That is the question that every man of good will must try to answer.

I think it can be found. The official leaders on both sides will not be pleased with the compromise. At any rate they will not sign it because they are too thoroughly shackled by their own maximalist propaganda. But the *people* of both sides, the great bulk of the plain Jews and Arabs, who have no hatred in their hearts for one another, will be happy and grateful for such a compromise. A reasonable compromise is poor incitement to an armed rebellion.

If I am asked what such a compromise would look like, I am prepared to give its general outlines here:

(a) *Government* in Palestine: Both peoples are to have equal political rights.

(b) *Immigration*: Agreements as to numbers are to be reached for periods of 10 to 15 years.

(c) *Federation*: A federal union is to be formed of the states which before the war constituted Greater Syria, including Palestine, Transjordan, Syria and the Lebanon.

(d) The union of the victorious free nations is to be responsible for the peace of the countries constituting the federative union of the four countries. The form of this control on behalf of peace would be dependent upon the form—the political, economic, spiritual form—which the New World took on generally. In any event, any trusteeship which the union of free nations assumed for its constituent parts—empires, federations, dominions, etc.—would *not* assume the form of granting mandates to single countries. Single countries have not proved their unselfishness as mandatories.

The above is, of course, but the roughest of surface sketches. There is much one could and must say under each heading; and others doubtless have other outlines which need to be considered.

The main thing is that the need of compromise be the guiding idea of those desiring a more or less peaceful, fruitful settlement here.

No statesman should at this moment, so it seems to me, commit himself to any particular scheme, but he should constantly inquire into the possibility of compromise. The *sine qua non* of a compromise is *no* Jewish State, and *no* Arab State, but some form of a Palestine cooperative body politic. No statesman should go further than this, so I think, at the moment. But everyone should get to work seeking the way of a compromise, which though perhaps not acceptable to the leaders (at least officially), would be welcomed by the Jews and the Arabs and the people generally of the free nations. Palestine must not be permitted to be a disturbing factor in the peace of the world.

100

To Rabbi Morris S. Lazaron
Baltimore

Jerusalem, October 6, 1942

Dear Dr. Lazaron:

I want to tell you how much I have enjoyed meeting Frank Kaufman. He was here recently a second time. He is intelligent and honest and from all accounts he is doing a very good piece of work. In general it is encouraging to see the type of some of the Americans now here, and I hope that those who come will measure up to their standards.

You may be interested in the organization called Ihud which has been established here recently, and I am enclosing a little material. It seems to me that there ought to be a similar organization or committee in America putting forward somewhat the same program, because the question of

Palestine affects American Jewry and, I believe, America at large just as much as it affects Palestine itself.

With kindest regards, I am

Sincerely yours, JLM

P.S. I had dictated the above yesterday and your very welcome letter of September 9 came this morning. I thank you especially for enclosing the Statement of Principles.

I am able to endorse this statement, but with questions as to the meaning of the passage in section (3) beginning: "But in the light of our universalistic interpretation of Jewish history" . . . to the end of the section.[1]

a. I also have a universalistic interpretation of Jewish history. But this for me is not in opposition to the national elements and hopes of the Jewish People.

b. You are unable to "support the political emphasis now paramount in the Zionist program." What does the word *emphasis* signify here? I am opposed to the political content of the program, not because it is political but because I think the content under present conditions likely to provoke civil war in Palestine and confusion abroad. Politics is one of the great spiritual concerns of mankind, as the Prophets of Israel showed. They were not cut off from life and they therefore did not oppose politics as such. But they were concerned with the kind of political principles the State was based upon, and upon the quality of the political action of statesmen and peoples.

c. It is true that Jewish nationalism tends to confuse people, not because it is secular and not religious, but because this nationalism is unhappily chauvinistic and narrow and terroristic in the best style of Eastern European nationalism. The factor of nationalism is also of great spiritual moment, and it cannot be answered by denying its existence. It depends upon what we make of it, and it is here where legitimate criticism is, unhappily, called for.

It is well that you and your associates have spoken, and I hope that you will keep on clarifying all aspects of your principles. "Research" is in style these days. Could you not set up a research committee for further delving into the bases and implication of your principles?

Might I suggest that you get into touch with Mr. Roger Straus of 120 Broadway, New York? I have written him at length, and perhaps an Ihud Committee might be set up in America so that we may all be working together.

Again with kind regards, I am

Sincerely yours, JLM

1. Section 3 of the Statement of Principles of the newly established American Council

for Judaism read: "In the light of our universalistic interpretation of Jewish history and destiny, and also because of our concern for the welfare and status of the Jewish people living in other parts of the world, we are unable to subscribe to or support the political emphasis now paramount in the Zionistic program. We cannot but believe that Jewish nationalism tends to confuse our fellow men about our place and function in society and also divert our attention from our historic role to live as a religious community wherever we may dwell" (*New York Times*, August 30, 1942, p. 26).

101

To Alexander Dushkin
New York

Jerusalem, January 7, 1943

Dear Dr. Dushkin,

I am very grateful to you and our friends Kaplan,[1] Pool,[2] Semel[3] and Schoolman[4] who with you signed the telegram of December 24, 1942.[5] I hope that I may always count on your friendship and understanding, however much our views may regrettably differ.

I cannot remember anything for which I am quite so sorry as that letter I sent to Lazaron. The reason is that it may raise the terrorist issue publicly, and that is something all of us should try to avoid. It is dangerous. It is the last issue I should have wished to raise publicly, and at this time, and in this way.

Moreover, the publication of my letter seems to have deflected a discussion of serious issues into a personal controversy. It passes me how a responsible person can publish extracts from a private letter without having secured leave for this. I have cabled Dr. Lazaron twice, and thus far have received no answer. I have also written him.

I wrote to him on October 7, 1942, because on that day I received from him the Statement of Principles signed by a large number of rabbis some of whom I know to be fervent Jews. I imagine that all of you would have subscribed to it with the exception of the same passages to which I took exception, those about nationalism.

I am sending you a copy of my letter to him so that you can see what my strictures were.

In general I should like to say that in my opinion the last word has not by any means been said about nationalism, this way or that.

My sentence about the Jewish national movement being terroristic was too general. I did not, of course, want to condemn the Jewish national movement. It was for this reason that I telegraphed the *Baltimore Jewish Times* concerning my attitude towards nationalism. I hope this has been published.

What I had in mind was not the few extremists mentioned by you, but rather, definite acts which some important leaders and groups have not repudiated and which thus take on the aspect of being, to say the least, not contrary to their national policy. Definite tendencies have thus been fostered among our youth which are causing many persons the gravest concern. There have been private meetings about this, but thus far without practical results. These tendencies are taking root in a youth inspired by the highest idealism and moral courage. But this is just another reason for deploring these developments.

I cannot give specifications in a letter in these days of censorship. I fervently hope that this miserable controversy will not take such a form as to lead to public statements on these questions.

You ask me to dissociate myself from Lazaron and his group because they are organized to destroy American Zionism. If what you say is a fact, this is the thing to do.

But is it a fact? You will pardon me for asking this question. Doubtless I am too little aware of what is transpiring in American Judaism. But one of my excuses must be that American Jewish publications, with but rare exceptions, have not been reaching us for close on to a year. As an indication of this you may be interested to know that no one here knew of the Biltmore resolutions of last May until Mr. Ben-Gurion brought them in his pocket upon his return to Palestine in November.

But there is another question involved which interests me much more than do Dr. Lazaron and his group, namely, what Ihud is to do in order to win to its program as many Jews in America as possible.

Ihud is a Zionist group here, and we want naturally to have the support of large numbers of Zionists in America who may agree or who can be won over to Ihud principles.

But I wish to go further and say that, as far as I am concerned, I should also like to see large numbers of non-Zionists in America adhere to the Ihud platform. I do not refer, of course, to people who want to destroy American Zionism, but to those who are really interested in Palestine.

I should like to quote from a letter under date of September 3, 1942, from a well-known "non-Zionist" whose active support I am sure everyone would welcome:

I just cannot go along with the Zionists, nor do I feel at home among the anti-Zionists. Although I call myself a non-Zionist, that does not mean much, and I am anxious therefore to get further information about Ihud.[6]

387

I should like also to quote my answer under date of October 1, 1942:

> The time has come once and for all, so I am convinced, to make a systematic, organized attempt to bring home a point of view which, as you properly indicate, is not anti-Zionist and is not non-Zionist, but, permit me to say, is Zionist if this term does not have to mean maximalist aims which in the opinion of many people cannot be achieved within our lifetime. It seems to me that there is no reason why those of us who have sympathy with a deep but moderate Zionism should yield this term to others who through their extremist views and actions are making it difficult for you and me and many good Jews and Zionists to carry out their full weight on behalf of the upbuilding in Palestine of a Jewish National Home.[7]

Non-Zionism is admittedly a clumsy and rather vague term, but it has official standing. The Jewish Agency is composed of Zionists and non-Zionists. That is one of the great achievements of the Jewish Agency — the coalition of Zionists and non-Zionists on behalf of the upbuilding of the National Home in Palestine.

Louis Marshall, Felix Warburg, Cyrus Adler, Cyrus Sulzberger and others were called non-Zionists. I had something to do with the favorable attitude of some of them towards Palestine, and I am interested in their children and their successors, i.e. in a large proportion of American Judaism. I would want to win them for Zion, in some such way as their forbears were won. Is the situation such that in your opinion it is necessary to break with them? This is not just a rhetorical question but one to which a carefully reasoned answer should be given.

Mr. Ben-Gurion and Dr. Weizmann have been very anxious to win their support, and I think rightly so. Is it only they who have the right to seek this support?

The question, therefore, is this: if non-Zionists accept the Ihud platform, should we repudiate them? Are we to reject Jews in America who agree with these principles but who may not be ready to join the Zionist Organization of America with its present program? I think it would be a positive, constructive asset for Palestine if in addition to many Zionists, all those so-called non-Zionist Jews could be won over to the Ihud program.

I think I need not dwell here on my attitude towards official Zionist policy. That is given in my article in *Foreign Affairs*.

I am glad to be in correspondence with you on these questions. They appear to me to be important. I assume you will give copies of this personal letter to those who signed the telegram with you, and also please to Mrs. Jacobs[8] and Dr. Schloessinger.

With kindest regards to all of you, I am

Sincerely yours, JLM

1. Mordecai M. Kaplan (see glossary of names).

2. Tamar de Sola Pool (1893–1981). Jewish community leader; born in Jerusalem and brought to the United States in 1904; president, Hadassah, Women's Zionist Organization, 1939–1943.

3. Bernard Semel (1978–1959). Merchant and Jewish community leader; born in Blechow, Galicia, and came to the United States in 1890. An active Zionist, he was a leading supporter of the New York Kehillah and the Jewish Education Association.

4. Albert P. Schoolman (1894–1980). Jewish educator; executive director of Central Jewish Institute, New York, and founder of Cejwin camp.

5. Lazaron published Magnes's private letter (document 100) in the *Baltimore Jewish Times*, which created an outcry against Magnes for designating Jewish nationalism as "chauvinistic and narrow and terroristic." His critics complained that he played into the hands of the anti-Zionist American Council for Judaism. The telegram from Magnes's friends pointed this out, expressed the hope that Magnes was refering "to only very small number of extremists," and appealed to him to dissociate himself from the Lazaron group.

6. Roger W. Straus to JLM, September 3, 1942, MP, 215.

7. JLM to Roger W. Straus, October 1, 1942, MP 215.

8. Rose G. Jacobs (1908–1975). American Zionist leader born in New York City. She was a founder of Hadassah and was its president from 1930 to 1932 and from 1934 to 1937. She served on the executive of the Jewish Agency from 1937 to 1946 and was a member of the board of governors of the Hebrew University.

102

Toward Peace in Palestine

Many of the basic problems of life defy complete solution. The Jewish problem is one of these. It is made up of so many complex elements — religious, moral, political, economic, social, racial, historical — that it is a difficult task to even formulate it, let alone speak of "solving" it. Most of the solutions which are put forward are over-simplifications. But Jews and non-Jews can attempt to understand the problem and labor together for a free and just society. And in the measure society is just and free, in that measure Jews and Judaism will find their appropriate places and functions.

Palestine must occupy an important place in any consideration of the Jewish problem. It is unique among the lands of the earth — the Holy Land of the three great monotheistic faiths. It is also the Land of Israel, with which the People Israel have been associated from Bible time to this day. Would that it were large and empty enough to absorb millions of persecuted, wandering Jews and to be constituted into a Jewish state! Some object to this conception on the ground that politics and religion have nothing to do with one another. But politics is one of the most profound of mankind's spiritual concerns. How men are to live together and be governed is a spiritual question with far-reaching implications. The fact remains that Palestine is small and is not empty. Another people have been in possession for centuries, and the concept of Palestine as a Jewish state is regarded by many Arabs as equivalent to a declaration of war against them. To those who contend that Palestine is the Promised Land of the Jews, I would say that it is necessary to distinguish between Messianic expectations and hard reality. When the late Chief Rabbi of Palestine, Rabbi Kuk, was asked by the Shaw Commission in 1930 what his attitude was toward restoration to the Jews of the site of Solomon's Temple, where the Mosque of Omar now stands, he replied that he believed with a perfect faith that this would come about in God's own time, but that meanwhile violence in achieving Messianic ends could not be countenanced by Judaism.

Some important Zionist leaders* contend now — they did not always do so — that room can be created in Palestine "for something like 400,000 families, or nearly two million souls" in addition to those already there, and that "this is likely to be approximately the number of people whom Palestine will in fact have to take care of very rapidly after the war." The only way this can be achieved, they maintain, is "by establishing a state of their own," that is, by constituting Palestine into a Jewish state or commonwealth.

But to make sure that there will be room in this small country for these additional two millions, some influential Zionists have adopted the idea put forward by the Palestine Royal Commission in its report of 1937† that the Arabs of Palestine, now numbering about a million, should be exchanged or transferred in the event of a partition of the country.‡ The Royal Commission spoke (p. 392) of an arrangement "for the transfer, voluntary or otherwise, of land and population"; and in a book of essays published in Palestine last year, B. Kaznelson, one of the foremost leaders of the Labor Party in Palestine, which constitutes the dominant group in the Jewish Agency, welcomed this initiative of the Commission.

Mr. Kaznelson, addressing the Arabs, says: "We shall be ready not to be your foes and even to support your aspirations for independence and unification, provided you cease disturbing us and provided you recognize Palestine as a Jewish state. Upon this presupposition there can be

*Cf. Chaim Weizmann, "Palestine's Role in the Solution of the Jewish Problem," *Foreign Affairs*, January 1942.

†Palestine Royal Commission, "Report," 1937 (Cmd. 5479).

‡*Editor's Note*: For comment on the Report, see "Alternatives to Partition," by Viscount Samuel, and "The Arabs and the Future of Palestine," by H. St. J. Philby, *Foreign Affairs*, October 1937. For a general treatment, see "The Palestine Situation Restated," by Felix Frankfurter, *Foreign Affairs*, 1931.

mutual understanding." As to the transfer of Arabs, he adds: "The question of the exchange of populations is likely to become pressing in our days. I believe this question to be *essential* (italics by the author) for us and also for them."*

On the other hand, the late George Antonius says: "There seems to be no valid reason why Palestine should not be constituted into an independent Arab state . . . No other solution seems practicable, except possibly at the cost of an unpredictable holocaust of Arab, Jewish and British lives . . . No code of morals can justify the persecution of one people in an attempt to relieve the persecution of another. The cure for the eviction of Jews from Germany is not to be sought in the eviction of the Arabs from their homeland; and the relief of Jewish distress may not be accomplished at the cost of inflicting a corresponding distress upon an innocent and peaceful population."†

The antithesis is complete. These extreme aspirations are clearly incompatible.

This is not to say that there is a lack of reassurances from one side to the other. In his article in *Foreign Affairs*, Dr. Weizmann says that in the Jewish state of Palestine there will be "complete civil and political equality of rights for all citizens without distinction of race or religion, and, in addition, the Arabs will enjoy full autonomy in their own internal affairs." Mr. Antonius says that in an independent Arab state Jews "would live in peace, security and dignity, and enjoy full rights of citizenship . . . and the widest freedom in the pursuit of their spiritual and cultural ideals . . . Jewish values could flourish and the Jewish genius have the freest play to seek inspiration in the land of its ancient connection."

These assurances of tolerance are sincerely meant. Yet the basic contrast persists, in that the one assumes the Jews are to rule and the other is predicated upon Arab hegemony.

The purpose of this article is to warn of the danger of war between Jews and Arabs, and to offer an alternative based upon a reasonable compromise. The uncompromising who believe that this collision is inevitable are supposedly making their preparations. Those who believe in the necessity and the possibility of compromise should also be preparing. Nothing is more dangerous and enervating than the advice to postpone all thinking and planning until the end of the war. The war will not end and the peace will not come unless in every field the utmost exertions are made to think things through and to work things out now.

The indispensable prerequisite for a reasonable compromise is, I am convinced, that America's moral and political authority be thrown into

*B. Katznelson, "In the Furnace," p. 168-9.
†George Antonius, *The Arab Awakening* Philadelphia: Lippincott, 1939, p. 410.

the balance. In view of the intransigence of many responsible leaders on both sides the adjustment may have to be imposed over their opposition. Only organized world democracy, convinced of the truth and the necessity of the Atlantic Charter, can have enough authority to do this; and it is America, I submit, which must be chiefly responsible for the practical fulfillment of the principles of this great pronouncement.

Great Britain's authority, unhappily, has been impaired for the time being in Palestine and in the Middle East. The association of the United States with Britain in the Holy Land can help reestablish the authority necessary to keep Palestine from becoming a menace to the world's peace. America is greatly trusted. She has no territorial or imperialist ambitions here. She has served the Middle East generously and unselfishly on numerous occasions, and she should continue to do so. She must not leave it to perfidious Japan sanctimoniously to hold up ideals of freedom and union before the peoples of the East. She should join Britain in helping find out and, if necessary, impose a reasonable compromise. But if the American people are to be drawn into this task in Palestine they must know beforehand that it is not simple or one to be undertaken lightly. They may become involved in the controversies and even in the hatreds which, unfortunately, seem to be almost inseparable from the Palestine problem.

Palestine as a Jewish state: Palestine as an Arab state. The two conceptions leave little room for compromise. But a search for one should be begun. The first step — and the sooner it is taken the better — should be an announcement that the adjustment will not include either of these alternatives. Such an announcement might help dissipate the increasingly bellicose atmosphere and might, perhaps, turn both Jewish and Arab propaganda in the direction of peace and understanding. The ordinary Jew and the ordinary Arab have no hatred for one another. They will rejoice over the prospect of a reasonable settlement which might enable them to live together and to develop their common country in peace. The search for a compromise might well be furthered, too, by the selection of a few Englishmen and Americans to cooperate with Jews and Arabs in canvassing the possibilities. There is much material that could be studied usefully.

I shall try now to give the general outlines of the kind of compromise which I think might be imposed upon the Jews and the Arabs by a sufficiently high moral and political authority without giving reasonable cause for rebellion. It is the outcome of many years of study, for the past 20 years in Palestine itself. It is not, I must admit, the official program of any political party.* I am putting it forward now in the hope that it may

---

*I may be permitted to say, however, that there are Jews and Arabs of some consequence who are in accord with its general purport.

serve as material for anyone who is convinced that the search for a compromise is essential. The suggestion of other ideas would be advantageous.

The proposals which I bring forward are based on the great idea of union. Union must be the guiding political ideal of the United Nations if they are to achieve victory. The unbridled greed of those who have ruled hitherto, and the narrow chauvinism of so many nations, can be overcome only if a really free and really united world is created. The Palestine situation must be raised to the high plane where the gigantic struggle to build a mighty union of free nations is going on. Union for Palestine may be said to have three aspects:

1. Union between the Jews and the Arabs within a bi-national Palestine.

2. Union of Palestine, Transjordan, Syria and the Lebanon in an economic and political federation. These lands form a geographic unit and constituted a political and economic union at several times between ancient Semitic days and the First World War.

3. Union of this federation with an Anglo-American union which is assumed to be part of that greater union of the free nations now laboring to be born out of the ruins of the decaying world.

I should like to consider each of these aspects in some detail.

Experience in the new states set up by the Treaty of Versailles has shown that a successful bi-national arrangement is hardly possible unless the majority and the minority nations or peoples constituting the state have equal political rights. The conception of minority rights has broken down in practice. It has to give way to equal rights for nations and peoples within the state as well as for individual citizens. Palestine as a Jewish state would mean Jewish rule over the Arabs; Palestine as an Arab state would mean Arab rule over the Jews. Palestine as a bi-national state must provide constitutionally for equal political rights and duties for both the Jewish and the Arab nations, regardless of which is the majority and which the minority. In this way neither people will dominate the other. But a constitutional provision alone is not sufficient. There must be effective guarantees that this political equality will be carried out in practice. The nature of these guarantees will be determined by the nature of the federation of which Palestine is to be a member, and also by the nature of the union of the free nations of which this federation is to be a part. I shall return to this point later.

If the political equality of the two peoples in Palestine is accepted as a part of the compromise we are seeking, there seems to be no good reason why a beginning should not be made now with a bi-national administration, so that officials may be trained as soon as possible for the great tasks which confront them. On more than one occasion Britain has held out hopes that the people of Palestine would receive an increasing share in the government of the country. These hopes have not been realized. If it be objected that the Palestinians are politically immature, the democratic way to attain maturity would be to place political responsibility upon them. The time has come to put Palestinians, both Jews and Arabs, in charge of non-controversial government departments and to make them members of the Executive Council of the Government. That would be a step forward of the highest educational and political value.

A modest way of associating the population of Palestine with the war effort has also been suggested. It has been proposed that a consultative body of representative citizens be appointed under the chairmanship of the High Commissioner. He would call the group together at intervals to make statements on the war and to consult on such matters as supplies and rationing, recruiting, the cost of living, agricultural and industrial production, profiteering and social welfare. But nothing has come of this suggestion.

It is a mistake to think that new arrangements will come into being automatically after the war. The time to begin to prepare the Jews and the Arabs for responsible duties in the bi-national Palestinian body politic is now.

Immigration is in many ways the crux of the problem and it is on this issue that agreement will be most difficult. There are 17 million Jews in the world. Understandably, the Jews want to admit hundreds of thousands of the homeless and persecuted to Palestine. But a long time would be required to settle even the two million whom some think the country could absorb. The astounding advances which the scientific knowledge and the devotion of the Jews have brought about in the agriculture and industry of Palestine might conceivably shorten this period. But today the country does not grow enough food to support its present population; and in order to import food, particularly from neighboring countries, peace between Jews and Arabs is necessary. If the capacity to absorb immigrants is to be increased by making Palestine largely industrial rather than agricultural, this will increase its dependence upon the Middle East for markets; and in this case also there must be peace between the two peoples.

The problem is dual. Taking into account both the country's economic absorptive capacity and the political situation, how can as large a Jewish population as possible be settled in Palestine? How is this to be accomplished within the framework of the suggested compromise? We begin again wih a negative aspect of the proposed adjustment in order to reach a positive conclusion. No Jew can agree to a fiat which would arbitrarily stop immigration into Palestine, the Land of Israel. This is the main reason why Jews have been unanimous in opposing the British

Government's White Paper of 1939.* Of the many arbitrary decrees included in that unhappy document, the one to permit no further Jewish immigration after five years from 1939 unless the Arabs are prepared to acquiece in it was the most unfortunate. The Arabs will not agree to unrestricted Jewish immigration. It would build up a Jewish majority and might mean Jewish dominance in Palestine. We must recognize that this is a genuine impasse and that a way out must be found.

The establishment of a federation would help resolve the problem. If and when the federation came into being, the whole question of numbers in Palestine would lose its present primary significance for the Arabs. For a federation of the four states in question, whatever its form, would include an Arab population of several million. The Arabs would be relieved of their present fear of being swamped and dominated by a majority of Jews. A Jewish majority in the federation is hardly conceivable.

It should also be borne in mind that since the outbreak of war Jewish immigration into Palestine has been practically at a standstill. This means that the proportion of Jews to Arabs in Palestine is growing progressively smaller, for the annual rate of natural increase of the Arabs is much higher (2.7 percent) than that of the Jews (1.3 percent). The present Arab population is estimated at about a million; in five years' time it might number rather more than 1,200,000† The Jewish population is estimated to be about 500,000; if there is no important Jewish immigration in the next five years the rate of natural increase will bring this to only about 540,000. In other words, the Arab population in 1947 would be larger than the Jewish population by more than 600,000. If, therefore, the political controversy between the Jews and the Arabs were composed, as it might be through the establishment of a federation, several hundred thousand Jewish refugees could be admitted to Palestine with advantage to the country and without disturbing the political balance. The establishment of a federation might also be advantageous to the Jews, as well as to the federation itself, by making possible agreements under which the Governments of Transjordan, Syria and the Lebanon would permit a given number of refugee Jews to settle in those countries without extending the Jewish National Home beyond the borders of Palestine.

Thus it seems clear that a federation would make it possible for many thousands of Jewish refugees to find room in Palestine and other parts of the federation, and this with Arab agreement instead of Arab animosity.

As to the economic absorptive capacity of Palestine, it should be pointed out that the Jews have given definite proof that it is greater than

---

*"Palestine Statement of Policy," 1939 (Cmd. 6019).
†Report of the Palestine Royal Commission (Cmd. 5479), p. 281.

had been supposed. The Jews have shown that there is more water in the country, more arable land, better land, the possibility of raising more diversified crops, more raw materials for industry, more chances of establishing industries both for home consumption and for export, than had been imagined. Whereas formerly the maximum population of present-day Palestine had been estimated at about three million, with agriculture as its chief economic activity, today responsible authorities admit that this maximum can be raised to four million.

The economic absorptive capacity both of Palestine and of the federation ought to be determined from time to time. This would be useful not only in selecting immigrants and determining their numbers, but also in drawing up any large-scale plan for the country's development. One of the first constructive tasks of the federation, under the aegis of the free nations and with their financial and scientific help, should be to work out such a plan of development for all the constituent parts of the federation, and to put it into execution. An Anglo-American undertaking of this sort in the name of the union of the free nations would go a long way toward bringing the compromise to fruitful success.

If for some unfortunate reason the federation should not come into being, the immigration question in Palestine alone would be made — as I think I have shown — that much more baffling. Even so, we should have to try to face that difficult eventuality as well as possible. For example, a proposal might be offered somewhat similar to that made in 1936, after the Arab rebellion had begun. At that time it was suggested that the number of Jewish immigrants be so calculated that at the end of a ten-year period the Jews would constitute no more than 40 percent of the total population. The Jewish population then numbered 400,000. It was estimated that under the plan, which was sponsored by a number of responsible Jews and Arabs, this figure would be doubled by 1946.

A similar procedure could be used now. It would have two basic provisions. First, whatever percentages and periods might be fixed, the Jewish population would never be permitted to become more than one half of the total population; and second, instead of dividing Jewish immigration into equal yearly quotas, as large a number as economically possible should be admitted in the years immediately following the close of the war to mitigate the fate of thousands of homeless Jews. This is a method which should be adopted, however, only after all hope of finding a better way has been abandoned. It has the fault that it again raises the majority-minority complex to primary political importance, as at present; whereas federation would reduce it to a secondary place.

In the preceding paragraphs I have attempted to show that a reasonable compromise is possible on the two chief points at issue — a bi-national government and Jewish immigration. Obviously, other matters of

tional government and Jewish immigration. Obviously, other matters of great importance remain to be settled also, such as land, employment and agricultural settlement.

The Jews are able to help as no other people can or will to build up the proposed federation as an integral part of a union of the free peoples. Their help can be scientific, financial, social, industrial and agricultural. But even before the start of the delicate and complicated process of establishing a political federation there can be an economic union of Palestine, Transjordan, Syria and Lebanon, and these countries can join with their neighbors in economic agreements.

These developments are possible because of the war. The four small states in question will be less and less able to stand the rigors of the war unless they form themselves into an economic bloc for the production of food and the manufacture of other goods and to arrange to receive supplies in common. One way of forming this very desirable economic union might be to develop the Middle East Supply Center to its full capacity for usefulness. This wartime organ is based on two ideas: its make-up is Anglo-American, which means that it pools Anglo-American resources for conducting the joint war effort in the Middle East; and it is giving blood and bone to the conception that the Middle East is a unit formed of contiguous countries with economic needs so vital in time of war that differences over their political borders and other matters become of secondary importance. This conception ought to be carried over into the peace, and I believe it is possible if the basic ideas of the Middle East Supply Center are worked out with efficiency and vision.

Another factor in the suggested compromise is Jerusalem, Holy City of three religions, which might become the federal headquarters or capital. Geography and history alike fit it for this great destiny. Should it once again become a center of spiritual and intellectual exchange, it will restore contact between Judaism, Christianity and Islam. So far these three faiths have failed in their efforts to create a society based upon ideals of righteousness and mercy. Yet despite the afflictions visited upon Israel in the Christian West, we may not despair of the West. And Israel, which once achieved great things for mankind in the Middle East, can acquire renewed youth and deeper wisdom if it is re-invigorated and rooted once more in the ancestral soil. The new Jerusalem, then, would symbolize a new relationship between Judaism, Christianity and Islam in the cradle of their origin; and in the New Jerusalem they would work out together part of their common problems with the old-new East which contains among its other elements the vast, vibrating, spiritual powers of Russia, India and China.

A compromise settlement of the Palestine problem such as I have outlined above would be doubly guaranteed: by the federation and by the

397

union of the free nations. But will this latter union be created? And how can we be sure that it will be any more effective or that its members will do their duty toward peace through it any more truly than they did through the League of Nations? Millions of men and women are asking these questions. When Vice-President Wallace and Mr. Sumner Welles speak eloquently and sincerely of the free world that is to be made, millions take courage. But afterwards they begin to ask themselves if, after all, it is only words. No answer can be found for this historic question except in the heart and the determination of each one of us individually. By now we should have learned that peace is indivisible and that there is no chance of political understanding in the world unless organized world democracy assumes responsibility for it by assuming responsibility for the security and the economic well-being of every nation, regardless of race, creed or color.

In making our Palestine compromise work we can learn much from the mistakes of the mandatory system. The principle of trusteeship which was implicit in that system is sound. But let the mandatories ask themselves if they have always acted like true trustees. Whatever the nature of the guarantee or trusteeship which is adopted after this war, experience has taught us that it should not assume the form of mandates granted to single countries or to groups of countries which have imperialistic, military or other selfish interests in the region involved.

Israel is an imperfect instrument through which universal religious and moral principles have been communicated to mankind. These principles call for the creation of a visible, tangible society founded upon justice and mercy. The utterances of the Prophets of Israel contain as powerful revolutionary ferment as mankind has ever known. Until Israel and the nations of mankind succeed in establishing a universal society based upon those ideals there will continue to be a Jewish problem. That is Israel's destiny.

103

Journal: Notes on Conversation with Omar Salih Barghuthy

Jerusalem, February 8, 1944

February 9, 1944. 4–4:45 P.M. At his house. We went out together to Miss Landau's building,[1] he to the law classes where he teaches twice weekly, and I to Miss Landau where we met with Av. Levin[2] and Mrs. Levy[3] about the Stoller girl.[4]

I said that I had not seen him and others of my Arab friends in a long time because I had lost hope that the Arab leaders and the Jewish leaders could come to an agreement. He could understand that it was hard for me, who had all these years worked for an agreement, to say this. But my friends Kalvarisky and Aaron Cohen[5] had told me that he was hopeful of an agreement, and I had come to hear what he could tell me. He said he thought an agreement not impossible but that it would have to be arrived at by the right people and in the right way. The Palestine Arabs themselves would never come to an agreement if left to themselves. There was no man or group among them with enough authority. The agreement with the Jews would have to be dictated to the Palestine Arabs by some outside Arab authority. He had recently reminded Awni that Feisal[7] had said in their presence the last time he was in Palestine: "You must come to an understanding with the Jews." The man who is to bring this about must be big enough to bear all kinds of abuse — that he is a traitor and has been bought by the Jews and by the English; and he would be threatened with death. But if bold enough to hold out, he would one day be proclaimed as a benefactor of the Arabs. I said, pointing to Feisal's picture on the wall: "It is a tragedy that that man died. Our whole situation here would be different had he lived." He agreed. (It might be of interest to note that the other picture on the same wall was that of Kaukji,[8] MacMichael's[9] friend. Omar probably meant Wauchope's.[10])

As far as he could see, the man best fitted to bring about such an understanding was Nuri [al-Sa'id]. Nahas[11] did not really understand the problem. He could not see why there should be any difficulties. Let the Jews in Palestine be like the Copts among us in Egypt, was his attitude. What should happen was that as a result of the Unity Conferences in Cairo[12] and with Nuri's support, all the Arab governments should impose an Arab-Jewish agreement upon the Palestine Arabs. "What would this imposed agreement be?" I asked. "Like the proposals of Dr. Magnes," he answered. I asked: "Did you see my recent letter to the *Economist*?" "An excellent letter. Just that: parity of numbers and of political rights and duties, but provided, of course, that there be a Federation."

He had been suprised to find Mr. Bentwich, who was a very fine man, such an extremist. He had told him that he was as bad as Ben-Gurion (Bentwich had told me that Omar Saleh had said the same thing about me). Bentwich had insisted that the gates of Palestine must always be open to Jewish immigration even after parity was reached, here as he understood that my point of view was parity in intention and in fact. I said that that was correct as far as I was concerned. But a question: if at any

399

time the larger Arab birth rate left a margin would the Jews be entitled to immigrants to make up this margin and thus restore parity?" "Of course," he said. I continued, "This is indeed my point of view. On the other hand, one could never tell what changes might come about if the Jews and Arabs lived together in political, economic and social peace and cooperation over a period of years. It might very well be that with Federation a fact, a new agreement with the Arabs as to a large Jewish immigration would be possible. But it would have to be in agreement with the Arabs, whereas bringing the Jews up to parity now might have to be imposed." Did he think the imposition of parity would stir the Arabs to revolt and the whole Arab and Moslem world into protest and agitation? He did not. He thought that with a Federation in existence, the idea of parity in Palestine would appeal to all thoughtful and reasonable Arabs.

"How about partition?" I asked. He said he knew that partition was being discussed among the Jews and English. He was sure the Arabs would fight this tooth and nail. It would destroy the chance of friendship between the Jews and the Arabs. Nuri had not discussed partition with them. But he had heard from a high English source that a plan had been proposed (and discussed with Nuri? I do not remember if he added this) whereby north of a line between the sea and Nablus would be Arab, and south Jewish, and the southern part would not belong to the Federation. But Omar Saleh thought this so absurd that it could hardly be discussed.

I told him that the idea of a Jewish Commonwealth, i.e. of a government with the majority in Jewish hands was, so it seemed to me, gaining ground in America and perhaps (though I did not know this) in England. What was his opinion of this? — This would mean war, he said, for a hundred years. I asked him what support his own views had. He said that he had a long talk with Nuri, and he found Nuri very receptive.

The question had also been brought up at a meeting of fourteen Arabs. They had divided into three groups. His own group which he called the Moderates contained Shawa of Gaza,[13] Feyhum of Nazareth,[14] Awni, Ibrahim Al-Shanti[15] and some others. There were also a number of younger lawyers thinking in this direction. When I expressed my surprise that Awni was among the moderates who would favor parity he said, "Awni will certainly not be a leader in this direction, but he will accept the inevitable if imposed. He will be a Forward but he could be made into a Goal Keeper if the authority was sufficiently strong. Awni wants to finish with the question. He wants to be a Minister."

The second group contained some of His Eminences (the Mufti's) followers. Their attitude was: if the Jews want to live here with us all right, but no more of them. The third group contained people like Khelmi,[16] Rashid Ibrahim[17] and Dr. Ḥusayni Khaldi. They wanted "Dr. Magnes's old program of 40 percent." I asked him how many Arabs he thought the country now had, and he said about 1,200,000. "If the Jews had 600,000," I said, "in order to achieve parity they would be bringing 600,000 more into the country." "Yes," he said, "but only if there is Federation." "What about Musa Alami?" I asked. "Musa is one of the finest of men," he said. "Honest and a clear mind and a moderate. But he does not want to have anything to do with politics. When Nuri asked him why he did not throw himself into it more, he said, 'I am glad to have you for a good dinner and to discuss things, but I am not a politician.' " Omar Saleh used an Arabic word which he said meant "between a man and a woman." He said his friends were weak — no newspaper, no funds, and all of them too busy to be doing political spade-work. They would not take funds from either the Jews or the English — that could not even be discussed.

As far as the English were concerned, it was interesting to hear Nuri's opinion about them. "What is to be done with these *awlad el kif* (sons of bitches)? They never listen, and when they act it is usually too late. Up to the present day Baghdad has any number of Axis agents but the English refuse to move against them." He had warned them and warned them during the years before the Rashid Ali revolt. He had gone to Ankara, to Cairo, to other places to speak to the English ambassadors — no results. They simply place all their reliance on the man on the spot even though the Empire is threatened.

As to Riad al-Sulh,[18] Nuri said that he would be somewhat difficult in regard to Federation, but would finally come around. More difficult was Shukri al-Kuwalty[19] because he was a friend of Ibn Saud.[20] I asked why Nuri always connected the Federation with Iraq. Surely this was one of the reasons for the difficulties with Nahas and Ibn Saud. His answer was that Nuri is only talking about Greater Syria — the four countries — for the present. Later on they would join up with Iraq.

As to some of the Jews: he did not like Sasson[21] — a tricky, unreliable man who never said what was really on his mind and who liked to play on words. Kalvarisky was a fine person, but was now too old. He had not made a good impression on Nuri. He liked Aaron Cohen despite his radical views — honest and straightforward. Shamush[22] was good.

1. The Evelina de Rothschild School; Ann Landau was the principal.

2. Abraham Levin. Lawyer; born in Jerusalem, where he practiced law until 1949.

3. Ethel Levy (1893–1977). Educator; assistant principal and then principal of the Evelina de Rothschild School.

4. Stoller received a large inheritance. Landau, executor of the bequest, consulted with Levin, Levy, and Magnes.

5. Aaron Cohen (1910–1980). Zionist leader, expert in Arab affairs, and author. Born in Russia, he emigrated to Palestine in 1929 and was a founding member of the Ha'shomer Ha'tsair kibbutz, Sha'ar Ha'amakim. He served as secretary of the League for Arab-Jewish Rapprochement and Cooperation between 1941 and 1948 and was a member of the Arab Department of the Histadrut.

6. Awni Abd-al-Hadi (1889–1970). Palestinian lawyer and political leader born in

Nablus, Palestine. He practiced law in Jerusalem for many years; was a founder of the Palestine section of the Istaqlal party; was a member of the Arab Higher Committee; represented Palestinian Arab interests abroad. After 1948 he held high diplomatic posts in the Jordanian government and served as foreign minister in 1956.

7. Feisal ibn Huseyn (1883–1933). King of Iraq from 1921 to 1933. Son of Huseyn, Sherif of Mecca and King of Hedjaz, he was a leader of the Arab nationalist movement. Expelled from Damascus by the French in 1920, he was crowned king of Iraq with British support. He represented Arab interests at the Versailles peace conference, where he came to an understanding with Weizmann on Arab-Jewish cooperation.

8. Fawzi al-Qawuqji (1890–1976). Syrian army officer. He commanded Arab guerilla forces during the 1936–1939 disturbances in Palestine and led a volunteer army in the Arab-Israeli war of 1948.

9. Sir Harold MacMichael (1822–1969). A British civil servant; he entered the colonial service in 1904, serving in the Sudan and Tanganyika. He was High Commissioner for Palestine from 1938 to 1944, rigidly implementing the 1939 White Paper's restrictions on immigration and land sales.

10. Sir Arthur Wauchope (see glossary of names).

11. Mustafa al-Nahas Pasha (1876–1965). An Egyptian statesman born in Cairo, he became the leader of the Wafd party in 1927 and served as Prime Minister for brief periods during the 1930s and from 1942 to 1944 and 1950 to 1952.

12. With British encouragement Nahas Pasha inaugurated talks in January 1944 with the intention of establishing a league of Arab states. A preliminary conference took place in September 1944, and the league was formed in March 1945.

13. Rushdi Shawa (1890–1971). A Palestinian Arab leader, he was mayor of Gaza from 1939 to 1946, when he was active in furthering political collaboration among Arab mayors.

14. Fa'id or Yusuf al-Fahum, members of a prominent Nazareth family with sympathy for the moderate Nashashibi political faction.

15. Ibrahim al-Shanti (1909–1979). A Palestinian Arab leader and journalist; a member of the Istaqlal party, he was imprisoned by the British in 1936 for participating in the Arab uprising. He founded and edited al-Difa. In the 1940s he supported the Mufti.

16. Ahmad Hilmi Abd al-Baqi (1882–1963). A leading figure in the Arab nationalist movements; born in Lebanon, he helped Abdallah consolidate his rule in Trans-Jordan following the First World War. One of the leaders of the Istaqlal party, he helped establish the Arab National Bank in Jerusalem; he was appointed treasurer of the Arab Higher Committee in 1936. He was interned by the British in the Seychelles Islands from 1937 to 1939. In 1945 he joined the new Arab Higher Committee and in 1948 briefly headed the Egyptian-sponsored Palestinian government in Gaza.

17. Rashid Ibrahim al-Hajj (18871953). A banker and Palestinian Arab leader born in Haifa; he was one of the founders of the Istiqlal party and manager of the Arab National Bank in Haifa. In the 1940s he took an active part in efforts to create a unified Arab political directorate.

18. Riad al-Sulh (1894–1951). A leader of the pan-Arab movement, he was Prime Minister of Lebanon from 1943 to 1945 and from 1946 to 1951.

19. Shukri al-Kuwalty (1892–1967). A Syrian politician, he led the struggle against France for independence; was President of Syria from 1943 to 1949 and from 1955 to 1958.

20. Abd al-Aziz ibn Sa'ud (1880–1953). Founder of Saudi Arabia and its first king.

21. Eliyahu Sasson (b. 1902). A Jewish expert in Arab affairs, he was born in Damascus and settled in Palestine in 1927. He was head of the Jewish Agency's Arab Department from 1933 to 1948 and then director of the Middle East Department of the Israeli Ministry of Foreign Affairs. Sasson was a cabinet minister from 1961 to 1969 and a member of the Knesset from 1965.

22. Isaac Shamosh (1912–1968). A Semitic scholar born in Aleppo, Syria, he studied law at the University of Beirut and Arabic literature at the Hebrew University. In 1937 he was appointed teacher of Arabic language and literature at the Hebrew University, where he received his Ph.D. in 1951.

104

To Mrs. Setty Kuhn
Cincinnati, Ohio

Jerusalem, May 30, 1944

Dear Mrs. Kuhn,

I was exceedingly glad to get your letter of April 20, and even gladder to know that you and Hans Kohn were talking things over and that you also were thinking of me. It is just as well that you did not telegraph me to come to America, because that is not so simple as it looks, either as to the journey itself or, what is perhaps more important, also if this is the appropriate time and what is to be the main object of my journey.

There are those who think that I ought to go to America on behalf of several causes; the University, Hadassah, the JDC, and I am sure that it would be possible for me to be of help to them. On the other hand, I am, as you know, very deeply concerned with the political problem, and there are those who say that I should go primarily for this. There is indeed somewhat of a contradiction between going to America on behalf of these three constructive enterprises, and going with the political problem in the center of my heart and weighing upon me. Some would say I had no right to speak on behalf of these institutions if I also spoke about the political situation, and it will be simply impossible for me not to deal with this latter in the freest possible way. Maybe you and Hans Kohn could exchange a note or two about this. I would be interested to hear what some of my friends think.

I have not quite been able to get through my head how it happened that I have been left more or less high and dry here without real help, either financial or moral, from my friends in America. I still flatter myself in thinking that there are many of these, and I should like to believe that there are ever so many people who also more or less share my approach to the political problems here. But judging from the almost complete absence of letters or checks one might think at this distance that everything had changed, perhaps for the better, and that only I, way out here, to be sure rather closer to Palestine than those in America, had not changed and that I had remained an old-fashioned obscurantist.

However this be, I become more and more convinced, as I see how things are developing, that the path which I and my few friends here have laid out for themselves ought to lead, if it is not too late, to some kind of an answer that would give some satisfaction to everyone concerned.

I am enclosing here a one-page statement on my views on the Palestine situation. Although my friends in America may be silent — a thing that can, I am glad to see, hardly be said of my opponents — ever so many people who pass through here interrogate me, and I have written this page as a kind of brief answer.[1] I should be interested to know what you and Hans Kohn think of it. Would you be good enough to have it copied and sent to him? Perhaps you and he might consider if some public use could be made of it in some suitable form.

I never seem to forget that you were here in the Library Hall in 1929 at the time I delivered what was then regarded on one side as an address by a traitor, and on the other side as the address of a man with some insight. I have reread this address recently, and how calm I find it and not revolutionary at all, either in this direction or that.[2] If you were here now I am sure you would find not only the atmosphere of our Library Hall charged with emotion but almost every corner of our life here.

It appears from your letter that you had not received mine of 30 January 1944. Please find enclosed a copy of the letter I sent you then.

It is a great comfort to have Nelson[3] here. Despite the fact that we do not see each other very often we can always pick up without any exertion just where we left off the last time. That for me is always the test of understanding. Please tell Helen[4] that Nelson is in fine health, and will you please also remember us to Gertrude Friedlaender?

My wife, who knows that I am writing to you, wishes to be most kindly remembered, and with the best regards, I am

Sincerely yours, JLM

P.S. I am returning Mr. Rennie Smith's letter.

1. In his summary statement Magnes formulated the central issue in terms of "how to give the Jews the chance of a larger immigration and at the same time take away from the Arabs their fear of being swamped by large numbers of Jews." He proposed numerical parity, the tempo of Jewish immigration to depend upon the economic absorptive capacity of the country. Because of the higher Arab birthrate limited Jewish immigration would be allowed periodically to maintain parity once it was reached. Arab fears of Jewish domination would be met by establishing a binational government in Palestine, and Palestine would join a union including Trans-Jordan, Syria, and Lebanon. A Middle East regional body and the United Nations would guarantee the agreement reached by the Arabs and Jews and would aid in the economic and social development of the "union of four countries."

2. Judah L. Magnes, *Addresses by the Chancellor of the Hebrew University* (Jerusalem, 1936), pp. 95–103.

3. Nelson Glueck (1900–1971). An archaeologist, biblical scholar, and educator born in Cincinnati, he graduated from Hebrew Union College in 1923; received his Ph.D. from the University of Jena in 1928; was director of the American School of Oriental Research in Jerusalem, 1932–1933, 1936–1940, 1942–1947, president of Hebrew Union College, 1947.

4. Dr. Helen Iglauer Glueck (b. 1907). A physician and the wife of Nelson Glueck.

105

To Paul Baerwald
New York

Jerusalem, July 25, 1944

Dear Mr. Baerwald,

Dr. Schwartz[1] is leaving for Egypt this morning and we hope that he will get an immediate connection for North Africa and Lisbon so that he may be there by the end of this week.

You doubtless are aware of the telegram which caused him to cut short his stay in Istanbul. Both in Istanbul and in Lisbon telegrams have been received concerning the possibility of transferring 1700 Hungarian Jews from Germany to Spain and then further. This is connected with a conversation which has been proposed for the end of this week between Dr. Schwartz and one other person on the one hand, and a non-Jewish representative on the other.[2]

Mr. Hirschmann[3] with Dr. Schwartz's help prepared a long telegram which was sent to the War Refugee Board a few days ago giving the whole history of the proposals for the exchange of Hungarian Jews. This further proposition for the rescue of 1700 Jews seems to be something different. Doubtless by the time Dr. Schwartz reaches Lisbon he will have received an answer as to the attitude of the War Refugee Board.

The situation is changing so rapidly in Europe that it is difficult to make plans. It is a question of what the next day will bring. Even since I was in Istanbul two weeks ago the situation has undergone a radical change, and that for the better as far as Hungary is concerned. There would really seem to be the opportunity of getting considerable numbers of Jews out of Hungary.[4] The question is in what direction. The Rumanian and Bulgarian governments have now for several weeks been disposed to give Jews facilities for leaving, particularly the Rumanian governmenmt. The first of five boats reached Istanbul while we were there. Why others have not followed as yet is a question that gives everyone concern. It may be because the Turkish government has closed the Black Sea to traffic for Turkish ships, and at least two of those now waiting at Constanza are Turkish. Moreover, there are rumors of important events impending in Turkey in about a week's time. Will all of this shut the door to the exit of Hungarian, Rumanian, Bulgarian Jews to Istanbul?

The change in Bulgaria in reference to the Jews there seems to have been so marked that it is not known how many of the Jews there will be wanting to leave at all. Although the desire of the Jews in Rumania to leave is much deeper, still, if Rumania is not included actively in the war zone the Jews there might also find the possibility of starting a new life there.

This would not be true of the Hungarian Jews, and the question is in how far they might be brought out of Hungary westwards. It is for this reason that the conversation which has been proposed to Dr. Schwartz is of even greater importance than the rescue of 1700 Hungarian Jews, however deeply important that may be.

Dr. Schwartz has taken with him a copy of the stenographic report of my statement to the Vaad Hahatzalah here, that is, the Rescue Committee of the Jewish Agency.[5] It is in Hebrew, and if you are interested in it you will doubtless be able to find someone in New York without any difficulty to translate it. Although my report at the time was the most up-to-date statement which the Palestine Rescue Committee had as yet received, the changes in the past two weeks have made it more of an historical document than one containing actual proposals. You may nevertheless be interested in it.

I am enclosing herewith a copy of a letter sent to Dr. Schwartz from Budapest on June 13, 1944, by the man there who has been active in JDC work. Doubtless Dr. Schwartz will get it to you but I am sending it herewith in order that you may be perfectly sure to get a copy as soon as possible.

I am enclosing herewith also a statement, which Dr. Schwartz will be transmitting to you as well, concerning the methods of putting Jews to death in the gas chambers. It is a dry and, as it would appear, factual statement and is all the more terrible on that account. It seems to me that a statement of this sort ought to be given the widest publicity in the USA.[6]

I also brought back with me a few photographs. If possible I shall try to include them in this letter. They are terrible beyond words. The one particularly, picturing the German soldier, is symbolic of the Germany of today. It should, I think, be reproduced throughout all the world. The publication of such a picture is, I know, a matter that must be considered from every point of view, and I do not pretend that all sides of the question are clear to me. It would, however, be possible for the JDC to take the matter up with competent authorities and decide.

Dr. Schwartz has asked Mr. Passman[7] to go to Istanbul as the JDC representative. Mr. Passman has agreed to do this provided, (a) the organization with which he is connected agrees, and (b) that his presence there be regarded as of an emergency character and that some other American go there as soon as possible. Last evening, before Dr. Schwartz left, we were talking about the possibility of having Mr. Pilpel[8] go there. Mr.

Passman would be just the man to break him in. One of the chief advantages of having Mr. Pilpel go would be that he could get there quickly, and this is a question of days and weeks, or of a very few months, so it would appear.

Mr. Passman has just returned from his long absence in connection with the parcels service. He was also in Bombay. The parcels service gives promise of developing into an even larger enterprise than we had contemplated. There are now more than 10,000 parcels a month being sent to the refugees in Russia, and if the arrangements with the Polish Red Cross which Mr. Passman will inform you about can be carried through, the service ought to be sending 20,000 a month. The JDC office gets at least a hundred letters and telegrams a day from refugees in Soviet Russia acknowledging the receipt of parcels, or asking that parcels be sent to relatives and friends. The difficulty at the present time is connected with the Soviet-Polish problem. Mr. Passman has been exceedingly careful and skillful thus far in keeping the JDC out of this bitter quarrel.

More than half of the JDC camp at Aden has been evacuated. The 650 refugees remaining are there because no immigration certificates for Palestine can be secured for them as yet. We applied to the Palestine Government for these, informing them that our contract with the nurses and the physician in charge of the camp would expire on September 1. Nevertheless the answer which we got was negative. We also proposed to the Aden Government to permit those in the camp to seek work in the Aden labor market. This was refused because the labor market there is already overcrowded, so it is said. We have decided to inform the Aden Government that our obligation is to cease on October 1, and we are informing the Jewish Agency of this also, thus giving the Jewish Agency time to make such arrangements with the Aden Government as may be possible.

The plan for the kitchens of the Yeshivot has begun to operate. We shall be sending a report in due course.

Enclosed please find also copies of two letters I wrote to Dr. Schwartz concerning the position of our Committee generally. We had a discussion on this question with Dr. Schwartz at two meetings of the Committee. We hope that we may be able to work the problem out, but there would be no use in concealing from you the fact that the members of the Committee are not entirely comfortable under the present arrangements.

I hope that you are well and with kind regards, I am

Sincerely yours, JLM

P.S. We are enclosing herewith a copy of this letter for Dr. Schwartz. Would you kindly forward it to him? Mail from here to Lisbon direct takes a very long time.

1. Joseph J. Schwartz (1899-1975). A Jewish community leader born in Russia and brought to the United States in 1907. He was executive director of the Federation of Jewish Philanthropies of Brooklyn, N.Y., 1931-1938; director of JDC's European operations, 1940-1949; director general of JDC, 1950-18951; executive vice chairman, United Jewish Appeal, 1951-1955; vice president of Israel Bond Organization, 1955-1970.

2. A transport of 1,684 Jews left Hungary on June 30, 1944, in exchange for ransom paid to Nazi SS commanders in Budapest by leaders of the Jewish relief committee in Budapest. Part of the group reached Switzerland in August and the remainder in December. Concurrently other proposals for ransoming Jews and stopping the deportations from Hungary were under discussion.

3. Ira Hirschmann (b. 1901). A department store executive, he was in charge of the War Refugee Board's office in Turkey from February to November 1944. His request for authorization to allow Kurt Becher, an SS officer in Budapest, and Joseph Kasztner of the Budapest Jewish relief committee to fly to Lisbon to negotiate with Schwartz was denied by the War Refugee Board in Washington.

4. In July 1944, when news of the mass deportations of Hungary's Jews became known, diplomatic pressure by foreign states and church leaders and the worsening military situation led the Hungarian government to stop further deportations of Jews.

5. Magnes investigated rescue operations conducted from Turkey in early July 1944. His report summarized information on the conditions of Jews in Hungary, Rumania, and Bulgaria; meetings with Ira Hirschmann of the War Refugee Board, representatives of the Jewish Agency, JDC, and clandestine rescue workers; transportation problems in bringing refugees from Rumania to Palestine; and his attempt to establish a coordinating authority among the organizations and government agencies active in rescue work. See "Report on Visit to Turkey at the Meeting of the Jewish Agency – Vaad Leumi Rescue Committee, July 14, 1944, Jerusalem," MP, 2137.

6. Magnes refers to a detailed report prepared by two Jews, Rudolf Vrba and Alfred Weczler, who escaped from the Auschwitz extermination camp in April 1944. Magnes opened his address at the beginning of the academic year of the Hebrew University on November 1, 1944 by quoting from the Auschwitz report. See document 106.

7. Charles Passman (1882-1971). Community worker in the United States and Palestine; born in Russia and brought to the United States in 1892. He first settled in Palestine in 1920; returned to the United States to manage the American Zion Commonwealth, a land investment company. He headed the Palestine office beginning in 1924. During the Second World War he undertook various missions for the JDC in the Middle East. Following the establishment of the State of Israel he headed the JDC's Malben program for aged and handicapped immigrants.

8. Robert Pilpel (b. 1905). A Jewish communal executive, he was general counsel of the JDC, 1939-1952, and secretary of the American Jewish Joint Agricultural Corporation, 1945-1952. He has been on the board of directors, General Bureau for the Jewish Aged, since 1953 and general counsel, division of aging, Federation of Protestant Welfare Agencies since 1968.

106

Opening Address of the Academic Year of the Hebrew University
November 1, 1944

FOR THY SAKE ARE WE KILLED ALL THE DAY LONG (PSALM 44:23)

About four months ago a document was handed me in Istanbul. Forgive me for reading from so harrowing a statement:

> Persons branded with the consecutive numbers, 38,000-38,600: 600 naturalized French Jews. These Jews arrived with their dependents, in all about 1,600 souls. Of these about 400 men and 200 women branded with the above consecutive numbers entered the camp. The remaining 1,000 French Jews, women, older men, children, were taken by a side track into the birch woods and there gassed and burnt.
>
> From this time on, every transport of Jews was dealt with in a similar manner. About 10% of the male and 5% of the female deportees were brought into the camp and the rest immediately gassed and burnt.
>
> The gassing and the cremation were carried out by the so-called "Sonderkommando," which worked in two shifts day and night. At this period, Jews were being gassed and burnt in numbers reaching hundreds of thousands. The "Sonderkommando" troop lived in separate quarters. The cadaverous smell issuing from them was sufficient to keep us from contact with them. They were always dirty, completely savage and brutal.
>
> The newly built crematory and gas-chambers were opened in February, 1943. At the present moment 4 crematories are operating at Birkenau. They consist of 3 parts:
> (a) Furnaces
> (b) "Bathing Halls"
> (c) Gas-chambers
>
> From the middle of the furnaces there projects a tall chimney, around which 9 ovens have been erected with four openings each. Each opening has a capacity for three normal bodies, the cremation of which lasts about an hour and a half. The daily capacity of the furnaces is about 2,000 bodies. Alongside is a large waiting hall, constructed so as to give the impression of baths. The hall holds almost 2,000 persons and there are allegedly other, similarly large, waiting rooms underneath this. From here a door and a few steps lead to a lower, very long and narrow gas-chamber. The walls of the gas-chamber are fitted with imitation showers, giving the chamber the appearance of a huge bath. There is a window in the flat roof of the chamber, hermetically closed by three valves. Rails lead from the gas-chamber through the hall to the furnaces. The victims are led into the hall where they are told that they are to bathe. There they undress, and in

order to strengthen them in this belief, they are given a towel and soap. Then they are driven into the gas-chamber. When the doors are shut, S.S. men scatter a powder from metal containers through the opened valves into the room. The containers are marked "Zyklon zur Schaedlingsbe-kaempfung" and have the trade-mark of a Hamburg firm. This seems to be a preparation of cyanide which becomes gaseous at a given temperature. In three minutes all are dead.

In all of human history there has never been anything like this either in extent or in the methods employed. Even now, as proofs continue to pile up, our minds prefer to reject the truth. The hunt for myriads of human beings created in the Image is organized scientifically, and they are transported to these gates of hell and destroyed scientifically. One of our University chemists said, after reading this document: "As though it had been prepared for a scientific text-book, objectively, calmly."

I think we have all come to realize the tragedy of science put to such uses. It is to the struggles and sacrifices of thousands of heroic spirits that science is due, and it is to such a pass that the world has been brought by modern man. Is this our progress over other more barbarous ages? What carrion foulness, what a stench of burnt bodies arises from these camps and fills the void of the world — that same world wherin so much of beauty is, light, love and joy. Man created in the Image proves to be the wildest and cruellest of raging beasts — man, who at times is but little lower than the angels.

Is it possible that this can happen under God's heaven? I must raise this question, even though I have no adequate answer. It gives millions of men no rest. The world to-day faces many fateful problems, but none so momentous as this. Is there a living God for whom all this has meaning? Is there design and purpose? Or, is the universe ruled by a blind, un-moral force, by some *deus absconditus*, who created the world and is no longer interested in its fate — withdrawn, asleep, or gloating over the writhing of his creatures upon the earth? I try to evade this question, and cannot. "And it was in my heart as a burning fire shut up in my bones, and I was weary with forbearing, and I could not."

This question is asked everywhere and always, and there are various answers, also in Israel. That of Genesis is different from that of Job, and Job's answer is different from that of Ecclesiastes. The Sadducees denied the idea of divine providence, and the Essenes that of free will, while the teachers of the Talmud sought to reconcile these opposites — God's pre-knowledge of everything and man's freedom to good or evil, as he chooses. There is answer after answer up to the present day.

I am not privileged to be among those who have found an answer. Yet there is an approach to the matter about which I wish to speak. This ap-proach or attitude may — so I should like to think — be called religious.

410

As with every basic position, so this approach involves metaphysical assumptions. Our attitude must also take account of the presuppositions and achievements of science. But it is not scientific, it is religious.

Although not competent to go over the multitude of philosophic answers to our problem, I should like to indicate two or three of our own postulates.

The chief of these is that the world of the senses does not constitute or exhaust the whole of being, but that there are unseen levels and modes of being which are nevertheless very real. The judgments we form, the values we create — mental, aesthetic, moral, religious — are the product of forces which are more than our senses alone. These forces are a part of a spiritual order, and in this spiritual order there is an abundance of possibilities, alternatives, contradictions, between which the human being must decide.

The judgments of philosophy upon all this evil and wickedness — this kingdom of Satan — are arrived at through reason, through speculative methods. The religious approach, however, insists that in order to arrive at a conclusion concerning evil and the evil-doer in God's world, not the rational powers only are required, but rather a man's entire being; and the decision must emanate from all the sources and roots of the human soul. Arriving at a judgment concerning evil and the evil-doer is almost an act of heroism, and as with every such act, choice and decision require all the strength of a man's spirit and not the reasoning faculties alone.

There is a further sense in which our religious approach is not philosophic — its inability to content itself with formulas alone, be they ever so majestic. The history of philosophy not only shows one system giving way to another, but also a certain ossification setting in when the aim of the speculative process is reached, namely, formulation. This is the height of philosophic attainment. Yet it is in the nature of formulas sooner or later to divert the attention from reality. The philosophic formula is a very great and important achievement. But it runs the danger of representing these tortures and these torturers not as actual and ever-present, but as a kind of abstraction.

In some philosophic theories, evil is not an actually existing positive thing, but only the negative of the good. As there is no light without shadow, so there is no good without evil. But, in order that the good may have its proper setting, is it really in need of this holocaust of millions of innocents?

Some contend that man is purified through suffering, and that through sin and misery the personality is exalted. Can it be, that man requires all these abominations in order to cleanse his soul, to discipline his

411

character? The contrary is the case. The very possibility of such atrocities, the massiveness of the thing, the depravity of its forms, are likely not to lift us to a higher plane of being, but to degrade us. You can find a rationale for your own suffering, for those of the individual. But what possible rationale can there be for the bodily and spiritual agonies of these hundreds of thousands? Were their souls exalted when they were led to the place of slaughter, when with towels and soap they were driven into these gas-chambers? Rabbi Akiba, so the tradition tells us, prolonged the recital of "The One," at the terrifying moment when he was martyred. But even his attending angels cried out: "Is this the Torah and this its reward?"

It is said, too, that if we could reach the place of the Most High — the *ens absolutissimum et perfectissimum* — we should perceive that evil only seems to be evil, and that for the Absolute Being there is no room for the distinction which mortals make between good and bad. But what man of flesh and blood can reach the Absolute? And meanwhile such a formula helps to obscure the boundaries between good and evil.

The world of the Stoics was all reason, and suffering had no place in it except to be mastered as though it did not exist.

There are others, again, who contend that ours is the best of all possible worlds. The argument is, that we cannot know what might result from even the slightest alteration in the world's fabric. This leaves us again with an abstraction and with nothing much that we can do to alter this unalterable world.

Of course, the mighty temple which the reason of man has reared throughout the ages has given refuge and encouragement to large numbers of mankind's greatest personalities. But in that temple it is all too possible for the spirit to dwell in such tranquillity that evil is not real but is mere seeming.

These great efforts of the rational faculties to discover something concerning the nature of evil constitute an essential part of mankind's substance. But they are only a part; whereas the religious approach demands the joining together of all a man's faculties into a single unit, into an ultimate burning point.

Nor is this religious approach scientific, if we accept a definition of the scientific method contained in a recent book of a distinguished biologist who says:

The Scientific method refuses to ask questions that cannot be answered.*

This would mean not that the scientist does not know how to ask cer-

*Julian Huxley, *On Living in a Revolution*, p. 44.

tain questions, but rather, that he must refrain from asking, and above all from attempting to answer them.

He denies in advance the very possibility of an answer as to the meaning of evil and the evil-doer in the world, and so there is no sense in putting the question. This is a species of ultra-negative agnosticism. It is not atheism. The atheist knows for certain there is no God in heaven or on earth, and he can prove it. The man of science is more modest. He can come to no decision because he does not possess all the evidence. And he never will.

It is the glory of science to be able to utter objective and sure judgments on all kinds of facts and phenomena. But can moral and religious phenomena wait until all the factual material is in hand? When the scientist arrives at what he regards as his own scientific truth, no amount of sceptical argumentation can shake him. But when he refuses, because not all the evidence is before him, to pose these ethical and religious questions, much less try to answer them, he is in reality deciding against any possibility of an affirmative conclusion.

The religious approach asserts that it is impossible to be a neutral, a non-partisan in problems as basic as these. Life itself is constantly calling for decisions. Must we really hold back, in these days of desolation and pollution, from going beyond the borders which the scientific method sets? There is spirit, there is moral character, there is will. There is an order of things based upon ethical and religious judgments and values, and for the creation of these man requires all of his powers, his reason, the scientific method and that spiritual quality which dares a yes or a no on such momentous realities as evil and the evil-doer in the world.

As in philosophy, so in religion, there are approaches which deny the reality and potency of evil and wickedness, and these approaches, too, rely upon the efficacy of formulas. These formulas embody exalted and often sacred truths. But they, too, are apt to still the conscience.

Our religious approach cannot content itself with formulas, even though they be taken from Scripture. Take the great words of Isaiah:

For my thoughts are not your thoughts, neither are your ways my ways, saith the Lord.

Yes, the abyss between the Creator and His creatures is immeasurable, terrifying; and it is the very essence of the religious problem to struggle unceasingly with the question: Is it possible to bridge this chasm, dare flesh and blood set foot upon this bridge? If to-day the answer be yes, tomorrow doubts creep in. To-day "he beholds the light and whence it flows," tomorrow the eye is without seeing, and there is cloud and thick darkness and the shadow of death. The struggle renews itself within the soul each day, each night.

It is easy enough to quote Isaiah's profound words as a formula, and thus ease the conscience in the face of life's tragedy. Small wonder that it has been said that religion is but opium for mankind.

Or, take the words of our tradition: "Because of our many sins." The first man sinned, and there is no righteous man that doeth good and sinneth not. Israel is a sinful, backsliding people, and all of us as individuals and as a people must be ready to accept our punishment. But who can say with a clear conscience that this "liquidation" of millions of the sons and daughters of Israel is chastisement commensurate with their sins, however heavy these may have been? Is there any proportion here? The heart protests against such a thought. Retribution will overtake their murderers, we trust, although no punishment, however stern and realistic, can be made to correspond to these deeds. But our real anxiety is not the question of punishment. What overwhelms us is the fact that there *are* such things in God's world, that men created in the Image have the power to inflict this misery upon other men—and exult in it.

Judaism has always said that God created evil. "I make peace and create evil." Our teachers have never ceased trying to reconcile the thought of a good God with all this evil. In rejecting dualism the problem for Judaism became that much more difficult and serious. But when you hear some of these great things quoted complacently and without anguish of spirit, you come to realize that there is a religious approach which you cannot share. It is the attitude of religious Quietism which would guarantee your peace and which enjoins quiet acceptance of everything going on about you. Some of the most moving of the Psalms have arisen out of this spirit. But encountering it in these awful days, it is difficult not to protest.

The non-quietistic religious attitude and that of pessimism have a common factor. They both face evil as a monstrous reality. Man is evil from his youth. Neither of them can permit abstract or sanctified formulas, or a lack of will, to disguise the ever-mounting power of this evil. Pessimism is itself a kind of religious challenge. It is overpowered by the knowledge that all's not well with the world. It shares all the questions and engages in the same reproaches as does this related religious attitude. But pessimism has lost all hope, "so that a man hath no pre-eminence above a beast." It cannot gird itself with strength. It cannot summon all a man's powers to cross these borders which confine him. The Pessimist has given up. But the religious attitude will not give up: "'Gird yourselves and ye shall be broken in pieces; gird yourselves and ye shall be broken in pieces." It may well be that nothing will result from not giving up. But

414

the essence of this religious attitude lies in just this: We will not cease trying to gird ourselves with all our strength, though we be broken in pieces.

Job faced the same question.

But Job did not receive an answer to his pleadings. True, he was healed from his loathsome disease, but that is no answer. The reply from out of the whirlwind is no reply, for Job had already known that God is all-powerful.

The reference to Nature in these chapters of Job are without parallel. But the first question that springs to the lips is: Why does not the All-powerful, who is more than Nature, put an end to this slaughter and these killings? Mankind has suffered from generation to generation. How long? It is not only from out of the whirlwind that the All-powerful speaks, but also through the still, small voice. A few weeks ago I was witness to the flowering of a night-blooming cactus, awaking from its long sleep, breathing, trembling slowly folding back its petals, with their soft shades and delicate tints, and a tiny flower in the center as like to the larger flower as an infant to its mother. The power which can bring this about is All-powerful.

Relying for support, however, upon the wonders of nature is not an answer to our problem. The heavens do indeed declare the glory of God and the firmament His handiwork, and from whom does not a "Bless the Lord, O my soul" break forth, at the sight of the majesty in heaven and on earth, "the springs, in the valleys that run among the hills," and who would not "sing and sing praises while he has his being"?

But our question is: Is the God of Nature a moral God concerned for the life of man? For, Nature all too often reveals itself as indifferent to man. "To cause it to rain on the earth where no man is; in the wilderness where there is no man"; and when the Face is hidden, all of Nature is seized with fury and confusion—cataclysms which destroy worlds with fire and brimstone, and floods which cover the earth and desolate cities and drag man into the bottomless pit.

There is a further weak point in this story of Job. He rises against God because of his own sufferings. He insists that he is a righteous man and that he has not merited this bitter punishment. When he tells of how throughout his life he helped the weak and the poor, it is clear that he was, in truth, perfect and upright. But like many who regard themselves as righteous, he was satisfied with the order of things in the world. He had sons and daughters, and his substance was very great. Yet at the time when God's blessings were resting upon him individually, might he not have known that all was not right with the world—suffering and sorrow,

415

and cruelty and the torture of the innocent? He did not rise up against his Creator then, or curse his day.

Job's rebellion would have had greater significance had it come from a man in health. We ourselves, through chance, have not been cast into those gas-chambers and furnaces. Does the problem on that account not stare us in the face? This question is not only for the sufferer. On the contrary, it is more urgent for those who are not the sufferers. There are many who throughout their lives have never known a day of hunger, a single day without work or love or companionship. They have had only to stretch forth their hands, and it was given them. When young they rejoiced in their youth, and in their age, despite its infirmities and life's sorrows and disappointments, they have been able to say with a full heart, that they are not worthy of the least of all these mercies. A special providence seems to have watched over them. *Their* condition, not even their own death, is of chief importance, but rather the very possibility that what is happening to these myriads and millions *can* happen under heaven. Is it not the unscathed who are called upon to be the true insurgents against God, and is it not out of the deepest depths of *their* being that the question breaks forth: Is there meaning to all this loathsomeness?

If there is to be an answer at all, it must come through the upsurging and the conjunction of a man's powers all together. We have assumed that there are diverse levels and modes of being, some of which are not merely identical with the world of sense or of abstraction; that, indeed, there are planes of being which are spiritual, aesthetic, moral, religious, and that to penetrate these, there is need of a union of all the diverse forces of the complete man.

We added that there are manifold possibilities, various alternatives, between which, men are called upon to choose. There is the possibility of a kingdom of heaven and that of a kingdom of iniquity and depravity, and we may not content ourselves with formulas, or stand to one side and take up a neutral, a so-called scientific position. We are bound to be partisan; and when we finally decide this way or that, this power of decision within us is a very complex substance. It is compounded of all that has happened to us as individuals and as a group. At the moment of decision, it is the course of history streaming through us, and everything we have learned from the great in mind and spirit, from prophets and saints, from philosophers and artists. When we make our fateful choice, all the souls's forces are brought into union at a single focus and all at once.

More especially, when we contemplate our nature and our experiences as Israel—with what obstinacy we have chosen to say, Yes! This stiffnecked people, which has turned its back so often and fallen away so monstrously, and which has drunk the cup of trembling to its dregs, and suffered as no other people in history, has, notwithstanding its fierce protestations and rebellions, nevertheless remained stiffneckedly faithful to the Most High.

What courage and grandeur creative Jewish thinking has manifested! The creation of the world by the Creator of evil and of good; the first man and the oneness of the human race; Abraham, the symbol of perfect faith; redemption from Egyptian slavery, symbol that man can be redeemed; revelation on Sinai, the sign that man can know God and listen to His voice; Moses and the possibility of a just social and political order; the prophets, the psalmists, Job, Ecclesiastes; the written Law, the tradition; exile and deliverance, the different expulsions and the struggle with higher and lower cultures; the idea of Zion from which shall go forth the Law, and the House which shall be a house of prayer for all the peoples; the Messianic idea; and Israel's great decision, which precedes and follows all the rest: the living choice of a living God.

I have said that I do not know *what* the meaning is of this desert of thick darkness that shuts us in. But by means of this religious approach I find myself facing in the positive direction, and not the reverse. It is as though two men were together standing on a narrow, obscure path. This path is the pessimism common to both. Then the one turns with all his might in the direction of No, and there he remains standing, while the other turns with all his might in the direction of Yes, — yes, there *is* a meaning to all this.

Thus turned, this man cannot stand still. He has started on a long and weary road. He wants with all his will to be among those who seek the Face and pursue righteousness. But from that man God hides His Face. An opaque screen holds him asunder from the living God. For all his trying to come nearer and to touch the outer fringe, he cannot. It will not be given him to appear before the presence, to hear the voice, or to understand the meaning of these massacrings, this wanton butchery. Yet, he can do no other than to persist in his quest to the last, to keep on inquiring, struggling, challenging. He will not be granted tranquillity of soul. But if it be given him to renew the forces of his being day by day and constantly to be among the seekers, the rebellious — that is the crown of his life and the height of his desire.

It is said of Rabbi Isaac Levi of Berdichev that he spoke thus:

I do not ask, Lord of the world, to reveal to me the secrets of Thy ways — I could not comprehend them. I do not ask to know *why* I suffer, but only this: Do I suffer for *Thy sake*?"*

*Buber, Gog u-Magog, p. 143.

417

For us, too, it would be enough to ask, not *what* is the meaning of this anguish, but that it *have* a meaning; and that our need of asking be so sincere that it becomes a prayer:

Teach us only this: Does man suffer for *Thy sake*, O lord?

107

To Paul Baerwald
New York

Jerusalem, December 13, 1944

Dear Mr. Baerwald,

We wired you yesterday that despite your rejection of our proposals for a Middle East office with proper authority and with Mr. Passman as Director, we have nevertheless advised Mr. Passman to fly to London in order to meet Dr. Schwartz. He left yesterday, the 11th.

Your telegram came on the tenth. Mr. Passman, Mr. Simon and I discussed the question as to whether his trip might not be just a fool's errand. We came to the conclusion that no effort should be spared in making clear what was in our minds, and we are grateful to Mr. Passman for taking this additional burden upon himself.

I do not want to go into past history. If we have looked to the JDC for more effective and more expeditious work, this is due to the knowledge that "better organization" is not just a phrase, but means the difference between life and death, despair and security for thousands and thousands.

Let me take some of the things that happen to be before us at this very moment.

You have asked Mr. Passman to go to Bucharest. Do you realize that up to this moment the JDC has not succeeded in securing permission for him to do this? Had the matter been left to him and to us, he would have been there three months ago, as he and we proposed. When the JDC answer came in November it was very vague, and it was not a hearty acceptance of his offer to give six months to the Balkans. The loss of these months means the loss of life, more disease and hunger and exposure, more despair. It means also that the JDC is not rushing to the help of large Jewish populations who need this help, and this means in its turn a lessening of the confidence the Jewish people had in the JDC.

We have been informed casually that the JDC is doing relief work in Rumania, money being sent to Mr. Filderman.[1] That is all we know about it. Yet on the other hand you now propose that Mr. Passman go in and draw up a *plan* of relief. There is lack of coordination here, and it is in the hope that some coordination may be established generally between East and West that we find Mr. Passman's meeting with Dr. Schwartz to be necessary.

We proposed long ago that a staff of workers be recruited here. The answer to this also is half-hearted. The JDC says yes, go ahead, but to let them know before any commitments are made, because they are to recruit American personnel. We can hardly look for responsible workers, if in the same breath we have to say that nothing may come of it at all. Does JDC policy require that American workers be recruited? We have no notion, nor do we know anything as to the size or the kind of staff you expect to engage in the United States, and when. It is therefore impossible for us to try to secure workers, and all of this means delay at a time when every day counts.

As to the purchase of Lend-Lease supplies in Teheran, your delay in answering Mr. Passman's cable from Teheran the middle of November caused the loss to needy Jews of $115,000 worth of supplies — overcoats, caps, etc. — which were purchased by the Iranian Government. In order not to lose the remainder, on which we had an option up to December 2, we informed Teheran, without waiting for your consent, to close the purchase. Subsequently the option was extended until December 9, and meanwhile your consent came along.

We exceeded our authority also, i.e. we have not had your consent, in ordering tea in India, and other Lend-Lease goods in other parts of Iran.

In negotiating for the purchase of further Lend-Lease supplies, Mr. Passman had secured the agreement of the representatives of the London Polish Government in Teheran to participate as heretofore, as he wired you from Teheran. They now feel that a confirmation from London may be necessary, for reasons which Mr. Passman has since explained to you. It is not out of place to remind you that of the $2,000,000 spent for USSR parcels, about one half has been contributed by the Poles, and it would be a pity if, because of defective JDC organization, they were now to go back on that agreement.

We were suddenly confronted with instructions from you to send 50 tons of supplies to Sommerstein,[2] whom you had informed of this. You are of course at liberty to dispose of JDC goods as you please. But effective organization might have prompted the JDC to ask us first if the 50 tons were on hand, and then to inquire what the status was of Mr. Passman's negotiations with both Polish parties and the Russians. Our purchase of additional Lend-Lease goods, without prior consent, gave the assurance of being able to continue the USSR parcel service, and also to send supplies to Sommerstein. As to Sommerstein, Mr. Passman has given you his opinion that he was in a much more favorable bargaining position vis à vis the Lublin-Poles before you sent your despatch to Sommerstein than after.

You seem to have overlooked entirely Mr. Passman's statement that the Russians and both Polish parties wanted him to go to Poland. Had we had proper authority here we would have suggested that he go to Moscow from Teheran, and then to Lublin for a quick survey, for consultation and impressions. As it is, Dr. Schwartz seems to be planning to go to Poland in several weeks' time, if he gets permission. We think this another instance where valuable weeks and months have been lost, and where greater coordination would have helped thousands of suffering human beings.

We asked some time back about the need for shoes. We mentioned 20,000 pairs. We have had no answer. On our own responsibility, we have decided to order 30,000 pairs. If your consent is withheld, we can sell these shoes or turn them over to the South African or Australian Relief Committees.

We cabled you some time back about medicines. We have had no answer, and we have therefore decided to order medicines, even without your authorization.

We are not happy about doing such things. But it takes so long, and sometimes requires so much argument, that we simply cannot reconcile inaction with our responsibilities. You may answer, as your cable emphasizes, that we are only an Advisory Committee, and that we are taking too much responsibility upon ourselves, or, as one of your high officers recently put it, "injecting" ourselves unwarrantedly into affairs that are not ours. That may be, but it is just here where the issue lies. We have no objection to the term Advisory, provided that a person with substantial authority be here on the spot. Without this we do not see, to our great regret, how we can continue to carry on.

We have been appealed to from various sources in connection with the Greek relief situation. We have answered that the JDC has not referred it to us. Suddenly we heard that Belle Mazur was to report to us, but that is all we have heard about this. We have received further telegrams from Mr. Pilpel. But we do not know to this moment if we are asked to do anything. Cairo is but a couple of air hours distance from here, and Cairo is the headquarters for Greek relief.

We heard quite by accident last week that the JDC-UNRRA unit had been in Cairo twiddling its thumbs for weeks; and the young woman who came here was surprised and glad to learn that there was a JDC committee here. They are more than anxious to be given JDC work to do.

I have touched upon such things only as are before us at this moment, and by no means on all of them.

There are also matters of major policy we ought to be discussing with you. But we hesitate.

One of the things that concerns us greatly is the relations between the JDC and the Jewish Agency. Our general view is that it would be good for the Jewish people and good for the difficult period of relief and rehabilitation lying ahead, if these two organizations could work together harmoniously and with understanding. There are a number of questions which should be elucidated together, such as gathering together the children and orphans in liberated countries and giving them a good *Jewish* education, the reeducation of adults for productive work wherever their lot may cast them, the disposition of Jewish property which may be available for use if the former owners can not be located. The JDC and the Agency have found a way of cooperation in relation to emigration. This is not always simple, but the way has been found, and suitable modifications can be proposed form time to time. In some such way there ought to be cooperation, in any event understanding, in other fields, each question to be taken up on its own merits, and an answer to be sought not dogmatically, but corresponding with the needs of each given situation.

Dear Mr. Baerwald, we have known each other and have worked together for years and years, and I hope I have not written a single word in this letter which would even seem to indicate that I am merely wanting to be critical. I honor and respect you and your devoted labors too much for that, and I am, I think, aware of the immense good the JDC does. All that I and my associates are anxious for is that it do the maximum good through improvements in your organization. Just as all of you in New York are busy, so each one of us here has plenty to do. But we have regarded it as an extraordinary privilege to be able to serve our stricken people through serving the JDC, and we should regret it beyond words if we could not come to an understanding with you. I am sure that this would be because of the distances between us and not because of lack of good will on anyone's part. We are convinced that our proposals would strengthen the JDC, and might lead you to have a Western office, not necessarily at Lisbon, in charge of the best man you could find, and an Eastern office in Jerusalem in charge of the best man to be found, and that Dr. Schwartz would be General Director, coordinating, visiting from place to place, and concerting plans with his regional directors for presentation to you.

We fervently hope that Mr. Passman's trip will have constructive results; also that this letter may help to make you feel that it is only the interests of the thousands of needy and suffering human beings, that animate us, as we know they animate you.

With kindest regards, I am

Sincerely yours, JLM

P.S. Since writing this letter two of the JDC-UNRRA young men have been to see me, Mr. Skorneck and Mr. Laub. They are splendid types and exceedingly eager to be at work. They ask if they could not be loaned back to the JDC.

1. Wilhelm Filderman (1882–1963). Rumanian Jewish communal leader born in Bucharest; he studied law in Paris. He was the Rumanian representative of the JDC from 1920; was elected president of Union of Rumanian Jews in 1923 and elected to Parliament in 1927; was member of Jewish Agency from 1929. During the Second World War he was a member of the underground Jewish council and after the war was elected president again of the Union of Rumanian Jews and was a JDC representative. In 1948 he fled Rumania and settled in Paris.

2. Emil Sommerstein (1883–1957). Galician and Polish Zionist leader and chairman of the Galician Zionist Federation and member of Polish Sejm, 1922–1939. He was arrested by Soviet authorities in Septemberr 1939 and imprisoned until early 1944, when the Soviet government invited him to represent Polish Jewry in Moscow. He was a member of the Polish Committee for National Liberation; was a founding member of the Central Committee of Polish Jewry; played important role in repatriation of 140,000 Polish Jewish refugees from the Soviet Union at the conclusion of the war.

108

To the Editor of the *New York Times*
February 17, 1945

Compromise for Palestine

The year 1945 will probably be a year of fateful decision for the world, and it behooves those of us who are concerned for the fate of the Holy Land to offer constructive suggestions, if we have any. It is clear that Palestine will not be constituted as either an Arab state or a Jewish state. It is clear also that the White Paper of 1939 offers no hope for future peace development.

It is therefore necessary to seek compromise, and the first task of all men of good-will is to teach and preach compromise and to elaborate such forms of compromise as they believe to be reasonable and practicable.

The very idea of compromise — the word itself — has been made abhorrent to too many of the inhabitants of Palestine. Their political education has not yet taught them that political compromise is the very breath of life of the Western democracies.

I have talked with many Jews and many Arabs during my twenty-two years in Palestine. Upon this basis I venture the assertion that a compromise can be found which will be acceptable to the ordinary Jew and the ordinary Arab. The compromise I speak about is one upon the basis of which no Arab leader could again get Arabs to revolt and "take to the hills," and no Jewish leader could get Jews to put pressure upon the rest of the world. The compromise I speak about is not easy to work out and does not offer a solution overnight. But it is a reasonable answer and is possible of being put into practice.

This compromise contains a number of elements, each of which requires careful study and detailed elaboration. On some points this had been done, on others not. What I shall attempt here is but a cursory glance.

There are three worlds interested in Palestine — Jewish, Christian and Moslem. For this reason any answer to the Palestine question must have inter-religious and international character. Politically, the international background may be said to consist of three main factors — the United Nations, the union of Arab states now coming into being, and the Jewish people.

A Middle East Regional Council, the setting up of which by the United Nations, one is bound to assume, would have specific functions in relation to Palestine, and for this purpose its Palestine section would consist of representatives of these three international bodies. The Jewish representative would be chosen by a reconstituted and strengthened Jewish Agency. The Regional Council would be the guarantor of any compromise arrangements that are made. Among other things this Regional Council would be responsible for security and armed forces, and it would act as the final authority in disputes on basic issues.

This Regional Council would have its seat preferably in Jerusalem. Jerusalem is the Holy City of these three great monotheistic faiths. A historic mission will be fulfilled if Jerusalem can be made increasingly the seat of interreligious, international organizations.

The administration of Palestine should be on a bi-national basis — namely, partly between Jews and Arabs in government, so that·neither would rule the other. It is not easy anywhere in the world to work out administrative machinery for a multinational council. The most successful example is, of course, Switzerland, which has been at peace for generations. But though practical bi-national constitutions are difficult to achieve, they are not impossible. Some plans have been prepared in this direction, and it is essential that the aid of experts and men of experience be enlisted in this basic task.

One way of meeting some of the difficulties is to give the Middle East Regional Council the power of appointing a High Commissioner and a few additional key men who are neither Jews nor Arabs. How long such an arrangement would continue would depend on how a binational constitution for Palestine worked generally.

Partition of the country? But that is a compromise that settles nothing. All it will do is to create two irredentas, irreconcilable and activist, on either side of the borders. That is the way to never-ceasing warfare, the kind that made the Balkans a byword. Partition also mutilates and cripples the living Jewish conception of the land of Israel, the Holy Land. Partition, furthermore, reduces the area available for Jewish settlement in Palestine. Partition may appear to be a rough and ready way of cutting the Gordian knot, but this surgical operation would kill the patient. If there be no mangling by partition, there is a chance of bringing the diseased body to health, even though this task be difficult and long drawn out.

If partition were carried out because of a declaration by some statesmen concerning a Jewish state or commonwealth, that would be nothing short of misfortune.

A fruitful way of compromise is to seek a solution in the whole of Palestine which will commend itself as reasonable to the ordinary Jew and Arab and to Christians everywhere, even if some political leaders do not acquiesce. The one or the other among these leaders may have engaged themselves deeply in state solution on either side—have burned their bridges behind them. That may be regrettable but is not irreparable. Their peoples can be trusted to recognize a reasonable, feasible compromise when they see one.

But one should be quick to add that a break ought to be made now with the present system in Palestine, where there are hundreds of British officials of all kinds in posts which could be filled satisfactorily by Jews and Arabs. Aside from the higher British salaries, which are an unnecessary burden on the budget of this small country, what is of fundamental importance is that the presence of so many British officials deprives the population of its natural right to participate more fully in its own government. If mistakes are made they should be made by the population. That is the way in which political responsibility is taught and learned.

I speak not only of the large number of lesser government posts in districts and municipalities but more especially of higher offices. No Jew or Arab is a district commissioner, head of a department, president of a court or a member of the executive council of government.

It is time that a substantial beginning be made in this direction. There are certain departments where having an Arab or a Jewish head would present no insurmountable difficulty. In offices where complications at the moment are too great, Jews and Arabs can be appointed as deputies and thus prepare themselves for a more normal future.

A very great additional advantage in appointing Jews and Arabs to responsible positions without further delay would be the creation in this way of a corps of men of two communities who would learn to know and respect one another through being engaged upon essential tasks for the good of their common country, Palestine. This would be a potent means of bridging the chasm which constantly widens between Jews and Arabs and between them and the British.

It it be asked what non-Palestinians are to be appointed by the Regional Council, I would answer that they be preponderantly British, for the following reasons: first, it is impossible to disregard the fact that of all the United Nations the British have had and now have more important interests here than any others.

Secondly, the British have greater administrative experience, and though one cannot say that they have been over-successful in Palestine, still under the proposed new dispensation it would be reasonable to suppose that they would propose to the Regional Council some of their best men.

Thirdly, since international administration has nowhere been effective, one nation has to be entrusted with the main burden of administration. Whereas the Regional Council should be responsible for the major policy, the chief responsibility for actual administration as sketched here must be committed to one of the United Nations.

It is hardly necessary to point out that the regional Council is something far different from the Mandate Commission, which has but advisory powers, and that the position of Great Britain as tutelary administrator is very different from that of Great Britain as the ruler of Palestine.

Jewish immigration, which is a large crux of the situation, should be permitted up to parity; that is, up to one-half of the population. Present official figures show that there are more than five hundred thousand Jews and more than one million Arabs in the country.

Nazi persecutions have massacred so many hundreds of thousands of Jewish men and women that it is thought there may be only about one and a half million left in all Europe outside Russia and the non-invaded countries. For tens of thousands emigration is a crying physical and spiri-

425

tual need. The young almost without exception want to come to the new life of Palestine.

If, as Dr. Weizmann has advocated particularly, immediate stress be laid upon bringing into Palestine as many as possible of the 100,000 children who may be left, all too many without parents, then the whole Jewish and Christian world and — I make bold to say — much of the Islamic world would back such a project. It might be more practical if formulated thus: the tempo of immigration to Palestine is to be dependent upon the economic capacity of Palestine to absorb new immigrants. A generous and gallant attempt to rush immigrants into the country regardless of the economic situation would result in catastrophe.

One task of the Regional Council would be to determine and help develop the economic absorptive capacity of the country from time to time. Jews have already proved that this capacity is far greater than has been believed, if given a fair chance they will increase this through patience, love and self-sacrifice. But this should not be their task alone. The Regional Council should work out and be responsible for the development of a plan for the whole country — Jews and Arabs alike.

Immigration up to parity would free the Jews from the minority status which is theirs in other parts of the world. It would not, however, produce a Jewish majority and therefore would not upset the political balance in Palestine.

One often hears the question asked: What about Jewish immigration after parity has been attained? In the first place, in order to maintain parity, Jews would have the right to additional immigration each year to make up for the difference between the lower Jewish birth rate and the higher Arab birth rate. But more important that this, our whole argument is based on the conviction that if there be a number of years of cooperation between Jews and Arabs and peaceful development of the country for the benefit of all its inhabitants, the chances are that further understanding between Jews and Arabs as to number would be achieved.

I have been trying to outline some of the terms of a reasonable, feasible compromise which I am convinced the two peoples interested can safely accept, even though many of their leaders may not be able to do so.

Yet not compromise comes to pass by itself. This or any other compromise must be labored for. The time has come for this. Time is passing quickly and the opportunity must be seized. For this reason the establishment of an Arab union at this juncture is of the greatest importance.

Nations are now to have a responsible address to whom they themselves and others can be referred; and as to the Palestine problem, the chances for compromise are thus made much brighter because discussion is lifted out of the narrow parochialism of Palestine politics and put on the higher and wider plane of international interests.

I have shared hope for many years that a political union of the autonomous lands of Palestine, Trans-Jordan and Lebanon might be effected. I have hoped for this because it would be a step forward in Arab unity generally, and this is sooner or later a historical necessity, and an Arab union would be the cornerstone union in the Middle East generally. All of this seems to me to offer greater possibilities for Jewish-Arab understanding and an atmosphere of mutual confidence.

But whatever momentary form an Arab union is to take when the time is ripe, it is not yet too late for Jewish leaders and Arab leaders to come together to discuss possible compromise—this or any other. Arab union and Jewish Agency—let them find ways of meeting informally and then officially. If they meet, a compromise can be found.

In order to hammer out compromise, ground is to be prepared. Leaders must be given a chance to adjust their mind, the hearts of two peoples must be softened, statesmen in whose hands decisions rest must be persuaded, political theorists and economists must be called in. Time is running short and there is much work to do.

What a task before the British and others to make up for lost opportunities and to bring two peoples together! I do not share the theory that the British have deliberately held them apart. But the British have not really exerted themselves, certainly never systematically and as a matter of major policy, to bring the two peoples together.

An Egyptian Arab recently put forward the following considerations: "Civilization," he said, "began in large measure in the eastern Mediterranean, including Egypt, Babylon and Greece.

"The wheel of history has now come to a full turn, and the new civilization of which mankind is in such desperate need can find its beginnings here again. Two of us together, Arabs and Jews, can do it. We need each other. We Arabs do not need your money so much as your great experience and your great schooling. Let us sit down together and view our problem from this larger point of view. Numbers and machinery are certainly of importance and we must extend ourselves to the full in order to work out satisfactory arrangements.

"We can do this only if we look upon such arrangements as ancillary to the main spiritual problem of finding our soul again. Together we can develop this important part of the world for the benefit of mankind. This has become again a center of communications—not caravans and camels any more, but airplanes and lorries carrying men and goods and ideas. Have we not leaders of large enough outlook and enough courage to face this task?"

His question is indeed the basic question.

109

To Eugene Untermyer
New York

Jerusalem, March 1945

Dear Eugene,

Your lively letter of February 16 reached me on March 23rd.

When I handed it to Beatrice I said: "Here is a letter from Eugene written in a fine spirit." Whereupon your aunt declared: "He always writes that way." As you see, she has a very soft spot for you, and for Elise and your girls.

We could see the twinkle in your eye, and we enjoyed your letter. Your proposals are excellent. I only regret that I am unable to accept them.

If the American Friends[1] really think I can be of help, perhaps they will agree to take me as I am. Moreover, I no longer have the strength or the time for diplomatic finesse. I tried that in 1931, and my trip was a failure.

Moreover, I doubt if your proposals have practical value. My views are, so it would appear, rather well known and my keeping silent about them would not help to conceal them. Those who throw stink-bombs would throw them anyway, and those who do not object to my having political views would hardly be attracted by my efforts at side-stepping. Indeed, the stink-bombers have never done much for the University; and what they might be persuaded by my silence to give now, would probably be offset by what others would refrain from giving.

I read an article about me the other day by Al Segal—syndicated and appearing in several papers. I was most interested to hear him say that, in his opinion, the majority of American Jews would, if polled, be of one mind with me. I do not know if they are the majority, but I am sure they are numerous. They have permitted the others to shout them down. This is due to a deplorable lack of leadership.

It has been disappointing that none of the American Friends have stood up and said, "Whatever be our own views, we rejoice and are proud of the fact that the Hebrew University stands for freedom of speech. We rejoice also that the President of the University is so ardent an advocate of friendly relations with the neighboring world, and so vigorous an opponent of narrow nationalisms." If some of the Friends could say something like that, they would be making a positive contribution to the fame and standing of the University.

I could understand that Hadassah or the Joint Distribution Committee might balk at saying such things. The Hadassah is definitely a Zionist organization and the JDC primarily a money-raising organization. But the *University*, whereas it certainly requires money, has a spiritual message to Jews and to the world, and its weakness during the past ten years and more is primarily due to the absence of any such message. I have been able to collect large sums in my day, and it was only because I thought I had a message, and others thought so too. Some of the chief contributors were men who could not agree with my views but who believed in me.

Why not try, and I should like to try with you, to find someone with a message, who would at the same time be satisfactory to the noisy section of the American Jewish public? Until such a man, or some other with a message, appears, the University is bound to lag in the rear of every other cause, despite its inherent attractiveness.

One of the reasons why the Zionists in England opposed me from the very beginning was, because I kept the University from becoming a part of the Zionist political organization, a position not always easy to maintain. I still feel that way about it.

There is serious talk again of making the University part of the Zionist Organization. It may be that the man with the message could then more easily be found and financially as a Zionist institution, the University might benefit, seeing that the Zionists do collect enormous sums. But I have thought of the University in terms of the whole Jewish people and in terms of a larger, freer humanity. Yet, why should there not be a Zionistic Nationalistic University, just as there is a Bulgarian Nationalistic, etc.?

I hope you will forgive this long letter, and I hope too, that I have been able to make you see that it would be pointless to ask me to come to America and open only one side of my mouth.

If we were to go to America, we should like to see all of you and to stay for six months, and visit some of the old places, and see something of the new heart and mind of America, and learn something from it. It would not be simple to finance our trip, but we would hope to find the way. If, while we are there, the University, or Hadassah or the JDC, or someone else thinks I can be of help, I can give the matter consideration — but as a free man. Any other way is not becoming to me, and besides it just won't work.

Remember me to Ira Hirschmann. That is the kind of fresh, vigorous mind and character the University should enlist. I do not know the others you mention. Please thank my good old friend Elisha Friedman[2] for his steadfastness and devotion.

Beatrice wants to add something.

Give my love to Elise and the girls.

Yours, JLM

1. The American Friends of the Hebrew University was established in the United States in 1925 to collect funds on behalf of the Hebrew University.

2. Elisha Friedman (1889–1951). Investment banker, author, government adviser; born in New York City. He was influenced by Brandeis to join the Zionist organization; was a member of the Advisory Commission of the Council of National Defense during the First World War; was secretary of the American Committee for the Hebrew University.

110

To John Haynes Holmes
New York

Jerusalem, April 18, 1945

Dear Holmes,

You really put me to shame. Here you are, one of the busiest of men in the busiest of cities going to all that trouble sending me those clippings and your comments. How can I thank you? and more especially for the encouragement you give me. I do hope that what you say is right, that there may be some good result from these efforts, after all.

You suggest in your letter of Feb. 27, which came today, that a further statement from me may be in place. I am writing to see what the San Francisco conference brings.[1]

I cannot free myself from the depression the death of President Roosevelt has laid upon me. Just at this moment! If he could have been spared another year for the making of the peace the world might be different. Or am I exaggerating? At this distance he has been a towering figure. His political and moral authority with the American people was never greater, and a forward-looking, generous liberal America is probably what the world requires more than anything else.

One of the favorite arguments for Zionism here is the growing anti-Semitism in America. It does seem to be growing. But I keep telling those who will listen that there is a greater and nobler America—the America of Lincoln and the America that Roosevelt came to personify. Woe betide Zionism if the world be such as to have an America one of whose ruling forces is anti-Semitism. In such a world, what chance is there for the Jewish homeland in Palestine, or for just causes anywhere? I know how powerful the forces of greed and hatred can be in America, and it was one of Roosevelt's greatest achievements to have held them in check sufficiently to give those other great forces of humanity in America a chance to summon their strength.

You will forgive me if I tell you how I feel about Germany and the Germans. As a Jew I have learned that hating a whole people is one of the gravest injustices. Indeed, I doubt if hatred is the feeling I have as to any German. But I feel deeply, even passionately, that the Germans ought to suffer—both innocent and guilty—for these unspeakable persecutions. Perhaps through suffering they may come to realize the responsibility all of them bear. That is, of course, not certain. I do not know how much the rest of us have learned through suffering.

Remember us to Mrs. Holmes.

Sincerely, JLM

I have the following letters from you:

February 21, February 27, March 8, March 12. Just to list these gives me an overwhelming sense of gratitude.

Thank you for what you wrote about Miss Szold.[2] I shall be sending you something I said about her.

1. The conference to draft a charter for the United Nations opened in San Francisco on April 25, 1945.
2. Henrietta Szold died on February 13, 1945.

111

To Norman Thomas
New York

Jerusalem, May 21, 1945

Dear Norman Thomas,

I am very grateful to you for your letter of April 4 which came yesterday. It gives me renewed courage to know that old friends are still friendly, and that our minds keep marching with one another despite the years.

I gather you are not much concerned with the religious problem. It gives me no peace. I met a banker the other day on the street — not a Jew. He carries a Bible in his hip-pocket and he charges 10 percent. What well-nigh enraged me was his smugness — "the important thing is that the individual should be right with God," whatever that may mean; the hope of the next world, and the victory at El-Almein due to the prayers he and thirty others offered up day and night in the barn near his house. "Spiritualizing" religion, making it something of a future world, is the death of it. Rendering to God what is God's and to Caesar what is Caesar's is, in any event, hardly a Jewish conception. If religion means anything at all, it has to be woven into the fabric of all of life.

From what one gets to hear about proceedings in San Francisco, there does not seem much inclination to yield to the demands of the official Zionist program. Indeed I am beginning to feel that my own proposals, which have been cried down as too moderate, are assuming the character of impossible maximalist demands. If some decent, workable compromise is not found, things here will be blowing up to a fine storm.

What you say about anti-Jewish feeling in America taking cover under a kind of pro-Zionism is very disturbing.

I am hoping to be able to come to America in October. I feel the great need of again touching the soil where I have such deep roots.

I hope you are well, and with kindest regards to you and your family I am,

Sincerely yours, JLM

112

Notes: Conversation with Azzam Pasha

Cairo, May 18, 1946

I met him through Yolanda Harmer[1] who took me there in her car. Though she is Cairo correspondent of Palco,[2] she nevertheless sympathizes with Ihud program. She was at the YMCA the day I testified.[3] She came to me that day quite thrilled. She met me at the hotel here — Shepherds — the day we arrived, as far as I know by chance. She arranged the meeting with Azzam on the phone. She says she is on good terms with most of the leading personalities concerned with Palestine.

We first talked of a number of non-political topics: the relation of Hebrew, Arabic and Aramaic, Persian civilization (pre-Islamic); his expulsion from Palestine in 1931 when he attacked the Italians at the Pan Moslem Congress at Jerusalem;[4] Joe Levy,[5] whose wife is here and whose oldest boy he calls King David; the Sulzbergers; his desire for Egypt's neutrality in the war. (I said it was hard for me to think of any neutral in that war.)

I began the political conversation by asking about Cyrenaica—Tripolitania. I wanted to know what the facts were. British policy in the Mediterranean seemed all of a piece; neutrality with Egypt, new treaty with Iraq, new treaty with Trans-Jordan, France out of Syria and soon out of Lebanon; India like before. Bevin's first proposal that Cyrenaica and Tripolitania join in an independent Libya; then all of a sudden Bevin's proposal that there be an Italian mandate. The latter did not seem to me to fit into the picture. He said my description was right. The latest was that Britain have a mandate over Cyrenaica regardless of what happened to Tripolitania. Bevin's proposal was made because he could not carry the idea of an independent Libya. Russia wanted Italian mandate over both Cyrenaica and Tripolitania; America wanted international mandate and independence after 16 years. The matter has been kept in that state.

The next question I put brought us into the very middle of the Palestine question: Why do not the Arabs propose something constructive as to Palestine? His first answer was that the White Paper had something constructive, an independent Palestine after 10 years. Meanwhile the Arabs were to be assured that they would not be swamped by foreign immigrants, and during that period the Arabs would learn to take a more constructive attitude towards the Jews. Why did I not favor the White Paper? Because, I said, it stopped Jewish immigration and forbade land sales in parts of Palestine. Had it not been associated with these things, there were some Jews who might have been attracted by the constitutional side of the White Paper. Moreover, I had lost faith in the efficacy of guarantees for minorities. The only hope for minorities was to give them equal political powers with the majority. In addition to that, great things had happened; the greatest war in history and the greatest massacre in history—6,000,000 Jews. Such things made a difference, and political programs necessarily underwent change. He agreed with that. There was a great deal of talk back and forth, but his main point, which he elaborated at length, was as follows: the Zionist attitude has been all wrong. Their propaganda has made both themselves and the Arabs believe that they wanted to become the majority and rule, whether they achieved this by force or otherwise—instead of making their peace with the Arab world and joining the Arabs as Oriental brothers, making common cause against European aggression. The Zionists were on the side of those who wanted to hold the Arab world down. He told of hearing a Jew in Hyde Park describing the Arabs as degenerate. They may be ignorant and backward, he said, and it may take them longer to get out of that state, but they are capable of better, and the Jews instead of wishing them better wanted them worse. He was invited to a debate at Cambridge, and the Jewish speaker instead of talking to the point spent half an hour in attacking Egypt. Such instances could be multiplied, and the Arabs were gradually getting to believe that the Jews were their enemies. If this kept up, and he was afraid it would, there would be engendered among the Arabs a fierce anti-Semitism which would do neither the Jews nor the Arabs any good.

Suppose for a moment the Zionists could achieve their objective: they would conquer the Arabs by force of arms and rule Palestine. Do they really think they would last very long in the atmosphere thus engendered in the Arab world? England had been in Egypt 64 years, and she was not to get out; and if these negotiations broke down there would be real bloodshed. He told of how as a young man he spoke against England in the mosques. The older men said: Do these youngsters think they can get England out? England is providing us with food. He then fought the Italians in Tripolitania for years. When he came back to Egypt he found that he was considered a moderate because he talked of peace by treaty negotiations instead of by fighting. The Jews might remain in the saddle for a time, but it would be constant warfare, and in time they would be defeated. The only hope he saw was if there could be a Jewish-Zionist *movement* for cooperation between Jews and Arabs. Efforts like my own, about which he knew, were very commendable, but they were not enough. They remained the efforts of a few individuals and had not much effect on Zionist aggression. My stand for parity between Jews and Arabs, which was regarded as moderate, should really be the maximalist position among the Jews. One could see how far the spirit of Jewish aggression had gone if the proposals for parity were regarded as too moderate. If there could be a Jewish movement of the kind he mentioned then many an Arab could exercise a moderating influence on the Arabs. Otherwise they would be condemned out of hand.

My answer was that a large part of his analysis was correct. But without going into details I would like to ask a double question: What could the Jews do to help the situation, and what could the Arabs do? If there was not something done now on both sides the situation might in a short time become almost helpless. I should like to say that there were very many Jews who felt as my friend and I did. (At one point he said, I really would like to know the truth; and I said, I am trying to give it to

434

you.) We had had many evidences of that since our testimony. Now with the problem of absorbing 100,000 refugees, the hands of most Jews would be full and I thought there could be a corresponding lessening of the Jewish state propaganda. Indeed I thought this the most favorable moment in a long while, and it ought to be utilized. I did not know if I could create a movement — I did not think so. I did think it was possible to enlist the sympathy of many Jews. But I did not think a movement was possible until the Arabs on their side did something to help along. I was always being asked: Where are the Arabs who think like you do? I would not want him as Secretary of the Arab League to make a declaration. (He protested that he had plenty of courage when it came to it, i.e. when he was convinced it would do some good.) But what I would want is that some Arab professor or doctor — only one man — would stand up somewhat like my friends and I are doing. This one man would have enormous influence. That is what I meant when I suggested that the Arabs propose something constructive. I thought the most constructive thing was to advocate self-government. I told him of our memorandum to the Anglo-American Inquiry Commission (he had read only the testimony; I am to get him a copy of this memorandum), and I described the three stages of self-government: now a truce, trusteeship, independence. I thought that perhaps some Arabs in America might be gotten to make the first move. He did not think there were such Arabs there. He wished me all success — it was important. When he came to Palestine I was the first person he would inform. He wanted to see the settlements. That was important for Arab society. I told him something of the Arabic studies at the University.

When we left I told Miss Harmer that there was a man I could come to an understanding with, and I asked her to tell him I had said this.

We both mentioned Joe Levy cordially. He had told Joe Levy he would answer the letter I had written him, but he did not answer. Later we were in entire accord about finding concrete things and tasks — e.g. self-government — to place before the two peoples. That was, I pointed out, a fundamental difference between the Palestine report and the recommendations for India. There the round-table failed and then the cabinet mission placed the Hindus and Moslems before great common tasks, and it is possible this will meet with success. He laughed rather scornfully when repeating what "they said," that the Arab League is a British tool. In any event he is not.

On the way here Miss Harmer had said that the meeting of Arab heads of state convened for next week by King Farouk was a "British success," i.e., it showed Farouk was now ready to fall in with British policy. He had achieved his two great desires — the removal of Killearn,[6] and the evacuation negotiations. Azzam said the Arab offices were Palestine

Arab offices, and not Arab League. It had first been proposed that they be Arab League, but Iraq had favored Palestine offices, and Musa Alami was in charge.

I had a few minutes talk with Morera. He is going to Paris and may or may not return to Palestine before going to America. I asked him what the connection was between the Arab Office in Washington and that run by Dr. Totah.[7] He said none, they were not working together. Totah's bureau was run by Americans of Arab stock. I thought such Arabs might be good intermediaries. He answered quite solemnly, with his hand on my shoulder: "There is no longer room for intermediaries, what is needed is a change of heart." I said, "Yes, otherwise there might be war." He agreed. I asked if there were any American Arabs of any size. He said no.

Haim Nahorian: The Moslem Brotherhood was getting to be the chief force. They now had 1 1/4 million members of whom 1/2 million in Egypt. The leader was a teacher of handwriting in a school. When he talked he had the same kind of influence on his hearers as Hitler. The majority of members are workers, and now petty government officials are joining. The rate of accession is about 25,000 weekly. The Jewish community of Egypt greatly under the influence of Zionist state propaganda.

1. Yolanda Harmer, a journalist, had close ties with Egyptian political leaders. During the Second World War she maintained contact with the Jewish Agency's political department.

2. Palestine Correspondence, a news agency founded in 1934 and dissolved in 1948.

3. Magnes testified before the Anglo-American Inquiry Committee on March 14, 1946. The meeting took place at the YMCA in Jerusalem.

4. The Palestine government expelled Azzam Pasha when he attacked the Italian government for its "barbarous" suppression of the Senussi revolt in Libya.

5. Joseph M. Levy (1901–1965). Journalist, public relations counsel; born in New Brunswick, N.J., and taken to Jerusalem as an infant, where he spent his youth. He attended the American University in Beirut; served as political secretary to Sir Ronald Storrs; was *New York Times* correspondent in the Middle East, 1928–1947; public relations counsel for French Embassy in Washington after 1947. He was active in aiding Jews living in Arab countries.

6. Sir Miles Wedderburn Lampson, Lord Killearn (1880–1964). A British diplomat; high commissioner for Egypt and Sudan, 1934–1936, he was ambassador to Egypt and high commissioner for the Sudan, 1936–1946.

7. Khalil Totah (1886–1954). An Arab educator and publicist born in Ramallah, Palestine, he received his Ph.D from Teachers College, Columbia University, New York. He was principal of the Arab College in Jerusalem, and the American Friends Boys School, Ramallah. From 1945 he was executive director of the Institute of Arab-American-Affairs.

113

Journal Entry

Kent House, Greenwich, Conn., May 26, 1946

We are expecting to drive into New York this afternoon with Benedict and Frances in Alfred Rossin's Hudson car. I should like to note a few things before getting into the New York vortex.

We have had a very fortunate introduction to America. On the plane our neighbors across the aisle were Mr. and Mrs. Storton on their way from Bahrein to Berkeley. He had kept his watch San Francisco time during the whole three months of his trip. He is an oil engineer—plain, matter-of-fact, courteous, hard-working. He kept going over his reports and maps and making notes. They have a married son and a daughter going to the University of California. He traveled extensively by plane during the war; she was a nice, soft-spoken modest lady. In front of them were Mr. and Mrs. Ohlgren (?). He is general manager of the American-Arabian Oil Co. — Saudi Arabia. He was a bit more ebullient than the other — younger. He wanted his company to do something for the Arabs, not just exploit the oil riches. He wondered if it was possible for America to work out a long-term policy of being helpful. He would come to Jerusalem to learn something of what was being done in Palestine.

There were a few hard-boiled TWA men on the way to New York. Some of them had been planning TWA routes beyond Cairo. The pilots and navigators for the various flights were good-looking, quiet, courteous. One of the stewardesses, Sally, was a competent, helpful lady. Faunes, the steward, was talkative and really desirous of making people comfortable in body and mind. He turned out to be a Jew. Indeed two of the other stewards seemed to me to be Jews. There was another oil engineer, Perry (?), a stoutish, professorial looking man — à la Halberstädter —who read good books — one was on the development of the Hadith — and who bought a book at the Madrid airport on Picturesque Spain and whose baggage was full of the gayest *abayas* [Arab cloaks] which some of the customs officials tried on jauntily. Then these customs officials themselves at LaGuardia Airfield — really hard-worked, quiet, business-like — and then Leon,[1] greatly aged, and Benny and Frances,[2] very like herself only more serious than her letters; and Alfred Rossin's car; and a much, much cleaner New York; and the drive through the beautiful parkways and the stately Greenwich trees.

It has been a true joy to be here at this Kent House. Beatie's insight has been justified. She felt that we ought to rest first after the air trip and to have Benny and Frances to ourselves, and to ward off family and friends and plans and work until we had had a bit of time to adjust our minds to our new situation. She has not been in America since 1931, and I since 1934.

I am greatly moved seeing Beatie here. I realize how much more deeply *this* America is part of her substance than it is of mine. She need hardly evoke anything from the past — it is as though she were returning to a past-present which was the more real and unified because of long absence. The experiences in Palestine seem to make *this* America deeper, truer, more genuine. I doubt if she compares the one with the other — they seem to be on different planes. *This* is natural, simple, direct; Palestine is conscious, created, maintained with effort. I do not want to say that one is better than the other. I am trying to see into the soul of my dearest friend, my companion, my wife. Her step on the lawn here; her listening to the robins; her going up to a bush or tree or flower and calling them by name; her tasting of the Southern food; her admiration of the genteel colored waiter; visiting the old haunts at Cos Cob and Chappaqua; accommodating herself to the house of the place, its colors, its rhythm, its guests and personnel. All of this seems so easy, sure, I should like to say beautiful, that I cannot help sighing when I think how complicated and difficult it often is to make the adjustments in Palestine. I am sure Beatie would object to some of what I have written; and in "evaluating" it all, I know that her *ḥeshbon* [reckoning] would have a debit and credit in both accounts. I am inclined to think, too, that she will want to return and not because of the grandchildren alone.

I had a peculiar feeling while approaching the air-field. I had been plane-sick since Portland, Maine. But I did look out of the window at times, and suddenly it seemed to me I had never been away. That happens to everyone after returning from a vacation or some other trip. But here, after 12 years, and with the interval of this war! I think this feeling may have been due to the lack of a gap in time and space between Jerusalem — Cairo and New York. Cairo — Rome — Madrid — Lisbon — Shannon all in the same day; and then the seemingly effortless flight over the Atlantic without a single jar or bump, and New York that afternoon. This two-day interval was no interval at all, and it is no wonder that I was under the illusion for the moment of having remained in the very place — New York — where I found myself then.

Knollwood,[3] June 27, 1946

Beatie and I arrived here yesterday morning. We both enjoyed the travel from New York by night train. The same uppers and lowers, and the same technique. We had the drawing room and were comfortable. Porter $1. He would like to get out of the porter trade. He was in the "German theater" during the war. We stopped at a station in the morning, and I told Beatie there was a chimney, a kind of factory. "Tupper Lake!" she said in a flash, "and that's the sawmill."

Since then she has been back home and one thing after another comes back to her. She knows where the electric switches in the house are, those behind the birch bark door; and the low closet in the bedroom where I gave my head a nice bump. One of the first things she noticed was that the big beech between the Marshalls and Guggenheims was down, and that led to a grand pow-pow on trees with Bernie Barbar who doesn't hear well and who works for Irma Bloomingdale and who is to do various things for us. We are occupying the downstairs bedroom which Beatie occupied in 1908. Mrs. Ryan is to come in each day to do the cleaning. Mr. Jos. Walsh who is arthritic is general manager of the Club. Beatie and I walked to the "Guide's House" yesterday towards evening and met Mrs. Walsh (May, she being the second wife) and Lillian, "my step-daughter." We had a nice chat in their parlor which had many electric lamps and also a picture of Napoleon on the wall. In a kibbutz there would be many books and a totally different picture.

They doubtless felt all of Beatie's age and importance when she told them that she had come here in 1900 before the houses were finished — they were still hammering the nails then. Beatie's name is no. 1 in the guest book beginning 1900 — written in Florence's[4] hand. To me the guest book was a sad affair — so many of those gone who once were here, who indeed built the place. Of course children inherit what their forebears leave them. But I almost resent the thought that the various Marshalls and their wives and their offspring come into so glorious a place without any effort or creative work on their part. Beatie and I are of course beholden to them for letting us come and enjoy their "property." But I feel myself to be Beatie's guest here, and hers alone, and the "property" is hers really because only she knows almost every stone and tree and house and road, and all the stories connected with the origin and growth of the place, and the traditions of the neighborhood which she had from the first settlers at Knollwood beginning with Ed Cagle.

Friday, June 28, 1946

The children came this morning ahead of time, as we did. It was a real pleasure to see them — young and full of plans. Fancy's[5] stage photos are glamorous, as required, and the throw-aways are about ready. These contain her picture and the program and Henrietta Kaplan is to run a card catalogue. Mamma Molyneaux[6] seems highly pleased, and we talked about how to get an advance "feature story." Bendah[7] is to be in town again on Monday for an appointment with Mr. Posner (alias "Arnoff") of MGM. Mr. Zimmerman who wanted Bendah as his assistant has evidently been unselfish and given Ben a boost, and there may be the chance of Bendah's going through an MGM "course" for six months in all departments, and then being sent to Cairo (!) to open a studio. We are all duly thrilled. If he takes this job he will see or write to Mrs. Thackrey. — Fancy is winding a ball of baby pink wool for a shawl for Beatie to take the place of Helen Glueck's pink rag in the mornings. Bernie Barbar has just given an exposition of how to skin bass and perch. Beatie caught five of them yesterday afternoon and I one off the boathouse dock. Ladies need no license and mine was an illegal. You should have seen Beatie hook the worms Bernie had dug; and throw the line. The first sound of the reel was a thrill. Beatie found a stick to dig up the worms from the bottom of the can. For a basket I found a kind of trash box with a glass bottom which turned out to be one of those arrangements for looking through into the water. Beatie immediately spotted the fire line on the opposite shore, and she named the islands and the mountains beyond. The Carlos Whitney place, the Tanglewood Trail, the names of flowers and trees — we should like Florence and David Billikopf here to hand the traditions down to them. They seem to be the only Marshall grandchildren really at home here.

Knollwood, July 3, 1946

The road travellers take;
Then the path in the woods,
And then the trail, narrowing, narrowing
The forbidding forest, and not even the narrowest trail.
Only the intrepid enter, or the thirsty
Or the searcher after a clearing —
Perhaps, perhaps in the light of the clearing
    He will see something he has not
    seen before.

Wednesday, July 4, 1946

This morning Florence Billikopf and her friend Ulrich Schwarze arrived. Ben, Frances, David Billikopf and the new two are preparing and eating breakfast. Mrs. Ruper has just arrived so the house is full. Beatie and I had our breakfast in that "Good Morning" room, just like yesterday. Even though the front porch be a fine place for breakfast, this room with Beatie in bed, her green shawl over her shoulders, and the two tables alongside and the trays, is an even better place. Moreover, it is quite cool out, and the sun shines into the room here since the big trees are down.

Yesterday, Tuesday A.M., I took a stroll over to the "beach" and found a small bench and had a nice time there for two hours away from the endless talk and voices filling the place since David B. arrived on Monday morning. He was on the same train as Bendah who had gone to New York to discuss things with Mr. Posner, MGM. Fancy and I met him at the station. We had gone there with Mr. Walsh. David got off the same train and went to Knollwood with Mr. Walsh. The three of us went into town and bought things. What a wonderfully organized and stocked place the self-service grocery is. Hundreds and hundreds of canned and cartoned foods, also frozen foods and fresh fruit and vegetables. I got a fishing license at the town clerk's — $1.65. I was given a little pamphlet with all the rules as to hunting and fishing, also statistics. What a great thing it is that the State holds so much of natural reserve — over 3,000,000 acres = 12,000,000 dunams, the amount of so-called arable land in all of Palestine. The State lets people have camps free of charge under specified conditions — 4 nights a week at the camp, renewal of license every ten days. The camper has to build his own camp, and if he does not use it, someone else with a license may. Of course on this lake he has to have a boat.

David is a very bright and good person. He has a great deal of knowledge and is alive to everything. He does like this place, and he knows it, and this pleases Beatie very much. He himself said yesterday that he never stops talking, and I said he can learn a lot that way, just as a teacher learns from teaching. He is young and loud, and I suppose that is as it should be. But it does fill the space of the world, and we do want a bit of quiet.

Yesterday afternoon Beatie and I were out in *Robert* again just like the day before. But yesterday we ventured out further and went to the beach and then along the shore a distance and then across to one of the islands and then around it a bit. These two days on the lake have been just about perfect. A warm but gentle sun, a cool but gentle breeze, a slight ripple on the surface of the lake, the trees dark and sunflaked in turn, a put-put now and again but hardly another sound. It is something to see Beatie at the prow of the boat with a paddle. It seems as natural and "instruktiv" to her as walking on the Greenwich lawn looking at the trees and identifying the flowers. She paddles without a sound, or paddles a long stroke, lifts the dripping, shining paddle behind her head from one side to the other. She stops and steers the boat as she wills, almost without thinking. She said, "This is one of the reasons I have come to America, and this is what I have dreamed about for years." Ed Cagle was her master, and she has absorbed that old Adirondack tradition.

441

When I attempt to row it is always: find a sight and stick to it; or, when you shift your oars put them on the gunwhales and keep the boat dry and neat; or, if you want to see something behind you turn your head and not your body. The boat has to be kept steady; or, when you get into the boat or out of it hold on to both sides of the boat; or, if your oar falls into the water don't tip the boat in the excitement of trying to reach it; or when we are near the shore: the snag over there, the rock beneath or in front, or the water-lilies and the various trees — cedar, true pine, birch, hemlock — but where are the balsam and the spruce?

She knows the names of the distant mountain chain and of the nearer hills and islands and of the families who had camps around the lake. She tells of how, during a thunder-storm when they were out, they used to haul the boat ashore and tip it and lie under it. — She does not want me yet to row the boat onto the dock between the two white barrels — presumably I have not the skill for that. Her sorrow is that when she gets out of the boat or into it she has to be helped, and she then refers to her creaking bones of today and her great dexterity then. She hasn't even wanted to swim yet, that is, preferably to float and paddle with her hands while on her back. Irma Asiel [Bloomingdale] used to have her regular steady swim each day around Flag Island and back. If indeed she could have a month of this every year, she would be able to stand up even better under the cruel hammer blows of this war in Palestine. What a grueling prospect to look forward to there.

I have now come to my haven at the "beach." I have my overcoat on — it is chillier than yesterday. We finished the search for the pencil that vanished in the [. . .] Beatie and Bennie were down in the cellar with candle and flash and I poured water down the place where the pencil fell through. We finally saw the mark of the water which came through, but no pencil. Bendah thought the only way to find the pencil was to pull the house down.

As I left, Beatie was in the sun in a rocker on the porch next to our room, and the sounds of Fancy's practicing could be heard from cottage 6. She is a truly hard and systematic worker. What is striking about her practicing is not just the precision and beauty of her notes, but the methodic, economic manner of it. It all seems to mean something. It is not just fiddling, the playing of snatches, or random "playing." I suppose a good teacher is to be told by whether or not he has taught his pupil how to practice. Fancy has evidently been through a good school.

The lapping, the gentle lapping of lake water on the shore — that is one of things I am grateful to see and hear. In Palestine we have the sea, the surf — grand, violent — but no lakes and very little gentleness in anything. Beatie hung out two small flags this morning, and as I was coming over here I met Walsh and asked if we were to have the flag up on Flag

442

Island. "Why—yes," he said with a moment's hesitation and quickly added, "and right away, too." There are two robins who call gloriously in the woods in the early morning and the late evening. The bulbul comes nearest to it, but is not as clear or as varied or as prolonged. This morning I heard a bird whistling: Ben-e-dict, Ben-e-dict.

10:40 A.M. The flag is up.

1. Leon Lowenstein, the brother of Beatrice.
2. Benedict Magnes and his wife, Frances. This was the first meeting with their daughter-in-law.
3. The summer house of the Marshall family near Saranac Lake, N.Y.
4. Beatrice Magnes's eldest sister, the wife of Louis Marshall.
5. Frances Magnes, a professional violinist.
6. Anna C. Molyneaux, the director of the concert management bureau handling Frances Magnes's appearances.
7. Benedict Magnes.

114

To James Marshall
New York

Jerusalem, January 15, 1947

Dear James,

This is in answer to your kind letter of January the 2nd. Enclosed please find a copy of a letter to Alan Stroock, and from this you will have an idea of our latest news. Please keep up your interest in the American Association for Union in Palestine. That might be of decisive help for the whole cause.

I had a letter from Louis Fischer, in which he is good enough to quote his conversation with Gandhi about Palestine and about me. It may be that Gandhi is right in thinking that, if the Jews had committed mass suicide, they might have impressed the world more deeply than the loss of six million lives has done. Yet I do not see how in the world such an action would be physically possible. The few hundred in the Fortress of Masada were able to commit suicide because they were in a confined place and were up against a belligerent army. How could six million Jews, or one million or 100,000 do anything of this sort? And if they did, would the impression on the world be any more lasting than the annihilation of the six million has been?

Louis Fischer in his book,[1] which I have just seen, talks about me in an altogether extravagant way. He says that my "constant companions" are God and the "common people." That indeed would be my great aspiration; but I must say that I have very little companionship, if any, with God. When I see people, who believe that they are on some intimate terms with Him, I envy them and wonder if it is true. I find that He turned His face away from me many years ago. That has been for me probably the most fundamental problem of my life. As to the common people, well I have little more knowledge of them, and I do feel rather intimate with some of the hard-working people, whom I stop on the street sometimes for a little questioning or a little chat. Gandhi's strength is that he knows all about God and that the way to him is always open. How happy Gandhi must be!

Enclosed please find a statement concerning the Arabic-Hebrew Dictionary. You will recall that you were good enough to say that you would let us have the $4,000 we require, if I wrote to you after the first of the year.

Enclosed please find an exchange of correspondence with Julian Huxley. Have you any further suggestions? Is there any "imminent danger" that UNESCO will butt in to our carefully laid plans for having the plundered Judaica and Hebraica referred to a Jewish trusteeship corporation? If you want more information about this, please get into touch with Professor Salo W. Baron[2] at Columbia University, who is chairman of the commission on Jewish Cultural Reconstruction.

We were happy to learn of Florence's engagement.[3] There does not seem to be much chance of my being in America for her wedding. I had, as you know, been expecting to be present at the meeting of the Board of Governors of the University, which is scheduled to take place on March the 17th in New York. You will be getting a copy of a letter which I am writing, and which will explain to you why I am not to be present.

The more we think of our three weeks in Knollwood and of our coming in and going out of the Dorset Hotel, the greater is our longing for its repetition. But we have almost reached the conclusion that our trip to America, after so many years of absence and after all the kindness and affection which was showered upon us, is something more or less like a honeymoon which cannot be repeated. And for this reason you will understand why, if ever we think of returning, we hesitate.

Give our love particularly to Ellen,[4] from whom we expect to hear good news presently. This letter will be mailed to you in New York. Much love to Lenore.[5]

Judah

1. *The Great Challenge* (New York, 1946), p. 163.
2. Salo W. Baron (b. 1895). Doyen of Jewish historians; born in Tarnow, Austria, and migrated to the United States in 1927. He has been professor of Jewish History, Columbia

University, since 1930 and was chairman of the Academic Council of the Hebrew University, 1941–1950.

3. The niece of James Marshall.
4. The daughter of James Marshall.
5. The wife of James Marshall.

115

To I. F. Stone
New York

Jerusalem, February 14, 1947

Dear Mr. Stone,

Your *Underground to Palestine* came yesterday, and I want to thank you for it as well as for your encouraging words on the fly-leaf. I had read some of it in *P-M*.

You say you "can only record as a reporter." But what a reporter — keen, deep, and above all identifying yourself with the suffering.

It was a great disappointment to me not to have met you last summer in America.

I am considering going to London. At one moment it seems to me that I ought, and the next moment that the time has not yet come, or has already passed, or will never come, and that it would be futile anyway.

I have learned a great deal during the past year. That is encouraging, because it shows that I am not too old to learn. But what I have learned is most discouraging.

I have learned a great deal as to how policy is made or not made. In Washington they told me that the binational proposals were just the thing, but that being an election year, it was not the merits of the proposals that could be decisive but the prospect of losing or winning the Jewish vote in New York, Chicago and a few other places.

In Britain one politician after another (or statesman, if you prefer) was bowled over in favor of partition, because partition was supposed to be the most "practicable solution." Even men like Brailsford[1] and Laski[2], as recently as last month, wrote lamenting that the binational idea was not put into effect and that reluctantly they had come to the conclusion that partition was the most practical solution. With one thump on the table by a Palestine Arab at the recent conference in London, the partition idea fell like a house of cards; and the London *Times*, which had

445

been the most vociferous of all publications in favor of partition, suddenly found that Mr. Bevin's new plan was to be preferred. It would be a great study to have someone look into the origins and the progress and the forces behind this immense propaganda on behalf of partition.

As to practicability, it can, I think, almost be proved, in so far as such things are at all capable of proof in advance, that partition is not the practical and final solution it is cracked up to be, but on the contrary it is the beginning of more and more bitter strife, and one of the most impractical proposals that can be made. Anyway, what does "practical" mean? I suppose it means the way in which a proposal can most easily and with least opposition be put into effect. Partition arouses the passion of all the Arabs, and of at least half of the Jews, among the latter such strange bedfellows as the activists and the Ihudists. It necessitates a long drawn-out process of fixing boundaries; it requires the securing of new authority from the United Nations; it means dragging things out who knows how long; it means setting up two tiny principalities with chauvinistic education for the youth, their irredentisms, their hatreds, and their almost inevitable clash. It means further cutting off the Jews from entering and developing large parts of the Holy Land. Is this really practical?

On the other hand, the bi-national proposals would, so many of us who live in Palestine know, meet with the acquiescence of very large numbers of Jews and of considerable numbers of Arabs, and, at the very least, such proposals would stir up less opposition both among the Jews and among the Arabs than any other. This is due to the inherent reasonableness of this compromise. Is that not practical? To be sure the present leadership on both sides is so far committed to their intransigent state ideas that they would find it difficult to accommodate themselves to the turn-about-face involved in the bi-national proposals. But, if only given the chance, the two peoples would see to that in the course of time.

Whatever be the political answer now given, the need for an association such as Ihud is deeper than ever and must be apparent even to the extremist. But if an association like the Ihud is really to be more than a debating club, it ought to have considerable means. It ought to have newspapers — a Hebrew weekly, an Arabic weekly, an English weekly. It ought to have funds for other publications and funds for sending emissaries to different parts of the Arab and Jewish world for talks and speeches and education generally.

Towards this end there ought to be Ihud Associations in America, England and other places. In New York an American Association for Union in Palestine has been in the process of gestation since last August, and by this time it may have become registered as a legal body. Do you know Mr. Leon Crystal,[3] city editor of the Jewish *Forward*? He has been the moving spirit in this, and I am afraid that he has not met with the encour-

446

agement that he and the idea deserve. Will you not get into touch with him?

I am sending you under separate cover by surface mail a booklet which has just appeared called "Towards Union in Palestine," and I think you may find some of the material there of interest. I am sending you also a copy of two speeches which I gave at the University in November and December.

With best regards, I am,

Sincerely yours, JLM

1. Henry Noel Brailsford (1873–1958). British socialist writer and journalist; wrote for the *Manchester Guardian* and *Nation* and edited the *New Leader*, 1922–1926.
2. Harold Laski (1893–1950). British political philosopher and author. Born in Manchester, England, and educated at New College, Oxford, he was appointed professor of political science at the London School of Economics in 1926, holding the post the rest of his life; he was an active member of the Labor Party and its chairman in 1945.
3. Leon Crystal (1894–1959). A journalist and Yiddish publicist born in Shargorod, Russia; he was an editorial writer, city editor, and UN correspondent for the *Forverts* and served as the secretary of the American Association for Union in Palestine, 1946.

116

To Maurice B. Hexter
New York

Jerusalem, February 14, 1947

Dear Dr. Hexter,

I am enclosing copies of two letters, one to Mr. I. F. Stone[1] and the other to Mr. Crystal.[2]

What is to be done?

Whatever the political "solution," the next five years are of the utmost gravity. Either we shall be able through tremendous efforts to further Arab-Jewish understanding and cooperation, or the rift between the two peoples will grow deeper, destroying all chance for some kind of peaceful life here.

Cannot you, Mrs. Jacobs, and Dr. Senator convene the non-Zionist members of the Jewish Agency and have them stand up for one thing — Jewish-Arab cooperation — and have them supply substantial funds to those who are prepared to make sacrifices towards bringing that about in all walks of life?

I do not know what I feel angriest about: the silence and apparent self-satisfaction of the so-called non-Zionists, who have miserably fallen down on their obligations, or the ineffectiveness of those of us here who do our little best, but who, through lack of means and instruments and machinery, are more or less choked off, even before we have time to open our mouths. If we have something to say, no paper will publish it, except our struggling, gallant, little Hebrew monthly. And there is no such thing as a pulpit here as there is in America, and there is the thing called "national discipline," which does not hesitate to bring down the forces of its fanaticism upon the heads of the few persons ready to brave it. Here we are behind barbed wire, playing our poker game in London and elsewhere, destroying the ethical marrow of our youth, killing, lying, threatening one another and stirring up hatreds which will bedevil us for long years to come; and only a voice or two raised now and again here and there, and the echoes of these voices soon fading away. What a tragedy!

Here is this magnificent work of upbuilding going on; old and young giving of their best strength and producing fine results, and all of this threatened by this moral decay on the one hand, and by the hatred we are arousing in the neighboring peoples on the other.

I am sending you three copies of the booklet "Towards Union in Palestine," and I will ask you to be good enough to give one to Mrs. Jacobs and one to Dr. Senator.

I hope you and yours keep well, and with kind regards,

I am,

Sincerely yours, JLM

1. See document 115.
2. In his letter to Crystal (February 14, 1947), Magnes discussed various organizational problems connected with creating a body in the United States that would support the Ihud program (MP, 2557).

117

To David W. Senator
New York

Jerusalem, February 18, 1947

Dear Dr. Senator,

Your letter of February 7 came yesterday.

All arrangements have been made for me to leave for London on the plane starting from Lydda tomorrow morning. Unfortunately, I have a slight attack of flu and yesterday I had temperature, and Dr. Rachmilewitz[1] is to come over this morning to tell me, so I am afraid, that I cannot go tomorrow. That is a great pity. All arrangements had been made through Government here for me to see the Colonial Secretary on Friday the 21st, and they were asked to arrange a meeting for me with the Foreign Secretary.

The situation can be summed up in two sentences from Lord Samuel: "Since Government are now at last drawing nearer to the lines which you and I have been advocating for so long, they may be very glad of your assistance in working them out. If you are able to come, you will no doubt let me know when it will be."

From all appearances this would be just the time for someone to get to London with the kind of proposals which we have been making all this time. The conference with the Arabs and the talks with the Jews of course broke down, and it must appear obvious, even to the most intransigent, that there is no other way of peace and progress in Palestine, except through Jewish-Arab cooperation. How this is to be brought about is, of course, a tremendously complicated problem. But granting that the main objective of declared policy, whether by Great Britain or by UNO, would be Jewish-Arab cooperation in an undivided Palestine with two equal nationalities, I am convinced today more than ever that we would find the way.

It now becomes the function of each of us to try to think this problem through and to take genuinely practical and effective steps to convince those who make policy in England, America, France, Russia and in the UNO, that every other way, whether it be a full state or a half state, is doomed to failure and trouble, and that there is a great chance if the Holy Land be kept whole and the Jews and the Arabs be given this lead from above to try to adjust their life and their needs and their aspirations to one another.

It was this that I was expecting to talk about in London. I suppose they will let me go in a week hence. But it depresses me, because it seems that now is the time.

You are right in thinking that I hesitate to leave here, because, unfortunately, I seem to be at times practically the only one with access to the highest quarters in Government. I had to intervene latterly on behalf of the Chief Rabbi to secure an interview for him, which the Chief Rabbinate and the Mayor of Tel-Aviv and all the others were unable to secure. I have been told that, if any further terror breaks out, exceedingly severe measures will be taken. They will be of such a nature as to impede the progress of the country for years to come. I have tried to convey some of these things to some of our friends. But we still live with these dangerous illusions that have bedevilled us for years, and I notice that we are going through the same process again now that the UNO is in the picture.

I wonder why it is that the so-called moderates in America are so ineffective, even powerless. The one person who seems to have any courage at all is Lessing Rosenwald. But his organization has too unfortunate a history. The American Jewish Committee content themselves with pious resolutions about immigration but are afraid to take a stand on the basic burning political issue. The Jewish Labor Committee is the same. The American Association for Union in Palestine seems almost to have been stillborn, although I am still hoping that it may come into life. People like Mrs. Jacobs and Alexander Dushkin, than whom there are no finer persons or better Jews and Zionists, seem to content themselves with agreeing with me but without being able to make up their minds to act. The non-Zionist members of the Jewish Agency in America might at the present time have a genuine role to play. But can they be moved into systematic, vigorous activity; and who will do it? It really ought to be your task and that of Mrs. Jacobs and of Hexter. You, at least, resigned from the Executive; they did not.

There is one great thing that might bind together thousands and tens of thousands, and not only Jews alone — cooperation in the Holy Land of two equal peoples. If there was a sincere, vigorous group in America ready to fight for this, I think I should be ready to come and give a lot of time and energy to preaching this message and to organizing public opinion in its favor, so that by the time the UNO meet, there would be an organization which could stand up with some authority.

I am writing you another letter on University matters.

With best regards,

I am,

Sincerely yours, JLM

1. Moshe Rachmilewitz (b. 1899). Professor of internal medicine at the Hebrew University-Hadassah Medical School.

118

To the Editor of the *New York Times*
September 28, 1947

Report on Palestine: UNSCOP Partition Plan Is Opposed, Bi-Nationalism Urged[1]

Only yesterday I saw the full text of the report of the United Nations Palestine Committee, as printed in the *New York Times* of September 9.

I hope that what I am now writing may not be too late. According to statements in the Palestine press, practically all American newspapers, including the *New York Times*, are for the Majority report, which proposes the partition of Palestine. Mr. Marshall is also reported as having indicated the favorable attitude of the United States towards the Majority report for partition.

Nevertheless I feel it to be my duty to warn against adopting any such "solution." Partition will not stop the terrorist activities of Jewish groups. To the tension and warfare which now exist, partition will add the Arab front, which hitherto has been quiescent. Partition will arouse the resentment of large numbers of Jews, of almost all the Arabs of Palestine, and of the Arab world. The Majority report itself says that force "on an extensive scale may be necessary for some time . . . Imposing a solution on both Jews and Arabs would be a basic condition of any recommended proposal."

There is no other way of peace here and in the Middle East except through a clear-cut policy which fosters Jewish-Arab cooperation. This is easier to "impose." Here we are together, Jews and Arabs, and the attempt to hold us apart through artificial boundaries will indeed require extensive force.

There is much more good will and readiness to cooperate between Jews and Arabs than the Majority report seems to be aware of. Even the intransigent Jewish and Arab political leaderships have not been able to destroy this. The effort to arrive at cooperation and understanding in a unitary Palestine requires less force and is much more practicable and workable and less mechanical than drawing these elaborate borders and thus precipitating the irrepressible conflict, which today does not yet exist.

The UNSCOP majority admit that partitioning the country is not entirely to their taste. They seek to mitigate the evil by the formula: political partition — economic union. They call this "partial partition." Economic union *is* indispensable. But so is political union. The one without the other is almost meaningless. The board which is to run the economic union is, for example, charged with establishing the tariff policy of the two hostile states. Who knows better than the citizens of the United States what basic political conflicts are at the bottom of every tariff policy? The Arab state will be primarily agricultural, the Jewish state primarily industrial — in that fact alone there are the germs of political conflict.

The UNSCOP majority admit that the Arab state is bankrupt from the very start. The Arab state begins, in accordance with the majority's figures, with a deficit of over £9,000,000 in a total expenditure of over £18,000,000. The Jewish state, therefore, will have to help cover this Arab deficit.

The UNSCOP majority threaten that if one state — presumably the Arabs — refuses to sign the treaty of Economic Union, the General Assembly of UN will take appropriate action. What action?

Yet, the majority are right when they declare that these common economic interests cannot be partitioned since they "are in fact inextricably bound together." Why then partition the country territorially, and thus lead to a loosening of these common economic interests? Indeed, the majority declare that the economic union, although it may have its political implications, "is dictated by the necessities of the overriding interest of unity."

But this overriding interest of unity applies not only to the economic life and development of Palestine, but also to its Holy Places and to Jerusalem. Why not then also to its social and political life and development as well? Without the unity of the country you are on the brink of chaos. With unity, you have a starting-point towards order and development.

[A word as to Jerusalem. One can be grateful, that at least the Holy City is to be kept unpartitioned and demilitarized. That ought to be the pattern for the entire Holy Land — unpartitioned and demilitarized. If the United Nations were to declare the Holy Land to be a demilitarized territory, perhaps some of the great powers might lose their present interest in it, and perhaps the Jewish armies and the Arab armies might learn to convert their swords into ploughshares.]

What Jewish State — without Jerusalem! Jerusalem, the heart and soul of our tradition. Nominally a Jewish State — without Judaism. A Jewish State without Judea, without the greater length and the outlet of the Jordan, without western Galilee, where even today you can see the ruins of the beautiful synagogues built in Roman and Byzantine times.

Both Majority and Minority reports favor increased Jewish immigration. That is the great step in advance. Whatever the fate of UNSCOP's proposals, the Jewish refugees should not be left in the lurch. There should under all circumstances be a large compassionate immigration to Palestine and elsewhere.

But for anyone genuinely concerned with Jewish immigration, partitioning the country and forbidding Jewish immigration, settlement and land purchase in the area of the Arab state would deprive the Jews of those larger immigration possibilities they require. In this regard the minority proposals, despite their opposition to partition in principle, are as truly restrictive and as thoroughly in the nature of partition as those of the majority.

But even a Jewish majority in the Jewish state does not dispose of the "Arab problem" here. Doubtless one of the first things we shall be hearing of is the "Arab underground" there; then of repressive measures against it; then of the answer from the Arab side of the border. Thus the war of the irredentas will have begun even before the independence of the two states has been proclaimed. [The Jewish army? The "token forces" of UN, if ever they come into being? Has not the history of the war and of the past two years in Palestine shown, that comparatively small underground forces, if backed by a considerable section of the population, can undermine the position of large, well-equipped regular armies?]

It is largely the Jewish terror groups which have made the people of Britain weary of their task in Palestine. Having secured the partition proposals through terror, they are now prepared to secure the rest of the country for the Jews in the same way. If the Jewish State opposes them, that creates an additional front. [Both the Jewish and Arab youth have been taught that violence, terror "pays." The Peel Commission proposed partition in 1937 after the Arab revolt. The Arabs refused to accept partition and, as a consequence, renewed their revolt. Then as a result of this came the White Paper of 1939. UNSCOP proposed partition in 1947 as a result of the Jewish revolt. To say, as the Majority do, that there is "finality" in partition is simply fatuous. It is but the beginning of intensified conflict. In view of this, it is interesting to find the UNSCOP Majority hoping for "reductions on Police expenditure" as a way of lowering the deficit of both states.]

The majority are aware of the weakness of their proposals, and they finally admit that, when all is said and done, the real advantage of their "partial partition" is that it "satisfies the aspirations of both groups for independence."

But even that, by their own showing, is not correct. In another section of their report they say that their partition proposals only meet "in part the claims and national aspirations of both parties." The wide powers of the proposed Joint Economic Board and of the Governor of the City of Jerusalem are clearly in derogation of the national aspirations and the sovereignty of these so-called independent states.

Palestine is not just a Jewish land or just an Arab land. It is a common Jewish-Arab land, an international, interreligious land of Jew, Christian and Moslem. There can therefore be no such thing as full national independence for the Jews and full national independence for the Arabs of Palestine, partition or no partition. Why then partition the country?

The UNSCOP Majority keep emphasizing the "irreconcilable" claims and differences of the Jews and Arabs. Yet they themselves say "there are no fundamental incompatibilities among them." Indeed the final passages of their commentary on partition are a paean to the whole idea of Arab-Jewish cooperation, of bi-national understanding and outlook. But why? Why not keep the bi-national Palestine whole, and work towards understanding and cooperation in all of the country?

That brings me to the minority report. But I have no time or space in this statement to analyze it as it deserves. This report seems to me to have many weaknesses, particularly in its practical proposals, which do not always accord with its principles.

But the Minority report has the outstanding virtue of believing Jews and Arabs *can* cooperate and of proposing that they build up a common citizenship in their common country.

For this reason I would urge that the Minority report be taken as the basis of discussion, and that changes be made in it somewhat along the following lines:

1. The boundaries between the Jewish state and the Arab state should be abolished. These boundaries constitute a form of partition, despite the federal nature of the state as a whole.

2. Instead of these almost sovereign boundaries, the unitary Palestine should be divided into counties, not necessarily contiguous, for purposes of local administration and no more.

3. The two peoples, Arabs and Jews, should be declared to have political parity, irrespective of who is the majority or the minority. This seems to be implied through the provision in the Minority report of an upper legislative chamber constituted "on the basis of *equal representation* of the Arab and Jewish citizens of Palestine"; and by the provision that "legislation shall be enacted when approved by majority votes in *both* chambers of the federal legislative body."

4. That the Federal Court of Appeals on constitutional matters be composed of an equal number of Jews and Arabs, and not of an Arab majority. This court is of decisive importance, as a reading of its proposed functions will show. If necessary, the chairman might be an appointee of the United Nations in some such way as is proposed for the International Commission on Absorptive Capacity.

5. That Jewish immigration be permitted in all parts of Palestine up to parity with the Arabs. This seems to be implied when the Minority re-

port excludes the possibility that the Jews, "by means of free mass immigration would become the majority population in Palestine."

This is the moment when the less intransigent among the Jewish and Arab leaders should get nearer together in view of the common danger of partition.

[A few days ago a young Arab labor leader, Sami Taha, was assassinated. He and his considerable following had not been satisfied with the policies of the present Arab leadership. Despite the inner Arab terror, many thousands of Arabs from all walks of life attended his funeral.

We are often asked if there are Arabs who are in favor of the binational Palestine. I should like to quote from an address by Fawzi Darwish al Husayni, another younger Arab leader who was done to death by Arab political assassins. He was the leader of a newly established party called "The New Palestine." He had been detained in 1936 for his active participation in the Arab revolt. Since then, he and many of the younger Arabs had learned a great deal and had changed their attitude towards the Jews. This is what he said shortly before his lamented death:

> There is a way towards understanding and agreement between both peoples in spite of the many obstacles. Agreement is necessary for the development of the country and for the liberation of both peoples. The condition for agreement is the principle of non-domination of one people by the other, and the establishment of a bi-national state based upon political equality and cooperation between both peoples in their economy, their social and cultural life. Immigration is a political problem, and in the framework of a general agreement it will not be difficult to solve the question of Jewish immigration according to the economic absorptive capacity of the country. The agreement of the two peoples should receive international confirmation by UNO; the agreement should assure to the Arabs that the independent binational Palestine will join a union with the neighbouring Arab countries.

This is the voice of an Arab brother, the authentic voice of our common Semitic tradition. It is as though he had heard the voice of the Hebrew Prophet:

> For Zion's sake will I not hold my peace,
> And for Jerusalem's sake I will not rest,
> Until the righteousness thereof go forth as brightness,
> And the salvation thereof as a lamp that burneth.

It is this voice which speaks out of the hearts of multitudes of Jews, Moslems and Christians. This is the true vision of the Holy Land to guide the United Nations, not the despair of the defeatists and the chauvinists.]

Do not dismember the country. Do not estrange Jews and Arabs from one another. Lay down a generous bi-national policy and make Jewish-

Arab cooperation the chief objective of this policy. Give the two peoples the chance they have never had of self-government *together*, and through systematic work day by day, year by year, their response will be increasingly joyous and constructive.

JLM

1. Text in brackets appeared in the original draft submitted by Magnes, which he entitled "Do Not Dismember the Holy Land" (JMP).

119

To Ernst Simon
New York

Jerusalem, November 12, 1947

Dear Dr. Simon,

Only now have I found the opportunity to read the copy of your letter to Natan Hofshi which, according to him, and I agree, "is interesting and a cause for concern." I hope you won't mind random comments as a matter of "personal privilege."[1]

A. *Tactics.* There is no social life without tactics, and certainly no political life. I believe I have never made a proposal intended solely to save my own soul, but rather my intention was to achieve something practical and concrete. A person may err and cause others to err by his tactics; one may accuse me of this far more than you can imagine. There are, however, limits to tactics, even those of the wisest and slyest of tacticians. For me partition marks such a limit; for you not. There are even tactics in the American proverb, "honesty is the best policy." But without speaking of such lofty notions as honesty, as long as partition remains an uncertainty my tactics are to oppose it — at the opportune moment publicly, and when times are not propitious then not publicly. Of course, one must ask when silence is best for Zion's sake, and when it is not. It is possible that honest men will differ on this. On the very day that partition becomes a fact it will be necessary to consider other tactics, seriously and not rashly, on the basis of the facts that will obtain then and which we have no way of knowing now and which are unknown even to those resident in America. And you will pardon me if I don't see any connection between the problems of "tactics" and the problems of "lyricism and drama," "Recht haben und Recht behalten," and similar matters.

B. Tell us, if you will, whom do you accuse of desiring an *Arab State*?

C. *The Minority Program.* In my article in the *New York Times* — did the editors include my recommendations for changes so that the minority program could serve as a basis for discussion?[2] As yet I have not received a copy of the paper. You fail to mention one word concerning my proposals. I made them for "tactical" reasons, undoubtedly poor and worthless "tactics" in your eyes.

D. *Our failure.* Yes, we failed at the critical moment. We did not fail in the case of the Anglo-American Committee of Inquiry. Now we have failed. Why? You know apparently. Perhaps you will tell us why? Possibly our basic idea is wrong, or our tactics are wrong, or we are inept, or because of other factors? In any event, it is vitally necessary to analyze the objective and subjective situation and to do it seriously and with pitiless thoroughness, and your colleagues here have begun to do so. However, it will be possible to do this in a manner in keeping with the needs of the hour only after we know what the proposed plan of partition and the methods of implementation are, and England's response to the recommendations.

E. "How shall we act after our defeat? Simply continue on as though nothing happened?" No, my friend. Believe me, none of us think so. We are thinking of our role, if there is one, in the unclear future. Perhaps it will be a greater one than until now, and perhaps it will mean disbanding the Association, permitting each one to join some existing organization thus enabling him to influence that organization from within. At the time that we established the Ihud there were those who thought it a mistake. Why another institution? Tactics — perhaps ours were unrealistic and there is a need to correct them.

F. Why not say what you think publicly if you have something to say "for Zion's sake"? Your comrades will understand and will be sympathetic.

G. *The organization.* No one is satisfied that we are strong in intellectual resources and weak in organizational and administrative talent. This you, too, have known. And the professional workers are the least satisfied. If we will have a task to perform in the future we must not begin new undertakings before we have faced these very basic problems.

Yours, JLM

1. Simon, then on leave in the United States from Hebrew University, wrote to Hofshi, a veteran pioneer, pacifist, and member of Ihud; Hofshi sent a copy of the letter to Magnes. Simon raised the issue of the propriety of the individual dissenter continuing to attack the decision of the majority even though it was "for the sake of Zion." Such behavior, Simon wrote, carried the quality of the "lyrical": "If the intention is to reach the realm of actuality, lyricism must turn into drama; one has to consider the other actors, as well. This we call tactics. Anyone who would affect the course of events has to make use of tactics . . . Our group belongs to that category of organizations of whom it will be said, 'They were right,

but they did not have the strength to convince their contemporaries'. This is the tragic difference between, 'being right' [*Recht haben*] and 'prevailing' [*Recht behalten*] . . . We have failed in that our ideas have been appropriated by the anti-Zionists. We were wrong in depending upon them" (New York, October 26, 1947). This letter has been translated from the Hebrew by the editor.

    2. See document 118.

7

A Mission
of
Peace
1948

T HE ISOLATION OF MAGNES and his Ihud associates increased in the early months of 1948. In America the Jewish community's support of the Zionists during the UN debate over partition broadened into an outpouring of compassion and material aid for a hard-pressed yishuv fighting for its survival. Magnes's American base shrank (document 121). Financial aid from the United States, which had sustained the Ihud and supported its weekly journal, *Ba'ayot*, dwindled. Arthur Hays Sulzberger, Maurice Wertheim, and Herbert Lehman, among others, declined to renew their substantial subscriptions (document 120). The American Jewish Committee, a group in which Magnes's name still carried weight, supported partition. In a March meeting of the committee's executive, Alan Stroock, vice-president of the committee, David Sher, and Frank Altschul, all of whom shared Magnes's views, urged the committee to temper its propartition position, but without success. At a time when various UN initiatives to end the fighting were being discussed, Magnes bitterly noted, the American Jewish Committee refused to pass a resolution encouraging the peace efforts (document 125).

For his part Magnes was prepared to grasp at every possibility that carried the faintest hope of ending the fighting. When Virginia Gildersleeve, dean of Barnard College, announced the organization of the League for Justice and Peace in the Holy Land, Magnes hastened to inquire whether or not a basis for collaboration existed between the league and the Ihud, although the new organization was clearly pro-Arab. The one Jew on the league's executive committee was Rabbi Morris Lazaron, a leading figure in the anti-Zionist American Council for Judaism. Yet Magnes utterly rejected the notion that his position as president of the Hebrew University required that he be circumspect in his political associations (document 122).

In Palestine, Ihud's political activities (mild in themselves — press releases and posters condemning mob action and calling for an end to the spilling of innocent blood) were denounced as defeatist and treasonous. For Magnes the escalation in the fighting proved the bankruptcy of parti-

461

tion. The situation was most precarious in Jerusalem, where the Jewish populace faced the well-equipped Arab Legion and a hostile British administration and army. The food supply depended on Hagana convoys breaking through the Arab blockade of the road from Tel Aviv — operations that were only sporadically successful. Entire Jewish sections of the city, such as Mount Scopus and the Jewish quarter of the Old City, were cut off. Magnes was not alone in questioning how long the Jews could hold out and what fate awaited a defenseless population (documents 127, 128). He was prepared to go to any length to prevent the chaos and destruction he feared.

These were the circumstances under which Magnes greeted what appeared to be the momentous turning point of March 19, when Warren Austin, America's chief delegate to the UN, announced the new United States position on the Palestine problem. America now favored postponing the implementation of partition, proposing instead a temporary UN trusteeship. To this end Austin called for a special meeting of the UN General Assembly (document 123). In early April, in preparation for the General Assembly, the State Department circulated its trusteeship proposals to European and Arab capitals. The United States consul in Jerusalem was requested to solicit Magnes's views as well (document 124). On April 9 Loy Henderson, chief of the Near East desk, received Robert Lovett's permission to invite Magnes to come to the United States as soon as possible. Henderson's message to Magnes read in part: "At no time has there been a greater need for courageously conciliatory attitude such as yours on part of both Arabs and Jews. If such attitude is to prevail cooperation on part of moderate and conciliatory Arabs and Jews is essential." (Henderson intended to bring in a "moderate" Arab counterpart; he had in mind Azzam Pasha, secretary of the Arab League.)[1]

Henderson's plans coincided with those of a group of Magnes stalwarts — Maurice Hexter, Edward Greenbaum, James Marshall, and Alan Stroock. After consulting with Henderson an ad hoc committee of Magnes's friends — Lessing Rosenwald joined the group — invited him to come to the United States. He arrived on April 21 with two political goals in mind: bringing about a cease-fire in Jerusalem, which he believed could then be extended to the entire country; and mobilizing support for the trusteeship plan, which he saw as the first step, at long last, in the direction of Arab-Jewish rapprochement. He had arrived in America while Jewish statehood hung in the balance and the yishuv was preparing for full-scale war with its neighbors. He wanted peace at nearly any price, surely at the price of statehood.

1. Henderson to Lovett, Acting Secretary of State, April 9, 1948; Henderson to Wasson, April 10, 1948; *Foreign Relations of the United States, 1948* (Washington, D.C., 1976), vol. 5, part 2, pp. 804–805, 811.

Magnes's meeting with Secretary of State Marshall on May 5 and with President Truman the following day were the high points of his personal diplomacy. In his talks with them and with Department of State officials he stressed his Jerusalem strategy: concentrate, first of all, on arranging a cease-fire in Jerusalem by appointing a UN governor of stature; a suffering population would rally to his support. Peace in Jerusalem could then lead to an armistice in the country, provided a center of power and authority were established. As a last resort Magnes raised the possibility of applying economic sanctions to both sides (documents 129, 130).

Magnes continued his diplomatic activity all through May and into June (document 131). Opposed though the Jewish Agency was to his activity it maintained liaison with him. He and Nahum Goldmann, one of the senior Jewish Agency diplomats in the United States, met from time to time in frank discussions. On June 10 Magnes suffered a stroke and was hospitalized for three weeks. Four days later he dictated a letter to his wife for Robert McClintock of the State Department. The letter contained a detailed plan for a confederation to solve the Palestine question: it called for two sovereign states, closely linked in questions of defense and foreign policy, with Jerusalem as the capital of the confederation (document 132). The plan was, in a sense, a compromise between binationalism and statehood, between partitioning Palestine and maintaining its unity.

Throughout the summer and early fall Magnes devoted his energies to two tasks: refining and disseminating his proposals and forming an American organization that would support his political program and Ihud's activities in Israel on behalf of Arab-Jewish reconciliation. Hannah Arendt, whom Magnes met in June, served as the chairman of the provisional group's political committee and in that capacity collaborated closely with Magnes. Magnes presented his proposals to Count Folke Bernadotte, the UN mediator in Palestine, and to Abba Eban, the representative of Israel to the UN. Magnes's fullest exposition of his views on confederation came, in fact, in the form of a letter to the editor of *Commentary* in October 1948, responding to Eban's article in the issue before (documents 133, 134, 136, 137, 138, 139). Despite Eban's rejection of confederation Magnes was hopeful that further discussion might soften the Israeli stand. A dialogue had begun that might have developed into a major political debate, now that a democratic state existed, had not death cut down one of the main protagonists.

One of the last entries in Magnes's diary, dated October 22, four days before his death dealt with the other theme that so occupied his thoughts: the moral dimension of politics. He referred to his success in persuading the JDC to consider extending aid to the Arab refugees. Two months earlier he had written in a similar vein to Ben-Gurion pleading with him to allow humanitarian considerations alone to determine the government's policy on the refugee question (documents 135, 140).

120

To Herbert H. Lehman
New York

Jerusalem, February 6, 1948

Dear Governor Lehman,

Mr. Alan Stroock's letter of December the 8th, in which he was good enough to send me yours to him of November the 18th,[1] reached me only two days ago.

I want to tell you how much I appreciate your straightforwardness in writing as you did.

That was before the partition resolutions of the United Nations Organization had been passed and before the events of the past two months in Palestine.

I wonder how you feel about it all now.

You are right in saying that I have been opposed to partition, and I believe in it less today than ever I did. I have said right along that it is merely a facile solution on paper, and that it can only be carried out through warfare over a period of many years. During that period I fear greatly for what will happen to this blossoming community here. In 25 years it was possible to build up the beginnings of a true and beautiful Jewish life. It is, in.my opinion, a great misfortune that since the adoption of the Biltmore Program in 1942 the minds and hearts of the Jewish people have been bedevilled by the mirage of a Jewish state.

Enclosed please find a copy of a letter which the correspondent of the *New York Times* is telegraphing to his paper today.[2] Do you not think that the Security Council should use every effort to bring about a truce and to seek ways of conciliation before attempting to send an international force here? Of whom will this international force consist? of Filipinos and Chinese, as rumor here has it? If so, Heaven protect us from our friends.

Nor can I refrain from saying that, in my opinion, the kind of pressure that was used at the UN Assembly to have the partition resolutions put through is as evil as partition itself. I do feel ashamed that this

Holy Land should have been made into a bargaining counter. One hears more and more of how the United States exerted the pressure, which this mighty government can, on countries dependent on it. Moreover, delegate after delegate stood up and said that they did not like partition, but inasmuch as they were told that partition was the only alternative to chaos, they would vote for partition. It is partition which is creating chaos. There were and there are other alternatives.

You may be interested also in a letter signed by Professor Buber, Dr. Senator and myself, which was published in the Hebrew daily, *Haaretz*. The editor of the *Palestine Post*, however, refused to publish it on the ground that it is "a Quislingism and a stab in the back of the Jewish cause." As you see, we are descending in the scale.[3]

I hope you are well, and with kind regards to you and Mrs. Lehman, I am,

Sincerely yours, JLM

1. Lehman, replying to Stroock's request for a renewal of his contribution to Ihud, declined to do so since he favored partition and Magnes opposed it. He believed that once the partition plan was carried out, Magnes could be effective in developing better relations between Jews and Arabs. He would then contribute to Ihud.
2. The letter, which appeared in the *New York Times*, February 9, 1948, p. 18, urged that the Security Council call for a cease-fire and mediate between the two sides.
3. The press release, dated January 29, 1948, appealed to "the people of Jerusalem" and "more particularly, to our Jewish brethren" to desist from mob violence and reprisals.

121

To Thomas Mann
Pacific Palisades, California

Jerusalem, March 1, 1948

Dear Mr. Mann:

I have just seen the memorandum "Could the Arabs stage an armed revolt against the United Nations?" submitted to the United Nations by The Nation Associates, of whom you are one.[1]

It is difficult for me to believe that had you gone over this memorandum carefully, you would have consented to have your signature appended.

Quite aside from the conclusion of the pamphlet, which has been falsified by events, that the possibility of an Arab revolt was "largely an empty threat," what amazes me about the memorandum is its deep cynicism.

The United Nations are reassured that they can safely resolve to partition Palestine because "the military strength of six of the seven Arab states is so slight as to constitute no danger whatsoever."

"Egypt has no war industry and insufficient raw materials for such an industry."

Syria has a "lack of officers," "no air force," "no navy."

"The armed might of the Lebanon consists of 5,500 men. There is no air force, no navy."

Iraq. "Soldiers do not know how to read . . . only a small percentage of them learn to use a machine gun. The Iraqi soldiers, poorly fed, ignorant, exploited, are not good fighting material."

Saudi Arabia. "The present army does not exceed 5,000 trained soldiers equipped for modern warfare."

Transjordan's Arab Legion is "the finest military force in the Middle East." But presumably it need not be feared because it "is entirely a British creation . . . It obeys only British orders."

Arab Palestine. "Few trained officers, no skilled technical experts, almost no armor depots and no arms-producing industry. They can construct primitive bombs, but cannot manufacture rifles and small arms. Their heaviest arms are sub-machine guns with a few machine guns. They have no mortars. Their explosives are of the most primitive type."

All of this seems to indicate an almost idyllic state of disarmament. The United Nations, which talks about peace and disarmament, should, one might think, be encouraged to do everything to perpetuate this situation. Instead, it is made a subject of mockery and a decisive reason why the United Nations can do what it pleases in this part of the world, without any fear.

The song is now, to be sure, coming out of the other side of the mouth. But that does not minimize the calculated cynicism of the Nation Associates document.

As to the Jews, they have "an organized modern defence army led by experienced officers who occupied important positions in the Allied armies . . . combat experience . . . trained as commandos . . . 70,000 members . . . well equipped with modern arms . . . maintains arms factories . . . has latest patents for Sten guns and other weapons . . . scientific apparatus."

The United Nations, therefore, need have no fear.

We are now in the midst of this bloody war, one of the immediate causes of which is the rivalry of New York newspapers to acquire a large Jewish circulation and the rivalry of political machines to acquire Jewish votes.

The partition resolutions were passed in disgraceful circumstances. Power politics had the upperhand and small states were coerced. Palestine was, for the most part, only a secondary consideration. The domestic and foreign politics of the great powers were the primary consideration.

I had hoped that you, with your great moral passion and your unrivalled insight into the motives which unleashed two world wars and threaten to unleash a third, would have been on the side of conciliation, compromise, understanding, cooperation between Jews and Arabs.

It is not too late for you to lift your powerful voice on behalf of a truce, of a conference, of determined efforts to bring about a settlement through agreement. This has always been possible. It is possible even at this late hour.

Kindly remember me to Mrs. Mann, and with best regards,
I am,

Sincerely yours, JLM

1. Nation Associates, Inc., *Could the Arabs Stage an Armed Revolt Against the United Nations? Memorandum Submitted to the General Assembly of the United Nations*, New York, 1947. The seventy-seven-page memorandum was made public in early October 1947 (*New York Times*, October 6, 1947, p. 4).

122

To Sir Leon Simon
New York

Jerusalem, March 16, 1948

Dear Sir Leon Simon,

Your telegram of March 5 reached me in due course. That was the first I had heard of "the Gildersleeve League."[1]

Your letter of March 7 came yesterday.[2] You should be satisfied. I have "not come out in support of the new League."

I am, however, doing my very best to convince Miss Gildersleeve and her associates of the justice and practicability of the Ihud's proposals as to Palestine. I sincerely hope I may succeed in this. I have tried to convince Arabs, British, Americans and others of the justice and practicability of these proposals. I brought them before the Anglo-American Inquiry Committee and before UNSCOP. I am looking for other opportunities, and I expect to make use of them.

Enclosed you will find copies of a personal letter I wrote to Dean Gildersleeve on March 8, and of a telegram I received on March 10 from the

467

Committee for Peace and Justice in the Holy Land, and my answer on March 14.[3] I have not made them public, but you are at liberty to do so. Doubtless Miss Gildersleeve's permission would have to be secured to publish my letter of March 8, since it was marked as not for publication.

Please find enclosed also a statement of mine which appeared in the *Palestine Post* on March 10.[4] This was also published in *Haaretz* yesterday. From this you will see how eagerly I advocate a truce, a stopping of this war, an end to the bloodshed, further attempts at conciliation between Arabs and Jews. Thousands and thousands of men and women, who are here on the spot, and not in some faraway land, fervently pray for this. I regret that such an attitude on the part of the President of the Hebrew University should make you "nearer than you ever were before to sympathy with the heresy-hunters."[5] You are doubtless aware that this attitude on the part of the President of the Hebrew University is regarded by others as reflecting credit upon the Hebrew University.

This morning's papers report that the United States, France, and China are to call upon the Jews and the Arabs to agree to a truce. Please God, that may be true. If I have had even the very slightest part in bringing this about, I shall be grateful always.

You use rather strong expressions concerning "Miss Gildersleeve and her friends."

"Not disinterested seekers after peace and justice."

"Notoriously represent missionary and pro-Arab interests."

"Not lift a finger to help Jews."

"Bitterly anti-Zionist . . . some of them anti-Semitic . . . at any rate anti-Jewish."

Even though all you say were true, that would be all the more reason for encouraging my efforts to persuade them to advocate the justice and practicability of a program which not even the wildest Zionist terrorist could characterize as missionary–pro-Arab–anti-Zionist–anti-Semitic–anti-Jewish.

Or is everyone, who, like myself, has opposed the official Zionist program since the fatal Biltmore resolutions in 1942 and who could foresee the catastrophe to which they would eventually lead, an anti-Zionist?

I must confess, to my surprise, that you, a comparative stranger from England, should venture to characterize distinguished Americans in such unbridled terms. For the sake of the University, I would strongly urge you to be a bit more moderate and not to rely upon the chatter of some of your propaganda informants. The Zionist politicians may think they have "the Jewish vote" of New York in their pockets and that, therefore, they can besmirch with impunity anyone not in agreement with them. They should be better advised. They have done more than their share in engendering anti-Semitism in Great Britain, and their truculence will, without doubt, recoil on the heads of the Jews of America. In any event, I should think that you might exercise a bit more restraint.

In addition to the names mentioned in the telegram to me, I have seen only the following: Harold Lamb, author; Allen O. Whipple, Clinical Director of Memorial Hospital; John A. Wilson of the University of Chicago; Walter L. Wright, Department of Oriental Languages and Literatures, Princeton University. Why you drag the red herring of Rabbi Lazaron across the trail, I do not know. Perhaps he is also among the 100 members of the Committee for Peace and Justice in the Holy Land? Suppose he is.

Perhaps, in fairness to yourself, you might consult *Who's Who* and try to discover for yourself who some of these mentioned above are. I have no *Who's Who* here. When the hundred names are available here, I shall also try to look up those I do not know.

Miss Gildersleeve was for long years Dean of Barnard College of Columbia University. Thousands of Jewish young women have gone through Barnard under her personal guidance. I have yet to hear that any one of them charges her with being anti-Semitic or anti-Jewish. She was appointed by President Roosevelt as a member of the U.S. Delegation to the Conference in San Francisco, where the Charter of the United Nations was drawn up. She is, next to Mrs. Roosevelt, probably the outstanding woman in American public life.

Henry Sloane Coffin is President of the Union Theological Seminary of New York, the most important Protestant theological school in America. It is associated with Columbia University. It has on its faculty H. E. Fosdick and Reinhold Niebuhr, whose names may be known to you. They are not anti-Semitic or anti-Jewish.

Kermit Roosevelt is the grandson of President Theodore Roosevelt. I met him in Jerusalem during the war. He had looked forward to an academic career in Semitic languages. He seemed to me to be trying to keep an open mind and to inform himself on the Palestine problem at first hand.

Dr. Whipple, who has connections with the Rockefeller Foundation, has had a distinguished medical career. The Memorial Hospital, of which he has been clinical director, is the most important cancer hospital in the United States. He has volunteered his services towards building up the Medical School of the American University at Beirut. "Missionary"? Most decidedly. I wish we had more like him. Perhaps our own medical school might then be farther along.

Professor John A. Wilson is the successor of James Henry Breasted as Head of the Institute of Oriental Studies at Chicago University. Ask Professor Mayer, who is now in the United States, what a distinguished and fine person he is.

In the same mail as your letter two others came from New York.

The one is from one of the oldest and staunchest supporters of Zionism among the non-Jews of America. He says: "I wonder if you have heard that Dean Gildersleeve organized a large and influential committee to give support to her viewpoint on the Palestine situation . . . Her plea is right along the line of urging, in accordance with Article 33, every possible means of understanding and conciliation before final resort by the United Nations to violent means . . . Clearer than ever stands out the truth of the position to which you have held from the beginning. I still dare to hope that it is not too late for the world to follow in the path which you have laid out." This is a man who has over and over again "lifted a finger to help the Jews." He is not anti-Zionist, or anti-Semitic, or anti-Jewish.[6]

The second letter came from a Jew who is a true lover of Zion. He writes: "I feel more sure than ever that your solution was the right one. It will come to that . . . Have you communicated with Dean Gildersleeve? While I am a little suspicious that her Committee may have a pro-Arab orientation it might for that reason be of special help if you could sell them your idea."[7]

This Jew has been and still is of considerable aid to the Hebrew University. He has given some of its problems time and thought. As far as I am aware, he has also contributed in money more, with the exception of Dr. Wechsler,[8] than any of the "Zionist" members of the Board of Directors or the National Council of the American Friends of the Hebrew University, as I find them listed on the back of the Friends' stationery.

I do indeed feel sorry for you, holding your hat for the money which the University so sorely needs and which the public is so reluctant to give in adequate measure.

Are you serious when you seem to indicate that this is due to "the alienation of Zionist support from the University because of the political views of its President?"

Will you have the goodness to point to a Zionist who has refused substantial support to the University because of my views?

A couple of years ago when the "old story" was repeated, I asked that an investigation be made by the Friends. The result was that one lone contributor had withdrawn his support on my account. He had been contributing all of five dollars a year.

Will you have the goodness also to produce any authoritative official of the Keren Hayesod or Keren Kayemet, either in America or in Palestine, who will declare that either of these Funds would have voted substantial sums to the University, or would not vote them, if the views of the President did not stand in the way?

Kindly ask those who are collecting funds for the Medical School if the views of the President are an interference. Indeed, ask the members of the Medical Reference Board generally if they agree or differ with the President. Ask those scientists and scholars whom you are trying to persuade to come here, if they would prefer to come to a University with a President holding my views or with a President holding views on the side of the heresy-hunters. Ask Professor Einstein, who, on the stationery of the Friends, is Chairman of the National Council, and Professor Baron, who is Chairman of the Academic Council, or the other scientific men listed on the stationery.

When it came to applying to the UPA [United Palestine Appeal], it was I who was asked by the American Friends to appeal to the Chairman of the JDC. I notice also on the stationery that Mrs. Felix Warburg and Dr. Rosenbach[9] are Honorary Presidents of the Friends. Kindly ask them. Please ask also Mr. Walter Meyer[10] who is Treasurer and Mr. Eugene Untermyer who is Vice-President. Also Mr. Sonneborn[11] and Mr. Greenberg,[12] Vice-Presidents, whose Zionism no one will impugn.

Perhaps also you would ask Viscount Samuel and Mr. Gollancz[13] in your own England, also Sir Montague Burton,[14] who is one of the very few Jews in England showing genuine interest in the University. There was a time when I was told that the members of "a family were going to do grandiose things for the University," if only they could turn their money over to others, not to me. I gave them that opportunity when I withdrew as Chancellor in 1935 and permitted myself to be kicked upstairs as President—all "for the sake of the University." You know better than I how paltry their contributions have been all these years.

Please ask also the men and women at the University here, some of whom travel the dangerous road to Scopus—the teachers, laboratory workers, librarians and other personnel, the wives who have to stand in line for hours for a can of kerosene, the mothers who have lost their sons or who fear to lose them—if they would want the President of the University to be less eager for a truce and conciliation and peace than he is. Can you tell them that, if there were a President with other views, the financial disaster which threatens their living, might be averted?

If you can, then I am ready to make you the following offer: if any Zionist or Zionists are ready to put up a million dollars within the near future, I am ready to withdraw as President of the University. This is about half of the annual budget. With $500,000 cash in hand in America, arrangements for borrowing can be made here, which will tide the University over the next difficult months. The second $500,000 would enable the University to proceed without a catastrophic deficit staring it in the face.

In this connection I would be ready to do my best with those contributors to the University who have given money because of me—I think

471

they make up the bulk of the American contributors — to continue their contributions, despite this blow to the freedom and the spiritual character of the University.

This would not be easy for me. In these dangerous days, more than ever, I have come to believe that it is providential that a man with my views is President of the Hebrew University. I think that my views are rooted deep in the religious and ethical tradition of Judaism. The charge is made against the University, that it is the stronghold of those who are against chauvinism and terror, and who are for peace, understanding and cooperation with the Arabs and other peoples. I think this is so, and it is this which gives me more genuine cause for thankfulness than anything in life. If it is, in however small part, because of me that men have been encouraged to be true to their higher selves, what a great thing it is to have been President of the Hebrew University!

It would be difficult for me to sell out to the highest Zionist bidder for another reason, because the new Jerusalem, Zion, needs the Hebrew University as the breath of its life. The great mission of Judaism to build up an ethical society in the spirit of the Prophets of Israel can be furthered by the Hebrew University in Zion. I think I can contribute to this as President of the University.

But the financial position of the University is so perilous and my feeling for my associates here who would suffer, should there be a financial collapse, is so deep that I am ready to make this sacrifice, if this might help guarantee the modest salaries they and their families are dependent upon.

"The Magnes question," "the old story" has become quite stale. It is time that it be given an airing. Indeed, you are at liberty to publish this letter.

The fact that I am writing about all of this — for the first time in all these years — to you, should be an indication to you that I value your efforts on the University's behalf and want to be of help to you. I cannot, however, forbear saying how sad I am to see the translator of Plato and of Ahad Ha'am howling with the pack.

I am,

Sincerely yours, JLM

1. Simon urged Magnes not to give public support to the League for Justice and Peace in the Holy Land "for the sake of the university."

2. Simon warned Magnes that his support for the league, which was considered anti-Zionist and pro-Arab, would alienate Zionist support for the Hebrew University.

3. Magnes's March 8 letter requested information concerning the league and outlined Ihud's position favoring a binationalist state. The March 10 telegram, signed by Virginia Gildersleeve, Henry Sloane Coffin, Garland Evans Hopkins, and Kermit Roosevelt, summarized the league's program. Magnes's reply of March 14 summarized the Ihud program and concluded, "Greatly hope your Committee will advocate similar program."

4. Magnes stated that he favored bringing about a cease-fire, initiating efforts at concil-

iation, and doing everything to bring about peace. The statement was a response to a rumor, which Magnes denied, that he had met a member of the Arab Higher Committee in Cairo to consider the possibility of moderates from each side opening negotiations with a view toward achieving a peaceful solution to the conflict.

5. Simon wrote in his letter of March 7: "I am naturally against any interference with freedom of thought and expression. But I should be less than candid if I did not say that your recent letter in the *New York Times* in support of Virginia Gildersleeve has made me nearer than I ever was before to sympathize with the heresy-hunters."

6. John Haynes Holmes to JLM, March 6, 1948 (MP, 2489).

7. James Marshall to JLM, March 4, 1948, MP, 222.

8. Dr. Israel Wechsler (1886–1962). Physician; president of the American Friends of the Hebrew University.

9. Abraham S. Wolf Rosenbach (1876–1952). Bibliophile and dealer in rare books. Born in Philadelphia, he received his Ph.D. from the University of Pennsylvania; he headed Rosenbach Co., dealers in rare books and manuscripts.

10. Walter E. Meyer (1882–1957). Attorney, investment banker born in Los Angeles. During the First World War he was a staff member of the Council of National Defence; he was director of the Public National Bank and Trust Company and a trustee of Hebrew University.

11. Rudolf G. Sonneborn (b. 1898). Businessman, Zionist, philanthropist. He joined his family's oil and chemical firm, L. Sonneborn and Sons of New York City, in 1920. He was president of the American Financial and Redevelopment Corporation for Israel; raised funds for Haganah for purchasing arms and ships for Haganah following Second World War.

12. David B. Greenberg (1892–1968). Businessman and writer on wildlife and conservation. Born in Yonkers, N.Y., he received his bachelor's degree from Columbia University and studied at Cornell and the University of Wisconsin. He was active in rescue efforts on behalf of European Jews during the 1930s, aided the Hagana during the 1948 war, and supported the Hebrew University's medical school.

13. Sir Victor Gollancz (1893–1967). English publisher and author. He founded his own publishing house in 1928; sponsored various humanitarian causes; from 1945 onward opposed the British policy of advocating admission of Jewish refugees to Palestine; he advocated reconciliation between Jews and Arabs; was a trustee of Hebrew University.

14. Sir Montague Burton (1885–1952). Garment industrialist; established Montague Burton Ltd., one of world's largest men's wear concerns.

123

To Warren Austin
New York

Jerusalem, March 25, 1948

Dear Senator Austin,

I tried to listen today to the broadcast from Lake Success. It was a disappointment not to have heard the formal motion you had expected to present for giving effect to your interim trusteeship proposals. They will doubtless be forthcoming at the meeting on Tuesday, March 30. I hope that what I am writing may not be belated.

With each year, and at the present time with each day, a Jewish-Arab agreement which is the great desideratum, is made more difficult. But it is altogether possible. The Zionist and the Arab Higher Committee leaderships may be intransigent. But the mass of people, both Jew and Arab, and many Jews and Arabs of importance both in Palestine and elsewhere, even today, bear no enmity towards one another. On the contrary, they hope and pray for a cessation of this cruel warfare and for an Arab-Jewish agreement.

This agreement can hardly be achieved if the present leaders are required to sign on the dotted line at Lake Success. There is no time for that. But the agreement can be brought about if the interim trusteeship, which you propose, is to have as its main objective the *immediate* cooperation of both peoples, as equal partners, in the government of the country. They have never had the chance of self-government. That, to my mind, has been the great drawback all these years. The interim trusteeship should hold out to them this great opportunity at once. This will afford them the basis, also, of cooperation in other walks of life. It cannot all be achieved overnight. It will take time.

The trusteeship should last until its main objective is achieved — the cooperation of the two equal peoples in self-government. This would also include an agreement as to a substantial quota of Jewish immigration. I do not think the trusteeship need be of long duration. When this happens, then, and only then, the country will be ready for independence.

My friends and I of the Ihud Association have made such proposals for a bi-national Palestine with two equal peoples, neither dominating the other. The form can be cantonal (counties) or federal. These proposals have met with the approval of many persons, including Jews and Arabs, both in and out of Palestine.

I am sending you the proposals we made along these lines to the Anglo-American Committee of Inquiry and to UNSCOP.

I cannot tell you how deeply grateful I am that it is the United States which is now sponsoring the attempt at conciliation and understanding. That is the one and only way which gives promise of lasting results.

The purpose of my letter is to encourage you to believe that even though it may not be possible to get the Arab and Jewish leaders to sign a document at the present time, this is of but secondary importance. The essential thing is to give the Arabs and the Jews the chance now and here and without delay — a chance they never have had — of themselves governing Palestine as two equal peoples.

Keep up your valiant efforts. It will be to the glory of the United States and the United Nations, and to your own great renown.

Kindly remember me to Mrs. Austin, and with best regards, I am,

Sincerely yours, JLM

124

To Thomas C. Wasson
Jerusalem

Jerusalem, April 6, 1948

Dear Mr. Wasson,

I am complying with your request and am giving you some hastily prepared comments on the 15 U.S. points for the trusteeship over Palestine.

There is not the slightest doubt whatsoever in my mind that at the very least one half of the Jewish community of Jerusalem would be in favor of what I have suggested. Agudath Israel and other religious bodies, which have within the very recent past indicated to me their agreement with the general point of view of the Ihud Association, form at least 25 percent of the Jewish population. I know the Jewish population here well enough, after my residence here of over 25 years, to venture the assertion that at least 25 percent of the rest of the population — professors, physicians, teachers, officials, merchants, mothers — would be in favor of this.

I cannot speak so convincingly concerning the Jewish population of the remainder of Palestine. Nevertheless there can be no doubt that large sections of the Palestine Jewish community throughout the country would be favorable to these views.

One of the reasons for their readiness to accept the trusteeship proposals is the evident determination of the United States to participate.

I am,

Sincerely yours, JLM

COMMENTS ON THE 15 INFORMAL SUGGESTIONS PRESENTED BY THE UNITED STATES FOR THE PROPOSED TRUSTEESHIP OVER PALESTINE

1. It is very important to have said that the trusteeship agreement would be of indefinite duration, subject, however, to prompt termination whenever the Arab and Jewish communities in Palestine agree on the future government of their country.

2. It is, however, equally important to insist that Jews and Arabs be associated, if possible in equal numbers, with government under the trusteeship from the first day. This is of importance for the following reasons:

a. It would show that the trusteeship is not meant to be government by foreigners.
b. It would bring Arabs and Jews together in a way that no other activity could.
c. It would be the school for training Jews and Arabs in self-government over against the time that the trusteeship was terminated.
d. It would show that the main objective of the trusteeship policy was the systematic, day by day, active effort to bring about Jewish-Arab agreement not in word alone, but in the real concerns of everyday life; and it would thus afford an impulse to Arab-Jewish cooperation in other fields.

3. It is of the utmost importance that the Governor General be appointed at once. He must be a man of large intellectual and spiritual calibre and must feel that his is an unparalleled historic mission.

4. As far as the cabinet is concerned, it should consist of an equal number of Jews and Arabs.

5. There should be a democratically elected legislature. The question is, however, what "democratically elected" means in a country like Palestine? Whereas in some countries, democracy means only elections upon the basis of individual electors, in multinational countries, that is in countries with peoples or nationalities legally recognized as such, democracy means that in the central government the nationalities are equal, regardless of who is in the majority or in the minority. This is true, for example, in Switzerland or in Yugoslavia, or in some of the other multinational countries of the world. In this way, the question of majority and minority in Palestine, which has formed one of the chief difficulties in the discussion, would be eliminated.

6. The fact that the United States was inclined to favor the two-chamber legislature indicates that in the minds of the United States representative, the question of majority and minority was not to play a decisive role. In the United States the Senate consists of an equal number of representatives of each of the States, regardless of population.

7. Before elections take place, however, the country should be more or less pacified. This might take six months or a year.

8. Pending the establishment of an adequate force for maintaining law and order, it might save the situation if the British troops could remain until July 15th, giving the Governor General and his cabinet the opportunity of organizing the required forces.

9. Jewish immigration should be upon the basis of the economic absorptive capacity of the country and should be permitted up to parity with the Arabs. Unfortunately, the reservoir of possible Jewish immigrants has been greatly depleted since the extermination of 6 million Jews

in Europe during the war. It should be announced that the 100,000 displaced Jews, on behalf of whom President Truman made his plea two years ago, were to be given priority. This would probably include the refugees now in Cyprus.

JLM
April 6, 1948

125

To Maurice B. Hexter
New York

Jerusalem, April 6, 1948

Dear Dr. Hexter,

Your letters of March 22nd, March 25th, and March 29th with their enclosures arrived yesterday. So also did three additional envelopes containing the clippings from the *New York Times* up to March the 29th, without anything for March 22nd, 23rd, 27th and 28th. It may be that nothing appeared on those days, and it may be that another envelope is on its way with them.

I was particularly glad to get the paper of the 29th, because in that issue the statement of the American Jewish Committee appeared, as did our own. It would be instructive if someone were to compare those two statements from the point of view of the realities of the situation, of political wisdom, and of human feeling. There is not a single word in the statement of the American Jewish Committee favoring a truce.[1] What can men of leading positions be thinking of when they permit themselves to be involved in wordy, legalistic arguments at a time when the dead and the dying are multiplying in the land they allege they are trying to help? I wish one of them might come to Jerusalem at this moment. He would find that almost the entire population, without regard to political affiliation, is hoping and praying for this truce. You can probably have no idea what an electric response there has been to the Ihud support of a truce. Various groups in the community have come to see me and have promised their public support. It seems likely that an appeal is to be issued today or tomorrow by a number of prominent rabbis—not, of course, Chief Rabbi Herzog[2] who learned how to be bloodthirsty in Ireland. Everywhere one goes the same story is heard: it is time to stop, very little food, the strategic position of the Jews impossible. There have been threats by certain sections that they would hoist a white flag—they have lived with the Arabs before and can do it again. The bitterness against the Agency, the Va'ad Le'umi, and the Va'ad Hakehilla [executive of the Orthodox Jewish community] knows no bounds. They are accused of incompetence, of not having taken precautions, of playing with the lives and the fate of the community.

The lawyers of the American Jewish Committee know just a little too much. In their document of March 26th, enclosed in yours of March 29th, they say: "If the seven votes are obtained, one may expect a veto from Russia." Even Russia voted for a truce, but not the American Jewish Committee. Moreover, Russia abstained in the voting for a special session of the Assembly, but not the American Jewish Committee. In the American Jewish Committee public statement they already know that "it is plain the parties in Palestine will not agree to a temporary Trusteeship." The parties will have to agree to a temporary Trusteeship. There is no other way.

I am sorry to read about Nelson's [Glueck] part in fixing policy. I had had some indication of it. I am sorry that so early in his difficult and responsible tasks he has permitted himself to be jockeyed into this untenable position. If the High Commissioner had said, "Let there be peace"—what innocence! This is all the more surprising in one who has lived through some of these tense situations. The receipt of some of my letters must have embarrassed him.

That editorial in *Life* of March the 29th was very well done again. Who is the person who writes this? I am anxious also to see the article in *Fortune* when it appears.

This morning we have the tentative outlines of America's proposals for the Trusteeship. They are exceedingly good. The one doubtful feature is when the term "democracy" is used. If only we could get them to take "democracy" in the sense in which we have been trying to explain it for years, most recently in my letter to Senator Austin, of which I sent you a copy! "Democracy" in America means democracy based on individuals. Democracy in multinational countries means democracy based on peoples or nationalities. The democratic way is to keep the majority people from dominating the minority people. That is a great conception of democracy. I only fear that education in this sense has not proceeded far enough in America to carry the day in the Palestine issue. If that could be done, ever so many obstacles would be avoided.

You say in your letter of March 29th that that morning you had my cable, which was sent from here on March 22nd, and that you will write about the possibility of forming an Ad Hoc Committee. This should be all the easier seeing that the American Jewish Committee has set itself up in opposition, this time, to the policy of the United States Government.

That is probably not a pleasant situation to find themselves in. A strong Ad Hoc Committee, adopting our point of view, including that of a democracy based upon two equal peoples, regardless of majority and minority, might make a great difference.

Will you be good enough to share this letter with others.

With best regards,

I am,

Sincerely yours, JLM

P.S. I am sending copies to James Marshall, Ernst Simon (Jewish Theological Seminary) and Jonathan [Magnes].

You will find enclosed a copy of Sir Leon Simon's answer to my letter to him of March the 16th. This came yesterday. I almost felt sorry for the man who wrote so weak and meager a reply.

1. The statement reiterated the American Jewish Committee's support of the partition plan.
2. Isaac Halevi Herzog (1888–1959). Chief rabbi of Ireland, 1921–1936; chief Ashkenazi rabbi of Palestine, 1937 to his death.

126

To Thomas Mann
Palisades, California

Jerusalem, April 12, 1948

Dear Mr. Mann,

It was good hearing from you, even though we seem, for the first time, to be on opposite sides of the fence.

I do not wish further to deal with Miss Schultz's[1] misleading and vicious pamphlet. It was merely part of the enormous propaganda, which cost millions, and for which the population of Palestine is now paying — more than 7,000 casualties thus far. Of course this is almost nothing in comparison with the loss in the great war, and from that point of view you are doubtless right in scoffing at the "warfare" here. Yet we who live here cannot take the matter so lightly.

Permit me to give you another instance of the same kind of propaganda. On October 10 several American newspapers published a letter signed by Messrs. Buxton Cassidy, Crum, Gervasi, Horin, McDonald and Mowrer "conveying to the American press and through it to the

American people our evaluation of these threats," i.e. of the Arab States. "The Arab threats are mere bluff."

The great god Propaganda carried the partition resolutions through the United Nations Assembly. It was there declared over and over again that the only alternative to partition was chaos. That was absolutely false. There were and there are other alternatives. But the partition propaganda had done its work. The United States "pinched the arm" of some U.S. satellites. It is now seen that partition is not the alternative to chaos, but the cause of chaos.

This result was as clear as the fingers on your hand. Ever so many people warned against it. But such persons were tarnished with the terms which American propaganda knows how to use so well: As persons, you have our respectful admiration. But you are "idealists" or "lacking in realism," or the various other epithets of expert American propaganda.

Yes, Propaganda is a great god — but he has clay feet. He almost rules the world, but not quite. He embellishes facts, threatens them, twists them, suborns them, he even creates facts. Yet one fine day he encounters reality, and his clay feet collapse. There are certain hard realities which no propaganda can subvert, actual things "die hart im Raum sich stossen."[2] In theological language — truth does sometimes prevail.

The inescapable fact of the Palestine situation is that millions of Arabs live in Palestine and all around Palestine. No propaganda can change that, nor can any propaganda shut off the Palestine Arabs from the other Arabs, any more than propaganda can shut off the Palestine Jews from the rest of the Jews of the world.

The question is, are the Jews to live here at war with the Arabs or at peace? If it is to be war, I, for one, do not see any chance of real development for the Jewish National Home. If it is to be peace, partition is just the way to destroy peace.

You think the reversal of the U.S. support of partition "the most humiliating and revolting political event since the treachery against Czechoslovakia in 1938." I, on the other hand, think it the most humane and the wisest decision which American statesmanship could have taken.

It is humane because it calls for a cessation of this "warfare," for a stop to this blood-letting.

It is wise because it is an attempt — long since overdue — to meet the problem through conciliation, compromise, understanding, cooperation between Arabs and Jews.

I think I know as well as many others what the power politics behind all this is — and what the power politics behind the pro-partition decision was. The U.S., Great Britain, Russia — the Eastern Mediterranean, oil (in the first place for the Marshall Recovery Program), bases . . . If a war breaks out between the U.S. and Russia, that appears to me to be the greatest crime of history. But we are now talking of Palestine, and I can only welcome the fact, the reality, that, whatever the reasons, the U.S. is for peace here, for compromise and understanding, and I want to help, if possible, with my limited powers.

With kindest greetings,

I am,

Sincerely yours, JLM

1. Lillie Schultz, who wrote on Middle East affairs for the *Nation,* was the principal author of the memorandum submitted to the UN (see document 121).

2. "Things in a room are wont to collide."

127

To General G.H.A. MacMillan
General Officer Commanding British Troops in Palestine, Jerusalem

Jerusalem, April 18, 1948

Dear General MacMillan:

I thank you for your kindness in writing me in detail about the tragic happenings at Sheikh Jarrah on April 13 when seventy-six Hadassah Hospital and Hebrew University workers lost their lives and twenty were injured.[1]

We are grateful that after Brigadier Jones took charge of the situation himself in the late afternoon it was possible to save the lives of twenty-eight persons, twenty of whom were injured.

I am ready to accept all you say as to the course of events. Yet that does not at all answer the question which is being put to hundreds of persons and which I shall have to put to myself for the rest of my life. That question is, why were not these victims rescued? Why?

The vehicles were immobilized by a mine and heavy shooting at 9:45 A.M. The twenty-eight persons were rescued in the late afternoon. Thus hours and hours elapsed. This was not out in the desert, but in plain sight of Jerusalem, not far away from the Central Police Depot and a few yards away from the Military Post. These men at the post did their best. Why were they not reinforced; or why was not something else done in all those hours to extricate the trapped victims?

It is greatly to be regretted that British soldiers are losing their lives, particularly while they are in the process of withdrawing from the country. But who should have prevented such a catastrophe, if not the British Army and the British police?

You may be right in saying that this outrage was a direct reprisal for the IZL [Etsel]-Stern outrage at Deir Yassin.[2] I think you know how I have tried to exert whatever influence I have against terror. But whereas that may explain the ferocity of the Arab attack, does it answer the question that haunts me and others: why were these victims not rescued in the course of those interminable hours? Why?

I am leaving for New York in the hope that I may contribute to the peace of Jerusalem and of Palestine. If you care to answer my question, would you be good enough to send the answer c/o Dr. Davis,[3] Deputy Medical Director, Hadassah Medical Organization?

I am,

Sincerely yours, JLM

1. MacMillan wrote to Magnes on April 15, 1948, defending the British army's conduct in coming to the aid of the ambushed convoy. The road from the Jewish part of Jerusalem to Mount Scopus passed through the Arab neighborhood of Sheikh Jarrah close to several British army posts.

2. On April 9, 1948, a combined force of Etsel and Lehi attacked the Arab village of Deir Yassin in the outskirts of Jerusalem; two hundred of the villagers were killed, including women and children. The Jewish Agency and the Hagana command denounced the action.

3. Eli Davis (b. 1908). Born in Birzai, Lithuania; he received his M.D. from the University of Manchester. He emigrated to Palestine, 1946; was deputy director, 1946, and director, 1948–1951, of the Hadassah Medical Organization.

128

Report on Arrival in the United States

New York, April 26, 1948

MINUTES OF MEETING HELD IN GENERAL GREENBAUM'S OFFICE, APRIL 26, 1948

Present were: Ju·lge Jerome Frank[1]
Mrs. Adele Levy[2]
General Greenbaum[3]
Mr. Alan Stroock
Judge Horace Stern[4]

Mr. James Marshall
Dr. Maurice B. Hexter
Mr. Harold Linder[5]
Mr. Frank Altschul[6]
Mr. Lessing Rosenwald
Mr. David Sher[7]
Dr. Louis Finkelstein's[8] name was mentioned,
    but he was not present.

(Mention was made of a previous meeting having been held within the past few days at which Dr. Hexter, Dr. Finkelstein, General Greenbaum and others were present.)

Dr. Hexter opened the meeting with a summary of recent contacts with Dr. Magnes, mentioning the various efforts to arrange for Dr. Magnes's coming. He stressed the general feeling that nothing be done which might "avoid" the American Jewish Committee. It was hoped that a way would be found to dissuade the American Jewish Committee from its present policies and commitments, possibly suggesting a form of ad hoc committee (in conjunction with State Department policy).

Dr. Magnes spoke next. He conveyed thanks to General Greenbaum, Dr. Hexter, Mrs. Levy and in general for the presence of everyone at the meeting. He expressed a feeling of great encouragement to know of those in the United States who are trying to find their way — without being affected by "propaganda." He spoke in some detail of the force of propaganda as contrasted to the "road of reality," rather than other ways of unrealistic, futile "romanticism."

The Hadassah Hospital tragedy was described, plus the press statement issued thereafter by Dr. Magnes, and he referred to the telegram received from the American Friends of the Hebrew University concerning this statement as an illustration of the negative force of propaganda. When facts begin to strike at propaganda, its entire machinery crumbles.

Among the facts Dr. Magnes wished to speak about were:

A. Concerning Jerusalem — the U.N. proposal to appoint a committee to safeguard the "holy places" and the "peoples" of Jerusalem.

The holy places are not a matter of concern — they will not be touched. It is the peoples which one must be concerned over.

Dr. Magnes described his experiences in Jerusalem during the past weeks, of receiving many letters, signed and unsigned, of talking to many people, known and unknown — his feeling, in general, of what a great and rare privilege it was for a man to experience human response to his own convictions. The tragedy of the times is most unfortunately responsible in large measure for this response. The great majority of Jerusalem's population are now on "our side." The personal Z'chut [privilege] of knowing this in one's own lifetime is indeed a great thing.

Dr. Magnes exhibited the weekly Ihud paper being issued in Palestine, and also posters that were being pasted up throughout Jerusalem. These posters, he said, are often torn down, then re-pasted. He was asked whether they did not receive threats from the people, and answered: "Of course we receive threats!"

B. Dr. Magnes described his home in Rehavia, a Jewish sector of Jerusalem, which is situated at the ridge of a gully. At one side of this gully stands the old monastery of "M'Salabe" and at the other, the residential sector of Katamon. He is in the habit of taking a walk at night, and the only safe place to walk is the area of a few yards directly in front of his house, since from all other directions the danger of stray bullets from snipers and from British two-pounders is very great.

He had formerly resided for many years in a predominantly Arab sector of the city, and due to an unfortunate incident involving the killing of a taxi driver outside his house, felt compelled to move. This Arab sector was in the very heart of the houses belonging to the two prominent and continually feuding Arab families, Nashashibi and Ḥusayni. Very often Dr. Magnes found himself meeting with members of one or the other of these families, and serving as a sort of information messenger between them. Dr. Magnes also described in some detail other relationships with various Arab leaders throughout the years.

He was interested to note in the American press for the first time the use of a phrase which he himself has often used: "fear of fighting in the streets of Jerusalem." This is a very real danger. He gave further details in describing conditions in the streets of Jerusalem, the shops, the battered buildings, etc.

C. To the question, "What measures can be taken for safeguarding Jerusalem?" Dr. Magnes emphasized that only through a truce at the earliest possible moment, and through a commission sent to Jerusalem for the purpose of setting up a provisional government, could this be achieved. *Not* by sending of troops, although the commission should have adequate protection for its own safety, and to enable it to carry out its functions.

D. As to the rest of Palestine, first came the problem of clearing the ways into Jerusalem. In Tel-Aviv, for example, life proceeds in an almost routine fashion, and such undoubtedly is the case in many other parts of the country. How much of the strife is actually felt in the rest of Palestine, Dr. Magnes could not venture to say. However, it would appear that there was a semblance of normal living and a different spirit in certain places outside of Jerusalem.

The Ihud has an active group in Tel-Aviv. Owing to the great difficulty in communicating with Jerusalem and other parts of the country, this group acts in a more or less independent way.

E. As to the Jews of Palestine generally, Dr. Magnes poses the question: "What do we want in Palestine?" wherever he goes. He is convinced that the answer from 100 percent of the population is: "Aliyah and B'niyah!" — or, Immigration and Upbuilding.

What then, about the "Medinah" — the State? Whereas he does not know the percentage in numbers, he would not hesitate to say that the great mass of the Jewish populace say that if only they could have their "Aliyah" and "B'niyah," — their Immigration and their Upbuilding for the next 20 to 30 years, one needn't have the "Medinah" — the State.

F. Mrs. Levy asked: did he mean that one needn't *ever* have a State? to which he replied: he did not mean ever but *now*.

Dr. Magnes and many other people have come to curse the Biltmore Program advocating statehood. The state can be achieved only through war, and war does not build up. Building up can be achieved only through cooperation. What would happen if we were given another 20 to 30 years for building up? It would mean 30 more years of fruitful progress, which is so evident today as a result of the past 30 years, despite all the difficulties which we have faced.

Yes, we can "take," Haifa, Tiberias, Jaffa, and many other points, but we'll be like the Germans — we'll lose the war. Professor Herman Cohen, a German historian, once compared the Jews to the Germans.

But we'll lose the war.

Why?

1. There are millions upon millions of Moslems in the world.

2. They have time. The timelessness of the desert.

3. We are in a hurry, because of our tragedy.

4. Arab life is cheaper. When a Hebrew University Professor of Psychology is burned to death, a personality is gone. When a student of the Hebrew University is shot, a personality is gone. When a man who has survived the agonies and tortures of a concentration camp, who has lost the members of his entire family, is killed, that is a deep tragedy.

On the other hand, when a simple Arab fellah, or peasant, is killed, he leaves a family behind in some obscure village perhaps, and his family gets used to it. It is a question of millions upon millions of Moslems being able to afford what for them is a relatively cheap sacrifice of lives as against the pitifully small remnant of world Jewry.

5. What will happen on May 16? If a provisional council of Jewish government is proclaimed, as has been announced,

(a) What will the international status of such a government be?
(b) What will the attitude of the neighboring Arab countries be? Such a government will have no real status. The United States has already declared that it will not recognize such a government.

485

To the question, "What about Russia?" Dr. Magnes replied that it may well be that Russia would recognize such a state, in which case the situation could only become a more complicated international affair.

In all probability the Arabs will declare a provisional council of government over all of Palestine on May 16, thus creating two rival states, one within the other. May 16 may very well become the very moment when the neighboring Arab states will send their regular armies into Palestine. Up until now, the many trained Arab soldiers who have been infiltrating from neighboring countries into Palestine have been for the main part mercenaries and adventurers. Although they have come there with the approval of those countries, they have not as yet been dispatched as regular organized armies.

6. It is possible that with the formation of two such provisional councils of government, or states, the United States government may impose economic sanctions with regard to Palestine. The United States is capable of refusing to permit any monies to be sent abroad from this country, and also ammunition. How can a war be fought without money and without ammunition? With regard to the oil concessions in the Middle East, the Arabs are greatly in need of United States dollars for this oil. The United States could impose economic sanctions upon the Arab states in refusing to buy such oil. Such a sanction could easily have serious international repercussions, inasmuch as it has been understood that in connection with the European Recovery Program, no oil from the United States proper be shipped to Europe. It is assumed that all shipments of oil for the ERP are to come from the areas in the Middle East.

7. Dr. Magnes criticized what he termed the "apologetic" attitude on the part of the American government in regard to Palestine. Granting that partition was accepted by many as an American policy, he feels that the American government at this moment at least, should be frank and admit that perhaps a mistake has been made. He, personally, believes that the present United States policy on Palestine is a good one, and should have been proposed at the very start. He dwelt at some length upon the methods of setting up a provisional government in Palestine, emphasizing that only through the insistence of admitting Jews and Arabs into key government positions from the very beginning could such a scheme be effectively feasible. He referred to his talk with Senator Austin, in which the Senator was enthusiastic about deleting from a draft of United States proposals in connection with Jewish and Arab government positions, the words "whenever practicable."

He stated, moreover, that publication of the Morrison-Grady Report[9] on Palestine at this time would be of great help. He referred to British unconstitutional procedure in her manner of relinquishing the mandate for Palestine as the greatest blunder committed. The U.N. charter states specifically that in turning over a mandated territory, the first step should be the setting up of a trusteeship, instead of which Britain simply threw the whole matter into the laps of the United Nations, or as he would rather put it, threw it into their faces.

When listening over the radio in Jerusalem to the voting on partition at Lake Success last November, he heard the Polish delegate say, "At last we have a success!" Dr. Magnes said to himself at that time, "Heaven help us from such a 'success.' "

He urged that the American government stop apologizing for what has been done before. He was greatly interested and encouraged upon hearing that the United Nations, through its Social and Economic Council, is considering the formation of a Middle East Commission. In conclusion, Dr. Magnes restated his conviction that, given another 30 years of upbuilding, together with compassionate immigration, Palestine can become *ours* — not by force of arms, not by force of statehood, not by conflict — but *ours* with cooperation.

There followed a series of questions:

If a truce is possible, will any attention be paid to it?

What about immigration?

Is it too late to use the proposal of the Lebanese delegate for a Near Eastern federation?

Can other Jews be helpful by stating their views in direct opposition to the present Zionist program?

Can the terrorists be contained?

What impact does the Russian "threat" have in the picture?

What is the attitude of the yishuv on Russia?

What about Russia and trusteeship?

Is Russia, or would she become, an ally of the nationalists?

What about American policy on Palestine in view of the coming elections?

The meeting then broke up and a few of the gentlemen stayed to talk with Dr. Magnes.

Another point discussed during the meeting was that of the position that the American Jewish Committee could take in this picture. It was argued that the President of the American Jewish Committee could "still" be dissuaded. However, the problem of dealing with Governor Lehman appeared to pose some difficulties. Inasmuch as a meeting of the leaders of the American Jewish Committee is to take place next Saturday, it was hoped that some solution might be reached.

1. Jerome N. Frank (1889–1957). Public administrator, jurist, and legal scholar. Born in New York City, he was an adviser to President Roosevelt, administering various New Deal programs. He was appointed to the United States Court of Appeals in 1941. He served on the executive committee of the American Council for Judaism, but in October 1947 he assisted the Jewish Agency in the negotiations at the UN over partition.

2. Mrs. Adele Levy, née Rosenwald (1892–1960). Born in Chicago, the daughter of Julius Rosenwald; civic worker and philanthropist. She was a member of the New York City Youth Board, 1947, and from 1956 a member of the New York State Youth Commission; first chairlady, National Women's Division of the United Jewish Appeal, 1946–1948.

3. Edward S. Greenbaum (1890–1970). Born in New York City; lawyer, public official. During the Second World War he was principal aide to Secretary of War; served on executive committee of Jewish Welfare Board, American Jewish Committee.

4. Horace Stern (1879–1969). Born in Philadelphia. He was appointed judge, Common Pleas Court of Philadelphia, 1930; elected to Pennsylvania Supreme Court, 1935, and served as its chief justice, 1952–1957.

5. Harold F. Linder (b. 1900). Born in Brooklyn. He entered industrial management and finance; was a partner, Carl Loeb, Rhoades and Co., 1933–1938; president, General American Investors Company, 1948–1955; president, chairman, Export-Import Bank, 1961–1968; U.S. Ambassador to Canada, 1968–1969; trustee, Institute for Advanced Study, 1949, and chairman of the board of trustees, 1969–1972.

6. Frank Altschul (b. 1887). Born in San Francisco; chairman, Board of General American Investor Co.; vice-chairman, Council on Foreign Relations; member, executive committee, American Jewish Committee.

7. David Sher (b. 1908). Born in Omaha. He became a lawyer; partner in Stroock and Stroock and Lavan since 1945; served on administrative committee of American Jewish Committee, and was vice-president, 1948–1952; president, Jewish Family Service, 1949–1954.

8. Louis Finkelstein (b. 1895). Born in Cincinnati; rabbi, scholar, educator. From 1931 he was professor of theology, Jewish Theological Seminary, and was president, 1940; chancellor from 1951; leading figure in Conservative wing of Judaism.

9. The Morrison-Grady plan, proposed in July 1946, envisioned dividing Palestine into four areas (Arab, Jewish, Jerusalem, and the Negev), with the British having exclusive authority over security and foreign affairs. An amended version was prepared in early 1947. The minority report of the United Nations Special Committee on Palestine incorporated features of the plan in its recommendations.

129

Journal: Interview with George C. Marshall

Washington, D.C., May 5, 1948

May 5, 1948. My interview yesterday (4.V.48) with Secretary of State Marshall lasted from 2:30 P.M. to 3:25 P.M. At the end he said he was sorry he had to stop. There was more to talk about.

We first talked about health. I said I was one of the lucky ones because my doctors really seemed to know what the matter with me was; and I followed their instructions. He said he had been avoiding doctors for seven years, and finally they whittled a big piece of him away. How did I stand high altitudes? I said flying across the Atlantic was no strain whatever. He said he was at Bogotá for six weeks and that was about

8500 feet up. He had an oxygen apparatus, and he would use it every once in a while. He was the only one not sick. Mr. McClintock of the UNO[1] desk who accompanied me asked what a fowler bed was. I described it, and the Secretary said: a hospital bed. I said it rented for $10 a month. The Secretary said $120 a year was too much. I said he could buy one probably for $50.

He then talked quite a bit about General Dill[2] without whom we would not have won the war. He knew everything that Dill wrote or received, and Dill the same with him. There was a relationship of absolute confidence between them. Each knowing everything the other did, it made no difference what the other members of the General Staff had to offer — some of Churchill's political suggestions, for example. A monument was being erected to him. I said that I knew Dill and had found him a man of great charm and knowledge. Of all the military commanders I had met in Jerusalem he seemed to me to be outstanding. I remarked that Jerusalem was 3000 feet above sea level. The Secretary said he did not realize it was so high. He had been there when the combined staffs had met — in 1944(?) — after President Roosevelt had determined to take over the command in the Mediterranean himself. (I do not know if I caught this right.) I said I remembered that the area of the King David Hotel had been blocked off at the time.

It was the lack of trust which was ruining the world. It was hard to establish a basis of confidence with Russia and others. That was the trouble in the Palestine issue, too. Besides, there was this great stream of propaganda — one hardly knew what to believe. Then there was politics. He himself was a soldier and did not go in much for votes — I said others did, thereat he smiled broadly: How could he be intimidated by the threats of either the Jews or the Arabs? On the military side he said he could foresee what was going to happen. The Jews had won the first battles like the Germans did; and they would lose the war. It would be well for them to make terms now. Besides, the economic strain of a war was very great, and the Palestine Jewish economy was largely artificial.

I said it pleased me to hear him say this about the war. I felt the same way about it. Besides the Arabs had plenty of time — if not this year, then the next or the next. Whereas we were in a hurry — we had thousands of displaced persons to settle. Inasmuch as he had mentioned the economic strain, I should like to take up a point which I did reluctantly but which might be decisive. The U.S. could exercise financial sanctions on both the Jews and the Arabs. We were largely dependent upon collections in America for both the beautiful things that were being done there and for the war. We had achieved fine things — farms, hospitals, a university. But the war was swallowing up our substance. The Arabs also were dependent on American dollars. He interjected, "Syria is pretty shaky." Mr.

McClintock added, "and Iraq." Doubtless the other Arab countries also were dependent on American financial collaboration. The Hagana had been costing $4,000,000 a month, and I did not know how much the upkeep of the Arab mercenaries and armies was costing. He asked if this proposed embargo applied also to commercial transactions as well. I said I hoped not. He said he thought it might be difficult to differentiate. I said I thought that financial sanctions should be applied only as a last resort, if there was no other way of stopping the warfare, and that they would have to be applied equally to the Arabs and the Jews. He thought the financial — as well as the arms embargo, if necessary — should be United Nations and not just U.S.A.

It seemed to be agreed, I said, that the main thing now was to try to get a truce. But the prospects of getting either a voluntary truce or an imposed truce 6000 miles away seemed rather slim. As to the voluntary truce, I understood that there were no prospects of getting agreement as to immigration. As to an imposed truce, it seemed that only the U.S.A. had declared its readiness to participate in enforcing an imposed truce. The question was, what was to be done in the few days at our disposal? I thought that the chief thing to be done was to have the UN appear in Palestine, i.e. that a man or men should appear there with the backing of the UN, speaking with the voice of the UN.

He asked how I meant that. I said I had three things in mind.

First Jerusalem. I had lived there for more than 25 years, and I thought I could speak for both the Jews and the Arabs. I had been particularly close to the community during the past several weeks. The people of Jerusalem were sick unto death of this conflict. They wanted it to end. They were praying for deliverance. I was afraid that that could not come from within the community. It had to come from the UN or the U.S.A. The people were ready. If I might use a military term, Jerusalem could be captured without firing a single shot. What had to be done and done at once was the despatch there promptly of a special UN representative. The people would welcome him and help him. All he needed was a secretary and a bodyguard — how large this should be I had not the competence to say — 10 men or 100. There were Jewish and Arab municipal police. He could begin with them, and he would quickly find the way on the spot of extending the truce to all parts of Jerusalem. I was sure millions of American citizens would applaud their government if such a step were taken.

The special representative should be a man out of the religious life. General Marshall asked if I had any names. I mentioned Bishop Oxman[3] and Charles P. Taft.[4] He thought the latter particularly good. The UN representatives would also have to see that certain municipal services were continued. He would have the help of the Jewish Council and the

Arab Council. If thought necessary, I was ready to go along with him to help him. Mr. McClintock asked if there was not danger from the Irgun and Sternists. My reply was that there was always this danger in whatever answer was given. Our terrorists were courageous, idealistic, ruthless, with a sense of mission. How they were to be handled I didn't know except that they were to be seized in some way or other.

As to the rest of Palestine, a governor general should be despatched without delay. He would have to be a man of action and of courage and decision. He should be sent even though the war was going on. The Secretary asked if I had anyone in mind. I said that a man like [Lord Louis] Mountbatten would be the type but that being a Britisher he was probably not acceptable. The Secretary agreed and said in addition that Mountbatten was pretty well worn down by all that he had been doing — first in Burma and then in India, where the loss of life had been so appalling. Mr. McClintock then asked the General if there might not be some men in his own army who might measure up to the task. The general asked, "Who?" The answer was General Mark Clark,[5] and that met with General Marshall's immediate approval. He had done a great job in Vienna. He was vigorous, courageous, and knew how to handle people. He had had a guard of about 12 nationalities. His mother was a Jewess and that would be of advantage. I said the fact I did not know he was half-Jewish indicated he wasn't much of a Jew. The Secretary was amused at this. The Secretary said he was available because he was now commanding about 22 men at the Presidio in San Francisco. The name of an Admiral was also mentioned. The Secretary said he was a good man, but rather quiet. Probably a more vigorous man was needed.

I stressed the Indonesian precedent. The war between the Indonesians and the Dutch was going on. But the Consular Commission was appointed and then the Truce Commission, and I recalled that one of the difficult problems was behind what line the two forces should retire in order to conclude the truce. The UN man should go to Palestine. His first task would be to effectuate the truce that was not brought about here. He could do this best if he appointed a cabinet or council of moderate Jews and Arabs — half and half. They would help him not only in the truce, but as a kind of central authority to keep certain essential services running such as food, electricity, ports.

I said I would permit myself to be somewhat frank in stating that American spokesmen had been rather too apologetic in their advocacy of the American trusteeship proposals, whereas the truce was the important thing at the moment. One of the purposes of the truce was to provide the opportunity for some kind of political settlement. I did not think that this political settlement could take place except within the framework of trusteeship. The essence of trusteeship was that there was some kind of authority at the center holding Palestine together as an integral land. This authority at the center could have a very light hand or large powers; that would depend upon the situation. Trusteeship was a flexible conception. It could permit a variety of governmental forms. Under trusteeship there could be a Jewish province, or canton, or even state, or an Arab province, canton, or even state, but they would be held together in a federal union. I said that the expression used by the American trusteeship proposals that temporary trusteeship should be without prejudice to the eventual political settlement, ought to be amended to read "without prejudice to the eventual political settlement to be worked out by the Arabs and the Jews." I thought that it was entirely clear that no settlement of the Palestine problem was possible unless the Arabs and the Jews could be gotten together to work out their own salvation. Trusteeship would offer them this opportunity.

I thought that the fundamental error of the British was that they had not carried out one of the chief purposes of the mandate, namely to associate Jews or Arabs more and more in government and in important positions so that there might at the end of the mandate be a large measure of self-government. Instead, the British had fewer and fewer Jews and Arabs in positions of central authority. During the past few weeks it is said that over 2,800 British officials, aside from the British police and army, had left the country. Surely it was possible to find 2,800 Jews and Arabs who might have filled these positions equally well. I didn't want to say that some of the Britishers had not done a good job. Some of them had. My favorite example was the Department of Archaeology of the Government. A fine young Britisher was at the head of the department. I asked him if he didn't think that Professor Mayer[6] of the Hebrew University could not fill his post equally well. His answer was, "He could do it better." "Why then," I asked, "are you in that post?" His answer was, "Why are all these posts occupied by Britishers?" The regime of the British at the center was more or less foreign to the people. If the special emissary to the United Nations were to go to Palestine, it should be made mandatory upon him to constitute a cabinet, or council, or staff, whatever it be called, of Jews and Arabs in equal proportions. In that way he could make headway, and I was convinced that he could not only bring about a truce, but that he could establish the beginnings of a central authority which would, at the very least, keep certain central services from disintegrating.

The Secretary said that this was the first account of the Palestine situation in which he could believe. Heretofore, he had always had the feeling that there was some partisan propaganda behind the accounts of which he had heard. He only wished that it were possible to find two or three or four Jews and Arabs with whom he could sit down and talk the problem over in this manner. What I had said had inspired his confidence. He said that he was sorry that the conversation had to end, and as he was taking me toward the door, he asked if I had seen the President. I said no, but that I should like to. He then asked Mr. McClintock to make arrangements for me to see the President. He said, "You talk to the President just like you talked to me."

As we were standing there taking leave of one another, I said: "Mr. Secretary, I should like to put a direct question to you: Is there any chance of imposing a truce?" He thought for a moment and said, "When you say 'impose', that means, does it not, the use of military force? I am very reluctant to take that step. As you are aware, the United States has offered to participate in a military force for Palestine, provided other governments did the same. Thus far, no government has come forward. That means that Uncle Sam would be left in the middle to bear the whole brunt. I do not think this advisable, but I shall give the matter further thought."

As he escorted me to the door and I went out first I overheard him say to Mr. McClintock who came out afterwards: "He wouldn't make a bad Governor General himself."

Naturally, I felt very flattered by what he said to me. On the other hand, it made me sad to think that this was the first talk on Palestine in which he had complete confidence.

After the talk with Secretary Marshall, Dr. Geiger[7] and I were with Loy Henderson[8] and a young man named Wilkins for more than an hour. We went over the same ground as that with the Secretary of State. He was greatly interested in our posters. I left the colored Arabic poster for photostating. He said it was encouraging to have me here. Sometimes they think at the State Department that what they know and do is all wrong because of the opposition it stirs up. I said, "America will have to say, 'We thought we were doing a good thing by advocating partition.' " ("We really did," he said.) We find bad results, therefore retrace our steps and take the course laid down by the constitution, i.e. the Charter, for the transfer of mandated territory. He thought English reinforcements were being sent in order to hold both the Arab states and the Hagana back. But the State Department was not in English confidence.

1. Robet M. McClintock (see glossary of names).
2. Field Marshall Sir John Greer Dill (1881–1944). He was assigned as the head of the British joint staff mission to Washington, 1941 to 1944; commander of British forces in Palestine, 1936–1937.
3. Garfield Bromley Oxman (1891–1963). Minister, Methodist Episcopal Church; president of Federal Council of Churches, 1944–1946; president, World Council of Churches, 1948–1954.
4. Charles P. Taft (b. 1897). Born in Cincinnati, son of William Howard Taft. A lawyer, he was president of the Federal Council of the Churches of Christ, 1947–1948.
5. Mark Clark (b. 1896). Commanding general Fifth Army, 1943–1945; commander-

in-chief, U.S. occupation forces in Austria and member of Allied Commission for Austria; commander-in-chief, UN forces in Korea, 1952–1953.

6. Leo A. Mayer (1895–1959). Orientalist; born in Stanislav, Austrian Poland. He settled in Palestine in 1921. He was inspector, Department of Antiquities, Government of Palestine, 1921–1929; librarian, Palestine Archaeological Museum, 1929–1932; professor of Near Eastern Art and Archaeology, Hebrew University, from 1932.

7. Alexander Geiger (1900–1963). Physician and professor of physiology at Hebrew University. He was Magnes's personal physician on his trip to the United States in 1948.

8. Loy W. Henderson (b. 1892). U.S. career diplomat; from 1943 to 1945 ambassador to Iraq; headed the Office of Near Eastern and African Affairs from 1945.

130

Journal: Interview with President Harry S. Truman

Washington, D.C., May 6, 1948

May 6, 1948. I was with President Truman, Wednesday morning, 5.V.48, from 10:35 to 11:05. I was told it would be fifteen minutes. It was an "off the record" appointment, i.e. it was not officially known to the reporters, and I was brought in by the side entrance (west side) and escorted to the east side where visitors come and go. I had been expected at the east entrance, but my cicerone, Mr. McClintock, made a shortcut into the west side entrance. After he had shown a paper and passed a police guard, we were greeted by a Mr. Simms (?), who asked why we had not come in from the east — old ?[1] was waiting for us there. Then we were taken through two other rooms, where some other guy (younger) shook hands. Dr. Geiger, Mr. McClintock, and I waited in a room with a very large table, red leather chairs and couch, plenty of paintings and prints on the walls. Suddenly I heard, "The President is ready to see Dr. Magnes." I was taken into an office-like room where another guy shook hands, and the door was opened into the President's beautiful, large, not too large, rather circular room — sunshine pouring in through the many windows overlooking lawn and gardens.

The President said that he had heard of our educational work in Palestine, and he wanted me to know that he was very deeply concerned about the whole problem. He thought it not exaggerated to say that there was probably no head of state who felt so deeply about the problem and who knew as much about it as he did. It was a question to which the answer had to be found — otherwise the peace of the world would be disturbed.

494

I told him in brief of my conversation with the Secretary of State. As far as I could make out, he had not yet had time to read the report of my interview which had been sent to him. Two or three times he asked, "Did you tell that to General Marshall?" I said that I did. At the end of my statement which I tried to make as brief as possible, and in which I tried also to emphasize Jerusalem as much as possible, he said, "Is not General Marshall a wonderful man? He is doing this job for me at a great sacrifice." Later I was told that the allusion was to General Marshall's health.

When I mentioned the names of Bishop Oxman and of Charles P. Taft as men out of religious life of America who might serve as special emissaries for Jerusalem, he said, "Not Bishop Oxman. He is a bigot. We don't want bigots to go to Jerusalem." He then explained that he had continued the policy of Mr. Roosevelt of having Myron Taylor as special representative to the Vatican. "Bishop Oxman was constantly at me to try to get me to revoke this appointment.

He said in relation to the Anglo-American Committee's Report, that that was a great document and he knew it almost by heart. Bevin had double-crossed him on that. Bevin had said that if the report were unanimous he would carry it out. He never thought it would be unanimous, but it was. I said, "It was a thousand pities that that report had not been carried out. We might have been spared much of this present misery." He said, "That report is right here in this drawer at my side. I take it out every once in a while and go through it." He then opened a drawer and remarked that that was a mighty precious drawer because it contained also the Charter of the United Nations and the documents on the European Recovery Plan. After going through a few papers in the drawer, he took out the Anglo-American Committee's Report which seemed to be prepared especially for him and which had a large number of tabs at the edge of various pages. He said, "Here it is. You see that it is a document that I could consult. I do consult it. But let's not talk of the past. What about tomorrow? I said there were but a few days left before May 15, one might say hours, and if anything was to be done it ought to be done at once. He then said, "The Jews refused my plane offer." I said, "I know they did, and I regretted that more than I could say because it was just along the lines that I was advocating, namely that by sending people to Palestine itself much more could be achieved than through these endless debates here, 6,000 miles away." When he said that the Jews had refused his offer of a plane, I did not ask him if the Arabs had accepted the offer.[2]

He said among his dreams had been that the peoples whose life was based more or less upon the same moral code might get to understand one another. Jews had a Mosaic code. The Christians had the same code and the Sermon on the Mount which really meant, "Do unto others . . ." The Moslems' moral code was also based on this moral code. He had dreamed that these peoples might get to understand one another better and might help to lift the world from the materialism which was holding the world down to the ground and might destroy it. If these peoples with a common moral code could understand one another and make some kind of common cause with one another, Russia would not have a spiritual leg to stand on. "But here it is — you Jews and you Arabs are spoiling things. You are not giving the Jews and the Christians and the Moslems of the rest of the world a chance to have confidence in one another. That is one of the reasons why I deplore so deeply this conflict in the Holy Land."

I mentioned the contribution which the Jews through their science and devotion and experience of the West might make towards the development of the whole Middle East, if only we could have peace between the Jews and the Arabs in the Holy Land. He said that was as he was always saying and he took me to a globe at the other end of the room, and laid his hand on Turkey and Iraq and said, "These waters used to feed at least 15,000,000 in antiquity. That is one of the things that we ought to try to do, to develop the great natural resources of this Middle East, so backward today, so remarkable in the past, and so full of hope for the future. If only you Jews and you Arabs will let us do it." He then said that when he was in Potsdam he wanted to have the old Danube opened up and all the great river ways and great straits opened up in order to afford the world opportunity of free commerce. I said, "In order to make a free world." He said, "That is exactly what we haven't got and what we require."

When we returned to his desk he said, "You see how close we are to one another. That is because we have similar views as to the Holy Land and all that great part of the world. That is the way we should all be in relation to this problem, close to one another, instead of as now, fighting one another."

As the time seemed to be drawing nearer for me to leave, I said, "Mr. President, there is one thing that I should like to leave with you. Do not give up. No matter what the obstacles, keep on trying. We must save the Holy City, we must save the Holy Land." He said rather emphatically, "Dr. Magnes, we won't give up! We shall hang on to this until we find a way. That is our duty."

Dr. Geiger had been waiting for me in the office and we were taken by an old darkie — he had been at the White House for 28 years — through other rooms and offices and through the portico into that part of the White House where visitors were coming and going. At the door some man shook hands with us and said, "I was waiting for you before. You came in on the west side and I was waiting here on the east side."

We were put into a car of the Department of State and driven to the hotel.

When I mentioned trusteeship, I said that the essence of it was to have some sort of central authority, some binding force to hold the parts of Palestine together. That was its essence. The rest was detail. He said yes, he understood that.

1. An official or attendant whose name Magnes evidently failed to recall.
2. On May 3, 1948 the State Department proposed a ten-day cease-fire, extending the British mandate for that period of time, and flying representatives of the Arab Higher Committee and the Jewish Agency to a site in the Middle East to negotiate an armistice agreement. The President placed his personal plane at the disposal of the two delegations.

131

Journal: Political Conversations

New York, June 1, 1948

Telephone conversation with Mr. Henderson at State Department at 9:30 A.M.

He said he would telegraph the U.S. Consul at Haifa mentioning the name of our son David Magnes of Natanya, age 38, born in New York and holding a U.S. passport and his wife Nora, born in England and holding an English passport. This was in connection with the report in this morning's press that Natanya had been occupied by Iraqi troops and that a ship had fired two shells into Natanya from the sea. We did not know what our son's intentions were or where he was, but we thought it our duty to mention his name in this way so that he and his wife might perhaps be helped in case of emergency.

He agreed that the proposed armistice for four weeks was a God-given opportunity for bringing about some kind of political settlement. If it is accepted by both states, I said I would be wanting to get into touch with various persons here in order to suggest a federal solution. He and I had talked this over when the policy of the U.S. Government had been trusteeship. If it were necessary to retain the term "State," the whole structure might be called the United States of Palestine. He agreed with this. I asked for suggestions as to procedure. He thought I ought to see Senator Austin. I asked if I ought to come to Washington again to bring the federal idea before the Secretary of State. He thought it would be most helpful if I worked the idea out a bit and had preliminary conversations before determining whether or not to come to Washington. I said

497

that I was of two minds as to whether I ought to be here or in Jerusalem. He understood the conflict but he thought that if the truce came about, I might find it advisable to be in Palestine to help Bernadotte.

Yesterday in a phone conversation with Mr. Power,[1] Deputy Secretary General of the United States Mission, he thought that I ought to try to see not only the United States Delegation but also the Delegations of France and Belgium as being the two countries on the Truce Commission together with the United States in Palestine. He added also the Canadian delegation although they had not been given much leeway by their government.

He said that Bernadotte[2] had changed his plans about staying in Athens and was arriving in Haifa whence he expected to motor at once to Tel Aviv.

As to Harold Evans,[3] he said that the telegram had come in just about ten minutes before to the effect that Dr. Ascarate[4] had been informed by the Arabs that Mr. Evans's presence in Jerusalem was no longer required. Dr. Ascarate had protested against this, and the answer had been that Mr. Evans should go to Amman to take the question up with higher authority there. I said to Mr. Power: "What a pity. He seems to have missed the bus." Mr. Power seemed to agree.

Conversation with Fawzi Bey,[5] Sunday, P.M., May 30

I expressed the hope that the Arabs would agree to the four weeks' armistice. He said that he himself was in favor of it and that he regarded it as perhaps the last opportunity for arriving at some kind of settlement without a protracted war. I said that now was the time to bring forward some kind of federal solution. If necessary the federal structure could be called the United States of Palestine. We had talked this over before and had been in agreement on it. I said I had been deeply impressed by what Dr. Malik[6] had said on Friday, May 28, at Lake Success as reported in the *New York Times*, and by what I had heard him say over the radio at Lake Success yesterday. This led him to the suggestion that if the truce were to be accepted by both sides it might be helpful if Fawzi were to invite me to meet with a number of his friends to talk the whole question over. He said that he himself had been considering the same idea and that he thought it was most likely that such a discussion would take place.

This morning, June 1, he telephoned to say that he was moving for the summer to Center Island, Oyster Bay, telephone 1585R and that he would be at my service at any time. He and his wife would very much like us to come to visit them. I said that I did not know that that would be possible. This week and next we were to remain in New York and beginning Friday, June 11, we had been invited to spend with a friend at White Plains. He said he was ready to visit us there. I then repeated the suggestion that if the truce come about, he invite me to a discussion with some of his friends so that we might canvass the possibilities of a federal solution, even calling it the United States of Palestine. He said he had not forgotten that. I said that no time ought to be lost. He said that every moment of these four weeks was precious and should be utilized to the fullest extent. I asked him if he did not think it useful if I were to get in touch with Dr. Malik whose speech at Lake Success had so much impressed me. He answered yes, but I should do this with the utmost discretion as I knew there had been reports about the lone stand of Lebanon as opposed to that of the other Arab states, and should know that Dr. Malik's speech was delivered with the full concurrence of the other Arab states. They wished just that atmosphere to be created. I asked him where Dr. Malik was to be found. He said either at the Ambassador Hotel or at the Lebanese Consulate in New York or at the Lebanese Legation in Washington. I said I preferred to get into touch with him only at the Hotel Ambassador. He said, yes, that was right, it should be entirely personal and be done with great caution.

He had received yesterday the answer from his government in reply to the telegram which he had sent the other day at my request asking that in case of emergency the Arabs take every possible step to safeguard the treasures of the Hebrew University Library, particularly its manuscripts and incunabula and the scientific collection and equipment of both the University and Hadassah. This was on Friday the 28th. He said he would telegraph that night. The answer which came yesterday was to the effect that his Government expressed great satisfaction that the matter had been called to its attention and that it would take immediate steps to guarantee the most meticulous care of the treasures and collections and equipment which had been mentioned. I told him I was very grateful for this. I wrote about it in a letter to Dr. Senator today. Whether my letter to Jerusalem will reach him I do not know.

On Sunday, May 30, I telephoned Dr. Eliash[7] in the morning.

I said that now that a four weeks' armistice seemed to be in the offing, I would like to urge upon him and his associates the necessity of considering some kind of federal solution to the whole problem. It might be in the direction of the United States of Palestine. I did not have to go into explanations with him on the telephone — he would know quite well what the implications of that were. He said I was going too fast. The truce had not been accepted. It was very doubtful if the Arabs would accept. I said that the Syrian delegate had declared the Arab acceptance "likely" and that Dr. Malik's speech had pointed in the same direction. Dr. Eliash replied that if the Arabs would accept, he was confident that the Jews would also. I said I did not see how it was possible for either side to refuse under all the circumstances. I added that I would be glad to discuss the whole question with him and his associates. I was ready to be of service to them if I might. He said he would convey this offer of co-operation to his associates.

1. Thomas F. Power, Jr. (b. 1916). U.S. career diplomat; deputy secretary general, permanent United States mission to the UN, 1946–1949.
2. Count Folke Bernadotte, the UN mediator for Palestine (see glossary of names).
3. Harold Evans (b. 1886). Lawyer, member of Society of Friends; born in Philadelphia. Appointed municipal commissioner for Jerusalem by the UN in May 1948.
4. Pablo Ascarate, Spanish diplomat; member of the secretariat of the League of Nations, 1932–1936, and then Spanish ambassador to Great Britain, 1936–1939; appointed deputy secretary of the Palestine Commission in February 1948.
5. Mahmud Fawzi Bey (1900–1981). Egyptian diplomat; served as consul general in Jerusalem, 1941–1944; member of Egyptian delegation to the UN, 1946, and delegate to Security Council, 1949–1951; minister of foreign affairs, 1952, 1967–1970; Prime Minister, 1970–1972.
6. Charles H. Malik (b. 1906). Philosopher, Lebanese diplomat; professor of mathematics and physics, American University of Beirut, 1927–1929, and professor of philosophy, 1937–1948; ambassador of Lebanon to the United States, 1945–1953; head of mission to the UN, 1945–1954.
7. Mordecai Eliash (1892–1950). Lawyer and diplomat. Born in the Ukraine and migrated to Palestine in 1919; legal advisor to Va'ad Le'umi; represented interests of Jerusalem Jewish community at the UN in 1948. In 1949 he was appointed first Israeli minister to the United Kingdom.

132

To Robert McClintock
Washington, D.C.

New York, June 14, 1948

Dear Mr. McClintock:

I have worked out the enclosed document with the assistance of some of my friends.

You may recall that at my meeting with the Secretary of State, you suggested the title "The United States of Palestine." This is recorded in the minutes of the meeting, which I was permitted to have "off the record" the following day. Would you be good enough to show the enclosed document[1] to Mr. Henderson. I would be greatly interested to know if he considers the idea to have any practical merit, and if he thinks that there is anything further I might do about it.

I talked it over with Dr. Philip Jessup,[2] who said he would give Senator Austin a report of our talk. Although Dr. Jessup did not say specifically if he was in favor of the idea or not, I nevertheless gathered that he would use it as a possibility.

I have talked it over in passing also with Fawzi Bey of Egypt and Dr. Malik of the Lebanon. Both seemed favorably inclined. I discussed it at some length with M. Parodi and M. de la Tournelle of the French delegation. From their questions in the course of the discussion, it was clear that they found great interest in it. It was indeed suggested that after I had discussed the matter further with others, there should be a meeting between me and M. de la Tournelle and perhaps others for a more thoroughgoing clarification of the whole idea. They were particularly interested in what the attitude of the United States might be. I said that I had no way of knowing.

If I do not miss my guess entirely, I would say that Mr. Eliahu Epstein,[3] representative in Washington of the State of Israel, would be on the lookout for some formula of political union which he knows is at least as important as the idea of an economic union for an acceptable settlement of the issue.

I continue to deplore the refusal to accept the Scopus evacuation in terms as proposed by Ascarate and confirmed by the Arab high authorities.[4]

I appreciate, of course, the contention that that would have been handing over Scopus to the Arabs. On the other hand, our main objective is neither military nor national prestige but rather the preservation of books and manuscripts and scientific treasures in the Scopus buildings.

If, indeed, their preservation should be due to the restraint and help of the Arab Legion, that might be a good augury for the future. It would help dissipate the all too prevalent notion that our Semitic cousins are nothing but marauders from the desert, in whose word no faith can be put.

The word of a desert king with a penchant for the inspired rhetoric of classic Arab poetry, may become an increasingly important factor in tranquilizing the cultural life of that part of the world.

You and Mr. Henderson may be interested to know that an attempt is now being made in New York to organize a group to promote Jewish-Arab cooperation. Among the organizers are General Edward S. Greenbaum, Mr. James Marshall, Dr. Maurice Hexter, Mr. Frank Altschul and Mrs. Arthur Sulzberger. A copy of their proposals is also enclosed.

I would urge you to send the substance of these two documents and of this letter together with a note about the situation on Mount Scopus to Count Folke Bernadotte at the earliest possible moment.

Would it be possible for you to put in the form of a telegram the main parts of my document and cable them to my friends of the Ihud Association, Jerusalem, in care of Dr. D. W. Senator, Administrator of the Hebrew University, Gaza Road, Jerusalem? Adding that in view of my thinking along these lines and that, knowing as I do what Dr. Senator and my associates have been thinking about, I have not hesitated to say that in my opinion, all of them would be in favor of this idea, and that, if this be the case, they get in touch with the United Nations Mediator, Count Bernadotte, and bring the idea to his attention. This may be done through the U.S. Consulate General in Jerusalem, through the courtesy of the U.S. State Department.

Could you send me a copy of a definition from some authoritative source book on the distinction between confederation and federation?

I hope you are well. With thanks for your courtesy and with best regards to you and Mr. Henderson,

Yours sincerely, JLM

P.S. I should like to ask if Dr. Senator received any of my letters. Kindly inform Dr. Senator that this morning, June 14th, his letter of May 10th reached me.

1. Magnes incorporated the document in his article in *Commentary*, October 1948 (see document 138).
2. Philip C. Jessup (b. 1897). Professor of international law, Columbia University, 1925-1961; United States delegate to the UN, 1948-1952. He was judge of the International Court of Justice, 1960-1970.
3. Eliahu (Epstein) Elath (b. 1903). Diplomat and Arabist. He migrated from Russia to Palestine in 1924; headed Middle East section of the Jewish Agency's political department, 1934-1945, and Jewish Agency's political office in Washington, 1945-1948. He served as Israel's ambassador to the United States, 1949; ambassador to the United Kingdom, 1950-1959; president of the Hebrew University, 1959-1962.
4. King Abdullah of Jordan agreed to allow Israeli forces to evacuate Mount Scopus, which was cut off from Jewish-held Jerusalem, guaranteeing to safeguard the Hebrew University's installations and library.

133
To Hannah Arendt
New York

Knollwood, N.Y., July 20, 1948

Dear Dr. Arendt:

I am sending you a translation of a letter from one of my former coworkers. Do you think it would have any interest for the members of our group? Also I enclose the translation of two articles from a recent number of *Ba'ayot*. Do you think they would have any interest for our friends?

Let me thank you for your letter of July 14th. The divergences between the different versions of the Asia Institute statement are so striking that one wonders what the purpose, if any, behind them might have been. I am sending copies of my answer to Mr. Pope[1] to Hans Kohn and Ernst Simon who, you have observed, are among the signatories. Your statement of the history and purpose of Ihud should serve a very useful end not only here but also in Jerusalem. I was particularly impressed by your analysis of the reasons why the Zionist leadership did not more actively pursue a policy of peace and understanding.[2]

Are you not mistaken on page 4 in ascribing to Sokolow the meeting with the Arab leaders in Damascus? I think it was Kalvarisky.

There is a small leader in *Ba'ayot*, May 13th, headed "Peoples Remain Forever." I shall try to translate it forthwith.

"It was on the eve of the First World War. The heads of the Arab national movement in Syria and in Palestine then endeavored to come to some understanding and cooperation with the Zionist movement which then began to strike root in the Homeland. But despite the endeavors of Kalvarisky, the pioneer of the movement for Jewish-Arab rapprochement, the Zionist leaders were chary about this. They cited as their excuse fear of the Ottoman government. Then one of the Arab leaders arose and said:

" 'Gentlemen, Zionists; Governments may come and go but peoples remain forever.'

"Kalvarisky was in the habit of repeating this prophetic word especially when he became indignant at our official leadership which continued to neglect the Arab problem in their exaggerated confidence in the generosity of the British government which meanwhile had replaced the Ottoman government. And now the British also are withdrawing from Palestine, leaving the two peoples locked in desperate warfare for life and death. Will the two peoples understand finally the wisdom of life of that aged Arab and of his Jewish friend — that governments come and go but peoples remain forever?"

It is not only flattering but also very instructive to have oneself and one's work objectified as you have done with me and with Ihud. Aside from ascribing to me more than I deserve, I think your representation quite sound. I agree with you that the press statement of our group should contain a cautious endorsement of Bernadotte's "Suggestions."

I hope you will receive shortly copies of the comments received by Mr. Goldsmith.[3] You will no doubt be able to make arrangements that such material reach you automatically.

I have been enjoying reading *The Federalist*. The type-face in the Modern Library Edition is very legible. A great deal can be learned both as to substance and as to terminology from a reading of the Articles of Confederation of 1777.

The discussion of the difference between the Articles of Confederation 1777 and the Constitution 1787 forms the main theme of the new book by Wheare on federal government.

You may be interested in the following extracts from my translation of a letter of June 13 from Dr. K. Wilhelm from Stockholm. Through our friend Professor S. H. Bergmann an important position in the Stockholm Rabbinate was offered to Dr. Wilhelm. Dr. Wilhelm had very great misgivings about leaving Jerusalem. I encouraged him to do this because I thought that he personally was greatly in need of a change. He and his wife had suffered a terrible shock when the explosions took place in Ben-Yehudah Street. Moreover I believe that Zion should send out its missionaries into the Jewish world. He writes:

> It may interest you to know that I had a very friendly talk with Ben-Gurion in Tel-Aviv. He congratulated me upon taking upon myself the task of going to Stockholm and he thought that an Ihud man would be able to do a great deal for Palestine. I had the impression that the atmosphere of our talk was much pleasanter than among some of my old friends. The position of the Aliyah Hadasha[4] is very strange to me. They are a kind of *meshumadim* [apostates] and the *meshumad* is always more dangerous than someone born a goy. It seems to me that the greatest danger now is a civil war in Jerusalem. Mr. Mendel Bergen[5] has moved to Jerusalem. There is hardly anyone of the Zionist leadership there. How shall we prevent the destruction of Jerusalem — by the Etsel who will find their allies among the martial clericals? Chief Rabbi Herzog is very much opposed to Ben-Gurion. Etsel has an unscrupulous propagandist in the novelist [Arthur] Koestler. His article about the ship carrying arms was published by the newspapers here in Sweden. I heard that an answer had been written but that the newspaper refused to publish the answer.

We are thinking seriously of returning to Jerusalem in case this is at all possible. Not being able to go to Lake Success, I wrote Count Bernadotte a letter.[6] When I get a copy of it, I shall send it on to you. (Enclosed please find the copy of the letter I sent to Count Bernadotte.)

I have had a talk with Commander Jackson[7] who was with Bernadotte in Rhodes. His view of the next steps is this:

1. That the UN provide the necessary number of observers in order that the truce may be maintained.

2. That the Jews and Arabs begin talking with one another as to the future.

3. That the policies of Great Britain and the United States as to Palestine be clarified and integrated.

He read a copy of the paper on Palestine Confederation in Rhodes which shows that the Swedish Consulate was as good as its word in sending it. I shall be sending you a copy of a letter from Dr. Silver[8] plus comments by Mr. Eban. What they write is exceedingly discouraging, almost as though it was not necessary to plan for tomorrow.

You may recall that I once mentioned that I had considerable material relating to some of the efforts I have made during the years to bring about Jewish-Arab cooperation. I should like to discuss with you the form in which this material ought to be worked up for possible publication in this country. If I personally were to get the material, it is the documents with notes which I should prefer to have rather than the text of the author of the book.

I am enclosing a copy of the translation made by Mr. Katz of an article which appeared in *Ba'ayot* entitled "The Spirit of Masada," a copy of which I will send to Mr. Elliot Cohen.[9] The article is very well translated. It was done by Mr. Samuel Katz. Perhaps he may be used for future translations.

Yours sincerely, JLM

1. Arthur Upham Pope, expert in Near Eastern art, was founder and chancellor of the Asia Institute.

2. Arendt later incorporated her statement in "Peace or Armistice in the Near East?" *Review of Politics*, 12 (January 1950), 56–82.

3. Arthur J. Goldsmith (1897–1964). Banker and philanthropist. Active in the liberal wing of the Republican Party.

4. Aliya Hadasha was a Zionist political party composed mainly of recent middle-class German immigrants.

5. The typist transcribing the handwritten letter apparently erred in rendering the name, which in all likelihood was that of Menachem Begin, the commander of the extremist Irgun Zeva'i Le'umi. Though the Irgun was incorporated into the Israeli army following the establishment of the state, it maintained its separate existence in Jerusalem. Begin (born in 1913, arrived in Palestine in 1943, and became Prime Minister in 1977) received a tumultuous welcome when he visited Jerusalem in the latter part of August.

6. Magnes sent Bernadotte his confederation plan, pointing out the similarity with Bernadotte's own proposals "with the notable exception of the provision for Jerusalem," which Bernadotte assigned to the Arab state. Magnes wrote, "In many ways Jerusalem seems to me to be the crux of the Palestine problem, that is, if Jerusalem could be internationalized and demilitarized and made the capital of the Federal Union, there ought to be a good chance for agreement and understanding between the Jews and Arabs of Jerusalem in the first instance, and then increasingly throughout other parts of Palestine" (JLM to Count Folke Bernadotte, July 14, 1948, JMP).

7. Robert G. A. Jackson, assistant Secretary General of the UN.

8. Abba Hillel Silver (1893–1963). U.S. Reform Rabbi and Zionist leader. Born in Lithuania, he was brought to the United States in 1902; ordained at the Hebrew Union College in 1916. He served as rabbi of The Temple, Cleveland, from 1917 to his death. In 1943 he became co-chairman of the American Zionist Emergency Council and then chairman of the American section of the Jewish Agency.

9. Elliot E. Cohen (1899–1959). Writer and editor. He was managing editor of

Menorah Journal from 1925 to 1931; director of public relations, Federation of Jewish Philanthropies of New York, from 1934 to 1945, and editor of *Commentary* from 1945 to 1959.

134

To Count Folke Bernadotte
Rhodes

Saranac Lake, N.Y., August 10, 1948

Dear Count Bernadotte:

I was delighted to get your letter from Rhodes under date of July 29th,[1] and thank you heartily for it.

Will you let me say that I was disappointed with the reasons outlined by you for your "Suggestions" concerning Jerusalem? I think that as far as the cost to the Jewish inhabitants is concerned if Jerusalem were to become the capital of the Palestine Confederation, they would be able to collect from the Jews of the world — Jerusalem is a unique word and has its deep hold everywhere — the difference between what they would pay in taxes and the amounts required from them to maintain the capital. Moreover, as capital of the Confederation, Jerusalem would produce a certain income through the presence there of important institutions and visiting travelers. Your second reason is, so it seems to me, more serious, and all I have to say about it is, "Let us try and see."

I gather from this morning's papers that despite all discouragements and difficulties you are still of stout heart and dogged in your determination to see things through. That is great.

The effort to form here a group which may be known as American Friends of Jewish-Arab Cooperation is making progress. The address is at the head of this letter and is that of the provisional office. Enclosed please find a copy of a statement I am issuing to the press within a few days.

May I call your attention to the fact that the Rev. Dr. K. Wilhelm, until recently of Jerusalem, has been called to an important post in the Rabbinate of Stockholm. He is one of the founders of the Ihud (Union) Association of Palestine of which I am Chairman. The Ihud (Union) Association has consistently stood for Jewish-Arab cooperation, and Dr. Wilhelm and I hold practically similar views.

My wife and I are hoping to be able to get back to Jerusalem within the not far distant future. When I am there, I hope to have the privilege of being able to help you in your devoted work.

With good wishes, I am

Sincerely yours, JLM

P.S. I am taking the liberty of sending Dr. Wilhelm a copy of this letter (Dr. K. Wilhelm, Mosaiska Forsammlingen, Wahrendorffsg 3, Stockholm, Sweden).

1. In his letter Bernadotte defended his proposal to assign Jerusalem to the Arab territory. He argued that the experience of having an international area within the boundaries of another state had been discouraging and the financial burden of maintaining an international organization was too great for a local population to bear. Bernadotte's other points were akin to Magnes's confederation plan (Bernadotte to JLM, July 29, 1948, JMP).

135

To David Ben-Gurion
Tel Aviv[1]

Knollwood, N.Y., August 19, 1948

Dear and honored friend,

I have the honor to enclose herewith a copy of a statement I gave to the press yesterday.[2] I hope you have the time to give this statement your attention. I think it is formulated in your own spirit. I permitted myself to mention your name twice: in connection with the agreement with the Arabs and in connection with Jerusalem.

I enclose here also copies of draft one and draft two for a Palestine confederation which were drawn up at the beginning of June. Number one is my original draft, while number two was edited without my knowledge. The resemblance between my proposal and that of the mediator of the UN is striking enough. I have learned that he issued his suggestions before he had seen my proposal. You will find here also copies of letters from Messrs. Silver and Eban (I shall have to send these under separate cover).[3]

I hope and pray that something constructive for the benefit of the Land and all its inhabitants will result from the discussions taking place on the basis of the mediator's suggestions. I appeal to you to settle the Arab refugee problem solely and alone on a humane basis and not through political bargaining. It is very good that you are inviting the

Arab countries directly for talks as to a peace settlement. Yet in my humble opinion indications are lacking as to the direction of the proposals it is your purpose to make.

To my deep regret, my health is somewhat weak, and it is doubtful if I shall be permitted to return home to Jerusalem soon. I suffer from this thought.

Kindest greetings to your wife. I hope her rheumatism is better.

A Happy New Year to you and to the whole People of Israel.

Respectfully, JLM

1. Translated from the Hebrew, probably by Magnes.

2. Magnes announced his support for a Palestine confederation of sovereign Arab and Jewish states with Jerusalem as the capital of the confederation. He mentioned Ben-Gurion's wish "to cooperate closely with the Arabs, both of Palestine and the neighboring countries," and Ben Gurion's view that the character of Jerusalem as "a spiritual center of world-wide importance be preserved" (news release, August 21, 1948, JMP; *New York Times*, August 23, 1948, p. 4).

3. Magnes titled his first draft "A United States of Palestine" (see documents 132 and 138). The second draft was entitled "Plan for a Palestine Confederation." Magnes sent this version to Abba Hillel Silver, the chairman of the American Section of the Jewish Agency. Silver replied that the plan "advocated the restriction of Israel's sovereignty and the dilution of its independence" and that the Jewish Agency deplored individual Jews' soliciting the support of the United States government or the UN delegations "for policies which run counter to those which the government of Israel is striving so gallantly to defend." Silver enclosed an analysis of the Magnes proposals that he had requested from Abba Eban, Israel's representative at the UN (Silver to Magnes, July 16, 1948, with enclosure, Archives of the State of Israel, Foreign Office Papers, Box 129).

136

To Hannah Arendt
New York

Knollwood, N.Y., August 31, 1948

Dear Dr. Arendt,

I thank you for your most interesting and valuable letter of August 28. I agree with you that Eban's article, as somewhat clarified by his letter, presents a well-reasoned, and perhaps hopeful point of view, despite the several details of his article with which one must differ.[1] Would you care to propose to Elliot Cohen then, that he publish my confederation proposal; and if he does, it would be most enlightening if your comments in paragraphs 3, 5 and 6 of your letter could be printed as well. That might be the beginning of a fruitful discussion.

As to *regional* cooperation, right through the war, beginning with my articles in *Foreign Affairs*, January 1943, I stressed the regional idea. But that was at a time when it looked as if the founders of the United Nations would take more account of the regional idea than unfortunately they did.

Would you be willing to supervise the typing of the two versions of the confederation plan in accordance with your next to the last paragraph? I am sorry I seem not to have made myself clear as to Eban's letter. I informed Miss Tobias she would get it from you for copying. I shall try to have it copied otherwise. Dr. Hexter was supposed to have left for New York yesterday. I hope that by this time you will have had from him my draft of a reply to Eban's letter.[2] If you think it adequate, would you please give it to Miss Tobias with the request that she type an original to be sent here as quickly as possible for my signature, and copies as well? Thank you for all your help.

We hope to be in New York at the Mayflower by September 13. There are two things which will occupy me — getting our organization going and trying to persuade my doctor that the improvement in my health is such that he can, with a good conscience, let me go back to Jerusalem.

With kindest greetings, I am

Sincerely yours, JLM

P.S. Do you think I might send the proof of the Eban articles to Jerusalem?

1. Aubrey [Abba] S. Eban, "The Future of Arab-Jewish Relations," *Commentary*, September 1948, 199–206.
2. JLM to Aubrey Eban, August 25, 1948, Archives of the State of Israel, Foreign Office Papers, Box 129. Magnes wrote that the Jewish-Arab cooperation they both desired could be achieved only by a "statutory confederation" and that no "looser form" would work.

137

To James Marshall
New York

Knollwood, N.Y., September 11, 1948

Dear Jim:

Thanks greatly for your most valuable letter of September 9. Its analysis and suggestions bring us a definite step forward in the process of organization.[1] I hope that each one of us will be bending all his efforts towards bringing about an effective organization without too much delay. Now is the time.

First let me say how happy and practical an idea yours is for a kind of *Handbook on Confederation* promptly and carefully done. You may know that the next *Commentary* is to have an answer from me to Eban's article. As to your analysis of the various elements in our present group, is there anyone except Lessing Rosenwald who is an avowed anti-Zionist? Of course a closely knit and homogeneous organization is ordinarily the best way to achieve results. Yet it is often the test of practical statesmanship to get results through the coordination of seemingly disparate forces.[2]

I am not one very prone to excommunicating anyone, primarily, I suppose, because I have been on proscribed lists myself all too often. Yet I am bound to admit in all frankness that if Lessing's name appeared as one of the Founding Fathers of the new group, it would be unfortunate because it would create the false notion that this was an anti-Zionist organization and the energy and time wasted in having to combat that are needed for more constructive purposes. That need not keep him or anyone else from coming in later on.

There are two further points which would prompt me to go slow about reading Lessing out of the ranks as an anti-Zionist. The question as to who is and is not a Zionist since the establishment of Israel has been occupying the official Zionists at their recent meeting in Palestine. Moreover, as far as I am aware, Lessing has been the one man in the country who has had the courage to buck the terror of the Zionist political machine. I think his has been rather a blunder in tactics and that is always to be judged mercifully. That is, he has been *anti-anti* Zionist, and being just anti, does not get you very far. But has it been anti-Zionism or rather the anti-Zionist *political machine here in the United States*? If it is the latter, I think I should be inclined to become anti—because I apprehend a severe reaction from which American Jews generally are suffering and will suffer from this establishment of this Zionist political machine with the Jewish vote in its pocket. Look at the JDC as an example. As to the other group—people who are pro-Magnes personally but against his ideas, I confess that I do not know who they are. But I think you should go very cautiously with them. The question to be asked there is what are those views and are their views publicly under the ban so that the new organization would have to be apologizing for itself too much on this account? In any event, the presence in our councils of some of the "intellectuals" and labor people might help us arrive at clearer and more practical conclusions, without involving us in too much delay.

Your ideological statement of which I have no copy by me now, might as I remember it, serve as a basis, i.e., anyone subscribing more or less to it is kosher. It might be the statement put before the public with greater emphasis on confederation and the return of Arab refugees than the original statement could have. You will find enclosed an extract from a letter to me from Jerusalem showing that our friends there are concerned with much the same questions. I had meant to type this letter, but got all bollixed up in the first page. Please send copies to those to whom your letter of September 9 went—also to Dr. Hexter. I think the views of Hans Kohn, Nelson Glueck and Prof. Finkelstein should also be sought. Beatrice is resting easily. We hope to be back at the end of the week.

Yours, Judah

1. Marshall, after consulting with Arendt, suggested that a group be formed consisting of Jewish intellectuals and labor movement people who shared Magnes's views and that a book be prepared presenting these views.

2. Marshall did not believe there was place in the projected organization for anti-Zionists, the most prominent of whom was Lessing Rosenwald.

138

To the Editor of *Commentary*
October 1948

For a Jewish-Arab Confederation

Major Eban's important article, "The Future of Arab-Jewish Relations," in the September *Commentary*, seems to me to be the best reasoned and in many ways most hopeful statement on this question which I have seen from an official Zionist source. It is to be hoped that it may become the starting-point for a fruitful discussion of this whole fateful problem of Jewish-Arab relations.

A substantial part of Major Eban's article is devoted to a critique of the approach to this problem on the part of the Ihud Association, of which I am proud to be chairman, and of some of my specific proposals for confederation between independent Arab, and Jewish states in Palestine. In discussing it, it might be useful to state more fully what the Ihud program recommends.

At the beginning of June, 1948, I drafted a paper, under the title of *United States of Palestine—A Confederation of Two Independent States*, the text of which follows:

A. *Political Union.* The question to be answered during the coming four weeks of truce, is, how to maintain the de facto existence of the State of Israel and at the same time reduce the Arab fears of partition or of this de facto state.

The one possible approach would seem to be the establishment of a confederation which would recognize the independence of the de facto State of Israel but which would on the other hand create a kind of federal union in political matters as well as in economic.

The resolutions of the United Nations Assembly on November 29, 1947 provided for a Federal Economic Board. The functions of the Board are described in detail in chapter 4D of the resolutions of November 29, 1947. There is, however, no chance of establishing this joint Economic Board if there is not also some kind of Federal Union in the political sense.

What may be some of the subjects reserved for the political center of a possible Confederation? Among these are: (1) foreign affairs; (2) defense; (3) international loans; (4) federal court; (5) protection of religious shrines and historical monuments and collections of cultural, artistic, and scientific importance.

Foreign Affairs. It might be dangerous to the peace of the Middle East if two tiny states, that of Israel and that of Palestinian Arabs (with or without Transjordan), were to have the privilege of deciding upon their foreign affairs policies without reference to one another. In this event, it might well be possible that one state would have its orientation towards one of the great powers and the other state towards another of the great powers, thus converting the Palestinian area into a hotbed of imperial political rivalries. It should be made mandatory upon the two states at least to consult with one another on their foreign affairs policies, and even perhaps to insist that they arrive at these policies together. In case of disagreement the subject would be referred to a higher tribunal, presumably to the appropriate organ of the United Nations.

Among the political difficulties of such a concerted policy on foreign affairs would be the question of consular representation and also their special representation in the UN. On the other hand, the British Commonwealth and Empire and the Soviet Union cover vast territories, whereas the State of Israel and the Palestinian Arab State are tiny in comparison.

It should be pointed out that in the old Austro-Hungarian state, Austria and Hungary were independent entities with separate parliaments, yet there were certain subjects reserved for the Council of Delegations. This consisted of delegates from the two parliaments who met for discussion and action on such reserved topics as foreign affairs, defense, and international loans. [Austria-Hungary is cited here as an interesting historical precedent and not necessarily as a model to be copied.]

Defense. Similar considerations apply to the problem of defense. It might be dangerous to the peace of the Middle East if these two states were to arm against one another, or if they were to be armed by rival imperial powers. It should, therefore, be made mandatory upon them at least to consult on their defense policies and activities, and it would be better if working out a common defense policy were made imperative.

International Loans. Reference is made here to such international loans as are of importance and of benefit to the entire population of the two states, as for example, in connection with a possible Jordan Valley Authority. In the provisions for economic union, it is stated that each state "may conduct international financial operations on its own faith and credit." This should be taken to mean international financial operations which have to do with the improvement of the entire area for the benefit of all its inhabitants without regard to race, creed, or nationality.

Federal Court. This might be constituted of three Jews and three Arabs and a United Nations appointee who is to be chairman.

Among the subjects coming within the jurisdiction of the Federal Court would be:

(a) the constitutional interpretation of all questions in dispute between the two states in reference to agreements between them or the international conventions entered into by them, or other constitutional questions brought up by one state or the other;

(b) it should be the court of appeals on all questions of religious and minority and civil rights. Any citizen or resident of either of the states is to be privileged to appeal to the Federal Court in cases where he contends that his religious or minority or civil rights are invaded;

(c) the Federal Court might also serve as the High Court for the International City of Jerusalem.

Jerusalem. Jerusalem is to be constituted as a *corpus separatum*, as an international, demilitarized, neutralized city.

Yet at the same time it should serve as the capital of the Confederation. To this end a special enclave should be set aside in Jerusalem as the seat of the Confederation, of the Joint Economic Board, of the Federal Court, and of the authority, whatever it be, which is to be charged with the protection of holy places and religious sites, to which may be added historical monuments including archaeological excavations and cultural, artistic, and scientific collections. There may be other international or Confederation bodies which should have their seat in Jerusalem as the capital.

B. The name United States of Palestine is proposed as being somewhat analogous to the name United States of America. Here there are sovereign states whose sovereignty is nevertheless limited by their adherence to the Federal Union. The United States of America is a federal structure in which the sovereignty of the individual states is much more limited than would be the case in the Palestine Confederation, which nevertheless should be called the United States of Palestine.

C. *Immigration.* Inasmuch as immigration is usually the crux of the problem, it might be well to state that immigration regulations are to be made by either state autonomously. Provision should nevertheless be made for the time when this subject is also to be taken up within the framework of the Confederation.

The same as to land sales.

This paper was submitted to a number of persons, among others to the Jewish Agency, and it contains, in my opinion, the long-range policy along whose lines a permanent settlement could be achieved. It also had a rather wide circulation in the form of a "Second Draft," but the text I have here cited is that of the original draft, and from correspondence between us and from his article, the difference between Major Eban's point of view and mine becomes clear. Major Eban sees no hope for Jewish-Arab cooperation through any kind of statutory political union, even Confederation, which in the Encyclopaedia of Social Science is defined as "A federation of existing governments without impairment of their sovereignty" (see article "Federation").

It would indeed be excellent and highly to be preferred, if there could be cooperation between the government of Israel and other governments in the same region without statutory political union. (As examples, the Benelux Union or the British Commonwealth.) One of the great achievements of history is the informal basis of union of the British Commonwealth and Empire as expressed in the Statute of Westminster. This is a union (despite the term "statute") by consent and without statutory obligations. The Benelux Union is a similar achievement. Is an understanding by consent and without formal statutory obligations now achievable as between Israel and neighboring countries?

In my opinion it is not. The psychological background for this is unfortunately lacking. Had the Jewish Agency all through the years made one single sincere and systematic attempt at understanding and conciliation and had it not rejected and frustrated the efforts made by others, and had this frightful, needless war with its legacies of hatred and ill-will on both sides not intervened, there might perhaps have been some slight chance of Jewish-Arab cooperation without formal and binding statutory obligations. As it is, we shall be very fortunate if we can bring about cooperation through some formal confederation, whether we label the idea of confederation as belonging to the 19th or the 20th century.

The idea of confederation has a special appeal to the American mind. The United States of America is the largest and most successful confederation of sovereign states in history. The constitution-makers of the new

514

Palestine may well use as primary sources both as to terminology and as to substance the American Articles of Confederation of 1777, which, because of defects discovered in practice, led to the Constitution of 1787. A thorough study of *The Federalist* of James Madison, John Jay, and Alexander Hamilton would be illuminating for the Palestine Confederation. The American tendency towards confederation is seen in the recent 20th-century vote in Newfoundland in favor of confederation with Canada. In announcing the United States government's support of the idea of an Assembly for Western Europe, the State Department declared: "This government strongly favors the progressively closer integration of the free nations of Western Europe."

It is to be welcomed that the Israel government has proposed direct negotiations with the Arabs for a peaceful settlement of the whole Palestine problem. They know, even if other patriots, particularly outside of Palestine, do not, that there is but very little chance for Israel if the war is to be kept up indefinitely. Yet the Israeli offer of a peace settlement is here again defective in that it is vague, not indicating to the Arabs along what lines the peace discussion is to be carried on. In this regard the proposals of Count Bernadotte, the UN Mediator, have the advantage of being clear and definite, "statutory" if you will.

It will be seen that my early June draft for a Palestine Confederation agrees very largely with the July suggestions of the Mediator. The chief difference is in regard to Jerusalem, which I propose should be the capital of the Confederation in addition to being demilitarized and neutralized as an international city.

Other points of possible controversy are my proposals for a concerted foreign policy and for common measures of defense. These would, it is true, restrict the sovereignty of the State of Israel; and it is understandable that a new and tiny state should be very sensitive about the necessity .of any self-limitation of its sovereignty. But the UN proposal for an Economic Union and for a Governor of the International Jerusalem was such a restriction.

In these days of striving towards the ideal of the United Nations and of the actual hegemony of the great powers, the small nations have not as a fact and in practice unrestricted sovereignty. The Benelux model, however desirable as an abstraction, does not solve the main difficulties of Palestine. A coordinated foreign policy is not an essential in Benelux because it is well-nigh inconceivable that two antagonistic great powers would ever try to play Belgium and the Netherlands off against one another. They do not require statutory coordination in their foreign policies because their own common interests in this domain have long been well established. This is not the case in the Middle East, where conflicting economic and political interests might at any moment incite and take advantage of national rivalries. In Palestine today the saying is current that the Jews have been more or less the pawns of American interests and the Arabs the pawns of British interests; and the question is asked if Russia's interest in unrest and instability in the Middle East is not clearer and perhaps more permanent than her present support of a Jewish state. In this connection a study of the establishment and the recognition of the various "independent" small states during the years of the war might be a profitable exercise.

Nor will it do to say that immigration is something which concerns only the Jews and the Jewish state. We see that it does concern the Arabs of Palestine and neighboring countries just as it concerns the countries which Jewish immigrants are leaving or those countries other than Palestine which they are about to enter, including the United States. The mass immigration of tens of thousands of men, women, and children does not take place in a vacuum. Such a movement of human beings has its military, economic, social, and political repercussions all over the world and not least in the countries neighboring Palestine.

In a recent statement of the Ihud, it was stated that some element of international regulation would be required in relation to immigration. This is necessary in view of the conflicts which might arise by reason of the two main elements in the problem: first, the incontestable need of Jews for immigration, and second, the equally incontestable fact that Jewish immigration to Palestine concerns not only the Jews and Jewish territory but also the Arab peoples.

For this reason Count Bernadotte's suggestions appear to me to be eminently reasonable: that there be free Jewish immigration for two years, during which time it may be anticipated that the Cyprus refugees and the DP's of Europe may, with international help, be integrated into the economy of Palestine, and that thereafter these questions be determined within the Confederation, or in case of irreconcilable conflict by the United Nations. The same as to land ownership.

In other words, questions of foreign policy, defense, immigration, and land ownership would in the last analysis be met under United Nations auspices if they could not be met, as is to be preferred, by direct understanding between the independent members of the Confederation.

Major Eban is right, it seems to me, in advocating a wide Middle East background as necessary and favorable to a permanent peaceful solution of the Palestine problem. He is right also in declaring that this background should be regional and not just racial, i.e., that Israel should be linked up not just with Arab and Moslem countries, but with all the various countries of the Middle East. It is to be regretted that the UN organization is not more generally built up on the regional idea. During the war, while the discussion concerning the United Nations was going on, the regional idea played a prominent part in the minds of those who eventually established the United Nations. There is every reason from the Jewish point of view to strive for a wide Middle East regional organization as part of the United Nations. Whereas there would be a great and perhaps decisive role for the Jews in this great undertaking, we should not forget that our first task is to try to bring about cooperation in all fields between the two peoples, the Jews and the Arabs, who alone remain as the descendants of the Semitic peoples of antiquity.

I should like to conclude with a word as to the question of the Arab refugees. There are many facets to the problem — military, political, humanitarian. Doubtless a very cogent case can be made out for meeting this problem from one of these points of view or another. It seems to me that any attempt to meet so vast a human situation except from the humane, the moral point of view will lead us into a morass. If the archives of the last war could yield all their secrets, we should doubtless find very able memoranda showing the advantage to certain countries of using displaced persons for the military, industrial, or political advantage of this or that state. I find it difficult also to reconcile the present attitude of the Israeli government in relation to the Arab refugees with its repeated statements that it is not the Arabs of Palestine, but only the neighboring Arab countries who are to blame for the outbreak of a Jewish-Arab war. If the Palestine Arabs left their homesteads "voluntarily" under the impact of Arab propaganda and in a veritable panic, one may not forget that the most potent argument in this propaganda was the fear of a repetition of the Irgun-Stern atrocities at Deir Yassin, where the Jewish authorities were unable or unwilling to prevent the act or punish the guilty. It is unfortunate that the very men who could point to the tragedy of Jewish DP's as the chief argument for mass immigration into Palestine should now be ready, as far as the world knows, to help create an additional category of DP's in the Holy Land.

Judah L. Magnes
New York City

P.S. My letter in response to Major Eban's article was written before the assassination of Count Bernadotte. I have today written the following personal comment, which I trust you will find space to print, and which I have also sent to the New York Times.

Count Bernadotte had come closer than any other man to bringing Jews and Arabs to an understanding, and his murder is a tragedy of historic importance for both peoples.

In a press statement issued August 23, 1948 I stated that Count Bernadotte had "done more to advance the cause of peace and conciliation in Palestine than all other persons put together," and I expressed the conviction that in all future discussions concerned with peace and reconciliation in the Holy Land, most of the suggestions advanced by Count Bernadotte would continue to serve as a basis for discussion.

At a crucial moment, this great task of peace-making has been deprived of Bernadotte's integrity of heart and mind and the great store of insight he had accumulated regarding personalities and other important factors involved.

It is very easy to join in the cry that Jewish terrorists are responsible for this attrocious crime. But who has been responsible for the terrorists? We all bear some responsibility. Certainly the large number of American supporters of terror in Palestine do — the senators and congressmen, the newspaper publishers and the large number of Jews and others who have supported terrorists morally and financially.

A large measure of responsibility must also fall upon those official circles in Israel who at one time and another carried on joint activities with terrorist groups, and instead of suppressing them, came to an understanding with them, incorporating them into the armed forces.

A large share of the blame is to be attributed to the recklessness of the charges made in Palestine and elsewhere against Bernadotte's honesty and good faith, charges which accused him of acting as the prejudiced agent of "the British" or of "British-American imperialism" or of "the oil interests."

Dr. Bunche has been burdened with an almost impossible task. He deserves the wholehearted support of all men of good will in carrying to completion Bernadotte's efforts at peace-making.

JLM
September 20, 1948

139

To Hannah Arendt
New York

New York, October 7, 1948

Dear Dr. Arendt,

Your article for the *New Leader*[1] is not only a rarely penetrating analysis, it might also be called a momentous article, i.e., it might have serious practical consequences if it were studied and taken to heart by anyone in whose hands decisions lay. You seem to have laid bare the inner meaning of Bernadotte's efforts and proposals; I very much doubt if that has been done in many places. Your story may be called tragic. Here was a great and good man who started full of hope and ended almost in despair. Suppose Secretary Marshall saw your article, with its alternatives of another form of UN trusteeship, or a continuation of the Jewish-Arab war, what would his conclusion be? In any event it ought to help clarify his mind and help him to a realistic conclusion. It is a grave choice, this way or that. Your article has depressed me, and I am asking myself, is there really no way out? I think every effort should be made to bring the article to the attention of those making decisions at Paris.

MacDonald isn't James but another, John J. who happens to be U.S. Consul-General in Jerusalem. I should like to hear what Mr. Landesco has to say. I should like to be able to introduce you to my wife. Could you come here some afternoon?

Sincerely, JLM

Your last paragraph is very moving. It has much of truth and beauty. I should some day like to discuss the Negev issue with you. I have permitted myself a few pencilled verbal suggestions.

1. "The Mission of Bernadotte," *The New Leader*, October 23, 1948, 8, 15.

140

Journal Entry: October 22, 1948[1]

New York

Marshall Plan for Middle East. I should discuss this with Landis.[2] Maybe through economic aid some chance of peace, otherwise war and hatred for decades.

Letter from Eddie Warburg[3] read to me by Steinbock.[4] Reason he didn't answer was because they were seriously considering the Arab refugee problem! Glad I am withholding resignation. When Morgenthau[5] returns we shall see. Letter from [illegible], October 19 to University office marked *Strictly personal*—please forward immediately. My letter to JDC one of my dramatic acts which make people take notice.[6] Seems to have worked at once, besides yesterday reply from Eddie W.: "J.M. has presented this problem to us and we are engaged in giving it serious consideration." Could I come to speak at their big meeting at Friends' House on 25? "Over here, at any rate, people do look to you for the lead." Enclosed the plan of the "Jewish Committee for Aid to Jews and Arabs" £10,000. Home near Jaffa for Jewish aged. For Arabs: clothing, medical supplies, team with station wagon.

1. Magnes died on the morning of October 27. The day before had been a normal one for him: a walk in Central Park, answering mail, meetings in his hotel room with friends and family. On the evening of October 26 he typed a letter to Dr. E. Bluestone expressing his views on relocating the Hadassah Hospital in Jerusalem.

2. James M. Landis (1899-1964). Legal scholar, educator, and governmental official; dean of Harvard Law School, 1937-1946. During the Second World War he served as consultant to Counsel of National Defense, director of Civil Defense, director of economic operations in the Middle East.

3. Edward M. M. Warburg (b. 1908). Philanthropist, Jewish community leader, son of Felix and Frieda Warburg. He was chairman of the JDC, 1941-1966; a member of the board of governors of Hebrew University; chairman of the executive committee, American Friends of the Hebrew University.

4. Max Steinbock, labor activist and editor of labor publications. He served as executive secretary of the ad hoc committee supporting Magnes's political activities during the summer of 1948.

5. Henry Morgenthau, Jr. (1891-1967). Government official and Jewish community leader. He was Secretary of the Treasury, 1934-1946; general chairman of the United Jewish Appeal, 1947-1959; chairman of the board of governors of the Hebrew University, 1950-1951; and chairman of Israel Bond organization, 1951-1954.

6. On September 2, 1948, Magnes wrote to Edward Warburg, chairman of the JDC: "What a wonderful opportunity is now before the JDC to do something which will help thousands of suffering human beings and which will at the same time redound to the glory of the Jews throughout the world, not least in Palestine itself." On September 29, 1948, he wrote to Warburg once more: "It is all too clear that within the JDC there is no feeling of urgency about the problem of the Arab refugees. This makes it incumbent upon me to withdraw as Chairman of the JDC Middle East Advisory Committee. How can I continue to be officially associated with a relief organization which can pass by so easily so great and urgent a relief problem . . . It was an opportunity of stretching out the helping hand of a Jewish brother to thousands in distress — in the same way the JDC has appealed to others to do for Jews in distress . . . It remains for me only to express my deepest regret that the JDC has not risen to this great opportunity and finally that my own connection with JDC of which I was one of the founders should end so ingloriously" (JMP).

THE DOCUMENTS AND THEIR SOURCES
GLOSSARY OF NAMES
SELECTED BIBLIOGRAPHY
ACKNOWLEDGMENTS
INDEX

THE DOCUMENTS AND THEIR SOURCES

1. To family, October 9, 1901, MP,10a.
2. To family, December 26, 1901, MP, 10a.
3. Journal entry, January 14, 1904, MP, 293.
4. To family, November 18, 1905, MP, 11.
5. To David Wolffsohn, June 19, 1906, CZA, Z 2/374.
6. Journal entry, September 1906– May 1907, MP, 295.
7. To the Editor of the *Tageblatt*, September 29, 1908, *American Hebrew*, October 2, 1908, p. 535.
8. "The Jewish Community of New York," February 27, 1909, MP, 1466.
9. "The Melting Pot," October 9, 1909, *The Emanu-El Pulpit*, vol. 3, 1909.
10. "Reformed Judaism – Plans for Reconstruction," April 24, 1910, *The Emanu-El Pulpit*, vol. 3, 1910.
11. To the President and Board of Trustees of Temple Emanu-El, May 16, 1910, MPWJHC.
12. To David Magnes, May 24, 1910, MP, 767.
13. To Solomon Schechter, February 5, 1911, SSP.

14. To the Executive Committee of the American Jewish Committee, November 6, 1912, MP, 1539.
15. Memorandum: A Yiddish Morning Daily, c. January, 1913, MP, 542.
16. To Oscar S. Straus, January 2, 1913, MP, 523.
17. To Chaim Weizmann, May 25, 1913, MP, 808.
18. To Walter Lippman, September 26, 1913, MP, 742.
19. Memorandum for the President and Members of the Executive Committee of the American Jewish Committee, for Meeting of the Committee at Temple Emanu-El, May 9, 1915, MP, 482.
20. To Louis D. Brandeis, June 30, 1915, MP, 720.
21. To Israel Friedlaender, August 31, 1915, MP, 1704.
22. To Louis D. Brandeis, September 2, 1915, MP, 720.
23. To Chaim Weizmann, January 28, 1916, MP, 1126.
24. To Louis D. Brandeis, July 25, 1916, MP, 767.
25. To Jacob H. Schiff, March 26, 1917, JHSP, Box 460.
26. Journal entry, October 2, 1917,

MP, 295.

27. To Scott Nearing, January 24, 1918, MP, 1236.

28. To the Members of the Executive Committee of the Joint Distribution Committee, March 11, 1918, MP, 1704.

29. Journal entry, June 29 [1919?], MP, 300.

30. Journal entry, c. November 1919, MP, 299.

31. "The Old America and the New," February 8, 1920, *War-Time Addresses, 1917–1921,* New York, 1923, pp. 82–90.

32. Journal entry, March 25, 1920, MP, 300.

33. To Dear Friend, May 1920, MP, 301.

34. To Members of the Executive Committee of the New York Kehillah, June 3, 1920, MP, 1459.

35. To Dear Friend, c. 1921, MP, 300.

36. To Mordecai M. Kaplan, January 14, 1921, MP, 462.

37. Journal entry, May 31, 1921, MP, 392.

38. To Beatrice Magnes, January 17, 1922, MP, 392.

39. Note, February 13, 1923, MP, 306.

40. Journal entry, May 3, 1923, MP, 306..

41. "Eretz Israel and the Galut," May 22, 1923, MP, 190.

42. Journal entry, June 16–18, 1923, MP, 306.

43. Journal entry, August 1–6, 1923, MP, 306.

44. Journal entry, September 11–13, 1923, MP, 306.

45. Journal entry, c. March 1924, MP, 308.

46. To Felix M. Warburg, April 11, 1924, FMWP, Box 220.

47. To Roger Baldwin, January 30, 1925, MP, 1939.

48. Journal entry, March 22, 1925, MP, 308.

49. To Ahad Ha'am, April 1925, MP, 2410.

50. Journal entry, May 28, 1925, MP, 308.

51. To Felix M. Warburg, Oct. 1, 1925, FMWP, Box 222.

52. To Julian W. Mack, November 4, 1925, MP, 310.

53. Journal entry, February 16, 1926, MP, 310.

54. Journal entry, February 18, 1926, MP, 310.

55. To Chaim Weizmann, October 5, 1926, MPWJHC.

56. Journal entry, May 21, 1927, MP, 315.

57. Journal entry, August 7, 1927, MP, 315.

58. Journal entry, February 13, 1928, MP, 1939.

59. Journal entry, March 7, 1928, MP, 310.

60. Journal entry, March 25, 1928, 310.

61. Journal entry, July 4–19, 1928, MP, 316.

62. Journal entry, September 14, 1928, MP, 312.

63. To Felix M. Warburg, April 28, 1929, MP, 1939.

64. To Chaim Weizmann, September 7, 1929, MP, 2414.

65. To Felix M. Warburg, September 13, 1929, MP, 2396.

66. "An International Enclave," November 24, 1929, *Like All the Nations?,* Jerusalem, 1930, pp. 34–41.

67. To Stephen S. Wise, February 6, 1930, MP, 2107.

68. To Chaim Weizmann, June 3, 1930, MP, 2396.

69. Journal entry, March 23, 1932, MP, 1939.

70. Journal entry, July 30, 1932, MP, 1939.

71. Note, October 29, 1932, MP, 1939.

72. To Chaim Weizmann, June 29, 1933, *Reply to the Report of the Survey Committee of the Hebrew University*, Jerusalem, 1934, pp. 149–151.

73. To Sir Philip Hartog, December 21, 1933, *Reply to the Report of the Survey Committee of the Hebrew University*, pp. 155–156.

74. Excerpts from the interview of Judah L. Magnes by the Survey Committee, January 1, 1934, *Report of the Survey Committee of the Hebrew University*, Jerusalem, 1934, pp. 136–159.

75. Journal entry, April 6, 1934, MP, 1939.

76. Note, June 1934, MP, 2308.

77. To Musa al-Alami, August 1, 1934, MP, 2436.

78. To Arthur Ruppin, April 18, 1936, MP, 2442.

79. To Reginald Coupland, January 7, 1937, MP, 2449.

80. To Felix M. Warburg, January 11, 1937, FMWP, Box 367.

81. To Felix M. Warburg, February 10, 1937, FMWP, Box 367.

82. Journal entry, February 22, 1937, MP, 317.

83. "Palestine Peace Seen in Arab-Jewish Agreements," *New York Times*, July 18, 1937, part 4, p. 9.

84. Address to the Council of the Jewish Agency, August 18, 1937, MP, 2452.

85. To Gladys Guggenheim Straus, October 14, 1937, MP, 2461.

86. Journal entry, December 18, 1937, MP, 317.

87. To John Nevin Sayre, January 12, 1938, MP, 2463.

88. Journal entry, February 6, 1938, MP, 318.

89. To Nuri al-Sa'id, February 23, 1938, MP, 2458.

90. To Sir Arthur Wauchope, February 25, 1938, MP, 2424.

91. To David Ben-Gurion, March 3, 1938, MP, 2458.

92. To Sol Stroock, June 5, 1938, MP, 2463.

93. To Benjamin V. Cohen, September 1, 1938, MP, 2462.

94. To Musa Abdallah al-Husayni, September 1, 1938, MP, 2462.

95. "War and the Remnant of Israel," October 29, 1939, *In the Perplexity of the Times*, Jerusalem, 1946, pp. 16–26.

96. Journal entry, June 15, 1940, MP, 340.

97. To Felix Frankfurter, November 12, 1941, MP, 213.

98. Journal entry, December 17, 1941, MP, 340.

99. Journal entry, August 30, 1942, MP, 2542.

100. To Rabbi Morris S. Lazaron, October 6, 1942, MP, 1958.

101. To Alexander M. Dushkin, January 7, 1943, MP, 2192.

102. "Toward Peace in Palestine," *Foreign Affairs*, January 1943, pp. 239–249.

103. Journal entry, February 8, 1944, MP, 2497.

104. To Mrs. Setty Kuhn, May 30, 1944, MP, 216.

105. To Paul Baerwald, July 25, 1944, MP, 2136.

106. "For Thy Sake Are We Killed All the Day Long," November 1, 1944, *In the Perplexity of the Times*, pp. 65–78.

107. To Paul Baerwald, December 13, 1944, MP, 2142.

108. "Compromise for Palestine," *New York Times*, February 17, 1945, p. 12.

109. To Eugene Untermyer, March 25, 1945, MP, 217.

110. To John Haynes Holmes, April 18, 1945, MP, 221b.

111. To Norman Thomas, May 21, 1945, MP, 217.

112. Notes: Conversation with Azzam Pasha, Cairo, May 18, 1946, MP, 2507.

113. Journal entry, May 26–July 4, 1946, MP, 1960.

114. To James Marshall, January 15, 1947, MP, 221b.

115. To I. F. Stone, February 14, 1947, MP, 221b.

116. To Maurice Hexter, February 14, 1947, MP, 2557.

117. To David W. Senator, February 18, 1947, MP, 221b.

118. "Report on Palestine," *New York Times*, September 28, 1947, part 4, p.10.

119. To Ernst Simon, November 12, 1947, MP, 2561.

120. To Herbert H. Lehman, February 6, 1948, MP, 222.

121. To Thomas Mann, March 1, 1948, MP, 222.

122. To Sir Leon Simon, March 16, 1948, JMP.

123. To Warren Austin, March 25, 1948, MP, 222.

124. To Thomas C. Wasson, April 6, 1948, JMP.

125. To Maurice B. Hexter, April 6, 1948, MP, 2529.

126. To Thomas Mann, April 12, 1948, MP, 222.

127. To General G. H. A. MacMillan, April 18, 1948, JMP.

128. Report to the Sponsoring Committee, April 26, 1948, JMP.

129. Journal entry, May 5, 1948, MP, 325.

130. Journal entry, May 6, 1948, MP, 325.

131. Journal entry, June 1, 1948, MP, 325.

132. To Robert McClintock, June 14, 1948, JMP.

133. To Hannah Arendt, July 20, 1948, MP, 2529.

134. To Count Folke Bernadotte, August 10, 1948, JMP.

135. To David Ben-Gurion, August 19, 1948, MP, 2529.

136. To Hannah Arendt, August 31, 1948, MP, 2529.

137. To James Marshall, September 11, 1948, JMP.

138. "For a Jewish-Arab Confederation," *Commentary*, October 1948, 379–383.

139. To Hannah Arendt, October 7, 1948, MP, 2529.

140. Journal entry, October 22, 1948, MP, 324.

GLOSSARY OF NAMES

ADLER, CYRUS (1863–1940). U.S. scholar and community leader; born in Van Buren, Arkansas, and moved to Philadelphia when he was a child. Adler received his Ph.D. in Assyriology from Johns Hopkins. From 1902 to 1905 he served as president of the board of trustees of the Jewish Theological Seminary, becoming president of the seminary in 1915 on Solomon Schechter's death. In 1908 he was elected president of Dropsie College, heading both institutions. He was cofounder of the American Jewish Committee and its president from 1929 to his death.

AHAD HA'AM. Pseudonym of Asher Zvi Ginsberg (1856–1927). Hebrew essayist, editor, and ideologue of cultural Zionism; born in Skvira, the Ukraine. He came to the notice of the Hebrew-reading public for his essays criticizing the early Zionist movement's settlement policy. He edited the important Hebrew monthly *Ha'shiloah* from 1896 to 1902 and was the most influential Zionist critic of Theodore Herzl's political Zionism, stressing the need for a spiritual and cultural revival of Jewish life. He lived in London from 1908 to 1922 and settled in Tel Aviv in 1922.

AL-ALAMI, MUSA (b. 1895). Palestinian Arab leader born in Jerusalem. He was educated in agronomy and law at the American University in Beirut and in England. He practiced law in Palestine and held various government positions until he was dismissed in 1937, when he fled the country, returning in 1941. He represented the Palestinian Arabs in the Arab League in 1945 and founded Arab information offices in Beirut, London, and Washington. Following the 1948 war he established an agricultural training school in Jericho.

AMERICAN JEWISH COMMITTEE. Established in 1906 to defend the civil and religious rights of Jews throughout the world, the committee drew its support from the upper strata of the German-Jewish community. It frowned on attempts to create a central coordinating body of Jewish organizations. The wealth and prestige of its supporters were the source of its influence in civic, government, and international circles.

527

AMERICAN JEWISH CONGRESS. Formed in 1917 of elected delegates representing Jewish communities and organizations, the congress sent a delegation to the Paris Conference to support Jewish minority rights in Eastern Europe. The American Jewish Committee, initially opposed to the congress, made its participation contingent on the congress's disbanding following the report of the peace conference delegation, which it did in 1920. Under the leadership of Stephen Wise, those who favored a permanent congress established an organization using the same name, but it no longer claimed to be the authoritative spokesman of American Jewry.

AMERICAN JEWISH JOINT DISTRIBUTION COMMITTEE. See Joint Distribution Committee.

ARAB HIGHER COMMITTEE. Formed in 1936 by representatives of four Moslem and two Christian Palestinian Arab parties under the leadership of the Mufti. In April 1936 the committee declared a six-month general strike. In the fall of 1937 its members were interred by the British or fled the country. Following the end of the Second World War it was reconstituted under the direction of the Mufti, who remained in exile in Egypt. It was supported by the Arab League.

ARENDT, HANNAH (1905-1975). Political scientist and philosopher. Born in Hanover, Germany, she received her Ph.D. from Heidelberg. In 1933 she fled to Paris, emigrating to the United States in 1941, where she was successively research director of the Conference on Jewish Relations, chief editor of Schocken Books, executive director of the Jewish Cultural Reconstruction, and visiting professor at a number of universities.

AUSTIN, WARREN R. (1877-1962). Lawyer, diplomat, and senator from Vermont. He served in the United States Senate from 1931 to 1947; was a member of the Senate Foreign Affairs Committee. He was UN representative from 1947 to 1953.

AZZAM PASHA (1893-1976). Egyptian diplomat. He was educated at the University of London; was Egyptian ambassador to Iraq, Saudi Arabia, Afghanistan, and Turkey, and was secretary general of the Arab League from 1944 to 1953.

BAERWALD, PAUL (1871-1961). Banker, Jewish community leader, and philanthropist; born in Frankfurt, Germany, and emigrated to the United States in 1896. He became a partner in Lazzard Freres, investment bankers, in 1907. A founder and then treasurer of the JDC, he succeeded Felix Warburg as chairman in 1932. He supervised the rescue work of the JDC during the Second World War.

BALDWIN, ROGER N. (1884-1981). Civil rights advocate and public law consultant; born in Wellesley, Mass. He was instructor in sociology, Washington University, from 1906 to 1909; chief probation officer, St. Louis, 1907 to 1910; and a founder and director of the American Civil Liberties Union, 1917 to 1950.

AL-BARGHUTHY, OMAR SALIH (1895-1965). Palestinian Arab lawyer and political leader born near Ramallah, Palestine. He was a leader of the Istaqlal party; lectured in the British Government Law School in Jerusalem; was a member of the Arab Higher Committee. From 1952 to 1954 he was a member of the Jordanian parliament.

BENDERLY, SAMSON (1896–1949). U.S. educator; born in Safed, Palestine, and emigrated to the United States in 1898. He received his M.D. from Johns Hopkins but did not practice medicine. In 1910 he was appointed director of the Bureau of Education of the New York Kehillah, where he introduced progressive methods of education and created the prototype of communal coordinating agencies for Jewish education.

BEN-GURION, DAVID (1886–1973). Socialist-Zionist leader and first prime minister of Israel; born in Plonsk, Russian Poland, and emigrated to Palestine in 1906. He was a founder of the Histadrut and its general secretary from 1921 to 1935. From 1935 to 1948 he served as chairman of the executive of the Jewish Agency. The moving force behind the Biltmore Platform of 1942 calling for the establishment of a Jewish commonwealth in Palestine, he supported the UN partition proposal, directed the yishuv's preparations for statehood, and in 1948, as prime minister of the newly-established state, led the successful defense of Israel in its war of independence.

BENTWICH, NORMAN DE MATTOS (1883–1971). British lawyer, Zionist, and professor of international relations; born in London. Bentwich served with the British Army in the Middle East during the First World War. From 1920 to 1931 he was attorney general of the Palestine Mandatory government. In 1932, he was appointed professor at Hebrew University. He shared the views of B'rit Shalom advocating Arab-Jewish rapprochement.

BERGMAN, SHMUEL HUGO (1883–1975). Philosopher and Zionist publicist; born in Prague. As a young man he joined the Bar Kokhba Zionist student organization and was influenced by Buber. He received his Ph.D. from the University of Berlin and in 1920 emigrated to Palestine, becoming the first director of the Jewish National and University Library. In 1928 he was appointed lecturer in philosophy at Hebrew University and professor in 1935. He was a founder of B'rit Shalom.

BERNADOTTE, COUNT FOLKE (1895–1948). Swedish nobleman and diplomat. He was president of the Swedish Red Cross during the Second World War. In May 1948 he was appointed UN mediator for Palestine and in September 1948 was assasinated by Jewish extremists.

BIALIK, CHAIM NACHMAN (1873–1934). Hebrew poet and editor; born in Volyn district, Russia. Bialik is known as the national poet of modern Hebrew literature. From 1900 to 1921 he resided in Odessa, where he began his literary activity. His major themes were the rebirth of the Jewish people and the return to Zion. He settled in Tel Aviv in 1924 and was a member of the board of governors of the Hebrew University.

BILLIKOPF, JACOB (1883–1950). U.S. social service administrator; born in Vilna and emigrated to the United States in the 1890s. He was a son-in-law of Louis Marshall and a nephew of Mrs. Judah Magnes. During the First World War he directed the major campaigns for Jewish war relief. In 1919 he was appointed executive director of the Federation of Jewish Charities of Philadelphia, where he was also active in labor mediation.

BRANDEIS, LOUIS D. (1856–1941). U.S. lawyer, social reformer, jurist, and Zionist leader; born in Louisville, Kentucky. Brandeis graduated from Harvard Law School and practiced law in Boston, where he gained a national reputation as a leader in social reform movements. In 1916 Woodrow Wilson appointed him to the United States Supreme Court. He became active in Zionist work in 1914, when he was elected chairman of the Provisional Executive Committee for General Zionist Affairs. He resigned his Jewish public offices soon after his appointment to the Court but continued to play an informal role in Zionist affairs.

B'RIT SHALOM ("Covenant of Peace") SOCIETY. Founded in Jerusalem in 1925 by a group of intellectuals and veteran Zionist settlers to foster good relations with the Arabs and to work out a mutually acceptable political solution. It proposed a binational state in which neither side would dominate the other. It ceased to function in 1933.

COHEN, BENJAMIN V. (b. 1894). U.S. lawyer and government official; born in Muncie, Indiana. Cohen served as attorney to the U.S. Shipping Board during the First World War. He was counsel to the American Zionist delegation that negotiated the terms of the Palestine Mandate from 1919 to 1921. A protege of Felix Frankfurter, he held a number of government executive positions during the New Deal and served as a presidential adviser to Franklin Roosevelt. From 1945 to 1947 he was counselor, Department of State.

COUPLAND, SIR REGINALD (1884–1952). British historian and diplomat. He was educated at New College, Oxford, where he was Beit Professor of British history from 1920 to 1948. He served on various royal commissions dealing with India and was a member of the Palestine Royal Commission, 1936 to 1937, where he was the dominant influence in formulating the recommendation for partition.

DUSHKIN, ALEXANDER M. (1890–1976). U.S. educator and community leader; born in Suwalki, Poland, and brought to the United States in 1901. Recruited by Samson Benderly to serve on the staff of the Bureau of Education of the New York Kehillah, Dushkin received his Ph.D. from Teachers College. He was inspector of Jewish schools in Palestine, 1919–1920; director of the Chicago Board of Jewish Education, 1922 to 1934; executive director of the Jewish Education Committee of New York, 1939 to 1949; and professor of Education at the Hebrew University from 1949.

EINSTEIN, ALBERT (1879–1955). Physicist; born in Ulm, Germany. He studied at the Zurich Polytechnic Institute and from 1916 to 1933 was professor at the Prussian

Academy of Science in Berlin, where he developed his famous theory of relativity. In 1921 he won the Nobel Prize. He supported various Zionist causes, touring the United States together with Chaim Weizmann on behalf of the Hebrew University. In 1925 he became a member of the board of governors of the university and chairman of its academic council. In 1933 he emigrated to the United States and joined the Institute for Advanced Studies in Princeton. In the early years of the Second World War he supported the development of the atomic bomb.

FRANKFURTER, FELIX (1882–1965). U.S. jurist and Zionist. Born in Vienna, Austria, he came to the United States as a child. He received his law degree from Harvard Law School, where he was a professor from 1914 to 1939. He was active in civil rights causes, was an adviser to President Roosevelt, and served as associate justice of the Supreme Court from 1939 to 1962. Louis Brandeis brought him into the Zionist organization. He attended the Paris Peace Conference in 1919 as a member of the Zionist delegation, where he met with Feisal, head of the Arab delegation.

FRIEDLAENDER, ISRAEL (1876–1920). Semitic scholar, educator, and U.S. community leader; born in Kovel, Russia. He obtained his Ph.D. from the University of Strasbourg and arrived in the United States in 1903 to become professor of biblical literature at the Jewish Theological Seminary. He was on the executive of the New York Kehillah, the American Jewish Committee, Federation of American Zionists, JDC, and Provisional Executive Committee for General Zionist Affairs. He was killed in the Ukraine while on a relief mission.

HAGANA ("Defense"). Jewish underground organization formed in 1920. It espoused restraint and opposed retaliation. Following the 1929 riots it became more centralized, storing arms and later manufacturing weapons. It had close ties to the Jewish Agency and was dissolved in 1948 upon the establishment of the state.

HARTOG, SIR PHILIP (1864–1947). British educator and administrator; born in London. A lecturer in chemistry, Hartog became registrar of the University of London in 1903. In 1917 he was appointed a member of the Viceroy's Commission on the University of Calcutta, India; served as vice-chancellor of the University of Dacca, Bengal, from 1920 to 1925; and headed the Commission of Inquiry of the Hebrew University, 1933 to 1934.

HEXTER, MAURICE B. (b. 1891). U.S. social service administrator; born in Cincinnati. He was superintendent of the United Jewish Charities of Cincinnati, 1917 to 1919; executive director of the Federation of Jewish Charities of Boston, 1919 to 1929; non-Zionist member of the Jewish Agency executive from 1929 to 1938, when he resided in Jerusalem; then assistant to and successor of Solomon Lowenstein as executive vice-president of the New York Federation for the Support of Jewish Philanthropic Societies.

HISTADRUT ("Organization"). The General Federation of Jewish Workers in Palestine; founded in 1920, it included, in addition to trade-union activity, mutual aid, social services, and the establishment of agricultural settlements and industrial, transport, and marketing cooperatives.

HOLMES, JOHN HAYNES (1879–1964). Unitarian minister; born in Philadelphia and graduated from Harvard Divinity School. He was minister of the Community Church of New York from 1907 to 1947 and a social activist and pacifist. He was a founder of the National Association for the Advancement of Colored People, a director of the American Civil Liberties Union, chairman of the City Affairs Committee of New York, and president of the War Resisters League.

AL-HUSAYNI, AL-HAJJ MUHAMMAD AMIN (1893–1974). Palestinian Arab nationalist leader. Born in Jerusalem to the influential Husayni family, he played a leading role in the April 1920 anti-Jewish riots. In 1921 he was appointed Grand Mufti (expounder of Muslim law) by Herbert Samuel in an attempt to appease the Arab nationalists. He used his religious role to consolidate his position as the most powerful Arab leader in Palestine, adopting an extremist anti-Jewish and anti-British attitude. He headed the Arab Higher Committee; collaborated with Nazi Germany during the Second World War. In 1946 he escaped from French detention and continued to direct Palestinian Arab affairs from his exile in Cairo.

AL-HUSAYNI, MUSA ABDALLAH (1914–1951). Palestinian Arab leader. A cousin of the Mufti, he studied at Al-Azhar University in Cairo, the University of London, and at Berlin and Jena Universities. He served in the Arab Information Office in London in the 1930s. From 1942 to 1945 he was in Germany with the Mufti. Following the 1948 war he was unsuccessful in establishing himself in Jordanian politics. He was hanged for plotting the assassination of King Abdallah.

IHUD ("Unity") ASSOCIATION. Established in August 1942 by the initiative of Judah Magnes, Ihud advocated an Arab-Jewish binational state in a self-governing, undivided Palestine, based on equal political rights for the two peoples of Palestine. In 1946 Ihud spokesmen appeared before the Anglo-American Committee of Inquiry and in 1947 before the UN Special Committee on Palestine, when they called for numerical as well as political parity between Arabs and Jews.

IRGUN ZEVA'I LE'UMI (National Military Organization), also IZL or ETSEL. A Jewish underground group that split away from the Hagana during the 1930s, favoring retaliatory actions against the Arabs during the 1936–1939 disturbances. In 1944 after a period of collaboration with the Hagana and the British, the Irgun adopted a policy of attacks and reprisals against the British. In 1948 with the establishment of the Jewish state the Irgun disbanded.

JEWISH AGENCY. The Mandate for Palestine provided for "a public body to advise and cooperate with the Administration of Palestine in such matters as may affect the establishment of the Jewish National Home." The World Zionist Organization was recognized as the Jewish Agency fulfilling these functions. In 1929 the Jewish Agency was enlarged to include non-Zionists willing to assist in establishing a Jewish National Home, the agreement stipulating parity between the non-Zionists and Zionists in the governing bodies of the Jewish Agency. In practice the Jewish Agency became coterminous with the executive bodies of the World Zionist Organization in matters dealing with Palestine. On the establishment of the State of Israel the Jewish Agency surrendered most of its quasisovereign functions to the state, dealing thereafter primarily with providing assistance to those immigrating to Israel.

JEWISH NATIONAL FUND. Fund for development and land purchasing in Palestine and, after 1948, the State of Israel. Founded by the Zionist organization in 1901, the fund raised its budget for land reclamation and purchase from contributions of world Jewry.

JOINT DISTRIBUTION COMMITTEE (JDC). The JDC was founded in 1914 to coordinate the overseas relief work of the American Jewish Relief Committee, supported largely by the established German Jews, the Central Relief Committee, which appealed to Orthodox Jews, and the People's Relief Committee, supported by the Jewish labor movement. Under its first president, Felix Warburg, the JDC supplied emergency relief, undertook rehabilitation programs in Eastern Europe during the 1920s and 1930s, and during the Second World War under the leadership of Paul Baerwald functioned as the main Jewish organization for relief and rescue work for European Jewry.

KALVARISKY, CHAIM MARGALIT (1868–1947). Agronomist and Zionist; born in Solalky, Russia, and emigrated to Palestine in 1895, aiding the agricultural settlement enterprises of Baron Edmond de Rothschild. One of the first Zionists in Palestine to establish close ties with the Arabs, he was a founder of B'rit Shalom and in 1936 of Kedma Mizraha (similar in its goals to B'rit Shalom). In 1939 he became president of the League for Jewish-Arab Rapprochement.

KAPLAN, MORDECAI M. (b. 1881). U.S. theologian and community leader; born in Svencionys, Lithuania, and brought to the United States in 1889. Ordained in 1902 at the Jewish Theological Seminary, he was appointed dean of the Teachers Institute of the seminary in 1910. He collaborated in the founding of the New York Kehillah and founded the Society for the Advancement of Judaism in 1922, remaining its leader until 1944. He established *Reconstructionist* magazine in 1934 and the movement known by that name, which defined Judaism as an evolving religious civilization. He was professor of homiletics and the philosophy of religion at the Jewish Theological Seminary.

KEREN HAKAYEMET; see Jewish National Fund.

KEREN HAYESOD; see Palestine Foundation Fund.

KISCH, FREDERICK H. (1888–1943). British soldier and Zionist administrator; born in Darjeeling, India. He served during the First World War in France and Mesopotamia. In 1923 he joined the Zionist Executive in Jerusalem and headed the political department. He resigned in 1931 but continued to advise the yishuv on security matters. He returned to active service in the British Army on the outbreak of the Second World War, serving as chief engineer, Eighth Army, with the rank of brigadier. He was killed in action.

KLAUSNER, JOSEPH (1874–1958). Hebrew essayist, historian, and Zionist; born near Vilna and grew up in Odessa. He received his Ph.D. from Heidelberg and succeeded Ahad Ha'am as editor of Ha'shiloah, which he edited from 1902 to 1926. In 1919 he settled in Jerusalem and with the opening of the Hebrew University was appointed to the chair of Hebrew literature. In 1944 he was appointed professor of Jewish history.

KLIGLER, ISRAEL J. (1889–1944). Bacteriologist and specialist in public health; born in Kaments-Podolski, the Ukraine, and brought to the United States in 1901. He went to Palestine in 1920 and worked for the Hadassah Medical Organization, undertaking research in malaria control. From 1926 to his death he was director of the department of hygiene of the Hebrew University.

KOHN, HANS (1891–1971). U.S. historian; born in Prague. He belonged to the Bar Kokhba Zionist group. From 1920 to 1921 he was secretary of the Comité des Delegations Juives, which functioned in Paris during the peace conference. After receiving his Ph.D. at the University of Prague, he worked for the Zionist organization first in London and then in Jerusalem. He resigned in 1929 in protest over Zionist policy on the Arab question. He was a founder of B'rit Shalom. In 1933 he came to the United States and was professor of history at Smith College from 1934 to 1949 and from 1949 to 1962 at the City College of New York.

KUHN, SETTY SCHWARTZ (1868–1952). Jewish philanthropist born in Cincinnati, Ohio; wife of Simon Kuhn, a banker, who was related to the Kuhn and Loeb families of Cincinnati and New York. She was particularly concerned with the Arab-Jewish question in Palestine.

LAZARON, MORRIS S. (1888–1980). U.S. Reform rabbi; born in Savannah, Georgia, and graduated from Hebrew Union College. Lazaron was rabbi of the Baltimore Hebrew Congregation from 1915 to 1949 and a cofounder and vice-president of the American Council for Judaism. He was associated with the National Conference of Christians and Jews, a director of the JDC, and a member of the National Council of the American Friends of the Middle East.

LEHMAN, HERBERT H. (1878–1963). U.S. banker, philanthropist, and statesman; born in New York City. He joined the family investment firm of Lehman Brothers. During the First World War he was special assistant to the Secretary of War. A cofounder of the JDC, he chaired its reconstruction committee in the postwar years. In 1928 he was elected lieutenant governor of New York and governor in 1932. Repeatedly reelected he resigned in 1942 to head the UN Relief and Rehabilitation Administration. He was elected to the U.S. Senate in 1949. A non-Zionist, Lehman supported free Jewish immigration into Palestine and in 1947 came out for a Jewish state as the only solution to the Jewish refugee problem.

LoḤAMEY ḤERUT YISRAEL ("Fighters for the Freedom of Israel"), also Leḥi; see Stern Group.

LIPPMAN, WALTER (1889–1974). Political essayist and editor born in New York City. He was associate editor of the *New Republic* from 1914 to 1917, when he left to become Assistant Secretary of War. From 1921 to 1967 he was a columnist for the New York *World*, New York *Herald Tribune*, and Washington *Post*, successively, publishing a number of books on political and social topics.

LOWENSTEIN, SOLOMON (1877–1942). U.S. rabbi and social service executive; born in Philadelphia. He graduated from the Hebrew Union College and served as superintendent of the United Jewish Charities of Cincinnati, 1901 to 1904; superintendent of Hebrew Orphan Asylum, New York, 1905 to 1920; executive vice-president and director, Federation for the Support of Jewish Philanthropies, New York, 1920 to 1942; and director of the AJC and JDC and vice-president of the American Friends of the Hebrew University.

McCLINTOCK, ROBERT M. (1909–1976). U.S. Foreign Service diplomat. After serving in Panama, Japan, Chile, and Finland, he was assigned to the Office of Special Political Affairs of the State Department in 1946 and served as political adviser to the United States delegation to the UN General Assembly in 1946 and 1947–1948. He was then successively ambassador to Lebanon, Argentina, and Venezuela.

MacMILLAN, SIR GORDON HOLMES ALEXANDER (b. 1897). British army officer. He held various posts and commands during the Second World War in Africa, Sicily, Normandy, Holland, and Germany, serving as General Officer Commanding, Palestine, 1947–1948.

MACK, JULIAN W. (1866–1943). U.S. judge and Zionist leader; born in San Francisco. He was a juvenile court judge in Chicago from 1904 to 1907; a professor of law at the University of Chicago, 1902 to 1911; and was appointed judge, U.S. Circuit Court, in 1913. He was a founding member of the American Jewish Committee; president, Zionist Organization of America, 1918 to 1921; and member, board of governors, Hebrew University. He also served on the National War Labor Board during the First World War and on the board of inquiry on conscientious objectors.

MAGNES, BEATRICE L. (1881–1968). Born in New York City, the daughter of Benedict and Sophia Lowenstein. She attended Hunter College; was a founding member of Hadassah. She married Judah Magnes in 1908, and they had three children: David, Jonathan, and Benedict.

MAGNES, DAVID (1848–1922). Born in Przedborg near Lodz, Poland to a hassidic family. He immigrated to the United States in 1863 and joined his older brother in San Francisco. He married Sophie Abrahamson in 1874, and they had five children: Judah, Isaac, Eva, Tess, and Rosalind. The family moved to Oakland in 1882, where David Magnes had a dry goods store.

MANN, THOMAS (1875–1955). German novelist and essayist; born in Lubeck, Germany. He published his first novel in 1901. Mann won the Nobel Prize for literature in 1929. With the rise of Hitler he left Germany in self-imposed exile and emigrated to the United States in 1936.

MARSHALL, JAMES (b. 1896). U.S. lawyer, civic leader, and author; son of Louis Marshall. He studied law at Columbia University and became a member of the firm of Marshall, Brattner, Greene, Allison and Tucker. He was a member of the New York City Board of Education from 1938 to 1952 and its president from 1938 to 1942. He was active in the American Jewish Committee, JDC, and American Friends of the Hebrew University.

MARSHALL, LOUIS (1856–1929). U.S. lawyer, Jewish community leader; born in Syracuse, New York. In 1894 he became a partner in the New York law firm of Guggenheimer, Untermyer, and Marshall. A founder of the American Jewish Committee, Marshall served as its president from 1912 to 1929. An outstanding figure in defending Jewish civil rights in the United States and abroad, he was chief spokesman for the German-Jewish elite. He was a cofounder of the JDC and president of the American Jewish Relief Committee. He was instrumental in forming the enlarged Jewish Agency representing the non-Zionists in negotiations with the Zionists led by Chaim Weizmann.

MOND, SIR ALFRED M. (Lord Melchett) (1868–1930). British industrialist and Zionist; born in Farnworth, England. He served as a Liberal member of Parliament, 1906 to 1926, and in various cabinet posts from 1916 to 1921. He was a key figure in forming the enlarged Jewish Agency in 1929, acting as associate chairman.

NEARING, SCOTT (b. 1883). U.S. educator, political radical, and author. He received his Ph.D. in economics from the University of Pennsylvania, where he taught until 1915, when he was dismissed because of his social reform activities. He was forced out of the University of Toledo in 1917 because of pacifism. He became chairman of the Peoples Council of America in 1917 and was identified with the militant wings of both the Socialist and Communist parties. He was expelled from the latter in 1930.

PROVISIONAL EXECUTIVE COMMITTEE FOR GENERAL ZIONIST AFFAIRS. Established in August 1914 to coordinate the activities of all Zionist groups and parties in the United States, the committee virtually absorbed the Federation of American Zionists. It raised funds to save the yishuv from economic collapse, transfered money to Jews in war-stricken Europe and Palestine, directed the activities of the Zionist organizations in the United States, and was instrumental in forming the American Jewish Congress. Louis D. Brandeis was the first chairman (1914–1916) and was succeeded by Stephen S. Wise.

ROSENWALD, LESSING (1891–1979). U.S. businessman and philanthropist; born in Chicago, son of Julius Rosenwald, a founder of Sears, Roebuck and Company.

He was chairman of the board of directors of the company from 1932 to 1939; president of Federation of Jewish Philanthropies of Philadelphia from 1930 to 1934; and first president of the American Council for Judaism from 1943 to 1945.

ROTHSCHILD, BARON EDMOND DE (1845–1934). Philanthropist and patron of Jewish settlement in Palestine; born in Paris. He became active in Jewish affairs in the 1880s following the pogroms in Russia. He took over the support and supervision of a number of Jewish agricultural settlements in Palestine in the late 1880s. In 1900 he established the Jewish Colonization Association (ICA) as a way of improving the management of the colonies, and in 1923 he formed the Palestine Jewish Colonization Organization (PICA), headed by his son James, which continued the settlement activity of its predecessor. Rothschild supported the Hebrew University and was made honorary president of the Jewish Agency in 1929.

RUPPIN, ARTHUR (1876–1943). Economist, sociologist, and Zionist official; born in Posen. He directed the Bureau of Jewish Statistics and Demography in Berlin from 1903 to 1907. In 1908 he was appointed head of the Palestine Office by the Zionist Organization and directed the Zionist settlement program in Palestine. He was a member of the Zionist executive from 1921 to 1927 and 1929 to 1931, and from 1933 to 1935 he headed the Jewish Agency's department for the settlement of German immigrants. His books on the sociology of the Jews were pioneer studies of their kind. He was a founder and chairman of B'rith Shalom.

RUTENBERG, PINHAS (1879–1942). Engineer and Zionist; born in the Ukraine. He took part in Russian revolution of 1905. Rutenberg was active in forming a Jewish legion during the First World War. He emigrated to Palestine in 1919. In 1923 he founded the Palestine Electric Company and was responsible for building the hydroelectric works in the Jordan Valley. He was a member of the Va'ad Le'umi and became its head in 1929. During the 1930s he was active in promoting Arab-Jewish understanding.

AL-SA'ID, NURI (1888–1958). Iraqi statesman and army officer; born in Baghdad. He fought in the revolt against the Turks during the First World War. From 1923 to 1930 he served as minister of defense and during the 1930s and 1940s served at various times as premier and minister of foreign affairs. He was instrumental in establishing the Arab League in 1946 and in forming the Baghdad Pact in 1954. He was assassinated in the revolt against King Feisal II's government in 1958.

SAMUEL, SIR HERBERT L. (1870–1963). British statesman, philosopher, and first high commissioner of Palestine; born in Liverpool, raised in London, educated at Balliol College, Oxford. Active in the Liberal party, he entered Parliament in 1902. He held various junior cabinet posts and in 1916 was promoted to home secretary. During the First World War he helped win Lloyd George's support for the Balfour Declaration. He served as high commissioner of Palestine from 1920 to 1925, thereafter supporting various proposals for compromise between Arab and Jewish political demands in Palestine. He was a member of the board of governors of the Hebrew University. From 1944 to 1955 he led the Liberal party in the House of Lords.

SAYRE, JOHN NEVIN (1884–1977). Minister and pacifist leader; born in Bethlehem, Pennsylvania, and graduated from Princeton and the Episcopal Theological School. Sayre edited *The World Tomorrow*, 1922–1924; was secretary of the Fellowship of Reconciliation, 1924–1934, and chairman, 1935–1946; and was cosecretary of the International Fellowship of Reconciliation, 1935–1955.

SCHECHTER, SOLOMON (1847–1915). Theologian and rabbinic scholar; born in Rumania. Schechter was reader in rabbinics at Cambridge from 1892 to 1899 before being invited to serve as president of the Jewish Theological Seminary in 1901. He was instrumental in expanding the seminary and influencing the development of the Conservative wing of Judaism, establishing the United Synagogues of America in 1913.

SCHIFF, JACOB H. (1847–1920). U.S. financier, philanthropist, and community leader; born in Frankfurt, he emigrated to the United States in 1865. He married the daughter of Solomon Loeb, head of the banking house of Kuhn, Loeb and Company, and was named head of the firm in 1885, turning it into one of the most powerful private investment houses in the United States. He was a munificent philanthropist to Jewish as well as general civic and charitable causes, and he took an active interest in the institutions and causes he supported. His sponsorship of the Jewish Theological Seminary, Hebrew Union College, Semitic Museum of Harvard, JDC, Bureau of Education of the New York Kehillah, Barnard College, and the Henry Street Settlement was notable. He was a founder of the American Jewish Committee.

SCHLOESSINGER, MAX (1877–1944). Semitic scholar, merchant, Zionist administrator; born in Heidelberg. He studied at the universities of Berlin and Vienna and at the Lehranstalt fuer die Wissenschaft des Judentums in Berlin. Instructor and librarian at Hebrew Union College, 1904 to 1907, he resigned because of the anti-Zionist stand of the administration. He established a flourishing export-import business in Germany and, following the First World War, in Holland, before moving to Palestine. A member of the board of governors of the Hebrew University, he served at various times as deputy to Magnes in the office of chancellor.

SENATOR, DAVID WERNER (1896–1953). Zionist administrator. Born in Berlin, he was secretary-general of the European office of the JDC from 1925 to 1930; was a member of the Jewish Agency executive from 1930 to 1935 representing the non-Zionists. He became the administrator of the Hebrew University. He was a member of B'rit Shalom and Ihud.

SHARETT (SHERTOK), MOSHE (1894–1965). Socialist Zionist leader and Israeli statesman; born in the Ukraine and emigrated to Palestine in 1906. He studied law in Constantinople and was commissioned in the Turkish army in the First World War. In 1933 he was appointed head of the political department of the Jewish Agency. Sharett was foreign minister of Israel from 1948 to 1956 and Prime Minister from 1954 to 1955.

SHOCHAT, MANYA (1880–1961). Socialist Zionist leader; born in Beylo-russia, she joined the Russian revolutionary movement as a young woman. In 1903 she became interested in socialist Zionism and emigrated to Palestine. She raised funds for Jewish self-defense in Russia and Palestine, visiting Europe and America for that purpose. A founder of the Hashomer self-defense organization in 1908 and the G'dud Ha'avoda in 1920, she participated in various efforts to bring Arabs and Jews together.

SIMON, ERNST AKIVA (b. 1899). Philosopher, educator, and writer; born in Berlin. He received his Ph.D. from Heidelberg; became an active Zionist in 1918, coediting *Der Jude* with Martin Buber. He emigrated to Palestine in 1928 and joined the faculty of the Hebrew University in 1935, where he became professor of philosophy of education. Simon was a founder of B'rit Shalom, on the executive committee of Ihud, and editor of its monthly, *Ba'ayot*.

SIMON, JULIUS (1875–1969). Merchant, Zionist, and administrator; born in Mannheim, Germany. He was a delegate to the Zionist Congresses from 1903 to 1921. He was called to London in 1918 to direct the Palestine department of the Central Zionist Office; was a founder in 1925 of the Palestine Economic Corporation and its president from 1931 to 1951. He lived in Palestine from 1933 to 1949.

SIMON, SIR LEON (1881–1965). British Zionist leader, civil servant, and writer; born in Southhampton, England. He entered the British civil service in 1904 and became director of telegraphs and telephones, 1931–1935, and director of savings banks, 1935–1944. He was a disciple of Ahad Ha'am and wrote extensively in Hebrew and English on Zionist thought, translating Ahad Ha'am into English. From 1946 to 1949 he served as chairman of the executive council of the Hebrew University.

SOKOLOW, NAHUM (1859–1936). Pioneer of Hebrew journalism and Zionist official; born in Poland. He was one of the editors of *Ha'zefira* and later of *Ha'olam*. From 1911 he was a member of the Zionist executive and collaborated with Weizmann during the First World War in negotiating the Balfour Declaration. From 1931 to 1935 he was president of the World Zionist Organization.

STERN GROUP (sometimes referred to as Stern Gang). Militant Zionist underground organization founded by Abraham Stern, who split from the Irgun in 1939, when the Irgun called off its campaign against the British military authorities for the duration of the war. Stern was killed after being taken prisoner by the British in 1942. In 1944 the group became active again. It was responsible for the assasination of Lord Moyne, British minister for the Middle East, in November 1944 and was allegedly responsible for the assasination of Count Folke Bernadotte, UN mediator, in Jerusalem in September 1948. It was disbanded following the establishment of the state of Israel.

STONE, ISIDOR F. (b. 1907). Journalist and author; born in Philadelphia. He was associated with the *New York Post*, *The Nation*, and *PM* and published the *I.F.*

Stone Weekly. His book *Underground to Palestine* (1946) described the illegal immigration of Jewish refugees to Palestine.

STRAUS, GLADYS ELEANOR GUGGENHEIM (1895–1980). Philanthropist and civic leader; born in Elberton, New Jersey, the daughter of Daniel Guggenheim. She married Roger William Straus, son of Oscar Straus. She served as vice-president of Mt. Sinai Hospital; president of the Daniel and Florence Guggenheim Foundation; and vice-president, board of governors, Women's National Republican Club.

STRAUS, NATHAN (1848–1931). U.S. merchant, philanthropist, and civic leader; born in Otterberg, Germany, and emigrated to the United States in 1854. With his brother Isidor he built R. H. Macy into one of the country's largest department stores. Active in public health projects in the United States, he also supported similar activities in Palestine, visiting the country four times.

STRAUS, OSCAR S. (1850–1926). U.S. merchant, diplomat, and philanthropist; born in Otterberg, Germany, brother of Isidor and Nathan; the family emigrated to the U.S. in 1854. After completing Columbia University Law School, he became active in politics. He was U.S. minister to Turkey, 1887 to 1889 and 1898 to 1900, and ambassador from 1909 to 1910. He served as secretary of commerce and labor, 1906 to 1909, and was active in the cause of international arbitration. A founder of the American Jewish Committee, he opposed political Zionism but supported philanthropic efforts to resettle Jews in Palestine.

STROOCK, ALAN (b. 1907). Lawyer and Jewish community leader; born in New York, son of Solomon Stroock. He served as law clerk for Justice Benjamin Cardozo from 1934 to 1936 and then joined Stroock and Stroock. He was chairman of the board of trustees of the Jewish Theological Seminary, president of the Federation of Jewish Philanthropies, a vice-president of the American Jewish Committee, and then chairman of its administrative committee.

STROOCK, SOLOMON M. (1874–1941). Lawyer and Jewish community leader; born in New York City. He was active in the New York Bar, a leading member of B'nai Jeshurun, and chairman of the board of directors of the Jewish Theological Seminary from 1931 to 1941. He was among the founders of the enlarged Jewish Agency. Chairman of the executive committee of the American Jewish Committee from 1934 to 1940, he served as its president in 1941.

SULZBERGER, ARTHUR HAYS (1891–1968). Newspaper publisher; born in New York City, the son of Cyrus L. and Rachel (Hays). He joined the *New York Times* in 1918 and assisted his father-in-law, the publisher Adolph S. Ochs, succeeding Ochs upon his death in 1935. In 1961 he turned the management of the paper over to his son-in-law Orvile E. Dryfoos. He married Iphigene B. Ochs in 1917.

SULZBERGER, CYRUS (1858–1932). Businessman and community leader; born in Philadelphia and moved to New York in 1877. Active in civic betterment movements, he was an early advocate of the Jewish federation movement, a publisher of the *American Hebrew,* president of the Industrial Removal Office, and a member of the executive committees of the New York Kehillah, American Jewish Committee, and the JDC.

SULZBERGER, MAYER (1843–1923). U.S. lawyer, jurist, and community leader; born in Heidelsheim, Germany, and emigrated to the United States in 1849, settling in Philadelphia. A Hebrew scholar, he was chairman of the publications committee of the Jewish Publication Society from 1888 to 1923 and was active in reorganizing the Jewish Theological Seminary in 1901. He served as a governor of Dropsie College and was first president of the American Jewish Committee and a trustee of the Baron de Hirsch Fund. He was appointed judge of the Court of Common Pleas in Philadelphia in 1895 and in 1915 was elected president judge of the court.

SZOLD, HENRIETTA (1860–1945). Community leader in the United States and Palestine; born in Baltimore. She received a Hebrew education from her father, Rabbi Benjamin Szold. She was secretary of the Jewish Publication Society editorial board, secretary of the Federation of American Zionists in 1910, founder and first president of Hadassah, and organizer of the American Zionist Medical Unit in 1916. In 1920 she settled in Palestine and became the director of the Medical Unit and later the Hadassah Medical Organization. She directed the Youth Aliyah program, which was responsible for transfering refugee children from Germany to Palestine beginning in 1933. She supported a binational solution to the Palestine question and was a founding member of Ihud.

THOMAS, NORMAN (1884–1968). Presbyterian minister, pacifist, and socialist leader; born in Marion, Oregon. He headed the American Parish, a settlement house in East Harlem; became an active pacifist and secretary of the Fellowship of Reconciliation, 1917; and joined the Socialist party the following year. He was active in the American Civil Liberties Union and was nominated for President by the Socialist party regularly from 1928 to 1948.

UNTERMYER, EUGENE (1893–1959). Lawyer and civic leader; born in New York City. He graduated from Columbia Law School and was a member of the law firm of Guggenheimer and Untermyer and its predecessor, Guggenheimer, Untermyer, and Marshall. He contributed his services to the Selective Service system for many years and served as vice president of the American Friends of the Hebrew University. His mother, Sadie Lowenstein, was the sister of Beatrice Magnes.

USSISHKIN, MENAHEM (1863–1941). Zionist official; born in Dubrovno, Russia. He was an early supporter of Hebrew University and participated in all phases of its organization. From 1923 to 1941 he headed the Jewish National Fund, residing in Jerusalem and serving on the executive of the Jewish Agency.

VA'AD LE'UMI (National Council). The executive body of the Knesset Yisrael, the statutory Jewish community operating under mandatory law and chosen by annual sessions of the Asefat Ha'nivharim (elected assembly) to administer the affairs of Palestine Jewry. It was recognized by the British Mandatory Government as the official spokesman of the organized Jewish community in Palestine.

VOORSANGER, JACOB (1852–1908). U.S. Reform rabbi; born in Amsterdam. He studied at the Jewish Theological Seminary in Amsterdam, emigrating to the United States in 1872. After holding several pulpits, he was called to Temple Emanu-El, San Francisco, in 1866 and served there until his death. Well versed in Jewish literature, he became the foremost rabbi on the West Coast. He founded the weekly *Emanu-El* and was a governor of the Hebrew Union College.

WARBURG, FELIX M. (1878–1937). U.S. banker, philanthropist, and community leader; born in Hamburg, Germany, and emigrated to the United States in 1894. A partner in Kuhn, Loeb and Company, he married Freda Schiff, the daughter of Jacob Schiff, the senior partner of the firm. His chief interests were philanthropy and culture. He supported the Jewish Theological Seminary, Hebrew Union College, and the Graduate School of Jewish Social Work; he was chairman of the JDC from 1914 to 1932 and aided the YMHA movement and the New York Kehillah's Bureau of Education. Though not a Zionist he aided Zionist activities in Palestine through the Palestine Economic Corporation and Hebrew University and as chairman of the administrative committee of the Jewish Agency, succeeding Louis Marshall.

WASSON, THOMAS C. (1896–1948). U.S. Foreign Service diplomat from 1925 to his death. He was U.S. consul in Jerusalem from April to May 1948.

WAUCHOPE, SIR ARTHUR (1874–1947). British soldier and civil servant; born in Edinburgh, Scotland. Following his service in the Boer and First World wars, he served as chief of the British section of the Military Inter-Allied Commission of Control from 1924 to 1927 and later as commanding general of Northern Ireland. He was high commissioner of Palestine and Trans-Jordan from 1931 to 1938.

WEIZMANN, CHAIM (1874–1952). Scientist and Zionist leader; born in Motol, Russian Poland. He studied in Germany and Switzerland before becoming lecturer in biochemistry at the University of Geneva and in 1904 reader in the same subject in Manchester. His discoveries during the First World War were important in manufacturing explosives and won him a worldwide reputation. Weizmann supported Zionist settlement activities together with diplomatic initiatives to win political recognition for Zionist aspirations in Palestine. In 1917 he was instrumental in procuring the Balfour Declaration, stating that Great Britain favored the establishment of a Jewish National Home in Palestine. After 1920 he assumed the leadership of the Zionist movement, serving as president of the World Zionist Organization from 1920 to 1931 and from 1935 to 1946. Weizmann became the first President of the State of Israel, holding the office from 1948 to his death. As early as 1902 Weizmann, together with Martin Buber and Berthold Feiwel, published a detailed plan for a university in Jerusalem. He was the key figure in the preliminary work that led to the opening of the Hebrew University in 1925.

WISE, STEPHEN S. (1874–1949). U.S. Reform rabbi, social reformer, Zionist leader; born in Budapest and was brought to the United States as a child. He was educated at Columbia University. After holding a pulpit in New York, he moved to Portland, Oregon, where in addition to his rabbinical duties he was commissioner of child labor. He was a founder of the Federation of American Zionists in 1898. In 1906 he returned to New York and established the Free Synagogue, taking an active part in civic reform movements. He was a founder of the National Association for the Advancement of Colored People and was active in various pacifist organizations, though he supported America's entry into the war. In 1914 he helped form the Provisional Executive Committee for General Zionist Affairs, succeeding Louis Brandeis as its head. He was president of the Zionist Organization of America from 1936 to 1938. He was a founder of the reorganized American Jewish Congress in 1920 and its president until his death. During the 1930s and 1940s he was the most prominent spokesman for American Jews.

WOLFFSOHN, DAVID (1856–1914). Merchant and Zionist official; born in Russian Lithuania. He supported Theodore Herzl's Zionist policy and succeeded him as president of the World Zionist Organization, serving from 1905 to 1911.

YISHUV. Hebrew term meaning "settlement," which denoted the Jewish community of Palestine prior to the founding of the State of Israel.

ZANGWILL, ISRAEL (1864–1926). English author, early Zionist and Territorialist; born in London. He became known as a chronicler of Jewish immigrant life. He believed in settling Jews forced to emigrate from Eastern Europe in territorial concentrations outside of Palestine.

SELECTED WORKS BY
JUDAH L. MAGNES

Books

Joseph ibn Aknin, A Treatise as to Necessary Existence, etc. Edited and translated into English by J. L. Magnes. Berlin, 1904.

Russia and Germany at Brest-Litovsk; a Documentary History of the Peace Negotiations. New York: The Rand School of Social Science, 1919.

War-time Addresses, 1917–1921. New York: Thomas Selzer, 1923.

Like All the Nations? Jerusalem, 1930. (Published also in Hebrew and German.)

Addresses by the Chancellor of the Hebrew University. Jerusalem: Hebrew University, 1936.

In the Perplexity of the Times. Jerusalem: Hebrew University, 1946.

Arab-Jewish Unity; Testimony before the Anglo-American Inquiry Commission for the Ihud (Union) Association. Judah L. Magnes and Martin Buber. London: Victor Gollancz, 1947.

Towards Union in Palestine; Essays on Zionism and Jewish-Arab Cooperation. Edited by M. Buber, J. L. Magnes, E. Simon. Jerusalem: Ihud (Union) Association, 1947.

Articles and Pamphlets

"Some Poems of Bialik." *Hebrew Union College Annual*, 1 (1904), 177–186.

"Evidences of Jewish Nationality." *The Emanu-El Pulpit*, vol. 1. New York, 1908.

"A Republic of Nationalities." *The Emanu-El Pulpit*, vol. 3. New York, 1909.

"The Melting Pot." *The Emanu-El Pulpit*, vol. 3. New York, 1909.

"Reformed Judaism: Plans for Reconstruction." *The Emanu-El Pulpit*, vol. 3. New York, 1910.

Zionism and Jewish Religion; Address Delivered before the Philadelphia Section of the Council of Jewish Women. Philadelphia, 1910.

The People Do Not Want War; Address Delivered at Madison Square Garden, March 24, 1917. New York, 1917.

"The Rights of the Jews as a Nation." *Annals of the American Academy of Political and Social Science*, 72 (July 1917), 160–164.

"*The Spirit of Peace and the Spirit of War; World Fellowship Through Religion.* London: The World Congress of Faiths, 1936.

"Toward Peace in Palestine." *Foreign Affairs*, 21 (January 1943), 239–249.

"Compromise for Palestine." *The Nation*, December 23, 1944.

"Jewish-Arab Cooperation in Palestine." *The Political Quarterly*, 16 (October–December 1945), 297–306.

"For a Jewish-Arab Confederation." *Commentary* (October 1948), 379–383.

ACKNOWLEDGMENTS

It is a pleasure to acknowledge the initial encouragement and continued interest of the directors of the Judah L. Magnes Museum in Berkeley, California, and particularly its executive director, Seymour Fromer. The following friends of the Museum provided financial aid in the publishing of the book: James W. and Lucille Abrahamson, Norman Coliver, Douglas E. Goldman, Madeline Haas Russell, Richard and Roselyne Swig, and the Memorial Foundation for Jewish Culture. Over the years I have accumulated a heavy debt to Professor Moses Rischin. His belief in the importance of the book, the advice he generously gave at every juncture of its progress, and his critical reading of the manuscript proved invaluable.

New York friends of Judah Magnes — James Marshall, David Sher, and Alan Stroock, all of whom have been long associated with the American Jewish Committee, of which Magnes was a founder — and the Jacob and Hilda Blaustein Foundation provided assistance in bringing the book to completion. Morris Fine of the American Jewish Committee took a special interest in the book and offered valuable counsel. Grants from the Israel National Academy of Sciencies and Humanities and from the Hebrew University's faculty of humanities enabled me to secure secretarial and research assistance. An appointment as the Joseph M. Levine America–Holy Land Research Scholar of the Hebrew University's Institute of Contemporary Jewry made possible a trip to the United States to examine archival material. On that occasion and on subsequent trips to New York, Professor David J. Rothman provided this wandering scholar with a place to work, sound advice, and, together with his wife, Sheila, warm hospitality. This book was completed at Columbia University, where as a visiting scholar I enjoyed the cordiality of the history department and its chairman, Professor Malcolm W. Bean.

Interviews with co-workers and acquaintances of Magnes and advice from scholars and specialists enriched my understanding of the man, influenced my selection of material, and solved a number of problems of annotation. Among the many I turned to I would like to mention the following: in Jerusalem, Professor Gershom Scholem, Professor Ernst Simon, Professor Yehuda Bauer, Professor Moshe Davis, Dr. Paul Mendes Flohr, Dr. Shlomo Slonim, and Yona Shiloh; in

New York, Dr. E. M. Bluestone, Paul M. Herzog, Maurice Hexter, and Dr. Ronald Sobel; in Philadelphia, Lessing Rosenwald; and in Boston, Max Gorenstein. James Marshall granted me a number of interviews, gave me permission to use the Louis Marshall Papers, and allowed me to examine his own files of correspondence with Magnes.

My work in various archives was facilitated by the knowledge and efficiency of curators in Israel and in the United States. Professor Jacob Rader Marcus and his staff made my stay at the American Jewish Archives in Cincinnati a productive one. Ruth Rafael guided me through the Magnes holdings at the Western Jewish History Center and tracked down obscure details concerning Magnes's family in Oakland. Dr. Menahem Schmelzer of the Library of the Jewish Theological Seminary in New York, J. Richard Kyle, curator of the Swarthmore College Peace Collection, Swarthmore, Pennsylvania, Luise Calef of the Weizmann Library in Rehovot, Israel, Dr. Michael Heymann, director of the Central Zionist Archives in Jerusalem, Margot Cohen, curator of the Martin Buber Papers at the Jewish National and University Library in Jerusalem, and Yehoshua Rivlin, archivist of the Hebrew University, were most helpful.

I owe my greatest research debt to the staff of the Central Archives of the History of the Jewish People in Jerusalem and to its director, Dr. Daniel J. Cohen. The documents that form the bulk of the book were drawn from the Magnes collection located at the Central Archives and are published with their permission. Over the years, Hadassah Assouline, the chief archivist, met my requests with incomparable patience. Her familiarity with the collection and the splendid catalogue she prepared greatly facilitated my work. Yaacov Tsabakh tracked down with unfailing courtesy the thousands of files I used.

Menahem Blondheim, Robert Fisher, Deborah Goldman, Howard Gootkin, Dr. Aryeh Maidenbaum, and Urit Uziel Meged were resourceful research assistants. Dr. Carol Bosworth Kutscher helped prepare the manuscript for publication, and Amanda Heller and Camille Smith of Harvard University Press handled a difficult text with dispatch.

Professor Yehoshua Arieli, with whom I discussed this work from the beginning, was always edifying in his comments. He read the entire manuscript and gave helpful criticism of an early version of the introduction. I benefited, as well, from Lucy Dawidowicz's and Professor Ezra Mendelson's incisive criticism of a later version. Professor Deborah Dash Moore read a number of the documents and the introduction and made valuable suggestions.

Documents 83, 108, and 118 are reprinted by permission from the *New York Times;* copyright © 1937, 1945, 1947 by the New York Times Company. Document 102 is reprinted by permission from *Foreign Affairs,* January 1943; copyright 1943 by the Council on Foreign Relations, Inc. Document 138 is reprinted by permission from *Commentary,* October 1948; copyright © 1948 by the American Jewish Committee.

I owe a special debt of gratitude to the Magnes family and particularly to Jonathan Magnes, for many years professor of physiology at the Hebrew University's School of Medicine. In 1968, on the death of his mother, he asked me to examine the family papers that had remained in her possession. When I later undertook to prepare an edition of his father's writings, he agreed that the choice of material to be included in the book be solely mine. I consulted with him frequently, as I did with his wife, Hava. His balanced and perceptive comments were matched by his graciousness and warmth. He died in August 1980 as the book was being completed. Another of Magnes's sons, David, who died in May 1981, followed the progress of the book with no less interest. Benedict, the surviving son, discussed his father and family life in Jersualem with me on a number of occasions and gave me access to family correspondence in his possession.

INDEX

Aaronson, Aaron, 15, 122
Abd-al-Baqi, Ahmad Hilmi, 400
Abd-al-Hadi, Awni, 41, 399–400
Abd-al-Hamid, Yasin, 339
Abelson, Paul, 19, 214
Abraham, Abraham, 71–75, 77–79, 80
Acheson, Dean, 48, 371
Adler, Cyrus, 133, 238, 239, 258, 280, 290, 388, 527
Adler, Saul, 231
Ahad Ha'am (Asher Zvi Ginsberg), 11, 12, 29, 35, 84–85, 213, 234–235, 240, 243, 283, 472
al-Alami, Musa, 36, 41, 42, 44, 305–306, 401, 436, 527
Altschul, Frank, 461, 483, 501
American Association for Union in Palestine, 47, 371, 443, 446, 450
American Jewish Committee, 15, 17, 46, 54, 95–100, 139–143, 147, 238, 257, 450, 527; and Kehillah, 20, 126–131; and American Jewish Congress, 21–22, 122, 144, 154–155, 264; and partition, 461, 478, 483, 487
American Jewish Congress, 21, 159, 264, 528
American Jewish Relief Committee, 140, 147–148
Anglo-American Committee of Inquiry, 39–40, 48, 370, 435, 457, 467, 474, 495
Antonius, George, 41, 391
Arendt, Hannah, 55–56, 463, 502–505, 508–509, 518–519, 528
Arslan, Shekib, 41, 306
Asch, Sholom, 15, 45, 332–333, 334
Ascarate, Pablo, 498, 501
Austin, Warren, 53, 55, 462, 473–474, 478, 486, 497, 500, 528

Azzam Pasha, 370, 432–436, 462, 528

Backer, George, 335
Baerwald, Paul, 50, 405–407, 418–422, 528
Balch, Emily, 26
Baldwin, Roger, 26, 230–231, 528
Balfour, Lord Alfred, 205, 231–235
Balfour Declaration, 27, 28, 40, 47, 184–189, 231–233, 235, 277, 282–283, 311, 319
Baneth, David Z., 338
Baron, Salo W., 444, 471
al-Barghuthy, Omar Salih, 41, 398–401, 528
Barth, Karl, 267–269
Benderly, Samson, 19, 128, 133, 192, 197, 216, 529
Ben-Gurion, David, 3, 41, 43, 45, 46, 56, 305–306, 309–311, 333, 349–350, 354, 387–388, 399, 463, 504, 507–508, 529
Bentwich, Herbert, 29
Bentwich, Norman, 34, 189n, 240, 247, 255, 266, 399, 529
Berger, Sophia, 229, 255
Bergman, Shmuel Hugo, 38, 50, 51, 272, 322–323, 504, 529
Berkson, Isaac B., 19
Bernadotte, Count Folkes, 56, 463, 498, 501–504, 506–507, 515–519, 529
Bevin, Ernest, 433, 446, 495
Bialik, Chaim Nachman, 12, 17, 240, 243, 358, 529
Billig, Levi, 338
Billikopf, David, 440–441
Billikopf, Jacob, 47, 290, 530
Biltmore Declaration, 46–47, 370, 387,

464, 468, 485
Bingham, Theodore A., 63, 94–98
Binyamin, Rav, 46
Biram, Arthur, 9, 216
Blum, Edward Charles, 72, 74–75
Blumenthal, Rosalind Magnes, 6, 64, 216
B'nai Jeshurun (New York), 62, 124–125,
    216, 221
Bodenheimer, Fritz S., 302
Bodenheimer, Max Isidor, 154
Bogen, Boris, 168–169
Bowman, Humphrey Ernest, 255
Brainin, Reuben, 254
Brandeis, Louis D., 3, 20–24, 122–123,
    144–152, 154–155, 159, 530
B'rit Shalom Society, 38, 39, 42, 46,
    205, 272–273, 312, 530
Brodetsky, Selig, 266–267, 295–296
Buber, Martin, 11, 38, 40, 50, 53,
    161, 240, 243, 249, 370, 465

Canaan, Tewfik, 340
Chajes, Zvi, 240
Chancellor, Sir John, 40
Chipkin, Israel S., 19
Cohen, Aaron, 399, 401
Cohen, Benjamin V., 353–357, 530
Cohen, Elliot, 56, 505, 508
Cohen, Emil, 9
Coupland, Sir Reginald, 43–44, 315–320,
    530
Crystal, Leon, 446–447

Danziger, Felix, 232
Davis, Eli, 482
Debs, Eugene, 26, 181
Dushkin, Alexander, 19, 197, 386–388,
    450, 530

Eastman, Crystal, 25
Eastman, Max, 26
Eban, Aubrey (Abba) S., 463, 505, 507–
    518
Eder, Montague David, 231, 243
Ehrmann, Rudolf, 240, 243, 247, 250
Einstein, Albert, 30–33, 203–204, 238–240,
    243–249, 265–267, 295–299, 301, 471,
    530
Elath, Eliahu, 501
Eliash, Mordecai, 499
Eliot, Charles William, 102, 236–237
Evans, Harold, 498

Fawzi Bey, Muhamed, 55, 370, 498, 501
Federation of American Zionists, 16,
    62–63, 82–83, 122, 145
Felix, Arthur, 297

Filderman, Wilhelm, 419
Finkelstein, Louis, 483, 511
Fischel, Harry, 147
Flexner, Abraham, 238, 295
Flexner, Bernard, 258
Fodor, Andor, 240, 243, 245–247, 250, 265
Frank, Jerome, 54, 482
Frankel, Lee K., 168–169
Frankel, Zecharias, 111
Frankfurter, Felix, 378, 531
Freud, Sigmund, 240
Friedenwald, Harry, 63
Friedlaender, Israel, 16, 19, 63, 128,
    145–148, 159, 168–169, 197, 531
Friedman, Elisha, 430

Geddes, Sir Patrick, 240, 257
Giffard, Sir George, 369, 372–377
Gildersleeve, Virginia, 461, 467–470
Ginzberg, Shlomo, 238
Glueck, Nelson, 371, 404, 478, 511
Gluskin, Ze'ev, 153
Goldman, Julius, 174
Goldmann, Nahum, 463
Gorki, Maxim, 88, 208
Gottheil, Richard, 92, 170n
Graham-Browne, Francis, 42, 339, 346,
    348, 350, 351, 353
Greenbaum, Edward S., 47, 54, 462,
    482–483, 501
Greiger, Alexander, 493–494, 496
Guggenheim, Daniel, 17

Haas, Jacob de, 146
Hadassah, 16, 47, 49, 50, 56, 215, 218,
    403, 429; hospital, 54, 481–483, 499
Hagana, 54, 369–370, 462, 482, 490, 531
al-Hajj, Rashid Ibraham, 400
Ha'ol, 50
Hartzog, Sir Philip, 295–303, 531
Hebrew Union College, 90–92, 215,
    221, 371; Magnes as student, 4, 6–8;
    Magnes as instructor, 11–12, 61–62,
    76–77
Hebrew University, 3, 9, 29–35, 39, 203–
    205, 228–230, 278, 280–281, 291–292,
    309, 321–324, 338, 370, 372, 377,
    403–404, 428–429, 461, 468–472, 481,
    499; plans for, 29–31, 136–138,
    236–251; opening addresses, 33–35, 56,
    357–365, 378, 409–418; opening, 205,
    231–235; Academic Council, 238, 246,
    267, 299, 301, 471; and Weizmann,
    265–267, 273–275; Hartzog Survey
    Committee, 295–303
Heller, Hayim, 199
Henderson, Loy, 48, 55, 462, 493, 497,

500-502

Hertz, Joseph, 240

Herzl, Theodore, 10-11, 254

Herzog, Isaac Halavi, 477, 504

Hexter, Maurice B., 47, 54, 320, 352, 447-448, 450, 462, 477-479, 483, 501, 509, 511, 531

Hillquit, Morris, 24-25, 168

Hirsch, Baron Maurice de, 68

Hirschmann, Ira, 50, 405, 430

Hochschule, 8-9, 61, 64-65

Hofshi, Natan, 456

Holmes, John Haynes, 25-26, 205, 430-431, 473n, 532

Honor, Leo, 19

Horovitz, Joseph, 231, 240, 243, 245, 250, 303

al-Husayni, al-Hajj Muhammad Amin, 40-42, 339, 345, 350, 352-353, 400, 532

al-Husayni, Ishaq Musa, 339

al-Husayni, Jamal, 41, 350

al-Husayni, Musa Abdallah, 353, 357, 532

Huseyn, Taha, 337-338

Hyamson, Albert M., 310, 344, 348, 350

ibn Huseyn, Feisal, 345, 399

ibn Saud, Abd al-Aziz, 40, 401

Ihud Association, 38, 40, 47-48, 57, 370-371, 384-385, 387-388, 432, 446, 457, 461-463, 467, 474-475, 477, 484, 501, 503, 511, 516, 532

Jabotinsky, Vladimir Ze'ev, 276

al-Jabri, Ihsan, 41, 306

Jackson, Robert G. A., 504

Jacobs, Joseph, 130

Jacobs, Rose G., 352, 388, 447-448, 450

Jessup, Philip, 500

Jewish Agency, 40-44, 50, 204, 238, 258, 282, 303, 373, 382, 423, 427, 447, 450, 463, 478, 514; enlarged, 32, 273-275, 277-280, 388; and partition, 309-311, 329-334, 390; Magnes meeting with Arab leaders, 344-352; and Joint Distribution Committee, 406-407, 421

Jewish Colonization Association, 68, 258

Jewish Defense Association, 14, 22, 63, 80, 97

Jewish Theological Seminary, 7, 15-16, 125n, 128, 132, 183, 321

Joint Distribution Committee (JDC), 3, 23, 28, 122-123, 159, 161, 173, 182-183, 215, 403, 429, 471, 510, 533; Middle East Advisory Committee, 49-50, 370, 405-407, 418-422, 463, 519-520; and Zionists, 242, 257-260; and Russian colonization, 252-253

Jones, Arthur Creech, 55

Kalvarisky, Chaim Margalit, 46, 370, 399, 401, 503, 533

Kann, Jacobus, 228

Kaplan, Mordecai M., 16, 19, 62, 125n, 160, 193-195, 386, 533

Kappes, Heinz, 337-343

Kehillah, 18-23, 26-28, 34, 63, 121, 126-132, 161, 172-174, 207; Bureau of Education, 121, 127-129, 133, 173-174, 197-198, 214; Magnes's resignation as chairman, 190-191

al-Khalidi, Husayn, 313, 400

al-Khayri, Khulusi, 339

Kisch, Frederick H., 255-256, 303, 533

Klausner, Joseph, 17, 30, 226, 286-287, 534

Kligler, Israel J., 240, 250, 534

Kohler, Kaufmann, 77, 91

Kohn, Hans, 38, 51, 272, 403-404, 503, 511, 534

Kohn, Leo, 238, 243, 248

Kuhn, Setty Şchwartz, 403-404, 534

al-Kuwalty, Shukri, 401

Landau, Ann, 219, 398-399

Landau, Edmund, 240, 243, 245, 248-249, 251, 303

Landis, James, 519

Lazaron, Morris S., 384-387, 461, 469, 534

Leach, Agnes Brown, 343

Lehman, Herbert H., 17, 258, 461, 464-465, 487, 534

Lehman, Irving, 17

Levi, Israel, 229

Levin, Shmaryahu, 15, 17, 52-53, 88, 154n

Levontin, Zalman D., 153

Levy, Adele Rosenwald, 482-483

Levy, Joseph M., 433, 435

Lewin-Epstein, Elias W., 83

Libman, Emanuel, 239-240, 243

Linder, Harold F., 483

Lindheim, Irma L., 287

Lippmann, Walter, 139, 535

Lipsky, Louis, 21, 260

Lochner, Louis, 26

London, Meyer, 121, 147

Lowenstein, Leon, 437

Lowenstein, Solomon, 47, 79, 216, 281, 336, 353, 535

Lubarsky, Abraham J., 92

McClintock, Robert, 55, 463, 489-494, 500-502, 535

MacDonald, Ramsay, 331
MacMichael, Sir Harold, 352, 354, 374, 394, 399
MacMillan, Sir Gordon Holmes Alexander, 481–482, 535
Mack, Julian W., 147, 154–155, 169, 237–239, 242–251, 254, 303, 535
Magnes, Beatrice Lowenstein, 14, 29, 55, 116, 122, 124, 171, 173–174, 197–200, 203, 207, 215–217, 229, 255, 267–268, 289, 304, 321, 323–324, 335–337, 428, 437–442, 511, 535
Magnes, Benedict, 7, 14, 219, 321, 323, 437–443
Magnes, David (father), 4–6, 64, 116–117, 535
Magnes, David (son), 14, 117, 124, 215–216, 219, 323, 336, 497
Magnes, Isaac, 6, 64, 117
Magnes, Johathan, 7, 14, 219, 232, 321, 323, 336, 479
Magnes, Sophie Abrahamson, 4–5, 64, 77–78, 255; death, 62, 71, 73
Malik, Charles H., 498–499, 501
Mann, Thomas, 465–467, 479–481, 536
Marks, Simon, 330
Marshall, George, 55, 463, 488–493, 495, 500, 519
Marshall, James, 46–47, 54, 336, 443–444, 451, 462, 473n, 479, 483, 501, 509–511, 536
Marshall, Louis, 14–15, 17, 21, 24, 26, 32, 85, 92, 94–95, 116, 124, 135n, 147, 168, 204, 215–216, 243–244, 257–260, 280–281, 303, 388, 536
Mayer, Leo, 30, 469, 492
Mohilever, Joseph, 273
Mohl, Emanuel Nehemiah, 256
Mond, Sir Alfred M. (Lord Melchett), 240, 250, 536
Morgenthau, Henry, Jr., 519
Morrison-Grady Report, 486
Motzkin, Leo, 17

al-Nahas Pasha, Mustafa, 399, 401
Nearing, Scott, 25, 29, 166–168, 226, 230–231, 536
Neumann, Emanuel, 260
Newcombe, Stewart F., 311, 344, 348, 350
Nordau, Max, 135, 213
Novomeysky, Moshe, 320

Ornstein, Leonard S., 240, 243–245, 251, 303
Oxman, Garfield Bromley, 490, 495

Palestine Royal Commission (Peel Com-

mission), 37, 43–44, 310, 315–320, 324–329, 331–333, 339, 354, 390, 453
Panken, Jacob, 26
Parodi, Alexandre, 55, 501
Passfield, Lord, 309
Passman, Charles, 49, 406–407, 418–422
People's Council of America for Democracy and Peace, 25, 160, 167–168
Philby, Harry St. John, 40, 282–284
Picard, Leo, 302
Pilpel, Robert, 406–407, 420
Pinchot, Amos, 26
Pinski, David, 15
Pollack, James H., 320
Pool, David de Sola, 197
Pool, Tamar de Sola, 386
Popper, Tess Magnes, 6, 116–117
Power, Thomas F., Jr., 498
Proskauer, Joseph, 46
Provisional Executive Committee for General Zionist Affairs, 20, 22, 144, 149–152, 536

Ratnoff, Nathan, 239
Roosevelt, Franklin D., 380, 430, 469, 489, 495
Rosen, Joseph A., 252, 258
Rosenwald, Lessing J., 54, 450, 462, 483, 510, 536
Rothschild, Baron Edmond de, 229, 537
Rothschild, James de, 240, 243
Rothschild, Simon F., 68, 72
Ruppin, Arthur, 17, 38, 42, 122, 139, 272, 312–314, 333, 537
Rusk, Dean, 55
Rutenberg, Pinhas, 320, 537

Sacher, Harry, 240
al-Sa'id, Nuri, 42–43, 344–352, 355, 399–401, 537
Salutsky, J.B., 132
Samuel, Lord Herbert, 232, 235, 240, 449, 471, 537
San Remo Conference, 27–28, 161, 184–187
Saphirstein, Jacob, 132
Sasson, Eliyahu, 401
Sayre, John Nevin, 342–343, 538
Schafer, Samuel M., 92
Schatz, Boris, 89
Schechter, Solomon, 15–16, 62, 81, 92, 111, 117, 123–124, 132, 538
Schiff, Jacob H., 14–15, 17, 19, 21, 116, 121, 124, 135n, 160, 162, 236, 538
Schiff, Mortimer L., 236
Schloessinger, Max, 9, 47, 67, 71–72, 94n, 240, 242–243, 247, 303, 320, 388, 538

552

Schocken, Salman, 322–323
Scholem, Gershom, 7, 38, 50, 53
Schoolman, Albert P., 386
Schwartz, Joseph J., 405–407, 418–422
Seligman, James, 92
Semel, Bernard, 386
Senator, David W., 447–450, 465, 499, 502, 538
Shamosh, Isaac, 401
al-Shanti, Ibrahim, 400
Sharett (Shertok), Moshe, 41, 43, 310–311, 345, 351, 354, 369, 373–377, 538
Shawz, Rushdi, 400
Sher, David, 47, 54, 461, 483
Shochat, Israel, 253
Shochat, Manya, 15, 92, 232, 252–254, 539
Shor, David, 252–254
Silver, Abba Hillel, 505, 507
Silverman, Joseph, 84–88, 90–93
Simon, Ernst, 38, 50, 370–371, 456–457, 479, 503, 539
Simon, Julius, 320, 352–353, 539
Simon, Sir Leon, 467–472, 479, 539
Smilansky, Moshe, 46, 320, 370
Society of the Jewish Renascence, 160, 193–195
Sokolow, Nahum, 136, 153, 240, 243–244, 249–250, 503, 539
Sommerstein, Emil, 419
Stern, Abraham, 369n
Stern, Gavriel, 370
Stern, Horace, 482
Stone, I.F., 445–447, 539
Storrs, Sir Ronald Henry, 256
Straus, Gladys Guggenheim, 335–337, 540
Straus, Lewis, 54
Straus, Nathan, 17, 122, 138, 540
Straus, Oscar, S., 15, 17, 135–136, 147, 540
Straus, Roger, 337, 385
Steinbock, Max, 519
Stroock, Alan M., 47, 54, 443, 461–462, 464, 482, 540
Stroock, Solomon M., 46, 351–352, 540
Sukenik, Eliezar, 54–56
al-Sulh, Riad, 401
Sulzberger, Arthur Hays, 44, 47, 337, 433, 461, 540
Sulzberger, Cyrus, 17, 388, 540
Sulzberger, Iphigene (Mrs. Arthur), 501
Sulzberger, Mayer, 81, 124, 133, 541
Szold, Henrietta, 16, 19, 29, 47, 49, 73, 81, 253, 370, 431, 541

Taeubler, Eugen, 9, 240

Taft, Charles P., 490, 495
Tannous, Izzat, 42, 346, 348, 350–351, 353
Tarazi, Wadi, 337–342
Teller, Eva Magnes, 6, 68, 81, 116
Temple Emanu-El (New York), 13, 15–16, 62, 79, 83–93, 107–116, 221
Temple Israel (Brooklyn), 13, 62, 71–80
Thomas, Norman, 25–26, 29, 231, 431–432, 541
Thon, Jacob J., 136n, 256
Thon, Osias, 243
Totah, Khalil, 436
Truman, Harry, 55, 463, 477, 493–497
Tschlenow, Yechiel, 153

United Hebrew Charities, 98–99, 129, 183
Untermyer, Eugene, 428–430, 471, 541
Ussishkin, Menachem, 17, 29, 45, 256, 273, 331, 541

Villard, Oswald Garrison, 26
Voorsanger, Jacob, 4, 6, 7, 64, 542

Wadsworth, George, 42
Wald, Lillian, 24
Warburg, Edward M. M., 519–520
Warburg, Felix M., 7, 17, 29, 46–47, 124, 168–169, 183, 215, 236, 254, 258, 260, 287–288, 310, 321–322, 388, 542; and Kehillah, 19, 121; and Hebrew University, 30, 32, 203–204, 228–230, 238–243, 291; and Arab-Jewish cooperation, 40, 44, 320, 331, 335; and Jewish Agency, 273–275, 277–281
Warburg, Freda Schiff (Mrs. Felix), 353, 471
Warburg, Otto, 17, 243, 250, 302
Wasson, Thomas C., 475–477, 542
Waterfield, Arthur Charles, 353–356
Wauchope, Sir Arthur, 41, 309, 325, 347–349, 352, 399, 542
Wechsler, Israel, 470
Weil, Gotthold, 9
Weitz, Naphtali, 153
Weizmann, Chaim, 3, 11, 12, 17, 123, 254, 542; and Hebrew University, 30–33, 39, 136–138, 203–205, 229, 232, 238–240, 243–244, 247–250, 265–267, 273–275, 291–292, 295–297, 301; and Jewish state, 40, 45, 55, 153–154, 257–260, 276–279, 288, 310, 331, 370, 388, 391, 426; and Nuri Pasha el•Sa'id, 344–345, 351–352
Weizmann, Moshe (Selig), 243, 266, 273
Weltsch, Robert, 40, 312
Wertheim, Jacob, 17

Wertheim, Maurice, 17, 46, 336, 461
Weyl, Bertha, 29, 216
Weyl, Walter, 26
Wilhelm, Kurt, 342, 504, 506–507
Wise, Stephen S., 3, 16, 23, 62, 85, 123, 159, 168–169, 260, 286–287, 543
Wolffsohn, David, 10, 82–83, 543
Wolfsshon Foundation, 228, 251
Wood, L. Hollingsworth, 343

Yahuda, Abraham Shalom, 297
Yassky, Chaim, 49

Yellin, David, 30, 256

Zangwill, Israel, 19–20, 69, 101–106, 186, 318, 543
Zhitlovsky, Chaim, 15
Zionist Organization, 10, 12, 17, 30, 122, 149–154, 238, 244–248, 257, 275, 277, 283, 303, 354, 370, 429; Small Actions Committee, 17, 82, 278; Congress, 44, 136, 149, 329; American, 145, 149, 388
Zuckerman, Baruch, 16
Zunz, Leopold, 76